Law and Parenthood

DATE DUE

AP 17 07			

DEMCO 38-296

Law in Context

Editors: Robert Stevens (Covington & Burling, London)
William Twining (University College, London) and
Christopher McCrudden (Lincoln College, Oxford)

Ashworth: *Sentencing and Criminal Justice*
Barron, Sherman and Bentley: *IP Law Text and Materials*
Barron: *IP: Copyright, Industrial Design and Trademarks*
Bercusson: *European Labour Law*
Birkinshaw: *Freedom of Information: The Law, the Practice and the Ideal*
Cane: *Atiyah's Accidents, Compensation and the Law*
Clarke & Kohler: *Property Law Commentary and Materials*
Collins: *The Law of Contract*
Cranston: *Legal Foundations of the Welfare State*
Davies and Freedland: *Labour Law Text and Materials*
Detmold: Courts and Administrators: *A study in Jurisprudence*
Doggett: *Marriage, Wife-Beating and the Law in Victorian England*
Dummett and Nicol: *Subjects, Citizens, Aliens and Others: Nationality and Immigration Law*
Goodrich: *Languages of Law*
Hadden: *Company Law and Capitalism*
Harlow and Rawlings: *Law and Administration Text & Materials*
Harris: *An Introduction to Law*
Harris: *Remedies in Contract and Tort*
Lacey, Wells and Meure: *Reconstructing Criminal Law – Text and Materials*
Lewis: *Choice and the Legal Order*
Moffat and Chesterman: *Trusts Law – Text and Materials*
Norrie: *Crime, Reason and History*
Page and Ferguson: *Investor Protection*
Picciotto: *International Business Taxation*
Ramsay: *Consumer Protection: Text and Materials*
Richardson: *Law, Process and Custody*
Snyder: *New Directions in European Community Law*
Twining and Anderson: *Analysis of Evidence*
Twining and Miers: *How to do Things with Rules*
Turpin:*British Government and the Constitution*
Zander: *Cases and Materials on the English Legal System*
Zander: *The Law-Making Process*

Law and Parenthood

Chris Barton
Reader in Law, Staffordshire University

Gillian Douglas
Senior Lecturer in Law, Cardiff Law School

Butterworths
London, Dublin and Edinburgh
1995

a Division of Reed Elsevier (UK) Ltd,
se, 35 Chancery Lane, LONDON WC2A
l Street, EDINBURGH EH2 3JZ

Australia   Butterworths, SYDNEY, MELBOURNE, BRISBANE, ADELAIDE,
                   PERTH, CANBERRA and HOBART

Canada   Butterworths Canada Ltd, TORONTO and VANCOUVER

Ireland   Butterworth (Ireland) Ltd, DUBLIN

Malaysia   Malayan Law Journal Sdn Bhd, KUALA LUMPUR

New Zealand   Butterworths of New Zealand Ltd, WELLINGTON and
                   AUCKLAND

Puerto Rico   Equity de Puerto Rico, Inc, SAN JUAN

Singapore   Butterworths Asia, SINGAPORE

South Africa   Butterworths Publishers (Pty) Ltd, DURBAN

USA   Northwestern University Press, 625 Colefax Street,
                   Evanston, Illinois 60208-4210

A CIP Catalogue record for this book is available from the British Library.

ISBN   0 406 04499 6

Printed in England by Clays Ltd, St Ives plc.

Preface

The law relating to the parent-child relationship has grown in theoretical significance and practical importance over the last decade, culminating in the major reforms of the law by the Children Act 1989 and the Child Support Act 1991. There has been increasing international attention to this subject as well, most notably in the 1989 United Nations Convention on the Rights of the Child. The academic literature on the subject has tended to emphasise the position of the child *vis à vis* the parents or the state. In reality, however, the law focuses far more on the role and functions of parents, or those to whom it entrusts parental responsibilities, than it does on the child. This is hardly surprising, since the delivery of care to the child can only be performed by adults. The first aim of our book is therefore to accord the role of parent the significance which it deserves, and which has been neglected hitherto, in our view.

Secondly, our aim is to redress the balance of previous accounts, in giving a greater degree of attention to the functioning relationship between parent and child, rather than to perpetuate the assumption that this is governed by what might be termed 'pathological' law.

The third aim, which follows on naturally from these, is to examine English law in order to discover the extent to which it can be said to offer a coherent, and consistent model of parenthood, both in relation to *status* (who, in law, is a parent?) and *role* (who is entrusted with parental responsibility?).

There is already a well-developed literature on, for example the development of the 'welfare' principle, and the increasing equality of mothers and fathers in relation to rights in respect of their children. Our aim is to go beyond this analysis to a more fundamental examination of the concepts of parentage and parenting in English law. We accordingly trace, through a broad social, historical and philosophical, as well as legal, account, the apparent transition from rights to responsibility; from a view of the parent as 'owner' of the child, to being the child's 'trustee';

from an emphasis on the biological, or genetic link between an adult and a child to the social or psychological bonds between them.

Whilst we are equally – and exclusively – responsible for *Law and Parenthood*, we received a lot of help. Secretarial help was provided by Kathryn Bates at Cardiff, and further administrative support was provided by Sarah Richardson at Staffordshire. Parts of the book were read by either Ursula Dobraszczyc (for sociology) or Nigel Lowe (for law). Chris Barton would also like to thank his friends Sheelagh Rowbottom and Alison Stubbs, tutor librarians at Staffordshire. We were each fortunate enough to be granted study leave by our respective institutions. Cardiff Law School Research Fund also financed the activities of two research assistants, Carolyn Goodall and Richard Hughes. Butterworths' editorial and production staff were extremely helpful and efficient in dealing with the manuscript. We are very grateful to all of them.

This book is dedicated to our respective children, Sally Barton, and Isobel and Duncan Rawlings.

Chris Barton
Gillian Douglas
March 1995

Contents

Table of statutes and statutory instruments

References in this table to *Statutes* are to Halsbury's Statutes of England (Fourth Edition) showing the volume and page at which the annotated text of the Act may be found.

List of cases

A

B

C

D

E

F

G

H

I

J

K

L

M

N

W

X

Y

PART I

Introduction

CHAPTER 1

Law, parenthood and society

1. INTRODUCTION

Family law concerns the recognition and regulation of certain relationships. In recent years, and particularly in the past decade, the focus of attention in family law has shifted from relationships between adults, and between adults and the state, to those between parents and children, and parents, children and the state. The reasons for this shift are not immediately obvious, although it is likely that they have something to do with actual changes in patterns of family formation. The number of people marrying in 1991 was nearly 50,000 lower than in 1961; with the marriage rate for men and women roughly halving from 1971 to 1991. The rate of marriage is higher for divorced men and widowers than it is for bachelors, while that for divorced women and widows is very low. At the same time, the divorce rate has increased enormously, from 2.1 per 1,000 married population of men in 1961, to 13.6 in 1991, and from 2.1 to 13.4 for women. Nearly 20% of men and women aged between 16 and 59 were cohabiting in 1992, and a third of births were outside marriage. Finally, one-parent families with dependent children nearly doubled as a proportion of all families with dependent children, from 10% in 1976 to around 19% in 1991.[1] Such changes mean that traditional stereotype images of 'the family' – the stable married couple with two young children – no longer reflect the life experiences of significant numbers of the population. Law, and legal commentary, must accommodate the change sooner or later.

Changes in social arrangements are probably not in themselves sufficient to explain the shift in focus of social, and legal attention. There is clearly much less social stigma attached to extra-marital sex, cohabitation and procreation than was the case 30 years ago, and there have been legal developments which take account of this, but it cannot be established

1 *Social Trends 1994*; see Ch 2.

whether this reflects the growth in these phenomena, or encourages such growth. There is probably a symbiotic relationship between the two.

It may also be that such changes, and legal interest, are influenced by a growing emphasis on the freedom of the individual, and the right to do as one pleases, so long as it harms no one else. Adults who choose to cohabit rather than marry or who choose to have sexual relationships with members of the same sex may have ceased to excite the same attention that they formerly did, except where their choices have implications for others. 'Society' may no longer be accepted as a sufficient 'other' for this purpose. Such an approach has become the subject of political and philosophical dispute as to the extent to which it is legitimate to speak of society, or community, and how far what Western societies need is a shift from emphasis on civil rights to civic responsibilities.[2] But it is not regarded as problematic that children, who may be affected directly by the choices of adults, should be recognised as having sufficiently significant interests and needs to justify interference in and regulation of their family by the state.

Another influence may be an increasing interest in, and awareness of, the processes involved in the psychological development of children, stimulating attention to the quality of care given by adults to children and recognition of the potential need to take measures to seek improvement where quality is poor. Of particular significance here have been first, in the immediate post-war period, the work of John Bowlby on maternal deprivation,[3] and secondly, in the 1970s and 1980s, that of Goldstein, Freud and Solnit.[4] Bowlby's view that the child requires a single, unchanging primary caregiver to whom the child can attach and develop bonds of love was built on by Goldstein, Freud and Solnit. They emphasised the child's need for stability in family ties and that it is the child's psychological parent (the person who fulfils the child's 'emotional demands for affection, companionship and stimulating intimacy'),[5] rather than a blood relative *per se*, who is important for the child's emotional well-being. They also argued that the child's 'sense of time' is quite different from that of an adult; children are much less able than adults to sustain emotional relationships at a distance over time. These theories proved enormously influential in shaping social work policies and judicial attitudes towards children at risk of neglect or abuse and towards the need to avoid delay in decision-making and planning for the

2 See, eg, C Murray, *The Emerging British Underclass* (1990)   (with critical commentaries); D Selbourne, *The Principle of Duty* (1994).

3 *Child Care and the Growth of Love* (1965) discussed further below.

4 J Goldstein, A Freud and A Solnit, *Beyond the Best Interests of the Child* (1973, 1980); *Before the Best Interests of the Child* (1979).

5 *Ibid* (1980) at p 18.

child's future.[6] Ironically, notwithstanding their preference for minimal state intervention in family life, and for the psychological parent's autonomy in determining whether a child should continue to see an absent parent, their theories have been used to *justify* the reverse of both. For example, they were used to support a social work preference for sustaining, or creating social/psychological parenthood through the adoption of children from the public care system (with or without the consent of the birth parents), and they bolstered the emergence of the 'new father' who has a closer emotional relationship with his children which necessitates continuing contact after marriage breakdown, regardless of the feelings of the caretaking mother.[7]

In the context of these influences and factors – social, philosophical, political, psychological – we propose to explore the parent-child relationship as recognised and regulated in law. The focus of much recent attention in family law has been on the *child's* position. Theories of children's rights have been developed, of both libertarian or liberationist types, and more qualified, limited paternalist models.[8] The role of parents in the procreation and rearing of children has received less attention. Yet this remains a central issue for legal and social policy. Politicians' rhetoric about the desirability of 'traditional' family life, which came to the fore particularly during the Conservative governments of the 1980s and 1990s places *parents*, and their failings in particular, at centre stage. Thus, cruelty or neglect of children may be found to produce a 'cycle of violence' transmitted down the generations; single parenthood may be blamed for rising crime rates; selfish parents (and especially working or, still worse, career mothers) may be blamed for rearing children fit only for playing video-games and cheeking their elders. The sins of the fathers may no longer always be visited upon the children, but the sins of the children are always blamed upon the parents.

Parent and child are frequently discussed as if placed in opposite camps. This is especially demonstrated in discussions of children's rights – if the child has a right to decide something, then it may be argued that the parent cannot have the same right.[9] But parenthood and childhood are not co-relative concepts. Parenthood denotes a relationship with a

---

6 See, eg, the anti-delay principle in s 1(2) of the Children Act 1989 (Ch 8).
7 See the critiques in C Smart and S Sevenhiujsen (eds) *Child Custody and the Politics of Gender* (1989).
8 For the former, see eg, R Farson, *Birthrights* (1978) and J Holt, *Escape from Childhood* (1975). For the latter, see M D A Freeman, *The Rights and Wrongs of Children* (1983) and J Eekelaar, 'The Emergence of Children's Rights' (1986) 6 OJLS 161 (Ch 2).
9 Andrew Bainham has criticised this dichotomy and argued for dual recognition of parents' and children's rights – see 'Growing up in Britain: Adolescence in the Post-Gillick era' in J Eekelaar and P Sarcevic (eds) *Parenthood in Modern Society* (1993).

child: one cannot be called a 'parent' unless one stands in *some relation* to a person of a succeeding generation. Although the parents *may* have *created* the child through procreation, parental status is *derivative* – it depends upon a child's existence (or previous existence perhaps).

The concept of childhood is different. If a person is described as a 'child', this may mean that he or she is of tender years, *or* that he or she stands in a particular relation to an adult who is or was a parent (and in this sense, one is one's parents' child all through one's life). But while parenthood denotes the state of being a parent and fulfilling the roles expected of parents, childhood means a state of being young.

Parenthood is itself a fragmented concept however. It is possible to distinguish various roles within it, any or all of which may be played by the parent figure. For example, the procreative or biological role is distinct from the social role; a person may provide the genetic material for a child's creation but play no part in the child's upbringing. With the development of embryo transfer techniques and surrogacy arrangements, it is also possible for a woman to act as the gestational mother – ie carry the child to term, even though she is not the genetic mother and will not be the child's carer after birth. The social role may be performed by a person genetically unrelated to the child. We have already noted that the 'psychological parent' provides the *emotional* bonding with the young child.

In addition to parenthood, there are further quasi-parental roles, most notably that of step-parenthood.[10] The step-parent occupies an ambiguous and problematic position somewhere 'in between' the child's 'real' parents, especially where there has been a marriage breakdown rather than a death. We shall see in later chapters the extent to which the different roles of parenthood have been accorded legal recognition.

There has been relatively little philosophical discussion of the family:

'Family arrangements are regarded as below the level of attention of political theory, familial decisions as involving no ethical problems distinct from those which may arise between any two individuals. A territorial division of normative questions into political theory and ethics has left questions about the family in no man's land, which, perhaps significantly, is often regarded as woman's sphere.'[11]

Onora O'Neill and William Ruddick blame Locke for this situation, since he argued that there was little connection between familial and

---

10 The 'word "step" has its roots in the Anglo-Saxon English word "astepan" which means deprived or bereaved' – C Hughes, *Step-Parents: Wicked or Wonderful?* (1991) p vii.

11 O O'Neill and W Ruddick (eds) *Having Children: Philosophical and Legal Reflections on Parenthood* (1979) p 3. A similar bias towards the public sphere is reflected in sociological theory and writing: see the critique by M Stacey, 'The Division of Labour Revisited: Overcoming the Two Adams' in P Abrahams *et al* (eds) *Practice and Progress – British Sociology 1950–1980* (1981).

political institutions, demolishing the concept of the sovereign as the father of the nation, and hence turning political theorists' attention away from the domestic sphere. To some extent, this paucity of thinking on the family has been redressed in recent years by the emergence of feminist critiques. It has been argued by feminist scholars, as an explanation for family and social policies, that liberal thinking envisages a public and private dichotomy, with family issues relegated to the private and hence beyond the reach (or outside the gaze) of legal or moral theorists.[12] Michael Freeman, for example, has argued that

'It may be from liberal economic thought that we get the distinction between the economic world of the market (the public) and the non-economic sphere of the home (the private "haven"). But it is in liberal political thought that we find the normative conclusions which have had such enormous implications for the regulation of the family.... Liberals question the legitimate extent of governmental authority: the public sphere, they believe, is properly subject to governmental regulation but not so the private. The state should refrain from intervention in the "private" lives of individuals... '.[13]

Such an analysis has been criticised by John Eekelaar as being irrelevant to our understanding of family law. He suggests, instead, that what is important is exploring the *public interest* in family life, for the state 'intervenes' (in a variety of ways not confined to legal mechanisms) in the family when the public interest is threatened:

'provided that the public interest is efficiently served by the proper functioning of the family system, the law plays but a small role in the definition or enforcement of those values... it is misleading to set up familial obligations as expressed in their legal form as if they were in opposition to the less "caring" precepts of public law. They can be viewed as integral parts of the public law system as a whole.'[14]

We regard both of these analyses as of value in explaining the legal concept of parenthood, its place in society, and its role in the state. The family as a treasured part of one's private life is proclaimed as a valuable aspect of (liberal) democracy. It is not accidental that Article 8 of the European Convention on Human Rights protects a person's right 'to respect for his private *and* family life, his home and his correspondence'.[15]

---

12 In this country, see M D A Freeman, 'Towards a Critical Theory of Family Law' (1985) *Current Legal Problems* 153; 'The Private and the Public' in D Morgan and G Douglas (eds) *Constituting Families: A Study in Governance* (1994) 22; K O'Donovan, *Sexual Divisions in Law* (1985). In the United States, see C Pateman, *The Sexual Contract* (1988); S Moller Okin, *Justice, Gender and the Family* (1989).
13 M D A Freeman (1985) op cit 168.
14 J Eekelaar, 'What is "Critical" Family Law?' (1989) 105 LQR 244, 256.
15 For discussion of Article 8 and its placement of the family in the private sphere, see K O'Donnell, 'Parent-Child Relationships within the European Convention' in N V Lowe and G Douglas (eds) *Families across Frontiers* (forthcoming).

It is well understood, in the context of modern European history, that the freedom to choose a sexual partner, to bring up children and to live with them without harassment are essential freedoms. At the political level, family privacy, and privacy for one's activities in creating and living in a family, are values which are proclaimed, and worth proclaiming in a democracy. At the same time, Freeman and others have clearly illustrated how a refusal by the state to protect the weaker members of the family, because it would be 'wrong' to 'interfere' in 'the family', has been used to justify the exploitation and coercion of women and children. Today, there is a clearer (though not perfect) recognition of the need to respect the rights and interests of *all* family members as distinct *individuals*. But the public/private dichotomy can be said to explain the nature of the *political* discourse surrounding the family more than it does the times and ways in which the *law* is directed towards the family and family members. Eekelaar's argument that it is the public interest which determines the nature and extent of 'intervention', and not the often arbitrary classification of something as public or private, helps to explain the ways in which the relationship of parent and child is recognised, regulated, and in some instances, privileged, by the law in a given society. The task for the family lawyer then, is to explore what shapes that public interest. We attempt such an exploration in this book.

2. SOCIOLOGICAL THEORIES OF FAMILY AND PARENTHOOD

We now examine the relevance of sociology, the 'scientific and more particularly the positivistic, study of society',[16] to the structure and role of parenthood in society as reflected by law. In view of the public propensity to hold them both in disdain, it is ironic that lawyers and sociologists continue to view each other with suspicion. The lawyer may be accused of profiting from family breakdown and the sociologist of pontificating about it.

(a) Definitions of the family

Modern sociologists might well laugh at contemporary legal struggles to define the term 'family', or at least at judicial efforts to do so. Even in the modern Australian case of *Mehmet v Mehmet*,[17] the court was content to

16 D Jary and J Jary, *Collins Dictionary of Sociology* (1991).
17 (1987) FLC 91-801; for a collection of inter-disciplinary materials, see S Parker, P Parkinson and J Behrens, *Australian Family Law in Context* (1994).

rely, at least in part, upon two nineteenth century English Masters of the Rolls: Romilly MR '... the primary meaning of the word "family" is "children"';[18] and Jessel MR, 'The word "family" has various meanings ... In [one] sense, the word includes children only; thus when a man speaks of his wife and family, he means his wife and children. Now every word which has more than one meaning has a primary meaning ... What then, is the primary meaning of "family"? It is children.'[19]

By contrast, sociology, although a more recent discipline than law, has given more express thought to the meaning of parenthood and the family.[20] The latter has been defined as 'A group of people, related by kinship or similar close ties in which the adults assume responsibility for the care and upbringing of their natural or adopted children'.[1] This flexible, and perhaps rather vague, definition may stem from the apparently greater awareness of sociologists of the historically changing nature of family relationships than is possessed by, in particular, politicians who, for many years, have proclaimed a stereotyped view of 'the family', either explicitly or implicitly, and who see any deviations as fundamental threats to society.[2] A more precise, and limited definition has been offered by G P Murdock, based on his study of 250 societies from which he claimed that 'the family' is a universal phenomenon:

> 'The family is a social group characterized by common residence, economic co-operation and reproduction. It includes adults of both sexes, at least two of whom maintain a socially approved sexual relationship, and one or more children, own or adopted, of the sexually cohabiting adults.'[3]

It is usual to compare the 'nuclear' family model, which consists of parent(s) and dependent child(ren), with the 'extended family', in which more than two generations live in very close proximity; modern examples of the latter may be drawn from Chinese or Indian society. While the former appears a closer reflection of currently prevailing norms in the West, the question of whether it is a relatively recent development which arose as a response to the need for mobility of the workforce associated with industrialisation or whether it has been the primary model of family

18 *Re Terry's Will* (1854) 19 Beav 580, 581.
19 *Pigg v Clarke* (1876) 3 Ch D 672, 674.
20 But reference should again be made to Stacey's discussion of the gender blindness of classical sociological theory (see p 6, n 11).
 1 *Collins Dictionary of Sociology.*
 2 Antony Giddens, in *Sociology* (1989) at p 143, cites examples of fears about changing family structures dating back to 1859: 'The family, in its old sense, is disappearing from our land ... the very existence of our society is endangered' which are echoed by politicians in every generation (see, eg Margaret Thatcher in her address to the 1986 Conservative Women's Conference, 'Our policy starts with the family, its freedom and its wellbeing)'.
 3 G P Murdock, *Social Structure* (1965) p 1.

household structure is an ongoing and unresolved one.[4] We need to contrast also the 'family of orientation', in which the child is raised and which, as we explain below, is the chief agent of his or her *socialisation*. Later, he or she may find a partner to continue the process, in their own 'family of procreation'.

As regards the modern hankering after a golden age of parenthood,[5] Lawrence Stone[6] has argued that emotional warmth between parent and child is no more long-rooted in our social history than is companionate marriage. In all social classes, the infant mortality rate discouraged too much sentimentality. So far as the poor were concerned, the cost of their offspring softened any emotional blow when they quit the household for the labour market. The upper classes had domestic staff for the early childhood of their young, far-off schools for their adolescence and two universities for their 'higher' education. *Tremain's Case*,[7] in which a young man who preferred Oxford was *twice* returned by the court to Cambridge, his guardian's choice for his education, may well have illustrated an unusual degree of inter-generational concern. Sir Robert Walpole barely saw his parents between the ages of six, when he was banished to school, and 22, when he was summoned back from Cambridge on the death of his elder brother.

Stone's thesis has been criticised as overstated and ignoring other sources.[8] Similarly, Philippe Ariès' argument that there was until the eighteenth century little concept of 'childhood' and little recognition of children's interests, has been controversial.[9] But in any event, it is accepted that by the eighteenth century, greater recognition of the needs of children was apparent: swaddling clothes disappeared; children's toys were manufactured; and the practice of breaking a child's will, at least through flogging, had received its first challenges with the Children's Petition – 'A modest remonstrance of that intolerable grievance ... of the School discipline of this Nation ... wherein our secret parts ... must be the anvil exposed to the immodest eyes and filthy blows of the smiter' – being presented to Parliament in 1669.

---

4   See L Stone, *The Family, Sex and Marriage in England 1500-1800* (1977) (but see below). Compare P Laslett and R Wall, *Household and Family in Past Time* (1972) who argue that the average size of family households has changed little over the centuries.

5   See generally, C Barton, 'Legal Family Favourites: the Man, then the Couple – now the Child' (1989) 2 *Journal of Child Law* (1) 29 at 30.

6   Stone *op cit*. See generally, W Murphy, 'Come Whoam to Thi Childer An' Me' (1983) 46 MLR 363.

7   (1719) 1 Stra 167.

8   L Pollock, *Forgotten Children: Parent-Child Relations from 1500-1900* (1983).

9   P Ariès, *Centuries of Childhood* (1962, 1979). For a concise account of the debate, see M Abbott, *Family Ties* (1993) Ch 1.

'In our own society ... where life expectancy is high, childhood is a prolonged phase of life compared with some cultures where the physically viable child was, and still is, treated as an adult ... In our society, children wear different clothes to adults, have special artifacts, such as toys, created for them and are largely absolved from the obligations of adult life.'[10]

We now turn to what sociologists perhaps see as the most significant element of the parent-child relationship.

(b) Socialisation

In the nineteenth century, Auguste Comte proposed what was to become a constant theme in sociology: that the family is primarily instrumental in the conversion of the individual into a social being. This is the process of 'socialisation', whereby the individual learns to adjust to the prevailing order, and takes on the norms (standards of conduct in given situations) and values (group beliefs as to the comparative desirability of things) in his or her set. By being socialised, the individual can predict the likely course of events in most situations because he or she has the appropriate expectations. Socialisation is the means whereby individuals learn the 'culture' of their society 'the way of life of its members; the collection of ideas and habits which they learn, share and transmit from generation to generation.'[11]

This process may be described in rather darker fashion, as being a means of ensuring conformity with norms through the collective control of behaviour, achieved by individuals internalising such controls through exposure to example and education. It continues throughout one's life, although attention has been concentrated upon the childhood stage where the process is at its most intensive and the role of the family as a socialising agent is at its most influential. Socialisation in childhood is thought to be critical in determining the person's social identity as both child and adult, with specific upbringing practices (toilet training is a notorious example) having ascribed to them particular consequences, such as authoritarianism (belief in a system in which some individuals control whilst others are controlled).

The question of how *morals* are inculcated has also been of considerable political interest. One school of thought, headed by Durkheim and Freud, argues that the vital factor is the relationship with *parents*, whose cultural values are subsequently reflected in their child's individual personality.

---

10 J Gahagan, 'The Foundations of Social Behaviour' in J Radford and E Gover (eds) *A Textbook of Psychology* (1980) at p 583.
11 R Linton, 'Present Conditions in Cultural Perspective' in R Linton (ed) *The Science of Man in World Crisis* (1945) at p 203.

On the other hand, George Mead, who was concerned with the intellectual aspect of socialised morality, argued that it is the relationship with *peers* through which individuals acquire principled reactions to events in society.

The learning involved in socialisation develops the *social self*, the totality of attitudes that a person makes of him- or herself. This in its turn can be explained by reference to the idea of the *looking-glass self*, ie the 'person' that one imagines others in the same group see in oneself. Thus, children appraise themselves, with varying degrees of accuracy, by reference to a combination of how they think they appear to others, together with their perception of how those others evaluate what the children think those others see. Mead suggested that, in their early development, children react only to *significant others*, specific individuals who have the greatest influence on the development of the social self, like parents. The children learn to accept their attitudes, but to take part in a wider life, they must learn how to react to the *generalised other*, representing the broader communal view.

Mead postulated a two-part division of the social self: the 'me', an individual's socialised and predictable responses to the expectations of others; and the 'I', the unique, independent, creative part. The former ensures order, the latter, change. These classifications are reminiscent of two of the three, perhaps better known terms introduced by Freud. The *id* ('I') is the unconscious primitive self which corresponds to our instinctive desires in the areas of life such as sex and aggression. The *ego* develops out of and attempts to control the id, mediating between the id and the *superego* ('me'), which represents the largely unconscious internalising of society's norms and values.

Both Durkheim and Talcott Parsons explained the process of socialisation by reference to the theory of functionalism, ie that societies have innate tendencies towards harmony and self-regulation, in a manner analogous to living organisms. Societal characteristics cannot be attributed to the choices of individual 'actors' because those choices are themselves the product of socialisation. More recently, others have become reluctant 'to view people as happy robots, acting out predetermined roles'.[12] Two psychiatrists who have had a major influence on the sociology of the family, R D Laing[13] and David Cooper,[14] have depicted the family, and the parent-child relationship, as being positively harmful. Laing argues that the latter engenders an unremitting demand for mutual concern which can create considerable potential for harm. The son whose father is ashamed of him cannot dismiss the matter lightly, and runs to his

---

12 T Bilton *et al*, *Introductory Sociology* (2nd ed, 1987) p 21.
13 'Series and Nexus in the Family' in D Worsley (ed) *The Politics of the Family* (1976).
14 *The Death of the Family* (1972).

mother for protection: 'A family can act as gangsters, offering each other protection against each other's violence.'[15] Cooper analyses the matter along Marxist lines, arguing that the socialisation of children by their parents teaches them not how to survive the society but to submit to it. They are merely prepared for subsequent exploitation in capitalist society.[16]

The starting point of the process of socialisation is the fact that the newborn baby is helpless, being not merely physically dependent upon older people, but lacking necessary behaviour patterns. A child responds to approval or disapproval, and follows parental example. If the child is deprived of care, socialisation will not take place. Thus, the 'wolf children of Midnapore', two girls aged two and eight, were supposedly found in a wolf den in Bengal in 1920. They walked on all fours, ate raw meat, howled like wolves and could not speak. More recently, poor Isabelle spent most of the first six years of her life in a darkened room with her deaf mute mother:

> 'Her behaviour towards strangers, especially men, was almost that of a wild animal, manifesting much fear and hostility. In lieu of speech she made only a strange croaking noise.... At first, it was hard even to tell whether or not she could hear, so unused were her senses. Many of her actions resembled those of deaf children.'[17]

It is important to recognise that the child's need for adult care is not necessarily focused on parents, be they genetic or social, or whether they be single or dual. Life in an Israeli kibbutz may demonstrate this (as presumably might life in a children's home). Kibbutzim are collective farms, founded on socialist or communist principles. Typically, children lived[18] in communal dormitories cared for by a nurse, rather than in their parents' homes. Contact with parents was purely social and for pleasure. The parental role in socialisation was transferred to the community.

15 M Haralambos and M Holborn, *Sociology – Themes and Perspectives* (3rd ed, 1990) p 467.
16 See also J Donzelot, *The Policing of Families* (1979) and C Lasch, *Haven in a Heartless World: The Family Besieged* (1977) discussed in Ch 10. Whereas Marxism sees the oppression derived from capital's long-term needs for future labour power, as suffered equally by both parents, radical feminism, as propounded by Shulamith Firestone in *The Dialectic of Sex: The Case for Feminist Revolution* (1979) sees it as an example of how men/husbands/fathers benefit from the daily services of women/wives/mothers. She argues that pregnancy, breastfeeding and child care, even more than menstruation, childbirth and the menopause, are the causes of women's dependence upon men, and that only when conception and development of babies outside the womb become possible will mothers be freed from inequality with fathers.
17 K Davis, *Human Society* (1970) p 206. See also A Giddens, *Sociology* (1989) who refers to the 'wild boy of Aveyron' (1800) and to Genie, a Californian girl who, in the 1960s and 1970s, was kept virtually incommunicado by her father between the ages of about 18 months and 13 years.
18 Such upbringing is increasingly out of favour and many parents are assuming more conventional roles today.

Alvin Toffler has suggested an even more radical alternative: in his proposed system, there would be professional social parents who would simulate family groups and specialise in child rearing as a paid occupation. This would end the present haphazard system of amateur caretaking and break the conventional, inadequate nexus between procreation and upbringing.[19]

It is open to question whether the kibbutz model of child-rearing is still a *family*-based model, albeit a very large extended family. In any event, kibbutz children's socialisation and emotional stability have not been found to have been adversely affected by communal upbringing, and the kibbutz is far removed from that nadir of parenthood once found 'in the more arid parts of Australia [where] female infanticide was practised to reduce the population in times of famine, and occasionally the baby was eaten'.[20]

It is a commonplace that the early years are crucial to the child's socialisation:

> 'At this stage the foundations of personality are laid .... Most authorities agree that the early childhood years are crucial for learning to integrate effectively in social situations. The type of socialisation a child receives, and hence his chance in life, are thus greatly dependent on the type of family into which he is born and on the aspects of the culture which are transmitted, and the means by which this is done. Mental, physical, moral and emotional development may all be retarded in the absence of suitable social stimuli; and poverty, infection, emotional insecurity and inappropriate parental example are all cultural hindrances to satisfactory socialisation.'[1]

Clearly, care, such as that involved in the availability of adults capable of providing appropriate stimulation, is crucial. The words of Lord Hailsham LC in *Richards v Richards*[2] to the effect that 'the court ought not to confine itself to a consideration of purely material requirements or immediate comforts' would seem to involve an awakening legal cognisance of the sociological view that 'To be born into a high socio-economic stratum does not guarantee a propitious child-rearing *milieu*'.[3] But the physical environment in which the child is brought up will still be influential, with much dependent upon whether the family income is sufficient to generate the proper nourishment, housing, clothing and play space:

> 'other things being equal, middle and upper-class children have advantages, the suburb over the slum, Hampstead over Hackney'.[4]

19 *Future Shock* (1971). Plato proposed something similar; see Ch 2.
20 M Haralambos and M Holborn, *Sociology – Themes and Perspectives* (3rd ed, 1990) at p 3.
1 M Farmer, *The Family* (2nd ed, 1979) p 98.
2 [1984] AC 174, 205.
3 Farmer *op cit* at p 99.
4 *Ibid.*

Adopting the definition of the family put forward by Murdock, and cited earlier in this chapter, it becomes apparent that sex,[5] reproduction,[6] and economic support[7] are all highly visible matters which have prompted legal sanction and regulation. On the other hand, socialisation has the lowest legal profile. Only a handful of recent English cases[8] make express reference to the concept, often in the context of criminal behaviour which is 'explained' by the accused's poor socialisation:

> 'She [a psychologist appearing as an expert witness in a case concerning the residence of a 13 year old boy] says that ... he is manipulative, has little or no self-control, constantly displaying outbursts of uncontrollable and violent anger at his peers for slights real or imagined, but usually arising from lack of socialisation skills ...'.[9]

Judicial allusions to socialisation generally arise only in the case of those few children whose upbringing chances to attract the attention of the court. The primary focus of the law is on that minority of families which suffer formal failure (usually through divorce, more rarely through compulsory care proceedings)[10] and it plays little part in buttressing the functioning family and the parent-child relationship. It is open to question whether, were the state to take a more active role in socialisation, there would be fewer 'failed' families and 'better' parenting. However, the importance of socialisation to the state *has* been recognised in so far as education (mainly for the work-place?) has become primarily the state's responsibility. We discuss this in Chapter 11.

(c) Nature versus nurture

Heredity also plays a part in the child's development and personality, although the degree of its influence has long been a particularly controversial question:

5 Eg, the duty to consummate the marriage (failure to do so may lead to annulment under s 12(a)(b) of the Matrimonial Causes Act 1973) and to keep sexual relations exclusive within marriage (failure may lead to divorce under s 1(2)(a) of the 1973 Act).

6 Eg, the Human Fertilisation and Embryology Act 1990, which regulates aspects of assisted reproduction treatment. For a discussion of the extent to which notions of kinship and the 'normal' family underlay the debate surrounding this legislation, see M Mulkay, 'Science and Family in the Great Embryo Debate' (1994) 28 *Sociology* (3) 699.

7 Eg, the Child Support Act 1991 and s 15 and Sch 1 to the Children Act 1989 which enable assessments and orders for maintenance and other financial relief to be made in favour of children (see Ch 9).

8 See, eg, *R v Raghip, Silcott and Braithwaite* (1991) Times 9 December, CA.

9 *Re M (a Minor) (Child Abduction)* [1994] 2 FLR 126, [1994] Fam Law 366.

10 See Chs 8 and 13.

'The sperm cell carries 23 minute structures called chromosomes which it releases into the ovum where they join 23 further chromosomes .... It is these chromosomes which are the carriers of the child's heredity. Each bears somewhere around 20,000 smaller particles, complex chemical chains called genes .... The disease phenylketonuria provides an example of a genetic defect which can lead to mental retardation. The lack of a gene associated with the production of a critical enzyme leads to over-production of phenylpyruvic acid which attacks the central nervous system.... While heredity is thus known to act directly on individual biological characteristics, the evidence linking it with psychological traits is much less clear.... Like height and weight, intelligence is normally distributed in the population, and this suggests the interactive involvement of large numbers of genes.'[11]

After conception, but even before birth, it is clear that the mother can influence the development of the child *en ventre sa mère*:

'the placenta does not form a barrier against the harmful contents of the mother's bloodstream. The effect of drugs in the maternal bloodstream has been dramatically demonstrated by the birth of deformed children to mothers who used the sedative drug, thalidomide during pregnancy.... Malnutrition during pregnancy ... is ... associated with deficit in size and weight at birth. More serious is the possibility of limitation of brain development, the effects of which are irreversible. The most rapid increase in the size and number of brain cells occurs between conception and birth; six months after the child is born there is no further increase in the number of brain cells.'[12]

At birth, nurture assumes primary significance. But even where children's material needs are being met, their best interests can only be served in a home where the emotional atmosphere is one of consistent love with all that this implies in terms of a framework for socialisation. John Bowlby put forward the thesis[13] that maternal deprivation in the early years produces an affectionless personality resistant to later redemption.[14] Later researchers argued that equally significant may be *partial* maternal deprivation, arising from a low quality of mothering, despite continuous physical presence, and others queried his research sample of already-deprived children as being atypical.[15] Indeed, Bowlby himself recognised that some separation might be beneficial to the child who needs exposure to playmates and others. At the same time, Bowlby emphasised the importance of understanding the meanings which their attachments have for children if one is to understand the effects on them

11 J Radford and E Gover (eds) *A Textbook of Psychology* (1980) p 472.
12 *Ibid* at p 474.
13 In *Child Care and The Growth of Love* (1965).
14 More recently, 'reactive attachment disorder' has been 'diagnosed' in certain adopted children who have been severely emotionally deprived in earlier life and who exhibit antisocial behaviour (see *Adoption & Fostering News*, October/November 1994). It may be queried whether attaching the label to such children has any value. It is akin to labelling certain criminal offenders as 'psychopaths' and says no more than that such people are damaged or dangerous.
15 M Rutter, *Maternal Deprivation Re-Assessed* (2nd ed, 1972).

of loss of those attachments. In so doing, he counteracted the image of the child as the passive object of socialisation, and presented instead a picture of the child as participant in social relationships, through which he or she learns a cultural and social identity.[16]

The objections to Bowlby's theories were perhaps compounded by his view that fathers have little more significance for children's development than as economic providers for the family. It is now fashionable (if no more than that) to argue that full child development may also require fathers to play a more integrated role within the family, providing a role model of male behaviour for both boys and girls to learn from. The evidence that the absence of a father figure is damaging to children's development is not clear-cut, and is bound up with the issue of family poverty.[17] Most children in one-parent families are living with their mothers rather than their fathers.[18] Single mothers earn relatively little money and are much more dependent upon state benefits, whereas 'single fathers' are not only likely to have jobs – and better paid jobs – but also, since society expects them to be at work, to receive more help in their parenting role than mothers do. Single mothers, struggling with parenthood in poverty, may become isolated from the network of friends they had built up during the marriage or relationship. Whatever the true position may be, the 1985 view of Ellis Cashmore[19] that it is often preferable for a child to live with one caring parent than with one caring and one uncaring parent (particularly if the parents are constantly quarrelling), is heard less often nowadays.

This leads us to a final point; whether in a single-parent or dual-parent household, the experience of parenting and parenthood will be different for mothers and for fathers. Notwithstanding the supposed advent of the 'new father', either as primary or as equal caretaker of his children, the reality of contemporary family life in Britain is that mothers are still expected to, and do, play a much more involved part in their children's upbringing. The difference, in everyday language, between 'mothering' and 'fathering' – the former implying care, the latter implying procreation – is reflected in prevailing social arrangements, attitudes and mores,[20] and in turn in the shaping of legal rules and legal attitudes to parenthood.

---

16 We are grateful to Ursula Dobraszczyc for this perspective on Bowlby's work.
17 See generally, N Abercrombie and A Warde, *Contemporary British Society* (2nd ed, 1994) pp 299-301.
18 In 1991, just over 17% of families with dependent children were headed by a lone mother, compared with just over 1% headed by a lone father: *Social Trends 1994* p 36.
19 'Re-writing the Script', (1985) *New Society* December p 511.
20 See Ch 6. For discussion, see L McKee and M O'Brien (eds) *The Father Figure* (1982); D Richardson, *Women, Motherhood and Childrearing* (1993).

CHAPTER 2

Perspectives on the rights and duties of parenthood

1. PHILOSOPHICAL PERSPECTIVES

Having outlined sociological theories of parenthood and the family, we now turn to considering philosophical perspectives on parenthood.

The philosophical and legal significance of parenthood has generally been discussed in the context of rights. This has been criticised as eliminating the possibility of other moral bases for parenthood, or as promoting a male-centred view of what is morally significant, compared to a female-centred view of an ethic of caring as opposed to rights.[1] Such an argument may be particularly telling in the context of the differential roles that 'mothers' and 'fathers' play in our society. Further, concentration on rights does not tell us *which* 'rights' we should recognise, or why. As Eekelaar has suggested:

'Unless some prior moral principle was to stipulate otherwise, the claims of the racist or the child pornographer would become a constituent element of morality.'[2]

Nonetheless, the essence of parenthood, when translated from the moral to the legal sphere, lies in consideration of the rights and duties which may flow from the status, and so we focus upon such considerations here. Do parents, as opposed to others, have *rights* in respect of, and over their children, as well as any rights that the children themselves may enjoy, or any duties that parents may also owe?[3] This discussion is

1 M Midgley, 'Rights-talk Will Not Sort Out Child-abuse: comment on Archard on parental rights' (1991) 8 *Journal of Applied Philosophy* 103; S Moller Okin, *Justice, Gender and the Family* (1989); C Gilligan, *In a Different Voice* (1982).
2 'Parenthood, Social Engineering and Rights' in D Morgan and G Douglas (eds) *Constituting Families: A Study in Governance* (1994) 91.
3 For a full discussion of these questions, see D Archard, *Children: Rights and Childhood* (1993) especially Part III.

sometimes broadened to the more abstract question of how the parental relationship is to be characterised. Do parents in some way own or possess their children? Or are they somehow their children's trustees, and if so, are they responsible to the children, or to the state for the discharge of their trust?

(a) Rights of parenthood

(i) Children as property?[4]

In ancient Rome, the father, as paterfamilias, had the power of life and death (*jus vitae necisque*) over his children. He could sell his children into slavery, give them in marriage – and divorce them from their spouses, have them adopted or emancipate them.[5] The right to take the child's life originally extended to killing grown children for their misdeeds, but later in the Roman era, the power was reduced to that of exposure of new-born infants.

> 'Exposure was the right of the *pater* and only his. It is to be hoped that in most cases where a family could not or would not bring up another child, the father secured his wife's consent. In one famous instance, however, the foundling... who ended up as a librarian in Augustus' service, had been exposed as the result of a quarrel between his parents.'[6]

Children were, in a very real sense, the father's property, disposable as he saw fit. Such a view of parenthood would be regarded as anathema in modern Western societies, where children are, at least in some respects, regarded as persons, as individuals and worthy of protection *from* as well as *by* their parents. The idea of the child as the property of the parent appears to affront our sense of the equal worth of every person.

Why, in any case, *should* parents be regarded as having a proprietary right in the child? Is it because they created the child through an act of procreation? Is the child the fruit of their labour which they have the right to own? There are at least two difficulties with such a view. First, if the right to property in the child derives from the fact of procreation, adopters who are not biological parents could not be said to have the moral right to possess the child who, legally, is regarded as 'theirs'.[7]

---

4 Included in the term 'rights' are the various categories of rights expounded by Hohfeld, viz, rights, privileges, powers and immunities. For a valuable analysis of the 'property' view of parental rights, see J Montgomery, 'Children as Property' (1988) 51 MLR 323.

5 A Borkowski, *Textbook on Roman Law* (1994) pp 102–105.

6 J Gardner, *Women in Roman Law and Society* (1986) p 156.

7 Equally, it would have to be conceded that unmarried fathers, who lack the automatic *legal* right to possess their children, have the moral right to do so. Indeed, many would argue that this is precisely the case. See Ch 5.

Edgar Page has argued that this is not, in fact, a difficulty with the proprietary model, but an essential truth.[8] He argues that it is right to distinguish adoption from what he calls 'natural' (meaning genetic or biological) parenthood, because the latter is bound up with *both* procreation and with child-rearing. Adoptive parenthood is only *modelled* on biological parenthood – adopters can choose whether they want a particular child or not, biological parents cannot. One may query the accuracy or completeness of his explanation, since, while adopters have a choice over whether to accept a child, once they have been granted parental status, they stand in virtually the same position to the child as biological parents, and owe the same duties to the child. Furthermore, biological parents today can usually plan whether to have a child, and even where a birth is unplanned, they can always give up the child for adoption, in which there is a ready market for healthy babies. In any event, adoption is generally valued as a desirable alternative means of creating a family, and it ought therefore to be possible to find a way to regard adopters as being in an equal moral position with biological parents.

Viewing the child as one's property has been criticised by David Archard, on the basis that:

> '[i]f begetting did generate ownership, then it is hard to see why ownership should not be lifelong, how we would apportion property rights between mother and father, and how we might acknowledge the productive contribution of medical staff'.[9]

But before we recoil from Page's argument, and gratefully seize on Archard's refutation, we should pause. In many ways, the presumption of ownership, or at least possession, is at the core of the liberal conception of the family and of parenthood. Imagine that a child is born in a hospital, and is abducted from the nursery. When, a few hours, or days later, the child is found and returned to the parents, this is because he or she is regarded as 'their' child. The baby is not the child of the 'state', to be placed in a community nursery until the genitors, or perhaps others who might make better parents, are entrusted with caring for him or her. The baby is regarded as *belonging* to the parents. We are concerned here with contrasting the parents' position with that of the state, and of the importance of parenthood and family in the liberal state; we accept the moral abhorrence of viewing children as property to be fought over by the parents themselves when their relationship has broken down, most dramatically evidenced in abduction cases, as we discuss in Chapter 8. Indeed, one does not need to envisage so drastic an illustration. It is, after

8   E Page, 'Parental Rights' (1984) 1 *Journal of Applied Philosophy* 187.
9   D Archard, 'Child abuse, parental rights and the interests of the child' (1990) 7 *Journal of Applied Philosophy* 183, at 186.

all, normal for hospitals to allow the parents to take 'their' baby home once mother and child have recovered sufficiently from the birth – and it would be regarded as highly abnormal if this were not to happen.[10] As Hugh LaFollette puts it, many people think that 'parents, particularly biological parents, own or have natural sovereignty over their children'.[11] He argues that this is why the prior vetting, or licensing of those seeking to become parents is regarded as abhorrent, at least where 'natural' parenthood is concerned. We consider the vetting of non-biological would-be parents in Chapters 3 to 5.

Nor are Archard's objections insuperable. We can envisage forms of ownership or possession which may be time-limited – ownership of land may be lost through adverse possession; short-term leases may be granted. The House of Lords regarded parental rights themselves in a similar way in the *Gillick* case,[12] and the Children Act concepts of residence and contact, discussed in Chapter 8, are also concerned with sharing the time children spend with parents and other family members. The law can easily accommodate joint ownership and enjoyment of property (and does recognise and encourage multiple parental responsibility for a child under ss 2 and 3 of the Children Act 1989). The role of the midwife in delivering a child, or even the role of the geneticist in placing egg and sperm in vitro and then transferring the resulting embryo to the womb, are not creative in the same way that providing the genetic material is creative. The publishers of a book are not its authors, even though their role is vital in ensuring that it is produced. But how then, if parenthood does betoken some form of ownership or possession, can it encompass the parental status of adopters, or of others who are not the genetic parents of a child (as in the case of embryo donation)?

Page suggests one reason, although he does not see it as applying to adopters. For him, parenthood is desired for its own sake, as a 'distinctive form of activity and with a special place in human life and among our basic values'. It is a good in itself, first, because many, if not most people, wish to experience it and secondly, because:

'parenthood is a basic dimension of human existence which conditions and structures our perceptions and conceptions of ourselves and others, and thus affects all our lives whether or not we become parents'.[13]

10 Where the baby is thought to be at risk of abuse or neglect, the parents might indeed be prevented from taking the baby home , but this requires legal sanction, see Ch 13.
11 'Licensing Parents' (1980) 9 *Philosophy and Public Affairs* 182.
12 *Gillick v West Norfolk and Wisbech Area Health Authority* [1986] AC 112, eg Lord Fraser 'the father's authority [is] a dwindling right' (at 172H); Lord Scarman 'parental right yields to the child's right to make his own decisions when he reaches a sufficient understanding and intelligence to be capable of making up his own mind' (at 186D). See Ch 6.
13 'Parental Rights' (1984) 1 *Journal of Applied Philosophy* 196, 197.

Parenthood then, carries with it rights, including that of possession, because otherwise, the desirable activity of parenthood could not be protected. We could argue that, if this is so, *all* forms of parenthood valued by society, biological or not, require that protection.

Nonetheless, conceiving parenthood as a form of proprietary right feels uncomfortable. It smacks of selfishness on the part of the parents, and emphasises the inequality of children simply because they are children. In recent years, children have sometimes been regarded as the latest fashion accessory for upwardly mobile young couples, but this is not a new development:

'The Edwardian socialite, Mrs Willie James, setting out for church, would ask their Nanny which of her five children would go best with her dress.'[14]

Yet having children *is* a 'selfish' activity. It is usually very difficult for people to explain, still less to *justify*, why they have become, or wish to become, parents. Archard dismisses as worthless the following possible reasons, some demonstrably selfish, others not:

'to bring about a life that avoids the errors of its begetter, to create a companion and an assistant for one's dotage, to add another soldier to the army of the motherland or another true believer to the ranks of the faithful, to prove it can be done, to spite another adult'.[15]

He fails, however, to consider others which might be more acceptable. For example, in many cultures, the desire for an heir to carry on the family name, or to *support* the parents in their old age would be regarded as highly praiseworthy. At one time, it might have been thought that having a child would 'cement' a marriage. Such reasons would, however, be criticised as infringing Kant's principle that people should be seen and valued as ends in themselves. Perhaps instead, the desire to have a child upon whom to bestow one's love (and one's wealth) might be seen as not unreasonable.[16]

(ii) Children in trust?

While the ancient Romans may have adopted a proprietary view of children, this was not the universal position in ancient civilisations. The Stoics took what might be seen as a more modern approach, although their non-proprietary model was directed towards encouraging a healthy detachment from affection which would not sit well with the modern Western emphasis on emotionally committed and lifelong relationships:

'if you kiss your child, ... remind yourself that the object of your love is mortal; it is not one of your possessions; it has been given to you for the present, not

14 M Abbott, *Family Ties: English Families 1540-1920* (1993) p 63.
15 D Archard, *Children: Rights and Childhood* (1993) p 105.
16 Archard himself seems to think this would merit protection, *ibid* at p 188.

inseparably nor for ever, but like a fig, or a cluster of grapes, at a fixed season of the year ...'.[17]

An alternative justification for granting rights to parents, which recognises this reality of temporary possession only, would be to argue that, either as a matter of fact, or, more likely, as a matter of social preference, we regard parents as *presumptively* best placed to bring up children they have produced (usually, these days, deliberately), or, in the case of adopters, children they have voluntarily agreed to care for. They have the motivation, or they have the close natural bond of affection, to do what is best for the child. The difficulty here is that we know, from daily reports in the media, that parents frequently fail to bring up their children adequately, so that the presumption, or intuition, is not borne out in practice. We then have to qualify parental rights by insisting that they cannot be exercised in such a way as irreparably to damage the child's development, since this would infringe the *child's* rights.[18] This brings us to the main modern justification for the rights of parenthood; that they exist *in order*, and only so far, that children can be protected and nurtured until they reach independence and adulthood.[19] In fact, this is not a particularly novel view, dating back at least to Locke:

'The power then, that parents have over their children, arises from that duty which is incumbent on them, to take care of their off-spring, during the imperfect state of childhood. To inform the mind, and govern the actions of their yet ignorant nonage, till reason shall take its place, and ease them of that trouble, is what the children want, and the parents are bound to.'[20]

On this reasoning, parents have no interest inherent to themselves which parental rights serve to protect. At this point, parental rights seem to turn into duties, to be exercised only in the interests of the child and not in order to fulfil parents' own desires or claims. John Eekelaar has analysed legal parental rights precisely in terms of, among others, 'duty-rights',[1] and Alexander McCall Smith has argued that parental rights fall into those which are child-centred and those which are parent-centred, the former having as their purpose the advancement of the child's welfare.[2]

17 Epictetus, quoted by B Almond, 'Human Bonds' (1988) 5 *Journal of Applied Philosophy* 3 at 5–6.
18 J Bigelow *et al*, 'Parental Autonomy' (1988) 5 *Journal of Applied Philosophy* 183.
19 The *Gillick* case again illustrates this reasoning: eg Lord Fraser, 'parental rights to control a child do not exist for the benefit of the parent. They exist for the benefit of the child and they are justified only in so far as they enable the parent to perform his duties towards the child' (at 170D).
20 *Second Treatise of Civil Government* para 58 in P Laslett (ed) *Two Treatises of Government* (1963).
 1 'What are Parental Rights?' (1973) 89 LQR 210.
 2 'Is Anything Left of Parental Rights?' in E Sutherland and A McCall Smith (eds) *Family Rights: Family Law and Medical Advance* (1990).

Such analyses suggest that parenthood should be seen as a form of trust, and a number of writers have advocated this view. It has the benefit of appearing to recognise the child's personhood, and need for protection. It places the child at the centre of our attention.

The most sophisticated treatment of this argument is that presented by Connie Beck *et al*.[3] Using the trust as a model or analogy, they argue that the corpus of the trust would be the body of rights which are or should be ascribed to the child, to be held by the parents or the state until the child develops the full rational powers of an adult. The parents or state, as trustees, are to be seen as responsible both *for* and *to* the child for decisions taken during the child's minority. Such decisions must be taken solely in the interests of the child as beneficiary.

Adopting a similar approach, Dingwall, Eekelaar and Murray have argued that just as trustees have rights over property which they must use in the interests of the beneficiaries, so parents have rights which they must use to promote the object of their trust, in this case, the promotion of the child's welfare.[4] (It will be seen that the emphasis in this account is on the child's welfare rather than on his or her *rights*.) Katherine O'Donovan has put forward yet a further variant of the argument. She notes that legal acknowledgement of the violation of the 'trust' already exists through the possibility of invoking the criminal law or civil actions for damages against parents for harm they have caused to their children, and suggests that the idea of a trust 'is attractive, if only because it expresses our cultural attitude to children as priceless'.[5] We will also see in later chapters that the trust model is implicit in the modern legal statements of parental rights, both in case law and statute.

But again, before we become over-enthusiastic, three difficulties of the trust concept should be noted. First, concentration on the welfare of the beneficiary may lead to an emphasis on the quality of parenting which our society might find contrary to its ideas of freedom. Not everyone is deemed qualified to act as a trustee of property, and their trusteeship can be removed. Is the same to be true of parenthood? Will Kymlicka argues that 'the parental trust principle is an extremely strong principle which is hard to contain, and most liberals... have invoked it rather selectively.' It leads 'to an Orwellian world of parental licences and judicial restrictions'.[6] If we think about the ways in which the powers of trustees are hedged around with limitations and safeguards for the beneficiaries, it is not obvious that we would wish to treat parenthood similarly. We

3   C Beck, G Glavis, S Glover, M Barnes Jenkins and R Nardi, 'The Rights of Children: A Trust Model' (1978) 46 *Fordham LR* 669.
4   R Dingwall, J Eekelaar and T Murray, *The Protection of Children: State Intervention and Family Life* (1983) p 224.
5   *Family Law Matters* (1993) pp 103–105. See also Ch 7.
6   'Rethinking the Family' (1991) 20 *Philosophy and Public Affairs* 77 at 91.

will see in Chapters 3 and 4 that the acquisition of parental legal status is generally *not* dependent upon proof of parental fitness, although it is true that once biological parenthood is abandoned as the criterion for legal status, there are increasing attempts by the state to scrutinise the abilities of those who seek parenthood.

Secondly, the trust metaphor may be incoherent. Who is the object, who the settlor, and who the beneficiary? Beck *et al* argue that the state is the settlor, but it is not obvious that democracies would accept children as being at the disposal of the state which this analogy implies. Are the parents trustees for the state, which has an interest in the child who is, or will become, a citizen? Or are they trustees for the child, and if the latter, can the child be the creator of a trust to benefit him or herself? Is the child the beneficiary, or the property which is the subject of the trust? Can the child be both? Perhaps it is unnecessary to become so over-refined. It may be enough to argue, as O'Donovan does, that utilising the trust concept serves to encourage us to view the parent-child relationship in a different, less proprietary way.[7]

But thirdly, and perhaps most awkwardly, the trust concept ignores a category of parental rights which need not be based on the child's interests or welfare. The right to possession is one of these, for we noted above that there might be many people who could make a better job of bringing up a child than the parents. Eekelaar argues that the parents' presumptive right of possession is grounded in a *social* choice, and does not follow from biological parenthood as a fact of nature, any more than, until the nineteenth century, the rule of custody of children applied by the courts favouring fathers over mothers was a natural inevitability.[8] While we agree with him that the social context will determine the extent to which *legal* rules favour parents' rights, we doubt his view that there is no innate moral basis for those rights. His argument would suggest that, if a totalitarian (or entirely democratic) regime required all women to give birth in maternity hospitals, from which all babies would be removed to state nurseries or re-allocated to more deserving or fit carers, the birth parents would have no moral justification to argue for their return. This would scarcely be a new idea; Plato advocated it as the best means of ensuring that his ideal city was peopled by those who would identify their own interests with everyone else's:

'As the children are born, officials appointed for the purpose ... will take them....
The children of good parents they will take to a rearing pen in the care of nurses

7   William Ruddick adopts a similar view of the value of the trust model; see 'Parents and Life Prospects' in O'Neill and Ruddick (eds) *Having Children: Philosophical and Legal Reflections on Parenthood* (1979).
8   'Parenthood, Social Engineering and Rights' in D Morgan and G Douglas (eds) *Constituting Families: A Study in Governance* (1994) at pp 92–93.

living apart in a certain section of the city; the children of inferior parents, or any child of the others born defective, they will hide, as is fitting, in a secret and unknown place.... The nurses will also see to it that the mothers are brought to the rearing pen when their breasts have milk, but take every precaution that no mother shall know her own child...'.[9]

McCall Smith's analysis, by contrast, recognises a residual space for 'parent-centred' rights. He argues that these cluster around the parents' interest in moulding a child in the way that they wish. This certainly explains why, as we discuss later in this book, parents are given legal rights to determine the education and religious upbringing that their children will have, with, in the latter case, virtually no possibility for the state to assert that the parents may be damaging the child's emotional or psychological development.[10] On the other hand, education is the area where, in many ways, parents have been left with the *least* scope for autonomy, because although the family is the primary site of socialisation, educating the future workforce and citizenry is deemed too important to be left to individual initiative.

A further difficulty of McCall Smith's scheme is that it is not clear why certain rights should be regarded as parent rather than child-centred,[11] or why moulding the child's personality should be regarded as acceptable as the moral basis for a parent-centred right. (This takes us back to the initial caveat we entered in discussing parenthood in terms of rights in the absence of an expressed prior moral principle.) Why *should* parents have the moral right to bring up a child within, say, a religious tradition which might teach exclusivity and intolerance of other beliefs? Almond argues that one reason might be because this limits the power of the state to indoctrinate and curtail cultural and religious autonomy,[12] which brings us close to a view, favoured in particular by the Right, of the family as a bastion of freedom against the otherwise overweening power of the state.[13] Another argument, that parents have the right to shape the child because they produced the child, brings us back to the proprietary model we outlined above.

9 Plato, *The Republic* Book V 460b-d (trans G M A Grube: 1981). Similar attempts at communal upbringing have taken place, inspired by Marxist theory, in Israeli kibbutzim for example, as discussed in Ch 1.

10 For an American perspective drawing out a similar theme, see B Bennett Woodhouse, '"Who Owns The Child?" *Meyer* and *Pierce* and the Child as Property' (1992) 33 *William and Mary Law Review* 996. Parental *responsibility* for the child's crimes may be traced to the same rationale.

11 Andrew Bainham notes the difficulty of categorising the two; *Children – The Modern Law* (1993) p 104, n 153.

12 'Parenthood – Social Construct or Fact of Nature?' in D Morgan and G Douglas (eds) *Constituting Families: A Study in Governance* (1994) p 105.

13 F Mount, *The Subversive Family* (1982) is a good example, Such views are explored further in Ch 10.

We suggest that there are elements in both these arguments which are of value. Whereas Page emphasises the procreative aspect of parenthood, we regard the rearing task as more fundamental. It is the extent to which a child develops into a happy, well-adjusted adult who has the opportunities to experience the goods of life, and to fulfil his or her potential, which is important to the child (and to society) and by which parents are judged. People who *accept* the role of parenthood, either through their procreation of a child, or through their demonstrated intention to act as social parents, (eg, by going through the procedures to adopt) have a moral right to the child as an aspect of their freedom, not from state interference in families, but to take on a project of human development which society values and must therefore respect.[14]

Recognising a residual category of parent-centred rights also makes it possible to draw a distinction between two situations where parental rights might be in issue. Parents may argue that they have rights to determine what is to happen to a child, regardless of the child's own views on the matter; the primary example in the English case law is the *Gillick* case – the question of whether parents had a right to veto a child's consent to be prescribed contraceptives. The issue here is whether parents should be able to assert their own interests and ideas over those of the child him or herself. The second situation is where parents take a view of what should happen to a child, or act towards a child in a way which is different from that regarded as acceptable by the state (in the guise of a variety of organs, including education authorities, social services departments and medical services). For example, parents may decline medical treatment for a child because of religious beliefs, or refuse to force a reluctant child to attend school . Here, the issue is whether the parents have rights, as parents, to take such steps or whether the state has a sufficient interest in the child to override them. It might be desirable to argue that in the first situation, once the child has reached maturity, the parents should not be able to assert their own views of how the child should continue to develop – it is for the child now to do so. But in the second case, the residual interest that parents in a free society have in bringing up a child who reflects *their* cultural, spiritual and philosophical values may point to a continuing right, provided that the child is not harmed thereby, to assert that interest in the face of the state's objection.

In summary, we argue that parents possess moral rights in respect of their children, which, while certainly in large part justifiable as existing in order to enable parents to fulfil their duties and obligations to the child, go beyond this and may vindicate a claim or interest which is separate

14 A similar argument, which goes on to suggest that such parental autonomy cannot take priority over the child's interests, is developed by J Bigelow *et al* 'Parental Autonomy' (1988) 5 *Journal of Applied Philosophy* 183.

from those of the child, whether derived from a proprietary notion of the child, or from an argument based on freedom. To this extent, parenthood is more than, or different from, both ownership and trusteeship.

(b) Duties of parenthood

From the above discussion, it would seem self-evident that parents owe moral duties to their children to safeguard and promote their welfare. But this still needs independent justification. Why should parents, as opposed to other adults, or even other blood relatives, owe duties to children if, as many have argued, the *mere* fact of procreation is not generally regarded as an adequate moral basis for giving them *rights* in respect of children? We have argued, above, of course, that procreation *as evidence of the acceptance of the nurturing role* rather than *per se* is sufficient to ground rights. It should be noted, however, that mere procreation *is* regarded as an adequate *legal* basis for imposing duties of a financial nature – the social security system, and the Child Support Act 1991 are predicated upon the assumption that those who produce must support (unless the child is adopted or the offspring of gamete donors); see Chapter 9.

John Eekelaar[15] suggests that there are two sources which combine to establish the moral basis for parental duty. The first is an *a priori* duty to promote human flourishing, which exists independently of the actual organisation of any society. But this duty applies to everyone, and not just to parents. The fixing of the duty in particular upon parents depends upon society's decision to allocate the responsibility in that way. Thus, there may be cultures where all members of the tribe assume a responsibility to bring up children, or where uncles assume the role which in our society is allocated to biological fathers (or, in a significant number of cases, to step-parents who adopt). Eekelaar's argument helps explain why gamete donors may have no (legal) duty to support their biological offspring – society, through legislation, has relieved them of that duty because it chooses to impose it upon those who have indicated their intention to assume the task of bringing up the child – the social parents. This appears convincing, but it ignores the meaning that any society may attach to parenthood itself. It may be true that other cultures allocate the duty to care for children differently from our own – but this may be because they allocate *parenthood* itself differently. In other words, it is not that they do not regard *parents* as bound to care for their children, but that they do not regard, for example, biological fathers, as *parents* in the first place. On this basis, social decisions may determine

15 'Are Parents Morally Obliged to Care for their Children?' (1991) 11 OJLS 51.

who are parents, but the duty flowing from that decision may derive from a moral, not social imperative.

We would argue that the key to the moral basis of parental obligation lies in recognition of the significance of the acceptance of the social role of parenthood. Parents can, contrary to Edgar Page's opinion noted above, choose whether they wish to continue to fulfil their parental role as *carers* for their children, and it is the duty to care with which we are concerned. Parents can give up their children for adoption (or, in certain instances, abort them before birth). Non-biological parents can acquire parental status through adoption – a form of accepting their duties to their children. In the same way that we suggested parental rights may be justified as supporting parents' freedom to take on the valued role of parenthood, we suggest that the moral basis for parental duty lies in this voluntary acceptance.

What of the unwilling genetic parent? For example, the woman who is raped and does not wish to bring up the child produced as a result? She may have a conscientious objection to abortion and therefore go through with the birth. We would argue that she is *not* under a moral duty to care for the child as a *parent*.[16] However, in the same way that a passer-by who finds an abandoned baby in a telephone box would be morally obliged to take the child to shelter, so the rape victim is morally obliged to do what is necessary to ensure that the child is cared for. What of the man who has intercourse with a woman who falsely assures him that she is taking contraceptive precautions? There is a world of moral difference between forced and voluntary sexual intercourse, and it can be argued that, in having such voluntary intercourse, he cannot morally divest himself of his responsibility to the child, society and the woman, in his acceptance of the possibility, however remote, of procreation, on the assurance of the woman.

There is a further aspect of parental duty which we need to consider. There are limitations on the extent to which the parental duty to the child's welfare predominates over parents' individual interests and claims. Parents' own autonomy interests permit them to perform acts which may in fact damage their children's development. It is here that Eekelaar's emphasis on social choice determining attitudes resonates particularly loudly. The best example is of separation and divorce. Parents are regarded, in Western society at least, as morally free to choose to separate from each other, regardless of the emotional and other harm which this might cause to their children. The individual's interest in self-fulfilment, or in sheer physical protection, takes priority over the

16 At present in English law, it is the rapist who, if unmarried, lacks parental responsibility (though he does have the liability to support), rather than the mother; see Ch 5.

desirability of preserving the family unit for the children. Perhaps only a few years ago, this would not have been the case.

In recognising this acceptance, it is important to note that society is far more tolerant of men's desires for self-fulfilment than of women's. Social concern about the 'latch-key' children of the 1960s and 1970s, whose mothers were at work instead of at home when they returned from school, has been replaced by media panics about the 'home alone' children of the 1990s, whose parents leave them to go off on holiday, or to work, or to the pub. Of course, there is anxiety at children being left with no one at all to care for them in such situations. But the bulk of criticism is still directed at the mothers rather than the fathers. It is clear from this example that, in *social* terms, *mothers* are not regarded as having the same freedom as *fathers*. It is *socially* more difficult for a mother to leave her children than for a father to walk out, not just because of the financial implications for women, but because an absent mother is regarded as more fundamentally having failed in her obligations than an absent father. We trace in Chapter 9 the equation between absence and financial obligation. Until recently, fathers' duties to children have been seen primarily in financial terms, whether they are present in the home or not, while mothers have been expected to take a much wider responsibility for their children's well-being. We do not see how *morally* this can be justified. The decision as to which parent is under an obligation to fulfil which parental task 'has traditionally not been a matter of reasonable argument, but of little more than social prejudice'.[17]

Parents then, have moral duties to their children, deriving from their intention to act as parents, when demonstrated by their *assumption* of the role of parenthood. We next consider the children's rights debate before considering how far the rights and duties of parenthood have been identified and sanctioned in international law, as natural, or human rights and duties.

2. PARENTING AND CHILD-RIGHTS THEORY

In recent years, there has been an enormous outpouring of discussion concerning whether children can be said to have, or ought to have, rights. Ascribing rights to children is problematic because doing so must involve someone, parents and/or others, in co-relative burdens and enforcement. There is also the major question whether it is justifiable to give children rights which might be exercised in ways inimical to their

17 V Held, 'The Equal Obligations of Mothers and Fathers' in O'Neill and Ruddick (eds) *Having Children: Philosophical and Legal Reflections on Parenthood* (1979) p 232; see Ch 6.

welfare. The debate has been well-summarised in other works,[18] and since the focus of our interest is on the position of parents rather than children, we consider the issue of children's rights only briefly here in order to put our broader discussion into perspective.

Both Neil MacCormick and John Eekelaar have noted the difficulty of applying the 'will theory' of rights to children. The will theory sees the rights-holder as able to choose to enforce or waive the right. This is in opposition to the 'interest theory' which focuses upon protection of the holder's interests rather than choices. An infant or even an older child may be incapable of consciously choosing a course of action, of expressing that choice, or of exercising what others may objectively regard as a sensible or desirable choice. MacCormick[19] therefore concludes that such a child can have rights only on the basis of the protection of the child's interests, such as in being cared for and reared. Having identified this basis of a child's rights, he concludes that parents (or others, not always easily ascertainable) have a corresponding duty towards their children.

John Eekelaar has added to this analysis by seeking to categorise the interests which children may have which would form the basis of their rights. He argues that to do this, one should consider what the child, having reached adulthood, would have wanted to happen to him or her while a child. This enables one to distinguish between the child's interests, and those of the parents. He identifies three categories of such interests which a child, now adult, would have wished to have: 'basic' interests, or those necessary for the nurture of the child, and primarily laid at the parental door or the state in lieu; 'developmental' interests, concerned with maximising one's potential, sustainable against the wider community but probably not classifiable as legal rights, but rather moral rights; both of these could be seen as 'welfare' interests of the child. Finally, he identifies an 'autonomy' interest, or the freedom to choose a course of action.[20] The last of these might conflict with the child's developmental or basic interests, and would have to yield to these. More recently, Eekelaar has argued that one could reconcile welfare interests with greater recognition of the child's autonomy by allowing scope for what he terms 'dynamic self-determinism' – or encouraging the child to draw on a wide range of influences as he or she matures which can then enable the child to make rational contributions to decision-making about his or her life.[1] However, since Eekelaar does

18 See, eg, A Bainham, *Children: The Modern Law* (1993) pp 76-94.
19 N MacCormick, 'Children's Rights: A Test-Case for Theories of Right' (1976) 62 *Archiv fur Rechts und Sozialphilosophie* 305.
20 J Eekelaar, 'The Emergence of Children's Rights' (1986) 6 OJLS 161.
 1 J Eekelaar, 'The Interests of the Child and the Child's Wishes: The Role of Dynamic Self-Determinism' (1994) 8 *International Journal of Law and the Family* 42.

not equate such self-determinism with delegating decision-making to the child, even where the child is legally competent to make the decision (a test which we discuss in Chapter 6), his reconciliation of welfare and autonomy is arguably little more than a plea to parents and others to 'remember the child' for whom they take responsibility.

Eekelaar's categorisation of interests was influenced by an earlier discussion by Michael Freeman.[2] The latter's list of children's rights contains four groups: to welfare; to protection; to be treated like adults; and rights against parents. His basket of welfare rights includes entitlement to what might be called identity, for example name and nationality, and carries on to embrace freedom against racial and other forms of discrimination; and the right to social security, incorporating nutrition, housing and care. Such rights are social manifesto rights which permit of societal differences in application. Secondly, protective rights include protection from abuse or neglect from parents or from others. The third and fourth categories move away from concentration upon welfare towards autonomy. So far as the right to be treated like adults is concerned, his starting point, echoing the approach of the United States Supreme Court in *Re Gault*[3] is that children, in sharing personhood, share with adults an entitlement to a measure of common legal treatment. But in deciding the extent of that measure, the child's capability to take decisions like an adult would have to be weighed on a case-by-case basis. Freeman reaches this conclusion as a means of relieving the tension between the reality of the growth in children's abilities and the danger of a blanket legal incapacity which balks those children who can reach sound decisions about themselves, by themselves.

So yet again, the debate touches the everyday dilemma of whether children should be allowed to do what they want or whether parents, or others, should decide. Freeman's final cohort of rights, those against parents, brings this possible four-way tension into even sharper relief. Interestingly, he does not confront the matter by way of the comparative seriousness of the particular conflict – we might give the example of when the younger child should go to bed, as opposed to with whom the older should go to bed – but instead by whether the child should be able to act independently as of right, or only by successful appeal against parental refusal,[4] perhaps to a court. His approach is first, that where parents and child are in accord, then no problem arises. (But we might note that the state may have its own independent interest in what happens to the child, regardless of parent-child harmony, for example, where the child refuses medical treatment because he or she has been brought up as

2 See generally, *The Rights and Wrongs of Children* (1983).
3 87 S Ct 1428 (1967).
4 See Ch 7.

a Jehovah's Witness.) Freeman proceeds to argue that disagreement between parents and child may indicate that the parent has ceased to represent the child's interests. Where there is such disagreement, he would uphold the parental view provided that it is at least consistent with a neutral view of Rawls' 'primary social goods', ie the objectives such as good health which it would be perverse not to want to pursue. If not so consistent, Freeman concludes, then 'representativeness' ceases, and intervention on behalf of the child is justified.

Such analyses of children's rights clearly continue to give greater weight to children's objective welfare interests than t o their autonomy, and in so doing, maintain the real focus of attention upon who will be called upon to safeguard those interests – parents, others or the state? We now consider how far this question has been addressed in international law.

3. INTERNATIONAL HUMAN RIGHTS AND DUTIES OF PARENTHOOD

The developing collection of international statements of rights to be claimed and respected is beginning to provide a new dimension to the consideration of legal norms regulating family relationships. Several such rights may be better seen as 'manifesto' rights which set out aspirations to shape the conduct of governments in the long term. Indeed, within international law discourse itself there is a clear distinction drawn between, on the one hand, civil and political rights which may, in theory at least, be claimed immediately, and on the other, social, economic and cultural rights which are dependent upon the available resources of individual states for their implementation.[5] The value of international conventions may lie not so much in their immediate effect upon the quality of people's lives as in their potential to influence thinking in all the organs of a state and to bring about changes which may enhance future lives.

There are, furthermore, various kinds of international conventions. At one level, there are multilateral agreements intended to harmonise laws and practices and to provide mechanisms whereby international families can be adequately protected regardless of borders.[6] Into this category fall

---

5 For the difficulties of implementing these different types of rights, see D McGoldrick, 'The United Nations Convention on the Rights of the Child' (1991) 5 *International Journal of Law and the Family* 132 at p 138.
6 For an indication of the range of such measures simply within one region – Europe – see M Killerby, 'The Council of Europe's Contribution to Family Law' in Lowe and Douglas (eds) *Families across Frontiers* (forthcoming).

agreements such as the two Conventions on international child abduction, and the Hague Convention on Inter-Country Adoption, drafted in 1993.[7] These are directly applicable (once enacted into domestic law) to disputes relating to children. They reflect the agreed views of individual states on how such disputes should be handled and states will generally only become signatories if they are prepared to implement the detailed provisions required to make the mechanisms effective. At the next level up, as it were, are international conventions which state broader aspirations, but which do contain an enforcement mechanism. For example, the United Nations International Covenant on Civil and Political Rights is supervised by the Human Rights Committee to which individuals may complain about alleged violations of their human rights and freedoms protected by the Covenant, where the states concerned have accepted an Optional Protocol.[8] If the Committee finds a complaint (called a 'communication') well-founded, states must amend their laws to bring them into line with their obligations under the Covenant.

(a) Parents and the European Convention on Human Rights

For the United Kingdom, the key instrument of this type is the European Convention for the Protection of Human Rights and Fundamental Freedoms.[9] Although this has not been incorporated into domestic law, findings by the European Commission or European Court of Human Rights that the United Kingdom's laws are in breach of the terms of the Convention have prompted legislative changes and have also begun to influence judicial approaches to issues concerning the family.[10] The Convention guarantees certain fundamental human rights, some of

---

7 On the workings of the Hague Convention on Civil Aspects of International Child Abduction and the European Convention on Recognition and Enforcement of Decisions Concerning Custody of Children, see G Van Bueren, *The Best Interests of the Child – International Co-Operation on Child Abduction* (1993) and Ch 8 below. On inter-country adoption, see Department of Health, Welsh Office, Home Office and Lord Chancellor's Department, *Adoption: The Future* (1993) Cm 2288, Ch VI.

8 For a discussion of the Human Rights Committee's work, see D McGoldrick, *The Human Rights Committee: Its Role in the Development of the International Covenant on Civil and Political Rights* (1991).

9 Discussed by G Douglas, 'The Family and the State under the European Convention on Human Rights' (1988) 2 *International Journal of Law and the Family* 76; L Smith, 'Children, Parents and the European Human Rights Convention' in J Eekelaar and P Sarcevic (eds) *Parenthood in Modern Society* (1993); K O'Donnell, 'Parent-Child Relationships within the European Convention on Human Rights' in Lowe and Douglas (eds) *Families across Frontiers* (forthcoming).

10 See, eg, Child Care Act 1980, Pt 1A; Education (No 2) Act 1986; *Re KD (a minor) (ward: termination of access)* [1988] AC 806.

which have a bearing on the regulation of families by the state. There are three provisions of clear relevance to parenthood; Article 8 provides:

'(1) Everyone has the right to respect for his private and family life, his home and his correspondence.
(2) There shall be no interference by a public authority with the exercise of this right except such as is in accordance with the law and is necessary in a democratic society in the interests of national security, public safety or the economic well-being of the country, for the prevention of disorder or crime, for the protection of health or morals, or for the protection of the rights and freedoms of others.'

Article 12 provides:

'Men and women of marriageable age have the right to marry and to found a family, according to the national laws governing the exercise of this right.'

Article 2 of the First Protocol to the Convention provides:

'No person shall be denied the right to education. In the exercise of any functions which it assumes in relation to education and to teaching, the State shall respect the right of parents to ensure such education and teaching in conformity with their own religious and philosophical convictions.'

There is no definition of 'family' in the Convention, and there was little discussion of its meaning when the Convention was being drafted. It is therefore uncertain how wide a family grouping is intended to be encompassed. It appears from the jurisprudence that a rather conservative and traditional view of what constitutes a family has been adopted by the Commission and Court, although there is a trend to greater liberalism as diverse family forms receive increasing recognition in the individual member states (see below). Article 8 has been held to include a nuclear family formed outside marriage,[11] and to protect the ties between grandparents and their grandchildren.[12] However, the relationship between foster-parent and child has been held to be protected by the right to respect for her private rather than family life.[13]

It is also unclear what family 'life' is intended to mean. Biological ties of themselves have been deemed insufficient to establish a 'family life'. In *G v Netherlands*,[14] the European Commission upheld Dutch courts holding that a man who acted as sperm donor for a lesbian couple, and who had had contact with his daughter when she was first born had no family life with her. The mere fact that he was the biological father was inadequate, and his position was in no way analogous to that of a married father. Such an approach is compatible with the moral justification for parental rights which we suggested above – that it is the assumption of

11 *Marckx v Belgium* Series A, Vol 31 (1979–80) 2 EHRR 330; *Johnston v Ireland* Series A, Vol 112 (1987) 9 EHRR 203.
12 *Marckx* (above); *Price v United Kingdom, Application No 12402/86* 55 D & R 224.
13 *Application No 8257/78* 13 D & R 248.
14 (1993) 16 EHRR Part 7, CD 38.

the parental role which is significant. It would appear that for protection under the Convention there needs to be a form of caring or dependence between family members – in the *Nielsen Case*, the European Court stated that:

> 'family life in the Contracting States encompasses a broad range of parental rights and responsibilities ... The care and upbringing of children normally and necessarily require that the parents or an only parent decide where the child must reside and also impose, or authorise others to impose, various restrictions on the child's liberty ... the exercise of parental rights constitutes a fundamental element of family life'.[15]

Although relatives other than parents may have a family life with children, the Commission has considered that they are not entitled to the same degree of involvement in the child's life. Hence, in *Price v United Kingdom*,[16] the Commission considered that access by grandparents to a child would normally be at the parents' discretion, and when a child was in care, the authorities would not be required to consult or involve grandparents in their decision-making in the same way that they would the parents. Such cases suggest a prioritisation of certain family relationships over others based on a traditional nuclear model of family life.

As regards the right to found a family, guaranteed under Article 12, it has been accepted by the European Commission that adoption of children is covered, as well as 'natural' procreation. However, the right is subject to national laws, and hence, a law prohibiting adoption by an unmarried person, for example, does not breach the Convention.[17] It is open to doubt whether a right to procreation through assisted reproduction would yet be held to be protected under the Convention, given the wide variation in what is regarded as acceptable in the different member states.[18]

John Eekelaar and Robert Dingwall have argued that the main thrust of concern in upholding the right to respect for family life has been on the parents', rather than the children's right.[19] A similar emphasis is particularly apparent in the formulation and interpretation of the right to education in Protocol 1. Most famously, perhaps, the European Court held that suspending pupils from school because their parents refused to let them be subject to corporal punishment was an infringement not only of the children's right to education under the Protocol, but also of the parents' right to ensure that the education their children received was in conformity with their religious and philosophical convictions.[20] The provision

---

15   Series A, Vol 144, para 61 (1988) 11 EHRR 175.
16   55 D & R 224.
17   *Application No 6482/72* 7 D & R 75.
18   See G Douglas, *Law, Fertility and Reproduction* (1991) pp 21-24 for a discussion of this issue.
19   *Human Rights, Report to the Council of Europe* (1987) pp 17 and 21.
20   *Campbell and Cosans v United Kingdom*, Series A, Vol 48 (1982) 4 EHRR 293.

demonstrates the weight placed upon the moral right of parents which we discussed above to shape their children's upbringing and very identities; the Protocol was intended after all to prevent political indoctrination of children by the state. At the same time, the European Commission and Court have been alive to the resource implications of upholding *positive* rights to educational facilities. Thus, in an early Court decision, the *Belgian Linguistics Case (No 2)*,[1] it was held that, so long as no discrimination is practised, a state is not required to respect the preference of parents for children to be taught in a particular language, for example, their language of ethnic origin. Parents desiring such teaching may always choose to have their children educated privately.

In the United Kingdom, aspects of the powers of the state to remove children from their parents because of perceived risk to the children's welfare were altered pursuant to the European Court finding that there were breaches of the parents' rights under both Article 8, and under Article 6 which guarantees a right to a fair trial in the determination of one's civil rights. In condemning restrictions upon parents being able to visit their children in local authority care, and to challenge administrative decisions taken by local authorities to assume parental rights over the children and to determine what was to happen to them, the European Court could be seen as reasserting an emphasis on the quasi-proprietary right of parents to possess their children, or, at least, to sustain a relationship with them, which had appeared to have become downgraded by the English courts.[2] In so doing, the European Court has recognised a claim to compensation for the emotional harm suffered by parents as a result of losing their children, which the English courts have rejected. In *F v Wirral Metropolitan Borough Council*,[3] on facts very similar to those in the European Court cases, the Court of Appeal held that parents have no right of action for damages arising out of any interference with their rights to their children. The Court of Appeal considered that, in so far as any parental right had been recognised in the case law, it

'stems from the parental duty towards the child to care for and protect the child, and is subservient to the welfare of the child. It does not give any rights beyond this in favour of the parent *qua* parent upon which a right of action in damages against an interfering stranger could be founded'.[4]

The European organs appear to have been more ready to give weight to parents' interests, while at the same time accepting, through the operation of Article 8(2), that parental rights will have to yield to the

1 Series A, Vol 6, (1968) 1 EHRR 252.
2 *H and O v United Kingdom, B, R and W v United Kingdom* Series A, Vols 120, 121, (1987) 10 EHRR 29, 74, 82, 87, 95.
3 [1991] 2 Fam 69. See also *McMichael v United Kingdom* (1995) Times, 2 March; compensation awarded by European Court to Scottish parents denied access to reports concerning their child's being placed for adoption.
4 At 135E.

child's needs. This approach has continued in a number of cases involving Swedish laws relating to removal of children from their parents, where the Court has criticised the adequacy of the laws and practices under which state authorities have operated, but has not criticised the *merits* of their original decisions to remove children or to restrict contact.[5] However, more recently, a greater recognition of the child's position and views can be detected, and interestingly, this appears to derive from a children's *rights* as well as welfare perspective. In *Olssen v Sweden (No 2)*,[6] the Court noted that the children, who had been removed from the parents some years earlier, did not want much contact with them now, and certainly had no wish to return to them from their foster-parents. The Swedish Government, which had already been found in breach of Article 8 for its earlier procedural mishandling of the case,[7] argued that it would have been incompatible with the children's rights under the United Nations Convention on the Rights of the Child to have required them to have greater contact with the parents. The Court did not directly address this point, but did note the need for national authorities to strike a balance between the parents' and the child's interests and rights. This appears to be the first time that the Court has directly considered children's rights in contradistinction to those of the parents. In other judgments, it has either focused upon the parents' rights only, or has regarded children's rights as effectively the same as those of the parents. Ironically, three dissenting judges also relied upon the United Nations Convention, but to bolster their view that the parents' 'most sacred rights' to their children had been infringed by the authorities' dilatoriness in not rehabilitating the children.[8]

(b) Parents and the United Nations Convention on the Rights of the Child

If the United Nations Convention can be used to assert both children's and parents' rights it therefore becomes important to examine its terms. It falls into a third category of international instruments. These, of less direct effect, but of potentially equal long-term significance, are international conventions which do not contain an enforcement mechanism which can be invoked by individuals,[9] but which set out the rights which

---

5 *Eriksson v Sweden* (1989) 12 EHRR 183; *Andersson v Sweden* (1992) 14 EHRR 615; *Nyberg v Sweden* (1992) 14 EHRR 870 (European Commission).
6 (1994) 17 EHRR 134.
7 *Olssen v Sweden* (1988) 11 EHRR 259.
8 Para 90 and p 191.
9 The United Nations Convention on the Rights of the Child, however, provides an indirect compliance mechanism, by requiring signatories to submit to a Committee

states signatories must endeavour to respect through their own internal laws and practices. They may be of limited regional scope, such as the European Convention on the Legal Status of Children Born out of Wedlock, intended to minimise the discrimination suffered by children whose parents are not married. They may also have a potentially world-wide impact, and the United Nations Convention on the Rights of the Child 1989 is the most important of these.[10] While this Convention is, as its title makes clear, intended to enhance recognition of *children's* rights, and in so doing marks a further stage in a global approach to families and the individual members of those families, it has considerable effect, both explicit and implicit, as the *Olssen* decision (above) demonstrates, on international attitudes to the role of parents and the functions and nature of parenthood.

The Preamble to the Convention states that signatories are:

> '*Convinced* that the family, as the fundamental group of society and the natural environment for the growth and well-being of all its members and particularly children, should be afforded the necessary protection and assistance so that it can fully assume its responsibilities with the community' and '[*Recognise*] that the child, for the full and harmonious development of his or her personality, should grow up in a family environment, in an atmosphere of happiness, love and understanding'.

Such statements underscore the view that children are first and fore-most members of families, not resources of a state, and that children are best brought up in families. Since the Convention is a global one (although its drafting was accomplished mainly by delegates from Western states)[11] it must envisage a variety of family types within which such upbringing is accomplished, and there are provisions which recognise the role of the extended family or local custom in child-rearing. Nonetheless, parents are clearly recognised as the central and primary carers of children.

We can divide those of the Convention's provisions which affect parenthood into four types: articles which recognise the rights of parents; articles which impose or recognise the duties of parents; articles which

---

> on the Rights of the Child (set up under Article 43) a periodical report on their progress in implementing measures to give effect to the terms of the Convention: Article 44. See *The UK's First Report to the UN Committee on the Rights of the Child* (1994).

10 For discussion of the drafting of the Convention, and the significance of its provisions, see D McGoldrick, 'The United Nations Convention on the Rights of the Child' (1991) 5 *International Journal of Law and the Family* 132; B Walsh, 'The United Nations Convention on the Rights of the Child: A British View' (1991) 5 *International Journal of Law and the Family* 170; and, for feminist perspectives, see F Olsen, 'Children's Rights: Some Feminist Approaches to the United Nations Convention on the Rights of the Child' in P Alston *et al* (eds) *Children, Rights and the Law* (1992).

11 On this point, see M G Flekkoy, *Children's Rights* (1993) pp 430-435.

offer support to parents in their child-rearing functions; and finally articles which offer children protection from their parents.

(i) Parental rights under the Convention

As might be expected in a Convention on children's rights, it appears to take the prevailing modern view of parental rights which we noted above, as existing for the benefit of the children, rather than for some interest inhering to the parents themselves. For example, Article 3, which requires the best interests of the child to be 'a primary consideration' where public or private institutions take actions concerning children, requires states 'to ensure the child such protection and care as is necessary for his or her well-being, taking into account the rights and duties' of the parents (and others). Thus, states must have regard to parental rights, but can override these where the child's well-being is at stake. Similarly, Article 9(1) requires that states ensure that a child is not separated from his or her parents against their will, except when it is determined, subject to judicial review, that this is necessary for the best interests of the child. However, it is the *parents'* will which is to be respected, again subject to the child's needs. There are provisions (such as Articles 7 and 8) which guarantee the child's right to know and be cared for by his or her parents, but these do not appear to import the same safeguards of judicial review of state decisions. There is then at least a hint in the Convention of a recognition that parents may have rights, or interests which go beyond those of safeguarding the child. Of particular significance in this respect are Articles 5 and 14. The former provides that states:

> 'shall respect the responsibilities, rights and duties of parents ... to provide, in a manner consistent with the evolving capacities of the child, appropriate direction and guidance in the exercise by the child of the rights recognised in the present Convention'.

Article 14 reiterates the 'rights and duties of the parents ... to provide direction to the child in the exercise of' his or her right to freedom of thought, conscience and religion. Both of these Articles reflect a view that parents do have a right (or, interestingly, a duty) to mould the way their children grow up and the sort of people they will become.

(ii) Parental duties under the Convention

Recognition of the parents as the primary carers of children is underscored by reference to their duties and responsibilities. If, as the Preamble asserts, children should be brought up in families, the main task of child-rearing must therefore be imposed upon families. The key provisions are Articles 18 and 27. The former states that:

'Parents, or as the case may be, legal guardians, have the primary responsibility for the upbringing and development of the child. The best interests of the child will be their basic concern.'

Of particular interest here is the requirement that carers have the child's best interests as their 'basic' concern. This may be contrasted with the imposition on state authorities to have such interests as a primary consideration. It is open to debate to decide what the difference between these two formulations may import. State institutions may clearly be able to outweigh the child's interests by reference to other factors – financial resources might be an obvious example. In respect of parents too it appears to be recognised that first, it is not always possible for them to put their children's interests first, and secondly, that, as we noted above, parents' own autonomy interests may lead them to take actions which do have harmful effects upon their children. In any event, the requirement upon parents would appear to be unenforceable, although it forms part of the general scheme of the Convention to enable children to be protected *from* as well as *by* their parents.

Article 27 reaffirms that parents 'or others responsible for the child' have the 'primary responsibility to secure... the conditions of living necessary for the child's development'. However, it is recognised that they may need assistance in meeting this responsibility.

(iii) Support for parents under the Convention

It is perhaps in supporting the parental role that the contrast between civil and political rights on the one hand, and economic, social or cultural rights on the other, becomes important. It is easy to proclaim parents' 'primary' position as carers of children. It is harder to enable them to fulfil the general obligations under the Convention to ensure to childhood special care and assistance if they lack the economic wherewithal to achieve this. But the requirements upon states to assist parents in their task are themselves subject to economic realities. For example, Article 18 requires states to 'render appropriate assistance' and to take 'all appropriate measures to ensure that children of working parents have the right to benefit from child-care services and facilities for which they are eligible.' The word 'appropriate' allows a wide margin of appreciation to individual states to determine what should be provided, and the word 'eligible' provides a further means of limiting what is provided to certain, unspecified, categories. Similarly, Article 27(3) requires states 'in accordance with national conditions and within their means' to provide material assistance and support programmes. Inevitably, poor countries will therefore fall short of what should ideally be done for children and their parents. However, there is no excuse for a rich country such as the United Kingdom to fail in such obligations, and it is at least arguable that, in such a society, what is 'appropriate' should be pitched at a high and generous level.

(iv) Protection from *parents under the Convention*

The key recognition that children are individuals with interests distinct from those of their parents or other family members may be the most important aspect of a 'children's rights' perspective. One dimension to this is the granting to children of autonomy rights, such as the right under Article 12(1). This requires states to:

> 'assure to the child who is capable of forming his or her own views the right to express those views freely in all matters affecting the child, the views of the child being given due weight in accordance with the age and maturity of the child'.

It is significant that this right is *not* expressed to be subject to a parental right of guidance, as Article 14 (the child's right to freedom of thought, conscience and religion) is. It fits in well with developments in English law which we discuss in Chapter 6, which have recognised the growing competence of children as they near adulthood to make decisions for themselves. An important dimension to such a right is the possibility that children may need to be protected from their parents' views, by being given their own voice in judicial or other proceedings,[12] or simply by being legally able to decide upon courses of action without parental interference. The Convention does not deal in much depth with this, arguably the most important aspect of the parent/child relationship. In particular, the interrelationship between Article 12 and Article 14 is not articulated – in which circumstances must states respect a parent's right to direct a child's intellectual freedom (Article 14(2)), and in which might the child's view take priority?

What the Convention clearly recognises is the need for procedures whereby the primary right and responsibility of parents to assume the care and upbringing of their child can be overridden. Articles 9 and 19 require states to take appropriate measures to protect children from abuse or neglect suffered while in their parents' care. No doubt different cultures will take widely differing views on what amounts to appropriate measures, or what can be defined as abuse or neglect. Frances Olsen,[13] for instance, notes that, while the Convention attempts to limit child military service (which affects mainly boys) in Article 38, it says nothing about child marriage. In many cultures, such practice may not be regarded as abusive, in which case, children (mainly girls) will not be protected from

---

12 See Chs 7 and 16.
13 'Children's Rights: Some Feminist Approaches to the United Nations Convention on the Rights of the Child' in P Alston *et al* (eds) *Children, Rights and the Law* (1992).

it. There is thus enormous scope for differential standards and approaches to children's interests, which will be determined not simply by economic factors, but by much more deeply rooted cultural beliefs.

There is a tension in the Convention which no doubt reflects these differences and which might, at a very crude level, be identified as a tension between Western and other ideologies. The whole concept of children's rights might be seen as part of a Western tradition of rights talk which does not graft easily onto other political traditions (although we might note that the initial impetus for the Convention came from the ambassador to the United Nations of the then communist Poland). While the input of developed nations may have been greater than that of less developed states, there was clearly a concern to enable as many states as possible to sign the Convention, and hence to provide a generalised set of rights which could be widely adopted, and adapted to different cultural familial traditions and models. It may be for this reason that different Articles refer, almost casually it seems, at some points to parents and legal guardians (for example, in Articles 14(2) and 18), at others to parents and others responsible for the child (Article 27(2)), and at still others to members of the extended family or the community (Article 5). The Convention may, in this regard, be contrasted with the European Convention which demonstrates an arguably greater level of cultural cohesion and homogeneity in its conception of the family and of the human rights which civilised states should respect. That conception is now showing signs of age, and of requiring an updating through the developing jurisprudence of the Commission and Court.

It may mean that, although in so many respects an aspirational document, at closer inspection the rights guaranteed under the United Nations Convention represent only a minimum standard of what children should expect from states (and from their parents or other carers), and without the possibility of renewal through an equivalent enforcement mechanism to that provided by the European Convention, in time the United Nations document may appear outmoded and irrelevant. In the short term, however, all states can expect to be subjected to increased scrutiny to discover how far they fulfil these international standards.

PART II

Parentage

CHAPTER 3

Automatic parental status

1. WHAT DO WE MEAN BY PARENTAGE?

In this chapter, we consider the extent to which biological or genetic parentage (amongst other possibilities) underpins the attribution of the legal status of parent.

We might assume that all human beings begin life with two parents – the genitors, or persons whose egg and sperm lead to the creation of further human life. But the development of assisted reproduction renders even this certainty problematical. The embryo in the test-tube may have been created from sperm collected from a man years before, and frozen until needed. The man may have died in the meantime. Although the embryo can only be created from genetic material of two parents, there may be no such parent in existence at that time of creation. Historically, it would not have been at all uncommon for a man to die while his child was still in the mother's womb; laws of succession were developed to cater for such an eventuality.[1]

At one level, parentage is always a matter of biology, and even the most advanced scientific techniques have yet to find a way of dispensing with the need for the genetic components to come from two people of the opposite sex. But at another level, parentage is a matter of social understanding, as we noted in Chapter 1. Marilyn Strathern argues that in 'Euro-American society':

'the child is recognised; the parent, by contrast, is constructed... the child is regarded as autonomously produced by biological processes ... To see a child is thus to "recognise" a natural fact. Yet ... persons are not presumed to be parents unless there is some way of knowing they have had children. Whether socially or legally, by contrast with the child, parenthood is thus always "constructed" as an object of knowledge.'[2]

1 For details, see C H Sherrin *et al, Williams on Wills* (6th ed, 1987) Ch 72; see also Ch 7 infra.
2 M Strathern, *Reproducing the Future: Essays on Anthropology, Kinship and the New Reproductive Technologies* (1992) p 148.

In many societies, including our own, parentage and lineage may be traced other than through direct genetic parentage. It has been traditional to look at very different societies to perceive this. For example, Lucy Mair describes how, in the Lobedu tribe, a woman with no son to whom her brother may marry a daughter, marries the daughter herself. The daughter must provide a son to take the woman's son's place as her descendant. A man is chosen to act as the genitor, but he is not classed as the daughter's husband, nor as the child's father.

'These rules achieve two ends which are similar but not identical; the desire to have *descendants* and the desire to have *children*.'[3]

Such rules look very different to those operating in our own contemporary society, but when we explore our own laws, we can find similar complex provisions designed to achieve the end result of providing adults with certain children to fulfil particular functions, and of providing children with adults designated to be responsible for them. (Sometimes, of course, unintended procreation may provide children whom the genitors did not want.) Increasingly nowadays, the main motivation for those seeking to have children will be to provide them with an object of love, but, notwithstanding ethical reservations, which we noted in the previous chapter, providing a descendant to carry on the family name is still a not unknown motivation. For example, some couples experiencing difficulty in conceiving may be prepared to try artificial methods of reproduction such as insemination, or in vitro fertilisation, but do not wish to use donated gametes (let alone adoption). Fears have also been expressed that the development of sex selection techniques, whereby a child of a particular sex can be created or brought to term, will result in an imbalance of males in the population, as males carry on the family name and are assumed (in part at least) therefore to be more desirable than females.[4]

Recognition of certain people as the *parents* of a child may depend upon different aspects of the parenting role. Mair distinguishes the 'genitor', the actual begetter of a child, from the 'pater', the man to whose line the children belong.[5] We noted in Chapter 1 that Goldstein, Freud and Solnit lay stress upon the 'psychological parent', the person to whom the child relates emotionally in early life. The 'social parent' may be described as the person who performs the caring role for the child. In the

---

3 *Marriage* (1971) p 60. See also R Thandabantu Nhlapo, 'Biological and Social Parenthood in African Perspective: The Movement of Children in Swazi Family Law' in J Eekelaar and P Sarcevic (eds) *Parenthood in Modern Society* (1993) p 35, although the mechanisms there described are more akin to adoption and fostering.

4 Discussed in G Douglas, *Law, Fertility and Reproduction* (1991) pp 201-202; HFEA, *Sex Selection: Public Consultation Document* (1993).

5 *Marriage* (1980) p 59.

past, the concept of being *in loco parentis* expressed this idea, and was usually used in relation to a teacher's ability to discipline a pupil.[6] Nowadays, one might cast adoptive parents as the chief examplars of social parenthood. 'Surrogate mothers' are surrogates in the sense that they are not intended to perform the caring function once the child is born, but they may still be the genetic mothers of the children they bear, and are by definition the gestational mothers.[7] Strathern also demonstrates how the idea of the 'natural' parent is undergoing a change:

'The "natural" father was once the progenitor of a child born out of wedlock; the "natural" mother was once the progenitor of a child relinquished for adoption... Contemporary possibilities of artificial procreation introduce a new contrast between artificial and natural process ... The "natural" parent of the future ... may well turn out to be the one for whom no special techniques are involved and the one on whose behalf no special legislation is required.'[8]

This may help to explain why increasing reference is made to the 'birth mother' when speaking of the woman who gives up her child for adoption, and to the 'unmarried father', when discussing the man whose child is born outside marriage. Neither expression is satisfactory. The birth mother may not now be the genetic mother, and the unmarried father may in fact be married to someone other than the mother of his child.

The ascription to a person of the term 'parent' is clearly not straightforward, and can imply a variety of different functions and attributes. Those functions are explored in later chapters. We are concerned here with the question, who is regarded in law as a parent? This may, or may not be the same person as the biological parent, or the person regarded by society at large as the parent of a given child. The law distinguishes between legal parenthood – the status of being a parent – and parental responsibility – the power to act as a parent. The former concept derives a certain shape from the biological necessity of having two parents, in that the law never recognises a child as having more than two legal parents at a time.[9] This was clearly demonstrated in *Johnson v Calvert*[10] where the Supreme Court of California declined to accept the argument of the Americal Civil Liberties Union that a child, born as a result of a womb-leasing arrangement (whereby a couple's egg and

6 See H Crook, "In Loco Parentis: Time for a Reappraisal?" [1989] Fam Law 447.
7 See G Douglas, *Law, Fertility and Reproduction* (1991) Ch 7.
8 *Reproducing the Future: Essays on Anthropology, Kinship and the New Reproductive Technologies* (1992) p 20.
9 Though note that an adopted child remains within the prohibited degrees of the birth family, as well as being prohibited from marrying an adoptive parent: Marriage Act 1949, Sch 1; Adoption Act 1976, s 47(1).
10 Cal LEXIS 2474, 851 P 2d 776 (1993), discussed by G Douglas, 'The Intention to be a Parent and the Making of Mothers' (1994) 57 MLR 636; D Morgan, 'A Surrogacy Issue: Who is the Other Mother?' (1994) 8 *International Journal of Law & Family* 386.

sperm were fertilised in vitro and then transferred to a surrogate for gestation), should be held to have two mothers.

> 'Even though rising divorce rates have made multiple parent arrangements common in our society, we see no compelling reason to recognise such a situation here... To recognise parental rights in a third party [ie the gestational mother]... would diminish [the genetic mother's] role as mother.'[11]

The latter concept of parental responsibility does indeed envisage the possibility of a multiplicity of people being able to exercise parental functions for a child.[12]

2. WHO IS REGARDED IN LAW AS A PARENT – A DOCTRINE OF INTENTION?

Although the United Nations Convention on the Rights of the Child refers frequently to 'parents', it does not offer a definition of parentage or parenthood, thus implicitly recognising the culturally diverse meanings attached to the status, as we have noted.

In English law, parental status may be achieved in a variety of ways, ranging from automatic ascription of the status to the woman who carries and gives birth to the child, to court-ordered recognition by means of an adoption order. This multiplicity of mechanisms has been described as operating on a continuum of state regulation, from minimal, if any, control in the case of the carrying woman who happens to be unmarried, to lengthy state investigation into the applicant's suitability to be a parent in the case of adoption.[13]

DIAGRAM ONE

Our analysis will draw on this scheme, which provides a horizontal analysis of parentage. One can also add a further dimension to the

---

11 *Per* Panelli J.
12 Section 2(5) of the Children Act 1989 provides that: 'More than one person may have parental responsibility for the same child at the same time' and imposes no maximum number of such persons.
13 See G Douglas and N V Lowe, 'Becoming a Parent in English Law' (1992) 108 LQR 414.

scheme, ranging from an emphasis on biological or genetic parenthood at one end to social parenthood at the other.

DIAGRAM TWO

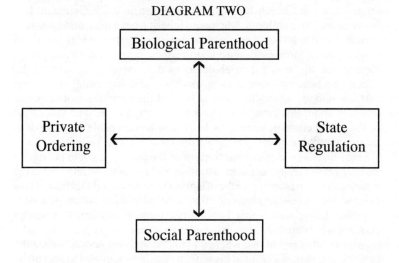

We argue that the extent to which legal recognition is given to a person's intention or desire to be regarded as a parent, and to fulfil the functions of a parent, has increased over time, so that it is now the *primary* test of legal parentage.[14]

Historically, intention was not perceived to be a strong factor in determining parentage, and it was never relevant to mothers, who, by virtue of giving birth, were immediately and irrevocably fixed as one of the legal parents of the child. The position of fathers was different. For example, the child of parents who were not married to one another was originally classed as *filius nullius* (no one's child). However, the putative father could be required by the church to contribute to the support of the child.[15]

---

14 For views which advocate intention as the normative criterion for parenthood, see J Hill, 'What does it mean to be a "parent"? 'The claims of biology as the basis for parental rights' (1991) 66 *New York University Law Review* 353; M Shultz, 'Reproductive technology and intent-based parenthood: an opportunity for gender neutrality' (1990) *Wisconsin Law Review* 297.

15 Although it has been argued that affiliation proceedings in the ecclesiastical courts were rare – R H Helmholz, *Canon Law and the Law of England* (1987) Ch 10. Compare the evidence presented in P Laslett *et al* (eds) *Bastardy and its Comparative History* (1980) especially K Wrightson's description of attempts to punish for fornication etc by both the ecclesiastical courts, which could order maintenance, and the justices of the peace, who could bind over for good behaviour to avoid the parish having to maintain the child; see also Ch 9.

Jack Goody has shown that the concept of legitimacy arose through the influence of the Christian church in discouraging concubinage and downgrading it from a different, albeit lesser, form of marriage. He argues that the Church turned the distinction in early Germanic law between freeborn children, who could inherit from a man, and his slave-born children, who could not, into the distinction between legitimate and illegitimate children. Children born to a concubine, who was a recognised member of the man's household, ceased to be able to inherit; the concubine became classed as a mistress, and her children became bastards. Goody argues that part at least of the Church's motivation in bringing about this change was to limit the way in which an individual or kin-group could determine its heirs, and hence enable the Church to receive more donations of wealth from those with no heirs.[16]

Since marriage requires the consent of the parties, it could be argued that even historically, as a demonstration of the man's commitment to the woman and, in particular, to the offspring they produced together, it was evidence of the couple's intention that he be classed as a father. However, the extended approach that English law took to legitimacy, whereby children who were born to married women were strongly presumed to be legitimate, also meant that where a man doubted that he was indeed the biological father of a child of his wife, he could be required to accept the child as his, and thus his intention and willingness to be the parent of his wife's children were not important.

But the desire to be a parent, in the sense of carrying out the parental role, has been increasingly accommodated by the law, with new ways being developed to give recognition to that desire through parental status and by the concept of parental responsibility. The womb-leasing case we noted above illustrates the increasing recognition of intention in the acquisition of parental status. Panelli J, delivering the majority judgment of the Supreme Court of California, considered that resolution of the dilemma as to who was the legal mother of the child lay in looking at the parties' intentions, as manifested by their surrogacy agreement. The commissioning parents:

'are a couple who desired to have a child of their own genes but are physically unable to do so without the help of reproductive technology. They affirmatively intended the birth of the child, and took the steps necessary .... But for their acted-on intention, the child would not exist .... We conclude that although [the law] recognises both genetic consanguinity and giving birth as means of establishing a mother and child relationship, when the two means do not coincide in one woman, she who intended to procreate the child – that is, she who intended to bring about the birth of a child that she intended to raise as her own – is the natural mother under California law.'[17]

16   J Goody, *The development of the family and marriage in Europe* (1983) p 77.
17   At Cal LEXIS 2474, 16-17.

(a) The blood tie

Traditionally, the blood tie has been regarded as the best and fundamental basis for parentage, but it may have a different meaning in different societies. Janet Finch notes that 'traditional kinship systems in Jamaica are based on the belief that "mother-blood is stronger than father-blood"'. Thus, she concludes that even 'the effect of biological relationship is mediated and modified through the *social* meaning of kinship'.[18] In English society it is the father's blood-tie which has been accorded greater significance. It was originally seen as important to ensure that the correct child inherited the man's property (and name). Its significance was not to provide a means to give the father rights over the child, but to attach the right child to the father. Indeed, Engels argued that while in primitive societies, descent through the mother is the only sure means of determining kinship, the transition to patrilineal descent 'entailed the overthrow of "mother right", a revolution that was "the world historical defeat of the female sex" '.[19] The difficulty was that there was no means of *reliably* establishing a genetic relationship; indeed, no such means existed until the development of DNA testing in the 1980s. Hence, 'the monogamous family emerged for the sole purpose of propagating children of undisputed paternity, which meant that it was imperative to ensure the wife's fidelity.'[20]

(b) Presumptions

We begin discussion of the modern importance of the blood tie by examining the development of the presumptions of legitimacy and parentage which were used by the common law courts to overcome the lack of any reliable method of proving a genetic link between adult and child. It is necessary to discuss mothers and fathers separately: 'the mother is constituted in her connection with the child, whereas the father is constituted in his relationship to the mother'.[1]

(i) Mothers

The technology now exists to enable a woman to donate her egg to be fertilised and implanted in the womb of another, who will carry it and

18 J Finch, *Family Obligations and Social Change* (1989) p 220, emphasis added.
19 See the discussion of Engels's thesis, published in 1884 in *Origin of the Family, Private Property and the State* by D McLellan, *Engels* (1977) pp 33-37.
20 C Shalev, *Birth Power: The Case for Surrogacy* (1989) p 24.
 1 M Strathern, *Reproducing the Future: Essays on Anthropology, Kinship and the New Reproductive Technologies* (1992) p 148.

deliver the resulting child. It was never established in the common law whether the legal mother of a child was the genetic or gestational mother, since the problem could not arise until recently. There were, however, dicta to the effect that gestation was the key factor. In the *Ampthill Peerage* case, Lord Simon said 'Motherhood ... is based on a fact, being proved demonstrably by parturition.'[2] This *obiter dictum* derived from the saying, *mater est quam gestatio demonstrat* (motherhood is proved demonstrably by parturition), but since it is most unlikely that his lordship would have imagined that any alternative were possible, it is not a particularly convincing citation. Indeed, it has been argued, that:

> 'it is possible that the common law viewed genetic consanguinity as the basis for maternal rights. Under this... interpretation, gestation simply would be irrefutable evidence of the more fundamental genetic relationship.'[3]

Section 27 of the Human Fertilisation and Embryology Act 1990 now provides that:

> '(1) The woman who is carrying or has carried a child as a result of the placing in her of an embryo or of sperm and eggs, and no other woman, is to be treated as the mother of the child'.

This provision achieves the objective of most assisted reproduction treatment, which is to give the couple desiring treatment a child, but it severs the blood tie in so doing. But it does not achieve the objective in surrogacy cases, where the woman who gestates the fetus is not intended to perform the social function of mother after the birth. Insofar as it thereby discourages surrogacy arrangements, it is in keeping with the general legislative disapproval of these, but in womb-leasing cases, which are regarded as less objectionable because they use the gametes of the intending parents, it causes difficulty by denying the intending mother the status of parent. We have seen that the Californian court has recognised the importance of intention in the ascription of parental status. There was an opportunity for the English courts to rule on the question raised in *Johnson v Calvert*, in *Re W (minors) (Surrogacy)*[4] but ultimately the issue was avoided because of legislative intervention, which we discuss in the next chapter.

(ii) Fathers

The presumption based on marriage. The position in relation to fathers is much more complex. The view that it is 'a wise child that knows its own

---

2 [1977] AC 547, 577.
3 J Hill, 'What does it mean to be a "parent"? The claims of biology as the basis for parental rights' (1991) 66 *New York University Law Review* 353 at p 370.
4 [1991] 1 FLR 385.

father' can be traced back at least to Homer,[5] and the canon law and common law wrestled for hundreds of years to establish rules and procedures to determine whether a child was the offspring of a particular man. The starting point is to examine the law relating to legitimacy, for it was this, rather than parentage, which determined who, in law, would be regarded as the father and with what consequences.

Baker states that:

'Bastardy, or illegitimacy, was a condition imposed upon a child by the Church as a punishment for the sin of parents who conceived it by illicit connection.'[6]

The definition of bastardy at common law was complex. It distinguished between 'general bastardy', where the parents did not marry after the child's birth, and 'special bastardy' where they did later marry. Where general bastardy was disputed, it could be tried in the ecclesiastical courts, but special bastardy was a matter for the common law courts, because canon law did not recognise it as bastardy at all. Rather, all those born of parents who married each other, no matter when the marriage took place, were legitimate.[7]

The common law, however, drew a sharp distinction between birth inside and outside wedlock. A child might be treated as legitimate, even where the parents married only a few weeks before the birth, as in *Gardner v Gardner*.[8] This was a remarkably sad case, decided on appeal by the House of Lords from Scotland, and which epitomises the hypocrisy of Victorian family values. A man married his wife some six weeks before she gave birth to a daughter. Two days later, the child was placed with a nurse, and although the husband/father maintained the daughter during her infancy, neither he nor the mother ever saw her. Eventually, when in her 20s, she learnt of their existence and claimed them as her parents. The father offered to make a settlement on her if she would renounce all claims to be his daughter but she refused. He thereupon brought an action seeking a declaration that she was not his child, and an order that she desist from so asserting. Although the mother accepted that this was her daughter, she claimed she had been raped by a stranger. The House held that the father had failed to prove his case, for there was a strong presumption in both English and Scottish law that, knowing the condition of his bride, and failing openly to repudiate the child immediately at birth, he must have believed himself to be the father. The inference is that no betrothed man would 'romantically' marry a fallen woman purely in order to save her character. But it was not until the Legitimacy Act

5 *The Odyssey* (1946 edition) p 30, Telemachus to Athene.
6 J H Baker, *An Introduction to English Legal History* (3rd ed, 1990) p 559.
7 A Macfarlane, 'Illegitimacy and illegitimates in English history' in P Laslett *et al* (eds) *Bastardy and its comparative History* (1980).
8 (1877) 2 App Cas 723.

1926 that the law classed as legitimate those children whose parents married *after* their birth (provided that neither had been married to anyone else at the date of the child's birth), and not until 1959 where the parents had contracted a void marriage[9] or had conceived the child through adultery.

If the child were legitimate, then the husband of the mother was regarded as the father and he had parental rights (and any corresponding duties). If the child were illegitimate, as we have noted, he or she was classed originally as *filius nullius*, belonging to no one. The practical significance of this was to settle inheritance rights.[10] A 'bastard' could not succeed to real property except by will or deed, according to Swinburne in the eighteenth century.[11] Illegitimacy also became important after the sixteenth century to determine disputes between parishes over their poor law liabilities. For example, in *R v Kea*[12] the question concerned the legitimacy of a child of seven. If the child was legitimate, the parish where the mother's husband was legally settled would be responsible for the child, but if illegitimate, the parish where the mother now cohabited would be responsible. It was held that the mother could not give evidence of non-access to her by her husband, since this would 'bastardise' the child and was contrary to public policy. The husband's parish was therefore responsible for the child. More recently, ascertaining who was the father of a child could help to establish adultery on the part of the wife and hence provide grounds for divorce.[13]

In modern times, the status of legitimacy has lost its significance, as we discuss in Chapter 5, and instead, the presumptions developed by the law have been used as the bases of parenthood alone. It remains the case that the basic presumption which operates in the law is that the husband of the woman who gives birth to the child is that child's father.[14]

The presumption based on registration. A second presumption derives from the birth register.[15] Article 7(1) of the United Nations Convention on the Rights of the Child requires that a child be registered immediately after birth 'and shall have the right from birth to a name ... and, as far as possible, the right to know and to be cared for by his or her parents'. However, where the parents are unmarried, inclusion of the *father's*

---

9 Now see the Legitimacy Act 1976, s 1.
10 See R Helmholz, 'Bastardy Litigation in Medieval England' (1969) 13 *American Journal of Legal History* 360.
11 Cited in A Macfarlane 'Illegitimacy and illegitimates in English history' in P Laslett *et al* (eds) *Bastardy and its comparative History* (1980) p 73.
12 (1809) 11 East 132.
13 See, most famously perhaps, *Russell v Russell* [1924] AC 687, which came back to haunt the courts in the *Ampthill Peerage* case, above.
14 Or, as it might traditionally have been rendered, *pater est quem nuptiae demonstrant.*
15 *Brierley v Brierley* [1918] P 257.

name on the birth certificate[16] is subject to the agreement of both parents, or to the production of a court order showing that the man is the father.[17] In 1992, 31% of births in England and Wales were outside marriage, but three-quarters of these births were registered by both parents, and nearly half by parents living at the same address.[18] As cohabitation and birth outside marriage become ever more common, the appearance of the father's name on the birth register will increasingly be relied upon as his admission and acceptance of parentage. Nonetheless, there are still a significant number of children born each year whose father's identity is not revealed on their birth certificate. In 1991, of 211,300 births to unmarried parents (out of a total of 700,000 births) 54,100 did not record the father's name.[19] It is open to question how frequently such identity is actually *known*, and, where it is, how many of the fathers concerned play a part in their children's lives. The point is, however, that the child's right under Article 7 may not always be respected.[20] English law appears to give priority to the parent's right to acknowledge the parental link, rather than the child's right to identity, for apart from the orders requiring him to pay maintenance for the child, all these mechanisms of registration show the father's *intention* to accept parentage of the child and to be acknowledged as a parent, and will be accepted as such if the matter is disputed in court. They are therefore one indication of the increasing reliance by the law on the intention to act as parent as the key to the ascription of parental status.

(c) Proving or disproving fatherhood

The question arises as to what evidence could be used to rebut these presumptions, or, in the absence of either applying to a particular situation, how biological fatherhood might be proved. There are two basic ways to do this. One is by showing that sexual intercourse or conception did or did not, or could or could not have taken place at the relevant time, for example, that the husband was away at sea for the

16 Which does not give him parental responsibility: see Ch 5.
17 Births and Deaths Registration Act 1953, s 10.
18 *Social Trends 1994* Chart 2.21.
19 OPCS, *Birth Statistics 1991* (1993) Table 3.9. See the discussion by J Masson and C Harrison, 'Identity: Mapping the Frontiers' in N V Lowe and G Douglas (eds) *Families across Frontiers* (forthcoming).
20 See also *Marckx v Belgium*, Series A, Vol 31 (1979–80) 2 EHRR 330 and *Johnston v Ireland*, Series A, Vol 112 (1987) 9 EHRR 203 (both from the European Court of Human Rights), where discrimination between legitimate and illegitimate children, including in the way in which legal ties between parent and child are recognised, was ruled a breach of Article 8 of the European Convention on Human Rights – the right to respect for one's family life.

period during which the child could have been conceived. The other is to show that the child is or cannot be genetically related to the husband; this is now done by means of scientific tests.

(i) Circumstantial evidence

As to the first method, until 1949, evidence by a spouse that the husband and wife had not had an opportunity for sexual intercourse could not be admitted in proceedings concerning the legitimacy of a child born during marriage, including proceedings for divorce based on adultery.[1] The reasons given for such exclusion were 'public policy, decency and morality'. 'It is not decent that husband or wife should give evidence to bastardise the issue of the wife during the marriage, however decorous the evidence might be in itself.'[2] The awful stigma which attached to being regarded as illegitimate was to be avoided wherever possible, and this led to some strained versions of biological reality as well as legal fictions, in the case law relating to the issue. For example, in *Gaskill v Gaskill*[3] it was held that a pregnancy lasting 331 days could not be ruled out as impossible, while in *Hadlum v Hadlum*[4] a period of 349 days was similarly regarded as possible. However, this appears to have been the point of no return, since in *Preston-Jones v Preston-Jones*[5] the House of Lords held that a court was entitled to take judicial notice of the fact that a normal pregnancy lasts no more than 280 days, and that if a husband proved that a child had been born 360 days after he last had an opportunity to have intercourse with his wife, and that the birth was a normal one, he had proved his case beyond reasonable doubt.

This approach was intended to ensure that the child apparently born to a married couple should be classed as legitimate wherever possible, and makes very clear that the genetic link was secondary to this purpose. It was lowered by s 26 of the Family Law Reform Act 1969 to the balance of probabilities, although this has been held to mean more than *mere* probability. In *Serio v Serio*, Sir David Cairns held that the proper standard of proof was that 'commensurate with the seriousness of the issue involved'. In so holding, the Court of Appeal rejected the view of the first instance judge that the statutory change had produced a 'relatively mild legal onus of establishing that it [was] more probable than not that' the husband was not the father of the child.[6] Again, by requiring proof which goes beyond the bare balance of probabilities, the courts appear to

1 Reversed by the Law Reform (Miscellaneous Provisions) Act 1949, s 7(1).
2 *Per* Viscount Finlay in *Russell v Russell* [1924] AC 687 at 706.
3 [1921] P 425.
4 [1949] P 197.
5 [1951] AC 391.
6 *Serio v Serio* (1983) 4 FLR 756, at 763G and 761E.

accept that it may be more important to uphold the child's legitimate status as a child of married parents, than to discover the biological truth.[7]

The other form of proof was to adduce different evidence that the husband or other man was or could not be the genetic father. For example, photographic evidence of facial resemblance was admitted, although with a warning that the court should keep in mind the 'perils' of so doing, in *C v C and C (legitimacy: photographic evidence)*.[8] If the married couple were both white, and the child and alleged father black, the genetic link between husband and child might be disproved.[9]

(ii) Blood testing

In modern times, proof or disproof of the genetic link is provided by the use of scientific tests. The much greater reliability of blood testing and in particular the use of DNA profiling has made this method of paramount use today, and renders the question of the standard of proof largely irrelevant. The advent of more reliable testing provides the paradox in the modern law of parentage – we can now be sure of genetic parentage, but may no longer attach so much weight to the genetic link anyway.

Blood testing before the development of DNA[10] profiling could *exclude* a certain person as a genetic parent, but could not *prove* their parentage. Nonetheless, scientific refinement of blood testing produced what looked like very high degrees of probability. In *Serio v Serio*, for example, the court had evidence from a serologist that the degree of probability that the husband was not excluded from being the father was 88.5%, and in *Turner v Blunden*,[11] the serologist reported that 998 out of 1,000 men chosen at random could be excluded from paternity of the child. Not surprisingly given these probabilities, the courts were prepared to accept such evidence as highly cogent, but still, blood testing of this type could not be completely conclusive. DNA profiling filled the gap by enabling a positive finding of genetic parentage to be made.[12] It works by means of a print of a person's DNA which resembles a bar code. This is then matched with prints from the mother and alleged father(s). Bands in the 'bar code' prints of the child are first matched with those of the mother. Those which do not match must come from the father. Prints from the 'father(s)' are then compared to see if either matches the remaining

---

7 A Bradney, 'Blood Tests, Paternity and the Double Helix' [1986] Fam Law 378.
8 [1972] 3 All ER 577.
9 See *Slingsby v A-G* (1916) 33 TLR 120, *W v W* [1972] AC 24.
10 Deoxyribonucleic acid – the material which makes up the genes.
11 [1986] 2 FLR 69.
12 Discussed by A Grubb and D Pearl in *Blood Testing, AIDS and DNA Profiling* (1990) Ch 6.

bands. Grubb and Pearl describe a case where either of two men could have been the child's father. The DNA profiles taken from them and the child showed that all 20 of the paternal bands found in the child's sample matched that of one of the men, while the other man's print matched with only four bands. The probability of the coincidence of bands occurring by chance in anyone but the true father was one million million to one against.

If all the relevant parties agree to the taking of a sample for the purpose of carrying out the DNA test, there is no problem, but if one or more refuses, the question is whether a court could *order* a test to be carried out in order to settle the issue. Section 20 of the Family Law Reform Act 1969 governs the position. It provides that in any civil proceedings in which a person's parentage falls to be determined, the court may give a *direction* for the use of blood tests to ascertain whether such tests show that a party to the proceedings is or is not the father of that person.[13] The court cannot order a person of full age and capacity to undergo a test against his or her will, the reason being that 'English law goes to great lengths to protect [the person] from interference with his personal liberty'.[14] However, if an adult declines to comply with a direction to undergo a test, then under s 23(1) of the 1969 Act, the court may draw such inferences, if any, from that fact as appear proper in the circumstances. Indeed, in *Re A (a minor) (Paternity: Refusal of Blood Test),*[15] the Court of Appeal held that it would infer that the man who refused DNA testing was the child's father, since the technique is so reliable that any man unsure of his own paternity can set all doubt at rest by submitting to a test.

The position is more complex in relation to carrying out a test on a child. By s 21(3), a sample may be taken from a person under 16, 'if the person who has the care and control of him consents'. The court has a discretion whether to make a direction for a test to be carried out on the child, and in deciding whether to do so, the leading case remains *S v McC; W v W*.[16] There, the House of Lords had to decide whether a test should be directed to be carried out on two young children which would have the effect of determining whether they were legitimate. The Official Solicitor,

---

13 The reference to blood tests was amended to 'scientific tests' by s 23 of the Family Law Reform Act 1987 to take account of the increasing ability to obtain DNA from samples other than blood, and the section was also amended to allow the genetic motherhood of a party to be established, but the changes have not been brought into force.

14 *Per* Lord Reid in *S v McC: W v W* [1972] AC 24, 43E.

15 [1994] 2 FLR 463.

16 [1972] AC 24.

representing the two children, objected to an order being made on the basis that it would not be for the children's benefit. Lord Reid considered that the court ought to permit a blood test to be taken unless satisfied that it would be against the children's interests. While noting that the stigma of illegitimacy might still exist, he took the view that, where a husband is disputing paternity of a child (as in the cases before the Lords), to prevent the blood test would be to suppress evidence.

> 'The person most affected by the refusal is the husband .... Suppose the case goes against him in the absence of a blood test. He will still maintain that he is not the father and may well refuse to do more for the child than the law compels him to do. But suppose a blood test shows that he can be, or probably is, the father. One might reasonably hope that in that event he would accept the decision and treat the child as his child .... The court must protect the child, but it is not really protecting the child to ban a blood test on some vague and shadowy conjecture that it may turn out to its disadvantage: it may equally well turn out to be for its advantage or at least do it no harm.'[17]

His lordship reasoned that carrying out the test was as likely to benefit, as to disadvantage the child. In later cases, courts have had to decide whether the advantages would indeed outweigh the disadvantages of testing.

For example, in *Re F (Blood Tests: Parental Rights)*[18] the Court of Appeal declined to direct a blood test to be taken on the application of a man with whom the mother had had a relationship. During the relevant period, she had been having sexual relations with both the applicant and her future husband. She and her husband brought the child up as theirs, but the other man applied for parental responsibility and contact with the child. The Court held that the child's welfare depended upon her relationship with her mother and on the stability of the family unit which included the husband. Anything which might disturb that stability was likely to be detrimental to the child's welfare and therefore unless this could be counter-balanced by other positive advantages to her of ordering a test, it would be wrong so to direct. The case is significant for its emphasis on recognition of the value to the child of the relationship forged with the husband who, even if he were not in fact the genetic father, had clearly performed the *social* role of father and had willingly done so. It is therefore an example of the growing importance of the social, as opposed to the genetic aspect of parenthood. On the other hand, in rejecting the other man's attempt to assert his genetic relationship, the case may be said to represent a rejection of the mere *intention* to act as parent as being crucial.[19] But this is because the mother had formed an

17 At 45C,D.
18 [1993] Fam 314. See J Fortin, '*Re F*: "The Gooseberry Bush Approach" ' (1994) 57 MLR 296.
19 It may also be incompatible with the right to respect for family life under Article 8 of the European Convention on Human Rights: in *K, Z and S v Netherlands,*

intact family unit with the other man, so that there were two competing claims to fulfil the father's role.[20] However, even where there is no stable family unit remaining, it has been held that, where the person with care and control adamantly refuses to give consent for a child to be tested, then even though adverse inferences could be drawn against him or her, directing a test is not in the child's interests since it would simply prompt further acrimonious litigation between the 'parents'.[1]

Where this is not the case, courts may be more likely to direct testing to be carried out. An argument which appears to carry weight with the courts is that if a man were convinced of the biological link to a child, he might be more prepared to accept the social role of father. For example, *Re J (a minor) (Wardship)*[2] concerned unmarried parents. The mother was mentally ill and could not care for her baby son who was taken into care and placed with foster parents. As Sheldon J put it, the 'putative father for his part is willing, and indeed would like, to care for the boy, provided he is satisfied that he is in fact the father'.[3] The court directed tests to be carried out, but the mother then decided to leave the jurisdiction before DNA profiling could be arranged. The court held that it could grant an injunction restraining the mother from leaving the country until the testing could be carried out. In this kind of case, the man's willingness to be regarded as the father is conditional on the genetic link being proved, and courts appear willing to accept this reasoning,[4] even though it could be argued that it might betoken a certain meanness of spirit on the part of someone who will have had an intimate relationship with the mother, possibly of long standing (eg, in *Re J*, the man had cohabited with the mother and the tenancy of their council flat had been transferred to his sole name).[5] In *S v McC; W v W*, the House of Lords also appears to have accepted the importance to the husband of discovering if his wife had indeed cuckolded him, though in more recent cases, courts appear to

Application No 18535/91, cited by J Fortin in '*Re F*: "The Gooseberry Bush Approach" ' (1994) 57 MLR 296 at n 41, the European Commission apparently declared admissible an application brought because the marital presumption of paternity in Dutch law prevented an unmarried father from establishing legal ties to his child whose mother was married to someone else.

20 A similar approach was taken in *Re J S (a minor)* [1981] Fam 22.

1 *Re CB (a minor) (Blood Tests)* [1994] 2 FLR 762.

2 [1988] 1 FLR 65.

3 At 66H.

4 A similar approach can be detected in the Matrimonial Causes Act 1973, s 25(4) – in deciding whether to exercise its powers to make financial provision orders for a child who is not the child of a party to a marriage, the court shall have regard, *inter alia*, to whether the spouse knew that the child was not his or her own: see Ch 9.

5 R Deech makes a similar point, and notes how the case demonstrated that increased paternal rights can curb mothers' liberties, including freedom of movement: 'The unmarried father and human rights' (1992) 4 *Journal of Child Law* 3.

have accepted their lordships' view that they should decline to permit husbands to engage in 'fishing expeditions' by means of blood-testing in order to determine adultery. But where the wife is prepared to accede to testing on both her own and the child's behalf, then the courts are prepared to uphold a direction.[6] The legal position of the 1990s therefore appears to be that while DNA testing can effectively provide positive proof of a genetic relationship, and the stigma of illegitimacy carries little if any weight,[7] courts will still hesitate to direct a test which would not affect the outcome of legal proceedings, but which might disrupt the stability of an intact family. In so doing, they have been criticised by Jane Fortin[8] for failing to pay heed to the child's psychological need to know the truth about his or her genetic identity, an issue which we consider further in the next chapter.

(d) Assisted reproduction

(i) Mothers

Legislation was passed in 1990 to accommodate the increasing numbers of people resorting to assisted reproduction treatment to have children.[9] We have already discussed s 27 of the Human Fertilisation and Embryology Act 1990 which provides that the legal mother of a child carried as a result of embryo or egg donation is the carrying woman and no other. This gives recognition to the intention, or choice, to act as social parent on the part of the woman undergoing the treatment. However, the law imposes a degree of state regulation on this choice. Several attempts were made in Parliament to prohibit the use of assisted reproduction techniques for unattached women because of dislike of the prospect of women choosing to have a child without being in a relationship with a man who could act as the father. These attempts failed, but s 13(5) of the 1990 Act requires that a woman may not be provided with treatment services unless 'account has been taken of the welfare of any child who may be born as a result of the treatment (including the need of that child

---

6 *Re T (a minor) (Blood Tests)* [1993] 1 FLR 901. Cf *Re G (a minor) (Blood Tests)* [1994] 1 FLR 495: mother asserted that the child was not that of her former husband but of her current partner. Blood tests were directed despite her opposition, the judge stressing that the child was conceived when the marriage was breaking up and that the husband's position was not akin to that of a mere intruder into the marriage having an affair.
7 Balcombe LJ in *Re F* [1993] Fam 314 considered that the first instance judge may have given more weight to the child's benefiting from the presumption of legitimacy 'than is appropriate in modern circumstances' (at 321F).
8 '*Re F*: "The Gooseberry Bush Approach" ' (1994) 57 MLR 296.
9 See G Douglas *Law, Fertility and Reproduction* (1991) Ch 6. See also Ch 8, *infra*.

for a father)'. This is a clear recognition of the social function of fatherhood. All children have a genetic father, because he donated the sperm which helped create the embryo. But what Parliament was concerned about, and deemed to be generally essential, was the social and psychological relationship between a child and a man. The extent to which this concern was based on prejudice against women as parents, as compared with evidence about the adequacy of upbringing in lone-parent families, may be open to question, and we explore such evidence in later chapters. For now, we can see that women who want or need egg donation in order to achieve motherhood will have to satisfy the test in s 13(5). There is little conclusive evidence on whether single women experience difficulty in satisfying it. The limited research carried out suggests that the main difficulty lies in persuading clinics to consider taking the woman as a patient for treatment at all. If the clinic is prepared to do this, the scrutiny which the woman has to undergo will certainly be greater than if she were part of a conventional married (or unmarried but cohabiting) couple.[10]

(ii) Fathers

Yet again, the position in relation to fathers is more complicated, due in part to the continuing legacy of the marital presumption. Sperm donation is much more common and still easier to achieve than egg donation, and has been practised in Britain since at least the 1940s (the first reported instance of human sperm donation was in the late nineteenth century). The Law Commission, in its original working paper on illegitimacy[11] explored the law relating to donor insemination which pertained at the time. Although a child born to a married woman would be presumed to be that of her husband, blood testing could provide evidence to rebut that presumption so that the child would be illegitimate. There was a strong temptation for married couples to register the child as that of the husband, thus committing an offence under s 4 of the Perjury Act 1911. The Commission accordingly felt it proper to ask:

> 'whether the law should be so framed that, in proper cases, it gives effect to the social reality (that is, that the child is the offspring of the husband and wife) rather than the genetic truth (that is, that he is the offspring of the wife and donor)'.[12]

Their conclusion was that donor insemination could be distinguished from "natural extra-marital conceptions" because:

10 G Douglas, 'Assisted reproduction and the welfare of the child' in M D A Freeman and B A Hepple (eds) *Current Legal Problems* (1993) p 53. Prospective adopters may similarly face difficulties, although there, the problem may not relate to a woman's sexual relationships, so much as to her ethnic and racial origin. See Ch 4.
11 WP No 74 (1979).
12 *Ibid*, para 10.3.

(a) there is no personal relationship between the mother and donor so that ethically insemination differs from adultery;
(b) the husband could usually be assumed to be willing from the start to treat any resulting child as his own;
(c) the anonymity of the donor prevents any attempt by him, or the child, to develop a relationship with each other (be it one of maintenance or affection); and
(d) a doctor would have considered the stability of the couple's marriage before agreeing to do the insemination, while adultery may be a sign of the instability of the marriage.

Section 27 of the Family Law Reform Act 1987 catered for the limited situation where a married couple had a child through donor insemination. However, egg and embryo donation, and other techniques such as GIFT[13] were not dealt with by that legislation, and the 1990 Act, s 28 repealed and provided a more comprehensive measure.

'(1) This section applies in the case of a child who is being or has been carried by a woman as the result of the placing in her of an embryo or of sperm and eggs or her artificial insemination.
(2) If—
(a) at the time of the placing in her of the embryo or the sperm and eggs or of her insemination, the woman was a party to a marriage, and
(b) the creation of the embryo carried by her was not brought about with the sperm of the other party to the marriage,
then, subject to subsection (5) below, the other party to the marriage shall be treated as the father of the child unless it is shown that he did not consent to the placing in her of the embryo or the sperm and eggs or to her insemination (as the case may be).'

This therefore enacts that the husband will be the legal father, subject to two conditions. The first is contained in s 28(5) and provides that the marital presumption of legitimacy (and paternity) still applies even apart from s 28(2). The second is that the husband must be able to show that he did not consent to the treatment given to his wife. The effect is that if the husband wishes to avoid legal parentage, he must prove lack of consent *and* rebut the marital presumption.[14] In practice, clinics offering treatment would seldom treat a married woman without evidence of her husband's consent, even though the legislation does not make this a requirement of treatment.[15] The Law Commission rejected the view that

---

13 'Gamete intra-fallopian transfer' – where the sperm and eggs are inserted directly into the fallopian tubes.
14 Under s 27 of the Family Law Reform Act 1987, proof of lack of consent by the husband was the only way of avoiding legal parentage of a child born as a result of donor insemination of the wife.
15 The Human Fertilisation and Embryology Authority Code of Practice advises clinics always to obtain consent and research shows that they would be reluctant to treat without it – G Douglas, *Access to Assisted Reproduction – Legal and Other Criteria for Eligibility* (1992).

the husband should have to give his consent before the blood tie between child and donor be broken, on the basis that this would require a complex scheme of implementation and would put in jeopardy the legal relationship between child and husband if any elements of the consent scheme had not been complied with. But insemination may be carried out without medical or scientific help. If a married woman made use of it without her husband's knowledge, then even if he proved his lack of consent, he would still have to go on to rebut the presumption arising from marriage, which he could do by recourse to DNA testing.

The Act went further than any other legislation in demoting the significance of the blood tie *and* of the marriage bond, by enabling the non-marital partners of women who receive donated sperm or embryos also to achieve the legal status of father. Up to now, we have assumed that the law will recognise only a genetic link, or a willingness to assume parentage evidenced by the commitment to the mother through marriage. But s 28(3) provides that if no man is treated as the father of the child by virtue of either s 28(2) or of the common law marital presumption, then where the embryo or sperm and eggs were placed in the woman, or she was artificially inseminated 'in the course of treatment services provided for her and a man together by a person to whom a licence applies' that man shall be treated as the father of the child. This is a bold innovation. It is the first legislative example of a person with no genetic link to a child, and no legal link with the child's mother, being accorded automatic parental status. It goes further than the law has been prepared to go in recognising the social role of, for example, step-fathers who may acquire parental responsibility, but who cannot acquire the status of parent short of adopting the child, as we shall discuss in the next chapter. Secondly, the section does not require that the man and woman be cohabiting, let alone have shown settled cohabitation for any particular minimum period, for the man to be accorded parental status. All that is required is that the 'treatment services' have been provided by a licensed person for the man and woman together. Section 2(1) of the Act defines such services as 'medical, surgical or obstetric services provided to the public or a section of the public for the purpose of assisting women to carry children'. It can be seen that 'DIY' insemination will not suffice to bestow parental recognition on the man – the treatment must be offered to the public or section of the public by a person licensed to provide it. So whereas the *husband* of a woman who is inseminated outside of treatment services will still be regarded as the father, a *partner* of such a woman will not be, and the donor will remain the legal father. Parliament may well have assumed that clinics would not accept unmarried couples for treatment unless they were satisfied as to the stability of their relationship first.[16] By discriminating against unlicensed treatment, the

---

16 Douglas *ibid* suggests that clinics' exploration of the stability of relationships does not extend very far.

section encourages couples to go to licensed clinics for insemination so that the state can, albeit very tenuously, operate some form of control over the resort to such treatment by 'unconventional' prospective parents.

We noted above that the law appears unable to contemplate the possibility of a child having more than two parents at a time. The Human Fertilisation and Embryology Act 1990 provides mechanisms to enable non-biological fathers to achieve legal parenthood, and s 28(6)(a) provides that where a donor gives the requisite consent and his sperm is used in accordance with that consent, he is not to be treated as the father of the resulting child. This enables the father created by virtue of s 28(2) or (3) to be the sole legally recognised father.[17] But it also means that, in the unusual though not unknown case where a single woman is treated by a licensed clinic, the resulting child will have *no* father in law. The child will, in these circumstances, be in the same position as the illegitimate child whose birth register entry contains no details of the father, or of the child adopted by a single person who is recorded as having only one parent. For these children it seems, no father may be better than any father.

Of course, since most people receiving licensed treatment will be couples, the section achieves their objective of granting them, and no other person, parental status (leaving aside the complications of surrogacy arrangements for the moment). More striking though, because it operates to *counter* the desire of those seeking treatment, is s 28(6)(b), which provides that where the sperm of a man, or any embryo created with his sperm, is used after his death, he is not to be treated as the child's father. All sperm used in licensed clinics is frozen,[18] and it is possible to preserve sperm and embryos for several years without damaging them. It is common for men about to undergo cancer treatment which will render them infertile to have their sperm stored in case they wish to have children later in their lives. Sadly, some such men do not recover from their cancer, and die. Cases have arisen where they and their wives or partners wish to have the sperm used after their death.[19] The Warnock Committee, whose report led to the passage of the 1990 Act, disapproved of such posthumous use, on the basis that it allegedly betokens a psychological refusal on the part of the woman to come to terms with the man's death, and also, more practically, that it may cause problems

---

17 It also embraces the approach taken by the European Commission of Human Rights in *G v Netherlands* (1993) 16 EHRR Part 7, CD 38, that a biological tie *per se* does not give a donor a right to respect for family life with the child under Article 8 of the European Convention (noted in Ch 2).

18 This is partly because it is necessary to carry out tests on the donor for diseases such as AIDS and these require a time gap of some months for effective diagnosis. Cryo-preservation of eggs has also become possible, but s 27, which makes the woman who gives birth the legal mother in all cases, avoids a similar complication which might otherwise arise from posthumous use.

19 See Douglas *Law, Fertility and Reproduction* (1991) p 125.

concerning the winding-up of estates.[20] Where sperm is used in these circumstances, the child will therefore again have no father who could be registered as such, and express provision for the child would have to have been made by will.

The only exception to the statutory scheme which sets the intention to act as parent over the genetic link is in relation to inheritance of titles of honour. The House of Lords stood firm against the possibility of children born from donated gametes inheriting such titles. For the nobility, therefore, the emphasis remains upon the need to trace the genetic link through the generations.

While this could certainly be achieved today with DNA testing to resolve any doubts, it may be wondered if there were not the occasional lapse in previous generations, with adulterine offspring able to inherit because of the inability to rebut the marital presumption of paternity.[1]

---

20 *Report of the Committee of Inquiry into Human Fertilisation and Embryology* (1984) Cmnd 9314, paras 4.4 and 10.9.

1 Indeed, we know this was regarded as a problem – hence the development of the causes of action for alienation of affections and criminal conversation: see L Stone, *Road to Divorce* (1990) Chap IX. Even where illegitimacy was acknowledged, it did not always harm the child: the prefix 'Fitz', which betokened illegitimacy, was also a sign of membership of the nobility.

CHAPTER 4

Ascribed parental status and the child's identity

1. INTRODUCTION

So far, we have examined methods of achieving parental status which do not involve the *prior* scrutiny and sanction of a court. Douglas and Lowe[1] have argued that the acquisition of parental status operates on a continuum of increasing state regulation, with the woman who gives birth outside marriage at one extreme of no state sanction, to adoption at the other where legal status is not granted without close scrutiny and approval of the lifestyle and other attributes of the proposed adopter(s). In almost every case of the woman giving birth outside marriage (or inside, of course), except for the still rare use of donated eggs, the woman giving birth will be a genetic parent as well. In the majority of adoptions, there will be no genetic link between child and adopters.[2] Judicial proceedings are an essential part of the process of scrutiny for adoption, and also for surrogacy, which perhaps marks the mid-point along the continuum. In this chapter, we examine the way in which parental status can be obtained through such proceedings, which recognise that the child's legal parents should be his or her social or psychological, rather than genetic parents. We also consider the implications of recognition of social parentage for the child's right to discover his or her genetic identity.

2. PARENTAL ORDERS IN FAVOUR OF GAMETE DONORS

We saw that s 27 of the Human Fertilisation and Embryology Act 1990 provides that, notwithstanding egg donation, the carrying woman is the

---

1 G Douglas and N V Lowe, 'Becoming a Parent In English Law' (1992) 108 LQR 414.
2 But approximately half of adoptions are by a genetic parent together with a step-parent or by a family relative. See below.

69

legal mother of the child, and s 28 provides that her husband or partner will presumptively be the legal father. This produces the wrong result for those people who commission a 'surrogate' to carry the child for them. The true incidence of surrogacy is unknown. It was reported in the press in 1990 that over 70 couples were known to have had children through surrogacy.[3] Others may well not be known about. Whatever the true figure, it is unlikely to be large. There has been a strong incentive to conceal the true circumstances surrounding a surrogate birth, given societal disapproval, demonstrated by Parliament's passing an Act which made criminal its commercial manifestations – the Surrogacy Arrangements Act 1985 – and by declaring unenforceable any surrogacy arrangement, whether commercial or not (s 1A of the 1985 Act). But during the passage of the Human Fertilisation and Embryology Bill, a case of 'womb-leasing' reached public attention and persuaded Parliament to change its stance, at least in part. A commissioning couple recruited a woman to act as a surrogate. Two of their embryos, created by in vitro fertilisation, were successfully transferred to her, and twins were born. They were cared for from birth by the commissioning parents. The local authority for the area where the commissioning parents lived sought a declaration as to the legal parentage of the twins and also made them wards of court. The concern of the authority was as to whether the twins should be regarded as having been privately placed with the commissioning parents, who would then have to give notice to the authority and seek to adopt the children. Their solicitor wrote to *The Times*[4] suggesting that it would be absurd to expect the couple to adopt 'their own' children (which begged the question, of course), and their MP raised the matter in Parliament. An amendment was hurriedly drafted to the Bill to provide a mechanism to enable courts to make 'parental orders' to cater for this sort of case. The action between the local authority and the couple was settled on the latter's undertaking to apply for an order as soon as the Bill became law.[5]

The relevant provision is now s 30 of the Human Fertilisation and Embryology Act 1990. It provides that parties to a marriage may apply for an order of the court which will provide for a child 'to be treated in law as the child' of the parties, if the child has been carried by a woman other than the wife as the result of assisted reproduction treatment, and the gametes (eggs or sperm) of the couple, or either of them, were used to bring about the creation of the embryo, and a number of conditions are satisfied. We may note that only spouses may seek an order; cohabiting couples or single commissioning parents are barred, though there seems

---

3   *The Observer*, 24 June 1990.
4   *The Times*, 28 February 1990. The case became known as the 'Cumbria case': also reported as *Re W (Minors) (Surrogacy)* [1991] 1 FLR 385.
5   The provision did not come into force until 1 November 1994.

no reason why this should be so, given the acceptance of couples and even single women, taking advantage of ss 27 and 28, and that it has always been possible for a single person (although not an unmarried couple) to adopt. Secondly, there must be a partial genetic link – one at least of the commissioning parents must be a genetic parent of the child. It will not be possible under this section for a couple to commission *another* couple to produce an embryo for them and have a surrogate carry it to term. This is an odd denial given the acceptance by Parliament of the lack of any genetic link in embryo donation where the intending parent carries the child. It suggests that there is still some assumption that a blood tie is preferable if at all possible, and that given the dubious morality of surrogacy arrangements, as evidenced in the provisions making them unenforceable and sometimes criminal, the blood tie is operating as a means of 'rescuing' the arrangement from total unacceptability. We discussed in the previous chapter how the law has recognised either the blood tie *or*, failing proof of this, the marriage bond as generally sufficient to establish parenthood. This section requires *both*.

It goes on to lay down several conditions designed to ensure that the agreement of the surrogate (and any man deemed to be the child's father by virtue of s 28) has been given unconditionally to the making of the order, re-emphasising the extent to which intention, or deliberate decision, has become a key to the grant (and renunciation) of parental status. In order to limit the possible financial exploitation which can be inherent in surrogacy arrangements, s 30(7) requires the court to be satisfied that no money or other benefit (other than for reasonable expenses) has been given or received for or in consideration of the making of the order, the giving of the agreement to it, the handing over of the child or the making of any arrangements with a view to the order, unless authorised by the court. This means that if the court were not so satisfied, and refused to authorise any money or benefit extra to expenses, the order could not be made, although this would leave all the parties, and the child, in a difficult situation as regards their future.

The regulations governing the grant of orders apply the relevant provisions of the Adoption Act 1976 (which we discuss below) to the proceedings, which also rank as family proceedings under the Children Act 1989. This means that the court could choose to make a different, or additional order to that sought by the commissioning parents, for example, an order for contact with the surrogate. The whole mechanism therefore combines aspects of state regulation, epitomised by adoption, with recognition of the blood tie as giving the commissioning parents standing to seek an order in the first place. It therefore straddles a point between genetic (and hence often automatic) recognition, and social parenthood (hence often sanctioned by the state). The commissioning parents' *intention* to act as social parents is given partial sanction, but the circumstances – surrogacy – are deemed to require outside control by the court.

3. ADOPTION

Until the enactment of s 30 of the Human Fertilisation and Embryology Act 1990, the best example of state regulation of the acquisition of parental status based on the intention to fulfil the social role of parent, was adoption, and it remains the mechanism subject to the closest control through the law and administrative process. Adoption is the:

'process by which the legal relationship between a child and his or her birth parents is severed and an analogous relationship between the child and the adoptive parents is established'.[6]

Adoption was a well-known legal mechanism in ancient civilisations, including India and Mesopotamia, and was of particular significance in Rome.[7] Its purpose was to provide an heir for a childless man, and it was not concerned with the welfare of the child. But it disappeared from Europe remarkably quickly:

'The change was radical. There is no entry for adoption in the whole thirteen volumes of Sir William Holdsworth's *The History of English Law*. Its absence from the legal systems of Europe was striking and long-lasting.'[8]

Goody argues that the reason for the disappearance was the influence of the Christian Church. He suggests that the Church discouraged adoption as part of its strategy, described in the previous chapter, to persuade adherents to leave their wealth to the Church if they had no heirs. The strategy worked, and legal adoption did not reappear in the Euro-American world until the nineteenth century, with Massachussetts the first American state to legislate for it, in 1851. This is not to say that other means were not found to transfer the upbringing of children from one set of parents to another. Goody posits wet-nursing, nannying and apprenticeship as alternatives to adoption, although the first two of these were not intended to displace the formal family relationship between parent and child. The latter was sometimes used as a means of obtaining

---

6 Department of Health *Inter-departmental Review of Adoption Law, Discussion Paper No 1, The Nature and Effect of Adoption* (1990), para 2.

7 J Goody *The development of the family and marriage in Europe* (1983) pp 72 *et seq* and Economic and Social Committee of the European Community, 'Opinion on Adoption' *Official Journal of the European Communities* No C 287/18, 4 November 1992, paras 1.3.1, 1.3.2.

8 Goody, *Ibid* at p 73.

an heir to a business where the owner had no sons of his own; often the lucky apprentice would marry the daughter of the house to enable a continuation of the owner's blood-line in the business.[9] When adoption was reintroduced in Europe, the possibility of using it, or a form of it, to provide an heir, was also recognised, and such special kinds of adoption remain possible in many countries. For example, in France, the author, Somerset Maugham, tried to adopt his adult secretary, Alan Searle, so that he could inherit Maugham's estate in preference to Maugham's daughter. The adoption was declared void because of the attempt to disinherit her.[10]

In this country, the legal introduction of adoption came with the passage of the Adoption of Children Act 1926.[11] The impetus was a perception that there were many children left fatherless as a result of the 1914–18 war (either through the death of the father, or because they were illegitimate 'war babies'), who would benefit from being brought up in a new family.[12] There was accordingly a greater, though not exclusive, focus upon adoption as a child welfare mechanism rather than as a means of providing satisfaction (or an heir) for an adult.[13] The Act was preceded by reports from two governmental committees, which took sharply differing approaches to the desirability of introducing a legal mechanism for adoption. The Hopkinson Report enthusiastically urged the introduction of legal adoption as a matter of urgency. There were, it said, an increasing number of people who wished to bring up a child as their own. The Committee recognised that while the welfare of the child was of paramount importance, it was:

9 See M Abbott, *Family Ties: English Families 1540-1920* (1993) p 85.
10 See T Morgan, *Somerset Maugham* (1980) pp 607-608. See also I Shimazu, 'Japan: Trailing the West in Family Law' (1988-89) 27 J Fam Law 185 pp 188-193. The Economic and Social Committee of the European Community (see n 7 above) define 'simple adoption' as: 'A legal provision essentially applicable to intra-family situations. For example an uncle adopts his nephew without the latter losing his blood ties with his natural family. The uncle looks after and brings up his nephew who may take on his uncle's name and become his heir, with the same rights as a natural child. The child continues to maintain links with its biological family'. The Opinion also compares adoption laws in all the member states of the Community.
11 For a brief summary of the history of adoption law since that time, see the *Report of the Departmental Committee on the Adoption of Children* (the Houghton Report) (1972) Cmnd 5107, paras 9-14 and for a more detailed account of the purposes of the original Act, see the *Report of the Departmental Committee on the Adoption of Children* (the Hurst Report) (1954) Cmd 9248, para 12.
12 Although it was thought that those who had 'marked physical or moral defects are generally best provided for in an institution'. *Report of the Committee on Child Adoption* (the Hopkinson Report) (1921) Cmd 1254, para 11.
13 For a discussion of the various purposes of adoption, see M Hill, 'Concepts of parenthood and their application to adoption' (1991) 15 *Adoption and Fostering* (4) 16.

'right also to recognise that if the natural desire of many persons, who have no children of their own, to have the care and bringing up of some child could find legitimate satisfaction, that too is a proper object to aim at'.[14]

While welfare motivations were important, the Committee therefore accepted that the desire to act as social parent to a child was something which the law might recognise as warranted. The question of whether adoption is a method of providing a child for those wishing to be parents, or of providing parents for a child, is one which remains at the heart of the debates over how adoption should be regulated. The tension between the two was clearly brought out by the Hopkinson Report, which propounded what might appear today to be either very progressive, or very strange views on who should be allowed to adopt. For example, the Committee proposed that married couples aged over 25, individual spouses with the other spouse's consent, and single people aged over 30, should be allowed to adopt, provided that they were at least 20 years older than the adopted child. The Committee apparently viewed with equanimity the possibility of single men and women adopting children. But in the case of:

'a single woman, for example, [who] might have adopted a boy in infancy and might find difficulties as he grows up, in regard to education and other matters on which, if she has no suitable friends of her own, the advice of a Judge sitting informally who had knowledge of all the circumstances might be of the greatest assistance'.[15]

The idea that a single woman would be a suitable adopter for a boy seems strange in an era where single women who seek to have a child by assisted reproduction or to adopt a child are frequently regarded as selfish and unable to provide a 'proper' upbringing because of the lack of a father figure for the child.[16] Admittedly, there is an exception where the child would not be wanted by anyone else, for example, the Government in its White Paper grudgingly noted that:

'[s]ome children, often with special needs, are successfully adopted by unmarried women, women no longer married or women widowed early. The devotion and care they can bring to children often rightly commands admiration.'[17]

The further idea that a judge would be in a position to advise the adoptive mother on coping with an adolescent youth might be regarded by some as even more far-fetched today!

---

14 At para 14.
15 At para 43.
16 Indeed, as a means of obviating the need for adoption in some cases, the Committee even raised the possibility of the payment of child allowances to women where the father was not contributing to the child's support (para 69(2)), thus pre-dating the proposals of the Finer Committee on One-Parent Families by 50 years. See Ch 9 below.
17 Department of Health *et al, Adoption: The Future* (1993) Cm 2288, para 4.38.

But the eagerness of the Hopkinson Committee was not shared by the second body set up to consider what was clearly highly controversial. The Child Adoption Committee (the Tomlin Committee) was much more dubious. It defined adoption as 'a legal method of creating between a child and one who is not the natural parent of the child an *artificial* family relationship analogous to that of parent and child'.[18] It assumed that *de facto* adoptions would continue regardless of any legal mechanism to facilitate them, but considered that the increase in such adoptions after the war had not been maintained. 'The people wishing to get rid of children are far more numerous than those wishing to receive them'.[19] (The position today, at least in respect of healthy white babies, is now reversed: 'there are undoubtedly many couples whose wish to adopt is bound to be disappointed by the decline in the number of children who need adoption.'[20]) Although it grudgingly considered that people who were caring for children in such arrangements might feel insecure knowing that they had no legal standing in relation to the child, it assumed that since courts would apply the child's welfare as the paramount consideration in any dispute as to the child's future between adopters and natural parents, such apprehension probably had a more theoretical than real basis. But the Committee also thought that the 'sentiment which deserves sympathy and respect, that the relation between adopter and adopted should be given some recognition by the community' did justify an alteration to the law to enable adoption, with proper safeguards, to take place.[1]

The problem of devising a mechanism which would satisfy both the welfare of the child *and* the desire to act as a parent by the prospective adopters, while at the same time giving due regard to the claims and interests of the biological parents, was and remains the dilemma for adoption law in this country. Indeed, the dilemma has become even more acute. First, changing social customs, in particular the decline in the stigma of birth outside marriage (both in respect of cohabiting couples and single mothers) and the increase in contraception and abortion, have led to a decreasing, but more problematical pool of children available for adoption. The overall number of adoption orders has fallen from 22,500 per year in 1974 to 6,751 in 1993. The number of babies adopted has dwindled from 23% of adoptees in 1977 to 12% in 1991.[2] Children adopted from the public care system now make up about half the total.

---

18 *First Report* (1924–25) Cmd 2401, para 4, emphasis added.
19 *Ibid*.
20 Department of Health *et al, Adoption: The Future* (1993) Cm 2288, para 3.12.
 1 *First Report* (1924–25) Cmd 2401, para 9.
 2 *Judicial Statistics 1993*, Table 5.6; Department of Health *et al, Adoption: The Future* (1993) Cm 2288, Ch 3.

Such children may have difficult emotional and physical problems which require specialist help to overcome; they may be of an age to remember their birth families and to wish to maintain links with them; and the birth families may strongly resist the loss of the child to another family. Almost half of adoptees are adopted as a means of integrating them into a step-family[3] – often as a means equally of breaking the legal link with an absent parent. Adoption is thus now far removed from the world envisaged by the Hopkinson and Tomlin Committees, or even the Hurst Committee of the 1950s, as a mechanism for rescuing orphans and illegitimate babies. Second, there is now increasing awareness of the sense of loss experienced by both adoptees and birth parents as a result of adoption.[4] Third, such awareness has been recognised by the growing emphasis upon the rights to knowledge and preservation of one's family identity under Articles 7 and 8 of the United Nations Convention on the Rights of the Child, albeit motivated by political events, such as the 'disappearances' of children in Argentina in the 1970s (where children of political opponents of the regime were abducted from their parents and 'given' to childless families in the military to bring up as their own), and the desire to do justice to the birth families, rather than by a paramount concern for the psychological health of such families and their lost children.

We consider the role of adoption within the public care system in Chapter 14. Here, we are concerned with the following issues, which relate directly to the acquisition of parental status and compare sharply with the automatic acquisition outlined in the previous chapter: how is the fitness to act as a parent of the prospective adopters to be assessed and who decides whether an adoption should take place?

(a) Prospective adopters

There are now few *statutory* restrictions on who may seek to adopt a child. The applicant(s) must generally be aged at least 21 and domiciled in a part of the United Kingdom, the Channel Islands or the Isle of Man.[5]

---

3 *Judicial Statistics 1993.* In 1993, 47.4% of adoptions were by step-parents.

4 See, eg, P Brinich, 'Adoption, ambivalence and mourning' (1990) 14 *Adoption and Fostering* (1) 6; F Scourfield and A Hendry *et al*, 'Unfinished business – the experience of a birth mothers' group' (1991) 15 *Adoption and Fostering* (2) 36. We discuss these issues below.

5 Unless the proposed adoption is by a married couple of a child of one of the spouses, in which case, that spouse must be at least 18 (s 14(1B)); or the application is for a Convention adoption under s 17 (for details of Convention adoptions, see P M Bromley and N V Lowe, *Bromley's Family Law* (8th ed, 1992) pp 453-454).

It is not possible under the current law for a married person to adopt by him or herself unless the spouses are separated or the other spouse is incapable of making the application due to ill-health, and couples who are unmarried may not adopt jointly.[6] A single person may adopt, and it is therefore possible for one member of a cohabiting couple, either heterosexual or homosexual,[7] to adopt, although research into adoption for the Department of Health by Murch *et al* found no examples of such cases, and only 2% of applications for agency-placed children were by single persons (all women).[8]

The law distinguishes between adoptions by relatives of the child, and adoptions by strangers. The former do not have to comply with all the detailed requirements laid down for the latter. Most importantly, where it is sought to adopt a child who is not a relative, the child must be placed with the prospective adopters by an adoption agency, unless the placement is pursuant to a High Court order. Otherwise the placement is unlawful under s 11 of the Adoption Act 1976.[9] The aim is to prevent unsuitable adopters obtaining care of a child with a view to later adopting, and also to prevent them putting pressure on a vulnerable biological mother to hand over her child. The Houghton Committee, which recommended the restriction in its 1972 Report, also feared that private adoptions arranged by doctors and matrons at maternity homes for unmarried mothers might be prone to abuse and deception. Indeed, a striking illustration of this danger emerged when an adult sought to have his adoption (which took place in 1959) set aside because his adoptive parents, Orthodox Jews, had been told he was of Jewish origin by the matron of the nursing home where he was born, when in fact, he was of Arab parentage.[10] But where the child is placed with a relative, greater recognition is given to the pre-existing biological or marital tie. Close regulation is deemed less important where the adoption is within the child's original family, reflecting the general stance of the law to 'intrude' as little as possible within an intact family.

A relative is defined widely by s 72(1) of the 1976 Act as including, amongst others,[11] the unmarried father. Oddly, the definition does not

---

6 Adoption Act 1976, ss 14 and 15. Article 6 of the European Convention on Adoption also prohibits adoption by unmarried couples.

7 For discussion of the position regarding adoption by homosexuals, see R Sandland, 'Adoption, Law and Homosexuality: Can Gay People Adopt a Child?' [1993] JSWFL 321.

8 *Pathways to Adoption* (1993) at para 2.6.

9 Unless the child was originally *fostered* only, and the foster parents later decide to apply for adoption. In such a case, the child must have lived with them for 12 months preceding the application (s 13(2)).

10 *Re B (Adoption: Setting Aside)* [1995] 1 FLR 1. The application was unsuccessful, since there had been no failure of procedure in the judicial proceedings.

11 'Grandparent, brother, sister, uncle and aunt, whether of the full blood or half-blood or by affinity and includes, where the child is illegitimate, the father of the child and any person who would be a relative within the meaning of this definition if the child were legitimate'.

include a child's step-parent. As we have noted, adoption by a biological parent and his or her new spouse is common but there appears to be no provision to permit a private placement of the child with a step-parent alone after the death or divorce of the natural parent. Furthermore, there is no definition of step-parent in the Act and it is open to doubt whether a person would be classed as a step-parent if he or she is not married to nor cohabiting with the natural parent.[12] We noted above that the law cannot cope with recognising more than two parents for a child at a time, and the failure to accord legal recognition to step-parents may be an indicator of this.[13]

Where the placement is not through an agency, notice of the intention to apply to adopt must be given to the local authority to enable it to investigate the suitability of the applicants and submit a report to the court. As we have noted, adoptions by step-parents (with a natural parent) and relatives make up a significant part of the total. In the Department of Health's research project, *Pathways to Adoption*, 34% of the 1,268 cases in the sample were step-parent applications and 7% by other relatives, and the proportion of step-parent adoptions has since risen.[14] The Houghton Committee disapproved of such adoptions, regarding them as severing, in law, an existing relationship, and creating an adoptive relationship in place of the natural relationship which in fact, though not in law, may continue unchanged.[15] Step-parent adoptions might be sought where a parent divorces and re-marries as a means of cementing the new family unit, but this will mean severing the legal ties with the absent parent which, as we shall see in Chapter 8, is generally disapproved. Such adoptions, or those by relatives such as grandparents, may also be used to disguise the true genetic parentage of the child (eg it was not uncommon some years ago for grandparents or a married sister to adopt the illegitimate child of a daughter). The Houghton Committee

12 Katharine Bartlett argues that, in the United States of America, 'because the step-relationship derives from the marriage of the natural parent and the step-parent, it is generally held by statute as well as under the common law that the relationship automatically ends upon termination of the marriage or on the death of the natural parent: 'Rethinking Parenthood as an Exclusive Status: The Need for Legal Alternatives When the Premise of the Nuclear Family has Failed' (1984) 70 *Virginia Law Review* 879, 914.

13 See G Douglas and N V Lowe 'Becoming a Parent in English Law' (1992) 108 LQR 414 above, for further comment on this point. The Government proposed in its White Paper, *Adoption: The Future* (1993) Cm 2288 that step-parents be permitted to adopt without the natural parent having to do so as well (para 5.22).

14 M Murch *et al*, *Pathways to Adoption* (1993) Table 2.3, and n 3, p 76 above. For the saga of attempts to limit such adoptions, and their failure and repeal, see P M Bromley and N V Lowe, *Bromley's Family Law* (8th ed, 1992) pp 420-421 and sources cited therein.

15 Houghton Report (1972) Cmnd 5107, para 97.

regarded these adoptions as potentially damaging to the child, and recommended a new mechanism whereby step-parents and other relatives might acquire parental responsibility without the status of parents. Houghton's approach implied an increased emphasis upon the genetic 'truth' as the basis of parentage, but the unpopularity of the recommendation and its eventual repeal by the Children Act 1989 show that the wish to achieve parental status by those who will care permanently for the child has proved of greater weight.[16]

Applicants who wish to be considered for agency placements are scrutinised by the agency (which may be a local authority or voluntary society[17] such as the Catholic Children's Society) in accordance with a highly detailed list of factors relating to their health, life-style, relationship etc as set out in the Adoption Agencies Regulations; police checks are carried out, and a 'home study' assessment is undertaken.[18] Agencies have their own additional criteria eg as to a *maximum* age of adopters,[19] that applicants be non-smokers, or that, perhaps most controversially, they be of the same racial or ethnic origin as the child. The Adoption Law Review recommended that there should be central guidelines to agencies regarding suitability of adopters to ensure consistency and to avoid what might be viewed as ideologically extreme requirements being imposed.[20] Publication of the Government's White Paper on Adoption was delayed in 1993, partly because of a public outcry at the revelation that a couple where the wife was Asian were rejected as prospective adopters of a mixed-race child because they told the agency that they had not experienced racial discrimination and were therefore assessed as 'racially naive'.[1] When the White Paper was finally published, it affirmed the rejection of a 'politically correct' approach to assessing prospective

16 *Ibid* para 115. The mechanism was introduced in the Children Act 1975, and was called custodianship. The relevant provisions of the Act were not brought into force until 1984. See E Bullard, E Malos and R Parker, *Custodianship: Caring for other people's children* (1991). Oddly, given the unpopularity of custodianship, the Government proposed a new version, to be confusingly called 'inter-vivos guardianship', it its White Paper *Adoption : The Future* (1993) Cm 2288, para 5.23. However, courts may still require greater persuasion to sanction an adoption by a relative or step-parent, and the alternative of a residence order under s 8 of the Children Act 1989 might be preferred – see G Douglas and N V Lowe 'Becoming a Parent in English Law' (1992) 108 LQR 414 at p 424. There has been anecdotal (but no statistical) evidence of an increase in resort to step-parent adoption as a means of sidestepping the operation of the Child Support Act 1991, discussed in Ch 9.

17 Section 1 of the Adoption Act 1976.

18 SI 1983/1964. See the description by M Richards, *Adoption* (1989) pp 59-64.

19 Department of Health and Welsh Office *Review of Adoption Law, Consultation Document* (1992), para 26.7 refers to limits varying from early to late thirties, with few agencies accepting applicants over the age of 40 for healthy infants.

20 *Ibid* para 26.3.

1 *The Guardian,* 12 July 1993.

adopters, except where such an approach, renamed 'common sense', was in line with the Government's own views of desirable family structures.[2] It argued that applicants for acceptance as prospective adopters are

'entitled to expect that throughout the assessment process they will be treated with courtesy and sensitivity; that the assessment made will be fair and objective; and that it will not be distorted by dogmatic attitudes on such matters as the suitability of trans-racial adoptions or the suitable age for adopted [sic] parents'.[3]

To this end, the Government proposed a new complaints mechanism whereby a rejected 'couple' (and presumably single applicants) would have the right to be re-assessed by another agency, the cost to be born by the first.[4] The assumption behind this proposal seems to be that an agency would be more careful about rejecting an applicant if it thought it would have to cover the cost of a second assessment, a strange means of ensuring an 'objective' assessment of suitability.

An adoption panel, made up of social workers, a medical adviser and nominees of the local authority or agency, recommends to the agency whether the applicant should be approved as suitable to adopt.[5] Some panels may invite the applicants to attend their meetings, although this is unusual.[6] Surprisingly, given the Government's desire to increase the sensitivity to be given to the feelings of such applicants, it did not propose making their attendance at panel meetings a requirement, although it did seek to increase the proportion of independent members on panels in its consultation document.[7]

There must then be further approval by the panel of the matching of applicants and child for a suitable placement. Once this is accomplished, the application may proceed to the court for a final judgment to be made, though not without the agency producing a report to the court.[8] Further, if the adoption is contested, then a guardian *ad litem* must be appointed for the child. The guardian's function is to safeguard the child's interests by investigating the case and making a confidential report to the court. There is therefore ample scope for duplication of information being

---

2 See, eg, paras 4.27-4.42 and 5.7-5.9 of *Adoption: The Future* (1993) and the discussion by S Jolly and R Sandland, 'Political Correctness and the Adoption White Paper' [1994] Fam Law 30.

3 *Ibid* at para 5.8.

4 Department of Health, *The Future of Adoption Panels, Consultation Document* (1994) para 7.5.

5 For a study of some applicants who were rejected by adoption panels as unsuitable, see J Selwyn, 'Applying to adopt: the experience of rejection' (1991) 15 *Adoption and Fostering* (3) 26.

6 L Bingley-Miller and D McNeish, 'Paramountcy or partnership? Applicants attending adoption panels' (1993) 17 *Adoption and Fostering* (4) 15.

7 *The Future of Adoption Panels, Consultation Document* (1994) para 5.1.

8 This is known as the Schedule II report (from the Adoption Rules 1984).

compiled and assessed by the agency, the panel, the court and the guardian. There is also ample scope for delay, with the *Pathways to Adoption* project finding that the average length of time from approval of the adoption placement (ie matching of the child and prospective adopters) to the date of application to adopt was five and a half months, and, that it took about nine to ten weeks after the application had been made for the court to receive the Schedule II report.[9]

All these mechanisms are intended to ensure that the placement and eventual adoption will be for the welfare of the child, and in deciding whether to make the adoption order, the court must, under s 6 of the Adoption Act 1976, give:

'first consideration ... to the need to safeguard and promote the welfare of the child throughout his childhood; and shall so far as practicable ascertain the wishes and feelings of the child regarding the decision and give due consideration to them, having regard to his age and understanding'.

This test is not the paramountcy test which applies in other proceedings relating to the upbringing of children, although in practice it makes little if any difference to outcomes. It reflects the historically greater significance attached to the right of parents to keep their own child from being adopted, but Article 21 of the United Nations Convention on the Rights of the Child requires that the 'system of adoption shall ensure that the best interests of the child shall be the paramount consideration'. The Government translated this requirement in its White Paper into imposing:

'a clear and positive duty on the court to address itself to the needs of the child and to the scale of potential advantage to the child of having a new family; and to satisfy itself that the likely benefit of adoption is so significantly better when compared with other options as to justify an adoption order'.[10]

We examine the paramountcy test in more detail and also consider the position where there is a contest between the prospective adopters and the natural parents in Chapters 8 and 14.

The contrast with what happens in assisted reproduction is striking. There, in cases other than surrogacy, it will be recalled, such scrutiny of the prospective parents that takes place is carried out by the clinicians or other employees of the clinic who provide the treatment. The reason for the disparity between assisted reproduction and adoption is the view that, as the name implies, all that is happening in the former is that would-be parents are being *helped* to have a child of their own, while in adoption, again implicitly in the name itself, the prospective parents are taking on, and taking over, the care of a child from someone else – very often in

---

9 *Pathways to Adoption* (1993), paras 7.8 and 7.9.
10 *Adoption: The Future* (1993) para 5.4. This appears to conflate the criterion for making the adoption order with that for dispensing with the parents' agreement.

competition with other potential adopters. But logically, there is not such a clear-cut difference between the two procedures. In either case, the aim of the intending parents is to have a child to care for and bring up as their own. In assisted reproduction there need be no genetic link between the intending parents and the child, just as there need not be in adoption. Equally, there may often (or even usually) be a partial genetic link between the intending parents and the child, in assisted reproduction, and there will often be such a link in adoption. The distinction made by the law appears therefore to be based on a general perception of assisted reproduction as being a device for producing a child for parents, while adoption is a device for producing parents for an existing child who requires new ones. The emphasis in assisted reproduction is on satisfying the legitimate wish of the adults to have a child, but this can also be seen as a *selfish* wish if the adults do not satisfy our ideas of who is deserving of help (lesbian women, 'virgin mothers' or post-menopausal women, for example). In adoption, the emphasis is on fulfilling the needs of the child, and adopters are generally viewed as altruistic people who charitably volunteer to take on a child who would otherwise be at risk. This attitude to adoption has grown stronger over the years since the 1926 Act, as social workers and others in the field have successfully portrayed adoption in these terms. The degree of scrutiny and the elaborate procedures surrounding adoption reinforce the image of it as a child-saving mechanism. Indeed, so successful has the child-centred image of adoption become, that there may be public disquiet when those who appear to offer the chance of a good home to a child in need are turned down as unsuitable. Similarly, there may be considerable unease at the 'experts' determining, that a black child, for example, placed and well-bonded with white foster carers, should be removed from them to a black family because he or she may experience racism when older.[11] There may be equal incredulity at the argument that children in Romanian orphanages or Bolivian shanty towns should *not* be adopted by white Westerners and removed from their cultural heritage. The emotional response in such cases may tend to be that the child's immediate need to avoid starvation or neglect is best served by placement or adoption with white Western families if others are not forthcoming. Couples able and willing to take on such children are viewed as deserving congratulation rather than rejection.[12]

---

11 See O Gill and B Jackson, *Adoption and Race* (1993). For examples in the case law see *Re N (a minor) (Adoption)* [1990] 1 FLR 58; *Re P (a minor) (Adoption)* [1990] 1 FLR 96; *Re JK (Adoption: Transracial Placement)* [1991] 2 FLR 340.
12 See *R v Secretary of State for Health, ex p Luff* [1992] 1 FLR 59, for example.

(b) Who decides?

Both the Hopkinson and Tomlin Committees recommended that adoption should be by court order, and this is still the case. However, the *Pathways to Adoption* research found that 75% of agency adoption applications were uncontested, and that orders were granted in 95% of *contested* cases,[13] and mooted the possibility that non-contentious cases could be dealt with through a registration procedure rather than through a court.[14] Before the application can be decided upon by the court, a degree of scrutiny from social workers will, as we have shown, have taken place to assess both the fitness of the proposed adopters, and the welfare of the child. Adoption is the best example of 'licensing parents' before they can be entrusted with the care of children.

4. DECLARING AND DISCOVERING PARENTAGE

Reference to the child's ethnic and cultural background leads us on to consider the matter of the child's genetic identity. It should be noted that identity has a meaning which goes beyond genetic inheritance and which embraces psychological completeness, and a sense of cultural belonging. These may obviously be influenced by discovery of genetic background – indeed, the rationale for facilitating such discovery lies at least in large measure with the significance attached to such dimensions of identity.[15] We have already noted the rights of children under Articles 7 and 8 of the United Nations Convention to 'know' their parents and to preserve their identity. These rights may be used to justify the procedures which exist to determine or discover who is the child's genetic parent. Adults too may wish to discover who their genetic children are, although it is less clear that they can point to a human right recognising this wish. It is arguable that Article 8 of the European Convention, which declares the right to respect for one's family life, might be prayed in aid, although there is no Convention definition of 'family'. As regards gamete donors, however, the European Commission held, in *G v Netherlands*,[56] that merely acting as a donor does not give a right to respect for the donor's family life with the resulting child which should be recognised by granting contact with

---

13 M Murch *et al*, *Pathways to Adoption* (1993) Table 2.15(c). The proportion of uncontested applications in which an adoption order was made was 99%.

14 *Ibid* p 245.

15 For a valuable discussion of these issues, see J Masson and C Harrison, 'Identity: Mapping the Frontiers' in N V Lowe and G Douglas (eds) *Families across Frontiers* (forthcoming).

16 (1993) 16 EHRR Part 7, CD 38.

the child. It is doubtful that the European Court would hold that a birth parent who relinquishes the child for adoption has a right to discover the present identity of the child because of the voluntary giving-up of parental status, but where the adoption is against the birth parent's will, there might be a stronger claim.[17]

At this point, legal recognition of the social role of parenthood may well clash with rights protecting genetic identity. Our concern here is to consider first, when parentage might be in issue and what legal procedures exist to determine it, and second, since it is clear that legal parentage is not always the same as genetic parentage, what rights there are for a person to discover his or her genetic parentage.

(a) When parentage might be in issue

Legal proceedings involving a child may require that a finding of the child's legal parentage be made. For example, if a man claims to be the father of the child, and applies for an order under the Children Act 1989, s 4 for parental responsibility[18] his application cannot proceed unless and until he is established as the child's father.[19] A child might seek to succeed to a title, or claim an interest in an intestacy and need to prove his or her parentage in order to qualify. Finally, proof of *genetic* parentage may be vital in immigration cases, where DNA testing has been used to overcome the perceived weaknesses of foreign legal mechanisms for establishing family relationships.[20]

(b) Declarations

Proceedings such as those just described may be initiated by a 'parent' or by the child, and while they may lead to a finding of parentage, such a finding will be a judgment *in personam*, and only binding on the parties themselves or those claiming through them. It would obviously be

---

17 The trend of decisions regarding continuing contact between parents and their child in public care is to uphold parents' rights to seek rehabilitation with their child; see, eg, *Eriksson v Sweden* (1989) 12 EHRR 183; *Andersson v Sweden* (1992) 14 EHRR 615 and *Olsson v Sweden (No 2)* (1992) 17 EHRR 134 (all from the European Court of Human Rights), discussed in Ch 2. Cf *Re H (Adoption : Disclosure of Information)* [1995] 1 FLR 236 (court order to permit disclosure of otherwise confidential information to allow tracing of adoptee by natural relative).
18 Discussed in Ch 5.
19 See the previous chapter.
20 See the discussion by A Grubb and D Pearl, *Blood Testing, AIDS and DNA Profiling* (1990) pp 159-172.

preferable in disputed cases if there were a mechanism which could lead to a determination which would settle the controversy once and for all, and this is provided by a declaration. It may also be valuable for the child to be able to obtain a legal judgment of his or her parentage which is not dependent upon other proceedings being in train. A procedure for obtaining a declaration of legitimacy (and not parentage *per se*) was introduced into law in the Legitimacy Declaration Act 1858, and the modern law is set out in s 56 of the Family Law Act 1987, which provides that:

'(1) Any person may apply to the court for a declaration—
 (a) that a person named in the application is or was his parent; or
 (b) that he is the legitimate child of his parents.'

It will be seen that a person claiming to be a parent cannot use this procedure – it is the *child* who may apply – and also that the declaration can extend to establishing the child's legitimacy (but not *illegitimacy*) rather than his or her parentage *per se* .[1] So far, we have been mainly considering in this chapter the ways in which *parents* may *establish* a relationship with a child; what the declaration does is to permit the *child* to *obtain recognition* of a relationship with the parent, and it predates the more controversial ability of children to seek leave to obtain orders under the Children Act 1989 s 10(8) by over a century.[2]

(c) Discovery of parentage through the register

We can look further at the position of *children* in relation to the legal establishment of parentage by considering how they may discover their parentage without taking legal proceedings. We saw in the previous chapter that entry of a man's name on the birth register is *prima facie* evidence that he is the father of the child, and that all births must be registered within 42 days, by either parent, if married, and by the mother,

---

1 Jane Fortin argues that adults claiming to be parents should also have the right to seek a declaration, although on the basis that this would enable the interest of the *child* in knowing his or her true genetic identity to be vindicated where the caretaking parent declines to take action: see '*Re F*: "The Gooseberry Bush Approach"' (1994) 57 MLR 296, 304. There is a second kind of declaration, which however lacks the benefits of that just outlined. This is contained in s 27 of the Child Support Act 1991, which provides for the court to make a declaration of parentage on the application of the Secretary of State (in practice, an officer of the Child Support Agency) or the person with care (in practice, usually the mother) with a view to a maintenance assessment being carried out under the Act (see Ch 9). This declaration has effect only for the purposes of the Child Support Act, so that the *in rem* nature of a declaration is missing. It also cannot be sought by the child.
2 See Ch 7.

if she is not married to the father. The birth register may be consulted by any person, but it will usually only record the information given at the time of registration,[3] which may not be accurate. For example, a married woman might have committed adultery without her husband finding out, and given birth to a child. If the husband is registered as the father, and the adultery is never discovered by the child, the child's true genetic paternity will never be known by him or her. If a single woman gives birth and registers without including the father's name, or the child was conceived after licensed assisted reproduction treatment, the child may be legally fatherless, and in either case, may again never have a chance of discovering who the father was. If a couple conceived a child by means of donor insemination before the Family Law Reform Act 1987, and they chose to register the husband (or partner) as the father rather than the donor, the child would not be able to discover his or her genetic identity from the register, and since the 1987 legislation (and the more comprehensive Human Fertilisation and Embryology Act 1990), the intending parents would be entitled, and indeed required, to register the husband or partner as the father if s 28(2) or (3) applied, since there would be no other man who could be classed in law as the father. The register will therefore only tell the official version of the child's birth story.

Furthermore, the adoption of a child will be registered on the Adopted Children Register and, until the Children Act 1975, the child had no right to discover his or her original birth entry (disclosing the name of the woman who gave birth, and possibly the father, depending upon the circumstances).[4] Such information had been kept secret, to protect the child from the stigma of illegitimacy and to ensure the continuing anonymity of the natural parent(s), and to enable the adopters to present the child to the outside world as 'theirs'. The Houghton Committee recommended introducing a right of discovery, upon the adopted child's reaching the age of majority, because they were influenced by the findings of research carried out in Scotland, where adopted children had had such a right since 1930 when adoption was originally introduced into Scottish law. The research, by John Triseliotis, found that the majority of those he questioned who discovered the original birth record found it of some value in coming to terms with the fact of their adoption. Although there was concern that parents, especially women who had given birth outside marriage, who had given up their children for adoption would be severely distressed if the adopted child later traced

---

3   Unless the child is re-registered following the parents' marriage, entry of the father's name under ss 10 and 10A of the Births and Deaths Registration Act 1953 outlined above, or declaration of parentage.

4   Now see ss 50 and 51 of the Adoption Act 1976. A person adopted before 12 November 1975 must attend a counselling interview before information from the birth register may be disclosed (s 51(7)).

them, Houghton took the view that the fear of being traced may have been unduly magnified.[5] The Economic and Social Committee of the European Community, on the other hand, has been concerned that the birth mother, who would be more easily discoverable from the birth record than the child's father, should not take all the 'blame' for giving up the child, and that therefore access to the record should not be an automatic right of the adopted child.[6] The assumption that a birth parent will be blamed is revealing of the attitude that giving up one's child for adoption is a failure of the parental role, and very different from the attitude taken to gamete, especially egg donors, who are seen as providing a valuable service to the infertile.

Triseliotis, among others, carried out further research into the workings of the 1975 change, and found that 'the calamities anticipated by sections of the media, politicians, and some organisations have not materialised'.[7] Far from thousands of adopted children knocking on the door of the birth mother, it has been estimated that no more than 15 to 20% of adoptees are likely to seek access to their birth records, and of these, probably no more than about half would wish to meet the birth parent or family, and even fewer be able to trace them successfully.[8] In any event, as we have seen, the original birth entry may be incomplete or inaccurate. Further, it was held by the Court of Appeal in *R v Registrar General, ex p Smith*,[9] that there is no absolute right to discover the original birth entry. In that case, a man who had been adopted had become a violent criminal and murdered his cell-mate under the delusion that he was the adoptive mother. He was obsessed with finding his birth mother, and there were fears for her safety should he do so. The Court held that public policy gives the Registrar General a discretion to withhold access to the original entry where there is a significant risk that providing it could result in the adopted person endangering the life of the birth parent.

In fact, by the time of the Adoption Law Review in 1990-93, the emphasis had shifted towards the desire of birth parents to find out what had happened to their adopted children. For example, many birth mothers interviewed by researchers revealed that adoption was like 'a bereavement without a death'; they had no way of knowing if their child was even alive or dead,[10] and they spoke of 'the torment of wondering whether their son

5 Houghton Report (1972) Cm 2288, paras 300-305.
6 'Opinion on Adoption' *Official Journal of the European Communities* No C 287/18, 4 November 1992, paras 1.4.6.1, 2.15.
7 J Triseliotis, 'Obtaining birth certificates' in P Bean (ed) *Adoption: Essays in Social Policy, Law and Sociology* (1984).
8 See the summary of research in Triseliotis, *Ibid* pp 49-50.
9 [1991] 2 QB 393.
10 Despite the registration arrangements designed to prevent the birth parent tracing the child through the registers, it is apparently possible, and has led to disruptions in adoption placements. In *Re X (a minor) (Adoption Details: Disclosure)* [1994] Fam

was in the disaster at the football stadium at Hillsborough, their daughter in the ferry at Zeebrugge'.[11] The Children Act 1989 went a little way to addressing these needs by establishing an Adoption Contact Register, whereby, assuming each has registered, details of the name and address of birth relatives are forwarded to an adopted person who then has the option to make contact. This therefore strengthens the position of the adopted child, but does not enable the birth family to initiate action which will lead to the contact. Yet in a survey of 262 birth mothers who had given up their child for adoption, all except nine wanted to see their child and to be found, and two-thirds had tried to trace their child. The majority considered that they should have the same rights to information as their child.[12]

It has been accepted in the case of adopted children, that they should have a general right to discover the 'truth' about their origins. Similar provision has been made for children born as the result of a surrogacy arrangement, who are the subjects of parental orders under s 30 of the Human Fertilisation and Embryology Act 1990.[13] It has also been held that a child brought up to believe, wrongly, that her mother's cohabitant was actually her father, had a right to be told the real identity of her father.[14] However, for children born as a result of assisted reproduction (apart from surrogacy), there is only a right, once they reach the age of majority, to seek information of a non-identifying nature about the donor of the egg and/or sperm.[15] It was thought that permitting the child to discover the identity of the donor would deter people from acting as donors at all, and there was also a sharp division of opinion as to whether it would be in the child's interests to learn of the fact of donation.[16] This leaves children born as a result of assisted reproduction in a different

---

174, the Court of Appeal held that the High Court could make an order under its inherent jurisdiction, to prevent a recurrence of such disruption, that during the child's minority, the Registrar General should not disclose the details of the adoption on the Adopted Children Register to anyone without the leave of the Court. The aim of the order was to prevent the child's mother from tracing the child, after she had forcibly abducted the child from other placements. On the other hand, an order may be made requiring the Registrar General to reveal information, otherwise kept confidential, to enable such tracing, where the court is satisfied that this is desirable: *Re H (Adoption: Disclosure of Information)* [1995] 1 FLR 236.

11 See P Bouchier, L Lambert and J Triseliotis, *Parting with a child for adoption* (1991), and A Mullender (ed) *Open adoption: the philosophy and the practice* (1991) p 113, 118.

12 As is the position in New Zealand under the Adult Adoption Information Act 1985. See S Wells 'What do birth mothers want?' (1993) 17 *Adoption and Fostering* (4) 22.

13 Parental Orders (Human Fertilisation and Embryology) Regulations 1994, Sch 1, para 4(b), SI 1994/2767.

14 *Re R (a minor) (Contact)* [1993] 2 FLR 762.

15 Section 31 of the Human Fertilisation and Embryology Act 1990.

16 See the discussion by G Douglas *Law, Fertility and Reproduction* (1991) pp 132-136.

position to other children, and the law in a complicated mess. Whether this matters depends upon whether one regards the genetic or birth origins of a child as a matter of importance. If one takes the view that the birth register itself may be an incomplete record of the reality, then inability to gain access to it may be insignificant. What counts is the relationship between the child and those people who undertake the upbringing of the child.

This does reflect the general trend in legal development, which we have traced throughout this and the previous chapter, to emphasise the value and importance of social parenthood carried out by those who voluntarily assume the role of parents. Yet how do we account for the increased recognition given to the needs of the adopted to discover their birth origins? The paradox is the same as the ability to fix genetic parentage through DNA testing while discounting the legal significance of that same genetic parentage. But perhaps there is no paradox after all. Instead, the law is recognising the *greater* importance of social parenthood and the reality that a child may have *several* people in his or her life who carry out various aspects of the parenting role. The genetic basis of parenthood is one aspect, and a child might be entitled to know the identity of those who provided that genetic basis. Thus, John Eekelaar argues that biological parentage should be established as a matter of routine, without its carrying any implications for the exercise of social parenthood through parental responsibility.[17] The difficulty with this is in devising ways in which this could be done – for there will still be occasions when the father's identity cannot be established because he is no longer on the scene to be tested, or when the mother declines to permit the child to be tested. In the meantime, in order to satisfy both the desires of those wishing to fulfil the social role of parent, and also the need of the child for security in a stable family unit, the law appears increasingly ready to bestow the title of legal parent on the social parents.

17 'Parenthood, Social Engineering and Rights' in D Morgan and G Douglas (eds) *Constituting Families: A Study in Governance* (1994).

CHAPTER 5

Unmarried fathers, former parents and non-parents

We have argued that the modern law increasingly grants the status of parent to those who have manifested an intention and desire to fulfil the social role of parent, ie to bring up the child. However, having established who, in law, is a parent, we need to consider two other aspects of legal recognition of social parenthood. First, where parental status is qualified because it does not import with it 'parental responsibility', the powers (and duties) of parenthood.[1] The parents concerned are unmarried fathers and those whose children have been 'freed for adoption'. Secondly, we examine the acquisition of parental responsibility by those who are not given parental status.

1. QUALIFIED PARENTAL STATUS

(a) Unmarried fathers

Historically, as we have seen, children whose parents were not married to each other were classed as illegitimate and considerable social stigma attached both to the child and the mother. This situation has changed dramatically in recent years. First there has been the growth in the number of children born outside marriage to over 30% of all live births.[2] Secondly, a realisation that the sins of the fathers should not be visited upon the children appears to have become a global revelation, as witnessed by the articulation of the international obligation to prohibit discrimination against those born out of wedlock. For example, Article 2(1) of the United Nations Convention on the Rights of the Child requires

---

1 See Chs 6 to 8.
2 *Social Trends 1994* Chart 2.21.

states to respect and ensure the child's rights, irrespective of, *inter alia*, the child's birth or other status.[3] The Law Commissions in both England and Wales and Scotland examined the legal position in the 1980s. The initial preference of the former was to replace the terms 'legitimate' and 'illegitimate' with 'marital' and 'non-marital'.[4] However, the latter considered that these labels would soon acquire the previous undesirable connotations and proposed that it would be preferable to distinguish between parental relationships rather than between children, so that express reference should be made to the parents' relationship where (but only where) this was regarded as of legal significance.[5] The Law Commission[6] re-examined the issue in the light of the Scottish report and adopted a similar approach, which led to the passage of the Family Law Reform Act 1987. Section 1(1) of that Act provides that:

'references (however expressed) to any relationship between two persons shall, unless the contrary intention appears, be construed without regard to whether or not the father and mother of either of them, or the father and mother of any person through whom the relationship is deduced, have or had been married to each other at any time'.

This means that the fact of marriage between parents is irrelevant unless statute provides expressly to the contrary. However, we suggest that the most important aspects of a child's legal relationship with his or her parents are first, which of those parents has parental responsibility for the child; secondly, which of those parents passes on citizenship and nationality; and thirdly, which parent can agree to the child's adoption by someone else or to the making of a parental order in favour of a gamete donor. The first is important because in our society, a person with parental responsibility is empowered to take most important decisions in respect of the child, is responsible for the care of the child and has presumptive possession of the child. The second is important because a person may be denied the right to enter or remain in this country unless he or she has British citizenship. The third is important because adoption or surrogacy are the only ways in which a person can give away (or, in the case of adoption, have taken away) his or her status as parent in respect of a child already born. In relation to all of these, the law

---

3 See also the European Convention on the Legal Status of Children Born out of Wedlock (1975); Article 8 of the European Convention on Human Rights (and the *Marckx, Johnston* and *Inze* cases before the European Court). For discussion of the human rights dimension to the issue, see R Deech, 'The unmarried father and human rights' (1992) 4 *Journal of Child Law* 3.
4 See Report No 118 (1982).
5 Scot Law Com No 82 (1984), enacted in the Law Reform (Parent and Child) (Scotland) Act 1986. The term 'marital child' was, however, incorporated into Isle of Man law – see the (Isle of Man) Family Law Act 1991, s 5.
6 Report No 157 (1986).

continues to distinguish between children born inside and outside marriage. By s 2(2) of the Children Act 1989, only the mother of a child whose parents were not married to each other at the time of his conception or birth has automatic parental responsibility for the child, although, as we discuss below, the father can acquire this by making a parental responsibility agreement with the mother, or seeking a parental responsibility order from a court, under s 4 of the Children Act. Under the British Nationality Act 1981, s 1(1), a person born in the United Kingdom shall be a British citizen if at the time of his birth, his father or mother is a British citizen or settled in the United Kingdom. However, by s 50(9):

> '(a)the relationship of mother and child shall be taken to exist between a
> woman and any child (legitimate or illegitimate) born to her; but
> (b) ... the relationship of father and child shall be taken to exist only between
> a man and any legitimate child born to him;'

Thus, even where the unmarried father has parental responsibility by virtue of s 4 of the Children Act, he is still not able to bestow British citizenship on his child. Thirdly, under the Adoption Act 1976, the agreement to the making of an adoption order is only required to be given by the child's 'parent', who is defined, in s 72(1) as 'any parent who has parental responsibility for the child under the Children Act 1989'. At least here, then, the 'unmarried father', by obtaining parental responsibility, may have legal standing in adoption proceedings, but otherwise, he does not rank as a 'parent'.[7]

The question of whether such fathers should be placed in the same position as those who are married to the mother remains controversial.[8] The Scottish Law Commission has proposed, as did the majority of its consultees, that unmarried fathers should be given automatic parental responsibility, along with all other legal parents.[9] Their reasons for this proposal were as follows. First, a 'bad', but married, father would otherwise have the parental responsibility denied to a 'good', but unmarried one. Second, the uninterested absent father presents no problem to the care giving mother, as parental responsibility may be exercised without consent by the other parent. Third, the *mother* is not denied parental status because the liaison was merely casual, so why

---

7 *Re C (a minor) (Adoption: Parental Agreement: Contact)* [1993] 2 FLR 260. A complaint under the European Convention on Human Rights concerning a similar provision in Swiss law has been held admissible: *D v Switzerland* (1993) 15 EHRR Part 7, CD 29.

8 For a compelling discussion of the argument in favour of giving unmarried fathers automatic rights, see Andrew Bainham, 'When is a Parent not a Parent?' (1989) 2 *International Journal of Law and the Family* 209, but for a rejoinder, see R Deech 'The unmarried father and human rights' (1992) 4 *Journal of Child Law* 3.

9 Scot Law Com No 135, *Report on Family Law* (1992) paras 2.36-2.51.

should the father be? In any event, parental responsibility is conferred for the benefit of the child, not the parent. Fourth, resentment felt by lone mothers should not inform the general law, nor should any fears that they might be harassed by the father, since court regulation is the answer to parental involvement against the child's interest. Fifth, discrimination against unmarried fathers may foster irresponsible paternal attitudes. Sixth, the child is currently disadvantaged in, say, a claim for compensation, for if a single mother is killed in a car crash, no one is automatically qualified to act as the child's legal representative. Seventh, the 'rapist father' – a man who rapes the mother and then demands rights over the resulting child – seems to be a phantom figure. Finally, given that so many births in recent years have been outside marriage, and the the number of cohabiting couples is now substantial, 'the balance has now swung in favour of the view that parents are parents, whether married to each other or not'.[10]

These arguments may be divided into three categories. First, there are those relating to the position of the men themselves. It is discriminatory and unfair to those men who wish to play a full part in the lives of their children that they are not classed as worthy of the status of parent, except when it comes to fulfilling their liability to support the child financially. It is particularly unfair where the man wishes to marry the mother, but she refuses. Secondly, there are arguments which focus on the children. It is discriminatory to deny them a father with normal legal responsibilities and rights; for example, if the mother is killed in a train crash the child would have no one *automatically* qualified to act as his or her guardian. It may also encourage an irresponsible attitude to children if the father knows that he has no legal responsibility for the child's upbringing anyway. Thirdly, there are arguments relating to the mother. It is true that women might fear interference by the unmarried father in how they wish to raise the child, but this would be equally possible in respect of *married* fathers anyway, and the child's interests and welfare should not be dependent upon the feelings of one parent. The argument which weighed heavily with the English Law Commission, that it would be wrong to permit a man who had raped the mother to have automatic parental responsibility, was dismissed. The Commission agreed with one consultee who suggested that 'the rapist father seems to be almost certainly a phantom whose existence should be discounted (unless it can be shown that such persons exist on any significant scale)'.[11] But since we do not

---

10 *Ibid* at para 2.48.

11 We might add that it is likely that the majority of such rapine children as do exist are legitimate, given that marital rape is more common than rape by non-husbands: K Painter, *Wife-Rape, Marriage and the Law* (1991). Her survey found that 'lawful rape [as marital rape then was] exceeds unlawful rape by acquaintances or boy-friends by 2 to 1 and stranger rape by 7 to 1', p 1.

know how many such cases there are, we cannot k now if the rapist is indeed a phantom. However, the Commission went further, arguing that to exclude the rapist from automatic parental responsibility would be unprincipled:

> 'The nature of the sexual intercourse (whether in or out of marriage) resulting in the conception should not affect the legal relationships arising from the procreation of the child.'[12]

It is true, as the Commission points out, that the absent, uninterested father is unlikely to seek to play a part in the child's life; there is far more of a problem in encouraging men (married and unmarried) to accept their responsibilities than to dissuade them from exercising them, as the experience of the Child Support Act, discussed in Chapter 9, perhaps demonstrates.

However, extending automatic parental responsibility to unmarried fathers would be more than a break with the traditional approach to the law. It would also reverse the trend towards recognition of the *intention* to act as parent as the key to parental status. Even though the Scottish Law Commission argues that it is precisely that which they wish to recognise automatically, what their reform would achieve would be full parental status *whether or not* the man had ever evinced a willingness to assume the social role of parent.

The value of marriage to parenthood is that it may constitute an express and public commitment to the partnership with the mother and to any children the couple have together. It can be seen as *evidence* of the intention to act as a parent. But clearly, with the growth of cohabitation and births outside marriage, it can be argued that an alternative mechanism for manifesting the intention to act as parent is required. The parental responsibility agreement provided for by s 4 of the Children Act is an equivalent and, given that the child must actually be in existence, possibly even clearer piece of evidence of such intention than marriage. Such agreements must be in prescribed form and filed with the Principal Registry of the Family Division. There is no fee for this service, and no scrutiny of the circumstances in which the agreement has been made. It is considerably easier in terms of paperwork, cost and effort, than getting married.[13]

If they do not agree to marry and the mother declines to enter into an agreement, the father has the alternative of seeking an order from the

12 Scot Law Com No 135, *Report on Family Law* (1992) at para 2.47.
13 It is arguably too easy; the lack of any scrutiny raises the possibility of the mother coming under pressure to sign the form, perhaps in return for maintenance for the child. There was also scope for fraud since anyone's name and signature could be entered on the form; the Parental Responsibility Agreement (Amendment) Regulations 1994 SI 1954/3157 now require that the agreement be witnessed by a justice of the peace or officer of the court.

court. Indeed, even where there is apparently no disagreement between the parents, an order may be sought. In one early survey of the working of the Children Act, of 68 applications for parental responsibility orders,[14] it appeared that 35 were not contested by the mother, leaving it unclear why proceedings for an order were felt to be necessary. Possibly, there was dispute as to other applications (eg, for contact with the child), or the mother was not willing positively to enter into an agreement but did not bother to resist the application for an order. This might explain why 21 orders under s 4 were made where the mother was not disputing the order by the end of proceedings. It may, alternatively, have been the case that legal advisers were not as aware of the possibility of the agreement route as they should have been. The number of agreements registered with the Principal Registry has grown steadily since the Act came into force, from around 1,500 in the second half of 1992 to nearly 3,000 in the equivalent period in 1994.[15] Even so, compared with the roughly 260,000 births outside marriage each year, of which, as we know, three-quarters are registered by both parents,[16] there is clearly still a huge shortfall in the number of agreements which could potentially be registered.

On this comparison, court orders are even more unusual, running at about two-thirds of the number of agreements made.[17] Nonetheless, it appears that courts may generally seem to regard s 4 orders as something that unmarried fathers are entitled to, unless clearly unfit. In *Re H (minors) (Local Authority: Parental Rights) (No 3)*[18] Balcombe LJ held that even a father whose children were in the care of the local authority and about to be placed for adoption was entitled to a parental rights and duties order (the forerunner of a parental responsibility order) provided that he could satisfy the court as to the degree of commitment he had shown towards the child, the degree of attachment existing between him and the child, and that he had valid reasons for seeking the order.[19] Similarly, in *Re H (a minor) (Parental Responsibility)*[20] a court granted the father a parental responsibility order because the mother and her husband had moved to Scotland and were contemplating adopting the

14 See I Butler *et al*, 'The Children Act 1989 and the Unmarried Father' (1993) 5 *Journal of Child Law* (4) 157.
15 *Children Act Advisory Committee Annual Report 1993/94* (1995) p 76.
16 *Social Trends 1994* Chart 2.21.
17 *Children Act Advisory Committee Annual Report 1993/94* (1995) p 76.
18 [1991] Fam 151.
19 Though compare *W v Ealing London Borough Council* [1993] 2 FLR 788: 'the principle that an order is not precluded merely because parental rights may not in practice be exercisable is no authority for the converse proposition that an order must be made in such circumstances' (*per* Sir Stephen Brown P at 796D).
20 [1993] 1 FLR 484.

child. The court wished to protect the father's position in the light of the adoption proceedings or in case the mother and husband suffered some misfortune. The father who can demonstrate his commitment to the child therefore has a means of obtaining full status and parental responsibility.[1]

To be consistent with the increasing legal emphasis on the intention to fulfil the social role of parent, it is sufficient to provide a mechanism whereby that intention can be demonstrated. As we have seen, s 4 of the Children Act 1989 may be utilised for that purpose. Further, once made, the order *or* agreement may only be brought to an end by a court, on the application of any person who has parental responsibility for the child, or with leave of the court, the child him or herself.[2] Of course, it could be argued that there are irresponsible mothers who do not deserve full parental status, as well as irresponsible fathers, so why should all birth mothers be given automatic parental responsibility? The short answer is that, by carrying on with the pregnancy when it could have been terminated, the mother has shown her intention to act as social parent, even if only for the short time necessary to make up her mind to give the child up for adoption. It must be conceded, however, that the *prima facie* denial of parental responsibility to unmarried fathers, if done on the basis that they are less likely than married fathers to be *de facto* carers, does not sit well with the principle that such responsibility necessarily survives parental divorce.

(b) Former parents – parents of children freed for adoption

Under s 2(9) of the Children Act 1989, a person who has parental responsibility for a child may not surrender or transfer any part of that responsibility to another (unless by way of adoption or parental order in favour of gamete donors). In adoption proceedings, a parent must either agree to the adoption, or have his or her agreement dispensed with, under s 16 of the Adoption Act 1976 . We consider the factors which may lead to such dispensation in Chapter 14. Here, however, our concern is to note that, under the current law, parents may agree to the *principle* of their child being adopted (or have agreement dispensed with) in advance of an actual adoption placement or order being made. This is known as 'freeing

1 The position is similar in the United States, see Bartlett 'Rethinking Parenthood as an Exclusive Status: The Need for Legal Alternatives when the Premise of the Nuclear Family has Failed' (1984) 70 *Virginia Law Review* 879 at pp 919-927. For an example of an order being refused, see *Re T (a minor) (Parental Responsibility: Contact)* [1993] 2 FLR 450, where the father had been violent to the mother and callous towards the child. He was also prohibited from making any further application for three years (cf the discussion in Ch 14).
2 Section 4(3).

the child for adoption'. The aim of freeing is to end any uncertainty regarding a child's availability for adoption, by providing a procedure whereby the birth parents' legal interest in the child may be extinguished. As the Houghton Committee, who originally recommended its introduction, put it, there were a sizeable number of children in care for whom no permanent future could be arranged, possibly because the parents could not bring themselves to make a plan for them, or refused to agree to adoption.

> 'Some of these children may have no contact with their parents and would benefit from adoption, but the parents will not agree to it. In other cases a parent may have her child received into care shortly after birth and then vacillate for months or even years over the question of adoption, thus depriving her child of the security of a settled family home life.'[3]

Under the prior law, there was no way of testing whether a court might dispense with the parents' agreement to the adoption short of placing the child with prospective adopters and bringing the adoption application. If the court refused to dispense with agreement, the child could not be adopted and much anguish and insecurity would have been suffered by both child and prospective adopters in the meantime.

Section 18 of the Adoption Act 1976 empowers a court to make an order declaring a child free for adoption, on the application of an adoption agency, provided that parental consent has been given, or dispensed with. The court must be satisfied that the parents have been given an opportunity of making, if they wish, a declaration that they prefer not to be involved in future questions concerning the adoption of the child.[4] The effect of the order is to vest parental responsibility for the child in the adoption agency and to extinguish parental responsibility in the birth parents.[5] They retain parental status in the sense of remaining on the birth register as the child's parents, but they are also classed as 'former parents', even though no adoption order has yet been made (and indeed, may never be made if suitable adopters cannot be found for the child). These 'former parents' may be given progress reports about the child, and may seek a revocation of the freeing order if no adoption order has been made within 12 months and the child does not have a home with a person with whom he or she has been placed for adoption.[6] For all other purposes, however, the parents rank as strangers to the child. This means

3 Houghton Report, Cmnd 5107, at para 221.
4 Section 18(6). It may be noted that, although a father without parental responsibility does not, as we have seen, rank as a parent for purposes of adoption, the court must be satisfied that he has no intention of seeking a s 4 order or residence order in respect of the child, or that if he did, the application would be likely to be refused (s 18(7)).
5 Sections 18(5) and 12(3).
6 Sections 19 and 20.

that if a birth parent seeks an order under s 8 of the Children Act 1989 while the child is waiting to be placed or adopted, he or she has no automatic right to seek the order, but requires the leave of the court to do so. [7]

The concept of freeing is an interesting illustration of the difficulty in establishing exactly what we think is meant by being a parent. By classing the original parents as 'former parents' once a freeing order is made, the law may be viewed as placing increasing emphasis on the social dimension of parenthood, and on the declining importance of the biological, or birth relationship. On the other hand, placing parental responsibility in the adoption agency alone means depriving the child of a legal relationship with a human family, let alone with the desired norm of two adults (of different gender). We have argued that the law has not yet come to grasp the idea of a child having more than two people with the status of parents at a time, but equally, it appears uncomfortable with the idea of the child having *no* human parents at all who could, if necessary or desirable, exercise responsibility in taking decisions for the child. Social parenthood and the intention to parent, are valued, but not when vested in the state. We shall see in Chapters 12 to 14 that the role of the state in regulating parenting or assuming parental functions has long been problematic, and freeing is merely a small illustration of such role. It has been proposed that parents should retain their parental responsibility until the adoption order is made.[8] This may be seen as something of a retreat to a more biological model of parenthood, but it is also a statement that any parents may be better than none, and a recognition of the *child's* interest in maintaining his or her family ties.

(c) Parents of children in care

Where a child is the subject of a care order, the parents retain their parental status and responsibility for the child, although this may be circumscribed. We discuss the position of such parents in Chapter 14.

---

7 *Re C (Minors) (Adoption: Residence Order)* [1994] Fam 1. *A fortiori*, if the child has been adopted, the birth parent will require leave to seek an order: *Re C (a minor) (Adopted child: Contact)* [1993] Fam 210.
8 Department of Health, *Placement Orders, Consultation Document* (1993) paras 14.4.b, 17.2.

2. PARENTAL RESPONSIBILITY FOR NON-'PARENTS'

We turn in the final part of this chapter to consider how the law bestows parental responsibility, short of parental status, upon persons seeking to care for a child.[9] Here, the social function of parenthood is the primary focus of attention, although the law still pays some regard to genetic ties. While a child is only allowed two parents at a time, the law will contemplate more than two holding parental responsibility, in theory at least, although in practice it is doubtful that multiple responsibility-sharing is at all common. We discuss in Chapters 6 to 8 the significance of having parental responsibility.

There are three mechanisms which exist to permit non-parents to acquire parental responsibility for a child. The first is by an act of the parent(s), the second is by order of the court and the third requires both court and local authority sanction.

(a) By act of the parent(s)

Under s 5(3) of the Children Act 1989, a 'parent who has parental responsibility for his child may appoint another individual to be the child's guardian in the event of his death', and by s 5(6), such a person 'shall have parental responsibility for the child concerned'. The appointment must be in writing, dated and usually signed.[10] While at common law (now abrogated by s 2(4) of the Children Act 1989), guardianship was bestowed upon the father of a legitimate child and basically gave him all parental rights, the purpose of guardianship under the modern law is to provide a substitute to fulfil the parental responsibility for the child in the event of the parent's death. The appointment as guardian does not come into effect until the death of the parent making the appointment *and* until there is no other parent with parental responsibility (if there is one), unless the parent who appointed the guardian had a residence order in respect of the child in his or her favour at the time of the death.[11]

---

9 We are not addressing here the power to perform certain aspects of parental responsibility, such as to educate, provide day-to-day care, or discipline the child. Such individual functions can be *delegated* by the parent under the Children Act 1989, s 2(9), without the delegate acquiring parental responsibility in full.
10 There are further requirements if the appointment is made in an unsigned will or signed at the direction of the parent (s 5 (5)).
11 Section 5(7)(8).

Testamentary guardianship is an interesting device, since there is no judicial or other scrutiny of the person chosen to act as guardian by the parent.[12] It is the closest that a parent can come to a unilateral transfer of his or her parental responsibility, although of course, it does not take effect at least until that person has died. The guardian has no right to a say in whether he or she is appointed by the parent, so that guardianship is *not* an example of intention on the part of the carer as the key to acquisition of parental responsibility. However, under s 6(5), such a person may disclaim the appointment in writing within a reasonable time of first discovering that the appointment has taken effect.[13] There is therefore a negative reliance on intention – the intention *not* to act as social parent will be recognised. Guardianship is similar to but not the same as a parental responsibility agreement made between the mother and unmarried father of a child, since it enables parental responsibility to be shared without outside scrutiny, but it does not require *agreement* between the parties. The *type* of parental responsibility given by guardianship is also closest to that acquired by unmarried fathers. The guardian, like the unmarried father (and other parents), but unlike others who obtain parental responsibility, is given the right to appoint another guardian to act in the event of his death,[14] to consent or withhold consent to the making of a freeing for adoption order,[15] and to agree or withhold agreement to the making of an adoption order.[16]

The Government in its White Paper on Adoption,[17] proposed a similar device for enabling a step-parent to acquire parental responsibility by agreement with the birth parents, or by order of the court. The aim was to provide an alternative to adoption which, as we saw in the previous chapter, remains a significant mechanism for step-families seeking to cement their legal ties. If this proposal were enacted, it might prove of much greater significance than guardianship, given the roughly 150,000 dependent children whose parents are divorced each year.[18] On the other hand, it is not clear that birth fathers would be very willing to enter into agreements while still responsible for child support maintenance under the Child Support Act 1991. Nor is it clear that courts would prove to be as willing to accommodate the wishes of step-parents by the making of orders, as they have been in the case of unmarried fathers, where the

---

12 See G Douglas and N V Lowe, 'Becoming a Parent in English Law' (1992) 108 LQR
     414 at p 428 for discussion of proposals to impose a measure of scrutiny.
13 See eg *Re S (minors) (Care Proceedings: Power to make Care Orders in respect of*
     orphans) [1994] Fam Law 356.
14 Children Act 1989, s 5(4).
15 Adoption Act 1976, s 18(1).
16 Adoption Act 1976, s 16(2).
17 *Adoption: The Future* (1993) Cm 2288, para 5.21.
18 Lord Chancellor's Department, *Looking to the Future* (1993) Cm 2424, Chart 4.

blood tie still appears to carry some weight. Finally, from the step-family's point of view, parental responsibility by agreement or order would not carry the same degree of permanence and security provided by adoption.

(b) By order of the court

It is not known how many parents appoint guardians to take on the care of their children for them should they die, nor how many such appointments take effect.[19] In situations where no appointment has been made, or in circumstances other than the death of the parents, such as the long-term illness of a sole parent, the bringing-up of a child by grandparents where the mother is herself still a child, or the private fostering of a child with carers on a paid basis, there may well be no legal recognition of the situation at all, meaning that the *de facto* carer has no parental responsibility for the child and therefore in law no capacity to take important decisions for that child.[20] Where the relevant parent is dead but no guardianship appointment was made, s 5(1) and (2) of the Children Act empower a court to appoint an individual to be the child's guardian and thus bestow parental responsibility upon that person. It is likely that the court would also make a residence order under s 8 to settle the arrangements concerning with whom the child is to live, and obtaining a residence order will be the only other way in which a person can obtain parental responsibility for the child.[1]

Although it will be the norm for proceedings to be taken under the Children Act 1989, it is still possible for any person (other than a local authority) to make a child a ward of the High Court, which could make a residence order as a means of resolving the issues raised in the wardship proceedings, including the need to allocate parental responsibility.[2] While the child remains a ward, the Court retains the final say in all major

---

19 'Guardian's allowance', which is a form of child benefit paid to those caring for children whose parents are dead, was payable in respect of 2,369 children in 1992: *Social Security Statistics 1993* Table G4.01. See the discussion in Ch 10.

20 Although by s 3(5), such a person may (subject to the provisions of the Act) 'do what is reasonable in all the circumstances of the case for the purpose of safeguarding or promoting the child's welfare'.

1 For an illustration, see *Re A, J and J (minors) (Residence and Guardianship Orders)* [1993] Fam Law 568.

2 Most use of wardship before the Children Act was by local authorities; this use was restricted by s 100 of the Act, and the number of originating summonses for wardship has declined from 4,961 in 1991 to 492 in 1992. It is likely that the latter figure is a closer reflection of the general volume of applications brought by private individuals in wardship: Children Act Advisory Committee, *Annual Report 1992/93* (1994) p 25.

decisions affecting the child, so that wardship would not usually be an appropriate mechanism for obtaining parental responsibility for the duration of the child's minority. It might be used, however, where, for example, there was an urgent need to prevent a child being removed from the country.[3]

A residence order gives the person in whose favour it is made parental responsibility while it lasts.[4] As with all orders granting parental responsibility, this will be shared with anyone else who already possesses it – usually, of course, the parent(s) of the child.[5] However, depending upon the relationship to the child of the person in whose favour the order is to be made, an application may be made as of right, or only with the prior leave of the court.

(i) Applying as of right

A parent (but not, as we have seen, a former parent) or guardian has the right to seek a residence order.[6] Where the parent is an unmarried father who does not already have parental responsibility under s 4 of the Act, if the court grants him a residence order, then it must also make a s 4 order at the same time.[7] This means that even if the residence order were later varied or discharged, the s 4 order could continue in effect. But other parents, or guardians, will already have parental responsibility for the child, so for them, the significance of the residence order is to settle the child's living arrangements.

A step-parent in relation to whom the child is a child of the family;[8] a person with whom the child has lived for a period of at least three years; or a person who has the consent of anyone who already has a residence order in his or her favour, the consent of the local authority in respect of a child in its care, or in any other case, the consent of each person who has parental responsibility for the child; are also entitled to apply for a residence order. This is an important recognition once more of the social

---

3 See *Clarke Hall and Morison On Children* (10th ed) Div 2[2] *et seq*. It has been held that where all outstanding issues can be resolved within the framework established by the Children Act 1989, wardship is not an appropriate jurisdiction to exercise: *C v Salford City Council* [1994] 2 FLR 926.

4 Section 12(2).

5 Section 2(5).

6 And any other s 8 order: s 10(4).

7 Section 12(1).

8 Defined in s 105(1) as 'in relation to the parties to a marriage ... (a) a child of both of those parties; (b) any other child, not being a child who is placed with those parties as foster parents by a local authority or voluntary organisation, who has been treated by both of those parties as a child of their family'.

role of parent. The person who has shown a willingness to perform that role, or who has the consent of those who do, is enabled to seek parental responsibility through a residence order, on the strength of that commitment.

(ii) Seeking leave to apply

Any other person seeking to acquire parental responsibility through a residence order must first surmount an initial hurdle of persuading the court to grant leave to make the application.[9] Under s 10(9) of the Children Act, the court must, in deciding whether to grant leave:

'have particular regard to—
    (a) the nature of the proposed application ... ;
    (b) the applicant's connection with the child;
    (c) any risk there might be of that proposed application disrupting the child's life to such an extent that he would be harmed by it ; and
    (d) where the child is being looked after by a local authority—
        (i) the authority's plans for the child's future; and
        (ii) the wishes and feelings of the child's parents.'

It has been held that the decision whether to grant leave is not a decision relating to the upbringing of a child and so is not governed by s 1(1) of the Children Act, which makes the child's welfare in such decisions the court's paramount consideration.[10] However, other matters including those set out in the welfare 'checklist' in s 1(3), such as the wishes and feelings of the child, may be taken into account as well.[11]

The test is not an easy one to satisfy. The courts appear reluctant to permit 'outsiders' to seek leave to apply for an order (or to seek leave to be joined as parties to pending proceedings), often on the basis that the applicant would be unlikely to succeed in obtaining an order, and the proceedings would be disruptive for the child and the immediate family. Unless there is a close and long-term relationship between the applicant and child, which goes beyond the mere blood tie, the application for leave is unlikely to be granted. What the courts appear ready to recognise is a case where the applicant can point to having played a significant part in the child's life already, but if the applicant is relatively new to the scene, for example, is an aunt with whom the child has never, or only briefly lived but who is willing to offer a home, this may not be regarded as

---

9 The requirement to obtain leave applies to any s 8 order, and not just to residence.
10 *Re A (minors) (Residence Orders: Leave to Apply)* [1992] Fam 182; see J Masson, 'Leave, Local Authorities and Welfare' [1992] Fam Law 443.
11 *Re A (a minor) (Residence Order: Leave to Apply)* [1993] 1 FLR 425; *G v Kirklees Metropolitan Borough Council* [1993] 1 FLR 805.

sufficient. Thus, while proof of having performed the role of social parent will be accepted, the *intention* to perform the role in future is not.[12]

(c) Foster carers

For some carers, the desire to acquire parental responsibility must be satisfied through the third mechanism provided by the law, the sanction of both local authority social services department, and the court. Even having acted as social parents may not be enough.

Foster carers are people who take on the day-to-day care of a child because the child's own parents are unable or unwilling to do so. It may be noted that while the term 'foster carer' is preferred by those who are responsible for providing fostering services in local authorities and voluntary organisations, the more traditional 'foster parents' is used in the legislation. Changing the term to 'carer' reinforces the non-parental relationship of the carer to the child, and underscores the fact that the purpose of fostering is perceived as being to provide a substitute *carer* but not a substitute *parent*. There are two types of foster carers recognised in English law; private foster parents and local authority foster parents.

Fostering on an informal basis has probably always been part of social life in Britain, with children being sent to stay with relatives, to act as servants, or to be raised by relatives after becoming orphans. Baby farming (discussed further in Chapter 10), whereby unwanted infants, usually illegitimate, were passed to women to 'care for', and generally died shortly thereafter, was another, undesirable side of substitute care. The statutory controls on private fostering date from the nineteenth century when such baby farming became a public scandal.[13] In this century, the image of fostering has become much more one of an altruistic activity, like adoption.

Fostering has long been regarded as preferable to placing a child in a children's home, because it provides a substitute family set-up in which the child can be cared for. Jean Packman[14] has described how, apart from the baby farms, fostering, or 'boarding -out' as it was known, was also used (both for benevolent reasons, and because it was relatively cheap) in the nineteenth century by both the Poor Law authorities and charities such as Dr Barnado's, and how it was seen by the Curtis Committee in the 1940s (whose report led to an overhaul of child care law and facilities

---

12 See the cases cited in the previous note, and also *Re M (minors) (Sexual Abuse: Evidence)* [1993] 1 FLR 822, where the Court of Appeal ruled that grandparents should not have been given leave to seek a residence order where their interests were identical to those of the children's mother.

13 See R Holman, *Trading in Children: A Study of Private Fostering* (1973) pp 2-5.

14 J Packman, *The Child's Generation* (2nd ed, 1981) Ch 2.

for deprived children) as the ideal method of providing care. She also notes that added impetus for the perceived value of fostering was given by the wide experience (of children, their families and their carers) of war-time evacuation and, the decisive factor, Bowlby's work on maternal deprivation. Bowlby argued that a child needs a continuous and intimate relationship with the mother, or mother-substitute, and that if the child had to be removed from home, the best alternative was another family, not an institution.

Thus, the need to be able to *recruit* foster carers, who can provide better care than that available in residential homes, has grown. At the same time has come a recognition that first, fostering may require highly-trained and skilled carers, and secondly, that they may need to be paid to take on what may be a very difficult task of caring for badly disturbed and hurt, or gravely disabled, children. According to one researcher, foster care 'now teeters uneasily between the traditional charitable model and the alternative model of a professional salaried service'.[15] Furthermore, the increasing stress on preserving children's links with their birth families, which we noted in the previous chapter in relation to adoption, requires that, so far as local authority fostering is concerned, the emphasis is on finding carers who will tolerate, and often encourage, continuing contact with birth relatives and who may also mirror the child's racial, ethnic and social origins. Thus, while in the past, the majority of foster carers were recruited from the comparatively comfortably off, the trend has been to seek more working-class and ethnic minority families, who may *need* financial support if they are to offer themselves as foster carers at all.

(i) Private foster carers

Section 66(1) of the Children Act 1989 defines a privately fostered child as:

'a child who is under the age of sixteen and who is cared for, and provided with accommodation by, someone other than—
(i)   a parent of his;
(ii) a person who is not a parent of his but who has parental responsibility for him; or
(iii) a relative of his'.

This definition excludes carers such as grandparents or other blood or marriage relatives of the child. What is the concern of the law here is the care of children by those outside the child's family. But the extent to which private fostering should be externally monitored has not been clearly addressed. On the one hand, parents may be regarded as having the right to choose the type of substitute care for their child, be it by a

---

15 P Rhodes, 'Charitable vocation or "proper job"? The role of payment in foster care' (1993) 17 *Adoption and Fostering* (1) 8.

nanny, a boarding-school, or a foster carer. On the other, the state accepts a responsibility for safeguarding the welfare of children and ensuring that they receive an adequate level of care. Private fostering rests uneasily in a twilight zone where these two considerations have not been balanced out.[16]

Private foster parents do not have to be registered to act as fosterers of a child, but they do have an obligation imposed by the Children (Private Arrangements for Fostering) Regulations 1991, SI 1991/2050, r 4 to notify the local authority for the area of their intention to foster or, if already doing so, of that fact. The parent(s) or others with parental responsibility have a similar obligation to notify. The aim of this requirement is to enable the local authority to ensure that the fostering arrangement is satisfactory for the child, by carrying out regular visits to the child, with a detailed list of factors relating to the welfare of the child to be taken into account.[17] Notification also provides the only official measure of the scale of private fostering, although it is doubtful that the measure is at all accurate. For example, the number of children notified as being privately fostered in England was 1,952 as at 31 March 1990.[18] This was a substantial decrease on the numbers ten years earlier (approximately 4,500), but unofficial estimates have put the numbers of children far higher, with up to 9,000 children in private foster care. Not only are the numbers therefore uncertain, but there is a further dimension which makes private fostering particularly problematic. It appears that private fostering in this country is overwhelmingly used by West African parents while they are studying here. Eighty to ninety percent of children fostered are believed to be West African.[19] Yet they are placed by their parents with white families, usually in semi-rural areas, often when very young and with relatively little visiting taking place between parents and child. The duration of placements might be uncertain, and parents might return to Africa leaving their children here for long periods. There are consequent difficulties in ensuring a stable placement, with a family which appreciates the child's cultural and ethnic background, and which will maintain good links with the parents. Indeed, all the aspects of child care now deemed most important and the focus of attention in local authority fostering, are most at risk of being neglected in the private fostering world.

A person may be disqualified from acting as a foster parent if he or she has had a child made subject to a care or supervision order or has

16 R Holman, 'The twilight zone' (1986) *Community Care* 28 August.
17 Regulation 2(2).
18 Department of Health, *Private Fostering and Place of Safety Orders* (1991) Table A.
19 *The Independent*, 18 June 1992; C Atkinson and A Horner, 'Private fostering – legislation and practice' (1990) 14 *Adoption and Fostering* (3) 17 at p 18.

committed an offence against a child.[20] Alternatively, under s 69 of the Children Act, a local authority which considers a person to be unsuitable to foster a child may prohibit that person from so doing. In either case, the person may seek to have the decision set aside by the authority, or by appeal to a court.[1] It is doubtful whether monitoring of private fostering is a high priority for local authority social services departments.[2]

It is clear that the primarily unofficial, and unregulated nature of private fostering could create legal problems where, for example, a child requires important (but not life-saving) medical treatment, for which consent must be given by a person with parental responsibility. By the nature of the arrangement, it is unlikely that parents and fosterers will have reached agreement on how such matters are to be handled in advance. It is equally unlikely that a foster parent would *wish* to acquire parental responsibility for the child, as in most cases it will be clear that, however uncertain the arrangement, it is only going to be a temporary one. Should he or she wish to do so, however, then leave to apply for a residence order would have to be obtained, as discussed above. Ironically perhaps, at that point, the issues of same-race placement, cultural identity and continuity which would in all likelihood have been ignored up to that point would then become highly pertinent.[3]

(ii) Local authority foster parents [4]

The second type of foster parent is the local authority foster parent. Section 23(2)(a) of the Children Act provides that a local authority looking after[5] a child may provide accommodation and maintenance for the child by placing him with a family, a relative of his, or any other suitable person on such terms as to payment by the authority and otherwise as the authority may determine. By s 23(3), any person with whom the child is placed who falls into those categories is a local authority foster parent unless he or she is a parent of the child, has parental responsibility for the child, or had a residence order in his or her favour. A person cannot become a local authority foster parent without being approved first, unless the immediate placement of a child is necessary in an emergency and the fosterer is a relative or friend of the

---

20 The Disqualification for Caring for Children Regulations 1991, r 2 (SI 1991/2094).
1 Sections 68(1), 69(4) and Sch 8 para 8 to the Children Act 1989.
2 Or even for Government. No statistics are presented for private fostering notifications or disqualifications in the *Children Act Report 1993* (1994) presented to Parliament.
3 For a good illustration, albeit in the context of an adoption application, see *Re N (a minor) (Adoption)* [1990] 1 FLR 58.
4 A person may also act as a foster carer for a voluntary organisation, but the procedures and requirements are the same. See s 59 of the Children Act.
5 See Ch 12 for further discussion.

child.[6] The process of being approved is similar to that which applies to prospective adopters, with a detailed profile of the fosterer and his or her family prepared for consideration by a panel. Disappointed applicants to foster should be able to make representations about their rejection.[7] Relatives of the child may be designated as local authority (but not private) foster parents, and indeed, as we discuss in Chapter 14, placement with family or friends of the child is regarded as desirable. However, Paula Rhodes has pointed out that when *relatives* take on the care of a child, they may not be deemed eligible for local authority payments:

'The present situation is ... one where non-kin cases are offered increasingly attractive incentives, while the resources offered to kin carers are severely restricted in order to uphold, unpolluted, the notion of family responsibility and kinship obligation'.[8]

The main difference between private and local authority foster parents is, of course, the degree of supervision and scrutiny to which they are subject. While private fosterers have made an arrangement with the child's parents to undertake the caring function, and would usually be paid by the parents to do this, the parental responsibility for the child rests with the parents (albeit aspects are delegated) and they are in charge of the placement. The local authority must monitor the situation, but it has no place in the initial arrangement between parent and foster carer. Local authority foster parents are subject to prior scrutiny and must be approved on an annual basis. Their agreement to care for a child is with the local authority, not the parent, and they must undertake to allow the child to be removed by the authority where it appears to the authority that continuing the placement would no longer be the most suitable way of safeguarding and promoting the child's welfare.[9]

It is the requirement to permit the child to be removed which distinguishes local authority foster care from other types of care by non-parents. While private fosterers will no doubt agree with the parents that the child can be removed, and could not prevent them from so doing, if a dispute arises, the private foster parent may utilise the procedures in Part II of the Children Act in the same way as any other person requiring leave, as outlined above. But the local authority foster parent has an additional test to satisfy. By s 9(3), a person may not apply for leave to seek a s 8 order if he or she is, or was at any time in the last six months,

---

6 The Foster Placement (Children) Regulations 1991, r 11.

7 There is no statutory requirement for this, but the Department of Health Guidance, Vol 3, *Family Placements* (1991) para 3.42 recommends it. As already noted in the previous chapter, the Government proposed introducing a similar mechanism for rejected adoption applicants.

8 'Charitable vocation or "proper job"? The role of payment in foster care' (1993) 17 *Adoption and Fostering* (1) 8 at p 12.

9 The Foster Placement (Children) Regulations 1991, rr 3(6)(b), 7 and Sch 2(9).

a local authority foster parent of the child, unless the authority consents,[10] or the carer is the child's relative, or the child has lived with the foster parent for at least three years preceding the application.[11] (If this last exception applies, the foster carer may seek an order as of right, suggesting that there is *some* recognition of the social role once the child has been in the carer's family for a sufficiently long period). The aim is to prevent the foster parent frustrating the local authority's plans for the child. But the effect is to reinforce the problematical nature of fostering, especially when done on behalf of the state, as in local authority fostering.

The dilemma for those placing children with foster parents, and for the fosterers themselves, is how to reconcile the child's need for a close and loving relationship with one (or a few) people, with the possibility (or probability) that the child will be removed from the fosterers and either returned home, or placed in some other more long-term arrangement. As Bartlett puts it:

'foster care is in principle a temporary custodial arrangement, the goal of which is purportedly the child's reunion with his legal family ... The temporary state-controlled nature of foster care prevents courts from recognising foster families as substitute nuclear families even when children do form strong emotional attachments with their foster parents. The institution is thus criticised both for perpetuating the child's uncertainty and for failing to give *de facto* long-term relationships the legal status and concomitant security that children need.'[12]

When those who foster children seek to acquire parental status or parental responsibility, therefore, because they initially took on the care of the child on the express basis of *not* acting as permanent substitute parents, they are regarded as having broken their undertaking, and to be treated with suspicion. If they could freely renegue on that undertaking, parents and local authorities might be inhibited from making otherwise desirable placements. Here, the intention and willingness, and even the experience of acting as the child's social parent, may not be enough. The basic presumption of the law is to uphold the 'family' relationship of the child with his or her 'parents'; they continue to have the prior claim to

10 See *C v Salford City Council* [1994] 2 FLR 926, where the local authority gave their consent and leave to make the application was granted to the Roman Catholic foster parents, notwithstanding the opposition of the Orthodox Jewish parents, of a Down's Syndrome child.

11 In such a case, there is a *right* to seek an order. The period need not be continuous but must have begun not more than five years before the making of the application (s 9(4)). Anomalously, a local authority foster parent may apply to adopt a child who has been living with the foster parent for 12 months, without the consent of the local authority: see, for example, *Re C (a minor) (Adoption)* [1994] 1 WLR 1220.

12 Bartlett 'Rethinking Parenthood as an Exclusive Status: The Need for Legal Alternatives when the Premise of the Nuclear Family has Failed' (1984) 70 *Virginia Law Review* 879 at pp 942-943.

possess the child, and although as we shall see, this claim can be displaced, the task is not an easy or straightforward one.

3. THE OVERALL PICTURE

We still attach weight to the blood tie as the key to the relationship between parent and child. There is still a depth of feeling which underpins the idea of a child *belonging* to a particular set of 'parents' when they are linked genetically. The law, however, has had to accommodate its historical inability to prove a genetic link by stressing other factors, most importantly, the fact of marriage between the child's mother and the husband. This relative lack of emphasis on genetics may have aided the development of the notion that the social role of parenthood and the intention to fulfil that role should be given legal recognition. Mechanisms such as adoption provide a means whereby a parental relationship can be forged between 'strangers'. But while the sense of a child belonging to certain parents is strong for those who can point to the genetic link, where that link is missing, it is for the person who has the desire and intention to act as parent to prove that he or she should be given parental status and hence to acquire the ' possession' of the child. Legal scrutiny, and more recently medical judgment, are used to test this proof. Irrespective of how many people have contributed in various ways to the child's creation, the law will still only contemplate a maximum of two people, of different gender, being recognised as the parents of a child, perhaps in an attempt to (re)create the nuclear family which the child should have had.

Parental responsibility may be held by more than two people, so that it does not necessarily mirror the two-parent model of family life which parental status seeks to produce. Parental responsibility may actually be harder for the non-parent to acquire than parental status, because, apart from guardianship, it will always be necessary for the person to gain court approval. In the next chapters, we examine what parental responsibility entails, and how the courts decide upon disputes as to its exercise.

PART III

Private law: parental responsibility

CHAPTER 6

Issues and influences

1. INTRODUCTION

Now that we know whom the law regards as parents, we move on to consider the powers and responsibilities the law bestows upon them. We start by identifying key issues which can arise.

First, there is the question of whether parents' standing with regard to their children is different to that of other adults and, if so, whether it is the same for every parent or whether the law varies, between mother and father perhaps, or with the gender or age of the child concerned, not to mention the unique needs and abilities of each child and parent.

Then, there is the question of family privacy. In the liberal state, as we noted in Chapter 1, there is a reluctance to intervene in the family relationship. How far does this produce a corresponding reluctance to lay down standards of parenting which must be fulfilled? And how are such standards to be monitored? Does the law encourage, or permit, the exceeding of any minimum standards of parenting which it may require? How far does the law reflect, or recognise, non-British dimensions and standards of parenting?

Third, we saw in Chapter 2 that there is a case for recognising parents as having a distinct right and interest in the way their children are brought up. To what extent is parental discretion permitted to be exercised in contradiction of the child's own wishes?

Fourth, it may be asked whether the increasingly child-centred focus of family law is simply a new way of trapping women as *mothers* instead of as *partners* in a dependent and unequal position.

The question also arises as to whether parents are legally entitled to anything from their children, if only in return for fulfilling their parental obligations. (In ancient Babylon, parents could use children as security for their debts.[1])

1 W Kelly, 'Evolution of the Concept of the Rights of the Child in the Western World' (1978) 21 *The Review* (International Commission of Jurists) 43,44.

Perhaps the most fundamental questions concerning the parent-child relationship have always concerned the balance of power in decision-making. Once, the legal tension lay between – it might now be amongst[2] – the parents, whereas today, there are three more sets of protagonists: parent and child, parent and state, and child and state.

Finally, it should not be forgotten that parents are people too, with their own expectations for themselves and for their partners, which may conflict with their duty to their child:

'It is an irony of the modern world that the couple relationship has become ever more fragile as a greater and greater weight of expectation has been placed upon it. But just as we now expect much more of our adult relationships we also expect much more of our own and others' parent-child relationships. These two sets of expectations are pulling in opposite directions and the least the law can do is to avoid driving them further apart.'[3]

If the legal agenda can be inferred from the conventional list of issues involving some or all of those with parental authority, it might be itemised, roughly by the age of the child, like this:

(1) physical possession, home, protection and contact;
(2) name;
(3) education and religion;
(4) discipline and punishment;
(5) medical treatment;
(6) travel and emigration;
(7) property and contracting;
(8) legal proceedings;
(9) services;
(10) marriage;
(11) disposing of the child's corpse.

The package may be transferred, as with adoption (*inter vivos*) or guardianship (posthumously). It may also be replicated, perhaps by parental responsibility orders or agreements. These moves may occur either with or without the agreement of the original holder(s); and parental responsibility orders and agreements may endure only temporarily and they involve only some of the items concerned.[4]

Similar lists are to be found in many of the sources mentioned below. They tend to an understandable self-perpetuation following the continued refusal of Parliament and the courts to be definitive. By family law standards these lists seem to have changed little over the years and, although the actual enumeration of categories has varied, the present

2 If more than two people have parental responsibility.
3 B Hoggett, 'Joint parenting systems: the English experiment' (1994) 6 *Journal of Child Law* 8, 11.
4 See Ch 5.

texts seem to have settled on 14 issues.[5] One county court judge was daring enough to suggest priorities, 'The crucial ones, the absolutely crucial ones... must be these. First, the care and control of the child or children. Secondly, the protection and discipline of them. Thirdly, the maintenance of them. Fourthly, the education and religious upbringing of them.'[6]

Should the state now produce a definitive legal list? So far as *spouses* are concerned, the (English) Law Commission has spoken encouragingly of the importance of legislation to define rights during marriage, and not merely upon breakdown.[7] Yet domestically, at least, the repeated calls for a statutory statement of parenting law remain unheeded. In the 1970s, JC Hall said:

> 'What would be welcome now would be a statutory reformulation of parental rights as well of course as parental duties. This would provide the surest answer to the rather bizarre suggestion recently made that children "need a charter to protect them against the constant violation of their basic rights by adults" '.[8]

Hall's latter stricture seems anachronistic given that he was writing nearly fifty years after the UN Declaration of Geneva 1924, also known as the First Declaration of the Rights of the Child, which contained a general exhortation against the exploitation of children, as well as specifics concerning shelter, food and medical aid. The Second Declaration, in 1959, was more concerned with the social and economic rights to housing, recreation and nutrition, rather than the even more fundamental civil rights of life and liberty.[9]

Hall's call for codification, however, still with the emphasis on parental rights, was repeated shortly afterwards by John Eekelaar, who identified 11 such 'rights'.[10] 'It is no easy matter to state with precision

---

5 Eg, A Bainham with S Cretney, *Children – the Modern Law*, (1993) Family Law, is content to acknowledge (at p 96) the list compiled in P M Bromley and N V Lowe, *Bromley's Family Law* (8th ed, 1992) at p 301 – a list which is itself not that different from the matters mentioned in the first edition (1957, pp 277-327). Our list (above) contains some amalgamations.

6 *Re H (Illegitimate Children: Father: Parental Rights) (No 2)* [1991] 1 FLR 214 (CA), quoted at 219. The Court of Appeal was silent on the issue.

7 Most recently in WP No 90 (1985) 'Transfer of Money Between Spouses – the Married Women's Property Act 1964' at para 3.4.

8 J C Hall, 'The Waning of Parental Rights' [1972] 31 CLJ 248, 265. The 'rather bizarre' suggestion was made by the Advisory Centre for Education: *The Times,* 8 April 1971.

9 See Ch 2.

10 'What are Parental Rights?' (1973) 89 LQR 210, 234. Fortunately, another problem with which Eekelaar was required to grapple at that time, namely the different parental 'rights' which obtained when the courts granted to non-parents such rights as 'custody' of the child, has been obviated. The Children Act 1989 now makes only one, clear, distinction: between parents and others with parental responsibility.

what rights pertain to parenthood.' Writing in the early 1980s, Susan Maidment (20 'rights and duties') said:[11]

> 'Countless commentators have called for a reassessment of parental rights. The vagaries of litigation are inadequate for the comprehensive review of the law that is so clearly timely. One must look to the legislators to grasp the nettle of a completely statutory codification in this area of the law.'

Presently, s 3(1) of the Children Act 1989 is content, as a means of defining 'parental responsibility', simply to acknowledge 'the rights, duties, powers, responsibilities and authority which by law a parent has in relation to the child and his property'. In choosing to beg the question, Parliament had followed the view of the (English) Law Commission that it is a practical impossibility for the law to be comprehensive, because of the need to be responsive to the individual needs of different children and to changing times.[12]

> 'To attempt to provide a complete list of all a parent's rights and duties would clearly be a large task involving consideration of many difficult and controversial areas. It would require consideration of the interrelationship between the child's own legal status and capacities and the powers of parents, not only to act on behalf of children who are too young to act for themselves, but also to direct or control the actions of older children. We doubt whether the list could ever be comprehensive, and if it were, this might be undesirable in the interests of flexibility and capacity to adapt to changes in social circumstances.'[13]

Ironically, one reason that the Scottish Law Commission has given for recommending a statutory statement is that the 'increased emphasis on parental responsibilities, rather than parental rights, in English law under the Children Act 1989 [had] met with very wide support and approval'.[14] Despite the objection that such statements are inappropriate in legislation as having more of an educational or declaratory function, the Scottish Law Commission recommended[15] as follows:

> 'It should be provided that a parent has in relation to his or her child a responsibility, so far as is practicable and in the interests of the child,
>
> (i) to safeguard and promote the child's health, development and welfare
> (ii) to provide, in a manner appropriate to the child's development, direction and guidance to the child
> (iii) if not living with the child, to maintain personal relations and direct contact with the child on a regular basis'.

The above are recommended to last until the child is 18; the next only until 16.

---

11 'The Fragmentation of Parental Rights' (1981) CLJ 135, 158.
12 'Review of Child Law: Guardianship and Custody', (1988) Law Com 172 at para 2.6.
13 'Review of Child Law: Guardianship' Law Com PWP No 91 (1985) at para 1.9.
14 'Report on Family Law' (1992) Scot Law Com No 135 at para 2.1.
15 *Ibid* at para 2.6.

'(iv) to act as the child's legal representative and, in that capacity, to administer, in the interests of the child, any property belonging to the child.'

We have chosen not to go down the path of an individual examination of these items, but rather to examine the more important ones holistically. Some of them, perhaps most notably that concerning education, are located at the border between parent, child and state, and are thus considered later.[16]

2. CHILDREN'S AUTONOMY VERSUS PARENTAL DECISION-MAKING

Article 12(1) of the 1989 United Nations Convention on the Rights of the Child states that:

'States Parties shall assure to the child who is capable of forming his or her own views the right to express those views freely in all matters affecting the child, the views of the child being given due weight in accordance with the age and maturity of the child.'

Today, despite the age of majority being 18, there is much greater scope than hitherto for the child, the state, and others, to invoke the jurisdiction of the court in challenges to parental authority even where the parents, at least, are living together in amity and even where there is no question of the matter attracting the attention of either the criminal law or care proceedings.[17] Section 10(8) of the Children Act 1989 permits the court to grant leave to the child him or herself to apply for a s 8 order – residence, contact, specific issue,[18] prohibited steps[19] – provided that the child has 'sufficient understanding'.[20] The state, through the local authority, may apply for a s 8 specific issue or prohibited steps order.[1]

16 See Ch 11.
17 In lowering the age of statutory entry to adulthood under the Family Law Reform Act 1969, Parliament was able simply to lop off three years of legal childhood, without the decades of agonising over tapering which has since been the unhappy lot of the courts and others. In *Hewer v Bryant* [1970] 1 QB 357, 369 Lord Denning MR was in fine form, 'youngsters of 18 and 19 fought the Battle of Britain... since which time pop-singers of 19 have made thousands of pounds a week and revolutionaries of 18 have broken up Universities. Is each of them in the custody of his father? Of course not.'
18 '... an order giving directions for the purpose of determining a specific question which has arisen, or which may arise, in connection with any aspect of parental responsibility for a child' (s 8(1)).
19 '... an order that no step which could be taken by a parent in meeting his parental responsibility for a child, and which is of a kind specified in the order, shall be taken by any person without the consent of the court' (s 8(1)).
20 See Ch 7 for a discussion of the relevant case law.
 1 But not a residence or a contact order: s 9(2).

Finally, any individual not entitled to apply as of right for a s 8 order may seek leave to do so[2], the court having particular regard under s 10(9) to: the nature of the proposed application; the applicant's connection with the child; and any risk that the application would cause harmful disruption to the child.

The leading case concerning the child's autonomy is *Gillick v West Norfolk and Wisbech Area Health Authority*.[3] It should be noted that, specifically, the issue dealt with medical matters, and that the wider application of its principles to general parenting may be unclear. What may be asserted with confidence is that Mrs[4] Gillick's aim ('a crusade'[5]) was to confirm the existence of a parent-state-court partnership to control children – and that the attempt proved not merely abortive but actually counter-productive to the cause of parental rights.

This famous case heralded the start of a sustained public and political interest in parent and child matters, with such issues as the Children Act 1989, the Child Support Act 1991, the Criminal Justice Act 1991, divorce and adoption reform all becoming part of the debate on those 'family values' which have been so ambivalently perceived. The facts were these. In 1980 the then Department of Health and Social Security issued to health authorities a revised version of part of a Memorandum of Guidance on the family planning service originally issued in 1974. It included the following passages:

'There is widespread concern about counselling and treatment for children under 16. Special care is needed not to undermine parental responsibility and family stability. The Department would therefore hope that in any case where a doctor or other professional worker is approached by a person under the age of 16 for advice in these matters, the doctor or other professional will always seek to persuade the child to involve the parent... at the earliest stage of consultation, and will proceed from the assumption that it would be most unusual to provide advice about contraception without parental consent.

It is, however, widely accepted that consultations between doctors and patients are confidential.... To abandon this principle for children under 16 might cause some not to seek professional advice at all. They could then be exposed to the immediate risks of pregnancy and of sexually-transmitted diseases, as well as other long-term physical, psychological and emotional consequences which are equally a threat to stable family life. This would apply particularly to young people, whose parents are, for example, unconcerned, entirely unresponsive, or grossly disturbed. Some of these young people are away from home and in the care of local authorities...

The Department realises that in such exceptional cases the nature of any counselling must be a matter for the doctor or other professional worker concerned

2 See Ch 5.
3 [1986] AC 112.
4 Before the Children Act 1989, it was not wholly clear that parental responsibility could be exercised at the sole behest of one parent: Lord Fraser at 163, 'Mrs Gillick's husband is not a party to the present proceedings, but we were informed that he is in full agreement with Mrs Gillick's contention and I proceed on that basis.'
5 So described by Lord Templeman at 206 in his dissenting judgment.

and whether or not to prescribe contraception must be for the clinical judgment of a doctor.'

A carefully-reasoned and, some might say, humanitarian document. As Lord Fraser said:[6]

'... it is perfectly clear that it would convey to any doctor... who read it that the decision whether or not to prescribe contraception for a girl under 16 was in the last resort a matter for the clinical judgment of a doctor, even if the girl's parents had not been informed that she had consulted the doctor, and even if they had expressed disapproval of contraception being prescribed for her'.

In 1981 Mrs Gillick wrote to the area health authority, purporting to 'formally forbid' any of its medical staff from giving any of her (then four in all; a fifth was born later) daughters any 'contraceptive or abortion advice or treatment whatsoever... whilst they are under 16 years without my consent'.[7] Within the week came the oblique, but unambiguous reply, 'treatment prescribed by a doctor is a matter for that doctor's clinical judgment, taking into account all the factors of the case'. Mrs Gillick sought a declaration that the notice 'gives advice which is unlawful and wrong, and which adversely affects... the welfare of the plaintiff's said children, and/or the rights of the plaintiff as parent... and/or the ability of the plaintiff properly and efficiently to exercise her duties as such parent'.

She lost at first instance,[8] won in the Court of Appeal,[9] and lost again in the House of Lords. A total of four judges decided against the plaintiff as opposed to five in her favour.[10]

One difficulty about the specific issue raised, if not decided, by the case, is the extent to which contraceptive advice or treatment to those under 16 can be said to constitute medical treatment and thus fall to be covered by the law regarding such treatment of children. A girl may be a patient, but she is not necessarily ill, nor about to become so; a doctor may be involved but he or she is not necessarily healing or preventing sickness. In fact, their Lordships acted as administrators, or even legislators, in formulating specific policy about the issue. Here, Lord Fraser laced his general observations about girls, their lovers, parents and

---

6   At 164.
7   '... there is no suggestion that Mrs Gillick's relationship with her daughters is other than normal and happy, nor is it suggested that there is any present likelihood of any of the daughters seeking contraceptive advice or treatment without the consent of their mother' – per Lord Fraser at 163.
8   [1984] QB 581 (Woolf J).
9   [1986] AC 112, 118 *et seq* (Eveleigh, Fox and Parker L JJ).
10 Eveleigh, Fox and Parker L JJ (Court of Appeal) and Lords Brandon and Templeman in the House of Lords, would have granted the declaration sought. In the House of Lords, Lords Bridge, Fraser and Scarman reinstated the decision of Woolf J at first instance.

doctors, with some highly specific law. He postulated a necessary link between contraceptive advice or treatment and healing for the purpose of legitimating the former's availability:[11]

> 'there may be circumstances in which a doctor is a better judge... than her [the child's] parents. It is notorious that children of both sexes are often reluctant to confide in their parents about sexual matters... to abandon the principle of confidentiality for contraceptive advice to girls under 16 might cause some of them not to seek professional advice at all...
>
> There may well be... cases where the doctor feels that because the girl is under the influence of her sexual partner or for some other reason there is no realistic prospect of her abstaining from intercourse... He should, of course, always seek to persuade her to tell her parents that she is seeking contraceptive advice... At least he should seek to persuade her to agree to the doctor's informing the parents. But... the doctor will... be justified in proceeding without the parents' consent or even knowledge provided he is satisfied on the following matters: (1) that the girl (although under 16 years of age) will understand his advice; (2) that he cannot persuade her to inform her parents or to allow him to inform the parents that she is seeking contraceptive advice; (3) that she is very likely to begin or to continue having sexual intercourse with or without contraceptive treatment; (4) that unless she receives contraceptive advice or treatment her physical or mental health are likely to suffer; (5) that her best interests require him to give her contraceptive advice, treatment or both without the parental consent.
>
> That result ought not to be regarded as a licence for doctors to disregard the wishes of parents on this matter whenever they find it convenient to do so.'

The fundamental issue in the case concerned the extent to which a parent has the right to the final say in all decisions regarding a child under the age of majority. Lord Fraser said:

> 'It is, in my view, contrary to the ordinary experience of mankind, at least in Western Europe in the present century, to say that a child or a young person remains in fact under the complete control of his parents until he attains the definite age of majority, now 18 in the United Kingdom, and that on attaining that age he suddenly acquires independence. In practice most wise parents relax their control gradually as the child develops and encourage him or her to become increasingly independent. Moreover, the degree of parental control actually exercised over a particular child does in practice vary considerably according to his understanding and intelligence and it would, in my opinion be unrealistic for the courts not to recognise these facts.'[12]

From that hint of determinism, Lord Fraser moved to a welfarist/ Freeman 'parent-as-representative' line:[13]

> 'The solution depends upon a judgment of what is best for the welfare of the particular child. Nobody doubts, certainly I do not doubt, that in the overwhelming majority of cases the best judges of a child's welfare are his or her parents.'[14]

11 At 173.
12 At 171.
13 See Ch 2.
14 At 173.

Lord Scarman combined recognition of children as persons with a degree of paternalism, perhaps sharing Michael Freeman's view that when parental 'representativeness' ceases, as being inconsistent with the pursuit of 'primary social goods', then court intervention may follow:

> 'Nor has our law ever treated the child as other than a person with capacities and rights recognised by law. The principle of the law, as I shall endeavour to show, is that parental rights are derived from parental duty and exist only so long as they are needed for the protection of the person and property of the child.... When a court has before it a question as to the care and upbringing of a child it must treat the welfare of a child as the paramount consideration[15] in determining the order to be made. There is here a principle which limits and governs the exercise of parental rights... it is also a warning that parental right must be exercised in accordance with the welfare principle and can be challenged, even overridden, if not.'[16]

Lord Scarman's (legal) genesis was Blackstone[17] whose authority he invoked in justifying the extent to which the law would treat children as adults:

> 'The underlying principle of the law was exposed by Blackstone.... It is that parental right yields to the child's right to make his own decisions when he reaches a sufficient understanding and intelligence to be capable of making up his own mind on the matter requiring decision.'[18]

Lord Denning had earlier expressed the tapering nature of the legal element of parenting in a vivid phrase, reminiscent of Lord Fraser's view of the 'wise parent' above:

> 'it is a dwindling right which the courts will hesitate to enforce against the wishes of the child and the more so the older he is. *It starts with a right of control and ends with little more than advice*' (emphasis supplied).[19]

Lord Denning did not say that there is a *right* to give advice!

Perhaps Lord Templeman, despite being in the minority in disallowing the appeal, best captured the consensus view on the balance (if the term is properly applicable to more than two entities) of power amongst child, parent and court:

> 'The practical exercise of parental powers varies from control and supervision to guidance and advice depending on the discipline enforced by the parent and the age and temperament of the infant. Parental power must be exercised in the best

---

15 In dropping the then statutory reference to 'first' and paramount, Lord Scarman anticipated s 1(1) of the Children Act 1989. This was not, perhaps, as progressive a change as it might appear. The purpose was merely to ensure that the child's welfare should be the court's 'only concern', (Law Com No 172 (1988), para 3.14) and there has been no suggestion in post-Children Act 1989 cases that the different wording has led to different results.

16 At 184.

17 *Commentaries*, (17th Ed, 1830) Vol 1, Chs 16 and 17.

18 At 186.

19 *Hewer v Bryant* [1970] 1 QB 357, 369.

interests of the infant and the court may intervene in the interests of the infant at the behest of the parent or at the behest of a third party. The court may enforce parental right, control the misuse of parental power or uphold independent views asserted by the infant. The court will be guided by the principle that the welfare of the infant is paramount. But subject to the discretion of the court to differ . . . the parent [will] decide on behalf of the infant all matters which the infant is not competent to decide. The prudent parent will pay attention to the wishes of the infant and will normally accept them as the infant approaches adulthood. The parent is not bound by the infant's wishes, but an infant approaching adulthood may be able to flout the wishes of the parent with ease."[20]

John Eekelaar has pointed out[1] that the United Nations may have given little thought to the differing of 'philosophers and jurists' when coining its statements of children's rights: their Lordships certainly made no express reference to such luminaries (Blackstone apart) in their judgments in *Gillick*. Omission of such extra-legal authority is also noticeable in their pronouncements on medical and social matters. For example, Lord Templeman, this time on the specific issue of whether the law should nod at the possibility of girls, and indeed boys, under 16, having sexual intercourse took the view that:

'The interests of a girl under 16 require her to be protected against sexual intercourse. Such a girl is not sufficiently mature to be allowed to decide to flout the accepted rules of society. The pornographic press and the lascivious film may falsely pretend that sexual intercourse is a form of entertainment available to females on request and to males on demand but the regular, frequent or casual practice of sexual intercourse by a girl or boy under the age of 16 cannot be beneficial to anybody and may cause harm to character and personality'.[2]

His Lordship, far from weighing these 'accepted rules', and the possible 'harm to character or personality', failed even to adduce evidence of them: 'These arguments have provoked great controversy which is not legal in character.'[3] (There is the one exception of his contention that 'Contraceptive treatment for females usually requires daily discipline in order to be effective and girls under 16 frequently lack that discipline'.[4]) Despite his general disapproval of intercourse for the under 16s, Lord Templeman acknowledged that their indulgence in safe sex, at least, was a matter for individual parental discretion:

'Before a girl under 16 is supplied with contraceptive facilities, the parent who knows most about the girl and ought to have the most influence with the girl is entitled to exercise parental rights of control, supervision and guidance and advice in order that the girl may, if possible, avoid sexual intercourse until she is older.'[5]

20 At 200.
1 'The Importance of Thinking That Children Have Rights' (1992) International Journal of Law and the Family 221.
2 At 202.
3 *Ibid.*
4 At 203.
5 At 202.

and:

> 'A doctor is not entitled to decide whether a girl under the age of 16 shall be provided with contraceptive facilities if a parent who is in charge of the girl is ready and willing to make that decision in exercise of parental rights.'[6]

He would clearly prefer the decision to be 'no'.

> 'On behalf of Mrs Gillick it was urged with some force that the practical effect... was to enable an inexperienced doctor in a family planning clinic, exuding sympathy and veiled in ignorance of the girl's personality and history, to provide contraceptives as if they were sweets withheld from a deprived child by an unfeeling parent; and that any parent who was concerned with the girl's immortal soul or with moral or religious principles might be said to be "entirely unresponsive" to a proposal that an unmarried girl under 16 should be provided with contraceptives.'[7]

Had Mrs Gillick obtained the declaration sought, would that have prevented doctors from giving contraceptive advice or treatment to all girls under 16? Or merely to that smaller number of girls whose parents did not consent? Or to that even smaller number whose parents positively dissented? Was it parent power or the perceived absolute interests of young girls which was at issue? In 1985, the year that the case completed its journey through the courts, a survey posed yet another question: should 'doctors be allowed to give contraceptive advice and supplies to young people [no gender specified] without having to inform parents'? Some 35% thought so, as against 50% who thought not. When asked in 1987, the same question elicited a higher, 60%, number of 'no's although by 1989 they had dropped to 55%.[8] In 1986, 36% of those members of the public who were canvassed said that when responsible for bringing up a child they would 'try hard' to get the children to share their own views about sexual behaviour.[9]

One issue central to the *Gillick* case, and which was rehearsed by the judges as well as by public opinion and commentators, was the effect which the decision would have on the abortion rate for girls under 16. Those who applauded the decision drew support for their stance from the fact of its descent from 5% in 1981 to 4.2% in 1986 – and from its more dramatic drop to 2.7% in 1991.[10] The numbers of girls under 16 in England and Wales who actually conceive – babies born before their mothers reached that age would by definition be non-marital – provide

---

6 At 205.

7 At 206. Later, in Ch 16, we look at criticisms of the *a priori* approach taken by the Law Lords in *Gillick*.

8 *British Social Attitudes* (1992) "Availability of Contraception for Young People", M.1–14.

9 *Ibid*, N.1–13.

10 *Social Trends 23* (1993) Table 2.28.

similar ammunition. They dropped from 9,649 in 1984 to 9,194 in 1986,[11] and thence to 7,829 in 1991.[12]

We do not, of course, know what would have happened had the *Gillick* decision gone the other way,[13] or whether more or fewer young girls are having sex nowadays (with or without parental knowledge or consent). Even if these things were known, 'we' are not in a position to balance out, for example, the possibility that more people (of whatever age) are enjoying sexual pleasure with any deleterious effect which that may have, including the effect upon their relations with their parents. But we can say that since *Gillick*, although we cannot say that it is because of *Gillick*, there have been fewer girls under 16 in our legal system who have conceived and who have had abortions.

3.   THE AFTERMATH OF *GILLICK*

Following the *Gillick* decision, it began to be assumed that a child who satisfied the test for maturity was capable of taking decisions for him or herself and of thereby replacing the parent as decision-maker entirely. Indeed some went so far as to argue that, if the parents ceased to have the power to decide for the child, neither could the court, acting in its *parens patriae* jurisdiction.[14] The *Gillick* concept of the 'mature minor' certainly influenced the extent to which the child's views and power to veto medical assessment and treatment were to be respected under the Children Act 1989.[15] However, in two Court of Appeal decisions relating to medical treatment, a distinction was drawn between the capacity of a minor to *consent to* and to *refuse* medical treatment with consequential implications for the corresponding powers of those with parental responsibility.

In *Re R (a minor) (Wardship: Medical Treatment)*,[16] a 15 year old girl who was mentally disturbed refused to take drugs prescribed at a

---

11 *Series FM1 No 20*, Birth Statistics 1991.

12 *Population Trends 73* (1993).

13 After Mrs Gillick won her case in the Court of Appeal, attendance at family planning clinics by under 16s fell from 18,600 to 12,400: C Standley, 'Confidentiality and the Immature Minor' (unpublished LLM thesis 1994, Cardiff Law School).

14 See J Eekelaar, 'The Emergence of Children's Rights' (1986) OJLS 161 at p 181.

15 See, eg, s 1(3)(a), ascertainable wishes and feelings to be taken into account in assessing welfare when the 'checklist' applies; s 10(8), child may be given leave to initiate proceedings for a s 8 order; s 22, child's views to be taken into account in local authority planning; s 38(6), child may refuse medical or other examination or assessment during interim care order; ss 43(8) and 44(7), child may refuse medical or psychiatric examination (but see below).

16 [1992] Fam 11. See A Bainham, "The Judge and the Competent Minor" (1992) 108 LQR 194; R Thornton, "Multiple Keyholders – Wardship and Consent to Medical

residential treatment unit. She was subject to a care order, and the local authority, who had parental responsibility for her by virtue of that order, made her a ward of court so that the High Court could rule on whether her refusal of treatment could be overridden. At first instance and in the Court of Appeal, she was regarded as incompetent because of her mental condition[17] and hence consent could be given on her behalf by the local authority. However, Lord Donaldson MR also held that the *Gillick* case did not provide authority for the view that, once a child is competent, the parents cease to have an independent right to consent to treatment for the child. He suggested that consent should be seen as:

'a key which unlocks a door... whilst in the case of an adult of full capacity there will usually only be one keyholder, namely the patient, in the ordinary family where a young child is the patient there will be two keyholders, namely the parents, with a several as well as a joint right to turn the key and unlock the door'.[18]

Against this view would appear to be the statement of Lord Scarman in *Gillick* that:

'As a matter of law the parental right to determine whether or not their minor child... will have medical treatment terminates if and when the child achieves a sufficient understanding and intelligence to enable him or her to understand fully what is proposed'.

But the Master of the Rolls concluded that while a parent's right to *determine* or, as he explained it, to *veto* treatment might be lost, a parental right to *consent* to treatment remains. This distinction between determining and consenting is unconvincing and is an 'explanation' of Lord Scarman's dictum which few would have identified from the judgment before Lord Donaldson appeared to discover it.[19]

Nonetheless, the case was followed, and extended, in *Re W (a minor) (Medical Treatment: Court's Jurisdiction)*.[20] While *Re R* had concerned a 15 year old girl, *Re W* related to a 16 year old who, by virtue of s 8 of the Family Law Reform Act 1969, had a clear statutory right to consent

---

Treatment (1992) CLJ 34; G Douglas, "The Retreat from *Gillick* (1992) 55 MLR 569. For a Scottish comparison, see K McNorrie, "Medical Treatment of Children and Young Persons" and J Haldane, "Children, Families, Autonomy and the State" in D Morgan and G Douglas (eds) *Constituting Families: A Study in Governance* (1994).

17 Lord Donaldson MR and Farquharson LJ considered that *Gillick* competence cannot fluctuate on a day-to-day basis, ie a child cannot be competent one day but not the next.

18 At 22.

19 The court held that a court may override the child's refusal. This is more defensible, since courts have many powers which individuals lack.

20 [1992] 4 All ER 627. See N Lowe and S Juss, "Medical Treatment – Pragmatism and the Search for Principle" (1993) 56 MLR 865; J Eekelaar, "White Coats or Flak Jackets? Doctors, Children and the courts – Again" (1993) 109 LQR 182; J Masson, *Re W*: Appealing from a Golden Cage" (1993) 5 Journal of Child Law 37.

to treatment.[1] But she was *refusing* treatment for anorexia, and again the local authority, who had parental responsibility, sought a ruling from the High Court, this time under its inherent jurisdiction rather than wardship,[2] as to whether her refusal could be overridden. Once more, Lord Donaldson, now in the clear company of his brother judges, ruled that it could. Rejecting his earlier analogy of the keyholder ('keys can lock as well as unlock'[3]), he preferred to regard consent as a:

'legal "flak jacket" which protects the doctor from claims by the litigious whether he acquires it from his patient who may be a minor over the age of 16, or a "*Gillick*-competent" child under that age or from another person having parental responsibilities which include a right to consent to treatment of the minor'.[4]

The position for parents and others with parental responsibility is therefore that they may give a valid consent for their children up to the age of 18 (except where the courts have ruled that the treatment is of a kind which requires court sanction, see Chapter 10), despite the child having full capacity to take decisions for him or herself. A child can consent to, but cannot bindingly refuse treatment. What is not yet determined is the scope of these rulings beyond the sphere of medical treatment, and it may be that, in reality, there is limited scope beyond that sphere.[5] For example, it is doubtful that the parent could force a *Gillick*-competent child to attend school against his or her own wishes, and nor could the state once the child reaches the statutory school-leaving age of 16. Parents could not *force* their child into an arranged marriage – and if they exercised such pressure as to overbear the child's will, the marriage could be annulled.[6] In practice, except in cases of such dire seriousness as those concerning *R v W*, most parents would seek to persuade the child to their way of thinking, and would have little real choice, in the case of older children, but to accept a child's steadfast refusal.

As regards 'children' over 16 generally, the question arises as to whether, in law, parental responsibility should exist at all.[7] The most

1 Unlike the girl in *Re R*. Section 8 provides: '(1) The consent of a minor who has attained the age of sixteen years to any surgical, medical or dental treatment..., shall be as effective as it would be as if he were of full age... (3) Nothing in this section shall be construed as making ineffective any consent which would have been effective if this section had not been enacted.'
2 Section 100(2) of the Children Act 1989 now prohibits wardship of a child in care.
3 At 635.
4 At 635. The case has been followed in *South Glamorgan County Council v W and B* [1993] 1 FLR 574, despite the clear wording of s 38(6) of the Children Act 1989.
5 In *Youth, Family and Citizenship* (1992), G Jones and C Wallace note the lack of sociological research on the relationships between adolescents and their parents, and suggest (at p 414) that the omission reflects 'a more general ambivalence about the position of young people in British society'.
6 *Hirani v Hirani* [1982] 4 FLR 232.
7 J Saunders, in her unpublished LLM dissertation (University of East Anglia, 1994) argues that there should be a 'formal transitional stage: one that has been properly

important events which signal adulthood – completion of formal schooling; entry into the full-time labour force; marriage; parenthood – are all possible, and legal, if not necessarily desirable, before the official age of majority. No court can usually make orders under s 8[8] of the Children Act 1989 with regard to children aged over 16, or which are to continue to have effect after that age.[9]

4. NON-LEGAL NORMS

The term 'parental responsibility' deployed by the Children Act 1989 implies a representative-welfarist approach to parental obligation, and begs the question of how well the legal requirements measure up to ideas of parenting advanced by other, better-qualified, disciplines. In fact, just as the law does not normally insist upon prerequisites to procreation, neither does it routinely monitor parenting after parturition. Even when its attention is attracted, the criterion for taking the child away and into care – significant harm, caused by a departure from such parental care as might reasonably be expected[10] – is clearly met only by a very low standard of caring. When parents part, legal enquiry is only automatic if they are married: and, should they agree on the arrangements for the care of their children, is only of perfunctory standard even then. (On parental divorce, the highest level of interference permitted to the court, by s 41 of the Matrimonial Causes Act 1973 as amended, is to delay the making absolute of the decree of divorce: this only in 'exceptional circumstances' where it appears to the court that the circumstances might require the exercise of its powers under the Children Act 1989, and that this requires further consideration.) But should the separating parents, marital or otherwise, involve the court in their disagreements over the children, then the law may well invoke standards of parental care as a device to resolve competition. On the other hand, it is a well-known irony that, for the much *lower* number of children involved in adoption, the combination of market forces – there is more likelihood of competition here[11] than in

---

considered rather than that has simply come about by historical chance.'. As we have seen, both Parliament and the (English) Law Commission have been reluctant to list definitively the incidents of parental responsibility.

8 For 'residence'; 'contact'; a 'specific issue'; or a 'prohibited step'. See Chapter 8.
9 Section 9(6),(7). The court may make such orders if 'satisfied that the circumstances are exceptional'.
10 Section 31 of the Children Act 1989: the harm may also be due to the child being beyond parental control. See Ch 13.
11 In 1993, some 53% (3,202) of adoptions were by persons other than step-parents (*Judicial Statistics*, Cm 2623, Table 5.6): it has been said that some 100,000 persons may have expressed an interest in becoming adoptive parents before falling 'at the first official hurdles' (*The Times*, November 5, 1993).

parental divorce – and social policy, allow for much *higher* criteria in the potential parenting standards required of applicants. The extent to which legal interest in parenting is inversely proportional to the numbers of children involved can be demonstrated as follows: in 1992, some 690,000 children were born;[12] another 160,000 saw their parents divorced;[13] perhaps[14] 52,000 had their futures considered by the court in private law proceedings; and just 7,000 or so were adopted.[15] As John Eekelaar has said:[16]

'[The courts'] former generalised goal of protecting children's welfare is now increasingly being confined to exceptional cases... There is... a danger that the marginalisation of the courts will lead to a belief that *the law itself* has only a marginal role to play. This could be a serious mistake.'

What *are* approved standards of parenting, even if direct legal interest in them is restricted to so small a number of individual children? Predictably, those disciplines that do take an interest in such standards may not be unanimous as to what qualifies:

'Courts... are continually required to make decisions about children.... Should a child remain with its own family or should a local authority intervene; should a child return to its natural parents or be placed in a new family; should parental rights be terminated... ? All these decisions necessitate a judgment about the quality of parenting – is it good enough? The criteria that are used, however, are often not explicit. Professionals have their own standards based on a combination of values, knowledge and case law but these standards are not usually shared. They are not

12 689, 656 in England and Wales in 1992: *Population Trends 73* (1993).
13 Whilst under 16: (1993) *Population Trends* (No 70).
14 This number has been arrived at by aggregating the number of s 8 Children Act 1989 applications made in 1992 which were disposed of other than by withdrawal: *Judicial Statistics 1992*, Table 5:10.

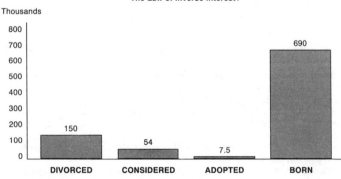

CHILDREN AND THE COURTS IN 1992
The Law of Inverse Interest?

15 7,452: *Judicial Statistics 1992*, Table 5.11. There were 8,894 originating applications.
16 'A Jurisdiction in Search of a Mission: Family Proceedings in England and Wales' (1994) 57 (6) MLR 839 at 858 (emphasis in original).

clearly described in text books on the law, medicine or social work. It is uncertain whether there is any consensus of professional opinion about a minimum sufficiently good standard of parenting.'[17]

Yet not many people – experts, parents and children – might be expected to dissent from the proposition that, 'All good-enough parents exert affection, compassion and control to promote their child's progress to maturity.'[18] In 1986, a public opinion survey[19] gave respondents a list of qualities 'which parents can try to teach their children'. Those who took part were asked to choose up to five that they considered 'especially important'. The list was: good manners; cleanness and neatness; independence; hard work; honesty; to act responsibly; patience; imagination; respect for other people; leadership; self-control; being careful with money; determination and perseverance; religious faith; and unselfishness. *Honesty* was first with over 85%, followed by *good manners* at 74% and *respect for other people* at 67%. As *leadership* was ranked least (2%), perhaps it may be said that we see the gentler, more considerate, side of socialising as being more within the desired range of parental influence.

Here are some specifics of parenting[20] identified by Polansky, which, again, many would find unexceptionable but to which our law, respectful of the privacy of the family and lacking the necessary monitoring and enforcing mechanisms, pays little attention.

Under the heading of *physical care*: parent has encouraged child to wash hands before meals; plans at least one meal a day consisting of two courses; plans for variety in foods; food is offered at fixed time each day; makes effort to get child to eat food not preferred but important for nutrition; special meals prepared for special occasions; sets bedtimes at about the same time each night; teaches child own address. Perhaps these examples of *emotional/cognitive care* are equally uncontroversial: child taken to see some well-known historical or cultural building, spectator sport, animals; parent is sensitive to child's indirect emotional signals; answers child's questions about how things work; plays with child; makes toys available; supplies designated play-area; is comfortable in demonstrating affection physically; guards language in child's presence; limits the watching of television.

One divorcing parent is reported as saying:

> 'There was no decision on things when I went to court... of things like who meets a child from school, takes it to the doctor and things like that, I mean those are the things which I would have thought important but the courts don't see it that way.'[1]

17 M Adcock and R White (eds) *Good-Enough Parenting* (1985) p 5.
18 *Ibid* p 77.
19 *British Social Attitudes Cumulative Sourcebook* (1992) N.1-35.
20 From the 'Childhood Level of Living Scale' in N A Polansky *et al, Damaged Parents: an Anatomy of Neglect* (1981).
1 J Brophy, 'State and the Family: the Politics of Child Custody' (1987) PhD Thesis, Department of Law, University of Sheffield.

That was the view of a mid-1980s parent. Since the Children Act 1989, her successors may well have gained an impression of even more cursory interest in view of the further relaxation of the supervision of parental divorce. Yet those (comparatively few) parents who *compete* to house their children may now be undergoing a more sophisticated, more realistic examination in order to resolve their disputes. *Re H (Illegitimate Children: Father: Parental Rights) (No 2)* [2] concerned a father who only wanted the court to award him parental responsibility – in line with that automatically enjoyed by his former partner – for their child. The Court of Appeal compiled this (non-exhaustive) list of factors to be weighed: the degree of commitment shown by father to child; the degree of attachment between them; and the father's reasons for applying. At first instance, Morton Jack J had found that the father had 'no understanding of how his desire for continued access to those children may affect their stability in the years to come'.[3] The judge made this comment about the father's visits to the foster parents, 'with all the present-giving and spree-taking, the occasional visitor who comes to play has none of the stress and difficulties of the day-to-day care of small children'.[4]

Discussion of the discipline aspects of *emotional/cognitive care* may at least *start* with a degree of consensus: the desirability of parental follow-through of both rewards and punishment; punishment not to involve the use of real or imagined fright objects, or, reaching controversy at last, smacking with implements. Those with parental responsibility may hit[5] their children in English law: so also in Scotland, where the Law Commission would outlaw[6] the use of implements intended to increase the severity of the punishment: south of the border the judicial view is, as some would see it, less squeamish: in 1993 McLean J reportedly saw it as 'potty' were a parent to be legally unable to slipper her child; he allowed a mother's appeal against her conviction for assault after so chastising her nine year old's bare bottom for stealing sweets.[7] Yet in her evidence to the Scottish Law Commission, Penelope Leach said that, in the Commission's words, the sort of 'moderate physical punishment allowed by the law and practised by many parents was particularly unlikely to be effective'; her own words were that, 'The scientific evidence suggests that if physical punishment is to be effective in modifying behaviour, it must induce a greater intensity of pain than would be acceptable to most parents.'[8]

2 [1991] 1 FLR 214.
3 At 218.
4 At 216.
5 See Ch 7.
6 'Report on Family Law' (1992) Scot Law Com No 135 at para 2.105.
7 *The Times*, 20 April.
8 'Report on Family Law' (1992) Scot Law Com No 135 at para 2.74.

We have quickly reached a sharp corner of that area where judges, parents and 'child-care professionals' are sometimes thrown together: the former may deny that they 'live in the past and have no time for psychiatrists and such new-fangled nonsense',[9] yet 'it is not to be assumed that social workers are always right'.[10]

5. MOTHERING AND FATHERING

In 1980, when Polansky's taxonomy of good parenting[11] (above) first appeared, it tended to specify 'the mother' as the performer of the tasks involved ('mother has encouraged child to wash hands before meals'; 'mother has encouraged child to wash hands after using toilet'). We have seen in Chapter 3 that technological advances have reversed the previously time-honoured assumption that the mother's identity is always self-evident but that the father's is not; but of a child's natural parents, it is the mother alone in whom the law *automatically* vests its package of parental responsibilities. Even the marital father's in-built advantage of sole guardianship was abrogated by the Children Act 1989,[12] s 1 (1) of the Guardianship Act 1973 having earlier ensured equality in the exercise of parental rights *even where there is no court order extant*.[13] When the parents become involved in disputes under s 8 of the Children Act 1989, even the modern court occasionally makes preferences based upon 'perceived' gender differences in parenting. In *Surtees v Kingston-upon-Thames Royal Borough Council*[14] Sir Nicholas Browne-Wilkinson saw a parent's responsibility to the child as not only surpassing that owed by other adults, but as one more usually borne by the mother rather than the father, 'The responsibilities of a parent, normally the mother, looking after children... far exceed those of other members of society'.[15]

The significance of breast-feeding was raised in *Re W (a minor) (Residence Order)*[16] in which Lord Donaldson MR made this (general) point about gender:

9 Cross J in *Re S* [1967] 1 WLR 396, 406.
10 Viscount Dilhorne in *B v W (Wardship: Appeal)* [1979] 1 WLR 1041, 1049.
11 'Childhood Level of Living Scale' in N Polansky, *et al*, *Damaged Parents: an Anatomy of Neglect* (1981).
12 Section 2(4).
13 Section 1 of the Guardianship of Minors Act 1971 had already enacted that the *court* shall not take into consideration whether 'the claim of the father... is superior to that of the mother, or the claim of the mother is superior to that of the father.'
14 [1991] 2 FLR 559.
15 At 583.
16 [1992] 2 FLR 332, 336. At first instance, Main J had said that 'If mother had been breast-feeding... I would have regarded that as very significant and... might have ordered the change of home [to the mother] requested'.

'At the risk of being told by academics hereafter that my views are contrary to well-established authority, I think that there is a rebuttable presumption of fact that the best interests of a baby are best served by being with its mother, and I stress the word "baby". When we are moving on to whatever age it may be appropriate to describe the baby as having become a child, different considerations may well apply.'

So it seems that *approved* gender stereotyping in parenthood seems to be on the decline in law[17] as in other disciplines. In 1968 [18] Sachs LJ felt able to say that:

'It is wrong... to proceed on the basis that because in the early years of the child's upbringing he had been with the mother, therefore he cannot be put into the custody of the father. Prima facie, a stage comes when it is better for him to be in his father's house'.

But two years later, Harman LJ, a member of a differently-constituted Court of Appeal[19], said:

'I do not at all agree with expressions of opinion which have fallen, perhaps *per incuriam*, from judges that a boy should, as a matter of *principle*, be with his father – just as much as I disagree with the other "principle", which has altogether been abandoned, that a girl of under three should, as a matter of principle, be with her mother' (italics in original).

In *Re S (a minor) (Custody)*[20], the court welfare officer thought that the mother would be better suited to deal with the nappy-rash suffered by a two year old girl. The justices decided that the girl should be with her father and the Court of Appeal held that the judge was wrong to substitute his judgment for theirs. Having agreed with Butler-Sloss LJ that 'it is natural for young children to be with their mothers', Lord Donaldson MR went on to say:[1]

'What is clear is that there is change in the social order, in the organisation of society, whereby it is much more common for fathers to look after young children than it used to be in bygone days. It must follow that more fathers are equipped to undertake these sorts of duties than was formerly the case.'

He also pointed out that the question of presumptions concerning young, particularly female, children being better off with their mothers, 'may be a matter of semantics as much as anything else'. In all these cases, the court is at pains to stress that the overriding issue is the welfare principle.[2] Section 1 of the Children Act 1989 provides that:

'(1) When a court determines any question with respect to—
    (a) the upbringing of a child; or

---

17 See Ch 15 for an account of *lawyers'* attitudes to gender in parenthood issues.
18 *W v W and C* [1968] 3 All ER 408, 409.
19 *Re C (A) (an infant)* [1970] 1 All ER 309, 311.
20 [1991] 2 FLR 388
  1 At 392.
  2 See Ch 8.

(b) the administration of a child's property or the application of any income arising from it,

the child's welfare shall be the court's paramount consideration.'

Further, the court considers that the judgment of the first instance court, which saw the parties, is not to be substituted unless an error of principle can be detected.[3] Yet in the passage quoted above, the Master of the Rolls may be acknowledging the trend to what sociologists have termed 'androgynous' parenting, ie roles that can be shared by both men and women and that have similar functions. Preparation for mothering may be ceasing to be so primary a goal in the socialising of girls. Women, perhaps through their increasing part in the labour force, are said to have achieved more balance between their 'expressive', ie affectionate, and 'instrumental', ie managerial, functions as parents. For the male on the other hand, parenting may be not so peripheral a role in society as it used to be, yet 'when he is the sole provider in the family, then his attitude about the quality of fathering he received as a child acts as a powerful predictor of his involvement in family work'.[4] In short, if he is holding the purse-strings in his 'family of procreation' he will carry on like his own father did.

We have at least moved away from the Victorian view that the man had an automatic weighting as *father*, whether the child was young or old, male or female. In *Re Fynn,*[5] life with father had left the children unwashed, ill-clothed and ill-fed, 'accustomed to using bad language... and... [appearing] to have no idea that they were doing wrong in using these expressions'. Not surprisingly, Knight-Bruce VC said that:

'To restore the boys to him will, as it seems to me, be in all probability to consign them to unsettled and irregular modes of life, adverse in the highest degree of culture, to discipline... to say nothing of the occasional or frequent, if not constant, privation of the ordinary comforts, perhaps decencies, of life'.

However:

'A man may be in narrow circumstances; he may be negligent, injudicious and faulty as the father of minors; he may be a person from whom the discreet, the intelligent and the well-disposed, would wish his children, for their sakes and his own, removed; he may be all this without rendering himself liable to judicial interference'.

3 In *G v G (minors: Custody Appeal)* [1985] 2 All ER 225, (HL) Lord Fraser said 'the appellate court should only interfere when they consider that the judge of first instance has not merely preferred an imperfect solution which is different from an alternative imperfect solution which the Court of Appeal might or would have adopted, but has exceeded the generous ambit within which a reasonable disagreement is possible'.

4 J J Bigner, *Parent-Child Relations – an Introduction to Parenting* (3rd ed, 1989).

5 (1848) 2 De G & SM 457. For an account of the law's journey from unthinking patriarchy to, at least, something different, see C Barton, 'Legal Family Favourites: the Man, Then the Couple – Now the Child?' (1989) 2 *Journal of Child Law* (1) 29.

Lieutenant Fynn, barrister-at-law, officer and gentleman, kept his children: their mother, his wife, was unable to persuade the court that his conduct was such as to 'render it not merely better for the children but essential to their safety... in some very serious and important respects that his rights should be treated as lost or suspended'.

Yet today, in perpetuating bilateral parental responsibility post-divorce (when the mother is likely to become or remain the primary carer), it may be that the Children Act 1989 will extend to *all* such cases the alleged weakness[6] of the previous 'joint custody' orders, ie that they empower men to exercise control over their former wives. They:

'may well return many mothers to the very power structures which they as mothers (as well as wives) experienced within marriage. This is a situation which can consist of substantial inequalities in the distribution of power and responsibilities between parents, whereby fathers retain the power to make final important decisions but continue to allocate to mothers major responsibility for children's daily care and needs. Ironically this may have been the very situation which drove such mothers finally to seek a divorce as a solution.'

Tyler v Tyler[7] may well be seen as an example of this. There, the mother, a divorcée, was prevented by the court from taking her two sons to live in Australia on the basis that the children's welfare required continuing contact with their father.

But when the law does grant the package to both mother and father,[8] or otherwise gives it to both a man and a woman,[9] does it give them different jobs. *Do* they, in fact, do different jobs and, if so, should they?

It is undeniable that 'no' is the answer to the first question, that 'often' is the likely answer to the second; and that, 'less than they do now' might best serve as a compromise answer to the third. It is quite clear, despite the refusal to give all fathers initial standing, and whatever might subsequently influence courts in resolving residence disputes between mother and father, that Part 1 of the Children Act 1989 does not divide its largesse, once bestowed, on the basis either of gender or anything else (such as, indeed, the gender of the child itself). Yet, to take the female parent first:

'"Mothering" refers to the daily management of children's lives and the daily care provided for them. Incorporated within the term "mothering" is the intensity and emotional closeness of the idealised mother-child relationship as well as notions of mothers being responsible for the fostering of good child development.... The

6 J Brophy, 'Custody Law, Child Care, and Inequality in Britain' in C Smart and S Sevenhuijsen, (eds) *Child Custody and the Politics of Gender* (1989), at 219.
7 [1989] 2 FLR 158.
8 Either as the mother's husband, s 2(2) of the Children Act 1989: or through court order or parental responsibility agreement, s 4.
9 Under s 12 (2) of the Children Act 1989 as a person in whose favour the court has made a residence order; the two are co-terminous.

institution of motherhood, explored... through meanings and ideologies, is inextricably linked with the experiences of mothering, which is explored... through practices.'[10]

There is much scientific evidence as to the actual division of labour involved in parenting. Much of it is not only recent, but recent enough to cast doubt on any suggestion that the division is becoming more equal, let alone that the jobs are more frequently co-performed. About half of parents surveyed in 1984[11] thought that women should be mainly responsible for looking after sick children, the other half plumping for joint responsibility. In fact the actual distribution – in the families of those surveyed – showed that the mothers did the job by themselves in 63% of cases, with only 35% sharing it equally with the father. A commercial survey in 1993 showed that not only did eight out of ten wives take sole or primary responsibility for cooking the main meal (with broadly the same ratio applying to unmarried couples), and that less than 1% of couples left the ironing to the man, but that:

'Like earlier studies, the... survey shows men start out with good intentions which evaporate with the arrival of children. Responsibilities are then abandoned, whether their partners are working or not.'[12]

So although Lord Donaldson's judicial optimism in the 1990s (see *Re S (a minor) (Custody)*[13] above) that more fathers are *equipped* to perform these tasks may well be justified, it seems that they are not all putting their new-found skills into practice. As early as 1984 a more satisfying position, perhaps, was discernible in matters of discipline which 80% believed should be a joint matter: an ideal which 77% of the same respondents had actually achieved in their own households. A pattern whereby (far) more parents believed in sharing responsibility than were actually practising it, was to be found in other aspects of their own partnerships, such as washing, cooking, cleaning and shopping.[14]

So far as parenting is concerned, there is evidence that mothers and fathers have different views of what it should constitute, let alone different views and practices as to which of them should perform it. It has been said,[15] for example, that mothers see discipline and control in terms of the importance of children showing respect for adults, that mothers

10 A Phoenix and A Woolton's Introduction to A Phoenix, A Woollett and E Lloyd (eds) *Motherhood: Meanings, Practices and Ideologies* (1991) p 6.
11 *British Social Attitudes Survey*, (1984) Table A.2, Social and Community Planning Research.
12 Reported in *The Guardian,* 22 December 1993.
13 [1991] 2 FLR 388.
14 *British Social Attitudes Survey* (1984) Table A2.
15 P Marsh, 'Social Work and Fathers – an Exclusive Practice?', in C Lewis and M O'Brien (eds) *Reassessing Fatherhood* (1987).

tend more to encourage by discussion and example the relationship which should exist between the child and the adult world. Fathers, on the other hand tend to see a more immediate link between punishment and control.

6. AN ETHNIC INFLUENCE?

In Chapter 2 we looked at the significance of supra-national laws and influences. We now turn to the matter of domestic multi-ethnicity, and whether the parental practices of the incomers have had any general impact on legal standards of parenting. In *R v Derrivière*,[16] where the headnote reads 'Immigrant parents must conform to English standards', the Court of Appeal (Criminal Division) dealt with an appellant 'from the West Indies' convicted of assaulting his 12 year old son. The boy had refused his father's order to apologise to his mother for coming home late. The father punched him several times, swelling his face, cutting his lip and hurting his jaw: some years before, he had fractured his daughter's wrists.

The statement[17] of Widgery LJ, in delivering the judgment of the court, that 'standards of parental correction are different in the West Indies from those which are acceptable in this country' has since been confirmed by empirical evidence.[18] Parents of Afro-Caribbean origin 'punish their children... more frequently and severely than do indigenous white parents'. The researchers wrote:

'It is perhaps salutary to remind ourselves that historically West Indies parents derive their values from a... social system which institutionalised... the physical beating of slaves by our own forbears'.

A parallel study[19] showed that parents in ethnic Punjabi households hardly ever hit their children.

In *Derrivière*, Widgery LJ continued:

'the Court fully accepts that immigrants coming to this country may find initially that our ideas are different from those upon which they have been brought up in regard to the methods and manner in which children are to be disciplined. There can be no doubt that once in this country, this country's laws must apply; and there can

---

16 (1969) 53 Cr App Rep 637.
17 At 639.
18 J and E Newson 'The Extent of Parental Physical Punishment in the UK' (1976) Paper presented to The Children's Legal Centre seminar on 'Protecting Children from Parental Physical Punishment'.
19 Each survey concerned the frequency of physical punishment of seven year old children in 200 families.

be no doubt that, according to the laws of this country, the chastisement given to the boy was excessive and the assault complained of was proved.'

The judgment is thus limited to the area of parental discipline, and to (corporal) punishment[20] at that, but the message would seem applicable to parenting law generally. It could not address the question of whether there were any currently-accepted 'English' parental practices which originated in one-time 'immigrant' examples: the impact of other cuisines and/or musical tastes, perhaps. In public law, we shall see that the Children Act 1989,[1] in detailing local authority support for children and families, imposes a duty to consider the racial group to which a child belongs. In *Re H (minors) (Wardship: Cultural Background)*[2] Callman J considered the future of two wards of court in the light of their 'past', the court again having to contend with differing cultural/ethnic attitudes to parental 'discipline'. A mother and her two children, aged eight and six respectively, were 'Vietnam boat people' who ultimately found their way to Britain in 1980. The mother was 'one of those people who can best be described as a "survivor", who quickly learn how to work a system and how to use even a strange system'.[3]

There followed a history of ill-treatment: in addition to frequent beatings, the little boy, when a three year old, was put out in the snow, naked from the waist down; his sister was left alone in the house at an even younger age. The social worker who attempted to serve the place of safety order, as the pre-Children Act 1989 device was termed, was threatened with a meat chopper. When the children were in the care of local authority foster parents, their behaviour improved dramatically, particularly after the court terminated 'access' to the mother. The authority sought direction as to the future of the children, whose short lives had thus far encompassed shipwreck, brutal motherly ill-treatment and now the ministrations of two psychiatrists and the wardship jurisdiction of the English High Court. The court addressed the limits placed by the English legal system on the punishment of children in the home, the significance to those limits of 'foreign ethnic origins and culture', and like-with-like matching for adoption purposes.

Callman J declared[4] a (perhaps insufficiently-publicised) limit on the parts of the body which may legitimately be beaten with implements during the exercise of 'parental responsibility':

'the physical beating of these children was excessive by way of its location – the hitting of the children in the face and on the head – for which no society finds any excuse when that beating is administered with an object such as a stick or other

20 See Ch 7.
 1 Sched 2, para 11; see Ch 12.
 2 [1987] 2 FLR 12.
 3 At 14.
 4 At 24-25.

implement so as to cause cuts and bruises in the face. Her beating was unritualised, uncontrolled and cruel, *even when judged by the standards of her own people.*' (our emphasis).

These standards permit[5] 'in... North Vietnam... chastisement with sticks, of a nature and degree which is not acceptable in Western society'. (Callman J also hinted that weight might be attached to social class, 'Such conduct may wholly offend the more educated Chinese society, as it does other sections of Western society.'.)

The appropriate weight to be attached was expressed thus,[6] 'I must consider the case against the reasonable objective standards of the culture in which the children have been brought up, so long as these do not conflict with our minimal standards of child care in England.' This has had as little publicity as the earlier passage, but perhaps more happily so: the latter, broader, ruling is rather less clear and perhaps less welcome. It seems open to two possible meanings, one that better standards of care are legally available for, and only for, children from 'better' backgrounds; or two, an uncomfortable admission that our legal standards are indeed 'minimal' – an equally low safety net for all.

7. THE STANDARDS OF CARE IMPOSED BY THE CRIMINAL LAW[7]

If the law's paradigm of its minimum expectation for parental care is merely the constraint imposed by the criminal law on *anyone* who presently chances to have 'charge' of the child, then there has been no substantive change for over 60 years. Section 1(1) of the Children and Young Persons Act 1933 provides (with subsequent incidental amendment) that:

'If any person who has attained the age of sixteen years and has responsibility for any child or young person under that age, wilfully assaults, ill-treats, neglects, abandons, or exposes him, or causes or procures him to be assaulted, ill-treated, neglected, abandoned, or exposed, in a manner likely to cause him unnecessary suffering or injury to health... that person shall be guilty of [an offence]...'.

In heightening the barrier to conviction by importing a *mens rea* element into the offence of wilful neglect, the House of Lords has concomitantly reduced the level of the duty to the child. *R v Sheppard* [8] involved parents who failed to procure medical aid for their child who

5 At 17-18.
6 At 17.
7 See also Ch 13.
8 [1981] AC 394.

died from malnutrition and hypothermia. Regarding the neglect implicit in that failure, Lord Diplock said:[9]

'Such a failure... could not be properly described as "wilful" unless the parent either (1) had directed his mind to the question whether there was some risk... that the child's health might suffer unless he were examined by a doctor and provided with such curative treatment as the examination might reveal as necessary, and had made a conscious decision, for whatever reason, to refrain from arranging for such medical examination, or (2) had so refrained because he did not care whether the child might be in need of medical treatment.'

Criminal lawyers might say that this is effectively *Caldwell* recklessness;[10] non-lawyers of any kind might say that, by exempting the 'merely' heedless, it only punishes those dangerous 'carers' whose conduct has bordered on the iniquitous. It might be said that criminal penalties, being intended to deter, are inappropriate for those who have not foreseen the harm which their conduct might cause. Yet in other strict liability offences, the knowledge that the unthinking have been punished is presumably intended to engender greater caution in others – the irony is that children themselves are often punished for forgetfulness! Perhaps a further irony is afforded by the fact of s 1(7) having specifically to legitimate (in a Part of the Act headed 'Prevention of... Physical Danger') 'the right of any parent, teacher or other person having the lawful control or charge of a child or young person to administer punishment to him'.

In fact s 1(2)(a) casts a further, higher, duty on a 'parent' or 'guardian' who:

'shall be deemed to have neglected him in a manner likely to cause injury to his health if he has failed to provide adequate food, clothing, medical aid or lodging to him, or if, having been unable otherwise to provide such food, clothing, medical aid or lodging, he has failed to take steps to procure it to be provided under the enactments applicable in that behalf... '.

Perhaps the little-known case of *Re P (infants)*[11] is worthy of greater attention. It concerned the court's discretion to dispense with parental consent to adoption on the ground of persistent failure without reasonable cause 'to discharge the obligations of a parent...'[12] which, said Pennycuick J:[13]

'refers in general terms to the obligations of a parent with no qualification; and it seems to me that in this sub-section the expression "obligations of a parent" must

9 At 404-5.
10 *R v Caldwell* [1982] AC 341; at 354 Lord Diplock said that a person is reckless 'if (1) he does an act which in fact creates an obvious risk... and (2) when he does the act he either has not given any thought to the possibility of there being any such risk or has recognised that there was some risk involved and has none the less gone on to do it'. See, eg, MJ Allen, *Criminal Law* (1991) at pp 59-67.
11 [1962] 3 All ER 789.
12 Under, as it was, s 5(2)(a) of the Adoption Act 1958.
13 At 793-4.

include first the natural and moral duty of a parent to show affection, care and interest towards his child... '.

The birth mother had parted with each of her two children a few weeks after 'it' (*sic*) was born, visiting them and making enquiries about their progress only infrequently. The court held that these failures were in breach of her 'natural and moral obligation' as a parent and that its discretion to dispense with her consent could therefore be exercised. Significantly, it is clear that Pennycuick J saw such 'affection, care and interest' as characteristic of parental duty *generally*.

A sobering disadvantage of dual parenting may occur when both 'carers' face criminal prosecution. The prosecution's inability to prove which one of them was responsible may result in the consequent acquittal of both. In *R v Lane and Lane*[14] the child of the accused had been fatally injured during a period when each parent had been partially present and partially absent, although throughout the period the child had always been in the presence of at least one parent. As it could not be proved who had injured the child, nor that each had been involved as principal or accessory, neither had a case (of manslaughter) to answer. If, however, the facts permit of a sufficiently clear inference that there was a concerted effort – including, eg, where the harm was done by one and the other stood by – convictions may follow.[15]

In this chapter we have been concerned with setting the scene for the function of parenthood in private law; in the next three chapters we look at its operation, in united and divided families respectively.

14 (1985) 82 Cr App Rep 5.
15 *Marsh v Hodgson* [1974] Crim LR 35.

CHAPTER 7

Dual parenting: anticipation and actuality

1. ANTICIPATING PARENTHOOD

Some, at least, of our legal knowledge of parenthood arises from the regulation of the functioning family. One example is the meaning of moderate chastisement,[1] where prosecutions for assault which establish the appropriate limits do not necessarily threaten the integrity of the household concerned. The court has also dealt with parental attempts to determine issues pre-emptively, by way of ante-nuptial agreement. *Andrews v Salt*[2] involved a marriage between a Roman Catholic father and a Protestant mother. Before their wedding they had made a verbal agreement whereby sons were to follow the father's religion and girls the mother's; which party was thought to have made the better bargain is not recorded. 'If there is any family it may make unpleasantness between us unless there is some arrangement made.' In delivering the judgment of the court, Sir George Mellish LJ said:

'We are of the opinion that such an agreement is not binding as a legal contract. No damages can be recovered for a breach of it in a court of law and it cannot be enforced by a suit for specific performance in equity. We think that a father cannot bind himself conclusively by contract to exercise, in all events, in a particular way, rights which the law gives him for the benefit of his children, and not for his own.... On the other hand... after the death of the father... the fact that the father before marriage promised the mother that girls... should be educated in her religion, is a circumstance to which in our opinion weight, and perhaps great weight, ought to be attached.'[3]

1 See below.
2 (1873) 8 Ch App 622, 636.
3 This temporising attitude, whereby the agreement is not guaranteed legal force, but nonetheless is seen as being highly influential, may well anticipate the modern court's general attitude to pre-marital contracts (at least until such time as these arrangements are governed by statute).

In a 1986 survey, 'religious faith' scored poorly in a 15-strong list of 'important qualities parents can try to teach their children'. Only around 9% of those asked placed it in their shortlist of five.[4] Article 14 of the United Nations Convention on the Rights of the Child temporises on the question of parent-child conflict in this area. Although 'States Parties shall respect the right of the child to freedom of thought, conscience and religion', they must also respect 'the rights and duties of the parents... to provide direction to the child in the exercise of his or her right in a manner consistent with the evolving capacities of the child'. 'Temporise' is perhaps too feeble a description, particularly as the Article concludes by stating that 'Freedom to manifest one's religion or beliefs may be subject... to such limitations as are prescribed by law and are necessary to protect public safety, order, health or morals'. Article 30 specifically acknowledges the right of children of minority communities and indigenous populations to enjoy their own culture, and to practise their own religion.

Today, both 'father' and 'mother' (as segregated by Sir George Mellish LJ in *Andrews v Salt*, above) would read 'parent' but even s 2(9) of the Children Act 1989, which prevents those with parental responsibility from surrendering or transferring it, makes no express provision for futuristic partnership contracts which attempt to predetermine the exercise of such responsibility. Yet in 1684, almost 200 years before *Andrews v Salt* and some 70 years before Lord Hardwicke's Act of 1753 effectively did away with common law marriage, poor Elizabeth Beecher was prepared actually to *have* her lover's child as a condition subsequent to the marriage she hoped to contract with him:[5]

'I do hereby promise under my hand that if I am not with child by you in two years to make void the contract which is now between us'.

Unfortunately, Elizabeth not only failed to persuade her lover to join her in executing the main marriage contract – which he gallantly kept, unsigned, until his death – but, having failed to become pregnant within the two years, eventually managed it after four years and again after six. In fact, Lawrence Stone explains that such conditions in marriage contracts were 'very unusual'.[6] Yet in 1989 those surveyed[7] as to whether 'a marriage without children is not fully complete' were fairly evenly split, the ayes being about 35% and the nos 32%. As regards who should

---

4 *British Social Attitudes Cumulative Sourcebook* (1992) N.1–35. The five most-favoured qualities were, in descending order: honesty; good manners; respect for other people; cleanness and neatness; and to act responsibly. Only 'imagination' and 'leadership' were ranked lower than religious faith. See Ch 6.

5 Bodleian, Rawlinson MSS B 382, fo 105.

6 *Road to Divorce: England 1530-1987* (1992)

7 *British Social Attitudes* (1992), N.1-7.

decide how many children a couple should have, about 90% of those asked thought it should be a joint decision of both parents, 4% thought the mother alone, and fewer than 1% the father alone.[8]

English cohabitants may be confronted by a comparatively blank legal canvas *qua* partners, but, *qua* parents, their *prima facie* responsibilities are as much imposed – although to different effect – as those of married couples.[9] By contrast, one unmarried American pair entered a purportedly binding contract which anticipated the entire gamut of parenthood, from procreation to separation. It covered: an acknowledgement that 'biology dictates a particular contribution to child-raising'; a preference for state schooling (unless 'it poses a threat to our child's physical or emotional security'); and the drawing of lots as a tie-breaker in custody disputes.[10]

In *Re W (a minor) (Residence Order)*,[11] the circumstances of the parents' attempt to anticipate their respective roles were not propitious. The expectant mother's marriage to a third party, with whom she had a three year old boy, had broken up, as had her relationship with the father. During the pregnancy the parents agreed that the new baby would be brought up by the father who, in reliance on the agreement, had engaged a nanny; a development on which a commercial lawyer might hope to base an estoppel. Some three days after the birth, despite an earlier change of heart, the mother entered into a parental responsibility agreement[12] with the father under s 4(1)(b) of the Children Act 1989. He took the child to his home. The mother changed her mind again and before the baby was one month old the Court of Appeal had made a residence order in her favour, on the basis of the rebuttable presumption that a baby is better placed with its mother. The court held that there could be no question of the parties being bound to the pre-birth agreement.

Choosing names during pregnancy is a more agreeable pursuit. True to form, the American couple (above) made the decision even earlier, their contract leaving only the names of their third and subsequent children (should they have proceeded to produce any at all) to the mercy of subsequent agreement. In this country, it is changing, rather than choosing, the child's surname which has attracted most legal attention,[13] mainly in the wake of parental divorce.[14] Yet, in the absence of strife,

---

8 *Ibid* N.1-11.
9 Only those men who are married to the mothers of their children at the time of the birth are automatically vested with parental responsibility: Children Act 1989, s 2(1), (2) (see Ch 5).
10 See L Weitzman, *The Marriage Contract* (1981) pp 319-324.
11 [1992] 2 FLR 332.
12 See Ch 5.
13 A very useful source of information, for children and others, is 'What's in a Name' (1993) 96 *Childright* May.
14 See Ch 10.

both initial choice and subsequent change are, in English law, comparatively free from constraint or formality. In the United Kingdom, parents have a duty to register a child within 42 days of birth,[15] and to give the Registrar the surname to be borne by the child. Forenames must also be supplied, if chosen. If none are registered then, or within 12 months of birth, the child will go through life without a 'Christian' name, or at any rate a registered one. So far as unsuitable choices are concerned, the Registrar only has a very limited power of refusal, however much he or she might wish to save the child from subsequent embarrassment: those born during successful cup-runs are therefore fair game for their fathers' fanaticism. Yet a sequence of numbers cannot be registered, nor can a name concocted from other than the traditional alphabet.

Article 8 of the United Nations Convention on the Rights of the Child gives a right to a name from birth, coupling this entitlement with other basic matters such as a nationality, and the right to know, and be cared for, by his or her parents. Article 9, in giving the *child* the right to preserve his or her name 'as recognised by the law', sees the name as a reflection of *identity* – a perception also found in psychology, if not in the law of contract.[16] Shakespeare, 'Who steals my purse steals trash... but he that filches from me my good name... makes me poor indeed'[17] surely had in mind something other than mere nomenclature. 'Names acquire special meanings and associations. A name becomes a very personal part of oneself. They are more than handy labels. The person and the name become associated in people's minds. Names are useful too – a reference point to distinguish one person from another.'[18]

The legal role in the initial choice of name, both the given and (in traditional Western society) the patronymic, is somewhat vague, given that most of us keep our parents' choice of first name throughout life, and that a man normally retains his father's surname. ('I should imagine, knowing modern children, the importance to them of the surname is very limited. In practice they do not use surnames very much.'[19]) In some cultures it is the grandparents who choose the name. Only convention, it seems, drives the usual practice whereby a marital child of either gender takes the paternal surname and a non-marital child takes the mother's.

15 Births and Deaths Registration Act 1953, s 2.
16 Cases such as *Lewis v Averay* [1972] 1 QB 198 indicate that, for the purposes of operative mistake, misapprehension merely as to the name of the other 'contracting' party may be seen as an attribute only, and thus insufficient to render the contract void *ab initio* at common law – cf *Militante v Ogunwomoju* [1994] Fam Law 17, where a mistake as to the man's *name* appears to have been accepted, at least in part, as grounds for a nullity decree.
17 *Othello*, Act 3, Scene 3.
18 'What's in a Name' (1993) 96 *Childright* May.
19 Per Ormrod LJ, *R v R (Child: Surname)* (1982) 3 FLR 345, 347.

Any 'unmarried' father who is not possessed of parental responsibility will not appear on the Register – and thus will be particularly unlikely to bequeath his surname – except, for example, where both parents attend the Registrar to request it.[20]

2. THE TWO-PARENT HOUSEHOLD

The law has tended to present two contrasting pictures of the parental role – either to live with and care for the child, or to be absent and pay. In the first of these the duties are limited to an unsupervised, normally low-level and ill-defined set of obligations, reminiscent in these respects of Lord Reid's dictum[1] on the rights of consortium: 'A bundle of rights some hardly capable of precise definition'. Indeed, Sachs LJ used exactly the same 'bundle of rights' expression to describe parent-child relations in *Hewer v Bryant*[2] almost 20 years later. Even so far as parental duties do not involve expenditure, they are minimal in standard. They are not 'means-tested'. The position is analogous to the wife's common law right to maintenance which was predicated on the principle that, so long as the spouses were together it was entirely for the husband to fix the standard of living.

(a) Caring by paying

In the American case of *Commonwealth v George*[3] the father, who was living in the family home with his wife and two minor children, was arrested on information laid by his wife[4] that he 'neglect[ed] to maintain his wife or children'. Her case was that he 'too strictly controlled the expenditure of his income'. She complained that 'the bills were not paid promptly, not that they were not paid; that he would give money directly to the children instead of to her so that she could give it to them'.

In giving the opinion of the court, Justice Patterson said:

20 Birth and Deaths Registration Act 1953, s 53, as amended by the Children Act 1989 Sch 12, para 6. The other circumstances are, first, at the request of the mother on production of a statutory declaration of paternity by the father, backed by a declaration by the mother that he is indeed the father, and, secondly, at the father's request on production of a statutory declaration by the mother that he is the father, together with his own declaration to that effect. Re-registration acknowledging the father is possible in the same circumstances.
1 *Best v Samuel Fox & Co Ltd* [1952] AC 716, 736.
2 [1970] 1 QB 357,353.
3 56 A 2d 228 (1948).
4 Under s 733 of the 1939 Pennsylvania Criminal Code.

'This record establishes that the appellant has provided adequate food, shelter, clothing and reasonable medical attention. It presents conflicting concepts of family financial management.... The arm of the court is not to be empowered to reach into the home and to determine the manner in which the earnings of a husband shall be expended *where he has* [not] *deserted his wife... and children....* The method whereby a husband secures to his wife and family the necessities of life is not a proper subject for judicial consideration and determination *in the absence of proof of desertion*' (emphasis added).

In English common law, it appears that a wife could not pledge her husband's credit for necessaries for their children whilst the spouses were cohabiting.[5]

Legal insouciance towards parental duty illustrated in *Hewer v Bryant* (above) gave Lord Denning MR the opportunity to add his own *imprimatur* to the wider issue:[6]

'For over 300 years anyone under 21 was not barred [from bringing legal proceedings] by lapse of time. He was not entitled himself to bring an action at law for damages: because... he was considered incapable of managing his own affairs, at least to that extent... he had to find someone to act as his next friend and bring an action on his behalf. But it was not everyone who was prepared to be his next friend, especially as a next friend is liable to pay all the costs if he loses. Even the most loving parent might hesitate, and a neglectful parent would not bother. No parent was under any duty to bring an action on behalf of his child. He was not even liable to maintain his child unless the neglect to do so would bring the case within the criminal law... all the more so, a parent was not bound to bring an action for him. The only thing the law did for a parent was to say that, if he did help his child to bring an action, he was not guilty of the criminal offence of maintenance.'[7]

Minors themselves have a contractual liability based upon their parents' station in life; law students of an earlier generation, when 21 was the age of full capacity, knew all about the idea of 'necessaries'[8] which by s 3(3) of the Sale of Goods Act 1979 include 'goods suitable to the condition in life of the minor... and to his actual requirements at the time of the sale and delivery'. So in *Peters v Fleming*[9] rings, pins and a watch-chain were famously held to be necessaries for an undergraduate blessed with a rich father. A number of ironies arise. The young men – all the reported cases involved males – had to pay for such purchases on the basis that traders would not otherwise give credit for essentials. One might otherwise have thought that minors might get away without paying for *real* necessities

---

5 See the original edition of P Bromley, *Family Law* (1957) at pp 311-2.

6 [1970] 1 QB 357, 367.

7 'Maintenance may nowadays be defined as improperly stirring up litigation and strife by giving aid to one party to bring or defend a claim without just cause and excuse', *per* Lord Denning MR in *Re Trepca Mines Ltd (No 2)* [1963] Ch 199 at 219.

8 One of the categories of contracts to which minor parties are bound. The term covers not merely articles essential to the support of life, but articles and services consistent with the minor's social and economic class. See any traditionally-minded contract text.

9 (1840) 6 M & W 42.

out of sympathy for their plight in not being able to afford them. Alternatively, that they should be be liable to pay for rings, pins, and the like as a punishment for profligacy,[10] and to discourage others from contracting to buy on credit what they do not need. Yet what concerns us here is that the parent's purse is not the measure of the parent's innate responsibility to the child, but merely the measure of the child's contractual liability to others.

On the face of it, Stephen Cretney's statement[11] that children's financial interests have not been well-served by the law, would seem to apply only when parent and child part. In truth it was reflective of the modest legal norm applicable when they were together (see *Mortimore v Wright*[12] below): now, the Child Support Act 1991 and the private family proceedings legislation may well require that much more be paid on, and after, parting; see Chapter 9. Admittedly, it may be possible to infer from the statutory ground for application for financial relief, 'failed to provide, or to make a proper contribution towards, reasonable maintenance for any child of the family',[13] a norm for the child in the functioning household. Such inference, which acts as an important qualification to the 'care or pay' doctrine, is strengthened by the Domestic Proceedings and Magistrates' Courts Act 1978. A financial provision order can be obtained under the 1978 Act even though the parties to the marriage are still living together at the date of the order.[14] A periodical payments order in favour of a *spouse* ceases to be enforceable if they continue to live with each other, or subsequently resume living with each other, for a continuous period of six months.[15] But periodical payments orders made in favour of a 'child of the family', on the other hand, do remain enforceable.[16]

In *Mortimore v Wright*[17] Lord Abinger CB was 'desirous to make the point absolute' that:

'In point of law, a father who gives no authority and enters into no contract, is no more liable for goods supplied to his son than a brother, or an uncle, or a mere stranger would be. From *the moral obligation* a parent is under to provide for his children, a jury are, not unnaturally, disposed to infer against him an admission of

10 In fact, s 3 of the Sale of Goods Act 1979 requires the minor to pay only a reasonable, and not necessarily the contractual, price.
11 A Bainham, *Children – The Modern Law* (1983) at p 291.
12 (1840) 6 M & W 482.
13 Domestic Proceedings and Magistrates' Courts Act 1978, s 1(c); Matrimonial Causes Act 1973, s 27(1)(b) (as substituted by the Domestic Proceedings and Magistrates' Courts Act 1978, ss 63(1), 89(2)).
14 Section 25(1).
15 Section 25(1).
16 Section 25(2)(a). Orders made in the superior courts under s27 of the Matrimonial Causes Act 1973 – including those in favour of a spouse – do not become unenforceable when the family reconvenes.
17 (1840) 6 M & W 482.

liability in respect of claims upon his son, on grounds which warrant no such inference in point of law' (emphasis added).

Mr Wright senior was thus not liable for 'necessaries' of board and lodging supplied to the young Joseph, who had fallen ill whilst working away from home. Crucially, he was still notionally in the parental household. The significance of such presence was later taken up by Blackburn J,[18] 'a father's legal obligation to support his child is not more than to supply such food and clothing as are necessary for health', but he went on to stress that just as the *husband's* liability to his wife increases on parting, so also does his liability towards his children. He expressed the comparison as follows:

'The wife of the richest subject in the realm, when driven from her husband's roof, is not obliged to have servants or clothes suitable to her degree. If she chooses to clothe herself economically, and dispense with attendance, she may do so; yet I apprehend it will not be disputed that she may bind her husband by ordering clothes, and hiring servants; and if her husband's station be high enough to make it reasonable, ordering liveries for those servants... not merely as the wife of a person in the station of the defendant, but as... *having the custody of the infant children of the marriage*'[19](emphasis added).

It is upon the division of the household that the more significant interest in the parental role arises, at least so far as the absent parent is concerned. We consider the question of separated parents (and their children) in the next two chapters.

(b) Children v parents

Thus far, we have been mainly concerned with those modest parental obligations which obtain whilst the children are *en famille*. When parents are housing their minor children their legal *duty* has always been light, but now their *power*, at least, can be challenged. In Chapters 2 and 6[20] we examined the development of children's rights by the courts, notably in the *Gillick*[1] case and we now deal with the anti-parent weapon provided by s 10(8) of the Children Act 1989, namely the child's right to ask for leave to apply for a s 8 order (for residence, contact, specific issue or prohibited step). After this provision came into force in 1991 it was sometimes extravagantly referred to as a means whereby children could divorce their parents.[2] In fact, the closest English law comes to sustaining

18 *Bazeley v Forder* (1868) LR 3 QB 559, 564.
19 *Ibid* p 563-4.
20 See Ch 16 for the *representation* of children in court.
 1 [1986] AC 112.
 2 See C Barton, 'Tell me off and I'll Phone my Lawyer', (1992) *The Times*, 17 November.

such a metaphor is when the court is influenced by the child's wishes in dispensing with parental agreement to adoption.[3]

No s 8 order made in favour of a third party can deprive parents of their parental responsibility, but it may curtail their exercise of it, as, by s 2(8), the possession of parental responsibility does not entitle the holder to act inconsistently with an order made under the Act. In *Re C (a minor) (Leave to Seek Section 8 Orders)*[4] the applicant for leave was the respondents' daughter who was almost 15 years of age. 'C has been given statutory rights by the Children Act 1989, and I must not seek to impede her in those rights.'[5] She sought a residence order to enable her to continue her stay at her friend's parents' house, and a specific issue order to go on holiday with them to Bulgaria (the necessary passport would only otherwise be available with the consent of her parents). In the event, she failed to obtain leave for either application, yet the apparent simplicity of the procedure may exacerbate the misgivings of those who disapprove of even the right to seek leave. Typically, a present-day child might have some awareness of the position, and the school teacher/social worker/ solicitor/legal aid connection – in *Re C* it was the last three only – may combine with the anti-delay principle of s 1(2) of the 1989 Act, and the rules regarding the allocation of business,[6] to have the matter brought quickly before a High Court judge.

The mechanism may seem hair-triggered, but the actual results may be less threatening to parental power than they appear at first sight. Sir Stephen Brown has said[7] that he does not expect applications by children under the 1989 Act to be made frequently, a remark which cautions solicitors and others against an over-ready recourse to s 10(8). Legal Aid Committees may be reluctant to support such applications in the first place,[8] and even if the solicitor is convinced of the child's capacity to give

---

3 See Chs 5 and 14.
4 [1994] 1 FLR 26.
5 Johnson J at 27.
6 Such cases are transferred for hearing by a High Court judge in accordance with a direction of Sir Stephen Brown: [1993] 1 FLR 668.
7 *Re AD (a minor) (Child's Wishes)* [1993] Fam Law 43 and 405. The President made his remarks in open court, following the case of a 14 year old girl who, feeling under pressure following her parents' divorce, had gone to stay with her boyfriend's family, at first with her mother's consent, and later on her own decision. The girl had instructed solicitors, and 'certain' orders were subsequently made under s 8 of the Children Act 1989, but the matter required further investigation and was transferred to the High Court. The mother issued a summons in wardship, and the court asked the Official Solicitor to act. Ultimately, the parties agreed that the wardship should continue and that the Official Solicitor should carry on as the girl's guardian *ad litem*. The President said that the case had become 'of a kind which the court in wardship had been dealing with for a very long time'.
8 See [1994] Fam Law 38 for anecdotal evidence of this.

instructions, the court may overrule him or her. In *Re H (a minor) (Role of the Official Solicitor)*[9] Booth J said that such capacity involves:

'much more than instructing a solicitor as to his own views.... He must be able to give instructions on many different matters as the case goes through its stages and to make decisions as the need arises.... The child also will be bound to abide by the rules which govern other parties, including rules as to confidentiality.'

In *Re C* (above) Johnson J refused leave for the residence application as it might have enshrined by court order a state of affairs which ought better to be resolved by C and her parents. Neither was leave given for the specific issue application, as the matter of the holiday was not important enough to invoke the jurisdiction and to grant leave might:

'be interpreted as a willingness of the court to entertain applications of children, even children of the age of C, in any matter in which they were in disagreement with their parents'.[10]

It is implicit in *Re C* that the court was 'satisfied that the child had sufficient understanding to make the proposed application' as required by s 10(8). In *Re SC (Leave to Seek Residence Order)*,[11] the court continued to take a cautious line with regard to children's rights by holding that such understanding did not necessarily mean that leave would be granted. The court still has to exercise its discretion and, as the initial application for leave does not raise any question regarding the upbringing of the child, neither the s 1(1) paramountcy of the child's welfare principle nor the s 1(3) checklist[12] are applicable. What is relevant to the court's exercise of its discretion is the likelihood of success of the proposed application. *Re SC* involved a 14 year old in care who lived in a children's home but who wanted to live with her friend's family instead. Because she was in care, both the local authority and the mother had parental responsibility, but only the mother objected to the application. Booth J granted leave on the basis that the child had the necessary understanding and that the proposed application had a reasonable chance of success.

(c) Punishment

English law is not prescriptive with regard to the wider issue of parental *discipline*, where the model of family privacy is at its strongest. The law contents itself with specifically permitting punishment, particularly

9 [1993] 2 FLR 552.
10 At 29.
11 [1994] 1 FLR 96.
12 See Ch 8.

corporal punishment, by way of the statutory acknowledgement[13] of 'the right of any parent... to administer punishment to [a child]'. It follows that English law[14] has yet to go down the road taken not only by Sweden (1979), but also Finland (1984), Denmark (1986), Norway (1987) and Austria (1989), all of which countries have either restricted or eliminated corporal punishment in the home. But with regard to parents, we still follow the Testaments both Old ('He that spareth his rod hateth his son; but he that loveth him chasteneth him betimes'[15]) and New ('For whom the Lord loveth he chasteneth, and scourgeth every son whom he receiveth'[16]). Not that the right to hit is restricted just to those *prima facie* imbued with parental responsibility. The long-standing right of such a parent to delegate the chastisement of his or her children would now seem to be covered by s 2(9) of the 1989 Act whereby a person 'who has parental responsibility...may arrange for some or all of it...to be met...on his behalf'. Presumably this is the only way in which a man can lawfully hit his cohabitee's children from a previous relationship, unless he is named with her in a residence order under s 10, probably following her divorce from the father. Permission under s 2(9) would even be needed by a putative father cohabitee, in the absence of a s 4 parental responsibility agreement with the mother. Finally, *any* person who has been granted a residence order 'over' a child thereby obtains parental responsibility – and thus hitting powers – even if he or she is neither parent or guardian (s 12(2)).

During the passage of the Children Bill through the House of Lords there was an unsuccessful attempt to render physical punishment by parents unlawful. The position therefore remains that laid down in *R v Hopley*[17] where it was held that 'moderate and reasonable' parental chastisement does not attract the attention of the criminal law. One hopes that it now takes rather less to exceed the limit than it did in *Hopley* itself, where a school teacher wrote to a boy's father asking whether he could chastise him severely, 'that if necessary he should do it again and again' and 'continue it at intervals even if he held out for hours'. The father did not 'wish to interfere with [the] plan and when the 'thirteen or fourteen year old' later died as a result of the ensuing assault – a secret two-hour

---

13 Children and Young Persons Act 1933, s 1(7); parents are thereby immune from prosecution under s 1(1) for cruelty to their children. In *R v Rahman* (1985) 81 Cr App R 349, a father's conviction for the common law offence of false imprisonment was upheld; such conduct was held to be unlawful where the detention was for such a period as to take it out of the realm of reasonable parental discipline.
14 See generally: P Newell, *Children are People Too* (1989); and C Barton and K Moss, 'Who can Smack Children Now?', (1994) 6 *Journal of Child Law* (1) 32.
15 Proverbs 13, v 24.
16 Hebrews 12, v 6.
17 (1860) 2 F & F 202.

night time flogging with a thick stick which led to a conviction for manslaughter – Cockburn CJ held that the parental authority actually granted had not been excessive. Whatever view is taken about abolition, it would seem desirable for the law to be more precise about when chastisement becomes unreasonable. Since *Gillick v West Norfolk and Wisbech Area Health Authority*,[18] it seems unlikely that it could be justified at all in the case of a child over 16. Yet surely the younger the child, the less the court would sanction hitting, at least in terms of severity.

It seems clear that Article 37 of the United Nations Convention on the Rights of the Child would now outlaw at least some of the sorts of parental beatings which were seen as legitimate in the past, 'No child shall be subjected to...cruel, inhuman or degrading treatment or punishment'. In their 1985 Paper,[19] the Committee of the Ministers of the Council of Europe merely *hoped* that member states would 'review their legislation on the power to punish children in order to limit or indeed prohibit corporal punishment'.

How much, or how often, are children hit by their parents in the United Kingdom? The most significant available information is that produced by John and Elizabeth Newson's long-term study of child-rearing habits in a random sample of 700 'indigenous' Nottingham families. It was reported[20] that 91% of the boys and 59% of the girls (three-quarters of the sample) had been smacked, hit with *or threatened by* an implement by the age of seven. Implements used, or with which children were threatened, were, in order of (parental) preference: belt or strap; cane or stick; slipper; miscellaneous objects (rulers, backs of hairbrushes, etc). By the age of 11, hitting had decreased considerably, involving 60% of children either less than once per month or not at all.

The abolitionists claim that physical punishmment is basically unjust, in the assumption that[1] 'it is acceptable to hit children, but that it is quite unacceptable for them to hit others, or for adults to hit anyone else'. It is said to be ineffective in that young children do not remember what they are being smacked *for*. Links have been drawn with child abuse, 'accidental' injury, the learning of aggressive behaviour, delinquency, and even extreme pathological behaviour. As early as 1886, Krafft-Ebing[2] felt able to condemn it as being sexually dangerous. A more

---

18 [1986] AC 112; see Ch 6.
19 Recommendation No 85(4), para 12.
20 In July 1986, they presented their paper, 'The Extent of Parental Physical Punishment in the UK' to the Children's Legal Centre.
1 P Newell, *Children are People Too* (1989) at p 12.
2 *Psychopathia Sexualis*.

contemporary view may be found in the submission of the British Psychological Society to the Scottish Law Commission:[3]

> 'an inefficient method of modifying behaviour, being situation-specific and of short-term effect, and with a possibility of providing undesirable side effects of both fear and learned imitative behaviour. More socially desirable attitudes would be encouraged by alternative methods of managing behaviour, such as the withdrawing of privileges and the rewarding of more desirable alternatives.'

We deal elsewhere with how corporal punishment is differently perceived by mothers and fathers (and in some ethnic communities),[4] and with state limitations in the education and child care spheres.[5]

(d) Failures of care

Where parents have been guilty of downright illegality in relation to their children, it is often the case that the latter only seek redress on adulthood, when they have left their 'families of orientation'.[6]

(i) Tortious parenting

The handful of reported domestic decisions on parental liability in tort all involve adult plaintiffs suing in respect of childhood injuries. Some may see such cases as an unwelcome ventilation of the legal family vacuum, perhaps risibly so in the potential for proceedings over trivial parent-child altercations of a decade or more earlier. On the other hand, others might say that parental liability for damage to life-chances caused by parental divorce, or from upbringing in an otherwise dysfunctional family, might rectify the harm done by the lack of direct legal constraints upon such matters. But even in America, the vacuum has been ventilated with care. In *Goller v White*,[7] a father was held liable in negligence when his son sustained injuries when riding on the towbar of a tractor, yet the Wisconsin Supreme Court indicated that there was a general immunity in tort as regards parental discretion in matters such as education, housing and medical services.

For nearly 300 years, *Ash v Lady Ash*,[8] in which the plaintiff-daughter won actions in assault, battery and false imprisonment against her

---

3 Scot Law Com, No 135 *Report on Family Law* (1992) cited at para 2.73.
4 Ch 6.
5 Chs 10, 11 and 13.
6 See Ch 1. In one survey, 87% of young people were found to be living at home on leaving school: M Buist and H Gentleman, *The Legal Capacity of Minors and Pupils – Experiences and Attitudes to Change* (1987) p 11.
7 20 Wis 2d 402, 122 NW 2d 193 (1963).
8 (1696) Comb 357.

mother, stood alone in this country, despite generating at least one overseas decision.[9] *Ash* has now been joined by the Court of Appeal decision in *Surtees v Kingston-upon-Thames Borough Council,*[10] although this was an action brought against foster parents and the local authority. There the court held that, whilst any duty of care bestowed upon the former is the same as that owed by 'legal' parents, such duty only arises from the facts and not from the parent-child relationship *per se*. As a two year old, the plaintiff suffered burns to her foot as a result of immersion in hot water, although she had no memory of how it occurred. Her action for negligence failed on the basis that the injury was most likely caused when she managed to turn on the hot tap, as opposed to the plaintiff's contention that she must have put her foot in a bowl of hot water whilst unattended.

The Court of Appeal nonetheless decided that a duty of care was capable of arising in such circumstances, and considered its nature. The duty only arises *ad hoc*, and not, as we have seen, from the parent-child relationship, but the standard is that of a careful parent in the circumstances. As regards this standard, the court took what might be termed a realistic attitude, Browne-Wilkinson V-C acknowledging that there is a limit to the care that even loving and careful 'mothers' can give in the rough and tumble of family life. Our domestic law, like that of America, has gone some way from the reluctance of the 1891 Mississippi Supreme Court ('The peace of society and... families... forbid to a minor child... civil redress... for personal injuries suffered at the hand of a parent'[11]) to open the family to justice, but parental duty in this area does not appear to be any higher than that of the responsible, but unloving, stranger.

(ii) Sexual abuse

Introduction: incest and marital exogamy. Our *criminal* law renders the incest taboo *reciprocal* between parent and child when each participant reaches adulthood (16 in the female's case[12]) when only full 'sexual

---

9 Eg, *McCallion v Dodd* [1966] NZLR 710, where the New Zealand Court of Appeal also relied on the more recent Scottish case of *Young v Rankin* 1934 SC 499, to establish that there was no rule of law precluding child versus parent actions for personal wrongdoing. In *McCallion*, a father was held contributorily negligent when his four year old son was hit by a motorist when the family was walking down a road in the dark; the child was holding the hand of his deaf mother who, as the father knew, was not wearing her hearing aid. In *Rankin*, a child-passenger was held to be entitled to sue his driver-father for negligence. For an account of these cases, and of the general issue, see J Wright 'Negligent Parenting – Can my Child Sue?' (1994) 6 *Journal of Child Law*, (3) 104.

10 [1991] 2 FLR 559.

11 *Hewellette v George* (1891) 68 Mis 703, 711.

12 Sexual Offences Act 1956, s 11(1).

intercourse'[13] is prohibited. *Mens rea* is required. In *R v Carmichael*[14] it was held that a man whose sexual partner was his own adulterine daughter, but whom he believed to have been fathered by his wife's then husband, thereby lacked the necessary mental element. When the participants are both adult, and the intercourse does not produce children, the taboo becomes unexpectedly difficult to justify, despite the long-standing and widespread feelings of repugnance inspired by its breach.[15] There are, or have been, cultures which have not imposed such bans, although the rare examples have tended to involve only the ruling classes such as the Royal House of Ancient Egypt. Further, even within the almost universal experience of the taboo, the range in the number of outlawed relatives has varied with time and place. Rationales proffered[16] include: the assertion that sexual indifference between close kin is a majority instinct; the need for the 'child' to direct his drive outside the nuclear family as an essential reflection of his need to learn his wider role as a member of society as a whole; the need to promote the advantages of collective security implicit in creating wider links; and that sexual competition within the family would destroy what is a crucial and valuable group. The uncertainty of the moral base on which adult, childless, incest rests has been recognised in countries such as France, where, to convict, it must be shown that one participant has abused his familial authority at the expense of the other. It seems that medieval Scottish law was not so equivocal: the Incest Act 1567 remarked that 'the abhominabill vile and fylthie lust of incest is swa abhominabill in the presence of God'.

So far as adverse social reaction is concerned,[17] mother/son incest (ironically, the least likely to produce offspring in view of the probable age difference) may well be the most condemned variant, perhaps because it is more in conflict with the expectations that older, bigger male partners will use their dominance to initiate a sexual relationship. The father/daughter taboo suffers, by far, the highest incidence of breach, certainly in terms of prosecutions, with incestuous fathers receiving the heaviest punishments (mainly, perhaps, as a reflection of the female's youth at the time of the offence). On the question of incidence, Judith Herman reports that a review of the five largest studies (worldwide) of parent-child incest reveal that the offender was the father in 97% of cases, the mother in only 3%. Herman goes on to say that:

13 *Ibid* ss 10(1), 11(1).
14 [1940] 1 KB 630.
15 See generally, C Barton, 'Incest and the Prohibited Degrees' (1987) 137 NLJ 502, and the references there cited.
16 See, eg, O Aberle *et al*, 'The Incest Taboo and the Mating Pattern of Animals' (1963) 65 *American Anthropologist* 15.
17 See generally, K Muselman, *Incest* (1979).

'Father-daughter incest is not only the type of incest most frequently reported but also represents a paradigm of female sexual victimisation. The relationship of father and daughter, adult male and female child, is one of the most unequal relationships imaginable.... The actual sexual encounter may be brutal or tender, painful or pleasurable; but it is always, inevitably, destructive to the child.... The horror of incest is not in the sexual act, but in... the corruption of parental love.'[18]

Marital exogamy only arises on 'adulthood' (the marriage of an under 16 year old being anyway invalid[19]) when, *a fortiori* of the sexual bar, any 'marriage' contracted between parent and child would be void *ab initio* as being within the prohibited degrees of relationship.[20] As seen in Chapter 4 this prohibition, unlike the law of incest, is equally applicable[1] to an adoptive couple, although it does not go beyond the parent-child link to include any of the adoptee's other new relatives.

Compensation for parental sexual abuse. In California (although not in some of the other States of the Union[2]) nemesis, in the shape of civil action, is now overtaking the parent who molests his offspring during childhood: statutes of limitations have been excepted by means of the doctrine of 'delayed discovery' whereby the trauma suffered by the now-adult plaintiff has caused them to repress their memories of abuse. In *Doe v Doe*[3] the California Court of Appeals held that a 24 year old daughter, whose father had stopped abusing her by the time she was five years old, could take advantage of the California Code of Civil Procedure whereby[4] 'Nothing... is intended to preclude the courts from applying delayed discovery exceptions to the accrual of a cause of action for sexual molestation of a minor.'

In Canada, plaintiffs time-barred in tort have claimed breach of fiduciary duty, benefiting from its equitable base and the comparatively lax doctrine of laches. In *KM v HM; Women's Legal Education and Action Fund, Intervener*[5] the plaintiff's father embarked upon a campaign of incest between her ninth and eighteenth years, her ordeal ceasing only when she left home. She only realised what had caused her subsequent psychological problems when she began attending a self-help group for incest victims ten years later. In the Supreme Court La Forest J said:[6]

18 *Father-Daughter Incest* (1981) p 4.
19 Matrimonial Causes Act 1973, s 11(a)(ii).
20 Matrimonial Causes Act 1973, s 11(a)(i).
 1 Since the Children Act 1975, Sch 3, para 8. Should the adoption have ended, the bar is nonetheless retained (as are, in any case, all the original bars which arose on birth: see Ch 4).
 2 See generally, N Clevenger, 'Statute of Limitations: Childhood Victims of Sexual Abuse Bringing Civil Actions Against their Perpetrators After Attaining the Age of Maturity', (1992) 30 *Journal of Family Law* (University of Louisville) (2).
 3 216 Cal App 3d 285 (1989).
 4 (West 1990) Cal Civ Proc Code 340.1(d).
 5 (1992) 96 DLR (4th) 289.
 6 At 323.

'It is intuitively apparent that the relationship between parent and child is fiduciary in nature... The act of incest is a heinous violation of [parental] obligation. Equity has imposed fiduciary obligations on parents in contexts other than incest, and I see no barrier to the extension of a father's fiduciary obligation to include a duty to refrain from incestuous assaults on his daughter.'

In England and Wales, in *R v Criminal Injuries Compensation Board ex p P,*[7] a woman claimed that her repressed memory of being sexually abused by her step-father between the ages of 5 and 14 had been revived when she learnt, as a 26 year old, that young girls were going to his house. One reason given by the Board for refusing her application for compensation was that the ten-year lapse was so long as to invalidate the reason for it.

The High Court's reason for refusing her application for judicial review was that compensation, under the scheme's rules as originally drafted, did not apply to 'same roof'[8] offences – the 'essay in bounty' (as Leggatt LJ termed it[9]) thereby putting the family beyond justice. Yet delayed action may be a defining characteristic of 'incest trauma':

'the classic psychological responses to incest trauma are numbing denial and amnesia.... Finding that the co-existence of these psychological and emotional disorders is unique to and characteristic of incest victims, experts have joined them under the heading of 'Post-Incest Syndrome'. Those suffering from this syndrome will persistently avoid any situation, such as instituting a lawsuit, that is likely to force them to recall and, therefore, to re-experience the traumas... until she can realise that her abuser's behaviour caused her psychological harm, the syndrome prevents her from bringing suit. Often it is only through a triggering mechanism, such as psychotherapy, that the victim is able to overcome the psychological blocks and recognise the nexus between her abuser's incestuous conduct and her psychological pain.'[10]

A self-serving collusion between therapists and lawyers, or an interdisciplinary breakthrough for the client-patient? To what extent has English law followed the United States and Canada in grappling with delayed civil actions against the bad parent, be it abusive (step)father or otherwise? In *Stubbings v Webb*[11] the matter was dealt with under the Limitation Act 1980. In 1987, when she was 30 years old, the plaintiff

---

7 [1993] 2 FLR 600; upheld by the Court of Appeal at [1994] 2 FLR 861.
8 'Offences committed against a member of the offender's family living with him at the time will be excluded altogether': para 7 of the Criminal Injuries Compensation Scheme 1964. A version of this rule continued until 1 October 1979. The reasoning of the court in the instant case was that the extension of the scheme did not betoken any previous deficiency of the scheme of which the applicant was entitled to complain.
9 At 604.
10 Jocelyn B Lamm, 'Easing Access to the Courts for Incest Victims: Toward an Equitable Application of the Delayed Discovery Rule' (1991) 100 *Yale LJ* 2189, 2194–5.
11 [1993] 1 FLR 714

sued her adoptive father and her adoptive brother for damages for the mental illness she had suffered, allegedly due to their ill-treatment of her during her childhood. She claimed that the father had sexually abused her between the ages of 2 and 14 and that the brother had twice raped her when she was 12 and he 17. These men denied that they had committed such acts. They also argued that her claims were now statute-barred; it was upon that cold preliminary issue that her claim foundered. Their Lordships held that her actions were for trespass against the person and thus subject to the six-year time-limit prescribed by s 2 of the 1980 Act. Although wholly suspended during her infancy, the period had nonetheless expired on her twenty-fourth birthday in 1981.

Lord Griffiths, in the one speech of substance, may have been relieved that the law was not that wrongly applied by both of the lower courts:

'It would obviously be a matter of grave difficulty for any court to determine where truth lies if this action was to proceed, for it would be investigating events that were alleged to have occurred in a period starting over 30 years ago and ending over 20 years ago.[12]

The plaintiff's case was that although she knew she had been raped... and... sexually abused... she did not realise that she had suffered sufficiently serious injury... until she realised that there might be a causal link between psychiatric problems she had suffered in adult life and her sexual abuse as a child... I have the greatest difficulty in accepting that a woman who knows that she been raped does not know that she has suffered a significant injury. The Criminal Injuries Board, ever since its inception almost 30 years ago, has been making substantial awards to the victims of rape, and since the enlargement of the scheme in 1979 this has included victims within the family setting.'[13]

The Court of Appeal[14] went into the matter (some would say) in greater depth. Nolan LJ said[15] 'Different considerations have arisen since [the drafting of the Limitation Act 1980]... such as the Cleveland Enquiry and Child Line and increased awareness of the mental scars which sexual abuse inflicts'. Sir Nicolas Browne-Wilkinson V-C added:[16]

'In my judgment it is important not to consider the question by reference to the social habits and conventions of 1991. Over recent years, for the first time, civil actions have been brought by victims of adult rape against their assailants. As to actions against child abusers, this is apparently the first case in which the alleged abuser has sought to sue her abusers. In the present climate and state of knowledge, it would, in my opinion, be very difficult, if not impossible, for a plaintiff coming of age in the late 1980s to establish that she acted "reasonably" in not starting proceedings alleging child abuse within three years of attaining her majority. But we are concerned with the reasonableness of the plaintiff's behaviour in the period

---

12 At 715.
13 At 719.
14 [1992] 1 FLR 296.
15 At 307.
16 At 307-8.

1975–8. At that time civil actions based on sexual assaults were unknown in this country.'

As we have seen, the Law Lords' opinion of this matter was consistent with their legal analysis. As it happens, a similar matching – albeit going in the other direction – occurred in the Court of Appeal.[17]

3. POSTHUMOUS PARENTING

(a) The status

Although posthumous *birth* is as old as human procreation, its potential has been extended – perhaps even beyond previous imagination – by late-twentieth century technology. Happily, fewer mothers now die in childbirth and live babies can be delivered from the wombs of those who have died – of unconnected causes – during pregnancy. The possibility of fathers dying before their children are born is a melancholy consequence of the fact of gestation, although increased life expectancy has no doubt reduced the incidence of these (some might say) most innocent of one-parent families. Private legal interest in such cases was mainly restricted to the presumption of paternity, whereby the husband of a married woman is *prima facie* taken to be her child's legal father. As seen in Chapter 3, this has required judicial notice to be taken of the vagaries of the human gestation period.

Most of the cases there mentioned involved parturition after decree absolute of divorce, or at least physical separation, but in *Re Heath*[18] Cohen J dealt specifically with the case of the posthumous child, 'I need not, however, decide whether the presumption [of legitimacy] applies, since I am satisfied that, if it does, I ought, on the facts, to find that it has been rebutted'.[19] If, as assumed, the daughter had been born at the end of the normal period of gestation, she was conceived a month or so before the husband's death, but between his stays in hospital and whilst the mother was living with another man. The latter, Mr Brookman, was registered as the father; he and the mother were subsequently married to

---

17 It was held that the plaintiff's action, for trespass of the person, fell within s 11(1) of the Limitation Act 1980, 'any action for damages for negligence, nuisance, or breach of duty', and that time therefore started to run under s 11(4)(b) when she knew that injuries were significant *and attributable to the acts alleged*. On the facts, the latter realisation only came to the plaintiff in September 1984 when she received psychiatric treatment which enabled her to make the connection. Her writ of August 1984 was therefore within the appropriate three-year limit.
18 [1945] Ch 417.
19 At 422.

one another. 'In my opinion, no reasonable jury could fail to conclude that the daughter is the daughter of Brookman'. She was therefore legitimated by her natural parents' later marriage and was thus entitled to her father's sister's estate upon the latter's intestacy, all preferential kin being predeceased.

Today, the intestacy rules take no account of (il)legitimacy; the significance of the presumption has been diminished to the point of negation by the availability of DNA testing; and other scientific advances can produce human life from the gametes of the now-dead.

(b) The function

So far as the parenting *role* is concerned, we might note that, on death, the position seems to echo the lighter duties of on-going parenthood rather than the heavier obligations which accrue upon divorce or separation.

(i) Guardianship and intestacy

Neither mother nor father is required to exercise, or even to consider the exercise, of their power to appoint testamentary guardians for the remainder of their children's minority. Jacqueline Priest's survey[20] of such appointments suggests that the matter is usually only raised by the drafting solicitor rather than the parent-client, of whom a 'significant minority' nonetheless fail to make an appointment, mainly through fear of provoking ill-feeling within the family as to who should be chosen. Apparently, only a 'negligible percentage' of such appointments as are made ever take effect as, happily, not many parents die during their children's minority. Perhaps more will be made now that this can be done by a simple written document, signed and dated, under s 5(5) of the 1989 Act.[1]

The same legal indifference has been discerned in the minimum level of material support required by intestacy law, which has been said to favour the widow(er) in lieu of the children:[2] not, perhaps, a view always shared by the surviving spouses themselves (particularly where the situation is complicated by the existence of children from earlier marriages). The legal facts are that, in addition to the deceased's personal

20 Of 26 solicitors in the North-East of England: her report appears as Appendix B in Law Com WP No 91, *Review of Child Law: Guardianship* (1985).

 1 Despite initial Law Commission hesitation (WP No 91 (1985) para 3 43) that 'a connotation of insignificance' might attach to a method of appointment previously used only for insubstantial property such as Post Office savings.

 2 S Cretney, in A Bainham, *Children – the Modern Law* (1993) at p 293.

goods, the surviving spouse obtains the current statutory legacy[3] of £125,000 and a life interest in one half of the balance, the children sharing the other half immediately and, ultimately, the capital amount of the widow(er)'s half. During their minority, the intestate's children may receive maintenance out of income under the statutory trusts, any balance being accumulated for their benefit for when they become entitled to their share of the capital when 18. So it does appear that parents have to be fairly well-off before their children are entitled to much on their intestacy.

Perhaps the moderate nature of these posthumous duties is an unconscious reflection of the lesser impact which bereavement is said[4] to have on a child, compared to the other routes to single-parenthood. There is not the same likelihood of hostilities between the parents, no separate households competing for support, and outside reaction is supportive rather than disapproving. Both materially and personally things are likely to be better: a lesser likelihood of economic difficulties; better accommodation;[5] and no increase in the rate of delinquency.[6] A dead parent is often idealised to children, and the surviving parent may increase his or her involvement in their care in order to compensate them for their loss.[7]

Yet it seems that whilst the parental duty to safeguard one's child after one's death is comparatively light, parental powers are strong: a legacy, as it were, of the old law on parent-child relations *inter vivos*. First, the power of a parent with parental responsibility to appoint a testamentary guardian[8] amounts to self-replacement by replication – in whatever number he or she chooses, and with or without their consent or knowledge, although disclaimers are now allowed.[9] In life, only adoption is comparable, when, as we have seen, specific appraisal and court order follow a competitive administrative process by the applicant(s) (other than in the case of 'private' adoptions) to achieve general eligibility.

> 'Given the gamut of... controls... to ensure that a transfer of parental responsibility to a non-parent is consistent with the child's welfare, their absence in the case of guardianship is striking.'[10]

3 Family Provision (Intestate Succession) Order 1993 (SI 1993/2906).
4 E Ferri, *Growing Up in a One-Parent Family* (1976).
5 *Ibid.*
6 M Rutter, 'Parent-Child Separation: Psychological Effects on the Children' (1971) 12 *Journal of Child Psychology and Psychiatry*. See generally B M Hoggett, *Parents and Children – the Law of Parental Responsibility* (4th ed, 1991) at p 95 and the authorities cited therein.
7 J Elliott and Martin Richards, 'Parental Divorce and the Life Chances of Children' [1991] Fam Law 481 at 484.
8 See Ch 5.
9 Children Act 1989, s 6(5). See Ch 5.
10 G Douglas and N V Lowe, 'Becoming a Parent in English Law' (1992) 108 LQR 414 at p 428.

In the case of a marital child there is no longer the added danger of conflict between the surviving spouse and the deceased's nominee: by s 5(8) of the Children Act 1989 the appointment only takes effect after *both* parents have, in Petronius Arbiter's mordant phrase,[11] 'joined the majority': a measure already established in every other member country of the Council of Europe. Under s 5(7)(b) the only exception is where there was a sole residence order in favour of the appointing parent at the time of his death. In fact Priest's (pre-Children Act) survey (above) suggested that the 'overwhelming majority of appointments... are positive appointments', ie to secure the smooth transition to a substitute home, and not 'negative', ie 'over-shadowed by a desire to deny a particular person (usually a non-custodial parent) any opportunity to assume the physical care of the children'. The survey also found that although potential testators often initially favour grandparents, solicitors tend to put them off the idea on the grounds that such appointees may be too old. Instead, the solicitors' influence often led to the appointment of aunts and uncles who were already blessed with children of their own.

Nowadays, when there are barely enough orphans to crew a pirate ship,[12] and most one-parent families are created by unmarried procreation or divorce rather than bereavement, there may be some excuse for our lack of knowledge about the practice of guardianship. Clearly, informal, consensual, *de facto* guardianship of orphans goes on: the social security 'guardian's allowance',[13] which is payable without contributions or means-testing, is open to such *de facto* carers even without benefit of legal status (although seemingly paid to very few people).

(ii) Disinheriting

A second illustration of the vigour of parental power lies in the strong, if not unqualified, capacity to disinherit (for which mere omission from the will suffices, rather than positive action): whilst parents are under no ostensible duty to leave anything to their children, the Inheritance (Provision for Family and Dependants) Act 1975 specifies the latter as one of the categories of persons who may apply for 'reasonable financial provision' from the estate. For this purpose, s 1(2)(b) lumps them with non-relatives (and indeed, parents), and not the widow(er), in that they must show that they need the provision for their *maintenance*. Although the 1975 Act does not make childhood an express factor (ie to be specifically considered by the court when hearing a claim) many of the most successful claimants have been mothers of the deceased's still-

---

11 Satyricon: Cena Trimolchionis 42.
12 A minimum requirement, of course, for the ship's company in Gilbert and Sullivan's *Pirates of Penzance*.
13 Social Security (Contributions and Benefits) Act 1992, s 77.

young children. Grown-up children may obtain an order despite their normal lack of any *inter vivos* claim on their parents. In *Re Debenham* [14] the applicant was a 58 year old epileptic, an unwanted child who had been rejected all her life by her now-dead mother who had willed her £200 whilst leaving the balance of her estate, over £170,000, to various animal charities. Ewbank J said:

'The difficult question is whether she owed any obligation and responsibilities to the applicant. She certainly did not owe any legal obligation, because the applicant was a mature woman of more than full age. I have to consider whether she owed any moral obligation or responsibility to the applicant.'

He ordered an immediate lump sum payment of £3,000 and annual periodical payments of £4,500: post-mortem, the mother's previously moral obligations thus became legally enforceable. Anomalously it was under s 25(1) of the 1975 Act that parents were given the same posthumous financial duty for non-marital children as for maritals, whereas it was not until the Family Law Reform Act of 1987 that the same parity was achieved (for their minor children only, at least) during lifetime.

Finally, we might note that applications under the 1975 Act may be made by step-children (whose numbers are unclear, although it has been estimated[15] that, following divorce, about half of all the children of the dissolved marriage live with the mother and her new husband). The right of such people to apply under the 1975 Act contrasts with their lack of standing under the rules of *intestate* succession. In *Re Leach, Leach v Lindeman*[16] illustrates this, as well as the vagaries of family form and the nature of adult relationships between (step)parent and 'child'. And, if that were not enough for one case, the passage[17] 'She said in evidence, "He'd trust Mary to see that I was alright"', might be worthy of note by the law student.

The witness was the plaintiff, Joan Leach. 'He' was Bertram Leach, her deceased father, and 'Mary' (another dead Leach) was her stepmother. The defendants were Mary's three siblings, *prima facie* entitled to all their sister's property under the intestacy rules. The question for the Court of Appeal was what proportion of the estate, if any, should come to Joan under s 1(1)(d) of the 1975 Act as being a 'person (not being a child of the deceased) who, in the case of any marriage to which the deceased was a party, was treated by the deceased as a child of the family in relation to that marriage'.

How had Mary 'treated' Joan, who only became her stepdaughter when the latter was 32? She had never maintained Joan, an action which

14 [1986] 1 FLR 404, 409.
15 J Haskey, 'Children in Families Broken by Divorce' in *Population Trends (No 61)* (1990) p 42.
16 [1986] Ch 226.
17 At 228.

would have been specifically relevant under s 3(3)(a) of the 1975 legislation. Slade LJ ruled out manifestations of what he seemed to see, on somewhat cynical grounds, as the mere civilities of the relationship 'mere display[s] of affection, kindness or hospitality... [as] reasonable step-parents can usually be expected to behave in a civilised and friendly manner towards their step-children, if only for the sake of the spouse'.[18] Yet what would – and did – suffice, may afford a rare legal view of parent-adult child relations *generally*. It involves an ongoing tandem of 'privileges and responsibilities', with the former eventually dwarfing the latter, 'If things take their natural course, the privileges of the quasi-parent may well increase and the responsibilities may well diminish as the years go by.'[19] So a posthumous requirement to provide for a family member on death can be based as much upon the idea of *repayment* by the deceased as it can upon a *continuing obligation* by him or her.

After Bertram's death, Joan continued to visit Mary, who entrusted her with personal confidences, helped her with business problems, and took her to visit her (Mary's) friends. The report tells us nothing of the relations between Mary and the three defendants, ie her sisters and her brother. The net estate was worth £34, 000. Joan was awarded £14, 000 of it – over 40%.

In the next two chapters we return to living parents – those who have parted during their children's minority.

18 At 235.
19 At 237.

CHAPTER 8

Separated parents (1): caring

1. INTRODUCTION

With around 150,000 divorces per annum and an increasing proportion of couples choosing to cohabit rather than marry, even after having a child, the chances of a child experiencing his or her parents' divorce or separation have increased considerably over the last two decades.[1] The extent to which legal procedures minimise or exacerbate the harmful effects of such an experience is a crucial question in assessing the validity of this area of the legal reputation of parenthood. In this chapter and the next, we examine that reputation.

(a) Care or pay?

On the division of a household, the legal interest in the parental role is likely to increase. This is because upon divorce or separation, the relationship between the former partners, far from being extinguished, often becomes more formal and specific (sometimes by court order) than it was beforehand; this process is likely to be accentuated when there are children. The law thus reserves its major interest for that small, if growing, minority of parents whose children[2] live in a so-called 'one-parent' family.

We should add that, as regards parental *duty* upon separation, the 'legitimacy' or otherwise of the children has limited relevance. Cohabitants – if the unmarried parents in question have ever been that – cannot divorce, but the financial obligations[3] owed to children by a

---

1 See the discussion of divorce and cohabitation rates in *Social Trends 1994* in Ch 2.
2 The percentage of dependent children living in one-parent families doubled to 18% in the 20 years from 1972: *Social Trends 23* (1993) Table 2.4.
3 See Ch 9.

departing parent are little affected by whether or not he or she is married to the other parent. On the other hand, there is a vital distinction with regard to the *assertion of parental authority*: it is upon separation that the 'unmarried' father and his children are most likely to feel the effect of his lack of automatic parental responsibility.[4]

In truth, there are two separate distinctions which must be drawn. One lies between the two and the one parent family[5] and the other, which is a sub-division of the latter, lies between the parent with care and the absent parent. We shall examine the nature of the absent parent's *financial* duty, 'paying rather than caring' in the next chapter. But it is important, for three reasons, not to represent the distinction between 'him'[6] and the parent with care as being more stark than it is, or as always being a matter of choice for the parent concerned.

First, it is fundamental that a *spouse's* parental responsibility is not forfeited upon departure, whether or not accompanied by matrimonial causes or family proceedings. Parental responsibility is unaffected by the making, or non-making, of a residence order under s 8[7] of the Children Act 1989 – although by s 2(8) it may not be exercised inconsistently with a court order – nor is it affected, as s 2(6) affirms, by the granting of parental responsibility to other(s), such as step-parents. It follows that in theory the 'caring' option continues unabated: in practice, it seems that the leaver (who may, of course, be the 'left' if the other has departed with the child) will not have much authority[8] given that he cannot, without invoking the court, overrule the carer who need not even tell 'him' what 'she' proposes (s 2(7)).[9] Conversely, he cannot be made to care for, or even to see, his child: in proceedings under s 8 of the Children Act 1989 he can only play the applicant role; neither the child nor anyone else may take such proceedings against him.[10] But, with court backing if need be,

4 See Ch 5.
5 As reflected in the division of contents between this chapter and the previous one (in which we noted the modesty of the standards – including that of maintenance – required of residential parent(s)).
6 The large majority of 'lone-parent' families are 'headed' by women: *Social Trends* 23 (1993) Table 2.9.
7 '... an order settling the arrangements to be made as to the person with whom a child is to live': s 8(1).
8 See Ch 6 for a list of the items concerned.
9 But cf in *Re G (Parental Responsibility: Education)* [1994] 2 FLR 964 where the Court of Appeal upheld the dismissal of the divorced mother's application (for a prohibited steps order under s 8 of the Children Act 1989) to prevent her former husband from sending their son to a boarding school. Glidewell LJ, after citing s 2(7) and (8), said, 'mother, having parental responsibility, was entitled to and indeed ought to have been consulted about the important step of taking her child away from the day school that he had been attending and sending him to a boarding school. It is an important step in any child's life and she ought to have been consulted' (at 967).
10 A 'contact order', eg, is defined by s 8 as one, 'requiring the person with whom a child lives, or is to live, to allow the child to visit or stay with the person named in the order'.

he may be able to exercise a *power* post-marriage. A dramatic and controversial example is to be found in *Tyler v Tyler,*[11] where, post-divorce, a caring mother and her children were prevented from moving from Leeds to the mother's original home in Australia (we noted earlier that 'travel and emigration' are examples of parental power) in order that the father's contact would not be prejudiced. She would 'survive', found Ewbank J; it was hinted that the absence of a step-father did not help. It has been suggested that the message given by this case (other than to find another partner) would appear to be to *behave badly*; the mother should stamp her foot and threaten to take it out on the children if she is not allowed to go. Alternatively, the father's enthusiastic support could be gained by threatening to dump them on him indefinitely.[12]

The position for non-marital parents and their children is radically different. As seen in Chapter 5, the father, in the absence of an agreement with the mother or a court order, will not have been seised of parental responsibility even when the family were together. It is therefore worth noting that if *she* quits *them*, she is effectively demoted to 'payer' status whilst he is left without the legal wherewithal for that 'caring' which the proper welfare of the child may well require of him. In the more likely case of the mother being left with the non-marital child, the father acquires paying duties without ever having had any caring status in law.

Secondly, for an unknown number of parents parted from their children, the concomitant duty of payment cannot fairly be described as one of choice, or as a financial penalty deservedly imposed as the price of rejecting their caring role. Such parents are mainly men[13] and may well be few in number but they do not all merit Carol Smart's condemnation[14] (of their pressure group *Families Need Fathers*) as being merely concerned with 'trying to reassert the authority of the father in the family' as part of the phenomenon whereby women's demands are 'trivialised, mocked and distorted'. It may well be true that, worldwide, the stress occasioned by divorce has[15] 'a disproportionate impact now on the women and children involved' but this does not mean there are no fathers who, through no fault of theirs, are parted from children with whom their main relationship is now one of financial provider:

11 [1989] 2 FLR 158.
12 C Barton, 'Emigration after Divorce (Not) the Children Act 1989' (1989) 24 JALT 81 at p 84.
13 Six months after the Child Support Act 1991 came into force the *Daily Mail*, 11 October 1993, reported that the first 'absent mother' (whose ex-husband and his new wife were earning more than twice her salary) had received a maintenance assessment from the Child Support Agency.
14 *The Ties That Bind* (1984) at p 130.
15 M Maclean and L J Weitzman, 'The Way ahead: A Policy Agenda' in L J Weitzman and M Maclean (eds) *Economic Consequences of Divorce – the International Perspective* (1992) at p 416.

'There are two possible scenarios to be sketched out here. One is optimistic and sees that fathers are becoming more involved in child care. It is felt that conflicts over custody that are erupting can be met by changes in legal procedures to give fathers greater rights. The other is pessimistic and fears that law will seek to impose a model of shared caring on separating couples, irrespective of fathers' actual involvement, and this will reduce women's autonomy and increase husbands' power to intervene in the lives of former wives. The former sees the problem as one of communication and compromise, the latter sees it as an issue of gender politics in which law plays a crucial, not impartial role.'[16]

Irrespective of gender, there are clearly parents who find themselves reluctantly and unfairly separated from their children and thus paying *for* them when they would rather be playing *with* them. There are a number of possible reasons for this: no-fault divorce; non-marital fathers not being vested with legal parental responsibility, coupled, on extra-marital breakdown, with the lack of such legal supervision as does occur on parental divorce; and the inability to compete in the accommodation stakes with the other parent. For such parents, the 'choice' is forced.

A third reason why the 'care or pay' roles on parental separation are not absolutely separate is that, as we shall see in the next chapter, a financial liability is notionally ascribed to the 'parent with care' for the purposes of calculating the absent parent's obligation under the Child Support Act 1991.

(b) Law and the parting process

We have referred earlier[17] to the desultory legal supervision of parental divorce. Once, such importance was ascribed to the role of the court that, even after introduction of the 'special procedure' in 1977, the judge made an appointment with the petitioner to discuss the arrangements proposed for the children of the family under 16. Research[18] carried out in the 1980s showed that these meetings were of little value. They often lasted less than five minutes. All that usually happened was that the judges ticked a box after the phrase 'the arrangements are satisfactory' or, 'the arrangements are the best that can be devised in the circumstances'. The courts hardly ever used their powers to delay the divorce. Now, the highest level of interference permitted to the court, by s 41 of the Matrimonial Causes Act 1973 as amended, is to delay the making absolute of the decree of divorce, but only in 'exceptional circumstances' where it appears to the court that the circumstances might require the

---

16 Preface by M Cain and C Smart to C Smart and S Sevenhuijsen (eds) *Child Custody and the Politics of Gender* (1989), at xii.

17 Ch 6.

18 G Davis, A MacLeod and M Murch, 'Undefended Divorce; should s 41 of the Matrimonial Causes Act be repealed?' (1983) 46 MLR 121.

exercise of its powers under the Children Act 1989, and that this requires further consideration. The reality is that a district judge will consider the arrangements to be made for the children, the proposals for which will have been submitted in writing and hopefully agreed by the spouses. If the judge, in considering the position under s 41, is dissatisfied with the plans, probably because of conflicting proposals, the parents may be required to appear.

The modesty of these measures represents an embarrassing tension between the privacy model of marital divorce – which the Children Act 1989 further accentuated – and more recent expressions of Governmental concern over the perceivedly deleterious consequences for children of single parenting, to which divorce is a major contributor. The truth is that the adult wish to separate and/or divorce has been afforded a higher priority. No statistics appear to be published of the current incidence of s 41 activated delays to decree absolute, and there has been some overstatement of the degree of supervision they involve; disturbingly, the following is taken from *Judicial Statistics*[19] for 1993:

'Where the couple has children, the court has to be satisfied with the arrangements for their welfare. Under the Children Act 1989, this is fundamental to a court's ruling, a central tenet of the Act being that the welfare of the child is paramount.'

Neither one of these statements is correct, particularly the reference to the 'welfare' principle (see below). John Eekelaar's remark that 'The protectionist mission of the court under the traditional court system has collapsed'[20] seems far more accurate.

Although state intervention in parental divorce can be seen as paternalistic, and criticised as an undue discrimination against divorced families,[1] there is now a great deal of evidence of the disadvantages which may await the children of divorce. In a famous study of 60 Californian families (admittedly untypical in terms of their social class and background) experiencing divorce,[2] the researchers, Judith Wallerstein and Joan Kelly, found that the divorcing process went through several stages for the family members. First, there was an initial period of high stress when the decision to separate was first taken; they found that there were high levels of conflict in the family, with deep unhappiness for all the protagonists. The children's own distress was not adequately addressed by the parents, because of their diminished capacity to parent whilst facing their own emotional crisis. Wallerstein and Kelly found that children of different ages at the time of the divorce responded

---

19 Cm 2623 at p 52.
20 (1994) 57 MLR 839 at 846.
 1 As concluded by the *Report of the Matrimonial Causes Procedure Committee* (1985) at para 2.24.
 2 *Surviving the Breakup: How Children and Parents cope with Divorce* (1980).

differently; the youngest were confused and fearful, and felt that their parents might dispense with them as they had with each other. Those older, aged between six and eight, were sad, angry with their mothers whom they saw as driving their fathers away. Those aged nine to twelve might identify with one parent against the other, whilst adolescents might become anti-social in their behaviour and experience conflicts of loyalty between both parents.

By the end of the first year, the children had recovered from their *acute* responses, with the girls recovering faster than the boys. They then went through a transitional phase, lasting up to three years, where they faced both practical and emotional adjustments to the changed situation. A third stage occurred when the family had reconstituted itself, perhaps through a remarriage. Not all the families had achieved stability and happiness. The researchers concluded that the eventual outcome for the children:

'depends, in large measure, not only on what has been lost, but on what has been created to take the place of the failed marriage. In full and proper perspective, the effect of the divorce is an index of the success or failure of the participants, parents or children, to master the disruption, to negotiate the transition successfully, and to create a more gratifying family to replace the family that failed.'[3]

The research finished five years after the original separation of the spouses, and the authors noted that *further* stages of adjustment could probably be identified if the study had continued. Perhaps most significant, however, was their finding that, five years on, over half the children did not regard the divorced family as an improvement over their pre-divorce family, and still wanted to turn the clock back: 'for all, a significant part of their childhood or adolescence had been a sad and frightening time'.[4] In contradiction of Goldstein, Freud and Solnit's arguments in favour of allowing the resident parent to have the final say in whether contact with the absent parent should continue, the research suggested that the relationship with the absent parent remained highly important for the children, and this particular finding has been crucial in the legal and social work attitude to contact arrangements post-divorce or separation, as we shall see.

Not only did the children go through a very unpleasant experience around the time of the divorce, but there is evidence to suggest that there are long-term disadvantages which they might suffer.

Judith Wallerstein, this time with another researcher, Sandra Blakeslee, went back to the California sample to explore the effects of divorce ten years on, and this time interviewed 52 families. They found that half the

3 *Ibid* p 305.
4 *Ibid* p 306.

children had seen a parent experience a *second* divorce in that time and 'half grew up in families where parents remained angry with each other'.[5] Three out of five felt rejected by at least one of their parents, and almost half 'entered adulthood as worried, under-achieving, self-deprecating and sometimes angry young men and women'.[6] Wallerstein and Blakeslee also identified a 'sleeper effect' of divorce whereby, when entering adulthood, the children experienced a sudden shock of anxiety or guilt which made them unable to succeed in their own relationships.

These findings have been very heavily criticised as unscientific and based on a tiny and unrepresentative sample, the criticism coming not least from Wallerstein's erstwhile collaborator, Joan Kelly.[7] Nonetheless, there is other evidence drawn from the British National Child Development Survey, a cohort of all the children born in one week in 1958. This research[8] found that only 14% of children of non-manual parents who divorced or separated obtained university level qualifications, compared with 32% of children whose parents remained together. It and other studies have also identified:[9] lower educational achievement; leaving home earlier; earlier heterosexual relationships; earlier marriage; poorer psychological health; higher divorce rates; and lower socio-economic status and income. On the other hand, as there is evidence[10] that the suffering (lower educational achievement, disruptive behaviour, feelings of anxiety) of children of unhappy marriages begins *before* their parents' divorce, it can be argued that increasing the amount of legal attention paid to children *during* the divorce proceedings would be of little help.

Yet paradoxically, as Jane Elliott and Martin Richards have said:[11]

'It is the behaviour of children at or around the time of separation, which may be used to determine future plans for their care. But there are few indications that the... immediate upset [has] any connection with the longer term outcomes... discussed here. We must raise our eyes to the horizon and consider decision-making on divorce from a perspective which stretches into the adulthood of children.'

5 *Second Chances* (1989).
6 *Ibid* at p 340.
7 See the review by Joan Kelly and Robert Emery at [1989] Fam Law 489.
8 J Elliott and M Richards, 'Parental Divorce and the Life Chances of Children', [1991] Fam Law 481 at 484.
9 *Ibid*, and see the references cited therein.
10 J Elliott and M Richards, 'Parental Divorce and the Life Chances of Children', [1991] Fam Law 481 at 481–3.
11 *Ibid* at 484.

(c) The paramountcy of the welfare of the child[12]

Article 3 of The United Nations Convention on the Rights of the Child requires only that the best interests of the child be '*a primary*[13] consideration', whereas the principle expressed in s 1(1) of the Children Act is that:

'When a court determines any question with respect to—
    (a) the upbringing of a child; or
    (b) the administration of a child's property or the application of any income
        arising from it,
the child's welfare shall be the court's *paramount*[14] consideration.'

As we have seen, this does not rule parental divorce; neither does it rule the financial obligations[15] owed to children on divorce and separation, nor a large number of other matters which may be vital to the well-being of children.[16] It is hard to avoid the conclusion that the interests of older people are to be preferred where it really matters,[17] although where a parent applicant is also a child, it is the child who is the subject of the application whose welfare is paramount.[18] But in applying to 'any question with respect to... the upbringing of a child', the welfare principle covers most of the 'caring' issues which may arise in the context of parental separation. As this context probably accounts numerically for most of the occasions in which the principle is invoked, we deal with it here.

Where it does apply, the welfare principle is innately neutral as between parental power and children's rights, but its main function has

12 See, generally, 'The Best Interests of the Child' (1994) 8(1)(2) *International Journal of Law and Family*, Special Issue; .
13 Emphasis supplied; see the discussion by P Alston, 'The Best Interests Principle: Towards a Reconciliation of Culture and Human Rights' (1994) *International Journal of Law and Family* 1.
14 Emphasis added.
15 See Ch 9.
16 Section 105 of the Children Act 1989 defines 'upbringing' of the child as including 'the care of the child but not his maintenance'. Neither does the welfare principle apply on adoption (see Ch 3) or for applications (eg, for ouster orders) governed by s 1(3) of the Matrimonial Homes Act 1983; see *Gibson v Austin* [1992] 2 FLR 437, and *Re M (minors) (Disclosure of Evidence)* [1994] 1 FLR 760. It is also inapplicable when considering whether to grant *adults* leave to apply for a s 8 order (*Re A (minors) (Residence Order: Leave to Apply)* [1992] Fam 182); or to applications for the restriction of publicity in circumstances not directly pertaining to the care and upbringing of the child (*R (Mrs) v Central Independent Television plc* [1994] Fam 192).
17 Although in *L v L (minors) (Separate Representation)* [1994] 1 FLR 156, the court ordered that the children of the family be separately represented in their parents' divorce proceedings; see Ch 7 and 16.
18 *Birmingham City Council v H (a minor)* [1994] 2 AC 212 (HL); *F (a minor) v Leeds City Council* [1994] 2 FLR 60.

always been to resolve disputes between the parents and to preclude any leaning towards, originally, the father. As regards the last, we have already noted (in Chapter 6) his declining status but, as a reminder of how things once were, we might mention here the early nineteenth century case of *Ex p Skinner*[19] in which the court refused to interfere with the 'right' of a father to have his six year old son brought daily to him in prison by his partner in adultery. Although the courts had already moved towards the welfare principle during the nineteenth century, mainly in 'custody' disputes, it made its first *statutory* appearance in s 1 of the Guardianship of Infants Act 1925. Minor amendments were wrought by the Guardianship Act 1973, the Domestic Proceedings and Magistrates' Courts Act 1978 and the Family Law Reform Act 1987, but it was only the 1989 legislation which excised the original statutory reference to 'first and' paramount. Despite Lord MacDermott's remark in *J v C* [20] that this formulation meant 'more than that the child's welfare is to be treated as the top item in a list of items relevant to the matter in question' some judges had 'balanced other considerations *against* the child's welfare rather [than considering] what light they shed upon it'.[1]

Whatever semantic skills are brought to the wording of the principle – the Law Commission's draft Bill[2] suggested 'the welfare of any child likely to be affected shall be the court's only concern' – the law's ability actually to recognise and serve the welfare of children is necessarily limited. It is a 'concept which allows for the maximum range of disagreement'.[3] Robert Mnookin[4] has criticised the indeterminacy of the welfare principle and has argued that it depends upon first, predictions of the future which can only be speculative, and secondly, upon the decision-maker's own value judgments. There is validity in these objections, which are in fact interrelated. For example, views on the desirability of infants or teenage boys living with their mothers after parental divorce, have changed as attitudes to fathers' abilities[5] to care

19 (1824) 9 Moore CP 278.
20 [1970] AC 668 at 710–11.
1 Law Com No 172, 'Review of Child Law – Guardianship and Custody' (1988) para 3.13 (emphasis in original)
2 *Ibid*; cl 1(2).
3 M Richards, 'Divorcing children; roles for parents and the state' from J Eekelaar and M Maclean (eds) *A Reader on Family Law* (1994) p 248 at p 260. Richards goes on to suggest that, in the resolution of residence disputes, the primacy of the children's welfare would be best met by the children living with 'whichever parent is able to convince the court that they (*sic*) are the parent most likely to foster and maintain the children's links with the other parent and the wider family'. He refers to this as the 'Solomon' principle.
4 R Mnookin, 'Child Custody Adjudication: Judicial Functions in the face of Indeterminacy' (1975) 39 *Law and Contemporary Problems* 226.
5 See Ch 6.

for children, and to homosexuality, to take but two issues, have changed. The welfare principle may therefore be regarded as unfair to children, since predictions may turn out to be mistaken, and unfair to parents, since it may import value judgments which discriminate against certain lifestyles or attributes.[6] Stephen Parker,[7] however, argues that localised conventions and understanding about family life and children may import degrees of predictability into the process; for example, notwithstanding *J v C*,[8] it is rare in the West, if not unheard of, for 'fit' parents to lose their child to a third party simply because that party asserts that he or she could do a better job of bringing up the child – rather, notions of family autonomy and, we would add, the presumption at least of a parental right of possession, limit the decision-maker's discretion.

The presence of certain values is clear in the statutory identification of the child's best interests detailed in s 1 of the Children Act 1989, which, for the first time in English law, attempted an elaboration of the welfare principle in the manner previously established in other family matters such as occupation of the home[9] or financial relief on divorce.[10] Such a 'checklist', as it has come to be called, clarifies what is involved in the welfare principle and should render its application more consistent. It should benefit all involved, in that the values implicit in the checklist may come to be seen as a template for good parent-child relations generally, as well as giving the courts a structure for their enquiry and a formula for their reasons in the event of an appeal.

The checklist items specified in s 1(3), to which the court shall 'have regard in particular', are not to be used in all cases. Although the checklist covers *all* applications for public law care and supervision orders under Part IV of the Act, it only covers s 8 applications if they are opposed.[11] When the latter are unopposed, the advantages alluded to in our previous paragraph would not obtain. On the other hand, time spent in considering the checklist might prejudice the anti-delay principle of s 1(2) (see below).

6 See the summary of such criticisms in J Eekelaar, 'The Interests of the Child and the Child's Wishes: The Role of Dynamic Self-Determinism' (1994) 8 *International Journal of Law and Family* 42 at pp 45–46.

7 'The Best Interests of the Child – Principles and Problems' (1994) 8 *International Journal of Law and Family* 26.

8 [1970] AC 668. The House of Lords held that the welfare principle was applicable to disputes between parent(s) and others, as well as to disputes between the parents themselves. See *Re W (a minor) (Residence Orders)* [1993] 2 FLR 625 for the application of the welfare principle to non-parents under the Children Act 1989.

9 Matrimonial Homes Act 1983, s 1(3).

10 Matrimonial Causes Act 1973, s 25.

11 Section 1(4).

In fact, the matters specified in s 1(3) are largely declaratory of indicators identified by previous case law. Section 1(3)[12] refers to:

'(a)the ascertainable wishes and feelings of the child concerned (considered in the light of his age and understanding);
(b) his physical, emotional and educational needs;
(c) the likely effect on him of any change in his circumstances;
(d) his age, sex, background and any characteristics of his which the court considers relevant;
(e) any harm which he has suffered or is at risk of suffering;
(f) how capable each of his parents, and any other person in relation to whom the court considers the question to be relevant, is of meeting his needs;
(g) the range of powers available to the court under this Act'.

Although an unexceptionable list – it would be difficult to cavil at any one particular item – the points raised are a mix of welfarism and self-determination (with the bulk favouring the former) and, in the absence of any weighting, are thus liable to conflict with one another. In *Re J (a minor)*,[13] for example, Thorpe J indicated that no significance was to be read into the fact that the child's wishes are the first element to be mentioned. In *Re P (a minor) (Education)*[14] the resolution of a post-divorce inter-parental dispute was much influenced by the views of the *Gillick*-competent youth concerned. The father announced that he could no longer afford the fees for the boy's private education at Stowe and the mother applied for the matter of his schooling to be determined judicially. The Court of Appeal, in deciding that the 14 year old should attend the local day school was much influenced by his wish to do so. Butler-Sloss LJ said:

'I form the view – not having met this boy who is obviously mature, sensible and intelligent and, no doubt being a musician, sensitive – that he has... now formed his own view as to what he wants to do and why he wants to do it... at this stage the degree to which he may have been influenced in order to come to that conclusion becomes irrelevant. What this court has to deal with is the result, not the way in which the result was achieved.'

Before leaving the welfare principle, we should consider two particular issues introduced by the Children Act 1989: the 'no-delay' and 'no-order' principles.

Section 1(2) states:

'In any proceedings in which any question with regard to the upbringing of a child arises, the court shall have regard to the general principle that any delay in determining the question is likely to prejudice the welfare of the child.'

---

12 The list is almost identical to that recommended in para 3.20 of Law Com No 172, *Review of Child Law – Guardianship and Custody* (1988).
13 [1992] Fam Law 229n.
14 [1992] 1 FLR 316.

The dangers of such delay have long been identified. Tardiness may reinforce the status quo, create insecurity for all concerned and distort the child's already-different perception of time: these factors had led the Law Commission[15] to recommend that 'the court should presume that delay is prejudicial to the child's interests unless the contrary is shown'.[16] Accordingly, it has been held that delay is not *always* detrimental as where, for example, time should be allowed for arrangements to settle down,[17] or where it is necessary to await the outcome of an assessment.[18] On the other hand, the anti-delay principle may mean that there is not always a right to an extensive oral hearing of issues.[19] Sadly, 'delay', 'lawyers' and 'courts' are notoriously associated matters, and there is evidence[20] of lengthy waiting periods with regard to child-related litigation. In 1995 the president of the family division, Sir Stephen Brown, issued a practice direction[21] designed to reduce delay. *Inter alia*, it gives superior courts a discretion to limit the length of opening and closing submissions.

The Law Commission concluded[22] that '... the most effective practical action which can be taken... is to place a clear obligation upon the court to oversee the progress of the case... ' and the 1989 Act now requires the court to draw up a timetable and to give appropriate directions for adhering to it.[1]

Section 1(5), in introducing the 'no-order' presumption, states:

'Where a court is considering whether or not to make one or more orders under this Act with respect to a child, it shall not make the order or any of the orders unless it considers that doing so would be better for the child than making no order at all.'

It has always been open to parents, married as well as unmarried, to part without going to court. Parents may well be able to make good arrangements for their children without external assistance, and the law should not seek to disturb these.[2] The effect of s 1(5) is that *all* orders

---

15 Law Com No 172, *Review of Child Law – Guardianship and Custody* (1988) paras 4.54-4.58.

16 *Ibid* para 4.58.

17 *S v S (minors: Custody)* [1992] Fam Law 148.

18 *C v Solihull Metropolitan Borough Council* [1993] 1 FLR 290.

19 Eg, *Re B (minors)(Contact)* [1994] 2 FLR 1.

20 See generally Ch 2 and Appendix 2 of the Children Act Advisory Committee Annual Report 1993–4; it appears (p 81) that, for example, the majority of public law cases can take up to 30 weeks from the start of proceedings to a final hearing in the county court.

21 *Case Management* Times, 31 January 1995.

22 Law Com No 172, *Review of Child Law – Guardianship and Custody* (1988) para 4.57.

1 Sections 11 and 32.

2 Law Com No 172, *Review of Child Law – Guardianship and Custody* (1988) paras 3.2-3.4.

must be justified, and that the court should consider each application in that light.[3] In 1993, the ratio of 'orders made' to 'orders of no order' in private law was in excess of 8 to 1.[4] Yet the combined total of 'applications withdrawn' and 'orders refused' was about one-third of the number of 'orders made',[5] and it is possible that the number of applications made in the first place is now being limited by the prospect of the 'no-order' presumption.

We now turn to some of the individual issues which may confront separated parents and their children.

2. HOUSING THE CHILDREN AND COMMUNICATING WITH THEM

Clearly, the minimum degree of connection between 'parenter' and child is some degree of propinquity or, failing that, communication. Article 9 of the 1989 United Nations Convention on the Rights of the Child envisages a full range of possibilities, from what might be termed residential double-parenting, to contact with a non-resident parent:

'(1) States Parties shall ensure that a child shall not be separated from his or her parents against their will except when competent authorities subject to judicial review determine... that such separation is necessary for the best interests of the child. Such determination may be necessary in a particular case such as... where the parents are living separately and a decision must be made as to the child's place of residence.'

There are *non sequiturs* bordering on the disingenuous here. To begin with, who is the 'their' in 'their will'? In the case of the parental separation envisaged in the second sentence, one, at least, of the parents has brought the situation about – it is the child, and often the child only, whose will to continue living with both parents – is being frustrated. It is an aphoristic commonplace that children would prefer their parents to stay together, yet even a Disney film would blench at making such wishes determinative, despite Article 12, in wording similar to that of the Children Act 1989,[6] assuring 'to the child who is capable of forming his

---

3 This principle does not apply so much to applications for financial orders under the 1989 Act; see Ch 9.
4 *Judicial Statistics* (1993) Cm 2623, Table 5.3; 61,650 as opposed to 7,332.
5 *Ibid* 20,471 to 61,650.
6 Section 1(4)(a) requires, in contested s 8 proceedings and all care or supervision proceedings, that 'a court shall have regard... to the ascertainable wishes and feelings of the child concerned (considered in the light of his age and understanding)' (s 1(3)(a)). Under s 10(8), the court is only permitted to grant the child leave to make a s 8 application on his own account – unlike a host of others specified in s 1(4)-(7) the child is not allowed to do so as of right: 'if it is satisfied that he has sufficient understanding' to make it; see Chs 7 and 16.

or her own views the right to express those views freely in all matters affecting the child, the views of the child being given due weight in accordance with the age and maturity of the child'. Furthermore the 'best interests' criterion (Article 9.1, above) only governs the issue of with which parent the child shall live, not whether he or she will be able to live with both: it is the parents, or one of them, who make the all-important decision to split. They do not require the permission of the court. And even then, in English law, 'competent authorities' only determine the residence/contact issue – and the welfare checklist in s 1(3) of the Children Act 1989 only then applies – when the matter is contested.

Para 3 of Article 9 goes on to state that:

> 'States Parties shall respect the right of the child who is separated from one or both parents to maintain personal relations and direct contact[7] with both parents on a regular basis, except if contrary to the child's best interests.'

This is particularly desirable in view of the received wisdom that 'children who fare best after their parents separate or divorce are those able to maintain a good relationship with them both'.[8] The right to respect for family life, enshrined in Article 8 of the European Convention of Human Rights, is also highly apposite here.[9]

The Children Act 1989, in substituting 'residence' and 'contact' for 'custody' and 'access' respectively, anticipated the use of the same expressions in the United Nations Convention.

(a) Housing

Where the parents separate, the ultimate expression of the right referred to in Article 9(3) above might be a 'shift system', whereby mother and father would take it in turns to live with the child, no doubt in the former family home. Such greater show of responsibility, whilst no doubt inconvenient for the adults, would be the best way of promoting continuity and stability, the antitheses of the twin dangers of upheaval and estrangement, for their child. They (the parents) could clearly make such an arrangement privately, although the court would have no power to order them to do so. (Perhaps the former couple could agree a similar time-share in a second property, returning to it by rotation during their non-residential periods.) In truth, were either parent to become part of

---

7   In *Re R (a minor) (Contact)* [1993] 2 FLR 762, 767, Butler-Sloss LJ pointed out that the Convention thereby underlines the principle of continued contact enshrined in the Children Act 1989 (see below).
8   Law Com No 172, *Review of Child Law – Guardianship and Custody* (1988) para 4.5 (and see the references cited therein).
9   *Re KD (a minor)* [1988] AC 806.

another family, the practicalities, already demanding, would surely become overwhelming.

The label 'time-share' has been attached to the (comparatively) more attainable, if less ambitious, system in which the child again lives with each parent in turn, but by moving between their homes rather than by them alternating at his or hers. Before the Children Act 1989, the Court of Appeal was afforded an opportunity to consider such an arrangement in *Riley v Riley*.[10] A nine year old girl, born before her parents' wedding, had experienced their separation when she was aged four, and their divorce at seven. For five years she spent a week at a time, turn and turn about, with her respective (and 'intelligent and sensible') parents at their homes, which were about one mile apart. Her school lay between the two. The mother, whose idea the 'time-share' had been, now sought to have her daughter live with her all the time, although she conceded that the original arrangement had done the girl no harm. Despite such presumption as may exist with respect to so long-standing a *status quo*, and the reluctance[11] of the appellate court to substitute its own judgment for that at first instance, the Recorder's decision was reversed. May LJ said:[12]

'In my judgment to keep a child of nearly nine, not far off puberty, going backwards and forwards each week between mother and father is prima facie wrong... the paramount interests of this child are that she should have a settled home.'

Nourse LJ added[13] that 'It must be in her best interests that, as she grows up, she should know where her home is'.

The child's view was not recorded, if indeed it was sought or known, and it is clear that the decision in favour of the appellant *qua* mother followed the perceived need to discontinue the 'time-share'.

It is clear from *A v A (minors) (Shared Residence Order)*[14] that the Children Act 1989 has overruled *Riley v Riley*, despite the need to interpret that statute 'in the light of the wisdom of the past distilled in many cases, and the fact that children's problems have not changed and the emotions of parents equally have not changed'.[15] Section 11(4) states that 'Where a residence order is made in favour of two or more persons, the order may specify the periods during which the child is to live in the different households concerned'. The Law Commission[16] gave the somewhat precious example of an arrangement for '... two out of three

---

10 [1986] 2 FLR 429.
11 *G v G (minors: Custody Appeal)* [1985] 2 All ER 225 (HL): 'exceptional circumstances' required.
12 At 431–2.
13 At 432.
14 [1994] 1 FLR 669.
15 Per Butler-Sloss LJ at 677.
16 Law Com No 172, *Review of Child Law – Guardianship and Custody* (1988) para 4.12.

holidays from boarding school with one [parent] and the third with the other' as being more realistically achieved by a residence order covering both parents, rather than by residence for one and contact for the other. The evidence from the United States[17] is that where they are practicable, such orders can work well. Here, they carry the specific benefit of giving the right to remove the child from local authority accommodation under s 20 of the 1989 Act, and may 'remove any impression that one parent is good and responsible whereas the other parent is not'.[18]

Joint residence orders are unlikely to become common because children will generally need the stability of a single home and, where shared care is appropriate, the no-order presumption of s 1(5) is likely to apply.[19] There is, however, some judicial uncertainty as to whether 'exceptional' or merely 'unusual' circumstances will be needed to justify such orders. In *A v A* above, Butler-Sloss LJ inclined[20] towards the latter, supposedly less-demanding line. In that case, the court made two sisters, aged seven and ten, the subjects of joint residence orders whereby they would spend about one-third of the year with their father (the applicant) and the balance with their mother. Crucially, despite the mother's resistance to the order, there were no other unresolved issues extant; no disagreements about education, for example, or the movements of the children between the parents. There was a necessary 'positive benefit'[1] to the girls, in the way the order reflected the working, well-settled arrangement, which allowed the father to play an important role in their lives.

Another 'unusual' aspect of *A v A* was that the girls' parents, despite using the court to resolve their differences, were still married to one another. In *Re H (a minor) (Shared Residence)*[2] the parents of the 14 year old boy involved had not married one another in the first place; all parents, be they unmarried, married or divorced, are entitled to make any s 8 application.[3] In *Re H*, Purchas LJ[4] stated that joint residence orders would only be made in 'exceptional' circumstances, the more stringent approach from which Butler-Sloss LJ expressly departed in *A v A*.[5] We suggest that this apparent difference of approach may be of little practical importance, and that the two cases can be easily reconciled with one another, given that in *Re H*, there were those very conflicts (between the parties) whose absence in *A v A* was so determinative. In *Re H,* the father

17 Law Com WP 96, *Custody*, (1986) para 4.45.
18 *The Children Act 1989 Guidance and Regulations, Vol 1*: Court Orders, para 2.28.
19 *Ibid*.
20 At 678.
 1 *Ibid* at 678.
 2 [1994] 1 FLR 717.
 3 Section 10(4).
 4 At 728.
 5 At 678.

believed that the mother was using their son as an emotional prop following the death of her mother and there were also tensions with regard to the boy's education.

It has always been, and is likely to remain, more common for the children to live most of the time with one parent, who, given prevailing social norms, is usually the mother. Whilst the *presumption* that mothers make better caretakers has been jettisoned (as we saw in Chapter 6) the courts still attach weight to the '*status quo*', ie that the child should not be moved from a *satisfactory* placement as this is disruptive to his or her welfare.[6] Such an attitude owes its rationale, in part at least, to the influence of Goldstein, Freud and Solnit, and is reflected in s 1(3)(c), the welfare checklist, which requires the court to have regard to the likely effect on the child of any change in his circumstances. In the United States, feminists have argued that this approach also pays due regard to the woman's previous commitment to the child, and hence recognises her just claim as primary caretaker, while being *prima facie* gender-neutral.[7]

But it would be a mistake to assume that children are guaranteed a place in at least one parent's household when their mothers and fathers part. Apart from the possibility that they may end up in care, or being accommodated by the local authority, or homeless,[8] the Children Act acknowledges the possibility of them living with a third party by allowing such a person[9] to formalise, or even to achieve, such an arrangement by way of a residence order. Anyone who has the consent of everyone with parental responsibility may apply,[10] but in most[11] other circumstances the prior leave of the court[12] is a condition precedent. In deciding whether or not to grant leave, the court must consider such matters as the nature of the proposed application, the applicant's connection with the child, and any risk that the latter may be harmed by the disruption caused by the application.[13] In *Re O (minors) (Leave to*

---

6 See, eg, *D v M (minor) (Custody Appeal)* [1983] Fam 33.

7 M Melli, 'Toward a Restructuring of Custody Decision-making at Divorce: an Alternative Approach to the Best Interests of the Child', in J Eekelaar and P Sarcovic (eds) *Parenthood in Modern Society* (1993).

8 A survey of young homeless people in London found that only 30% had lived with their parents up to or beyond their eighteenth birthday: *The Guardian*, 12 December 1994.

9 A person with whom the child has been living for at least three years may apply; s 10((5)(b). By s 10(10), the period need not have been continuous but must not have begun more than five years before, or ended more than three months before, the making of the application.

10 Section 10(5)(c)(iii). Similarly, a local authority may consent to the making of an application with regard to a child in their care; s 10(5)(c)(iii).

11 See s 10 generally.

12 Section 10(2)(b).

13 Section 10(9).

Seek Residence Order)[14] the two boys aged 13 and 10 were with their mother in England; their father lived in New Zealand. Three months after her marriage to an alcoholic, she and the boys went to lodge with another man. When she was hospitalised for cancer treatment this person reneged on his promise to look after the boys. The father's cousin agreed to look after them but, within days, the mother returned to the alcoholic husband with whom the boys did not want to live. The cousin successfully sought leave to make a residence application.

As regards residence orders generally, the number made in private law proceedings in 1993 rose by 59%[15] to 22,264. (There was an additional growth in contact orders; see below.) Despite the fact that 2,239 residence applications resulted in 'orders of no-order' in 1993,[16] the 59% increase does not appear to sit well with the 'no-order' presumption of s 1(5).[17]

(b) Communicating

English law has little to say about the *quality*[18] of the relationship between the separated parent and child. It concentrates more on the criteria for resolving the blunt, occasional, question of whether a given parent should be able to make 'contact' at all. These occasions are triggered either by the local authority and the parent(s) being unable, in public law cases, to agree on the matter when the child is in care,[19] or by private law disputes between the residential parent and someone else with parental responsibility. In the second of these cases, the likelihood is that the former has refused the latter's request for contact, and the latter has responded by initiating proceedings. So the resident parent can effectively, and with impunity, put the other in the position of having to supplicate for a right which both he or she and the child supposedly had already. Therefore, when it is the resident parent who is adamantly opposed to contact, 'she' can, in practice, negate the apparent advantage to the other marital parent of 'his' automatic possession of parental

---

14 [1993] 1 FLR 172.
15 From 1992; *Judicial Statistics* (1993), Cm 2623, Table 5.3 and p 45.
16 *Ibid.*
17 Yet the number of applications withdrawn (and the number made in the first place) may indicate that the 'no-order' presumption is having some effect; see above. Research at two major divorce courts in East Anglia showed that a very high percentage of cases involved no order being made on divorce: A Bainham, *Children – the Modern Law* (1993) at p 130, n 96.
18 Although the court may, as with any s 8 order, make 'directions as to how it is to be carried into effect': s 11(7).
19 See Ch 14.

responsibility; like the 'unmarried father', absent parents will have to make application to the court if they wish to see their children.[20]

The potential for children themselves to influence the matter is uncertain, in that the court will not entertain their own motion to require a reluctant parent to meet them, yet should they adamantly refuse to see the other parent, it is unlikely that the court will force them to do so. This is surprising in view of the wording of Article 9, para 3 above, not to mention the oft-repeated claim of English domestic law that contact is the right of the child,[1] the Children Act 1989 principle that the voice of the child be heard,[2] and the welfare principle generally. The issue is all the more worrying given the evidence that parents find it difficult to sustain contact arrangements and that contact diminishes over time. For example, John Eekelaar and Eric Clive found that while two-thirds of absent parents had contact in the first six months after separation, this had dwindled to one-third after five years (a further 10% had contact infrequently).[3] Martin Richards has argued that the reasons for diminishing contact are complex, including a mistaken belief (no doubt subject to re-examination in the light of the Child Support Act discussed in the next chapter) that if there is no contact, there need be no payment of maintenance; a wish to allow the children to 'settle down' to the new living arrangements; and finding contact for brief periods so painful that it is better to cease contact altogether.[4] It could be argued that a clear legal obligation to maintain contact could rectify some of these misconceptions and feelings.

A contrast may be found in employment law, whereby the rule that an injunction is not available if it would be tantamount to a decree of specific performance, does not apply where it would benefit the employee.[5] Similarly, the availability of reinstatement and re-engagement orders under the Employment Protection (Consolidation) Act 1978 indicates Parliament's willingness to insist upon the resumption of personal relations for the benefit of the weaker party.

The Children Act 1989, s 8(1), substitutes the more neutral term 'contact' for the old cold-hearted, property-based reference to 'access'.

---

20 Although the non-marital father would not automatically *gain* parental responsibility by way of contact order (as opposed to a residence order: Children Act 1989, s 12(1)) made in his favour.

1 Originating in *M v M (Child Access)* [1973] 2 All ER 81; in *Re H (minors)* [1992] 1 FLR 148, the Court of Appeal held that the same approach applies under the Children Act 1989.

2 See Chs 7, 14 and 16.

3 *Custody after Divorce* (1977).

4 M Richards, 'Post Divorce Arrangements for Children: A Pyschological Perspective' [1982] JSWL 133.

5 *Hill v C A Parsons and Co Ltd* [1972] Ch 305.

Given that it provides for the child 'to visit or stay with the person named in the order', as opposed to the parent having 'access to the child' as previously, it seems even more surprising that the child may not obtain the order against a recalcitrant parent. Furthermore, different again from access, the court may order communication – at the behest of the adult at least – by means other than meeting, by letter or telephone perhaps: 'or for that person and the child otherwise to have contact with each other'. Contact orders can be made in favour of non-parents, and more than one order may be extant at any one time.

In *Re D (a minor) (Contact: Mother's Hostility)*[6] the court found few, if any (other) differences in meaning between the former and present terms; the question is whether there are cogent reasons why the child(ren) in question should be denied contact with both their parents.[7] This approach is clearly consistent with the received wisdom that children fare better after divorce or separation when they maintain a (good) relationship with both parents:[8]

'Where children retain good relationships with both parents and subsequent upheavals are minimal, outcomes tend to be better. But breaks and continuing changes in these relationships can be associated with low self-esteem, depression and anxiety, and poor relationships with peers.'[9]

Re D involved the Court of Appeal in deciding whether a three year old boy should see his father, in view of the adamant opposition expressed by both the mother and the maternal grandparents. The parents came from very different backgrounds. The mother moved in with the father when she was 17 and moved back to her parents a year later when she was six months pregnant. Her parents gained the impression that he was a thoroughly bad lot although the first instance judge thought that he might well now be a reformed character. He sought 'access' to his child under the pre-Children Act 1989 law but there were 'unfortunate' delays in the obtaining of the court welfare report and over a year passed before the matter came to court.

The Court of Appeal held that the approach to contact had not been changed by the Children Act. Balcombe LJ stated[10] that, 'One starts with the premise that the child's right is to know both its parents but that there may be cases... where there are cogent reasons why the child should be

6 [1993] 2 FLR 1.

7 *Re H (minors) (Access)* [1992] 1 FLR 148. In *Re F (minors) (Denial of Contact)* [1993] 2 FLR 677, contact with a transsexual father was refused primarily because of the boys' (aged 9 and 12) own wishes.

8 See, eg, J Wallerstein and J Kelly, *Surviving the Breakup* (1980) and Law Com No 172, *Review of Child Law – Guardianship and Custody* (1988) para 4.5, both above.

9 J Elliott *et al,* 'Divorce and Children: A British Challenge to the Wallerstein View' [1990] Fam Law 309.

10 At 3.

denied that opportunity'. There was no evidence of the man's present unsuitability and even the general criticisms were solely on the word of the mother and her parents. At first instance, it was said that there was no evidence at all that the father had treated his [other] children badly. Nor was this a case, such as *Re SM (a minor) (Natural Father: Access)*,[11] where the mother had remarried and contact with the natural father might damage the new family unit.

Nonetheless, in *Re D,* the mother's implacable hostility went against the father. At the end of his judgment, in an *obiter dictum* which may merely have perpetuated the self-fulfilling effect of the mother's obduracy, Waite LJ expressed the hope that the mother would come to realise the advantages to her child of knowing both his parents. The other reason advanced by the court might also seem to encourage unco-operative behaviour on the part of a resident parent, and her family. It was that the father had had no contact with the child since birth, even though that was 'not a matter to be held against' him.

In 1993, the second full calendar year in which the 1989 Act operated, 27,780 contact orders were made in private law proceedings, an increase of 36% over the previous year.[12] This contrasted oddly with the 4,044 'orders of no order', given that under s 1(5) of the Act positive orders are only to be made where the court considers that they are better for the child than 'no order'.[13] Where contact is being sustained (only) by virtue of a court order it may be particularly prone to tension ('the most over-used word about contact must surely be reasonable'[14]) and nugatory of the supposed value to the child of continuing double-parenting. Good quality contact will surely involve recognition by the 'residence' parent of the child's need for the other parent; amicable handovers; a negotiating process that allows for changes of dates and times; not relegating the contact parent to the bottom of the child's social engagements; and encouraging the contact parent to keep abreast of the child's development, school progress, etc.[15] Potentially difficult cases may be helped by the existence of 'Contact Centres', where the non-resident parent can see the children on 'neutral' territory, thereby reducing the level of tension between the parents.

---

11 [1991] 2 FLR 333.
12 *Judicial Statistics* (1992), Cm 2268, Tables 5.9, 5.10.
13 *Judicial Statistics* 1993, Cm 2623, Table 5.3. The number of applications withdrawn (and the number of applications made in the first place) may provide a more favourable indication of how well the 'no-order presumption is working; see above.
14 A Johnson, 'Practical Guide to Contact' [1991] Fam Law 536.
15 *Ibid* at 536.

3. CHANGING THE CHILD'S NAME

Changing the child's name on parental divorce has generated more rules[16] than the original choice. Perhaps other domestic jurisdictions reflect a less insouciant attitude to name-change than does England and Wales. In Germany, it seems that children of parents who cannot agree will take the surnames of each parent.[17] In Nova Scotia, an order of the Supreme Court is always required for a post-divorce change of name, even if the other parent acquiesces. Such agreement may be dispensed with if, *inter alia*, the parent is a person 'whose consent in all the circumstances of the case ought to be dispensed with'.[18]

Generally, the simplest and cheapest method of name-change is to sign a statutory declaration, for which there is no age limit. The more famous 'deed poll', which is lodged in the central office of the High Court, is not only more expensive but may only be used on their own behalf by those over 16.[19] Parents who wish to change the names of their 16-18 year olds by this means must have their consent.

Under s 13(1)(a) of the Children Act 1989, if a residence order is in force, the leave of the court must be obtained for a change of name in the absence of the written consent of every person with parental responsibility. Irritatingly, there is no express provision to cover the normal situation (which the 'no-order presumption'[20] encourages even on separation or divorce) where there is no residence order in force. It would therefore seem that the situation falls under the general principle of s 2(7) of the 1989 Act whereby one person with parental responsibility 'may act alone and without the other', although it has been suggested[1] that an application to the court should still be made. In *Re F(Child: Surname)*,[2] where the divorced mother sought leave from the court to change the children's surname, there does not appear to have been a residence order in force. Perhaps she was not advised to adopt the tactic of unilaterally changing her daughters' names, which would have left the father with the option, and the need to take his own initiative, of seeking a s 8 Children Act 1989 'prohibited steps' or 'specific issue' order. When a child is in care,

---

16 A very useful source of information, for children and others, is 'What's in a Name', (1993) 96 *Childright* May. 1993 No 96: see Ch 7.

17 As a result of the German Federal Constitutional Court ruling that the previous law infringed the constitutional guarantee for equality between the sexes: see S Cretney's comment, at [1994] Fam Law 12–13, on *Re F (Child: Surname)* [1993] 2 FLR 837n.

18 SNS 1977, c 6.

19 Enrolment of Deeds (Change of Name) Regulations 1983.

20 Children Act 1989, s 1(5): the court shall not make an order under the Act 'unless it considers that doing so would be better for the child than making no order at all'.

1 D Hershman and A McFarlane, *Children Law and Practice* (1993) at A[13].

2 [1993] 2 FLR 837n.

neither the local authority nor anyone else may cause the child to be known by a new surname without, once again, the written permission of all with parental responsibility or the leave of the court.[3]

In *Re F (Child: Surname)*, a child of divorced parents attended a school where she had a different surname to that used by her mother and where she had been the subject of an 'unpleasant nickname derived from her existing, father's name'. The Court of Appeal refused the mother's application to use a double-barrelled concoction from her own (maiden) name and that of her new husband, Sir Ralph Gibson LJ saying:[4]

> 'We have been asked to bear in mind the change in public views of the importance of family relations which have been worked over the last 20 years or so. Doing the best I can to have regard to the current views of ordinary people, I see no reason to suppose that a little girl at school is going to be embarrassed or particularly unusual in being registered at the school in a name different from the current surname of her mother.'

Although the child's wishes in the matter are not determinative, s 10(8) of the Children Act 1989 would allow him or her to seek leave from the court to make an application for a name change by way of a 'specific issue' order under s 8, ie 'an order giving directions for the purpose of determining a specific issue which has arisen... in connection with any aspect of parental responsibility for a child'. To date, there seems to be no record of a child invoking s10(8) for this purpose. Embarrassment at school, arising from the child's surname differing from that of half or step-siblings, is often cited in those applications which have been made by residence parents following divorce and re-partnering: the child's view would seem particularly relevant in such cases, and s 1(3)(a) of the 1989 Act would require the court to take account of his 'ascertainable wishes and feelings'. Yet in *W v A*, Dunn LJ would '... not... attach decisive vital importance to the views of two young children of 12 and 10 who were about to embark on the excitement of going to Australia with their mother and new step-father'.[5]

There have been a number of cases involving the change of the child's surname upon the resident mother's remarriage. If the child is adopted by the mother and step-father, that disposes of the matter. But although children of divorcing parents are more likely to live with their mothers, and those mothers frequently re-couple, often by marriage, such adoptions remain the exception, and the matter may become cross-referenced under the related issue of the legal standing of step-families. An uneasy

3 Children Act 1989, s 33(7)(a). Such leave was successfully sought in *Re J (a minor) (Change of Name)* [1993] 1 FCR 74, where a 12 year old had evinced a clear desire to change her name to that of her long-term foster parents, who supported her wish. It was granted as being conducive to her welfare.
4 [1993] 2 FLR 837n at 838.
5 [1981] Fam 14, 21.

balance has obtained between, *per* Sir Ralph Gibson LJ in *Re F* above, first, 'the use when convenient of another name... in school' and, secondly 'permitting the name formally to be changed',[6] despite the warning that 'condoning the use of an informal name and a legal name is to arm the [residence] mother with the law of inertia [which] may add to the child's problems of identity'.[7]

In addition, legal policy has anyway wavered as to when formal change should be allowed. The issue may well be seen by the divorced father as being a threat to his dwindling link with his children, a potential dilemma variously described as 'between the principle of honesty in family relationships as against the needs of the new family'[8] or, 'weighing up embarrassment against preservation of family ties... the latter must win out every time if for no other reason than that it is in the child's interest to retain such ties. But in many cases the desire to maintain the original surname will reflect nothing more than sentimentality'.[9] More recently, it has been described as 'part of the wider debate about how far children should maintain their links with both sides of their genetic inheritance',[10] the writer proceeding to point out that, 'Unlike contact, however, it is much harder to see how children rather than the parent benefit from keeping this badge of belonging'. Relevant circumstances for consideration have been said[11] (prior to the compiling of the statutory 'checklist' in s 1(3) of the Children Act 1989) to include:

> 'seeing the witnesses, seeing the parents, possibly seeing the children, any embarrassment which may be caused to the child by not changing his name and, on the other hand, the long-term interests of the child, the importance of maintaining the child's links with his paternal family, and the probable stability of the mother's remarriage'.

The last item seems rather dubious. Unless the new family is already in trouble, in which case so odd an application should indeed be given short shrift, its 'probable stability' would hardly seem to be a justiciable matter.

Judicial willingness to change a child's name has oscillated between stances best typified by two cases in the early 1980s. The later case of *R v R (Child: Surname)*[12] displayed a more relaxed, utilitarian approach, leading to a greater amenability to change. The mother of the child,

---

6 At 838.

7 A Bissett-Johnson, 'Children in Subsequent Marriages – Questions of Access, Name and Adoption' in J Eekelaar and S Katz (eds) *Marriage and Cohabitation in Contemporary Societies* (1980) p 382 at p 387.

8 S Maidment, 'Step-Parents and Step-Children: Legal Relationships in Serial Unions', in, *Ibid* p 420 at p 425.

9 M Freeman, *The Rights and Wrongs of Children* (1983) at p 226.

10 B Hoggett, *Parents and Children* (4th ed, 1993) p 106.

11 *W v A (minor): (Surname)* [1981] Fam 14, *per* Dunn LJ at 21.

12 [1982] 3 FLR 345.

named Donna, had allowed the girl to be known around the neighbourhood and at school by her step-father's surname. Donna knew her 'real' name, and her 'real' father. He objected to the change, but the mother was granted judicial leave for the new nomenclature. Ormrod J combined 'pragmatism' as to the central issue with exhortations about the welfare principle and some general advice for parents:[13]

> 'The fact of the matter is that the court is a hopeless organisation for trying to interfere in the minutiae of a six year old child's life. It is quite impossible effectively to do anything.... How could [the mother] possibly stop children in the neighbourhood calling this child Donna T, I have yet to hear... I am afraid that this is one of these cases where the interest of the child has been lost sight of by the father, who perhaps has other concerns than the welfare of the child... she will find this kind of insistence by him is something against which she may well revolt, and revolt with some reason. Teenagers who revolt with some reason are rather difficult to manage.'

A criticism of the accepting approach to these initiatives is that they allow unilateral, pre-emptive action by the resident parent to become self-fulfilling. More recently, a more restrictive line has prevailed, Ralph Gibson LJ in *Re F* (above) feeling himself constrained by *W v A (Child: Surname)*.[14] In the latter case, the divorced mother and her new husband were granted leave to take the children permanently out of the jurisdiction to his home country, Australia. She now wanted to be released from her undertaking that the children would continue to bear their father's surname. Dunn LJ stressed not only that the welfare principle was determinative in such cases but that the question of name change was, *per se*, an important matter. Despite the wishes of the children, the fresh start in a new country, the father's two sons by his second marriage ensuring the survival in Gloucestershire of the family name and, finally, the children being able to revert to their original name later if they so chose, the Court of Appeal said no.[15]

4. ABDUCTION

The no-order presumption of s 1(5) of the Children Act embodies the hope and expectation that, upon division, the future arrangements for the children are best left to the family itself. Even if those arrangements exceptionally require the attention of the court by way of residence or contact orders, the disgruntled party will, it is hoped, be co-operative or, failing that, resigned to the situation. Dissatisfaction will not usually be

13 At 348.
14 [1981] Fam 14.
15 Whilst the child is a ward of court, no important step may be taken without the leave of the court, a constraint which would apply to a proposed change of name.

expressed by way of direct action. Yet if lack of contact with their non-resident parent is the fate of many children after divorce, a growing number (see below) suffer abduction at 'his' hands. Abduction is an example of the now outmoded and largely discredited view of children as parental property to be possessed, and, as such, is inimical to the child's status as an individual person. Although such behaviour is normally inexcusable, it can be represented as the antithesis of neglect. It may be motivated by feelings of deprivation and love, as well as jealousy and hate. It may even be regarded as a desperate attempt to re-unite the family. *International* child abduction, born of improved international communication (more marriages and easier travel) may be carried out in the belief that a return to the abductor's native country will serve the child's best interests. Older children have been taken to a parent's home country for the purposes of marriage.[16]

Article 35 of the 1989 United Nations Convention on the Rights of the Child associates the abduction of children with their *sale*: 'States Parties shall take all appropriate national, bilateral and multilateral measures to prevent the abduction, the sale of or traffic in children for any purpose or in any form'. Article 11 which states, 'States Parties shall take all measures to combat the illicit transfer and non-return of children abroad' is aimed more directly at the kidnapping parent and both provisions clearly recognise that the sudden and possibly forceful removal from family, home, friends and school is unlikely to be beneficial; one American survey[17] has estimated that between 10% and 40% of abducted children become 'severely disturbed'. The Solicitors Family Law Association code stated[18] robustly that 'Kidnapping of children both results from and creates exceptional fear, bitterness and desperation' and urged solicitors to take all steps to prevent it, and to inform parent-clients that they court imprisonment by such conduct. In *Ramsbotham v Senior*,[19] in 1869, it was held that a solicitor is obliged to disclose any information which will enable the court to trace a ward of court whose residence is being concealed from the court; in 1991 the Law Society suggested[20] that the same principle should apply to cases of child abduction.

Prevention is proverbially better than cure, and early warning signs of child abduction have been said[1] to include; shock over child residence

---

16 See generally, G Van Bueren, *The Best Interests of the Child – International Co-operation on Child Abduction* (1991).
17 G Frank, 'American and International Responses to International Child Abduction' (1984) *New York University Journal of International Law and Politics* 415, cited by G Van Bueren, *ibid.*
18 Para 6.5 as originally drafted (now omitted from 1994 edition).
19 (1869) LR 8 Eq 575.
20 *Guidance on Confidentiality and Privilege*, para A.2.(b)ii.
 1 G Van Bueren, *The Best Interests of the Child – International Co-operation on Child Abduction* (1991), at p 11.

decisions; a history of conflict over the child; and parental alienation from the society where the child lives. It seems that younger children are most at risk. They will find it harder to escape and the abductor may believe that it will be easier to cut the emotional ties with the other parent.

By definition, the more law-abiding the frustrated non-resident parent, the less likely he is to abduct 'his' (most abductors are fathers[2]) child. If the child is subject to a residence order under s 8(1) of the Children Act 1989, removal from the country requires *either* the *written* consent of every person with parental responsibility *or* the leave of the court. The parent with the residence order may remove the child for up to one month. Both these consequences are spelt out on the face of the residence order, which also states that any person with parental responsibility may ask the United Kingdom Passport Agency not to issue a passport allowing the child to go abroad without the knowledge of that person. Under s 1(1) of the Child Abduction Act 1984 it is a criminal offence[3] for a parent or person with parental responsibility to take or send the child under 16 out of the country without the consent of those with parental responsibility or leave of the court. He may be committing the common law offences of kidnapping a child, false imprisonment, or contempt of court. Such action is likely to prejudice any future applications he might make in civil family proceedings as regards the child.

Article 11 (above) of the United Nations Convention goes on to state that, in order to combat child abduction, States Parties 'shall promote the conclusion of bilateral or multilateral agreements or access to existing agreements'. In that the Child Abduction and Custody Act 1985 gives domestic force to the 1980 Hague Convention on the Civil Aspect of International Child Abduction, and to the 1980 European Convention on the Recognition and Enforcement of Custody Decisions, the United Kingdom has complied with this requirement, although the rise in the number of reported[4] abductions from 16 in 1986 to 191 in 1991 (in which year unofficial sources put the number at closer to 1,000[5]) suggests that it has had no pre-emptive benefit. The two Conventions themselves are open to the criticism that they do not give sufficient effect to two other aspects of the United Nations Convention. The emphasis in the Conventions is upon the speedy return of the children to the country from

2 As a result of them being more likely to be the non-resident parent.
3 Under s 1(5)(c), no offence is committed if the other person has unreasonably refused to consent; this defence is unavailable if there is a residence order in the latter's favour (s 1 (5A)(a)).
4 Figures produced by the Child Abduction Unit at the Lord Chancellor's Department; see G Van Bueren *The Best Interests of the Child – International Co-operation on Child Abduction* (1991) at pp 8-10.
5 Children's Legal Centre, 'Information Sheet on Child Abduction No 89' (1992) at p 9.

which they were abducted, rather than upon the best interests of the child (Article 3), and, contrary to Article 12, there are only limited obligations to establish and pay due regard to the child's wishes and feelings.

A British visitor's passport will not be issued to a child under eight, and a child's birth certificate may be annotated[6] on request, following which a solicitor will be notified if an attempt is made to obtain a duplicate copy of the certificate. This will prevent the issue of a visitor's passport even if the child is over eight. Under s 11(7) of the Children Act 1989 the court, in making a contact order in favour of the non-resident parent, could require the lodging of any passport relating to the child.

The unscrupulous parent might be balked by the 'port alert' system, whereby the police will send out an all-ports message on the police national computer, if they are satisfied that the danger is 'real and imminent'. But the free movement of persons within the European Community and the removal of border controls from 1993 pose a considerable threat to the system.

Where the relevant state is a signatory to one of the above-mentioned Conventions, the Child Abduction and Custody Act 1985 enables an abducted child to be returned summarily by co-operation between the central authorities (here, the Child Abduction Unit of the Lord Chancellor's Department) of the countries concerned. Generally, if the proceedings are commenced within one year of the wrongful removal[7] a child under 16 shall be returned 'forthwith'.[8] If more than a year has elapsed, return may not be ordered if 'the child is now settled in its new environment'.[9]

Unfortunately the 1985 Act only covers countries which are party to one of the International Conventions concerned. There remains within the non-members list a handful of not-unpleasant countries within which to settle, some of which possess the further 'advantage' of having no extradition treaty with the United Kingdom. Yet unscrupulous parents, and other would-be abductors, may be constrained by the prospect of their assets being sequestered, and sold. In *Richardson v Richardson*[10] it was held that the money raised could be used to pay the innocent party's costs of instituting proceedings abroad to recover the child. Where

---

6 By the Marriages Department at St Catherine's House in London.

7 From one Convention country where he or she is habitually resident to another Convention country. *In C v S (a minor) (Abduction: Illegitimate Child)* [1990] 2 AC 562, the House of Lords held that the cessation of habitual residence in one country does not necessarily mean that the child has become habitually resident in another; Lord Brandon (at 965) pointed out that it is possible to cease being habitually resident in country A within a single day, whereas a longer time may well be necessary for the child to achieve habitual residence in country B.

8 Article 12 of the Hague Convention (above).

9 *Ibid.*

10 [1989] Fam 95.

children are brought into England and Wales from a 'non-convention' country, it was held in *Re F (a minor) (Abduction: Jurisdiction)*[11] that their welfare is not normally best served by their abduction. Accordingly, where it appears that the foreign tribunal will apply principles broadly consistent with those employed in England and Wales, the court should adopt the same approach as that laid down under the Hague Convention. Should children be abducted *from* the United Kingdom to a non-convention country, then the only recourse is to take the appropriate court proceedings in that country and/or attempt the extradition of the abductor.

Internationally, 34 countries had ratified the 1980 Hague Convention by 1994. Its success, in returning children to their former homes for the resolution of 'custody' disputes, has been attributed,[12] in the first place, to its clear articulation of principles and goals, and its avoidance of traditional concepts such as jurisdiction and the enforcement of judgments. Consequently, courts of all countries have avoided the creation of loopholes, and confidence in the willingness of foreign courts to implement the Convention has prompted similar judicial decisions at home.[13] One British example is *Re R (minors) (Abduction)*,[14] which involved the return of French children to France. In January 1992 (all subsequent events occurred in the same year) the father of two non-marital children brought them to England, following a number of deferrals by the French *Tribunal de Grand Instance* of his application for parental authority. In May, the same court refused his application; found that his taking the children without the mother's consent was a tortious action against her; and ordered them back. The mother applied here under the Hague Convention for their return. After what the mother's English counsel called an 'inexcusable' delay, the French central authority contacted the Lord Chancellor's Department at the beginning of September. There followed an 'unfortunate' (Thorpe J) further delay until the issue of the originating summons under the 1985 Act on 9 October. Once before the courts things moved faster, and, on 30 October, Thorpe J ordered the return of the children to France on the basis that they had been brought here without the consent of the one person with parental authority, and had been kept here in defiance of the order of a foreign court of competent jurisdiction. These reasons alone sufficed to constrain the English court

---

11 [1991] Fam 25.
12 By C Bruch, 'The Anatomy of a Success Story; the Hague Convention on International Child Abduction' (Paper to International Society of Family Law 8th World Conference, 1994).
13 In *Re N (a minor) (Child Abduction) (Habitual Residence)* [1993] 2 FLR 124, the Court of Appeal held that proceedings are not even inquisitorial, let alone adversarial; as the court has a statutory duty to apply the Hague Convention, the proceedings are *sui generis*.
14 [1994] 1 FLR 190; and see the authorities cited therein.

under Article 12 of the Hague Convention. Even if there were scope for discretion, it was in the best interests of the children to return to their own locality and extended family.

Finally, until the Family Law Reform Act 1987, a parent could evade a 'custody' order by removing a child to another country within the United Kingdom. That legislation now provides for the original order[15] to be registered in the new jurisdiction, and for enforcement proceedings to be taken there. The 1986 Act also provides that an order made in any part of the United Kingdom, for the prohibition of the removal of a child from the United Kingdom, shall be enforceable throughout the United Kingdom.

We have now completed our consideration of some of the non-monetary aspects of separate parenting; the financial aspects now follow.

---

15 Now known as a 'Part 1' order, and including 'custody' and s 8 orders: s 1.

CHAPTER 9

Separated parents (2): paying

1. THE HISTORY OF CHILD SUPPORT

(a) Public obligation

As Stephen Cretney has said,[1] 'Historically, children's financial interests have not been well served by the law: there was, in theory, a common law duty on a father to maintain his legitimate children, but no procedure was available to reinforce the right'. On a closely-related issue, the very phrase, 'the poor law', continues to reverberate unpleasantly even at the end of the twentieth century. In 1974, the Report of the Committee on One-Parent Families (The Finer Report) put it thus:[2]

'the essence of the poor law system was that it was the means through which the public supported those who were unable to support themselves, but sought reimbursement by imposing a legal liability upon their relatives in accordance with early seventeenth century notions of kinship. The operation of the system in its later developed forms is best observed in its mid-Victorian application to unmarried mothers and their illegitimate children. Relief was provided to the mother in the workhouse. After childbirth and a period of nursing she was separated from her child, and she usually left the workhouse. The child remained there. Girls, in due course, were put out to domestic service and often ended on the streets. Boys were put out to the merchant service or other harsh trades. The mother could bring proceedings for an affiliation order against the putative father, but these could only take the form of a complaint to the magistrate. The maximum amount payable until the end of the first world war was five shillings a week. (It thereafter rose in stages until it reached fifty shillings in 1960; and the limit was altogether removed in 1968.) The poor law authorities could themselves lay complaint against the putative father – the "liable relative" – to recover the cost of the maintenance of his illegitimate child.'

---

1 A Bainham and S Cretney, *Children – the Modern Law*, (1993) p 291.
2 Cmnd 5629, Vol 1, paras 4.19,20.

We might add that 'five shillings' in 1920 was probably worth about £5 by 1992, in which year 'fifty' 1960 'shillings' reached a value of some £13.50.[3] So far as the Finer Report itself was concerned, the terms of reference laid down by Richard Crossman, the Secretary of State for Social Services were, *inter alia*:

> '1   To examine the nature of any special difficulties which the parents of the various kinds of one-parent families may encounter; the extent to which they can obtain financial support when they need it; and the ways in which other provisions and facilities are of help to them.
>
> 2   To consider in what respects and to what extent it would be appropriate to give one-parent families further assistance'.

This supportive approach to sole parents and their children was mirrored in the eventual recommendations (by which time Barbara Castle was Secretary of State): a guaranteed maintenance allowance for lone parents to be paid by the state; research to be carried out into the effect upon children of being brought up by one parent; and attention to be paid to the needs of such families with regard to employment and day-care. The needs of widowed families were given as much consideration as those sundered by a broken relationship. Yet by 1990, *Children Come First*,[4] the White Paper which led to the Child Support Act 1991 devoted 'a couple of sentences at the beginning to the welfare of children, while most of the rest of two volumes dwell on the cost to the taxpayer'.[5] (Ironically, the White Paper was one of the first of its ilk to have a glossy front cover adorned with pictures of good-looking children, some in the company of one or more equally attractive adults.) The 1991 Act itself represents the only attempt to address the major defects identified by the Finer Report: the lack of worthwhile gain in income by combining part-time work with income support (the poverty trap); the comparatively low level of income of lone parents; and the insecurity afforded by private law maintenance orders.

In a forerunner of the political debates of the 1990s, a Statute of 1601, 43 Elizabeth, legally underpinned the moral obligations not merely of the parents but also the grandparents and children of 'everie poore... blind lame and impotente person, or other poore person not able to worke', although in the case of non-marital children the liability was limited to mother and father. Echoes can also be heard today of the recommendations

---

3   *Whitaker's Almanac* (1994).

4   Cm 1264.

5   David Burrows, 'Anyone Remember Finer' [1993] Fam Law 699 at 670. Burrows probably had in mind the opening passage of the Introduction to Vol 1, 'Every child has a right to care from both his or her parents. Parents generally have a legal and moral obligation to care for their children until the children are old enough to look after themselves'.

of the Poor Law Commissioners in 1834.[6] They suggested that life in the workhouse would involve differing regimes of graded severity, appropriate to each resident's degree of culpability for his destitution. Whilst the 'able-bodied [would be] subjected to such causes of labour and discipline as will repel the indolent and vicious',[7] the helplessness of the aged and the young would also be acknowledged in that, 'the old might enjoy... indulgences without torment from the boisterous; the children be educated'.

In fact, the necessary resources were not made available for such segregation, which, so far as the young are concerned, is reminiscent of the continuing debate about the mix of children in local authority children's homes today.

Girls and non-marital children (together, in the latter case, with their mothers) fared worst. So far as the girls were concerned, Frances Cobbe said in 1865 that:[8]

'The case of the girls is far worse than the boys, as all the conditions of workhouse management fall with peculiar evil on their natures... we mass them by hundreds where they have no affection, no personal care, nay, hardly a personal existence at all save as units in a herd, no household duties, and as much degradation as hideous uniforms, and cropped hair and shoes which change the natural lightness of the step of youth to the shuffle of age, can possibly achieve.... The poor girls so trained go out to the humbler class of service where their ignorance... too often provoke[s] the harshness of their employers. In their errands in the street at all hours the secret of another and all too easy livelihood is revealed to them. No mother or friendly teacher is there to save them, no house to which to go when dismissed from service, save the weary workhouse again. Before they return hither they try that dread alternative.'

As regards the unmarried mother and her child, it was thought that men were at risk of blackmail and perjury by unscrupulous women: 'the shame of the offence will not be destroyed by its being the means of income and marriage'.[9] The Poor Law Amendment Act of 1834 therefore precluded the woman from charging a putative father before the magistrates. She had to use the Quarter Sessions, corroboration was required, and the mother's parish was liable for the full costs of an unsuccessful application. Any orders obtained ceased when the child reached the age of seven, and the father could not be imprisoned for default.

This was the Finer Report's conclusion with regard to non-marital children:[10]

6 *Report from his Majesty's Commissioners for Inquiring into the Administration and Practical Operation of the Poor Laws*, (44) XXVII.
7 At p 301.
8 *The Philosophy of the Poor Laws.*
9 Commissioners' Report for 1834, p 350.
10 Cmnd 5629, Vol 1, para 4.21.

'By the turn of the century, the Victorian poor law system was under assault. Its treatment of the illegitimate child, in particular, outraged a nascent public conscience that was fed from many sources, ranging from concern for the physical quality of the population as exposed in recruiting offices for the Boer war to a new kind of philosophical and emotional regard for the child as an individual.'

Yet the destitute, but marital, one-parent family might experience different treatment:[11]

'The treatment within the poor law of widows and deserted wives and their children followed a more diverse pattern, according to the policy of the particular poor law union. The husbands of the deserted women who were assisted were liable to reimburse the authorities, but the latter appear to have had a very limited success in making recovery. Up until 1914, in half the cases in which the poor law authorities obtained an order against a liable relative, the only result was that he went to prison for failure to pay.'

Why and how did the poor law demonstrate its comparative approval of the 'legitimate' one-parent family? The Local Government Board circular of 1914, *Relief to Widows and Children*, contains passages which may part-answer both these questions, as well as demonstrating the longevity of current ongoing debates about social and legal policy:[12]

'The value of true home life in the education of and training of the child is admittedly so great that... guardians would do well... to take such action in the granting of relief as will least interfere with the unity of the family... their action should be such as to tend to the early restoration of the family to a condition of independence and the establishment of the children in a position to support themselves in later life.... A widow's family, being deprived of the care of husband and father, necessarily lacks one of the essentials of the best home life, and for that reason it will sometimes be found desirable to provide for the training of some of the children in a well-equipped school or home.'

From this passage we gain a hint of the key distinction between the good and the bad one-parent family; outdoor relief in their own homes for those headed by widows and deserted wives – but the workhouse for fallen women and their *bastards*. In 1914, the year of the Report, some 235,000 children received poor law relief of whom 68,000 were in the workhouse. The rest were looked after in their own homes or were boarded out. Of that 170,000 or so, only 651 were 'with their mothers who were single women' as the Report, kindly, describes them.[13]

We must not leave this document without disinterring its typology[14] of (even) the preferred out-relief mothers:

'1 Women really above the average, capable and trustworthy, able to give their children an excellent training, to plan their future well-being, and to sacrifice a present gain for a future good.

11 *Ibid*, para 4.20.
12 At p 7.
13 At p 6.
14 At p 8.

2   Women of lower morale, good in intention, but less able to carry out their intentions, to look forward or to cope with their responsibilities. Often these are the women whose health has failed, whose force of character has not given them the power to rise above it.

3   The slovenly and slipshod women of weak intentions, and often of weak health, not able to make the most of their intentions.

4   The really bad mothers, people guilty of wilful neglect, sometimes drunkards or people of immoral character.'

The Board was not prepared to institute an absolute ban on working mothers if they were on outdoor relief, but held that it should not be permitted where home and children might suffer. And relief was not to be allowed to 'supplement the wages of sweated labour'.[15]

(b) Private obligation

Until the final decade of the twentieth century, it was easy for a parent (almost always, of course, the father) not merely to leave his or her children but to do so with at least some degree of financial impunity.[16] Not as easily as leaving a cohabitant, perhaps, but certainly easier than leaving a spouse.[17]

If the child were born outside marriage, then the longer ago he or she was born, the less likely it was that the father would ever have acted as a social parent, the more likely it was that he, not the mother, was the absentee, and the more likely still that he would have managed to evade payment altogether. As recently as 1985, the case of *Willett v Wells*[18] illustrated the inadequacy of the legal response to these men. In Grimsby, in 1981, the 'parties' had 'the child', whose name or gender (in a perhaps unconscious reflection of the lack of concern shown) appear not. They never lived together as a family and the father's contribution was limited to paying half the cost of the pram and later presenting the mother with a jumper and a pair of trousers. When Baby Willett was three years *and one day* old, the mother applied for an 'affiliation order' by way of

15   At p 11.

16   See below. Until the Child Support Act 1991, the resident parent was under little *obligation* to obtain money from the absent parent for the benefit of their children. Amounts actually ordered by the courts were often inadequate, as were enforcement provisions. In private law, s 35 of the Matrimonial Causes Act 1857 first gave the Divorce Court the power to make orders for the 'maintenance' of marital children, and the Poor Law Amendment Act 1844 first enabled the magistrates' court to make financial orders against putative fathers in affiliation proceedings.

17   It is fundamental that financial relief orders (for adults) are only available against marital partners (past or present): and even marital children only became the 'first consideration' of such orders under the Matrimonial and Family Proceedings Act 1884. See below.

18   [1985] 1 WLR 237.

'bastardy[19] proceedings' in the only forum then available to her, the magistrates' court. The magistrates were disinclined to help her because, for proceedings in respect of a child over three years old, s 2(1) of the Affiliation Proceedings Act 1957 required the putative father to have paid money for the child's maintenance after the birth. The pram was bought before that and it was not clear that the father himself had bought the clothes.

In fact the Divisional Court was prepared to presume, in the absence of contrary evidence, that he must have bought them. Nonetheless, the case amply illustrates the shortcomings of the law on financial support for such children which obtained until the Family Law Reform Act 1987. The 'respondent' was found to be the parent, a fact which he never denied. In the 1990s (and surely beyond) it would be difficult to find a serious commentator who would require anything further to make him liable. But pre-1987 the law was notoriously reluctant to 'punish', as many would have seen it, such a man. Further sexism was implicit in the fact that only the father was liable, and only then if the mother-applicant was a single woman. There were echoes of criminality in that the police were empowered to serve the summons, and indulgence of fatherly irresponsibility in that there were lots of loopholes for him to escape through. The attitude was reminiscent of the then prevailing attitude to drunken driving; he should be given a sporting chance to get away with it. Even where there was liability, there were no divorce court financial relief orders available, with the child's welfare the first consideration, as had been the case in parental divorce since the Matrimonial and Family Proceedings Act 1984. Whether born of a one-night stand or to parents whose relationship was as long and deep as many a marriage, there were no property adjustment orders, no secured periodical payments – and lump sum orders were restricted to £500. There was a personal injury style,[20] three year,[1] limitation on applications. The mother had to be unmarried, or to have forfeited the right to be maintained by her husband.

In asserting parental *status*, we have seen an increasing emphasis on social rather than biological parenthood, yet where financial support is concerned the trend has been the other way. The Family Law Reform Act 1987 equalised the private law financial opportunities for marital and non-marital children. By 1993, technological[2] advances had ensured a near-irrelevance of the presumption of paternity, and political concern about the financing of one-parent families had led to the implementation

---

19 'Bastard' comes from the old French, *fils de bast*, 'son of a pack saddle', and has long been used as a general, as well as a specific, term of abuse.

20 Limitation Act 1980, s 11(4).

1 Affiliation Proceedings (Amendment) Act 1972, s 2(1).

2 See Ch 3.

of the Child Support Act 1991, with its indifference to the nature of the parents' own legal relationship. In broad terms, the 1991 Act also ensured that parents could not, even with the connivance of the court, leave to the state what they could afford to do themselves.

In the meantime, the apparent enhancing (by way of the 1984 'first consideration' criterion) of the private law financial opportunities for marital children, had been severely qualified by the Court of Appeal in *Suter v Suter and Jones*[3] in which Sir Roualeyn Cumming-Bruce said that, 'The principle in point is that the husband should not be ordered to pay more for his wife's support than is just'. The result was that the wife's periodical payments were reduced to a notional £1 per annum on the basis that she could earn more, and/or that her cohabitant could contribute, and/or the Department of Social Security could make up the difference.[4] Although there had been no appeal against the children's periodical payments, the *real economics* of a single-parent household can only be based on a common fund: were the mother unable to extend her income, it cannot be supposed that the children's belts would have remained untightened.[5] We might note another matter, illustrated by the position of the cohabitant/co-respondent in the case: that a man who wishes to experience parenthood without having to pay for it, then or later, is best advised to form an extra-marital household with the mother[6] of someone else's children: financial liability for children can arise only by way of procreation, adoption or step-parenthood (by marriage), and not 'just' social parenthood.[7]

Today, in England and Wales, we are supposedly constrained by Article 27 of the United Nations Convention on the Rights of the Child, the unofficial 'summary' of which Article is headed 'Standard of Living':

> 1 States Parties recognise the right of every child to a standard of living adequate for the child's physical, mental, spiritual, moral and social development.

3 [1987] 2 All ER 336, 343.
4 G Douglas, 'Justice or Welfare in Financial Proceedings on Divorce' (1987) 50 MLR 516, demonstrates the inadequacy of that assumption in that, eg, if the former wife and her lover were to maintain their relationship, she would be at risk of losing what was then called supplementary benefit on the basis that they were living together as husband and wife.
5 See C Barton, 'Those who are First... shall one Day be Last' (1988) 1 JCL 24, for an account of how the sums ordered for the children compared badly with the real cost of looking after them.
6 Yet another, unsatisfactory, aspect is explored by Douglas (above): the 'assumption as to the proper role and behaviour of a divorced woman' who, 'ideally... should be supported by a man'.
7 But the statutory maintenance formula under the Child Support Act 1991 may now make *allowance* for the costs of supporting the step-children; see below.

2   The parent(s) or others responsible for the child have the primary responsibility to secure, within their abilities and financial capacities, the conditions of living necessary for the child's development....

4   States Parties shall take all appropriate measures to secure the recovery of maintenance for the child from the parent or other persons having financial responsibility for the child...'.

Procedurally, these international obligations would seem to be consistent, at least, with our present mix of public and private law. Yet as regards Article 12(4), this advance criticism of the Child Support Act, to which legislation we now turn, may have been prescient:

'likely to make no difference in most cases to the financial situation of lone parents on income support and their children, as any maintenance received will be taken fully into account in assessing benefit... implementation may cause additional problems for second families'.[8]

2. THE CHILD SUPPORT ACT 1991

(a) The background[9]

The first months of the Child Support Act 1991 (following its 1993 activation) probably generated more public and political attention to family law than any previous initiative, the Divorce Reform Act 1969 and the Children Act 1989 notwithstanding. It is clear that, even if the spectre of the 'maintenance assessment'[10] does not deter the severing of one parental partnership, it should certainly make each party think more carefully before he or she creates another. It has exacerbated the pay element of the 'care or pay choice',[11] in that it is fundamental that one or both parents be *absent*[12] 'in relation to' the child. The absent parent's maintenance bill is reduced if he has care of the child for more than 104 nights per year:[13] it may be argued that some mothers prevent contact for that very reason; *contra* that that is why some fathers seek it.

Another continuing theme sustained by the 1991 Act is the English legal preference that each child have two, self-selected, parents.[14]

---

8 P Newell, *The UK Convention and Children's Rights in the UK* (1991): we consider below the impact of the 1991 Act on second families.

9 See M Maclean and J Eekelaar, 'Child Support: the British Solution' (1993) 7 International Journal of Law and the Family 205; M Maclean, 'The Making of the Child Support Act 1991; Policy Making at the Intersection of Law and Social Policy' (1994) 21 JLS 505.

10 The calculation is explained below.

11 See the previous chapter.

12 Section 3(1).

13 Child Support (Maintenance Assessments and Special Cases) Regulations 1992, r 1(1).

14 See Ch 3.

Surprisingly, the perpetuation of this concept by the Child Support Act is not achieved by the mere identification of a, 'with care' and an, 'absent' parent. This is because it is not only possible for more than one person to be 'with care',[15] but also for more than one parent to be 'absent'[16] and thus for there to be no *parent* 'with care'. In fact, duality is upheld by s 3(1)(a) which, with reference to a 'qualifying' child, refers to 'both of his parents'. Interestingly, the more novel and ascriptive the type of parenthood, the more the Act is prepared to recognise it, and vice versa. Section 26(2) deals with the circumstances in which a child support officer may, indeed shall, make a maintenance assessment despite a denial of parenthood. 'Case A' is 'where the alleged parent is a parent of the child in question by virtue of having adopted him', and 'Case B' is 'by virtue of an order under section 30 of the Human Fertilisation and Embryology Act 1990' (parental orders in favour of gamete donors). Yet, in departure from, we might almost say in defiance of, the oldest legal and anthropological supposition, there is no presumption of paternity as regards a mother's husband, or, more predictably, as regards her cohabitant or lover. All these men are at liberty to invoke the prohibition in s 26(1) whereby, where there is a denial of parentage, 'the child support officer concerned shall not make a maintenance assessment on the assumption that the alleged parent is one of the child's parents'. Happily, such denials will not be undeservedly conclusive as, under s 27, the court[17] has the power to make a declaration of parentage, paternity effectively, and to this end can direct blood tests under ss 20-25 of the Family Law Reform Act 1969. Such attempts at false refutations are not even tactically advisable, other than in the very short term, as they will merely lead to an accrual of liability (although in the Act's early stages, mass repudiation was mooted as a means of overloading the system). In *Re E (a minor) (Child Support: Blood Test)*,[18] Stuart-White J held that s 27 gives the court a *discretion* to make a parentage declaration, and that, in deciding whether or not to exercise it by ordering a blood test, the criterion is that laid down by the House of Lords in *S v S*,[19] ie the test should be carried out unless it would be against the child's interests to do so.

The cartel between the separated parents – to which the courts themselves were sometimes privy – whereby the state was left to pay, is

15 Section 3(5).
16 Section 3(1)(b).
17 By the Children (Allocation of Proceedings) (Amendment) Order 1993, SI 1993/624; the procedure is the same as for public law cases under the Children Act 1989; the reference or application will commence in the family proceedings court, with the possibility of transfer in cases of, eg , complexity.
18 [1994] 2 FLR 548. From Spring 1995, it is intended that the Child Support Agency will ofer DNA tests to settle disputes about paternity with the man's costs being reimbursed if he is shown not to be the father; *The Times*, 29 November 1994.
19 *S v S; W v Official Solicitor* [1972] AC 24.

no longer the option that once it was. We have noted how, in *Suter* above, the court was happy, if mistaken, to imagine that public funds would be available to make up the shortfall between the needs of the child and carer and what it would be 'just' to make the absent parent pay. Perhaps *Reiterbund v Reiterbund*, in 1975, was the first case in which the superior courts evinced a knowledge of, and enthusiasm for, the significance of the social security system's response to family breakdown. At first instance, Finer J (Chair of the Report on the Committee on One-parent Families[20]) declined to disregard the availability of supplementary benefit in considering whether a decree nisi of divorce should be refused under s 5 of the Matrimonial Causes Act, ie that the respondent would suffer 'grave financial hardship':[1]

'in the Family Division at any rate, we should recognise that much of the law of [social security] is of the greatest possible importance in the daily work of the Division. None of us can afford, in this respect, to make the always suspect separation between lawyer's law that we have to know, and the other law which we have to look up when necessary. The law [of social security] requires as much study from practitioners as any other branch of the family law, of which it is, essentially, a part.'[2]

With reference to the genesis of the 1991 Act, it has been said[3] that 'the high water mark... was the decision of the Court of Appeal in *Delaney v Delaney*[4] ... where the welfare benefits to which the wife was entitled played a major part in the court's decision'. Mr Delaney, who was in work, successfully appealed an order that he pay £10 per week periodical payments for each of the three children of the family. Although the Court of Appeal 'deprecate[d] any notion that a former husband and extant father may slough off the tight skin of familial responsibility and may slither into and lose himself in the greener grass of the other side',[5] five pence per annum nominal orders were preferred:

'The court is entitled... to approach the case upon a basis that, if having regard to the reasonable financial commitments undertaken by the husband with due regard to the contribution properly made by the lady with whom he lives, there is

20 (1974) Cd 6478.
 1 [1974] 2 All ER 455. Upheld on appeal, [1975] Fam 99 (CA), where Ormrod LJ said (at 111) of the argument, proffered by counsel for the wife, that the court should ignore her social security benefits, 'Why, I am unable to understand; but he submits that this is the law. A law which produces the paradox that a woman who is in precisely the same financial position before and after the dissolution of her marriage has yet suffered, in law, grave financial hardship as a result of the divorce, requires no elaboration on my part to demonstrate its absurdity. What possible sense could there be in supporting such a paradox?'
 2 At 461.
 3 R Bird, *Child Maintenance – The Child Support Act 1991* (2nd ed, 1993) at p 20.
 4 [1990] 2 FLR 457.
 5 *Per* Ward J at 461.

insufficient left properly to maintain the former wife and children, then the court may have regard to the fact that in proper cases social security benefits are available to the wife and children of the marriage; that having such regard the court is enabled to avoid making orders which would be financially crippling to the husband.'[6]

Ward J saw the new couple's car ('the lowest in the range... being most modest of its kind'[7]) as essential to their working lives as well as for collecting the children for 'access'. His attitude may seem prescient to those who were to criticise the Child Support Act formula for its silence with regard to the expenses borne by the absent parent in seeing his child.[8]

Others were less sympathetic towards absent parents. These were the (reportedly untypical[9]) views of two Sheffield solicitors at the beginning of the 1980s:

'[Brain surgery] is the only answer with many men, you know, because they are little more than animals. They see life as in a very narrow and very selfish aspect, you know, they earn whatever they can, stick to as much of it as they can and pay out as little as possible to the wife and the children and they don't give a damn. And they go on from one woman to another...

I have a number of clients who have left strings, literally, of wives or (*sic*) common-law wives and children across Sheffield and they just move from place to place. They are on low incomes and really are immune from any of the consequences which involve other people.'

Another pair of solicitors had given some thought to how these matters might be resolved. This first idea avoids too rigid a formula whilst keeping everyone happy:

'So I know it sounds silly but one possibility would be for all deserted wives and children to be maintained by the state and let the husbands go and earn every penny they possibly can and spend it as they will, you know, secure in the knowledge that it will find its way back into the Exchequer some way or another, through indirect taxes, through other people's earnings and so on.'

Although its proponent might learn from the other's caution on matters of fiscal detail:

'we should have to pay a National Insurance stamp for this sort of risk, just as we pay for sickness benefit so perhaps we should pay it so as to provide the state maintenance benefit for wives, and husbands too if it's appropriate, and children. I don't know how it would work out economically, you'd need someone to produce some figures on it.'

---

6 Per Ward J at 462.

7 At 460.

8 Changes proposed in 1995 were to cater for this in certain circumstances; see below.

9 C Smart, *The Ties That Bind: Law, Marriage and the Reproduction of Patriarchal Relations* (1984) at p 175. See pp 181-189 for such solicitors' views about 'public or private' provision generally.

Although the work of the Child Support Agency (see below) got off to a rocky start, the data[10] which was incanted in support of the parent legislation should not be forgotten. The courts were in receipt of the National Foster Care Association's recommended rates of pay for foster parents, but there was evidence to suggest that the orders actually being made by the court were about half of what was recommended.[11] There were untenable variations from one case, and from one court, to another: of two fathers each earning £150 per week net, one was ordered to pay £5 per week and the other £50.[12] We should not forget the lax enforcement mechanisms, which allowed absent parents who were so minded to escape paying even where their co-parents had obtained court orders. A survey of orders in one court exposed a 55% arrears rate of which 57% had mounted up to sums in excess of £1,000.[13] Most determinative of change, there was the growth in the public funding of the growing number of one-parent families. Two-thirds, some 770,000 such families, were dependent on income support in 1989. In 1988–89 fewer than 25% were in receipt of private maintenance whilst their total benefits amounted to £3.2 billion. In the United States, a similar imbalance was said to obtain between the mother-and-child and absent father – without the same welfare culture safety net. Most notably, it was claimed that divorced women and the minor children in their household suffered an average 73% decrease in their standard of living in the first year of divorce, in comparison with a 42% increase enjoyed by the husband.[14]

The American example is significant in that experience there (and in Australia)[15] influenced the introduction of the Child Support Act here. The very expression 'child support' is a departure[16] from our own, long-lasting, terminology of 'maintenance' or, less indicatively, 'periodical payments' and from the Scottish 'aliment'. More importantly, the 1991 Act involves three radical substantive innovations to our system. These

---

10 Encapsulated in, eg: Ch 2 of R Bird *Child Maintenance – the Child Support Act 1991* (2nd ed, 1993); or E Jacobs and G Douglas, *Child Support: The Legislation* (1993) p 1 *et seq*.

11 £18 per week for any one child up to 18 in 1990 (*Children Come First* (1990) Cm 1264, Vol 1, para 1.5), as opposed to the then NFCA recommendation of £34.02 per week for a child under five.

12 *Ibid*.

13 S Edwards, C Gould and A Halpern 'The Continuing Saga of Maintaining the Family After Divorce' [1990] Fam Law 31.

14 L J Weitzman, *The Divorce Revolution – the Unexpected Social Consequences for Women and Children in America* (1985) at xii.

15 For a detailed account of the experience in some of the states of America, see L Weitzman and M Maclean (eds) *Economic Consequences of Divorce* (1992) Ch 10, and for the Australian Federal initiative, S Parker, 'Child Support in Australia: Children's Rights or Public Interest?' (1991) 5 IJLF 24.

16 E Jacobs and G Douglas, *Child Support: The Legislation* (1993) p 4.

are a rigid formula[17] to calculate the amount to be paid, an administrative rather than a court-based approach to assessment and calculation, and, where the parent with care, and thus effectively the child, is in receipt of state benefit, (generally) mandatory use.

(b) 1990–95 – A false start?

The Child Support Bill was passed *nem con* in the House of Commons, yet from the time of the Prime Minister's 1990 announcement[18] of the Government's intention to set up an agency which would trace absent parents and make them respect their financial obligations, through to the 1995 White Paper, *Improving Child Support*,[19] there was considerable public criticism. No doubt some of this came from men whose continuing desire to evade their responsibilities was threatened by the new law, but other, more legitimate, objections found their way into the postbags of, previously uncritical, Parliamentarians. From April 1993, when the Act first came into force, there followed two disparaging reports from the House of Commons Social Security Select Committee (the second[20] of which formed the basis of *Improving Child Support*), a third[1] from the Ombudsman (noting, for example, that the Department of Social Security had refused his request to compensate a married man wrongly accused of fathering an adulterine child), and a fourth from the National Audit Commission[2] (almost half the Agency's assessments wrong[3]). Even the Child Support Agency itself regarded its performance as unsatisfactory. The Chief Child Support Officer's Annual Report for 1993/94 showed that the Agency's level of accuracy in applying the formula was poor, with calculation of earnings incorrect in 25% of the 1,380 decisions sampled, and doubtful in a further 13%; incorrect dates at which payment was to commence in 18% of cases; housing costs wrongly or doubtfully

---

17 It is planned that, from 1996/97, there will be a limited discretion to depart from the formula (see below).
18 18 July 1990.
19 Cm 2745; presented to Parliament by Peter Lilley MP, Secretary of State for Social Security, on 23 January 1995.
20 *The Operation of the Child Support Act: Proposals for Change* (Session 1933-4) Fifth Report; See para 3 of *Improving Child Support* (1995), for an acknowledgement of its influence. (The earlier report was *The Operation of the Child Support Act* (1993).)
 1 Third Report from the Parliamentary Commissioner for Administration, *Investigation of Complaints Against the Child Support Agency* (1995).
 2 *Appropriation Accounts 1993/94*, Vol 9, Classes XII-III, Health and OPCS and SS.
 3 '... procedural failures in over half the assessments made and... possibly four cases in ten... contain[ed] errors resulting in incorrect maintenance assessments': *Appropriation Accounts 1993/94*, para 49 (and see Table 3 for a more detailed account).

assessed in 17% of cases; and doubt about payment of child benefit in 38% of cases.[4]

Despite some occasional changes of detail, such as, in February 1994, easing the transition to higher payments for some cases and making a few adjustments to the formula to benefit absent parents,[5] and the deferral *sine die* of previously unresolved cases concerning parents with care who had been in receipt of income support since before April 1993,[6] the Government resisted the calls for more fundamental change. But the 1995 White Paper eventually announced[7] two classes of intended *prospective*[8] changes. The first, requiring primary legislation and presaged for introduction in 1996/97, would allow either parent to apply for a 'departure' from the 'maintenance formula assessment' (see below) where the absent parent would otherwise face hardship or where there had been a 'clean break' (see below) before April 1993. The second group of reforms, whilst equally significant in many cases, involve 'only' administrative action, intended: (a) to reduce further the perceived unfairness of the formula; and (b) to improve the efficiency of the Child Support Agency.

(c) The formula

Ex hypothesi, any formula invites the controversy attendant upon the certainty/discretion dilemma – a fixed formula may well produce individual injustices whereas unfettered discretion is unpredictable and the enemy of rights – but the one actually selected was open to the further criticism of being too difficult to understand. Some of the warnings sounded during the passing of the Bill, and even during the two-year waiting period, proved wide of the mark[9] but Lord Simon, a former President of the then Probate Divorce and Admiralty Division of the High Court was ahead of most:[10]

> 'I ask your Lordships, how many maintenance debtors or creditors, how many citizens' advice bureaux, can possibly make head or tail of what it means? It is just as incomprehensible as the ancient Egyptian hieroglyphs must have been to an illiterate peasant in the Nile Delta.'

4 (1994) pp 3-5; and note the shortcomings identified in the National Audit Offices's
   Appropriation Accounts 1993/94, detailed above.
5 See *Improving Child Support* (1995) para 1.4 for a summary.
6 Announced on 20 December 1994.
7 See para 4, *et seq*.
8 None of the changes are retrospective; changes in assessment will apply only from the dates specified: para 5.
9 Most notably (see below) the fear that large numbers of women would be at risk from violent fathers whom they would be bullied into naming by zealous officialdom.
10 House of Lords, Official Report, 25 February 1991, col 817.

The formula's[11] starting point is to calculate the child's maintenance requirement, ie, the amount the Act defines as satisfying the child's minimum maintenance needs. The calculation is based on income support allowances, and, controversially, includes, where the child is under 16, a gradually decreasing amount intended to reflect the fact that the child is being cared for by the person with care, but which is seen by many absent parents as effectively maintenance for that person rather than the child.

The absent parent's 'assessable income' is then calculated. This is arrived at by allowing him to keep as 'exempt income', an amount to cover his subsistence needs based on the income support personal allowance plus reasonable housing costs,[12] including an allowance for any of his children now living with him, but housing costs only for step-children or a new partner or spouse.[13] Up to 30% of his remaining net income (take-home pay after tax, national insurance and half of pension contributions), is available to meet the child's maintenance requirement.[14] If the parent with care is also earning, the same calculation is carried out in respect of her. Persons with care who are *not* parents are not expected to have to support the child, reflecting the fact that this legislation takes a rather narrow view of parenting, confining liability to those recognised in law as parents and ignoring social parenthood. Where both parents are in receipt of benefits, their assessable income is calculated as nil (but the absent parent will normally be required to pay 5% of the adult personal income support allowance as a token payment unless he is supporting other children).

Having found the assessable incomes of the absent parent and, where relevant, the parent with care, these are added together and divided by two, to reflect the *equal* contribution which both parents are expected to make to their children's support. If the resulting amount is equal to, or less than, the child's maintenance requirement, the absent parent is presumptively required to pay half of *his* assessable income. However, to ensure that, where he is in fact living in and supporting a second family with a new partner and step-children, he can still continue to meet their needs, his 'protected income' is calculated, this time taking account of income support allowance figures for the members of his second family and allowing him an earnings disregard to give him an incentive not to

---

11 For fuller details of the formula, and the revisions made to it, see E Jacobs and G Douglas, *Child Support: The Legislation* (1993) and *First Supplement* (1994).

12 In *Improving Child Support* (1995) the Government announced its intention to allow (from April 1995) for travel-to-work costs at the rate of 10p per mile for any distance above 150 miles per week: see para 3.9 for further details.

13 The allowance for housing costs for a partner and 'step-children' was planned for April 1995: see *ibid* para 3.10.

14 *Improving Child Support* (1995) para 3.1.

become unemployed and claim benefit. Where paying half his assessable income would leave him below his protected income level, the amount due is reduced accordingly until he is left with that level of income.

Where the absent parent could satisfy the child's maintenance requirement without exhausting his assessable income, further formulae are provided to calculate what proportion of the excess should go to improve the child's living standards. A ceiling is imposed.[15] Where the absent parent could nevertheless afford to pay a higher figure, the person with care may have recourse to the private law, discussed below.

The innate complexity[16] of what is merely a skeleton formula was further compounded, as were many parents' (both 'with care' and 'absent') feelings of injustice, by way of some of the numerous regulations which, Lord Mishcon warned,[17] the Bill scheduled to be made under its powers. These were subsequently to provide, for example: a 100-word-plus statement of those factors which together constitute protected income;[18] when such things as an employer's loan to buy season tickets[19] might count towards a parent's income; and exhaustive insights into the vagaries of family form in modern Britain, whereby, for example a

---

15 Eg in 1994/95, the maximum amount payable for one qualifying child aged five was £143.40 a week, reduced to £104.85 from April 1995. The maximum amount of 'additional element' payable under the formula was to be reduced by half from April 1995 (*Improving Child Support* (1995) para 3.13).

16 One summary of the formula even resorted to parody:
    'So how much will the absent parent have to pay? Well you start with his "assessable" income which is his "net" income minus his "exempt" income. The definitions of these terms will be revealed under the Regulations yet to be made under the Act, but it is expected that NI will be his take-home pay, sort of, and EI will be his, er, income support plus his housing costs. Now make the same calculation for the caring parent. Then – you're sure you don't mind me holding up the action while I tell you all this? – add the two together and multiply it by P. Yes, P, which (Sch 1, para (1)) is, of course, "such a number greater than 0 but less than 1 as may be prescribed". (My contact at the Lord Chancellor's Department tells me it's likely to be 0.5 on the principle of equal parental liability). That gives you the "sum available". Now, if the Combined Honours people at the back have quite finished, you simply work out the "children's maintenance requirement", which is probably going to be based on Income Support scale rates for the child and the parent with care. Anti-climactically, all you have to do now is to make the "maintenance assessment" which, if the "sum available" is less than the "children's maintenance requirement" will be the "absent parent's" "assessable income" x "P".
    Here's one I prepared earlier.' (C Barton, *Law Teacher* (1992) Vol 26 at p 255.)

17 At col 780, where his Lordship pointed out that under clause 38 of the Bill only 12 of the planned regulations would need affirmative resolution by Parliament. 'That is very distressing: it is constitutionally objectionable'.

18 The Child Support (Maintenance Assessments and Special Cases) Regulations 1992 (SI 1992/1815) Pt 1, para 11.

19 An illustration suggested by E Jacobs and G Douglas, *Child Support: The Legislation* (1993) at p 214.

'partner', 'in relation to a member of a polygamous marriage' includes, 'any other member of that marriage with whom he lives'.[20]

Formula construction in such a near-infinite, shifting area as family life poses a challenge, particularly if no appeal is to be permitted on the formula, and politicians on all sides airily agree the principle before leaving the tiresome details to officials whose work receives inadequate Parliamentary scrutiny. A parallel may be found in 'cohabitation' and 'marriage contracts' and, to a lesser extent, consent orders on divorce: however many possibilities the draftsperson predicts and allows for, others will always arise. Indeed, those specified may actually spawn others. Significantly, most regimes postulated for domestic partnership contracts encourage the parties to include terms requiring the periodic review of the original agreement.[1] Of course, if the parents' financial circumstances change, so will the application of the child support formula. In her initial announcement, the Prime Minister assured that, 'Complicated cases may still have to be referred to the courts'.[2] In fact, para 2 of the Act reneged on any idea of residual *judgment*, despite the implication of discretion imported by the heading, 'Welfare of children: the general principle':

> 'Where, in any case, which falls to be dealt with under this Act, the Secretary of State or any child support officer is considering the exercise of any discretionary power conferred by this Act, he shall have regard to the welfare of any child likely to be affected by his decision.'

In 1994, Ewbank J rejected an application for leave to seek judicial review of an Agency assessment on the ground that the child support officer had failed to take para 2 into account as 'fanciful in the extreme'.[3] Nonetheless, this and the other attempts to induce an element of discretion into the formula eventually, bore fruit, as we have seen, in the 1995 White Paper, *Improving Child Support*. It contained plans for two sets of circumstances in which the Child Support Agency will have a *discretion*[4] to 'depart' from the formula assessment, although both sets will be 'tightly specified'.[5] They are both planned to take effect in the financial year 1996/97, following the promulgation of the necessary legislation.

20 The Child Support (Maintenance Assessments and Special Cases) Regulations 1992 (SI 1992/1815) Pt 1, para 1(2).
1 The Law Society's Family Law Committee, *Maintenance and Capital Provision on Divorce* (1991) recommended that 'marriage contracts' should be subject to automatic review/revocation on such events as the birth of a child, or the onset of permanent disability or long-term unemployment.
2 18 July 1990.
3 *The Guardian*, 16 August 1994.
4 '... the process is *not* intended to be simply the application of a series of mechanical rules; para 2.4 (emphasis in original).
5 *Ibid*.

One set will deal with the effect on the application of the formula of 'clean break' arrangements entered into before April 1993, and are discussed below. The other set are expected to involve cases where the absent parent faces 'specific additional expenses not taken into account in the formula and... that he would be unable to support himself (and any new family) if he were to pay maintenance at the level determined by the formula'.[6] These may include high costs of travel to maintain contact with the child, the costs of caring for step-children, and certain debts of the former relationship between the parents.[7] Parents with care are also expected to be able to seek a 'departure' if the absent parent has 'an extravagant lifestyle inconsistent with' his apparently low income or if he, 'has deliberately created... excessive costs'.[8] Perhaps these concessions to the mother (as the parent with care normally is) are intended to act as a counterweight to the generally pro-absent father tenor of the White Paper.

(d) The wary mother and other problems

The direction to 'have regard to' welfare in s 2 (above) is studiously not 'paramountcy' (or even 'first')[9] and in any case the Act confers little by way of discretion, portentously not so in the case of the formula (subject to the proposed 'departure'). Yet where such judgment *was* permitted, it allayed the major prospective fear in which the Act was held, namely that a parent with care and in receipt of social security benefit (the mother) would be punished for non-co-operation if she declined to identify the father, however prudent and understandable her silence. He might be violent or she might not wish to re-open a painful relationship. Initially, the clause permitting sanctions was defeated altogether in the House of Lords, despite Lord Coleraine's plea that 'it cannot be right for the single mother to refuse to name the parent of her illegitimate (*sic*) child',[10] before restoration in the House of Commons. Instead, and again in

6 *Ibid* para 2.5.
7 *Ibid* para 2.6.
8 *Ibid* para 2.8, (and see generally).
9 As in s 1(1) of the Children Act 1989. Before the Children Act 1989, the weighting to be attached to the welfare of the child was expressed as 'first and paramount'. That wording originated in the Guardianship of Infants Act 1925 and was re-enacted in the Guardianship of Minors Act 1971. But for present purposes 'first consideration... to the welfare while a minor of any child of the family' is the criterion for ancillary financial relief: s 25 of the Matrimonial Causes Act 1973. It should be noted, however, that for financial relief applications under the Children Act 1989, this criterion is not expressly included in the guidelines specified by Sch 1, para 4, of the Act.
10 House of Lords Official Report, 25 February 1991, col 540.

derogation from the welfare principle, s 6(2) provides that she will not be required to authorise the Secretary of State to recover child maintenance if 'there would be a risk of her, or of any child living with her, suffering harm or undue distress as a result'. In default of that, s 6(10)(b) provides that the obligation to provide information to enable the absent parent to be traced, 'may, in such circumstances as may be prescribed, be waived by the Secretary of State':

> 'we will make exception where rape and incest is involved.... Our proposals are aimed at putting the interests of children first, and their interests are not served if risk of violence to the caring parent is increased. So... if on the evidence before us we are satisfied that there has been a history of violence in a case or the parent has a well-founded fear that seeking maintenance will put her or the child at risk of violence that will be accepted as good cause.... A detailed and rigid list is neither possible or sensible. We do not want to add risk by spelling out just what an absent parent needs to say or do to avoid maintenance.'[11]

So no prescribed circumstances are contained in the regulations, which instead detail the 'reduced benefit direction' which may be made under s 46(11). The appropriate regulation[12] deducts 20% for the first 26 weeks and 10% for the next 26. We might recall the words of Lord Russell during the committee stage in the House of Lords:

> 'In this day and age I do not think that we can interpret the right to protection as meaning simply the right to protection from violent crime or external aggression. It also means protection from deprivation. I do not see any good reason for depriving people of benefit to the point where they get below subsistence level.'[13]

It is one thing to penalise a mother for suspectedly colluding with the father to cast the financial burden for the child on the state, and another to deprive the children for what their parents are supposed to have done. In the event, only some 22 parents with care (all mothers) were penalised for 'unreasonably refusing' to name the absent parent in the first seven months of the Act.[14] In this area, careful scrutiny by, at least, some members of the legislature managed to pre-empt subsequent disquiet, and they did so by leading a retreat from rigidity.

The perceived shortcomings of the Child Support Act – or its downright calamities as many parents and others believed – make for an interesting division between those criticisms which were levelled before, and those after, implementation. So far as the former are concerned, we have already mentioned the fearful mother (probably largely unrealised), a

11 Lord Henley, House of Commons Official Report, 14 March 1991, col 386.
12 Child Support (Maintenance Assessment Procedure) Regulations 1992, SI 1992/1813, r 36.
13 House of Commons Official Report, 19 March 1991, col 535.
14 Evidence given by Ros Hepplewhite, the first chief executive of the Child Support Agency, to the House of Commons Social Security Committee, *First Report of the Social Security Committee: The Operation of the Child Support Act*, Session 1993-94, HC 69, 1 December 1993.

complicated formula run by administrators (borne-out), the reliance on a coming plethora of regulations ill-examined by Parliament (ditto), and the retreat from giving 'first consideration', as in ancillary financial relief, to the welfare of children of the family (ditto again).

In addition, warnings were issued with regard to several other alleged flaws. First, that the Act was at odds with the Children Act 1989 principle that a family's problems should all be dealt with in one forum (if any, given the non-intervention principle[15]) and by the same criteria. Maintenance for the children was to become a fixed mechanism administered by civil servants and untouchable by the courts. Yet the latter, as we shall see below, retain jurisdiction over capital orders for the children, and also residence, etc, orders 'over' them, together with all forms of financial relief for spouses. So the *Families Need Fathers* lobby bemoaned the furthering of the division between a father's financial duty and the contact his children will have with him. *The Family Law Action Group*, in calling for a review of family law, 'in conjunction with the views of ordinary men, women and children and not with the professionals of the "divorce industry"' puts its (patriarchal?) ideology thus:[16]

'The joint effects of the divorce laws and CSA are... no less than a "social engineering" exercise in which the legally supportable "family" has become, not the traditional married family, but simply a mother and her children.

The changes in family law, including the activities of the Child Support Agency, are... not... a wholesome response to the changing needs of society but... a pathological retreat from the moral pressures placed on the legal system and created by material changes in society coupled with weakened social control mechanisms.'

Another advance criticism of the policy of the Act arose from the decision to exclude step-children from its ambit and the mother's husband from ascribed fatherhood: taken together these omissions seem(ed) to amount to a devaluing of marriage and social parenthood.

Ironically, objections to the exclusion of step-children from the category of 'qualifying' children, were drowned in, or perhaps withdrawn as part of, the outcry against the Act when implemented. But pre-1993 it could be seen as one example of the Government's failure to follow the best aspects of its Australian mentor legislation, the Child Support (Registration and collection) Act 1988 and the Child Support (Assessment) Act 1989. Two further examples of this departure may go a long way towards explaining the very different reception afforded to the Australian system. One is that under that system, payment is integrated into the internal revenue system; the Tax Office work on taxable income from previous years and the child support is collected automatically by deduction. The other is that *the formula may be appealed in the courts*. In *Bolton v Bolton*,[17] the wife was terminally

15 Section 1(5); see Ch 8.
16 Policy Paper No 2, *The Case Against the Child Support Agency* (1994).
17 (1992) FLC 92–309 at 79,322–3.

ill and her husband was found to have given up his job in order to avoid paying child support. The administrative calculation having produced a nil assessment, Cohen J held that it would be 'just and equitable and otherwise proper' to order the husband to pay the lump sum equivalent of two years child support in final discharge of his liability. And so far as appeals are concerned, it should be noted that, although the 'departure' system proposed in *Improving Child Support*, and described above, might cover the same situation as arose in *Bolton*, it is envisaged[18] that appeals will be made to an (albeit independent) Child Support Appeal Tribunal and not to a court.

Two advance rumbles grew to roars immediately on realisation of the Act. These were, respectively, the anxieties of those divorced parents who had previously entered a 'clean break' settlement and the role of the Child Support Agency.

(e) The clean break

We will deal firstly with the fears of those who, on legal advice, had agreed that the wife should have the former family home but that neither she *nor the children* should have any, or at least much, ongoing 'maintenance'. (This is, or was, an example of the private law of financial relief, particularly as regards 'clean breaks' and the future of the former marital home, to which we return later in the chapter.) Such settlements were initially deployed to meet the desire, which grew from the end of the 1970s, to permit each segment of the divided family to go its own way *via* a capital arrangement which would, typically, give the wife independence from the husband, and the latter the ability to recommence life unencumbered with old burdens – although perhaps with new ones brought by a second family. But it is important to remember that 'clean breaks' were always intended to be of particular relevance to 'childfree' marriages, and that the legal tools available were never otherwise capable of *guaranteeing* such severance.[19] Perhaps short, childless unions of younger persons with earning capacities are the only ideal background from which, in Lord Scarman's 1979 words:[20]

'to put the past behind... and to begin a new life which is not overshadowed by the relationship which has broken down... the specious reliance on public policy calls for an answer. There are two principles which inform the modern legislation. One

---

18 At para 2.3 (where it is acknowledged that 'there will be provision in the normal way for appeals on points of law from the CSAT to a Child Support Commissioner and, subsequently, the courts).

19 As since acknowledged in *Improving Child Support* (1995) at para 1.11.

20 *Minton v Minton* [1979] AC 593, 608.

is the public interest that spouses, to the extent that their means permit should provide for themselves and their children. But the other – of equal importance – is the principle of "the clean break". The law now encourages spouses to avoid bitterness after family breakdown and to settle their money and property problems.'

But he added that in the Matrimonial Causes Act 1973 as it was then worded, 'No plainer indication could be given of the intention of Parliament' that 'no previous dismissal of an application ... could displace the court's powers to make maintenance orders in favour of children'.

Para 2.1 of the Solicitors Family Law Association states that, 'The solicitor should advise, negotiate and conduct matters so as to encourage and assist the parties to achieve a constructive settlement of their differences as quickly as may be reasonable', but, by para 6.1, he or she should also 'encourage both his client and other family members to regard the welfare of the child as the... paramount consideration'. The suspicion has been that solicitors had colluded with, or at least advised, their clients to combine: (a) a consensual transfer[1] of the home to the mother-wife; with (b) a dismissal of her application for periodical payments, coupled 'with a direction that [she] shall not be entitled to make any further application' for such an order. As described thus far, such arrangement was, and is, entirely legitimate: the quoted passage is from s 25A(3) of the Matrimonial Causes Act 1973 which was inserted[2] in order to encourage adult self-sufficiency post-divorce.

But, crucially, that provision obtains only where 'the court considers that no continuing obligation should be imposed on either party... *in favour of the other*' (emphasis added). This, we may suspect, was being conveniently forgotten, by-passed (by *post hoc* rationalisation that the property or capital transfer was in part *commutation* of the liability to maintain the children), or even misunderstood[3] to the extent that no additional application *in favour of the child* was in fact being made. Critically, nor was it being made later when the wife was in receipt of state benefit – often including mortgage interest payments on the house she had 'gained'- for herself and their child(ren). The taxpayer was

1 Either directly, under s 24(1)(a), or, where they both had a current interest, by 'extinguishing' the husband's share under s 24(1)(d).
2 By s 3 of the Matrimonial and Family Proceedings Act 1984, following the recommendation of Law Com No 112, *The Financial Consequences of Divorce* (1982). In fact, the innovation only extended to making such order over the applicant's objection – previously, her consent was required.
3 Eg, the statement in K Standley, *Family Law* (1993) p 116 that 'the court can make a clean break where there are children' presumably refers only to orders in favour of a spouse on her own account. Yet (as Standley goes on to point out) the courts should be unwilling to sanction even that, as children may suffer a result of terminating spousal obligations. They will be sharing a household with their mother and their overall standard of living will be affected.

housing and feeding the man's children, as well as his former wife. We are back to the mischief the 1991 Act was lauded for deleting, that paternal financial support for children was dependent upon the mother taking a private legal initiative for which she had no incentive. These words might seem, to some, to 'blow the gaff':

'In some cases, the wife would increase the mortgage on the house so that she could make a lump sum payment to the husband, sufficient to enable him to pay a deposit on a house for himself and his new family. The outcome would be as follows: the wife would remain eligible for income support, and the costs of meeting interest payments on the mortgage would be added to her basic entitlement. The DSS would have no right to pursue the former husband in respect of income support payments made to the wife; and although the DSS would be entitled to recover income support paid in respect of the children, it may be that this right would not be vigorously exercised. The husband would have lost his interest in the former matrimonial home but he would have no on-going maintenance liability, and he would be in a position to buy another house on mortgage, and would be eligible for tax relief on the interest.'[4]

Although the Children Act 1989 and the Child Support Act 1991 differ over interventionism (s 1(5) permitting court orders under the 1989 Act only where they improve the lot of the child) both statutes serve parental continuity after separation, albeit in different ways. The one *permits and encourages the absent divorced parent to practise parental responsibility, whilst allowing the non-marital father to apply for it*, and the other *requires all absent parents to take financial responsibility*.

We suggest that this is a more accurate description of the relationship between the two statutes than that supplied by the Lord Chancellor, Lord Mackay, who said[5] of the Child Support Bill:

'Like the Children Act... it is informed by the two central principles or objectives, namely the giving of priority to the welfare of the child and the primary responsibility for securing that welfare even where the parents' own relationship has broken down'.

As we have seen, the extent to which s 2 imports the welfare principle into the 1991 Act is extremely limited.

Although the valid objection to ignoring 'clean breaks', namely that people should be entitled to rely on settled outcomes, was flagged before the Act was implemented, it was only when standing firm against subsequent complaints from those actually affected that the Government put the contrary view. In essence, this arises from the fundamental principle of s 6(1) of the 1991 Act, that it is mandatory for a parent with care to authorise the Secretary of State to recover child support

---

4 S Cretney, in A Bainham, *Children – The Modern Law* (1993) at p 303. The possibility of taking on a new or increased mortgage with the interest paid by the DSS was curtailed by measures in the 1993 and 1994 budgets: Income Support (General) Amendment Regulations 1994, SI 1994/1004.

5 House of Lords Official Report, 25 February 1991, col 773.

maintenance if 'she' (*sic*) is in receipt of benefit. No doubt it was this 'social security value orientation'[6] which, in 1993, led the House of Commons Social Security Committee[7] to accept, reluctantly, that the Child Support Agency should be concerned only with the parties' current finances on the ground that parental obligation is never settled. For the Government to 'unstitch those previous settlements and make some calculation for them in the maintenance formula has always seemed to us extremely difficult'.[8] One judge, at least, has subsequently declined the suggestion[9] that the courts be left to unscramble such previous settlements. In *Crozier v Crozier,*[10] Booth J would not accept that the former husband's new public law obligation to his child justified setting aside an existing clean break consent order for his former wife. The former wife, and the child, were now living in her fiancé's house. The former matrimonial home had been sold and the proceeds of £20,000, originally intended for the wife, were being held on deposit. Had the husband recovered 'his' half-share, the interest, it was calculated, would have been enough for him to meet his obligation under the 1991 Act. He argued that otherwise he would be paying twice. His former wife, on the other hand, said that she was going to invest that £10,000 for the son, and that on her remarriage, and with her additional income, she would not be entitled to income support. As a result, she said, her former husband might not then be liable under the 1991 Act. Nonetheless, he argued that the fact of his court order of £4 per week going up to an anticipated £29 per week child support was sufficient to undermine the basis of the clean break order. Booth J responded:

> 'I am unable to accept that submission. The fact that Parliament has chosen a new administrative method... to compel a parent to contribute towards the maintenance of a child... does not fundamentally alter the position... The parties were then unable to achieve a clean financial break in respect of their son. The legal liability to maintain him remained on them both as his parents. While the wife was prepared to assume that responsibility as between herself and the husband, she could not in fact fulfil that obligation without the assistance of state moneys. The state was never bound by the agreement or the order. At any time it could have intervened, through the Secretary of State, to seek an order through the courts, and the parties were not entitled to assume for the purposes of their agreement that it would not do so.'[11]

6 J Eekelaar, 'Third Thoughts on Child Support' [1994] Fam Law 99 at 101.
7 *The Operation of the Child Support Act*, First Report.
8 Alistair Burt MP (The Minister of State for the DSS) at *ibid* para 73. But their Second Report came out more clearly in favour of taking account of clean breaks in the calculation: *The Guardian*, 3 November 1994.
9 *Ibid* para 74.
10 [1994] 1 FLR 126.
11 At 135. Cf *Mawson v Mawson* [1994] 2 FLR 985 where Thorpe J held that a change in the regulations governing the formula was a matter which justified an appeal against an original settlement which had been predicated on a different child support assessment.

Before 1993, the court had declined to soft-pedal on its existing powers to make capital orders merely because of the forthcoming implementation. In *Wigney v Wigney,*[12] Butler-Sloss LJ rejected the husband's claim that the spectre of the 1991 Act should reduce the amount of capital transfer required of him. 'In my judgment that is not a matter for consideration by the Court of Appeal because the question... does not apply in respect of an Act not yet in force.' Earlier, in *Ballard v Ballard*[13] a husband sought to retain a deferred interest in the former family home. Balcombe LJ said that the effect of the Child Support Act 1991 coming into force 'is a further point which we cannot pursue to any extent'.[14]

There is the further matter of good practice for the future. How can property deals in parental divorce best be negotiated given that they cannot be offset against child maintenance liability? The suggestion, made jointly[15] by the Solicitors Family Law Association and the Family Law Bar Association, that private law cases which lead to capital (property adjustment or lump sum) orders should be locked outside the system, would allow a 'coach and horses' to be driven through the Act. John Eekelaar points out[16] that it would let parents return their child support costs to the public. His own idea (advanced to deal with the problem of existing settlements), that child support appeal tribunals be allowed to reduce the formula amount where the payer had so relied upon a previous settlement such that it would cause 'serious hardship or injustice', could apply prospectively. An equitable injection into the scheme could be achieved without the re-introduction of either judicial discretion or cost to the taxpayer.

In fact, the 1995 White Paper proposed two, phased, reforms to take account of 'clean breaks' made before April 1993. The first was recommended for introduction in April 1995, and envisaged that where an absent parent transferred property, usually, of course, some or all of the family home, worth at least £5,000, to his former partner, this should count as a contribution towards child maintenance by means of an allowance in his exempt income. For example, transfers worth £5,000 to £10,000 should carry an allowance in exempt income of £20 per week.[17] The White Paper acknowledged[18] that this 'broad-brush approach' would

12 (CA) (transcript, 6 May 1992).
13 (CA) (transcript, 21 Nov 1991).
14 See C Barton, 'Child Support Act 1991' (1993) 137 SJ 213 for a discussion of how these two cases might protect solicitors from claims for professional negligence.
15 [1993] Fam Law 700.
16 'Third Thoughts on Child Support', [1994] Fam Law 99.
17 See paras 3.2-3.6 for further details; eg, 'contemporaneous written evidence' will be required to show that the transfer, and its claimed value, took place: para 3.3. Interestingly, the parties will be assumed to have had equal shares in the property: para 3.4.
18 *Ibid* para 3.6.

not always produce the right result, and it was therefore proposed that, as part of the 'departure' system planned to take effect in 1996/97, further allowance should be made where such approach has failed to do justice.[19]

(f) The Child Support Agency

The other 'rumble which grew into a roar' was over the role of the Child Support Agency. True, the Bishop of Gloucester saw no reason even to rumble:[20]

'the creation of a single, powerful and well-publicised Child Support Agency could be significant of the nation's will to grapple with the problem of the children who are at risk and suffering as a result of family breakdown'.

Unlike Lord Houghton:[1]

'there are to be inspectors who will assess what [absent parents] shall pay, determine the method and the order in which they will pay it, and they have the power to enforce it. In short this tax is PAYT, pay as you are told. It is levied by a separate arm of the bureaucracy which is to be specially created for the task.'[2]

The Lord Chancellor's words, although less emotive, were consistent with Lord Houghton's: 'The agency will trace absent parents, investigate the parents' means and assess, collect and enforce means of payment'.[3]

It is the Agency, not mentioned in the Act[4] and constitutionally distanced from it as a 'next steps' entity, which (conveniently?) bore the brunt of much of the post-activation uproar. Lord Houghton's vision of phalanxes of out-of-control 'jobsworths' was certainly shared, accurately or otherwise, by some of those affected by it. But whereas the opening strategy (see below) of the Chief Executive of the Agency might have been open to criticism[5] discrete from the parent legislation, much of the

---

19 *Ibid* para 2.11 (which provides no further detail of substance).
20 House of Lords, Official Report, 25 February 1991, col 808.
 1 *Ibid* col 812.
 2 In practice, the child support officer will accept the information supplied by the absent parent if the latter completes the form.
 3 House of Lords Official Report, 25 February 1991, col 750.
 4 Section 13 is the statutory progenitor of the Child Support Agency by virtue of the duties it confers on the chief child support officer. The Child Support Agency was the first 'next steps' entity to have been created *de novo* rather than 'spun off' from the Civil Service.
 5 To an extent, some of the outrage, very heavily publicised and orchestrated, seemed disingenuous. Perhaps typical was a front page typesetting from the *Evening Sentinel* (a Staffordshire newspaper) of 4 April, 1994. 'Doctors' Fears for CSA Dad' was the chosen headline for a story about the Agency refusing, not surprisingly, to reduce a man's maintenance assessment despite pleas from both his GP and a psychiatrist. 'I am OK at the moment', readers were relieved to learn, 'but one more CSA letter could push me over the edge.' His (second) wife announced, 'I am worried. Bob has very explosive moods. We just don't know what's going to happen'.

transferred censure arose directly from the complexity and rigidity of the formula which Parliament and the Secretary of State had imposed on Agency and 'clients' alike.

One superficially effective criticism was that, in pursuit of the £530 million which it had been set by Government to save from public money in its first year,[6] the Agency had pursued existing payers instead of the non-payers[7] who, everyone was agreed, should be hunted down with vigour. Yet by definition these men's children (and their carers) were in receipt of benefit and not to have assessed their absent fathers immediately might have led to more cost in finding them later. Nearly 100,000 of the cases dealt with in the first year involved carers in receipt of family credit, who keep £15 per week of what the absent father will now pay; there were 20,000 carers, *not* on benefit, who kept everything.[8] When all previously divorced parents have been 'processed', this category will have grown, to the greater satisfaction of the man's 'ex' family if not, perhaps, to him and his 'current' one.[9]

(g) Balancing the first and second families

This latter point brings into sharp relief an issue which remained largely tacit during the planning of, and for, the 1991 Act but which has since been in the forefront of the debate. The balancing of the interests of a man's first and second (and indeed, subsequent) families had previously been addressed by the private law, but only unconvincingly: such principle as can be discerned had been ill thought-out and executed. We have already seen that it is difficult enough to disentangle the different interests of the former wife or partner from those of the child(ren) of the family: their budgets, for which she will take sole responsibility, are bound to merge, and in *Haroutunian v Jennings*[10] it was held that the amount of maintenance for a child may properly include an allowance for the parent with care. Yet when the absent parent forms another family,

---

6 It fell short by £112 million (Child Support Agency *First Annual Report* (1994)).

7 In the first year, about 200,000 maintenance assessments were made, of which some 60% involved clients who were not already receiving maintenance. The Child Support Agency located over 28,000 fathers for whom the mother did not have an address (*ibid*).

8 As given in evidence by the chief child support officer to the House of Commons Social Security Committee in 1993, *The Operation of the Child Support Act,* First Report.

9 But this day has been indefinitely deferred due to the inability of the Agency to take on all cases within the original timescale: *Improving Child Support* (1995) para 4.2.

10 [1977] 1 FLR 62. In *A v A (a minor: Financial Provision)* [1994] 1 FLR 657, Ward J acknowledged that both the mother and her *other* children might well benefit from the £20,000 per annum periodical payments order made against the putative father.

it may still be necessary to prioritise his financial responsibilities not merely *vertically*, ie as between the two families, but also *horizontally* – between the women and the children.

The private law[11] effort has been mainly restricted to weighing up the competing interests of a man's former wife (with those of the children only tacitly in tow) and his subsequent (usually marital again) partner. It has not discharged even that task very well. Whilst 'there is no doubt that many divorced wives feel that the law still fails to make adequate provision for them',[12] the Law Commission also acknowledged the claim that a second wife, 'is invariably forced to accept a reduced standard of living by reason of the fact that part of her husband's income is being diverted to support his first wife'.[13] In private law, it is not normally possible to stray too far from the fact that normally there 'is not enough money to go round',[14] a point which quickly leads to uniting both generations of the remainder of the first family against the whole of the second, as well as invoking the taboo against the use of public funds:

> 'Many [first] wives resent their dependence on what seems to them to be an inadequate level of state support and the drop in their living standards... particularly so where their husbands have remarried, and seem able to enjoy a high standard of living... it is often suggested that [such] wives should avoid dependence on [state] benefit by obtaining paid employment... but they may well experience difficulty in assimilating their working hours with the school hours and holidays of their children.'[15]

Yet the ensuing abandonment of the principle whereby the spouses should be placed in the financial position in which they would have been had the marriage not broken down, together with the encouragement of self-sufficiency,[16] shifted the balance away from first wives.[17] This must have prejudiced the children of the first family as well, even though 'first consideration' is to be given[18] to their welfare. Other private law provisions acknowledge an entire cast of possible stakeholders in a serial

11 We deal with private law *per se* in the next section of this chapter.

12 Law Com No 103, *The Financial Consequences of Divorce: The Basic Policy* (1980) para 27.

13 *Ibid* para 26.

14 *Report of the Committee on One-Parent Families* (1974) Cmnd 5629, Vol 1, para 4.90.

15 Law Com No 103, *The Financial Consequences of Divorce: The Basic Policy* (1980), para 27.

16 By the amendments wrought to Pt II of the Matrimonial Causes Act 1973 by the Matrimonial and Family Proceedings Act 1984.

17 Subsequent evidence from *Judicial Statistics* (*passim*) demonstrates that, eg, about half of the periodical payments orders made for spouses have been of the 'fixed term' variety, rather than 'until further order'. In *Judicial Statistics* (1993) Cm 2623, eg, Table 5.9 shows 8,351 of the former to 8,964 of the latter – and 10,082 applications dismissed.

18 *Ibid*.

breadwinner, making no attempt to form sub-group alliances from amongst their number. Section 25(2)(b) of the Matrimonial Causes Act 1973 includes amongst the matters to which the court shall have regard in making ancillary financial relief orders, 'the financial needs, obligations and responsibilities which each of the parties to the marriage has, or is likely to have in the foreseeable future'.[19] This has been held, on the dissolution of a subsequent marriage, to include the education of children from a previous one,[20] and a mother's responsibility to her extra-marital child:[1] it has been suggested that it also includes 'infirm parents, brothers and sisters unable to work, and any other person whom it is reasonable to expect either party to look after in the circumstances'.[2] It seems that 'obligations and responsibilities' may surpass the merely legal by embracing, for example, voluntary payments for the upkeep of an extra-marital child.[3] As worded, however, s 25(2)(b) is strictly even-handed as between the former spouses, and the fortune, or lack of it, that awaits each of them.

But the private law view of second and subsequent families is most significantly demonstrated by its lack of concern for parental divorce. As we pointed out in the previous chapter, our system does little or nothing to inhibit the parting or divorce *per se* of married parents. It is little better than if they were unmarried, when their parting, even assuming they had ever been together, is not subject to any automatic monitoring at all. And what supervision there is of parental divorce was reduced by the Children Act 1989. It leaves s 41 of the Matrimonial Causes Act 1973 minimally requiring that the court 'consider' the arrangements made for children of the family under 16. In sending the absenting father no message when he leaves, or is left by, his first family, the law gives no warning about him doing it, or its happening, again.

Yet these culpability and gender qualifications are irrelevant to the Child Support Act. It is 'absent parents' who pay and the vast majority of these creatures are men, however blameless some of them may be for the division of their families. Similarly, it is they who create (with another woman) second families whilst still liable to contribute, at least, to the financing of their first. At the outset of the Act in 1993 there were many men whose contributions to their first families were modest if any, particularly if their 'previous' children were non-marital. As such men, and their new families, were used to much, or all, of the formers'

---

19 Section 3(2)(b) of the Domestic Proceedings and Magistrates' Courts Act 1978 employs identical wording; s 27(3) of the Matrimonial Causes Act 1973 directly imports the s 25(2) criteria into applications for failure to provide reasonable maintenance.
20 *P (JR) v P (GL)* [1966] 1 All ER 439.
1 *Fisher v Fisher* [1989] 1 FLR 423.
2 P Bromley and N Lowe, *Bromley's Family Law* (8th ed, 1992) at p 774.
3 *Blower v Blower* [1986] 1 FLR 292.

earnings, the new distribution came hard. The formula and other adjustments made in the wake of the early protests may have mollified some of these men and their second families. The 'protected income level' was increased, the 'parent as carer' element of the formula was decreased, and increases for absent parents with second families and a previous formal agreement were phased in over 18 months.[4] The balance of the proposals (above) in the 1995 White Paper, *Improving Child Support* also favours the absent parent with the recognition of pre-April 1993 'clean breaks'; changes to the formula; and the deferring of pre-April 1993 non-benefit cases. But prospectively, their successors would be wise to consider themselves warned and their new partners would be wise to put themselves on enquiry. Sadly for the latter, existing parental obligation is not a matter of public record, and so another person may throw in 'her' lot with someone whose ongoing duties in this respect are unknown to her. Both members of the second partnership may be entirely blameless, one at least may even merit sympathy for the division of an earlier household, but, before they create a new family, the new couple should be ready to budget for it.

3. THE PRIVATE LAW

We have explained above how the private law was perceived, at least, to have failed. Voluntary arrangements apart, it consisted, and still consists, of some five separate routes: contract (and thus applications for variation/insertion of terms under the Matrimonial Causes Act 1973[5]); after divorce or other matrimonial cause;[6] upon failure to provide reasonable maintenance;[7] under the Domestic Proceedings and Magistrates' Courts Act 1978 in matrimonial proceedings in the magistrates' court;[8] and Sch 1 to the Children Act 1989 (the residuary route and the only statutory means for non-marital children).

The bureaucratisation of child 'support' under the 1991 Act was accompanied and achieved by side-lining, rather than repealing, the existing private law. It is difficult to escape the new law even when considering the 'old' because the latter exists only at the sufferance of the former. In cases where a child support officer has jurisdiction to make a maintenance assessment, s 8(3) provides that:

---

4 As from February 1994.
5 Section 35.
6 Sections 22-24.
7 Section 27.
8 Sections 2, 6 and 7.

'no court shall exercise any power which it would otherwise have to make, vary or revive any maintenance order in relation to the child and absent parent concerned'.

Where these powers are still extant, the court must (continue to) exercise them having regard to such matters as the child's 'financial needs', 'resources' and 'disability' (if any). The parents' finances are also to be considered, as are any expectations for the child's education.[9] We should, however, note the differences which exist between the guidelines in matrimonial proceedings as opposed to applications under the Children Act 1989. The Law Commission recommended that the criteria be only 'largely'[10] adopted from the present law, and in *A v A (a minor: Financial Provision)*[11] Ward J noted that under the 1989 Act, unlike the matrimonial legislation: the welfare of the child is not the first consideration; the family's standard of living is omitted ('no doubt because it is recognised that the mother and father may never have lived together as a family'); and no reference is made to any disabilities of the *parents*. We might add that the duration of their relationship is not mentioned; all these matters remain relevant to the marital family only. We return to the particular nature of financial relief orders made under the 1989 Act in the 'Exclusive powers' section of this chapter (below), but we should note at the outset that s 1(5), the 'no-order' presumption, has less application to these orders than to other parts of the Act. In *K v H (Child Maintenance)*[12] it was held that the courts should accede to the parents' invitation to make a financial order as agreed between the parties as this would be of benefit to the child.

What is the scope for obtaining money or property from a parent privately, upon family partition, since the 1991 Act?[13] We can categorise three sets of circumstances: transitional,[14] supplementary, and exclusive;

---

9 Section 25(3) of the Matrimonial Causes Act 1973 for ancillary financial relief; s 27(3A) for failure to provide reasonable maintenance; and s 3(3) of the Domestic Proceedings and Magistrates' Courts Act 1978 for financial provision applications in the family proceedings court. Authority for 'free-standing' applications is to be found in s 15 and Sch 1 of the Children Act 1989.
10 Law Com No 172 *Review of Child Law: Guardianship and Custody* (1988) para 4.64.
11 [1994] 1 FLR 657, 660.
12 [1993] 2 FLR 61.
13 For a working summary, see H Meadows, 'Child Maintenance After the 1991 Act – the Residual Functions of the Court' [1994] Fam Law 96.
14 An application filed before 5 April 1993 could subsequently be maintained if the parent with care so wished, and a maintenance agreement made before that date ousted the jurisdiction of the Act during the transitional period, unless the carer was in receipt of benefit.

 Another of the more significant transitional matters was that the court could still entertain applications for variation of those periodical payments orders made pre-Act. Where the parent with care sought a, presumably upwards, variation she would no doubt press the figure that would obtain under an Agency assessment, citing s 31 of the 1973 Act which requires the court to have regard to 'all the circumstances' of in addition there are what we might term 'ancillary' matters such as appeals from the child support appeal tribunal. The 'supplementary' and 'exclusive' categories are the most important. We turn to these now, but we should first acknowledge that, under the proposal in *Improving Child Support* that non-benefit cases involving court orders or agreements pre-dating April 1993 should be deferred *sine die*,[15] the courts would retain a jurisdiction originally intended for extinction.

(a) Supplementary powers

In what we have termed its 'supplementary' jurisdiction, the court continues to have authority additional to that of the Child Support Agency. The interests of the rich (to be fair, the interests of the *children* of the rich) are acknowledged, s 8(6) stating that a court which is 'satisfied that the circumstances of the case make it appropriate' may make periodical payments orders despite the payer's existing child support obligations. Under s 8(6)(b) this applies where the 'alternative formula'[16] (above) has been invoked, thereby limiting the amount of income fed into the formula. It operates when the absent parent's income enables him to pay above the upper 'ceiling' amount of child support maintenance, ie when 'his' income is at least £55,000 per annum. Perhaps it will fall to the courts to determine an optimum point at which the child's welfare (the 'first consideration'[17] for the making of private orders in matrimonial proceedings) requires no further funding, or even whether more riches might prove counter-productive to his or her happiness. It certainly seems that the number of periodical payments orders previously made for children under the 1973 Act (37,432 in

the case. Where a current maintenance assessment would have exceeded an old court order, could the carer, mindful of the fact that she might not otherwise approach the Agency until at least 1996, require the earlier attention of a child support officer by way of persuading the court to discharge it? Section 8(4) preserved the court's power to *revoke* a maintenance order and, again, 'all the circumstances' would be relevant. In one case, *B v M (Child Support: Revocation of Order)* [1994] 1 FLR 342, Bryant J allowed the father's appeal against such revocation. Without, he said, wishing to be prescriptive, it would normally be appropriate to seek an upwards variation rather than to attempt to avoid the transitional provisions.

15 Para 1.18.
16 Child Support Act 1991, Sch 1, para 4(3).
17 Section 25(1) of the Matrimonial Causes Act 1973 for ancillary financial relief; s 27(3) *ibid*, in applications for failure to provide reasonable maintenance in the superior courts; and s 3(1) of the Domestic Proceedings and Magistrates' Courts Act 1978 for financial provision orders in the family proceedings court. For financial relief applications under the Children Act 1989, the 'first consideration ' principle is *not* included in the 'matters to which the court is to have regard' under Sch 1, para 4.

1992[18], the last year before the Child Support Act came into force) is unlikely to be equalled in the future. In 1993 they dropped by some 30%.[19]

Section 8(7), which relates to school fees, is similarly unlikely to trouble those feckless council estate fathers who, it was hoped, perhaps particularly by those who bemoaned the high taxes which made it difficult for them to put their own scions through a private education,[20] were going to be the deserving losers under the Act.

A final example of a private order 'topping up' the Agency assessment is permitted by s 8(8), which covers the extra costs of caring for a 'disabled' child, one who is '... blind, deaf or dumb or is substantially and permanently handicapped by illness, injury, mental disorder or congenital deformity or such other disability as may be prescribed'.[1]

(b) Exclusive powers

We are back to rich parents, or at least to property owning fathers. The 1991 Act does not abrogate existing powers to make maintenance orders *by consent,* capital orders, lump sum and property adjustment orders, under the Matrimonial Causes Act 1973, nor those under the Children Act 1989, where now resides the authority to make such orders in favour of marital and non-marital children originally won (in the case of non-marital children) as recently[2] as the Family Law Reform Act 1987. It has been argued[3] that when such orders are made in favour of children, the purpose is to make proper provision for them as *dependants*, rather than as *persons*, with an interest in the assets of the family. Further, in dealing with a spouse/co-parent's own application for ancillary relief, it is suggested[4] that 'her' wish to make testamentary provision for independent adult children is irrelevant.

Any notion of children as 'preferential creditors in family bankruptcy', giving them first cut when their parents divide, by way of making capital orders in their favour is, as yet, more of a stimulating idea than a commonplace practice. There are no figures available as to the incidence of such orders but, as with those made in favour of husbands, the

18 In the county court: *Judicial Statistics* (1992) Table 5.3.
19 To 26,279; *Judicial Statistics* (1993) Cm 2623, Table 5.9.
20 The statutory formula envisages no input for this purpose.
 1 Child Support Act 1991, s 8(9).
 2 Section 2 of the Domestic Proceedings and Magistrates' Courts Act 1978 allowed for limited lump sums (to a maximum of £500, initially; now £1,000).
 3 See J G Miller, 'Children and Family Capital on Divorce' (1993) 5 *Journal of child Law* 113, and the authorities cited therein.
 4 *Ibid.*

suspicion must be that they are reported almost as often as they are made. ('Lump sums in favour of children, and in particular of children whose parents are of limited means, are rare'.[5]) Perhaps the most noteworthy are those orders made in favour of non-marital children, where the interest[6] gained by the mother, coupled with the carer allowance catered for by the Child Support Act maintenance formula, may combine to subvert the supposedly absolute differential between spouses and cohabitants in adjustive matters. One source even sees the orders available for the non-marital child *alone* as having 'the potential further to undermine the centrality of marriage in family law', without reference to these other gains recently made by the mother.[7] In *K v K (minors: Property Transfer)*,[8] the Court of Appeal held that it was empowered[9] to order the transfer of the father's share in a joint council tenancy) to the *mother* for the benefit of their children. They had once lived together as a family, and the order confirmed the council house as a continuing family home for the children: the Law Commission Report[10] which recommended the reform found little objection to the attendant maternal bounty. In *A v A (a minor: Financial Provision)*,[11] the non-marital father, a very rich man who lived abroad, was ordered to settle, on his ten year old daughter, the house in which the family had lived. The settlement was to terminate six months after the later of her 18th birthday or the completion of her tertiary education. Even though, 'The father [was] so rich he could transfer this property and not even be aware that he had done so',[12] such transfer should not be ordered in the absence of special circumstances requiring him to benefit his daughter beyond her independence.

As the proportion of non-marital children continues to grow,[13] and the number of such cases litigated (or settled) goes up, perhaps the *Mesher*[14] order and its forbears will be the exemplars of the likely outcome. Whilst that would be to import techniques developed in inter-spousal ancillary relief, their actual nature, particularly since the 1984 introduction[15] of the

5 *Per* Booth J, *Kiely v Kiely* [1988] 1 FLR 248, 251.
6 Section 1(2)(e) and Sch 1 to the Children Act 1989 permits a 'transfer to the applicant, for the benefit of the child'.
7 J Dewar, *Law and the Family* (2nd ed, 1992) p 150. He heads the passage, 'The end of marriage?'.
8 [1992] 2 All ER 727.
9 Technically under the Guardianship of Minors Act 1971. Nourse LJ, at 733, said that it would be the same under the Children Act 1989.
10 Law Com No 118 *Illegitimacy* (1982) para 6.6.
11 [1994] 1 FLR 657.
12 Per Ward J at 662; 'It is culturally accepted, even expected, that a man of the father's rank should have many children by many mothers.'
13 6% of all births in England and Wales in 1961; over 31% in 1992 (*Population Trends No 70* (1992) Table 8).
14 *Mesher v Mesher and Hall* (1973) reported at [1980] 1 All ER 126n.
15 See above.

'children's welfare is first consideration' principle, is largely child-based. The 'traditional' *Mesher* order provided for both spouses to keep or acquire an interest in the home as equitable tenants in common, deferring the trust for sale until, for example, the youngest child of the family reached a specific age, usually 17, or until all the children had completed their education. Included amongst the 'harsh and unsatisfactory'[16] results which this produces, are some, it has been said,[17] which militate directly against the children's interests, particularly of those who still need the place as a home when their schooling is over (as social security legislation presumes). Yet it must be conceded that the 'first consideration' principle of s 25(1) of the 1973 Act is limited to their welfare 'whilst a minor', a constraint consistent with the court not having the power to provide for children after their education or training, other than in 'special circumstances'.[18] This in turn may partly explain the court's reluctance[19] to settle the former marital home, on divorce, for the benefit of the wife and child(ren), perhaps by life interest to the wife with remainder to children. Such a tactic would also deny for ever the use of the capital by the parents. In truth, the existence of children of the family stretches both the ingenuity and goodwill displayed by the divorce court in deploying the property adjustment powers given by Parliament.

It has been estimated[20] that about half of all the children who, following divorce, are not living with both parents live with the mother and the man she has married: it has further been suggested[1] that the disruption to the personal development of 'divorced children' is exacerbated by parental remarriage, despite the pressures to be a 'normal' family. Perhaps the most important example of our 'exclusive' category of orders are those which benefit step-children, who are not, of course, 'qualifying children' for the purposes of the Child Support Act, a step-parent not being 'a person who is in law the mother or father of a child' under s 4.

A spouse is at *prima facie* risk of ancillary financial relief orders being made on behalf of his step-children if they qualify as 'children of the family', ie that they have been 'treated'[2] as such by both spouses although children 'boarded out' with them by a local authority or voluntary organisation are specifically excluded. This criterion seems to be easily satisfied. There must have been a family, so if the spouses separate before

16 Parker LJ, *Mortimer v Mortimer-Griffin* [1986] 2 FLR 315, 319.
17 P M Bromley and N V Lowe, *Bromley's Family Law* (8th ed, 1992) p 788.
18 Matrimonial Causes Act 1973, s 29(3)(b).
19 As in *Chamberlain v Chamberlain* [1974] 1 All ER 33.
20 J Haskey, *'Children in Families Broken by Divorce'* (1990).
 1 K E Kiernan, 'The Impact of Family Disruption and Transitions made in Family Life' (1992) *Population Studies*.
 2 Matrimonial Causes Act 1973, s 52(1).

the child is born, and never live together afterwards,[3] the spouse is safe. Other than that, some very short periods have sufficed, including as little as six months,[4] and even two weeks.[5] Ironically, there does not seem to have been the same reluctance to make these men liable for other men's children as was extended to men who fathered their own non-marital children, at least until the Family Law Reform Act 1987. This may be seen as a further example of the importance attached to the intention to fulfil the parenting role.

Even so, the position of the step-parent is not identical to that of the natural parent: the Matrimonial Causes Act 1973[6] mentions three additional (to those specified as relevant for *all* children (see above)) criteria to be considered before making orders against a spouse 'in favour of a child of the family who is not the child of that party'. The first of these criteria acknowledges the possibility that the child may be able to look to others for support: 'the liability of any other person to maintain the child'.[7] Following the implementation of the Child Support Act, the existence of such a person led to absent fathers complaining that the original formula did not allow for the cost to them of *their*, actual or *de facto*, step-children. The absent fathers saw themselves as disadvantaged by the Child Support Agency's alleged early failure to pursue the, perhaps less visible, biological fathers of these children.

The second criterion may also have potential relevance for all these children now 'of the family'. Estoppel-based, and reflective of the doctrine of intention, it requires the court to have regard to:

'whether that party assumed any responsibility for the child's maintenance, and, if so, the extent to which, and the basis upon which, that party assumed such responsibility and to the length of time for which that party discharged such responsibility'.[8]

Financial commitment to one's spouse's child from his or her liaison with a third party is thereby capable of being perpetuated beyond marriage. There is, however, something of a paradoxical relationship with the previous factor. There, the spouse is encouraged to find someone else to take responsibility, or at least to share it. Here, he is being discouraged from accepting any responsibility of his own. The 'estoppel'

---

3   *M v M* [1980] 2 FLR 39.

4   *Teeling v Teeling* [1984] FLR 808.

5   *W v W* [1984] FLR 796.

6   At s 25(4). The same criteria are imported into superior court applications for failure to provide reasonable maintenance under s 27 by s 3(3A), and into matrimonial proceedings in the family proceedings court by s 3(4) of the Domestic Proceedings and Magistrates' Courts Act 1978. Identical factors are applied to applications under the Inheritance (Provision for Family and Dependants) Act 1975, s 3(3).

7   Section 25(4)(c).

8   Section 25(4)(a).

factor would also encourage a well-prepared and/or well-advised fiancé, of, some would say, dubious moral commitment, to achieve disavowal by pre-marriage 'contract': a rare case of terms relating to children being potentially effective. The same device might be employed, even more pre-emptively, to deny any intention to treat the child as 'of the family' in the first place.

The final matter to which the divorce court must have specific regard when dealing with claims for ancillary financial relief against someone other than the natural parent, is a *negation* of the 'estoppel' issue. Section 25(4)(b) of the Matrimonial Causes Act 1973 asks 'whether in assuming or discharging such responsibility that party did so knowing that the child was not his or her[9] own'. It offsets any ascription of ongoing liability which would otherwise arise were a husband to maintain a child he wrongly believed to be his, whenever conceived and born. An uncomfortable matter: does it follow that the discovery will destroy his love, his 'affective relationship', for the child as well as his duty to maintain him or her? In a near inversion of the normal dissociation (in both public and private law) between contact and payment, such a man would be entitled to apply, at least, for a residence or contact order under s 8 of the Children Act 1989, as 'a party to a marriage (whether or not subsisting) in relation to whom the child is a child of the family'.[10] The issue demonstrates a reliance upon 'mcrc' biological parenthood.

Another circumstance in which the private law retains its exclusive jurisdiction has not, perhaps, been given sufficient publicity to realise its considerable potential. The scope of the Child Support Act, in England and Wales and Northern Ireland, is limited to the identification of each parent's liability to maintain his or her child, and to the enforcement of the absent parent's duty thus established. No child may take the statutory initiative which is variously offered to, or required of, the parent. The Act thus follows the income support scheme which (generally) limits eligibility to adults,[11] and not the Children Act 1989 which gives a voice, at least, to the child. Yet Scottish children are better served (as in some other legal respects[12]) in that s 7(1) of the 1991 Act allows them to apply for a maintenance assessment in their own right from the age of 12.

9 'Or her' seems remarkably punctilious, even at the present time of social gender-neutrality and scientific blurring of motherhood.
10 Section 10(5)(a).
11 The Social Security Contributions and Benefits Act 1992, s 124(1)(a), normally ensures that a person does not become entitled to income support in his own right until majority.
12 Not merely in the generally more adventurous recommendations of its Law Commission, but in parts, at least, of its current law: eg, the provision whereby children over 12 may veto their proposed adoptions.

In this regard, the 1991 Act follows the tradition in private, as well as public law. But it is a tradition from which the private law had already departed, at least in the limited case of adult children (who may also seek a variation of an existing order[13]) of a divorced family. The 'intervenor' in *Downing v Downing (Downing intervening)*[14] was ten when her parents divorced. Now, the mother was 'on' her third husband, the father his second wife, and the 'intervenor', having rejected the lot of them, had obtained a university place by her own initiative and was reading philosophy and linguistics. Neither parent would contribute, under the system then prevailing, to her county council grant. In a forerunner to the cases, two decades on, in which younger children sought to obtain s 8 Children Act 1989 orders over themselves, she consulted a solicitor and obtained a legal aid certificate,[15] 'on what evidence I know not, on what advice I know not'.[16] The court held that she was entitled to 'intervene' although happily, 'not without some encouragement from the court the parties decided not to continue this unhappy contest between members of the family'.[17]

The end of this chapter also completes our section on private law, and we now turn to the relationship between parents and the state.

---

13 Under s 31 of the Matrimonial Causes Act 1973.
14 [1976] Fam 288.
15 See Chs 7 and 16.
16 *Per* Payne J at 292.
17 We may complete the list of ways in which the private law takes the 'exclusive' responsibility for making orders regarding the financing of children by mentioning: those between 16 and 19 but not in education; persons over 19 (not 'qualifying children' under s 55(1) of the Child Support Act 1991); and those minors who (or one or both of whose parents) are not 'habitually resident' in the United Kingdom (Child Support Act 1991, s 44).

PART IV

Parents and the state

CHAPTER 10

State support for parents

1. INTRODUCTION

It is in the overt relations between parents and the state that the tension between the two main models of parenthood which we have discussed in earlier chapters (parent as possessor, and parent as trustee or guardian, of the child) becomes most obvious. This is so because notwithstanding the rhetoric of the primacy of the parental role, in certain aspects of a child's upbringing, the state may seek to assert the paramountcy of its own interests in contradistinction to those of the parents (or child); for example, by seeking to ensure that particular modes of behaviour or values are imparted to the child which reflect the approved model of conduct in the particular society.[1] Indeed, the concept of the Crown as *parens patriae*, made familiar through the jurisdiction of wardship, implies as much:

> 'The jurisdiction of this Court ... with regard to the custody of Infants rests upon this ground, that it is the interest of the State and the Sovereign that children should be properly brought up and educated; and according to the principle of our law, the Sovereign as parens patriae, is bound to look at the maintenance and education ... of all his subjects.'[2]

Yet, as we discussed in Chapter 1, it is the family unit, in which the child is brought up, which is usually regarded as the chief agency of socialisation: 'the family reproduces cultural patterns in the individual, imports ethical norms, shapes the child's character ...[and] colours the

---

1 See D Archard, *Children: Rights and Childhood* (1993) Ch 9. For a discussion of this conflict in the American context, see B Bennett Woodhouse, '"Who Owns the Child?": *Meyer* and *Pierce* and the Child as Property' (1992) 33 William and Mary Law Review 995.

2 *Hope v Hope* (1854) 4 De GM & G 328, 344-5, per Lord Cranworth LC. For the origins of wardship, see N V Lowe and R A H White, *Wards of Court* (2nd ed, 1986) Ch 1; J Seymour, '*Parens Patriae* and Wardship Powers: Their Nature and Origins' (1994) 14 OJLS 159.

child's subsequent experience'.[3] Perhaps parents should therefore be viewed as the *agents* of the state rather than the trustees of their children, the true owner, settlor, or possessor of children being the state itself.[4] The feudal origin of the *parens patriae* doctrine lends support to such a view.

Writers such as Christopher Lasch, or Jacques Donzelot, who have drawn attention most strikingly to this dimension of the state's social policy, are hostile to the 'capture' of the child from the family. Lasch, for example,[5] argued that capitalism exalts the family as the last refuge of privacy in a hostile and forbidding environment and the base in which individuals can be sustained emotionally to face the battles of the marketplace. Yet at the same time, it is capitalism itself which has destroyed the capacity of the family to fulfil this task. The state has therefore stepped in to take the place of the family, with a proliferation of experts, medical, educational and social, to advise the demoralised parents, and supervise their inadequate attempts to bring up their children.

Such radical thinkers form an odd coalition with New Right politicians and writers who have also argued that the state's role in the care and upbringing of children should be a minimal one.[6] By the 'New Right' we mean those on the right of the political spectrum who captured the policy agenda in the 1970s and 1980s from the left. They include both the neo-liberal economists advocating a totally free market in goods and services and dismantling of the role of the state in the economy (and for whom the market is 'private', compared to those critical legal scholars whose views we outlined in Chapter 1 who contrast the family – 'private' – with the market as the epitomy of the 'public'), and authoritarian Conservatives who seek a 'return' to the 'traditional' nuclear family model, which they see as the key both to economic well-being and social stability. In seeking to recreate the conditions for the resurgence of the traditional family, they have argued for the re-establishment of family privacy – free from state intervention, and family responsibility – with the family and not the state or society assuming the burdens of caring for the vulnerable. Indeed, the Children Act provisions designed to stress the primacy of parental responsibility which we have discussed in Chapters 6 to 8 are in some respects a watered-down version of that thinking.

---

3   C Lasch, *Haven in a Heartless World: The Family Besieged* (1977) p 3.

4   For a radical critique of such a view, drawing on the work of J Donzelot (below), see P Meyer, *The Child and the State: The Intervention of the State in Family Life* (1983) p 12: 'With its very functions delegated by the State, and able to exercise them only under State supervision, the family finds its activity limited to escorting its progeny to the institutions which have established a monopoly over apprenticeship, health, sport etc.'

5   C Lasch, *Haven in a Heartless World: The Family Besieged* (1977) p 3.

6   See R Levitas 'Ideology and the New Right', M David, 'Moral and Maternal: The Family in the Right' in R Levitas (ed) *The Ideology of the New Right* (1986).

The framers of that Act also appear to have been influenced by the thinking of Goldstein, Freud and Solnit, whose theories of the psychological needs of children were outlined in Chapter 1. It will be recalled that they argue that it is only through the continuous nurture of the child within the privacy of the family that the familial bonds needed for the child's healthy growth and development can be established and maintained. Furthermore:

> 'the state is too crude an instrument to become an adequate substitute for flesh and blood parents. The legal system has neither the resources nor the sensitivity to respond to a growing child's ever-changing needs and demands.... A policy of minimum coercive intervention by the state thus accords not only with our firm belief as citizens in individual freedom and human dignity, but also with our professional understanding of the intricate developmental processes of childhood.'[7]

But when it comes to aspects of socialisation (for example, the inculcation of law-abiding modes of conduct and attitudes) then even (and indeed especially) the New Right would wish to assert the state's interest. David Willetts, for example, who was Director of Studies at the Centre for Policy Studies before becoming a Conservative MP, has argued that

> 'the fundamental reason why the family matters is that it is the vehicle for the transmission of values and civilities which make it possible for us to get along together in society'.[8]

At this point, the ideology of the primacy of parents becomes mediated by the concept of a *partnership* between parents and state, where responsibility for the child is *shared*. This is a different aspect of the partnership principle embodied in the Children Act from that discussed in earlier chapters, which focused on the shared responsibility of disparate *individuals*.

2. THE CHILD AS INDIVIDUAL CITIZEN

It is possible to present the state's role in all this in a more positive light than Lasch or Donzelot suggest. We might view the state's assertions over the child as based on a view of the child as a citizen (either presently or in the future when adult) of the state, and hence deserving of the state's care and protection. The United Nations Convention on the Rights of the Child is a positive illustration of such an approach.[9] As Cass comments, what the Convention does is:

---

7 J Goldstein, A Freud and A J Solnit, *Before the Best Interests of the Child* (1980) p 12.
8 D Willetts, *The Family* (1993) WH Smith Contemporary Papers No 14, at p 17.
9 B Walsh, 'The United Nations Convention on the Rights of the Child: A British View' (1991) 5 *International Journal of Law and Family* 170 at p 171.

'to disaggregate the rights of children from the rights of "families", to constitute children as independent actors with rights *vis-a-vis* their parents and *vis-a-vis* the state'.[10]

There are two aspects to this conception of the child as citizen. First, the state may view the child as an asset, a future member of society, a future worker, who will make a contribution to the well-being of the whole society. Since the liberal capitalist state regards parents as best placed to bring up children, but at the same time is anxious to ensure that the full potential of this asset is realised, the state may privilege families financially or otherwise, and in return, albeit indirectly, hold itself entitled to impose certain obligations on the parents in the way in which they bring up their children. The state cannot afford to let them have a free hand. So, for example, child benefit may be paid to all those caring for children, irrespective of financial need, as a symbol of the importance attached by the state to children as a resource for the future. Parents may be required to see that their children receive education which will fit them to fulfil a future role in society. Parents may be held responsible for the delinquencies of their children, which mark a *failure* in their educative duty to the state.

The second aspect of viewing the child as citizen is a protective one. Since the child is an individual member of society, he or she is entitled to protection from physical or other harm, whoever inflicts it. A parent who proves unable to care for a child to the standard required by the state may be subject to state control, even the deprivation of his or her children. Such control or deprivation may be carried out where a parent fails to educate a child adequately, fails to control a child adequately, or positively harms the child through inadequate care or protection.

One of the most influential analyses of the development of the mechanisms for such control has been put forward by Jacques Donzelot,[11] whose thesis, developed in relation to France, has been applied to this country by Robert Dingwall and John Eekelaar.[12] The latter have shown how the concern of the state to ensure the care of the vulnerable and dependent was not a nineteenth century discovery, but has its origins in the Tudor Poor Law and possibly local church or community sanctions.[13]

10 B Cass, 'The Limits of the Public/Private Dichotomy: A Comment on Coady and Coady' in P Alston *et al* (eds) *Children, Rights and the Law* (1992) at p 142.
11 *The Policing of Families* (1979).
12 'Families and The State: An Historical Perspective on the Public Regulation of Private Conduct' (1988) 10 *Law and Policy* 341.
13 But see R Helmholz, 'And were there children's rights in early modern England?' (1993) 1 *International Journal of Children's Rights* 23, whose research shows that while children might be proceeded against in the ecclesiastical courts for abuse of their parents, the reverse was not so: the 'canon law enforced the duty of filial obedience to the exclusion of providing physical protection for abused children' (p 31).

However, as Mary Abbott points out, that concern was primarily motivated by a fear of public disorder, and not by humanitarian interest in children's welfare.

'Heads of families had an obligation to maintain and discipline their households.... This duty was all the weightier because, until the second half of the nineteenth century, there were no laws requiring children to go to school, and most communities were policed by unpaid constables. Those who failed to keep their families in order, therefore, failed in their responsibility to society.' [14]

The conception of children as threats to society has remained a powerful motivation in the development of British social and family policy; all the major pieces of legislation relating to child welfare (embracing child care, education and delinquency) have been justified as likely to improve the chances of children growing up to be productive, law-abiding citizens.

But the liberal view of the family as private and outside state control, coupled with fears of 'social engineering', produces a tension between the desire to take action and the need to limit interference in the private sphere.[15] Donzelot elaborates three mechanisms which could be used to diffuse this tension. The first is assistance, whereby help could be given to the needy through charitable rather than state agency, and made conditional on demonstration of appropriate commitment to moral values. The seemingly eternal distinction between the deserving and undeserving poor is an example of this: those who become distressed through no fault of their own are to be pitied and helped, those who get into this state voluntarily are to be stigmatised.[16] The second is normalisation, or the instruction in appropriate forms of behaviour – compulsory schooling is the prime example. Finally, there is tutelage, the surveillance of families on the basis that those who have nothing to hide will have no reason to object. Another manifestation of the tension is the requirement of proof of harm before the state can 'interfere' in the parent-child relationship by coercive removal or supervision. A simple paramountcy test does not suffice. Parents must in some way be found positively to have failed in their obligations to both child and state.

We now explore in detail the ways in which the child's status as citizen may be used by the state to regulate and supervise parental upbringing of

14 M Abbott, *Family Ties, English Families 1540-1920* (1993) p 2.
15 Compare an analysis of parenthood from the old Soviet Union, quoted by Freeman in *The Rights and Wrongs of Children* (1983) at p 244: 'In our country the duty of the father toward his children is a particular form of his duty towards society' which fits entirely with Abbott's understanding of pre-nineteenth century England, above, and with that of the New Right. See also J Eekelaar, 'Parental responsibility: State of Nature of Nature of the State?' [1991] JSWFL 37, for another analysis distinguishing parental responsibility *to* one's children, from responsibility *for* one's children.
16 For a celebration of the values of stigmatising the undeserving poor, see C Murray, *The Emerging British Underclass* (1990).

children. In so doing, we suggest another model to explain the position – a *reciprocal* relationship between parents and state, whereby the state provides certain facilities to parents or others caring for children, and in return, they are expected to fulfil certain expectations in how they bring these children up. In this chapter and the next, we concentrate on the positive aspects of the parent/state relationship and how the reciprocal rights and duties of each interact. In the following chapters we focus upon the more coercive or negative elements in the relationship, where the protection of the child *from* his or her family takes priority.

3. FINANCIAL SUPPORT FOR PARENTS IN THEIR CHILD-REARING FUNCTIONS

Article 27 of the United Nations Convention on the Rights of the Child requires states to 'recognise the right of every child to a standard of living adequate to the child's physical, mental, spiritual, moral and social development'. While the Article goes on to give parents the primary responsibility to secure, within their abilities and financial capacities, the conditions of living necessary for the child's development, the state is envisaged as having a duty to aid the parents in this task. The extent to which a state will willingly assume this duty and, in particular, make financial contributions to the upbringing of children, usually demonstrates its attitude to population policy and its view of children either as future productive assets who will form part of the workforce and add to the prosperity of the nation, or as present burdens on a hard-pressed economy.[17] States seeking to encourage population growth are more generous in providing incentives to parents to increase their family size. For example, France has traditionally had a generous system of allowances increasing in amount with the number of children in the family.[18] States wishing to limit population growth offer disincentives, with China's 'one child' policy the clearest example. In China, parents who decline to limit their family to one child may be penalised financially, losing the right to free schooling and health and other benefits for their children, and work privileges.[19]

In the United Kingdom, views on whether families should be encouraged to increase or reduce their family size have fluctuated. At the start of the century, eugenic theory, based on Darwinian evolutionary theory, that

---

17 G Douglas, *Law, Fertility and Reproduction* (1991) Ch 1.
18 See P Boisard, 'Le système français de prestations familiales' and B Fragonard, 'L'aide à la famille: Politiques de prestations et politiques fiscales' in M-T Meulders-Klein and J Eekelaar (eds) *Family, State and Individual Economic Security* (1988).
19 E Croll *et al* (eds) *China's One Child Family Policy* (1985).

the development of 'good' human stock required selective breeding, led to calls for middle-class families to be encouraged to increase their family size, and for working-class or immigrant families to be discouraged from reproducing.[20] After the 1939–45 war, a system of 'family allowances'[1] was introduced, in part with the intention of encouraging larger families, but also because of concern to ensure that families enjoyed a decent subsistence level of income. The allowance was paid to the mother, for second and subsequent children but not the first, so as not to relieve families entirely of their financial obligations for bringing up their children. But it received low priority in the social security system, and its value was uprated only spasmodically. Tax allowances were also made, including in respect of first children, and these were graduated according to the child's age. But tax allowances favour the better-off, and increase the take-home pay of the earner. Until the 1980s, this was much more likely to have been the father than the mother.[2] Fears that many fathers retained the extra money for their own spending rather than to improve the living standards of the family led, after many years of debate and argument, to the replacement of child tax allowances and family allowance with child benefit, in 1977.[3] More recently, in a further example of the 'new father' phenomenon, the Government opted out of European moves to introduce a right to paid or unpaid paternity leave on the birth of a new child. While those in favour of such a right argued that it would aid the psychological bonding of fathers with their children and thus strengthen their relationship in the future, the Government objected to the costs to industry.[4] In any case, its stance was compatible with its view of the desirability of the 'traditional' family of male breadwinner and female caregiver.

20 These calls were much stronger in other countries, especially the United States and Germany.

1 See P Hennessy, *Never Again: Britain 1945-1951* (1993) pp 129-130 for a description of the prime mover for the allowance, Eleanor Rathbone, and the passage of the legislation.

2 The proportion of married women who were economically active (ie working, or seeking work) rose from 48% to 59% between 1973 and 1992; for women aged between 25 and 34, the peak ages for having young children, the percentage rose from 44% to 70%: *General Household Survey 1992* (1994) Table 7.6.

3 The married person's tax allowance, which is not dependent upon having a child, remains nonetheless of some significance, since it is payable to *unmarried parents*, caring for and maintaining their own, or step-children: Income and Corporation Taxes Act, 1988 s 259.

4 *The Times,* 23 September 1994.

(a) Child benefit

Child benefit is a non-means tested benefit payable to a person 'responsible for' a child aged under 16 (or under 19 and in full-time education).[5] Being responsible for the child will normally mean having the child living with the person. Wives, or mothers, take priority over husbands or fathers in being entitled to receive the benefit, in order to address the complaint that payment to fathers could mean that the children never actually benefited from it.[6]

Interestingly, there need be no biological or legal parental relationship between the recipient and the child, thus demonstrating the state's recognition of the importance of social parenthood.[7] Child benefit was paid in respect of 12,485,000 children in 1992-93, making it the most universal of all the social security benefits.[8] The amount paid is not intended to meet the full costs of bringing up a child. The rate paid in 1994/95 was £10.20 for the first child and £8.25 for subsequent children, compared with £15.65 allowed for a child aged under 11, rising to £27.50 for a child aged between 16 and 18, whose parent was claiming income support.[9] The amount of child benefit paid does not vary according to the age of the child, ignoring the reality that older children cost more to maintain, but an extra amount is paid for the first child, on the basis that parents incur extra expense in acquiring equipment and clothing for a first child, which can be passed on for subsequent children in the family, and experience the greatest drop in income when the mother gives up work (if only during maternity leave) on having the first child. The proportionately greater poverty of lone parents[10] is recognised by payment

5   Social Security Contributions and Benefits Act 1992, ss 141, 142.

6   *Ibid* Sch 10, paras 3, 4.

7   Such persons responsible for a child whose parents are dead may additionally claim guardian's allowance. The term 'guardian' is not that defined in the Children Act 1989, s 5 but refers to anyone who is actually caring for the child: Social Security Contributions and Benefits Act 1992, s 77. This is in striking contrast to the position regarding the *recoupment* of state expenditure for children, as we saw in Ch 9. Indeed, the fact that the guardian can claim the allowance on top of child benefit reinforces the biological/legal parentage basis of financial liability in the public law sphere and the acceptance that the guardian is taking on an obligation which literally goes beyond the call of duty. (But only 2,369 children were covered by the allowance in 1992: *Social Security Statistics 1993* Table G4.01.)

8   *Social Trends 24* (1994) Table 5.9.

9   Child Benefit and Social Security (Fixing and Adjustment of Rates) Regulations 1976, SI 1976/1267 (as amended) r 2 and Income Support (General) Regulations 1987, SI 1987/1967 (as amended), Sch 2, Pt I.

10   40% of lone parents in 1992/93 had gross weekly incomes of less than £100, compared with 4% of married couples. Only 12% of lone parents had incomes of over £350 per week, compared with 59% of married couples: *General Household Survey 1992* (1994) Table 2.30.

of the child benefit increase, known as one parent benefit, worth £6.15 in 1994/95.

The actual financial support rendered by child benefit is therefore insignificant but its symbolic value is important in emphasising that the state recognises that it owes an economic duty to *all* children irrespective of their parents' own financial circumstances. But such recognition has not been readily accepted by all. Two objections may be made against child benefit. First, there is the view running through the Children Act and other recent legislation, of children as the responsibility of their parents, with a concomitant argument that if parents cannot afford the cost of having children, they should not have them. This consumerist approach to children fits in well with seeing them as the possessions of their parents and the family as private and autonomous. It ignores any state interest in its population. On this basis, child benefit should be abolished. An alternative and opposite objection, which implicitly accepts the state's concern for its citizens, is that only those who actually need the state's financial help should receive it, and this has led to calls for child benefit to become means-tested.

(b) Income-related benefits for families

Acceptance by the state of an obligation to assist those in need dates back, in this country at least, to the Tudor Poor Law, as we noted in Chapter 9. The system of social security and relief of need has undergone numerous changes since, of course, but it continues to bear traces of its origins. First, parents are held liable to support their children, and spouses to support each other (although familial obligation goes no further than this), with the risk of facing criminal or civil action if they wilfully refuse to do so.[11] Secondly, eligibility for some income-related benefits depends not only on low income or capital resources, but also on inability, for defined reasons, to work, so that a distinction continues to be drawn between the 'deserving' and 'undeserving' poor. Thirdly, benefit rates, in theory at least, are pitched at a level designed to encourage recourse to employment as a preferable alternative (although we should note the operation of the 'poverty trap', whereby taking up employment may result in disproportionate loss of income compared with remaining on benefit, once tax and national insurance are deducted, and 'passport' benefits such as free school meals and free prescriptions are lost).

Today, the two most important benefits currently available to parents to help meet the financial needs of their families are income support (supplemented by the Social Fund) and family credit. The former is the

11 Social Security Administration Act 1992, s 106.

modern version of 'national assistance', later 'supplementary benefit', introduced in 1948 after the Poor Law was abolished, and intended then to serve as a safety net for the few (it was assumed) who would lack an income through employment and their rights to contributory benefits paid for through national insurance contributions. The latter is a form of wage subsidy (but paid to the worker rather than the employer) for the low-paid.

(i) Income support[12]

Income support continues to reflect the old idea of poor law relief as the last resort for those with no other source of help. Although it is said to be available as of right (assuming the claimant fulfils the eligibility criteria), receipt may still carry a stigma, which, some would say, has occasionally been exploited by politicians seeking to find scapegoats for the country's economic difficulties. In May 1992, 5,088,000 people received income support, including 2.7 million children, and 957,000 single parent families.[13]

The rules covering income support provide that a person is eligible if aged 18 or over, with no income, or income below the 'applicable amount' and disposable capital below £8,000, and who is not engaged in remunerative work but is available for and actively seeking work.[14] The circumstances of those with children are catered for as follows. First, a lone parent who is responsible for a child under 16 is not required to be available for employment.[15] Secondly, the claim is made for the family unit – the claimant and his or her spouse or cohabitant and any dependent children aged under 19 living with them.[16] The needs and resources of the whole family are assessed together, with entitlement dependent upon needs exceeding resources. Needs are assessed according to allowances intended to cover the basic living requirements of the claimant him or

12 The Government announced in November 1994 that it intended combining income support with unemployment benefit in a new 'Jobseeker's Allowance' to be enacted in 1994/95. The description which follows will remain generally applicable when that is done.

13 *Social Security Statistics 1993* Tables A2.02, A2.03. N Oldfield and A Yu, *The Cost of a Child* (1993).

14 Social Security Contributions and Benefits Act 1992, s 124. Capital excludes the value of the family home. Capital between £3,000 and £8,000 reduces the amount of income support paid. A claimant may work fewer than 16 hours per week and still qualify, although any earnings above £15 per week reduce the amount of income support paid.

15 Income Support (General) Regulations 1987, SI 1987/1967, Sch 1, para 1.

16 The child need not be the biological or adopted child of the claimant; it suffices that the claimant is receiving child benefit for the child or, if no one is, that the child usually lives with the claimant, so that again, the law gives recognition to the reality of social parenthood: Income Support (General) Regulations 1987, SI 1987/1967, r 15.

herself plus any dependents (partner and/or children). As we have noted above, the amounts for children vary according to their age. 'Premiums', which are further allowances designed to reflect the particular circumstances of different types of claimants, are included in the calculation of the applicable amount; for example, there is a family premium, worth £10.05 in 1994/95 and lone parent premium worth £5.10.[17] Thirdly, young people aged 16 or 17 are generally ineligible for income support. This is because it is assumed that they are living at home with their families, who should take responsibility for them; and to encourage them to take up employment or youth training rather than become dependent upon benefits. Their financial needs are accordingly intended to be catered for by way of the state if they take up a training place; by their parents receiving child benefit for them if they remain in education; and by the amounts payable to the parents as child allowances if they themselves are receiving income support. Young people of this age who are lone parents are eligible but single parents under 16 are not eligible;[18] their needs are supposed to be met either by their families or by the state through local authority care of them or their children. Young people who would suffer severe hardship if they do not receive income support are also eligible under s 125 of the Social Security Contributions and Benefits Act 1992. The Government claimed, in its first report to the United Nations Committee on the Rights of the Child, that:

'This provision works – over 85% of those currently applying receive income support and on average the percentage is even higher for rough sleepers, care leavers and pregnant young women.'[19]

This constitutes an official admission that there are young people who are *not* receiving help. Furthermore, the success rate of applications had fallen to 81.1% by July 1994.[20] It is arguable that the severe limitations imposed on such children claiming income support in their own right break the obligation under Article 26 of the United Nations Convention to:

'recognise for every child the right to benefit from social security... taking into account the resources and the circumstances of the child and persons having responsibility for the maintenance of the child, as well as any other consideration relevant'.

Although intended to provide a subsistence level of income, it has been claimed that income support falls short of providing adequate financial support for bringing up a child. For example, research by the Food

17 Income Support (General) Regulations 1987, SI 1987/1967, Sch 2.
18 Income Support (General) Regulations 1987, SI 1987/1967, Sch 1A, Pt I, para 1.
19 *The UK's First Report to the UN Committee on the Rights of the Child* (1994) at para 6.95.
20 Parliamentary answer to Stephen Byers MP, *The Guardian,* 21 September 1994.

Commission suggested that the estimated allowance for food for a child under 11 on income support was insufficient to pay at current prices for the diet of a child in a London workhouse of 1876, consisting of bread and gruel, meat three times a week and no fruit, and fell some 70% short of that needed for the slightly less frugal diet recommended under the Poor Law Orders of 1913.[1] In 1993, the Family Budget Unit funded by the Rowntree Foundation, in a perhaps more sophisticated study, drew up two measures of support, one based on a 'modest but adequate' budget, and the other on a 'low cost' budget.[2] Both took account only of the direct costs of a child, and ignored indirect costs such as the loss of earnings which women face when they stop work to have a child.[3] The Unit found that, at 1993 rates, a child aged under 11 in a two adult, two child family, living in local authority housing, cost £59.10 per week at the modest but adequate level. This fell to £30.37 per week at the low cost level, but income support still left the family £5.74 per week short of reaching this.[4]

(ii) The Social Fund

Even those who reject the claim that income support is inadequate to live on accept that the levels of payment are too low to allow for saving to cover the cost of 'one-off' purchases of items such as furniture, baby equipment, or even clothing. The Social Fund exists to deal with such needs. Before 1988, persons receiving supplementary benefit (the forerunner of income support) could claim entitlements to 'single payments' for such needs, which were not repayable. The amount expended on such payments reached £335 million in 1985/86, which the Government regarded as unsustainable. Now, income support recipients may apply to a Social Fund officer for a 'community care grant' or for a crisis or budget loan.[5] In 1992/93, £231 million was spent on the Social Fund, after repayment of loans.[6] Community care grants, which are not

---

1 (1994) *Childright* March p 3.

2 The former represented a level sufficient to satisfy prevailing standards of what is necessary for health, nurture and participation in community activities; the latter was confined to items people should not do without, and the *opportunity* to participate in some community activities.

3 Eg, Heather Joshi estimated that a woman on average earnings may forgo £202,500 in lost earnings over her lifetime as the result of having two children, assuming eight years out of employment and a return to lower-paid part-time work: cited in Oldfield and Yu, *The Cost of a Child* (1993) pp ix and 1.

4 *Ibid*. See also Ch 9.

5 The Social Fund also pays a £100 maternity payment to any woman or her partner who is receiving income support or family credit for each baby expected, born or adopted: Social Fund Maternity and Funeral Expenses (General) Regulations 1987, SI 1987/481. This replaced, in 1986, a universal benefit, called maternity grant, of £25.

6 *Social Trends 24* (1994) Table 5.9. The Fund is cash limited, and grants and loans must be budgeted to ensure that each area has money available throughout the year,

repayable, are available, *inter alia*, to families suffering 'exceptional pressures', and may thus be seen as positive support by the state of family life. The circumstances envisaged include the break-up of a relationship, requiring a parent and children to move out of the family home; a move to avoid severe overcrowding in the home; or the re-establishment of the family unit after a separation. However, grants are given at the discretion of the officer, who is advised, in the Social Fund Officer's Guide, that all families face stress, and only *exceptional* pressures can attract a grant, so such examples would have to be supplemented by further extreme circumstances before they became exceptional. In 1992/93, of 1,184,000 applications for a grant, only 27% were successful.[7] A grant may be refused because other family members may be able to help (an effective widening of the usual 'liable relative' rules in social security).[8]

The working of the Social Fund is a perfect example of Donzelot's techniques of normalisation and tutelage. Help may be rendered, but only on condition that the family's intimate circumstances are investigated by officers of the state,[9] and, in the case of loans, that help is repaid through benefit deductions beyond the control of the claimant. The maintenance of lifestyles deemed undesirable or unusual is unlikely to be aided through the Fund.

(iii) Family credit

Concern that dependence upon means-tested benefits such as income support reduces the incentive to take up employment led to the creation of a benefit designed to supplement low-waged employees. This was originally called family income supplement, and was paid to families with children where the wage-earner was in full-time work. Like supplementary benefit, and now income support, it enabled the recipient to claim other benefits, such as free school meals for children, free medical prescriptions and free spectacles and dental treatment. However, relatively few families claimed it, and many parents found that, because of the relative rates of benefits paid, they would be worse off working and

resulting in inconsistency of decision-making depending upon the time of year and locality. It was reported that the net contribution (ie money not recovered from loans) of the Government to the Social Fund was down to £135 million in 1994: *The Observer*, 27 November 1994.

7 *Social Security Statistics 1993* Table A5.03.

8 *Annual Report of the Social Fund Commissioner for 1993/94 on the standards of reviews of Social Fund Inspectors* (1994) pp 57-59.

9 Eg, a Social Fund inspector remitted a case back for consideration requiring the claimant, who had applied for help to buy a pair of shoes, a pair of sheets and two towels, to provide information about the number of pairs of shoes her son possessed: 'a detailed list of all the sheets and duvet covers...[and] a list of all the towels available to the family', *Annual Report (ibid)* p 70.

receiving it than remaining unemployed. It was replaced by family credit in 1988, which was intended to provide a more generous and real advantage to those who qualified. The number of recipients did indeed rise, from 125,000 in 1981-82 to 420,000 in 1992-93.[10]

To be eligible, the claimant or his or her partner must be responsible for a child normally living in the same household who is under 16 (or under 19 and in full-time education), and be normally engaged in remunerative work lasting 16 hours a week or more.[11] A complicated calculation is carried out to determine entitlement, comparing the family's net income and prescribed 'applicable amounts'.[12] Like child benefit, it is generally paid to the woman of the family, emphasising the aim of ensuring that the money is used to benefit the family rather than the wage-earner. When the Government brought forward its proposals to improve the collection of child support maintenance after relationship breakdown, it made a specific attempt to recognise the special position of single parent families by enabling lone parents receiving maintenance payments to keep £15 per week of these before they are taken into account as net income in the family credit calculation. It was claimed that this would encourage lone parents to take up employment rather than remain dependent upon income support, but it seems to have been recognised that this was an insufficient incentive, and further encouragement was proposed in 1994 through an extra allowance in family credit[13] of up to £38.20 per week, intended to go towards the cost of child care for a child aged under 11 while a parent is at work. However, average childminding costs are estimated at £50 to £70 per week, and receipt of family credit does not act as a passport to benefits such as free school meals, representing a significant loss to some families.[14]

All these measures clearly demonstrate that the role of the state in providing financial support to families is regarded as a secondary one. The state in the United Kingdom will provide a subsistence standard of living for those who would otherwise suffer extreme hardship, and those recipients with highly developed money management skills could support their children adequately on the amounts paid. But many families find themselves with debts which eat into their limited incomes; for example, 443,000 income support claimants had Social Fund loan deductions averaging over £5 per week made from their benefit in 1991 – when

10 *Social Trends 24* (1994) Table 5.9.
11 This is not most people's idea of full-time work, but it was reduced in 1992 from 24 hours (itself not excessive) in order to enable more people to qualify and encourage them to come off income support.
12 Family Credit (General) Regulations 1987, rr 46-48.
13 The allowance also applies to disability working allowance, housing benefit and council tax benefit.
14 *The Observer,* 25 September 1994.

income support is pitched at no more than basic subsistence level anyway. A survey of 354 families with children on low incomes found that a fifth of the parents, and a tenth of the children, had gone hungry in the previous month.[15] It has been said that the ideology of family primacy which enabled the Government to cut back on young people's benefit entitlements and to ignore the fact that many may have no family that they can turn to has led to particularly acute injustice and hardship.[16]

4. HOUSING

Article 27(3) of the United Nations Convention requires states to 'provide material assistance and support programmes, particularly with regard to nutrition, clothing and housing'. Help in securing a home in which to care for children is an aspect of social policy which has been accepted by the Government since the early twentieth century, when measures were taken to control war-time profiteering by slum landlords.[17] Rent controls, security of tenure, the provision of council housing, subsidies and welfare benefits to help cover rent, rates and mortgage interest have all been developed to provide assistance with meeting the costs of a home.

The provision of housing itself involves other forms of assistance. There is no *entitlement* to be housed by the local authority. Housing authorities have a broad discretion to allocate any housing that they have, although they must give 'reasonable preference' to, *inter alia*, large families or those in overcrowded or insanitary conditions,[18] and they must publish a summary of their rules relating to allocation, which must be compatible with general administrative law principles of fairness.[19] The Government, noting that such provision 'sets out only in the broadest of terms the responsibilities of a local authority in the allocation of its housing', proposed replacement by a new basis for allocation which, nonetheless, would still be expressed in general terms and would specify only minimum requirements to be fulfilled by local authorities in

15 C Oppenheim, 'Families and the recession' (1993) *Childright* November, 11, Table 4 and p 14.
16 NCH Action for Children, *A Lost Generation?* (1993).
17 The first legislation was the Increase of Rent and Mortgage Interest (War Restrictions) Act 1915.
18 Housing Act 1985, s 22; *R v Canterbury City Council, ex p Gillespie* (1986) 19 HLR 7. See I Loveland, 'Square Pegs, Round Holes: The "Right" to Council Housing in the Post-War Era' (1992) 19 JLS 339.
19 *R v Port Talbot Borough Council, ex p Jones* [1988] 2 All ER 207. In *R v Tower Hamlets London Borough, ex p Mohib Ali* (1993) 25 HLR 218, a policy of offering inferior accommodation to homeless families compared with those on the waiting list was held lawful in principle.

exercising their discretion.[20] It is doubtful, unless detailed guidance were issued, that this would interfere significantly with the discretion of authorities to operate widely varying 'points' systems for choosing between applicants. Other authorities may simply allocate properties on a date-order basis, and still others might recognise factors other than the physical housing circumstances of applicants, such as marriage breakdown.[1]

There has long been a shortage of accommodation to provide suitable housing for all who need it. By 1994, there were an estimated 1.25 million people on council house waiting lists.[2] Loss of employment, family breakdown or domestic violence might also lead to families finding themselves unable to stay on in their homes.[3] Mortgage debts or rent arrears caused by a drop in income might result in eviction.[4]

The main response to this shortage was legislation enacted in 1977 to impose a duty upon housing authorities to assist people applying to them for accommodation, if they were homeless or threatened with homelessness. The relevant provisions are now contained in the Housing Act 1985, Part III. A person is homeless under the Act if there is no accommodation in Great Britain which he or she (together with any other person who normally resides as a member of the family or in circumstances in which it is reasonable for that person to reside with him or her) is entitled to occupy, or if the applicant cannot secure entry to the accommodation, or it is probable that occupation will lead to violence or threats of violence from some other person residing in it and likely to carry out the threats.[5] Any such person is entitled to advice and assistance to secure accommodation. However, the housing authority owe a higher duty where the homeless person has a 'priority need'. Such a need will be held to exist, *inter alia*, where the person has dependent children who reside, or might reasonably be expected to reside with him or her.[6] For such applicants, provided the housing authority are satisfied that they did not become homeless or threatened with homelessness intentionally, the authority must take reasonable steps to arrange for

---

20 Department of the Environment, *Access to Local Authority and Housing Association Tenancies* (1994) para 20.
1 J Bull, *Housing Consequences of Relationship Breakdown* (1993) para 3.141.
2 *The Guardian,* 19 January 1994.
3 See J Bull, *Housing Consequences of Relationship Breakdown* (1993).
4 The number of homes in the UK repossessed for non-payment of mortgages almost trebled between 1989 and 1990 and reached 75,000 in 1991: *Social Trends 24* (1994) p 116. However, it did then begin to fall back, in the wake of lower interest rates and different arrears management policies.
5 Section 58.
6 Section 59.

accommodation.[7] Under this scheme, such successful applicants take priority over everyone else on the authority's waiting list. In 1993/94, the Government proposed changing the law to provide that they would simply be entitled to be housed for up to a year (renewable should circumstances require).[8] This was proposed despite fears that such a policy would result in families being shuttled from one private let to another, and that children might have to move schools several times.[9] The ostensible rationale for the change was to redress the unfairness caused to those already on the waiting list who were kept from obtaining accommodation because the homeless could leapfrog over them. In fact, research found that 59% of those accepted as homeless were *already* on the waiting list.[10] The underlying reason for the move to a more restrictive attitude was the moral panic during 1993 and 1994 concerning the alleged increasing numbers of young women having children in order to leave home and be housed by the council.[11] But the changes would affect all those found homeless and in priority need, not just single mothers. The Government's new policy therefore had the potential to destabilise further all homeless parents with children, even where they conformed otherwise to the 'traditional' family model which the Government had hoped to advocate. In the face of widespread opposition and a slim Parliamentary majority, political expediency led to the shelving of these plans.[12]

A finding of *intentional* homelessness further weakens the position of families with children, since it prevents their receiving priority for any help in acquiring accommodation. A bold attempt to avoid such a finding was made in *R v Oldham Metropolitan Borough Council, ex p Garlick*[13] There, in two of the appeals, applications were made by the four year old sons of parents who had been evicted from their homes due to non-payment of mortgage instalments or rent. The House of Lords upheld the

---

7 The authority need not provide accommodation if the applicant or person residing with him or her has no local connection with the area, and *does* have such a connection with another area. The authority may then cast the duty onto the other relevant authority (but they may not do so if the applicant would run the risk of violence in the other area): s 67.

8 Department of the Environment, *Access to Local Authority and Housing Association Tenancies* (1994) para 6. The original proposals were altered slightly (but insignificantly) in the light of public reactions, see *The Guardian*, 19 July 1994. They also proposed redefining homelessness to require that the applicant be *roofless*; para 8.4.

9. *The Guardian* 19 January 1994.

10 See D Cowan and J Fionda, 'Back to Basics: The Government's Homelessness Consultation Paper' (1994) 57 MLR 610, at p 613.

11 Cowan and Fionda, *ibid* argue that there is no evidence to justify such a belief.

12 *The Times,* 31 October 1994.

13 [1993] AC 509. See D Cowan and J Fionda, 'New Angles on Homelessness' [1993] JSWFL 403.

lower courts' view that housing authorities owe no duty to such children directly. The Act presupposed that young children would be the dependants of their parents or other carers, and that any offer of accommodation had to be capable of being considered by the applicant – a four year old child could hardly do so.[14] However, Lord Griffiths pointed out that local authorities have a duty under s 20(1) of the Children Act 1989 to:

'provide accommodation for any child in need within their area who appears to them to require accommodation as a result of ... the person who has been caring for him being prevented ... from providing him with suitable accommodation or care'.

Furthermore, s 27 of the Children Act empowers local authorities to request help from other authorities in the exercise of their functions under that Part of the Act, and where such a request is made, the other authority are under a duty to comply if it 'is compatible with their own statutory or other duties and obligations and does not unduly prejudice the discharge of any of their functions'. An attempt to utilise these provisions to avoid the consequences of a finding of intentional homelessness failed in *R v Northavon District Council, ex p Smith*.[15] The House of Lords ruled that the duty under the Children Act does not require a housing authority to overturn their finding of intentional homelessness and to provide accommodation, especially where, as in the instant case, this would have the effect of exacerbating the wait of others on the housing list.[16] The House considered that, if the housing authority would not (or could not) accede to a request from social services to house the family,[17] the onus was on the social services department to protect the children of Mr Smith by providing financial assistance towards the accommodation of the family or by exercising the other powers available to them under the Children Act (discussed below in Chapter 12). This begs the question as to whether social services could in fact provide the assistance required without necessitating splitting up the family and placing the children with foster carers or in a children's home.

Direct assistance in the provision of housing for families is no longer a major concern for government. (The United Kingdom's First Report to the United Nations Committee on the Rights of the Child makes no mention of housing policy, despite express reference to the provision of housing in Article 27(3).) The rhetoric of support for the family has for

---

14 Compare a child under 16 who leaves home voluntarily: *Kelly v Monklands District Council* 1985 SC 333.

15 [1994] 2 AC 402: see G Holgate, 'Housing Dependent Children' [1994] Fam Law 582.

16 There were 2,632 people on Northavon's list, and families could expect to wait between two and a half and three years to be housed.

17 In considering this question, the authority must have regard to the code of guidance, *Homelessness, Code of Guidance for Local Authorities* (3rd ed, 1991), which advises that s 20 of the Children Act must be taken into account.

long not been matched by action to relieve the plight of those families who have no home or live in unacceptable conditions of overcrowding or squalor. Parents are left with the responsibility of finding some sort of accommodation for themselves and their children, with the intention increasingly obvious that the state will regard itself as obliged to provide only a safety net of temporary assistance, if that, where the alternative will be the break-up of the family unit. As with the old Poor Law, and with the rules on entitlement to income support for young people, the emphasis has become one of self-help, or help from other family members first; state aid as a last resort.[18]

5. HEALTH AND MEDICAL CARE

(a) The primacy of the state's interest

The principle that parents' rights should exist primarily for the benefit of their children came through a series of cases relating to medical treatment of young people. The *Gillick* decision[19] and its succeeding case law affirmed that parents' interest in their children's health and well-being is less determinative as the child reaches adulthood. But the state has an interest in the child's health and well-being, and this interest will not always be identical to that of either the child or the parents. For example, in *Gillick* itself, the 'policy' dimension in their lordships' reasoning is strong. The majority in the House of Lords recognised that, unpleasant as it might be for parents to contemplate their children having under-age sex, it was still more undesirable for society and the state to envisage them having unprotected under-age sex.[20] As part of that reasoning, the majority concluded that the disapproving parent could not veto her child's receiving treatment, provided that the child was of sufficient maturity to understand the consequences. Similarly, the courts have overridden parental refusal to consent to treatment for their children, where the refusal was based on religious belief, and where otherwise the child's welfare would be endangered.[1] Where the parents and child *both* agree that treatment should be refused, the courts may again override that refusal:

> "'Parents may be free to become martyrs themselves, but it does not follow that they are free in identical circumstances to make martyrs of their children before they

18 The reverse of the way most people view their kin: see J Finch, *Family Obligations and Social Change* (1989) p 240.
19 *Gillick v West Norfolk and Wisbech Area Health Authority* [1986] AC 112: see Ch 6.
20 Lord Fraser at 173F-174F.
 1 *Re S (a minor) (Medical Treatment)* [1993] 1 FLR 376.

have reached the age of full and legal discretion when they can make choices for themselves."... this court, exercising its prerogative of protection, should be very slow to allow an infant to martyr himself.'[2]

Indeed, according to Lord Donaldson MR, where the court disagrees with the competent child's decision, *either to consent to or refuse treatment*, it can override that decision.[3]

Such cases have usually been heard in wardship proceedings or, since the enactment of s 100 of the Children Act 1989 (discussed in Chapter 13), under the High Court's inherent jurisdiction. Both are aspects of the High Court's *parens patriae* jurisdiction. John Seymour has argued that it is unclear what is entailed in the exercise of this jurisdiction. Examining the pronouncements of the eighteenth and nineteenth century judges, he asks:

'Did [the judges] view the monarch – and hence themselves – as vested with the powers of a natural parent, or were they invoking the powers of a monarch who was much more than a parent-figure? .... It might be thought to be safer – and more consistent with the origins of the *parens patriae* jurisdiction ... for a court exercising that jurisdiction to see itself as a surrogate parent and hence limited to the exercise of parental powers.'[4]

But this would be to ignore the state's independent interest in the child as its citizen. If there are decisions which parents cannot themselves take, even where these are arguably in the child's best interests (sterilisation and the decision to discontinue treatment for the terminally ill are the prime examples in the case law[5]), it would seem undesirable to adopt the (dissenting) view of Brennan J in an Australian decision concerning sterilisation[6] that the court could not do so either. This would simply leave a child denied a course of treatment or action which would actually be in his or her best interests.

In fact, in the cases on this issue, the courts have considered proceedings as being concerned primarily to determine whether actions taken by medical staff will be lawful or unlawful, rather than what those actions should be. For example, *Re J (a minor) (Child in Care: Medical Treatment)*,[7] concerned a severely physically and mentally handicapped boy of 16 months, who was unlikely to develop further, who required constant care and frequent ventilation, and who had an uncertain, but

---

2 Ward J in *Re E (a minor) (Wardship: Medical Treatment)* [1993] 1 FLR 386 at 394, citing Holmes J in *Prince v Massachusetts* 321 US Rep 158 (1944).

3 *Re W (a minor) (Medical Treatment: Court's Jurisdiction)* [1993] Fam 64; see Ch 6.

4 J Seymour, '*Parens Patriae* and Wardship Powers: Their Nature and Origins' (1994) 14 OJLS 159 p 187.

5 *Re B (a minor)(Wardship: Sterilisation)* [1988] AC 199. We discuss termination of treatment below.

6 *Secretary, Department of Health and Community Services v JWB and SMB* (1992) 106 ALR 385.

7 [1993] Fam 15.

short, expectation of life. The medical professionals involved regarded
further treatment as futile and distressing for him. The Court of Appeal
held that where treatment was considered not to be in the patient's best
interests, it would be an abuse of judicial power to require a medical
practitioner to treat the child in a way contrary to his or her best clinical
judgment.[8] In *Airedale National Health Service Trust v Bland*,[9] the
House of Lords held that it would be lawful for doctors to discontinue
treatment (including artificial feeding) of an adult patient in a persistent
vegetative state. Lord Goff said:

> 'It is ... the function of the judges to state the legal principles upon which the
> lawfulness of the actions of doctors depend; but in the end the decisions to be made
> in individual cases must rest with the doctors themselves.'[10]

Nonetheless, the courts do retain the ultimate decision-making power,
since it is for them to rule on the lawfulness of the proposed course of
action, and, certainly in the most sensitive cases, they have required that
medical professionals seek judicial guidance before acting.[11] The state's
central interest in such issues is therefore upheld and demonstrated by the
role of the courts, and it takes precedence over the interests of family, and
the doctors. Of course, while the judges in these sorts of cases decide
upon the lawfulness of doctors' actions on the basis of the *patient's* best
interests, they inevitably assess those interests in the light of the values
they proclaim on society's behalf, and their exercise of judicial office
itself is an aspect of the interest that the state has in the matter.[12]

(b) The provision of health care by the state

Article 24 of the United Nations Convention on the Rights of the Child
requires states to 'recognise the right of the child to the enjoyment of the
highest attainable standard of health and to facilities for the treatment of
illness and rehabilitation of health'. Among other things, states must take
appropriate measures to diminish infant and child mortality, ensure the
provision of necessary medical assistance and health care for all children

---

8 See also, *Re J (a minor)(Wardship: Medical Treatment)* [1991] Fam 33.
9 [1993] AC 789.
10 At 871E-F.
11 In *Airedale National Health Service Trust v Bland*, eg, all their lordships regarded an
   application to the court as a prerequisite to the doctors deciding to terminate
   treatment, though cf *Frenchay Healthcare NHS Trust v S* [1994] 1 WLR 601, where
   the Master of the Rolls suggested that this might not always be the case.
12 For conflicting views on the extent to which the state should intervene in children's,
   or parents' health decisions, see K McK Norrie, 'Medical Treatment of Children and
   Young Persons' and J Haldane, 'Children, Families, Autonomy and the State' in D
   Morgan and G Douglas (eds) *Constituting Families* (1994).

and provide education and guidance for parents on child health and nutrition. This obligation is apparently met in the United Kingdom, where the provision of health care has been regarded, since the creation of the National Health Service in 1946, as a matter of central concern for the state. The concept of a National Health Service may be seen as the example, *par excellence*, of a universal benefit administered by the state for the welfare of all its citizens, regardless of their personal means or circumstances. Every person is entitled to be registered with a general practitioner for health care, and to receive emergency treatment from a GP, ambulance service or hospital. However, the reality has been a patchy service delivering a variable quality of care and unable to meet the health needs or desires of all those seeking to use it.[13]

Alongside such facilities, there is a panoply of further, more specialised services, many designed to promote the health of children. For example, health authorities have a duty to provide appropriate facilities for the care of pregnant women, new mothers and young children.[14] They employ community midwives and health visitors (who are qualified nurses, and frequently former midwives) to carry out this task. The community midwife monitors the health of a new born baby up to 28 days after birth, and the health visitor then takes over, and retains a monitoring role, carrying out periodical checks on the child's health and development until the child goes to school. Health visiting is a unique service, which developed from voluntary work at the start of the twentieth century intended to improve standards of child care and reduce the appallingly high levels of infant mortality. Contrary to the general trend in the provision of welfare services, it is a *universal* service which is provided automatically to all mothers and their children, and indeed, a refusal to permit the health visitor to see the child would be likely to trigger a child protection investigation. The system therefore operates both as a *facility* to parents who seek advice and reassurance on parenting, and as a form of surveillance.

'With their regular contact and access to children nurses [ie community nurses – midwives and health visitors] have a crucial part to play in protecting children. A nurse may be the first person to identify a child who is in need and who acts to bring the child to the attention of social services.'[15]

Family health needs are also met by the provision of school medical services, where the health of children can be periodically checked,[16] and free services such as dental or eye treatment and free prescriptions, for children under 16 and pregnant women and those who have given birth in the past 12 months.[17]

13 R Cranston, *Legal Foundations of the Welfare State* (1985) p 270.
14 National Health Service Act 1977, s 3(1)(d).
15 Department of Health, *Child Protection: Guidance for Senior Nurses, Health Visitors and Midwives* (1992) p v.
16 National Health Service Act 1977, s 5(1)(a).
17 National Health Service (Charges for Drugs and Appliances) Regulations 1989, SI 1989/419, r 6.

The state's provision of these services demonstrates its acceptance of a duty to take responsibility for children's health. But there is a tension in the system between providing a *service* to be used or not according to the willingness of parents, and providing a *mandatory* minimum level of health care of benefit to the community as a whole. For example, despite the overwhelming state interest in ensuring that all children receive inoculations against childhood diseases, there is no legal duty upon parents to have their children inoculated, and they may, and do, decline to do so.[18] Governments have sought to persuade, through education, rather than to coerce, paying in this instance more than lip-service to the *primary* role of parents to determine their children's health care, and providing another instance of the degree to which a minimum level of 'care' is required of the parent 'with care'.[19]

6. CHILD CARE FACILITIES

It might be regarded as axiomatic that whereas the state assists parents to care for their children by means of finance, housing and health facilities, the caring itself should be the primary responsibility of the parents. This is indeed the position in the United Kingdom. There is no statutory duty to provide child care facilities for parents who are working, even though Article 18(3) of the United Nations Convention requires states to 'take all appropriate measures to ensure that children of working parents have the right to benefit from child-care services and facilities for which they are eligible'. All that exists is a duty upon local authorities, under s 18(1) of the Children Act 1989, to provide such day care for children in need who are not yet at school or who require provision outside school hours or during school holidays 'as is appropriate'.[20] Limiting the duty to cover only those children 'in need' defines child-care as a matter for the state only where the child is in some way at risk or is disabled and therefore requires extra help. Once again, it is an example of a 'safety-net' service for those who cannot find help anywhere else. It also assumes that a parent is usually available to care for the child during the day. This ignores the high rate of working mothers in the United Kingdom. Sixty-five per cent of women with

18 Rates of vaccination for whooping cough have fluctuated depending upon public confidence in the safety of the vaccine: the percentage of children vaccinated was 78% in 1971, declined to 39% in 1976 and reached 88% in 1991-92: *Social Trends 24* (1994) Table 7.21.
19 See Ch 6.
20 'Day care' means 'any form of care or supervised activity provided for children during the day (whether or not it is provided on a regular basis)': s 18(4). The phrase 'children in need' is defined in s 17(10) and is discussed below and in Ch 12.

dependent children were working in 1992. Much of this employment is in part-time work, with 31% of women with children under the age of five in part-time jobs, compared with just 11% in full-time employment.[1] Nonetheless, 82% of such mothers had to make child-care arrangements to enable them to do their jobs, so for many parents, hours of working are not sufficiently flexible to allow them to avoid the complication of arranging child-care.[2] The extent to which lack of child-care facilities inhibits employment for mothers is shown most strikingly by the fact that lone mothers are much less likely to have either full or part-time employment; only 42% of them were working in 1992/93, and only 22% with children under five.[3]

Parents may make use of paid services, offered commercially or with a subsidy, such as day nurseries or after-school clubs. Alternatively, child-care may be offered in a person's home, either by a child-minder, who cares for the child in her home, or by a nanny, who cares for the child in the child's own home. The state has accepted a residual responsibility to children to ensure that they are cared for adequately by those other than their families since the 'baby-farming' scandals of the nineteenth century,[4] which led to a movement to press for the certification and registration of child-minders. The proposal was opposed by those who saw it as an infringement of parental liberties. For example, the Committee for Amending the Law in Points where it is Injurious to Women objected not to registration itself, but to the consequent obligation of parents to employ only registered minders:

'the State should forbear to limit their perfect freedom in this, as in all matters connected with the rearing and maintaining of their families'.[5]

Nonetheless, despite such objection, the Infant Life Protection Act 1872 made a limited inroad into this freedom by requiring anyone receiving for reward two or more children under the age of one year for more than 24 hours to register with the local authority, who could decline to register, or de-register them. The Act was aimed only at baby-farmers, excluding orphanages, Poor Law foster parents and also day-carers, but it was the precursor of more wide-ranging legislation, the descendant of which is Part X of the Children Act 1989.

This provides that day-care or child-minding offered for reward (except the employment of nannies) must be registered with the appropriate local authority.[6] The exemption of nannies from this requirement is only

1 *General Household Survey 1992* (1994) Tables 7.8, 7.9.
2 *Social Trends 24* (1994) Table 2.10.
3 *General Household Survey 1992* (1994) Table 2.29.
4 I Pinchbeck and M Hewitt, *Children in English Society* (1973) vol 2, pp 613-616.
5 *Ibid* at p 618.
6 It is an offence to provide day-care or child-minding within the terms of the Act without being registered: s 78. Child-minders must be served with an 'enforcement notice' requiring them to register first.

explicable on the basis that the Government did not intend to require middle-class career women to go to the inconvenience of having their nannies registered, and their homes therefore subject to inspection or refusal of the application by the social services department of the local authority. Local authorities must impose 'reasonable requirements' upon child-minders and other providers, for example, relating to the number of children they may look after and the facilities offered.[7] Refusal by the authority to register, or de-registration for a failure or refusal to abide by requirements may be appealed in the family proceedings court.[8] Authorities must be flexible in their approach to registration. In *Sutton London Borough Council v Davis*,[9] it was held that magistrates were entitled to query a local authority's policy of declining to register a child-minder who refuses to abstain from smacking the children in her care, even with the parent's consent. The authority had relied upon Department of Health guidance that corporal punishment should not be used by those providing day-care facilities.[10] The Department revised this guidance to permit smacking, but not shaking, so long as the parents have agreed to this form of discipline.[11] The decision and shift in policy may be seen as a powerful endorsement of a parent's right to choose a carer who will take care of the child in the privacy of a home (rather than a nursery) and whose views on child-care and discipline mirror his or her own. Together with the position concerning nannies, it is a relic of the importance attached to parental choice evinced in the nineteenth century.[12]

While these provisions are intended to provide a more effective monitoring system of day-care, they are still but a small interference with the parents' rights to arrange for their children's care, and as we have noted, there has hitherto been no attempt to make universal provision available. Although the Government reported to the United Nations Committee on the Rights of the Child that '9 out of 10 children will have gone to some form of group activity – nursery education, playgroup or day nursery – before they reach 5',[13] this masks the fact that the majority

7 Sections 72, 73.
8 Section 77. See C Barton, '"Guidance", Childminding and Smacking' [1994] Fam Law 284.
9 [1994] Fam 241
10 *Family Support, Day Care and Educational Provision for Young Children* (1991) vol 2, Guidance and Regulations, para 6.22. See C Barton, '"Guidance", Childminding and Smacking' [1994] Fam Law 284.
11 *The Children Act 1989: registration of child-minders* LAC (94) 23.
12 Compare *T (a minor) v Surrey County Council* [1994] 4 All ER 577 where Scott Baker J held that a local authority may be liable for negligent mis-statement in failing to warn a mother that a registered child-minder is suspected by them of child abuse. Local authorities can hardly be blamed for seeking to avoid registering child-minders who resort to physical punishment and thus to reduce their chances of liability under this ruling.
13 *The UK's First Report to the UN Committee on the Rights of the Child* (1994) para 1.21.

of such children attend for only a few hours per week, and their parents are dependent upon private sector provision. Fewer than 45% of the 1.5 million children attending registered day care were in public sector places in 1993, and the average duration of attendance was five to six hours per week.[14] Thirty-six to thirty-eight per cent of working mothers with children under five rely upon other relatives or friends to help them out with child-care.[15] A liberal democratic state would not wish to interfere in such arrangements through any form of inspection.[16] It is when arrangements break down and no substitute care can be provided that the state may be compelled to intervene in order to protect the child.[17]

7. HELP FOR PARENTS WHOSE CHILDREN HAVE DISABILITIES[18]

Where a child is born with, or later develops a disability, the need for state assistance may become paramount. In addition to medical care, there may be a continuing requirement for financial assistance to cope with the extra costs of caring for the child, for special therapy or educational provision, or for the child to live away from the family in a home or other facility where expert care and attention can be provided. It is the child with disabilities who perhaps brings home most forcefully the fact that the parent/child relationship does not terminate when a child reaches the age of majority. One of the greatest concerns for the parents of such a child will be to ensure that loving and protective care will continue to be provided for the whole of their child's life, which, for many, will mean after the parents' own deaths.[19]

Financial assistance is provided by the state through a range of benefits, which may be seen as symbolising the state's acceptance of its special obligation to ensure that a person with disabilities is able to live at a decent and humane standard, irrespective of the means of that person's immediate family. A parent may claim disability living allowance on behalf of the *child*, the amount payable dependent upon the degree of the child's disability. Where the child is aged over five, a 'mobility

14 *The Times,* 17 June 1994; Royal Society of Arts, *Start Right* (1994).
15 *Social Trends 24* (1994) Table 2.10.
16 Though Andrew Bainham notes that baby-sitters might fall within the legislation: *Children: The modern law* (1993) p 362.
17 We explore this in detail in Ch 13.
18 Provision of education for such children is discussed in the next chapter, in the context of special educational needs which may also affect children without disabilities of the kind dealt with here.
19 The sterilisation cases, eg, *Re B (a minor) (Wardship: Sterilisation)* [1988] AC 199; *Re F (Mental Patient: Sterilisation)* [1990] 2 AC 1, are a good illustration.

component' may be added to help cover the costs of transport where the child is unable or virtually unable to walk.[20] The parent may also claim invalid care allowance where he or she is engaged in caring for a severely disabled child (provided the parent is not also working for earnings of more than a prescribed amount per week).[1] Where the parent is receiving income support, disabled child premium (worth £19.45 per week in 1994/95) and carer premium (worth £12.40 per week) may be payable in addition to the benefits already described. Where the child has to have a special diet or extra laundry facilities or other special facilities, income support claimants may apply to the Social Fund.

Social work assistance is provided for children with disabilities under the Children Act 1989. Before its enactment, such children were dealt with primarily through powers contained in health and welfare legislation, which did not distinguish sufficiently between the needs of children and adults. This position was unsatisfactory, and disabled children were included in the Children Act in order to benefit from the services and safeguards which it provides for all other children needing extra social work help.[2] Under Part III of the Act, local authorities owe certain duties to children 'in need'. Section 17(10) includes disabled children within the definition of those taken to be in need, and s 17(11) defines a disabled child as one who is:

'blind, deaf or dumb or suffers from mental disorder of any kind or is substantially and permanently handicapped by illness, injury or congenital deformity or such other disability as may be prescribed'.[3]

We look in detail at the duties imposed upon local authorities by Part III in Chapter 12, but it may be noted here that extra duties are cast upon them in respect of disabled children, under Sch 2 to the Act. In order to identify those children who are disabled and plan and provide facilities for them, authorities must open and maintain a register of disabled children in their area and provide services designed to minimise the effect on disabled children of their disabilities and give them the opportunity to lead lives which are as normal as possible. Official guidance advises authorities that this may involve the identification, diagnosis, assessment and treatment of the children, with the funding and

---

20 Social Security Contributions and Benefits Act 1992, ss 71-73, Social Security (Disability Living Allowance) Regulations 1991, SI 1991/2890.
 1 Social Security Contributions and Benefits Act 1992, s 70 and Social Security (Invalid Care Allowance) Regulations 1976, SI 1976/409.
 2 See, eg, *The Law on Child Care and Family Services,* Cm 62, paras 15-17.
 3 This definition, which might be regarded as stigmatising, was used because it is the same as applies to adults with disabilities under the National Assistance Act 1948, but a report by the Association of Metropolitan Authorities recommended a new definition, more in keeping with current attitudes to disability: Association of Metropolitan Authorities, *Special Child, Special Needs* (1994).

provision of special equipment if required. Close co-operation with other agencies and authorities already involved with the child will be necessary.[4]

Where the authority provides accommodation for a disabled child, there is a duty, 'so far as is reasonably practicable, [to] secure that the accommodation is not unsuitable to his particular needs'.[5] This somewhat qualified duty extends not just to the provision of special homes for disabled children, but also, consistently with the general principle of the Act to promote the care of children by and within their families, to the provision of council housing for the child and his or her family.[6]

However, research carried out by the Social Services Inspectorate in England found that there was a sizeable mismatch between the demand for local authority services and their provision. Inspection of four local authorities in May 1993 found that their practice fell far short of what is required, with unreliable registers held by different agencies, such as health, education and social services instead of a combined register; assessments of children's needs carried out by individual agencies rather than combined; inadequate levels of services available, so that they tended to be provided when parents had reached crisis point; and a lack of adequate consultation with parents and the children concerned to identify what was needed.[7] Disabled children remain a severely disadvantaged group.

So far, we have examined the basic provision made by the state to enable and encourage parents to care for their children. In an international comparative study assessing the package of 'cash benefits, tax reliefs or services in kind which provides support for families raising children'[8] the United Kingdom emerged in the middle of a league table of Western countries, scoring higher for its package for one parent families and smaller families, and lower for larger families, those with pre-school children, those requiring special care, and those families who are the poorest. Such a score reflects the move to the safety net approach to family support which we have outlined. We look in the next chapter at the need to educate and socialise children for adulthood, and consider how far there is a reciprocal duty upon parents and the state in meeting this need, and how far the state's interest in its future workforce requires an approach which goes beyond the philosophy of the safety net.

---

4   *Family Support, Day Care and Educational Provision for Young Children* (1991) Vol 2, Guidance and Regulations, paras 2.17, 1.21

5   Section 23(8).

6   However, in *R v Brent London Borough, ex p S* [1994] 1 FLR 203, it was held that there is no duty to provide a home which is suitable in every respect for the particular child, still less a duty to buy or rent in the private sector if the authority has no accommodation of its own to offer.

7   *Children Act Report 1993* (1994) paras 2.28-2.38.

8   J Bradshaw *et al, Support for Children: A comparison of arrangements in fifteen countries* (1993) p 1.

CHAPTER 11

Educative duties

1. REINFORCEMENT OF VALUES AND CONDUCT THROUGH EDUCATION

(a) The right to education

Article 28 of the United Nations Convention on the Rights of the Child requires states to:

> 'recognise the right of the child to education, and with a view to achieving this right progressively and on the basis of equal opportunity...
> (a) make primary education compulsory and available free to all ...
> (b) encourage the development of different forms of secondary education ... make them available and accessible to every child, and take appropriate measures such as the introduction of free education and offering financial assistance in case of need;
> (c) make higher education accessible to all on the basis of capacity'.

By making primary education compulsory, such documents create a duty upon parents to see that their children receive at least some education, thus recognising the parental socialising function. But the need to balance state and parental interests is reflected by the further requirements that education must be directed, *inter alia*, to:

> 'the development of respect for the child's parents, his or her own cultural identity, language and values, for the national values of the country in which the child is living, the country from which he or she may originate and for civilizations different from his or her own'.[1]

---

1 United Nations Convention, Article 29(1)(c). As McGoldrick points out, it will not be easy to reconcile all these; see D McGoldrick, 'The United Nations Convention on the Rights of the Child' (1991) 5 *International Journal of Law and the Family* 132 at p 148 . See also, Article 5, which requires states to respect the rights of parents to 'provide, in a manner consistent with the evolving capacities of the child, appropriate direction and guidance in the exercise by the child of the rights' given by the Convention.

The importance attached to parental interests is illustrated even more sharply by Article 2 of the First Protocol to the European Convention on Human Rights, whose wording perhaps reflects the time at which it was drafted, with much greater emphasis placed upon the family rather than individual members within it. It provides that:

'No person shall be denied the right to education. In the exercise of the functions which it assumes in relation to education and to teaching, the state shall respect the right of parents to ensure such education and teaching in conformity with their own religious and philosophical convictions.'

In both the nineteenth and twentieth centuries in England and Wales, education has been a battleground of opposing ideologies and strategies centring upon the question of to what extent the state should take over from parents the right and duty to inculcate values and teach skills to children who will grow up to become productive workers and consumers. In the Victorian era, this debate focused upon whether it should be made a legally enforceable duty upon parents to provide education of some sort for their children. In the twentieth century, the emphasis was upon the delivery of education by the state and more latterly upon the content of that education. Yet although the focus has been different, the language and arguments used have been very similar.

Concern about the educational attainments of children relates first to an apparent failure to compete in the international market-place[2] – children are said to lack the skills and intellectual capacities needed in advanced capitalist societies in a global market where low-skilled jobs are done by third-world workers for low wages which it is impossible for British employers to match.[3] Secondly, children are said to be more unruly and disrespectful of others than in the past.[4] The educational remedies propounded for these two defects are first, greater control over what is taught, and how teachers teach it, and secondly, a return to the forms of discipline and socialisation which are alleged to have been more

2 The fear of being unable to compete with other countries for trade can be traced back at least to 1818, when Lord Brougham, chairing the Select Committee on the Education of the Lower Orders of Society, described England as the worst educated country in Europe. For the history of the development of state education, see K Evans, *The Development and Structure of the English School System* (1985).

3 In the nineteenth and early twentieth centuries, there was fear also that an ill-educated population could not cope with the demands of military service and that the interests of the Empire were being jeopardised.

4 The myth of the golden age of respectful and law-abiding children is explored (and exploded) in G Pearson, *Hooligan* (1983). Indeed, in recent years, calls to expand nursery education for pre-school age children have been buttressed by the argument that this can have a beneficial effect on the economy and the crime rate: *The Times*, 1 September 1993, reported a study in Michigan, USA showing that for every $1 spent on day care, the community recovered $7 in lower crime rates, greater taxation (through employed mothers) and improved employability of the children.

effective in the past. But since it is recognised that children spend only a relatively small amount of their time in school, parents must be co-opted in the drive for improvement, not only by being given greater responsibility to ensure their children attend school (or at least, a greater sense of that responsibility) but also by a greater say in which school they attend.[5] The most recent manifestation of this approach is apparent in the Parent's Charter, where there is a dual emphasis on consumer choice and parental responsibility. But it is the *parents* who are regarded as the consumers.[6]

The introduction of compulsory education for children in the nineteenth century was prompted by these concerns, and others.[7] Legislation limiting or prohibiting child labour in industry led to many children wandering the streets with the potential for mischief, disorder and exploitation, as exposed by Charles Dickens' *Oliver Twist*, for example. The expansion of the franchise to the industrial working class also led to fears of the likely political consequences of having an illiterate and ignorant electorate. As industrial processes developed in complexity, employers saw the advantages in having a disciplined and at least partly-skilled labour force and therefore supported the expansion of elementary education. (They wanted useful workers, however, not politicised intellectuals who might stir up discontent, a sentiment which perhaps still underlies distrust of the social sciences today.) The Elementary Education Act 1870 permitted the establishment of school boards which could set up schools for local children, remitting fees if required, to supplement any existing provision (hitherto haphazardly provided by church schools and other voluntary bodies). The Act did not make education compulsory, nor free of charge;[8] rather, it was intended to fill in the gaps left by voluntary provision to enable any parents who wished to have their children educated to do so. Compulsory education was not introduced until 1880, and even then, older pupils were required only to attend schools for part of the day, and

5 See N Harris, *Law and Education, Regulation, Consumerism and the Education System* (1993).

6 See, eg, the Welsh Office, *Education: A Charter for Parents in Wales* (1994) p 2: 'You have a right to a free school place for your child': the *child* is not expressed as having a right to such a place. 'Parent' is defined, for most purposes, in s 114 (1D) of the Education Act 1944 (as amended by the Children Act 1989, Sch 13, para 10), as including a non-parent who has pa rental responsibility, or who has care of the child. It does not appear to include an unmarried father, without parental responsibility, unless he has care of the child.

7 For a philosophical perspective on the growth of compulsory, and regimented, education, see M Foucault, *Discipline and Punish* (1975, trans 1977) as an aspect, along with prisons, factories, and hospitals, of increased state control over individuals.

8 The possibility of charging fees for attendance at elementary schools was not finally abolished until 1918. Free (as opposed to awards of scholarships) secondary schooling was not introduced until the Education Act 1944.

the school-leaving age was ten. There were tensions, first, between the needs of the economy for a skilled (or drilled) work-force and those of parents to support their families with the help of older offspring; and secondly, between the right of the state to assert what should be taught and the right of parents to control what their children learnt. Such tensions were reflected in the low leaving age, which permitted parents to turn their children into economically productive units, but only as soon as industry could make use of them, and the control over the curriculum by Her Majesty's Inspectorate[9] whose annual inspections led to a strong ethos of 'teaching to the test'. At the same time, there continued the rights of parents to withdraw their children from religious education classes and acts of worship or to send them to private schools, and the continuing existence (and state support) of church schools as alternatives to those run by boards or, later, by local authorities.[10]

(b) The parent's duty to ensure the child's education

The modern law of education remains based on the model created over a century ago, and it is based on parental rights and duties, with no emphasis placed on the rights or views of the child. Children have no legal right to a say in which school they will attend or whether they will attend religious or sex education classes, although they could seek leave to apply for a specific issue or prohibited steps order under s 8 of the Children Act 1989 to have the question determined by the court.[11] It has been argued convincingly that this position is not in conformity with Article 12 of the United Nations Convention.[12] Parents[13] are under a duty, under s 36 of the Education Act 1944, to cause a child of compulsory school age[14] to receive efficient full-time education suitable to his age, ability and aptitude and to any special educational needs he may have. Such education need not be received at a school, in which case the local education authority (LEA) must be satisfied that the duty is being met,

---

9 Set up as early as 1839, and with the outcome of inspections determining the amount of financial support received by schools – the 'payment by results' system; see K Evans *The Development and Structuring of the English School System* (1985) and L Rose, *The Erosion of Childhood* (1991) p 119.
10 See generally, Evans, *ibid*.
11 See Chs 6 and 7.
12 N Harris *Law and Education, Regulation, Consumerism and the Education System* (1993) p 195.
13 C Piper, 'Parental Responsibility and the Education Acts' [1994] Fam Law 146.
14 Currently from 5 to 16 years.

but Neville Harris argues that it has proved difficult to satisfy LEA education officers that suitable education can be provided outside the school setting, and 'well-nigh impossible' since the introduction of the national curriculum.[15]

Where a parent fails to do so, the LEA may serve a school attendance order requiring the parent to register the child at a particular school.[16] Non-compliance with the order may result in prosecution of the parent. Where a child is registered at a school but is not attending regularly without good excuse,[17] the parent is again guilty of an offence.

As an alternative, or in addition to such measures, the LEA may apply (after consultation with the local social services department) to the family proceedings court for an education supervision order.[18] The separation of non-school attendance from other grounds for concern regarding children's care and development necessitating state intervention was recommended by the Inter-Departmental Working Party reviewing child care law in the mid-1980s. It argued that the old law, whereby truancy by the child was a primary ground for granting a care order vesting parental responsibility in the local authority, operated in an arbitrary or unfair way, focusing attention upon the truancy rather than the reasons for it, and serving to draw more children into the net of compulsory care. The working party concluded that if the child's development were at risk because of lack of education, it would be preferable for local authority social services departments to obtain care or supervision orders concentrating directly on the child's welfare. School attendance could be achieved without such heavy-handed intervention, by means of a more limited process.[19]

---

15 N Harris, *Law and Education, Regulation, Consumerism and the Education System* (1993) p 209.

16 Education Act 1993, Pt IV.

17 The statutory grounds for justified absence from school are that the child has leave of absence from the school, is sick, has leave for a day of religious observance, that the child is prevented by some unavoidable cause from attending (which must relate to the child, not the parent – *Jenkins v Howells* [1949] 1 All ER 942 – parent's illness necessitating child's remaining at home to do housework not a legitimate excuse), or that the school is not within walking distance and no suitable arrangements have been made by the LEA for the child to attend the school. Parental objection that the *type* of schooling offered by the LEA is unsuitable is not a defence: *R v Dyfed County Council ex p S (minors)* [1995] 1 FCR 113 (parents objected to Welsh medium education at nearer school; LEA refused to provide free transport for children to attend further English stream school). See N Harris, *Law and Education, Regulation, Consumerism and the Education System* (1993) pp 208-212 for detailed discussion.

18 Children Act 1989, s 36. See *Guardians ad Litem and other Court Related Issues* (1991) Vol 7, Guidance and Regulations, Ch 3. 210 such orders were made in the year October 1992 to September 1993: *Children Act Report 1993* (1994) Table 3.1 .

19 *Review of Child Care Law* (1985) paras 15.20 and 12.21.

To obtain an education supervision order, the LEA must show that the child is not being properly educated, which is presumed if there is a breach of a school attendance order or a failure to attend regularly.[20] The order places the child under the supervision of the LEA, who appoint a person, usually an education welfare officer, to advise, assist and befriend the child and who is empowered to give directions to the family so as to secure the proper education of the child. The order is expressed to be intended to 'establish and strengthen parental responsibility, and to enable the parents to discharge their responsibility towards the child'[1] and the supervisor must act in consultation with the parents and the child. But persistent parental failure to comply with directions may be a criminal offence so that ultimately the order is coercive of parents and upholds the state's right to insist upon children receiving an education it deems appropriate. The order lasts for one year, with possible extensions up to three years at a time, and ends when the child reaches school-leaving age or is made the subject of a care order. If the child fails to comply with the supervisor's directions, the LEA must inform the social services department, who must investigate and who may then decide to bring care proceedings.[2]

(c) The state's duty to provide education

(i) Provision of schools

Local Education Authorities are supposed to ensure that there are, in their area, 'sufficient schools in number, character and equipment to provide for all pupils opportunities for education ... such as may be desirable in view of their different ages, abilities and aptitudes'.[3] This is a qualified duty, because the courts will be extremely reluctant to interfere in the LEA's provision and allocation of limited resources. As long as the LEA

20 Section 36(5).
  1 *Guardians ad Litem and other Court Related Issues* (1991) Vol 7, Guidance and Regulations, para 3.20.
  2 See Ch 13. Although truancy is not expressly one of the threshold conditions for a care order under s 31 of the Children Act, it will still be possible to obtain a care order on the basis that non-attendance at school will be likely to cause significant harm to the child's social, intellectual and educational development: *Re O (a minor) (Care Proceedings: Education)* [1992] 1 WLR 912
  3 Education Act 1944, s 8. Funding authorities, established to replace LEAs, may share this duty with LEAs when more than 10% of pupils in an area, at either primary or secondary level, are being educated in grant maintained schools (those state schools not administered by LEAs and funded directly by central government), and take over responsibility from LEAs once 75% are being so educated: Education Act 1993, s 12. In determining if sufficient schools are provided, independent and grant maintained schools in the area are included in the calculation.

are doing all they reasonably can, judicial review will not lie to require them to provide a school place where they have insufficient numbers of teachers to teach all the children requiring places.[4] Ironically, in recent years, the demographic trend in the population towards lower numbers of children of school age has led to rationalisation and closure of schools to reduce surplus places,[5] leading parents to try to challenge closures, either by court action, or, generally more successfully, by seeking to acquire grant maintained status for the school.[6]

(ii) Parental choice of school [7]

Parents have been able to take such action because of the much greater emphasis given in recent legislation to the concept of parental choice of school and parental say in the management of schools. While traditionally, parents were kept at arms' length by LEAs, pressure for greater involvement grew during the 1970s, resulting in the requirement that state school governing bodies comprise at least some parents[8] and, of greater impact for the mass of parents, in the enactment of provisions designed to strengthen parents' right to choose which school their child should attend.

Parents' frustration at the inflexibility of LEAs in allocating children to schools in their areas is a long-standing grievance, stemming from the old days of selection of children through the 11-plus examination for grammar, secondary modern or technical schools under the 1944 Act. Parents (and children) were strongly dissatisfied with the stigma of failure which attached to failing the 11-plus and having to go to a secondary modern school. Attempts to improve opportunity led to the gradual abandonment of selective entry and the advent of comprehensive schools. By 1979, the bulk of secondary schools had become comprehensives, and a new type of parental dissatisfaction came to the fore. This time, parents complained that comprehensives (in essence, those drawing children from deprived areas alongside more affluent

4 *R v Inner London Education Authority, ex p Ali* [1990] COD 317.
5 It has been estimated that there are up to 1.5 million surplus places; see N Harris, *Law and Education, Regulation, Consumerism and the Education System* (1993) p 38.
6 The possibility of acquiring grant maintained status for schools was introduced to enable schools to evade the policies and funding priorities of LEAs. But in many instances, parents of children at schools with falling rolls have used the process to avoid the schools being closed by the LEAs, who, in order to rationalise places, must then find alternative targets for closure: see *R v Secretary of State for Education and Science, ex p Avon County Council* and *ex p Avon (No 2)* (1990) 88 LGR 716 and 737.
7 See N Harris, *Law and Education, Regulation, Consumerism and the Education System* (1993) Ch 5.
8 See the discussion by N Harris and S Van Bijsterveld, 'Parents as "Consumers" of Education in England and Wales and the Netherlands: A Comparative Analysis' (1993) 7 *International Journal of Law and the Family* 178 pp 191-194.

ones) had lower academic standards than the old grammar schools and that therefore their children were being disadvantaged. Calls were made for a return to selective entry, or for a greater say in the decision on which comprehensive a child could attend at age 11 – or both. As the ideology of free market competition took hold during the Conservative Government of the 1980s and 1990s, it was also argued that if parents could choose which school a child attended, under-achieving, unpopular schools would be forced to improve or they would become unviable, and thus, standards of education for all children would improve.

The attempt to meet these calls and to respect parents' wishes in their choice of school for their child is contained primarily in the Education Act 1980. Section 6 provides that LEAs must allocate children to schools in accordance with their parents' expressed preference unless the school is a selective one and the child fails the entrance test, or it is a denominational school and the child belongs to another religion[9] or 'compliance ... would prejudice the provision of efficient education or the efficient use of resources'. For most schools, this will mean that provided the admissions limit[10] is not exceeded, preferences must be granted.[11] Where schools are oversubscribed, LEAs may set criteria (subject always to considering exceptional circumstances) for choosing amongst applicants; they may, for example, give priority to siblings of current pupils, and to proximity to the school, but they may not refuse admission simply because an applicant lives outside the LEA area.[12] A parent whose preference is rejected may appeal to an education appeal committee established by the LEA[13] but inevitably where there are more appellants than available places, such committees have a difficult task to perform and meritorious appeals may be lost.[14] It is the *parents'* preference

---

9 *R v Governors of Bishop Challoner Roman Catholic Comprehensive School, ex p Choudhury* [1992] 2 AC 182. Equally, it has been held that children of one religion, who have priority for places at denominational schools, may be considered for places at non-denominational schools *after* other applicants: *R v Lancashire County Council, ex p Foster* [1995] 1 FCR 212.

10 Education Reform Act 1988, ss 26, 27 provide that schools must not restrict their admissions to below their 'standard number', which is calculated according to the number of children admitted in 1979-80 or 1989-90, whichever is the higher.

11 The LEA may not refuse a parent's preference because they believe it to be based on racism: *R v Cleveland County Council, ex p Commission for Racial Equality* [1994] ELR 44.

12 Education Act 1980, s 6(5) and *R v Greenwich London Borough Council, ex p Governors of John Ball Primary School* (1990) 88 LGR 589.

13 There are equivalent bodies for voluntary schools (state-aided church schools) and grant maintained schools: Education Act 1980, s 7 and Education Act 1993, Sch 6. For children with special educational needs, there are independent Special Educational Needs Tribunals: Education Act 1993, s 169.

14 See N Harris, *Law and Education, Regulation, Consumerism and the Education System* (1993) pp 158-159 for the difficulties and the procedures which committees may follow.

which is relevant here, not the child's.[15] In fact, around 90% of parents succeeded in securing a place for their child at their first choice school in 1992 and 1993.[16]

(iii) Parents' say in the content of schooling

On the one hand, legislation during the 1980s and 1990s has strengthened the extent to which parents may determine how state schools are run through their involvement in the governing body, and the possibility of seeking to 'opt out' of LEA control by achieving grant maintained status for the school.[17] Yet, at the same time, the introduction of the national curriculum by the Education Reform Act 1988 led to much tighter central government control over the content of what is taught in schools.[18] This could be described as a return to Victorian values, since, with its emphasis on regular national testing of pupils and publication of league tables of the results to assess how well the curriculum has been delivered, it echoes the nineteenth century system which geared grant aid to the results of inspections. Section 76 of the Education Act 1944 provides that children are to be educated in accordance with their parents' wishes, so far as this is compatible with the provision of efficient instruction and training and the avoidance of unreasonable public expenditure. This provision is in line with the United Kingdom's international obligations outlined above, but it has proved ineffective in enabling parents to challenge the education policies of LEAs, being classed as no more than a general principle to be considered along with other factors.[19] Parents do, however, continue to have the right to withdraw their children from religious education classes and from acts of religious worship. The former must reflect the Christian tradition in Great Britain as well as taking account of other religions, and the latter must normally be 'wholly

---

15 Similarly, where a child is excluded (suspended or expelled) from a state school, the parents must be informed, and, where the exclusion is permanent, they, but not the child (unless over 18) have a right of appeal to the same education appeal committee as determines admissions: Education (No 2) Act 1986, ss 23, 26. The only remedy for parents whose children attend private schools is to sue in contract; *R v Fernhill Manor School, ex p A* [1993] 1 FLR 620.

16 (1994) *Childright* December, p 22.

17 N Harris, *Law and Education, Regulation, Consumerism and the Education System* (1993) pp 122-127.

18 An earlier, and perhaps more crude attempt to dictate content came in the notorious 'clause 28' – now s 2A of the Local Government Act 1986, which prohibits the 'promotion' by local authorities in their schools of the teaching of the acceptability of homosexuality as a 'pretended family relationship'. See P Thomas and R Costigan, *Promoting Homosexuality: Section 28 of the Local Government Act 1988* (1990).

19 *Watt v Kesteven County Council* [1955] 1 QB 408. The section applies also to the Secretary of State.

or mainly of a broadly Christian character'.[20] In a multicultural society such as Britain, one would expect significant numbers of parents to avail themselves of the right to withdraw their children from these, but it appears that few do so and many are ignorant of its existence.[1]

Parents also have the right to withdraw children from sex education classes, except in so far as these form part of the national curriculum.[2] This respect for parents' wishes does not stem from a desire to ensure compatibility with their human right to ensure that teaching is in conformity with their religious or philosophical convictions. It has been held by the European Court of Human Rights that making sex education compulsory in Danish primary schools was not a breach of the European Convention. While the Court recognised the parents' right to require the state to respect their religious and philosophical convictions, it regarded the setting and planning of the curriculum as within the competence of state authorities, as long as education did not become indoctrination, and the state presented information and knowledge to pupils objectively, pluralistically and critically.[3] Requiring British parents to permit their children to receive sex education would therefore have been lawful. But we suggest that the motivation for giving parents the right to withdraw their children derived from a desire to reinforce 'traditional' values of sexual morality on the part of the Conservative Government.[4] It is doubtful again that many parents would wish to exercise this right.

At a more general level, some parents did influence the delivery of education through resort to their rights under the European Convention. In *Campbell and Cosans v United Kingdom* it was held by the Court that exclusion of pupils from a school because their parents refused to permit them to receive corporal punishment infringed the parents' right to have their children educated in conformity with their philosophical convictions – not, it will be noted, the childrens' right to receive an education.[5] As a result of this ruling, corporal punishment can no longer be administered

---

20 Education Reform Act 1988, ss 7,8,9; see *R v Secretary of State for Education, ex p R and D* [1994] ELR 495. Each LEA must organise a standing advisory council on religious education whose task is to advise on education, decide if worship need not be mainly Christian, and, when constituted as a 'conference', draw up the religious education syllabus: see N Harris, *Law and Education, Regulation, Consumerism and the Education System* (1993) pp 206-207.

 1 See N Harris, *Law and Education, Regulation, Consumerism and the Education System* (1993) p 258.

 2 But this includes only the 'biological aspects' of human reproduction.

 3 *Kjeldsen, Busk Madsen and Pedersen v Denmark* (1976) 1 EHRR 711. See further, N Harris, 'Testing choice: parents, children and the National Curriculum' (1993) 5 *Journal of Child Law* (3) 125.

 4 K Stevenson, 'The provision of sex education in schools: the new DoE guidelines' (1994) *Childright* September, p 11.

 5 (1982) 4 EHRR 293.

in state schools.[6] But apart from these limited examples, there is no right for parents to determine the substance or manner of what their children are taught. If they are dissatisfied, their ultimate remedy will be to move the child to a private school, for which the national curriculum is not compulsory.

Where parents do seek to ensure that their children have limited exposure to the broader curriculum entailed within a civil, liberal education, by withdrawal from classes, or attendance at a private school (such as an Orthodox Jewish, or Islamic, school, or indeed at many independent schools) it has been argued that this may infringe the child's right to equality of opportunity to participate, both as a child, and later as an adult, (and, we would add, as a *citizen*) in all that society has to offer.[7] English law has scarcely begun to take account of such an argument; as we have noted above, there is no question of the children themselves having a legal *right* to determine their participation in aspects of the curriculum or attendance at a particular school. It may be that, as Carolyn Hamilton argues, the balance between respect for parental views, and children's rights, can best be struck by requiring *all* schools to follow the national curriculum.[8]

(iv) Parents with children having special educational needs

It has been estimated that up to one-fifth of school pupils have learning difficulties of various kinds.[9] Such difficulties may range from dyslexia to severe mental or physical handicap, and the help needed to overcome or minimise such difficulties may extend from extra time to write examination papers to intensive full-time one-to-one tuition over many years. Identifying these difficulties and providing help is a skilled and resource-intensive activity, and parents will therefore need extra assistance from the state to ensure that their children with these problems can reach their potential. The Education Act 1981 was enacted to attempt to meet this need, in particular by seeking to integrate these children into mainstream schooling where possible, but the working of the legislation

6 Education (No 2) Act 1986, s 47. The prohibition extends to children being paid for by the state to attend independent schools, see N Harris, *Law and Education, Regulation, Consumerism and the Education System* (1993) p 213, n 47. Inhuman or degrading punishment in independent schools is unlawful; Education Act 1993, s 293 (implementing *Costello-Roberts v United Kingdom* [1994] ELR 1, E Ct HR: see C Barton and K Moss, 'Who can smack children now?' (1994) 6 *Journal of Child Law* (1) 32).

7 See C Hamilton, 'The Right to a Religious Education' in N V Lowe and G Douglas (eds) *Families across Frontiers* (forthcoming) ; A Gutmann, 'Children, Paternalism and Education: A Liberal Argument' (1980) 9 *Philosophy and Public Affairs* 338.

8 C Hamilton, *ibid.*

9 Warnock Committee on Special Educational Needs (1978) Cmnd 7212, paras 3.16, 3.17.

was criticised.[10] Part III of, and Schs 9 and 10 to, the Education Act 1993 consolidate and attempt to strengthen its effectiveness in certain respects, but ultimately, limited resources will constrain the ability of the state, through LEAs, to make it succeed. There may also be serious differences of opinion between parents and LEAs on whether, and if so how, a child needs special educational provision. On the one hand, parents might see a child as stigmatised by a finding that he or she has special educational needs, especially where the learning difficulty is due to behavioural problems. Sending a child to a 'special school' may reinforce such feelings (and in part they lie behind the attempt to integrate children into mainstream schooling). On the other hand, parents worried about a child's speech development, or dyslexia, may find LEAs reluctant to accept these as problems requiring special provision at all.

The provisions depend upon a child being found to have 'special educational needs'. These are defined in s 156(1) as existing where a child has a 'learning difficulty which calls for special educational provision to be made for him'. A child is defined as having a learning difficulty if

> '(a) he has a significantly greater difficulty in learning than the majority of children of his age,
> '(b) he has a disability which either prevents or hinders him from making use of educational facilities of a kind generally provided for children of his age in schools within the area' of the LEA, or
> '(c) he is under the age of five years and is, or would be if special educational provision were not made for him, likely to fall within paragraph (a) or (b) when over that age.'

Special educational provision means educational provision additional to, or otherwise different from, that provided generally for children of the child's age in state schools. Harris cogently argues that:

> 'the combined effect of these provisions is that the question of whether or not a child has special educational needs depends not so much on the child's specific needs considered in isolation, but rather on the appropriateness or otherwise of existing provision'.[11]

Local Education Authorities and schools have a duty to identify pupils with special educational needs.[12] This will be done through an assessment process set out in the Act which requires a number of hurdles to be

---

10 See, in particular, *Third Report, Special Educational Needs: Implementation of the Education Act 1981* House of Commons Select Committee on Education, HC 201-1 (1987) and HC 287-1 (1993).
11 N Harris, *Law and Education, Regulation, Consumerism and the Education System* (1993) p 233.
12 Failure to do so is not actionable on behalf of the child as a breach of statutory duty, but may be in negligence: *E (a minor) v Dorset County Council* [1994] 3 WLR 853 (appeal against striking out of plaintiff's claim based on negligence allowed).

surmounted before a child is actually provided with the special educational provision he or she needs. The LEA carry out the assessment, either because their staff have identified the child themselves, or because the parents have requested them to do so. Parents have little option but to co-operate when the LEA instigate the process, as failure to comply with the requirements of a notice for a child to attend an examination may be an offence, demonstrating that the state's view of what the child needs may override that of the parents.[13] On the other hand, for parents who *do* wish an assessment to be carried out, s 173 gives a right to appeal to a Special Educational Needs Tribunal if the LEA have determined not to comply with their request.

After assessment, the LEA may decide whether a statement should be made determining what special educational provision the child's learning difficulty calls for. Parents may again appeal against the refusal to make a statement, or against the contents of the statement (which will include details of the LEA's assessment of the child's needs and the provision to meet them). Finally, where a statement is maintained, the LEA must arrange that the special educational provision specified in it is made for the child, and has a power to arrange any non-educational provision specified. The distinction between educational and non-educational provision has in the past proved to be a difficult one; courts have differed, for example, in their views of whether speech therapy is educational or non-educational provision.[14]

The greater difficulty with the scheme is its dependence upon resources which may be scarce or non-existent. LEAs have differed widely in the extent to which they accept children as having special needs, possibly because of their reluctance to see costs of provision rise. It appears that a child may be 100 times more likely to be 'statemented' in one authority than in another.[15] But there has also been an increase in the proportion of children identified as requiring special needs education, from 2% estimated by the Warnock Committee, to a 1993 figure of 2.5% expected to rise to 2.9%. In 1993, 179,132 school aged children received statements, some 37,500 more children than had been predicted.[16] This increase puts further strain upon LEA resources.[17] But the courts, as with other aspects

13 Education Act 1993, Sch 9, para 5.
14 Compare *R v Oxfordshire County Council, ex p W* [1987] 2 FLR 193 (non-educational) with *R v Lancashire County Council, ex p M* [1989] 2 FLR 279 (educational).
15 N Harris, *Law and Education, Regulation, Consumerism and the Education System* (1993) p 242. The Education Act 1993, s 157 requires LEAs to have regard to a Code of Practice which is intended to reduce inconsistency between authorities in their interpretation of their duties.
16 *The Guardian*, 22 September, 1994.
17 A survey by the Audit Commission found that only one English LEA, out of 60, had met the target of assessing a child within six months: *The Times*, 24 November 1994.

of education provision, will rarely intervene to require authorities to change their minds on whether provision should be given, or the type of provision it should be. As was pointed out in *R v Surrey County Council Education Committee, ex p H*,[18] Parliament has not required LEAs to provide a Utopian system or to educate the child to his or her maximum potential. The Special Educational Needs Tribunals can be expected to take a similar view. Yet it is in relation to children with special needs that the desire of parents to do what they think is best for their children may appear most frustratingly at odds with the limitations of state provision. While the development of competition within state education through parental choice of school and the creation of grant-maintained schools should theoretically improve standards for children, there seems little scope for such improvement where children have special needs. Indeed, there is a danger that the market ethos will lead to a decline in the provision available, and a reluctance by schools, conscious of league tables monitoring their 'performance', to take on the challenge such children offer.

(b) Reinforcement of values and behaviour – crime and parental responsibility

We have seen that one of the motivations for the introduction of compulsory schooling was to keep children off the streets and away from crime and disorder. Children were seen as both perpetrators and victims of crime, and the idea of a cycle of deprivation and delinquency is not a twentieth century one. As early as 1535, concern was being expressed at the danger of vagrants' children growing up knowing nothing other than how to beg.[19] The Tudor answer to this problem was a combination of education and punishment; pauper children could be removed from their parents and placed as apprentices or servants so that they could learn a trade or skill which would keep them safe from having to commit crime when they became adult, but if this failed, and they continued to beg or steal, they would be punished as severely as adults – including suffering the death penalty. This dual approach lends further support to the argument that the view of Ariès[20] that earlier societies had little concept of childhood may have been overstated. The fact that the common law age of criminal responsibility was seven,[1] but between that and 14, children were rebuttably presumed to be incapable of committing an

---

18 (1984) 83 LGR 219, 235.
19 I Pinchbeck and M Hewitt, *Children in English Society* (1969) Vol 1, p 95.
20 *Centuries of Childhood* (1979), discussed in Ch 1.
 1 The age was raised to ten by s 50 of the Children and Young Persons Act 1933.

offence (*'doli incapax'*), also shows that *some* distinction was made between children and adults in determining whether their anti-social acts required punishment.[2] Perhaps it was more the case that there was less recognition of *adolescence* as a distinct phase in growing up, and consequently more of a view that children could be regarded as possessing adult maturity and responsibility at a younger age than we would today. Once a child was found to have adult responsibility for his or her crime, there would be no reason to treat that child differently, in terms of punishment, than any other adult. Hence, there were no special measures for juvenile offenders.[3]

It was in the nineteenth century that greater differentiation between adults and juvenile criminals came to be made, at the same time that theories of criminality based on genetic or environmental factors, rather than a belief in 'original sin', began to e merge. As part of this trend, lower class parents' inabilities or unwillingness to set suitable examples for their children, or to exert proper control over them, were identified as contributing to juvenile crime.[4] If the parents could not, or would not, provide children with the appropriate moral and cultural values demanded by society, even on threat of suffering criminal penalties themselves (for example, for failing to ensure their children attended school), then the state would do so for them, by removing the children from the undesirable family environment and placing them in reformatories, if they had been convicted of offences, or in industrial schools, if they appeared to be at risk of doing so in future. Thus, the continuing association of deprivation and depravity – the assumption that children might be bad because they have been neglected or abused by the family or in some other way deprived – was reinforced. It has marked social policy concerning children ever since, to a greater or lesser degree. The high water mark of this approach in England and Wales came in the Children and Young Persons Act 1969. This Act enabled civil care proceedings, rather than criminal proceedings, to be taken where a child was suspected of having committed an offence; if the offence was proved, the juvenile court (now the Youth Court) could then make a care order, committing the child to the care of the local authority, in the same way that it might do so in respect of a neglected or abused child.[5] In fact, the Act's measures for dealing with juvenile offenders were never fully implemented, due to political hostility, later supplemented by concern from magistrates, that

---

2 The House of Lords, in *C v DPP* (1995) Times 17 March, upheld this presumption after the Divisional Court (at [1994] 3 WLR 888) had purported to abolish it as outmoded in an age of universal compulsory education.

3 A Morris and H Giller, *Understanding Juvenile Justice* (1987) Ch 1.

4 *Ibid*.

5 A supervision order could also be made.

such measures would leave them powerless to punish or deter determined and sophisticated young criminals. The magistrates in particular objected to the fact that, if a care order were made, it was for the social worker in charge of the case to determine whether the offender should be removed from home or not, thus apparently ignoring the fact that home and family influences might have contributed to the juvenile's criminality.[6] The juvenile courts retained alternative methods of disposal, and during the 1970s, increasingly used them; for example, whereas 20% of removals of juvenile offenders from home were to custodial institutions in 1965, by 1979, the proportion was 60%; 'The opposite to that intended by the 1969 Act had occurred – sentencing had become more penal than welfare orientated'.[7] This trend was reversed in the 1980s, not by greater recourse to care orders, but by the increased use of cautioning or community sentences.[8] In the 1990s, in the wake of the moral panic generated in particular by the James Bulger case, where a toddler was murdered by two ten year old boys, a return to a more punitive approach has been evident, in the doubt cast on the *doli incapax* presumption;[9] proposals for 'secure training orders' for persistent offenders aged between 12 and 14;[10] and revised cautioning guidelines whereby the youth of the offender is no longer of itself a justification for a caution rather than a prosecution.[11]

But the Scots went much further in the amalgamation of civil and criminal disposition of juveniles. Under the children's hearing system, a panel of people with knowledge or interest in social work and child care, rather than a court, except for the most serious offences, determines what is to happen to delinquent children or those in need of care or protection. A 'reporter' (employed by the local authority but acting independently of it) considers whether the child requires 'compulsory measures of care'. If the reporter thinks that the child does, the matter is referred to the hearing. If the parents and child accept that grounds for referral (which are similar to those which pertained under the Children and Young Persons Act 1969 and which include being guilty of an offence) exist, they then discuss with the panel how the matter should be dealt with. There is no legal representation at the children's hearing. If they dispute the grounds or guilt, the matter is heard by a sheriff, and, if the

---

6 Morris and Giller, *Understanding Juvenile Justice* (1987) pp 95-100.

7 *Ibid* pp 97,98.

8 The proportion of male indictable offenders aged 10-16 who were cautioned increased from 45% in 1979 to 70% in 1989: A Ashworth *et al, The Youth Court* (1992) p 20. The number of criminal care orders made in respect of such offenders fell from 1,000 in 1982 to none in 1991: *Criminal Statistics England and Wales 1992* (1993) Cm 2401, Table 7.6.

9 *C v DPP* [1994] 3 All ER 190, revsd (1995) Times 17 March.

10 Criminal Justice and Public Order Act 1994, Pt I.

11 Revised guidelines issued by the Home Office, 15 March 1994.

grounds are made out or guilt is proven, the case goes back to the panel. If the panel decides to impose supervision or a requirement that the child reside away from home, the child or parents can appeal to the sheriff's court. If the measure is upheld, or not appealed, the panel reviews the case annually.[12] In England and Wales, the trend after the 1969 Act was towards seeking greater formal protection for children and their families through increased procedural rights,[13] a growing distrust of social work decision-making, and a desire to re-establish the distinction between depraved and deprived children, which culminated in the abolition of 'criminal care orders' by the Children Act 1989, s 90.[14] Yet the Scottish system was long heralded as a triumph and no serious calls to change it fundamentally have been made, although a review of child care law in Scotland proposed some amendments to the system, and announced that a major study into its effectiveness was to be carried out, together with consideration of its compatibility with the European Convention on Human Rights.[15] Indeed, the United Kingdom Government entered a reservation to Article 37(d) of the United Nations Convention on the Rights of the Child, which grants to the child deprived of his or her liberty the right to legal or other appropriate assistance, because the system was regarded by the Government as incompatible with that provision.[16]

At the same time as the development of measures intended to offer delinquent children an environment in which they could be reformed, the other side of the coin – parental shortcomings which may have caused or contributed to their delinquency – was also addressed. The Children and Young Persons Act 1933, s 55 empowered juvenile courts to order that fines, compensation or costs be paid by the juvenile's parent or guardian, unless the court was satisfied that the parent could not be found, or that it would be unreasonable to make the order. In practice, such orders were rarely made. The Conservative Government attempted to increase their use first under the Criminal Justice Act 1982, by turning the power into a *duty* on the court. Parents have a right to be heard before an order is

---

12 These provisions are contained in the Social Work (Scotland) Act 1968, as amended.
13 See Ch 13.
14 The Youth Court may impose a supervision order with a requirement that the offender live in local authority accommodation for up to six months, under the Children and Young Persons Act 1969, s 12AA; the court must be satisfied, *inter alia*, 'that the behaviour which constituted the offence was due, to a significant extent, to the circumstances in which [the offender] was living': s 12AA(6)(d). Yet again, family influences are recognised as contributory factors.
15 Scottish Office, *Scotland's Children: Proposals for Child Care Policy and Law* (1993) Cm 2286, Chs 6, 7.
16 For the view that the reservation was unnecessary, see A Lockyer, 'The Scottish Children's Hearings System: Internal Developments and the UN Convention' and for an opposing view, see D Duquette, 'Scottish Children's Hearings and Representation for the Child', both in S Asquith and M Hill (eds) *Justice for Children* (1994).

imposed.[17] This change seems to have had only a limited effect. In 1985, about 26% of fines, and 35% of compensation orders were ordered to be met by parents, but by 1988, the proportions had dropped to 13% and 21% respectively.[18] The Government tried yet again by amending the 1933 Act further in the Criminal Justice Act 1991. In the White Paper, *Crime, Justice and Protecting the Public*,[19] they stated:

> 'Crime prevention begins in the home. Parents have the most influence on their children's development. From their children's earliest years parents can, and should, help them develop as responsible, law-abiding citizens. They should ensure that their children are aware of the existence of rules and laws and the need for them; and that they respect other people and their property ... when young people offend, the law has a part to play in reminding parents of their responsibilities.'[20]

This time, the Government could draw upon the public awareness of the concept of parental responsibility which had been such a feature of the recently enacted Children Act, to reinforce their message that parents should exercise proper control over their children. In fact, the legislation enables courts to do little that was not possible under the previous law. The main change was to impose duties, rather than powers, to impose certain penalties. Parents or guardians[1] are required to be present in court when their children are prosecuted unless this would be unreasonable in all the circumstances;[2] this enables the court to hear them there and then on whether they should be required to pay the child's fine or be subjected to other measures. In addition to the duty to make parents pay their child's fines, the court must, if satisfied that this would be desirable in the interests of preventing the commission by the juvenile of further offences, order the parent or guardian to enter into a recognisance in a sum not exceeding £1,000, to take proper care of and exercise proper control over the juvenile.[3] If the parent unreasonably refuses to consent to such a recognisance, the court may impose a fine. The recognisance may be forfeited if the juvenile commits further offences.[4] The initial effects

17 Children and Young Persons Act 1993, s 55, as amended.
18 Morris and Giller, *Understanding Juvenile Justice* (1987) p 181, and D Boyd, 'Blaming the parents' (1990) *Journal of Child Law* (1) 65 at p 66.
19 (1990) Cm 965.
20 At paras 8.1, 8.2.
1 Guardian includes 'any person who, in the opinion of the court ... has for the time being the charge of or control over the child or young person': s 107(1) of the 1933 Act. It also includes local authorities providing the child with accommodation: s 34A.
2 Children and Young Persons Act 1933, s 34A.
3 Criminal Justice Act 1991, s 58.
4 These are powers, rather than duties, where the juvenile is aged 16 or 17, it being accepted that parents may have little influence on the behaviour of near-adults. The Criminal Justice and Public Order Act 1994, Sch 9, para 50 added a power to s 58 to enable courts to bind over parents whose children fail to comply with the terms of community sentences, and a power to fine a parent where a child breaks the requirements of a secure training order: Sch 10, para 4, amending the Children and Young Persons Act 1933, s 55(1A).

were indeed to increase the proportion of children whose parents were required to meet their fines or compensation orders, particularly where the children were aged 10 to 13. In this group, the percentage required to pay fines rose from 22% in 1991 to 33% in the fourth quarter of 1992, and for those required to pay compensation, the proportion rose from 29% to 36%.[5] The Youth Court magistrates appear to have attempted to respond to Government exhortation to bring home to parents the sins of their children, although when set against a pattern of declining recourse to the courts to deal with young offenders, the impact may be marginal; the number of boys aged 10 to 16 sentenced for indictable offences fell from 13,600 in 1982 to 2,300 in 1992.[6]

These measures do not go so far as the Government originally wanted, which was to enact a new offence by parents of failing to prevent their children from committing offences. Such offences have been enacted in the United States, from where so much of the Conservative Government's social and family policy has been inspired. A striking example is the city of Dermott, Arkansas, which passed an ordinance in 1989 decreeing:

'a possible term of two days in the open-air stockade for parents whose children under 18 years violated the 11 pm to 5.30 am curfew. Further punishment could include the publication of a parent's picture in a local newspaper over a caption "Irresponsible Parent". If the parents maintain that they are unable to control their minor children, they must sign a statement to this effect, and the youngsters will be referred to the juvenile court as delinquents. The parents then will have to pay the city $100 for each child so designated or perform 20 hours of community service.'[7]

Apart from the formidable difficulties which might be expected in attempting to prove actual failure on the part of the parent to prevent his or her child's offending, other than the mere fact that the parent is guilty of 'having a kid who commits a crime', as an American Civil Liberties Union official has described such offences,[8] there is no evidence that measures of this kind, or even those which the Government did successfully enact in 1991, have any effect on levels of juvenile offending. Further, while it is recognised that family circumstances and parental upbringing do play a part in criminality, it has been cogently argued that the:

'parents most affected by the Government's proposals will be those with the fewest personal, financial and emotional resources.... It is a fallacy that in some way juvenile crime is more acceptable to ineffective parents who should therefore be made to attend court, agree to be bound over, pay fines, costs and compensation they can ill afford or act as gaolers policing and enforcing curfews as punishment in the community.'[9]

5 *Criminal Statistics England and Wales 1992* (1993) Cm 2410, Table 7D.
6 *Ibid* Table 7.6.
7 G Geis and A Binder, 'Sins of their Children; Parental Responsibility for Juvenile Delinquency' [1991] 5 *Notre Dame Journal of Law, Ethics and Public Policy* 303, at p 312.
8 *Ibid* p 315.
9 Boyd, 'Blaming the Parents' (1990) *Journal of Child Law* (1) 65, pp 66-67.

The continuing attempt by governments to bring home to parents through the operation of the criminal law the anti-social activities of their offspring seems unlikely to be more successful than in previous centuries. It is other aspects of social policy which are more likely to have effects, either for good or ill, on the ability of parents to instill the 'right' values and attitudes in their children.

So far, we have been concerned with the mechanisms available to support parents in the upbringing of their children, and the extent to which there are reciprocal rights and duties between parents and state in fulfilling this task. In the following chapters, we look at the state's interest in children as present or future citizens from another angle – its role in ensuring that children's care within the family is of an appropriate standard and, where necessary, in protecting them from their parents' or others' neglect or abuse.

CHAPTER 12

Protecting children through support and partnership

1. INTRODUCTION

In the previous two chapters, we were concerned with what might be described as the common interest which the state and parents have in the care and education of children. We saw that there may be differences of opinion in how such care should be provided, and on how far the state should assume primary responsibility for its various aspects of the child's upbringing. Nonetheless, an idea of partnership and common purpose can be identified, which may help to meet the criticisms of those who object to 'interference' in the privacy and autonomy of the family. In the next three chapters, we examine the powers the state may bring to bear to ensure that the values, attitudes and modes of behaviour which it wishes to inform a child's upbringing can be enforced in the teeth of parental lack of interest or opposition. Here, the intervention by the state can be coercive, although again, a philosophy of partnership is promulgated in an attempt to 'encourage' or 'persuade' parents to conform to society or state expectations and hence avoid the need for more coercive action.

The origins of the modern law and system of child protection lie in both state and private initiative, and the basic shape of that system still derives from the pattern laid down in the nineteenth century. The state, through the Poor Law, took a direct interest in pauper children, who might be orphaned, abandoned by their parents, or neglected. Concern to avoid a drain on the public purse led to the development of a range of measures intended to tackle these. For example, legislation was passed in 1868 empowering Boards of Guardians (who administered the Poor Law) to prosecute parents for wilful neglect which endangered their children's health.[1] This went further than the usual Poor Law emphasis on financial support for one's relatives, since it focused on risk to the child's health (the aim being to prevent pauperism from arising in the first place). Infant life protection legislation was also enacted, as we saw in Chapter 10, to stamp out the abuse of baby-farming, by introducing a system of registration of child-minders. Meanwhile, children dependent upon the parish because of pauperism were increasingly 'boarded out' with foster parents. This was partly building on the long tradition in English society of sending one's children to live with another family, to be trained and to work as servants or craftsmen. Foster parents were now paid an allowance by the guardians to take on such a role, whereas in the past, families themselves would have made the arrangements. Fostering was also cheaper than institutional care, although concern was expressed in the mid-nineteenth century that it was contrary to the principle of less eligibility, ie that children should not enjoy a higher standard of living with foster parents than with their own families.[2] To facilitate the placement of pauper children, the Poor Law Adoption Act 1889 permitted Poor Law guardians to assume all parental powers and rights in respect of any child who had been deserted by his or her parents and who was being maintained by the guardians. Versions of this power (which enabled a state body to supplant a parent, except in status, without court involvement) remained on the statute book, and were used, for a hundred years, until the Children Act 1989.[3]

Alongside the activities of the state, through the Poor Law machinery, a number of philanthropic organisations and pressure groups developed in the late eighteenth and nineteenth centuries.[4] One of the most famous of these was run by Dr Barnardo, who first opened homes for destitute children in the 1870s, and whose development of modes of care for the children, such as 'cottage homes' intended to imitate family life, rather than large-scale institutions, and emigration to the colonies, became programmes involving thousands of children over the years.[5] Other

1 Poor Law Amendment Act 1868. It had already been held a common law misdemeanour for a person under a duty to provide for a child of tender years to neglect to do so and thereby injure the child's health: *R v Friend* (1802) Russ & Ry 20, cited by P M Bromley and N V Lowe, in *Bromley's Family Law* (8th ed, 1992) at p 313, who add that cases were rarely brought.
2 I Pinchbeck and M Hewitt, *Children in English Society* (1973) Vol 2, p 523.
3 In Scotland, abolition of a similar power was proposed in the White Paper, *Scotland's Children: Proposals for Child Care Policy and Law* (1993) Cm 2286, para 3.8.
4 For an account of foundling hospitals in France, see J Donzelot, *The Policing of Families* (1980), and for discussion of the English equivalent, see R Harris, 'A matter of balance: power and resistance in child protection policy' [1990] JSWFL 332.
5 In retrospect, their invention and use was not an unmitigated force for good; see the criticisms of 'cottage homes' by the Curtis Committee, *Report of the Care of Children Committee* (1946) Cmd 6922, para 167 and, as regards emigration, see G Wagner,

organisations, such as the NSPCC, founded in 1889, sought to raise public awareness of cruelty to children. This was slow to develop. Until the late nineteenth century:

> 'both Parliament and the national press were largely unconcerned with the way in which parents treated their children, regarding even the most barbarous cruelty as beyond comment and beyond public intervention since children were not then regarded as citizens in their own right'.[6]

Not only were children's rights unrecognised, but parents' rights held as unchallengeable;

> 'The evils you state are enormous and indisputable, but they are of so private, internal and domestic a character as to be beyond the reach of legislation'.[7]

The rise of the charitable organisations fits well Donzelot's thesis that philanthropy filled the gap between the demands of the state and the preserve of family autonomy. Charity could be used to guide or supervise parents, without appearing coercive.[8] Ultimately, however, in the case of recalcitrant parents, compulsion might be needed, and hence there had to be an alliance between voluntary organisations and state authorities which could enforce the receipt of aid. Again, the legacy of this alliance remains, through the interaction of voluntary agencies and local authority social services departments.[9] Indeed, the trend of Government policy in the 1990s has been to increase recourse to the voluntary sector, as part of the drive to reduce the powers of local authorities, and to seek services at lower cost.[10]

Children of the Empire (1982); P Bean and J Melville, *Lost Children of the Empire* (1989); J Eekelaar, '"The Chief Glory": The Export of Children from the United Kingdom' (1994) 21 JLS 487, who all point out that many of the child migrants were not orphans, were kept ignorant of their family's whereabouts, were separated from siblings, and frequently subject to harsh treatment by those using them as a form of cheap labour in the Dominions.

6 Pinchbeck and Hewitt, *Children in English Society* (1973) Vol 2, p 611.

7 Lord Shaftesbury, the great reformer whose efforts prohibited many forms of child labour, such as chimney sweeping and mining, quoted by Pinchbeck and Hewitt, *ibid*, p 622. Similar reluctance to 'interfere' was displayed in relation to wife assault and marital rape.

8 Although Barnardo's requirement that parents sign an undertaking renouncing their parental rights before he would take their child might appear coercive to some. (Such an undertaking was unenforceable: *Barnardo v McHugh* [1891] AC 388.)

9 The NSPCC's contribution to child protection received statutory recognition for the first time in the Children Act 1989 by being named in s 31(9) as an 'authorised person' to instigate proceedings for a care or supervision order. Voluntary organisations may provide many of the services also provided by local authorities; eg, they may accommodate children in need. Where they do so, they are under the same duties as local authorities; see Part VII of the Children Act 1989. When we refer below in our discussion to the activities of local authorities, this should be read as including voluntary organisations as appropriate.

10 See the Children Act 1989, s 17(5).

The NSPCC lobbied for the passage of the Prevention of Cruelty to, and Protection of, Children Act 1889 through Parliament. This Act made it an offence for any person over 16, having custody of a boy under 14 or girl under 16, wilfully to ill-treat, neglect, abandon or expose such a child, in a manner likely to cause the child unnecessary suffering or injury to health. This provision, with some drafting amendment, remains the primary criminal offence relating to child cruelty on the statute book.[11] The Act laid a further foundation for the modern system, by enabling magistrates to issue a warrant to permit the police to enter a house and search for a child reasonably believed to be suffering ill-treatment or neglect and to detain the child in a place of safety. Such 'place of safety orders' were replaced by emergency protection orders under s 44 of the Children Act 1989. Finally, courts were given power to take a child out of the care of a parent convicted of neglect and ill-treatment, and to commit the child to the charge of a relative or other 'fit person', which term included charitable organisations and industrial schools. Local authorities were later included as possible fit persons, and they are now the authority in whom care orders vest parental responsibility.[12]

Notwithstanding several swings in policy direction in the intervening years,[13] the nineteenth century legislation contained all the elements which apply today to form a system, still perhaps not entirely coherent, of protection for children. There is the possibility of working with parents and families through the provision of services ranging from advice on how to deal with a crying baby to long-term accommodation for children whose parents cannot care for them; the removal of children from parents' care, with the child returning later when 'rehabilitation' has been achieved, or the finding of a permanent substitute home, and, in the case of adoption, a new legal family relationship, where such rehabilitation fails; and criminal liability to serve as a punitive and deterrent reminder of parental responsibility. Together, this package fulfils the obligation imposed by Article 19 of the United Nations Convention on the Rights of the Child to take all appropriate measures to:

'protect the child from all forms of physical or mental violence, injury or abuse, neglect or negligent treatment, maltreatment or exploitation, including sexual abuse, while in the care of parent(s), legal guardian(s) or any other person who has the care of the child'.[14]

11 Now the Children and Young Persons Act 1933, s 1(1), discussed in Ch 6.
12 Shared with the parents: Children Act 1989, s 33.
13 See J Packman, *The Child's Generation* (2nd ed, 1981).
14 Discussed by M Coady and C Coady, '"There Ought to be a Law against It": Reflections on Child Abuse, Morality and Law' in P Alston *et al* (eds) *Children, Rights and the Law* (1992).

Just as in the previous two chapters we saw that there is a two-way relationship of rights and duties between parents and the state in the provision of services to support the upbringing of children, so there is an interrelationship of support and coercion operating throughout the system of child care law, as it is known. Reliance upon the use of philanthropy to mediate between the direction of families and the rhetoric of autonomy has been replaced by an attempt, through the concept of partnership under the Children Act (and a part of the theory of social work practice before that Act), to treat the parents, child and family (although these have not always been clearly distinguished) as 'clients' of the social services department. This serves to mitigate, or to mask, the reality that sufficient failure to accept the service offered may result in more coercive measures. That reality is perhaps demonstrated by the fact that social work clients are one of the few groups of consumers of public services who have yet to receive a 'Charter' setting out their 'rights'.

We start by considering the genesis of the law which is laid down in the Children Act 1989.

2. THE DEVELOPMENT OF THE MODERN LAW[15]

The provision of assistance involving work with the families of deprived children, as distinct from work with children who had no families to call on, or work involving delinquent children, was the preserve of charities and philanthropic organisations until the Curtis Committee report of 1946. The focus of the report was on the needs of:

'children who from loss of parents or from any cause whatever are deprived of a normal home life with their own parents or relatives; and to consider what further measures should be taken to ensure that these children are brought up under conditions best calculated to compensate them for the lack of parental care'.[16]

The concern was primarily with the provision of accommodation for children away from their families, and the resulting legislation reflected this. Section 1 of the Children Act 1948 imposed a duty on local authorities to receive a child into care where he or she had no parent or guardian, or had been abandoned, or where the parent or guardian was unable to take care of the child, either temporarily or permanently.

---

15 For accounts of the development of the modern system, see J Packman, *The Child's Generation* (2nd ed, 1981), who examines the system which emerged after the report of the Curtis Committee in 1946 and the Children Act 1948; and N Parton, *The Politics of Child Abuse* (1985) who takes matters up to the mid-1980s, and then updates the story in *Governing the Family: Child Care, Child Protection and the State* (1991).

16 Terms of Reference of the Curtis Committee.

However, the Act also required the authority wherever possible to secure the child's discharge from care, to parents, relatives or friends. The reasons for this approach were two-fold. First, the aim was to encourage parents to utilise the local authority's services, rather than let the child suffer deprivation; to provide such encouragement, the emphasis was on the voluntary nature of what was provided, with parents able to take back the child whenever they wished. (This caused problems, as we discuss below.) Secondly, the legislation was brought forward at a time when it was being realised that care away from the family could be detrimental to the child's long-term development and John Bowlby's theories of child development and maternal deprivation were gaining recognition.[17] Family, rather than institutional or even foster care, was seen as the preferable option for the child. With this philosophy, the Curtis Committee and the Children Act 1948 laid the foundations for modern child care law. They also introduced modern social work administration and practice, by their emphasis on the appointment of a 'children's officer' to be responsible for the welfare of deprived children in the area. The children's officer would ideally be a graduate with social science qualifications, experience with children and good administrative ability. As Jean Packman puts it, she (and it was envisaged that such officers would be women) would be 'a one-woman, personal social work service'.[18] Subordinates of the children's officer, called boarding-out visitors, would require specialist social work training. This established the basis of an expert social work profession, trained to identify and respond to children's personal and familial needs.[19] Their work grew far beyond the confines of finding substitute homes for children who could not stay with their families, as it came increasingly to be felt that more good could be done if attention were placed on preventing children from having to leave home in the first place. The Children and Young Persons Act 1963, s 1 accordingly required local authorities to:

'make available such advice, guidance and assistance as may promote the welfare of children by diminishing the need to receive children into or keep them in care... and any provision made by a local authority under this subsection may, if the local authority think fit, include provision for giving assistance in kind, or in exceptional circumstances, in cash'.[20]

The children's officers, and the children's departments which developed as social work with children developed after 1948, did not survive the

---

17 His work, *Child Care and the Growth of Love* was not published until 1951, but he gave evidence to the Curtis Committee.

18 Packman, *The Child's Generation* (2nd ed, 1981) p 9.

19 While Donzelot's analysis of France focuses upon the central role of the 'psy' professions, in the United Kingdom, it is the rise of the social work profession which is most significant.

20 The provision later became s 1(1) of the Child Care Act 1980.

administrative reforms of the 1970s, which integrated different types of social work with different types of clients to form social services departments staffed by 'generic' social workers, with skills in tackling all kinds of social problems (at least in theory).[1] The reorganisation, however, merely continued the trend to attempt to prevent the removal of children from home altogether. Just as previous generations had argued that children were influenced most directly by the care and example they received from their parents, so there developed the view that intensive social work with the family as a whole would be more successful than focusing in isolation upon the child.

By the end of the 1960s, a re-evaluation of the approach to juvenile delinquency, and of the links between delinquency and deprivation had taken place. The Children and Young Persons Act 1969 recast the grounds for compulsory removal of children from their families because of abuse or neglect, but it did so in a statute primarily concerned with how to handle juvenile offenders. Nigel Parton argues that this had the effect, for a time at least, of removing any public sense of children as victims, but only as perpetrators of disorder and crime.[2] It also caused immense difficulties, both procedurally and substantively, by focusing upon the child's, rather than the family's circumstances (running quite contrary to the family-focused preventative approach which, as we have seen, had been favoured in the 1963 legislation). For example, the parents of a child found to be suffering ill-treatment were not parties to the proceedings, yet, under the original Act, they were permitted to represent the child – whose interests clearly conflicted with theirs.[3]

There was increasing dissatisfaction with the way the system was dealing with children in need. The (re)discovery of child abuse, as distinct from neglect, received enormous publicity, especially after the death of Maria Colwell, who was killed by her step-father after being returned to her mother from a happy home with foster parents.[4] Parton has noted how doctors were instrumental in the detection, or diagnosis of child abuse in the 1950s and 1960s. Their discovery of the 'baby battering syndrome' produced a medical, disease model of child abuse, which attributed its occurrence to the individual pathology of parents or carers, rather than to cultural or structural causes. Parents might perhaps be cured of their disease, either through punishment or treatment.[5]

---

1 *Report on Local Authority and Allied Personal Social Services* Cmnd 3703 (1968) (the Seebohm report). Specialisation re-emerged in the 1980s and 1990s.
2 N Parton, *The Politics of Child Abuse* (1985) p 45.
3 See the *Review of Child Care Law* (1985) Ch 14.
4 *Report of the Committee of Inquiry into the care and supervision provided in relation to Maria Colwell* (1974).
5 N Parton, *The Politics of Child Abuse* (1985).

But this model lost favour. In the 1980s, there was an apparent succession of deaths of children known to social services departments resulting in highly publicised inquiries into the reasons for the failure to protect them.[6] These fuelled a mounting concern that both the law and social work practice were inadequate to protect children. Even where action had been taken and children had been removed from their parents, research had shown that many children were subject to 'drift' – they were languishing in local authority care, with no settled substitute home, and no meaningful contact with their original families.[7] The Government responded to Parliamentary concern[8] by setting up an inter-departmental review of child care law to bring forward proposals for reform and later produced a White Paper.[9] Meanwhile, a further complication and dissatisfaction with the existing position resulted from the events in Cleveland in early 1987,[10] where 121 children were diagnosed by hospital paediatricians as having suffered sexual abuse. Most of the children were immediately removed from their families, and many remained away from home for several weeks. Fear of over-zealous social workers exerting too much, rather than too little, power, became the dominant media concern. The new focus was upon child protection, from abuse both by parents *and* by the state. Doctors' central role in the conception of child abuse became discredited, due to distrust of the Cleveland paediatricians' 'diagnosis' of sexual abuse. In particular, their alleged reliance upon 'reflex anal dilatation'[11] as a sign of suspected abuse was regarded as controversial. Yet non-physical evidence of sexual abuse, such as disclosure by the child, was equally problematic, because of distrust of children as witnesses, and fears that they could be led into making false allegations. It might have been thought that *clinical* physical proof of abuse would be treated in the same way that bruises and burn marks are – as strongly suggestive of non-accidental injury. Indeed, anal dilatation is an accepted sign of anal intercourse in *adults*. But the undoubted mistakes which were made in the handling of the cases strengthened the position of those who sought to roll back the state's 'interference' in family privacy. All of these factors were reflected in the eventual legislation.

6 Department of Health, *Child Abuse: A Study of Inquiry Reports 1980-1991* (1991).
7 See J Rowe and L Lambert, *Children Who Wait* (1973), and S Millham, R Bullock, K Hosie and M Haak, *Lost in Care: The problems of maintaining links between children in care and their families* (1986).
8 Second Report from the Social Services Committee, Session 1983-4, *Children in Care* HC 360, (the Short Report).
9 *The Law on Child Care and Family Services* (1987) Cm 62.
10 *Report of the Inquiry into Child Abuse in Cleveland 1987* (1988) Cm 413.
11 An explanation of both genital and anal abuse is given in Ch 11 of the Cleveland Report.

The Children Act 1989 was not a revolutionary break with the past, however, even though it was proclaimed as the 'most comprehensive and far-reaching reform of child law which has come before Parliament in living memory'.[12] In fact, it built upon the provisions of the 1948 and 1963 Acts rather than jettisoned them, although the Department of Health's Guidance suggested a change of emphasis:

> '[The old law] ... was formulated in a way that implied that the aim of supportive work is to prevent admission to care. This has contributed to a negative interpretation of local authority interaction with families. The direct link between preventive work and reducing the need for court procedures ... is reproduced in the Children Act in paragraph 7 of Schedule 2 but only as one of a range of local authority duties and powers... The Act gives a positive emphasis to identifying and providing for the child's needs rather than focusing on parental shortcomings in a negative manner'.[13]

The Act, and the accompanying guidance, reaffirm the principle that children should be cared for in their own family wherever possible, and that a partnership between family and state, through the local authority social worker, is both the effective way of achieving this, and a fair way. As the White Paper put it:

> 'the prime responsibility for the upbringing of children rests with parents; the state should be ready to help parents to discharge that responsibility especially where doing so lessens the risk of family breakdown... services to families in need of help should be arranged in a voluntary partnership with the parents'.[14]

Yet the word 'partnership' does not appear in the Act and is nowhere defined either there, or in the Guidance, and it may mean different things to different people. It can embrace both an idea of the empowerment of women and children, identified with the Left, and a New Right idea of family consumerism and choice. But, whatever its meaning, it breaks down because ultimately, despite the rhetoric, it will be for professionals – social workers and courts – to determine at what point voluntary partnership will give way to coercive control.[15]

---

12 Lord Mackay LC, 502 HL Official Report (5th series) col 488.
13 *The Children Act 1989 Guidance and Regulations, Volume 2, Family Support, Day Care and Educational Provision for Young Children* (1991) paras 2.13, 2.15.
14 Department of Health, *The Law on Child Care and Family Services* (1987) Cm 62, para 5.
15 S Braye and M Preston-Shoot, 'Honourable Intentions: Partnership and Written Agreements in Welfare Legislation' [1992] JSWFL 511. The tension between privacy, autonomy and partnership on the one hand, and compulsory intervention on the other, is illustrated by this statement in Vol 2 of the *Children Act 1989 Guidance and Regulations* (1991) para 2.7: 'Families with a child in need, whether the need results from family difficulties or the child's circumstances, have the right to receive sympathetic support and sensitive *intervention in their family's life*' (emphasis added).

3. PARTNERSHIP WITH PARENTS –
FAMILY SUPPORT

(a) Universal or selective services?

Article 18(2) of the United Nations Convention on the Rights of the Child requires states to:

'render appropriate assistance to parents and legal guardians in the performance of their child-rearing responsibilities and ... ensure the development of institutions, facilities and services for the care of children'.

We looked in Chapter 10 at the role of the state in the provision of child care, and how the United Kingdom has accepted that role half-heartedly. But state provision of advice and guidance to parents on the care and upbringing of children dates back to the beginning of the twentieth century when health visitors began to visit women who had recently given birth, to educate them in appropriate methods and standards of nutrition and hygiene.[16] Such women (they were always women) could also provide an inspection and surveillance system, which could be used to trigger further investigation should they have cause for concern, and they continue to perform both functions. Although the rise of social work as a profession and service has shifted the focus in child-care law away from health visitors' activities, they are still an important element of social control, with two distinctive features. First, they have a mandate to visit *all* new mothers and children up to five, thus 'intervening' in families regardless of social class, whereas social work is, albeit unintentionally, concentrated on the poor.[17] At the same time, and perhaps as a corollary, they have no coercive powers, and must depend upon co-operation. They may therefore appear less threatening and judgmental than social workers. Their identification with the *health* service, as qualified nurses and working as part of the primary health care team, rather than with the social services, facilitates this.[18]

Part III of the Children Act sets out the powers and duties local authorities have to provide support for children and families. Under s 17(1), they owe a 'general'[19] duty:

---

16   Chapter 10. For the origins of health visiting, see D Dwork, *War is Good for Babies and Other Young Children* (1987) Ch 5.
17   S Becker and S Macphearson, *Public Issues and Private Pain: Poverty, Social Work and Social Policy* (1988).
18   See R Dingwall, J Eekelaar and T Murray, *The Protection of Children* (1983) p 232.
19   The inclusion of the word 'general' has been taken to reverse a decision under the prior law requiring local authorities to consider the impact of policy decisions upon individual children rather than to the child population in general: *R v London Borough of Barnet, ex p B* [1994] 1 FLR 592.

'(a) to safeguard and promote the welfare of children in their area who are in need; and

(b) so far as is consistent with that duty to promote the upbringing of such children by their families, by providing a range and level of services appropriate to those needs'.

The duty is to a *category* of children in the area – to those 'in need' – rather than to all children. A child is defined in s 17(10) as in need if:

'(a)he is unlikely to achieve or maintain, or to have the opportunity of achieving or maintaining, a reasonable standard of health or development without the provision for him of services by a local authority under this Part;

(b) his health or development is likely to be significantly impaired, or further impaired, without the provision for him of such services; or

(c) he is disabled'.

We considered the services to disabled children in Chapter 10. Notwithstanding their inclusion within the definition in s 17, we regard their needs, and the relationship between parents and the state in fulfilling them, as distinct from those where deprivation or abuse may be in prospect, because of the usual absence of the possibility of coercive action being taken against the parents.

Section 17(11) elaborates the definition by providing that 'development' means physical, intellectual, emotional, social or behavioural development, and 'health' means physical or mental health. Andrew Bainham has described this definition as 'pregnant with indeterminacy'.[20] Official guidance states that the definition is 'deliberately wide to reinforce the emphasis on preventive support and services to families'.[1] However, local authorities, with limited budgets to provide services (although they are required to facilitate the provision of these by others, and in particular by voluntary organisations under s 17(5)), might interpret it in such a way as to limit their duty to cover only children who would otherwise be at risk of abuse or neglect. An overt policy of this kind would be unlawful, but in practice it does appear that services have been at least concentrated upon those children deemed most at risk. For example, a survey of local authorities found that highest priority in the provision of services was accorded to children 'for whom the local authority already have some responsibility, with children at risk of abuse or neglect and those in care or accommodated ranked highest'.[2] In an earlier analysis of this study, it was reported that of 60 returns indicating which categories of children were recognised as 'in need', 27 authorities

20 *Children, The Modern Law* (1993) p 338.

1 *Children Act 1989 Guidance and Regulations Volume 2* (1991) para 2.4.

2 *Children Act Report 1993* (1994) para 2.10. The Audit Commission also found a concentration of effort upon child protection rather than preventive and supportive work: *Seen but Not Heard – Executive Summary* (1994).

identified children with special education needs; 23, children with difficult family relationships; 17, families in bed and breakfast accommodation; 8, families whose gas, electricity or water had been cut off; and 4, children in independent schools. There is therefore enormous scope for regional variation in what is made available and to whom.[3] While John Eekelaar has suggested a division in the concept of parental responsibility in the Children Act, between the responsibility (ie duties) of parents *to* their children, and responsibility *for* those children,[4] and Nigel Parton has identified a further bifurcation in child care law, distinguishing children in need from those requiring *compulsory* intervention because they are suffering, or are likely to suffer significant harm,[5] there is another split here, between children in need, and the rest. The identification of the category enables further assessment and sub-classification to be carried out, as the survey returns suggest.

In addition to the general duty, authorities have a number of more specific duties set out in Sch 2, Pt I to the Act. They must take reasonable steps to identify the extent to which there are children in need in their area. This will enable them to plan the services they will provide. Having done so, they must publicise these services so that families can make use of them. The old preventive duty continues in paragraphs 4 and 7, which require authorities to take reasonable steps to prevent children within their area suffering ill-treatment or neglect, and to reduce the need to bring civil or criminal proceedings in respect of them. But a 'broadly consistent and somewhat worrying picture is emerging'[6] of authorities having little idea of the extent of need, beyond estimates based on past and existing referrals to social services and of little progress towards a proactive service being offered. There is present scepticism, therefore, at the extent to which these duties are being effectively implemented. A 'dark figure' of children and families who could benefit from support but who are not receiving it may therefore be postulated.

(b) The services to be offered

Support services for families covered by Part III of the Children Act 1989 fall into two main types; the first concerns children who continue to live at home and the second is the provision of accommodation for those who are unable to do so. Under the old law, the latter was regarded as a sign

3 *Children Act Report 1992* (1993) p 34.
4 J Eekelaar, 'Parental Responsibility: State of Nature or Nature of the State?' [1991] JSWFL 37.
5 N Parton, 'The Contemporary Politics of Child Protection' [1992] JSWFL 100, at 104.
6 *Children Act Report 1993* (1994) para 2.39.

that other social work intervention had failed and that the only course left was to let the child be taken away from home (even though parents could remove the child, subject to certain exceptions, at will). Classing accommodation as part of family support services is intended to emphasise its positive role.

(i) Services for children in need living at home

It may be noted first that, although the focus of the authority's interest will be upon the identified child in need, the service may be given to the child's family, or another member of that family, rather than to the child him or herself. For example, Sch 2, para 8 requires authorities to make appropriate provision for advice, guidance and counselling, occupational, social, cultural or recreational activities, home help, assistance with travel needs and assistance to enable the child and the family to take a holiday. One can note a blend of consumerism and of 'tutelage'[7] in this range of facilities. Mothers of large families, or with children with disabilities, for example, might be provided with a home help; alternatively, or additionally, they might be given guidance on child care. An element of surveillance may be present in the provision of such services; an apparent unwillingness or failure to accept what is offered, or to respond to the advice, may prompt a closer interest in the family and consideration of whether further intervention is warranted.

Surveillance in conjunction with help may be further facilitated by the establishment of 'family centres'. Under Sch 2, para 9, these must be provided as considered appropriate by local authorities for children (not just those 'in need') within their area. They are defined as centres where children, parents and other carers can attend for 'occupational, social, cultural or recreational activities' or 'advice, guidance or counselling', and they may be run as residential or drop-in centres. Department of Health Guidance identifies three types of centres: *therapeutic*, where intensive casework is carried out with families needing help in parenting skills and relationships; *community*, where neighbourhood groups provide a meeting place for families, and may run playgroups, adult education classes, baby clinics and other activities; and *self-help*, where groups run their own range of support services, often as a co-operative venture.[8] It adds that they may:

'provide accommodation where families can be observed for prolonged periods which may help to identify particular difficulties with parenting skills and what action to take to improve family function'.[9]

---

7 See Ch 10.
8 *Children Act 1989 Guidance and Regulations Volume 2* (1991), para 3.20.
9 *Ibid*, para 3.22.

There is inevitably a fine line to be drawn between benevolent observation and advice on the one hand, and scrutiny and evaluation of parenting ability on the other.

In addition to providing, or facilitating provision by the voluntary sector of these sorts of services, local authorities may provide assistance in the form of kind or, in exceptional circumstances, cash, but are obliged to consider the financial means of the child and the parents before doing so.[10] Furthermore where:

> 'it appears to a local authority that a child who is living on particular premises is suffering, or is likely to suffer, ill-treatment at the hands of another person who is living on these premises; and ... that other person proposes to move from the premises, the authority may assist that person to obtain alternative accommodation'.[11]

The rationale for this provision, which in one sense might be seen as rewarding an abuser by helping him or her find a new home, was the realisation that it is both unfair and potentially damaging to a child who is suffering, or at risk of abuse, to be removed from home rather than to have the abuser removed. However, the abuser cannot be *required* to leave by a local authority using the private law; in *Nottinghamshire County Council v P*,[12] the Court of Appeal allowed a father's appeal against a prohibited steps order preventing him from returning to the home where he had sexually abused his three daughters. The local authority had sought the order, rather than apply under Part IV of the Act for a care or supervision order, apparently to avoid 'excessive intervention in the life of a family'.[13] It might be queried whether a social services department's invocation of the court's power (assuming a prohibited steps order could indeed have been used as an ouster) to exclude a person from his home was not also something of an intervention in the life of a family. But in any event, it was clear that, under s 9(2) and (5), the local authority could not obtain a prohibited steps order if the effect of that order would have been achievable through the making of a residence or contact order. Further, although the court may make orders of its own motion, the Court of Appeal firmly ruled that local authorities have a duty to use the public law procedures laid out in Parts IV and V of the Act rather than attempt to use the private law route. The Court therefore attempted to introduce a rigid distinction between private law and public law powers and remedies, perhaps in order to emphasise the continuing autonomy of family life and the necessity of state intervention being

---

10 Section 17(6)-(8). People in receipt of income-related benefits are not required to make a contribution.

11 Schedule 2, para 5.

12 [1994] Fam 18. See also C Cobley and N V Lowe, 'Ousting Abusers – Public or Private Law Solution?' (1994) 110 LQR 38.

13 According to their counsel, quoted by Sir Stephen Brown at 37A

carried out by means of clearly defined and expected routes.[14] This can be criticised as, on the one hand, ignoring the potential for subtle intervention which, as we have suggested, permeates the Part III powers and duties; and on the other, as leaving a significant gap in the range of ways in which the state can protect children from abuse. There has been considerable official support for an ouster power: The Law Commission and the Children Act Advisory Committee both advocated the provision of a power to permit local authorities to seek orders to exclude an abuser from the family home, and the Government eventually accepted its value.[15]

The greater the provision of a range of support services where the child is living at home, the greater the need for careful planning and agreement between the authority and the parents, so that both are clear about what is to be provided, and what is perhaps expected in return. There will be even greater involvement when the decision is to be made to accommodate the child away from the parents.

(ii) Accommodation of children in need

The Children Act 1948 provided for the reception of children into local authority care at the parents' request when the latter were unable to carry on looking after them.[16] This process was known as 'voluntary care', because the parents agreed to it, and continued to enjoy their parental rights and duties in respect of the child, in contrast to the loss of those rights and duties by virtue of action initiated by the local authority, either through the courts, under care proceedings by virtue of s 1 of the Children and Young Persons Act 1969 or wardship, or by assumption of rights through passing an administrative resolution under s 3 of the Child Care Act 1980.[17] But the law could operate in such a way that the voluntary placing of a child into care could become an involuntary inability to recover the child,[18] and hence could be regarded with fear by parents

14 The restrictions on local authority recourse to wardship are motivated by the same desire, see s 100, discussed in Ch 13, (but note *Re S (minors) (Inherent Jurisdiction: Ouster)* [1994] 1 FLR 623, where, in similar circumstances, the High Court ousted the father under its inherent jurisdiction). As Nigel Lowe has noted (at [1994] Fam Law 10), there is an irony in this approach, given that the Act was intended *inter alia* to harmonise previously separate statutory schemes.

15 Law Com No 207, *Domestic Violence and Occupation of the Family Home* (1992) paras 6.15-6.22; *Children Act Advisory Committee, Annual Report 1992/93* (1994) pp 21-22; Scottish Office, *Scotland's Children* (1993) Cm 2286, para 5.19; Family Homes and Domestic Violence Bill Ch 17 and Sch 3.

16 There was also a duty to receive children who had been abandoned or who had no parents or guardians: Child Care Act 1980, s 2.

17 For a valuable discussion of the law before the Children Act, see A Bainham, *Children, Parents and the State* (1988) Chs 4, 5.

18 See, eg, the sequence of events in *F v Wirral Metropolitan Borough Council* [1991] Fam 69.

anxious to receive help for their children, but not to run the risk of losing them entirely. First, where a child had been in voluntary care for at least six months, parents could not remove the child without first giving the local authority 28 days' notice of their intention to do so. The House of Lords held, in *Lewisham London Borough Council v Lewisham Juvenile Court Justices*,[19] that the authority could use the 28 days as a breathing space in which to take action to keep the child away from home against the parents' wishes. Even where the child had been in voluntary care for under six months so that no notice period was required, the House's view of the law meant that provided children were not physically in the care of the parents, the authority could keep them long enough to take the requisite action. Further steps could take one of two forms. The local authority might pass a parental rights resolution, which could be done if certain grounds could be made out. The grounds generally related to parental fitness to care for the child, but one was that the child had been in voluntary care for at least three years, for whatever reason. A resolution could be challenged subsequently, but not before it came into effect, in the juvenile court. Alternatively, if no such grounds could be established, the authority could make the child a ward of court and ask the High Court to commit the child to local authority care.

One aim of these mechanisms, which might today appear draconian, had been to prevent the drift to which we referred above, with children lingering for long periods in voluntary care. As long as the parents retained their parental rights, the authority could not plan the child's long-term future properly, in case the parents suddenly decided to resume their care of the child and scupper the plan.[20] The influence of the views of Goldstein, Freud and Solnit, who emphasised that a child's sense of time is quite different from that of adults, and cannot sustain relationships at a distance over a long period, led to a desire to seek alternative long-term arrangements for children without having to show positive failure on the part of the parents; the fact that they had not had the care of the child for long enough in itself was to justify their loss of parental rights.[1]

Parental rights resolutions were eventually declared contrary to Articles 6 and 8 of the European Convention on Human Rights,[2] and the use of

---

19 [1980] AC 273.
20 Echoing the complaint, in the nineteenth century, that parents would abandon their children to the workhouses or charitable institutions, only to demand them back when they were old enough to be economically productive.
1 *Beyond the Best Interests of the Child* (1973).Ironically, Goldstein, Freud and Solnit argued that the state should rarely assume the power to remove a child from the 'psychological parent' precisely because of the damage caused by the removal and the difficulty of sustaining the relationship while apart: *Before the Best Interests of the Child* (1979).
2 *R v United Kingdom* [1988] 2 FLR 445, 10 EHRR 82.

wardship as a fall-back mechanism for local authorities unable otherwise to prove parental unfitness lost political support with the backlash against 'unwarranted' social worker intervention caused by the Cleveland affair. Furthermore, the possibility of using these mechanisms could be said to have *encouraged* drift, by allowing social workers the luxury of knowing that, at any time in the future, they could take emergency action to thwart the parents, so that there was no need to rush to obtain compulsory powers early on, although it may be that the pattern was more likely one of sporadic periods of voluntary care and return home, followed by a 'final straw' admission resulting in a resolution.[3] When the law came to be reformed, voluntary care was changed significantly to redress the balance which had apparently swung so far towards the state.

The local authority's duty to provide accommodation for children in need is now classed as one of the family support services under Part III of the Children Act, with the deliberate message that it is to be used, or not, at the parents' wish, in the same way as any other service, such as day care. To reinforce this message, local authorities have no power to acquire parental responsibility in consequence of them accommodating a child, and parents have no duty to give notice before removing the child, after any length of stay.

Section 20(1) of the Children Act provides that accommodation must be provided for a child in need who appears to the local authority to require it as a result of there being no person who has parental responsibility for him, his having been lost or abandoned, or:

> '(c) the person who has been caring for him being prevented (whether or not permanently, and for whatever reason) from providing him with suitable accommodation or care'.

This wording is similar to that which obtained under the old law, but the remainder of the section reinforces the emphasis on parental autonomy.[4] In particular, s 20(7) provides that the authority may not provide accommodation for a child under 16 if any person who has parental responsibility for the child, and is willing and able to provide accommodation or arrange for such accommodation, objects. Section 20(8) further states that any person with parental responsibility may at any time, and without notice remove the child from accommodation provided by the local authority. (Unmarried fathers and step-fathers without parental responsibility are therefore powerless to remove the child.) The only exceptions to these provisions are first, that a child aged 16 may be accommodated against the wishes of those having parental responsibility, if the child agrees to be accommodated.[5] Secondly, where

---

3 M Adcock and R White, 'The use of s 3 resolutions' (1982) 6 *Adoption and Fostering* 9.
4 But there are exceptions where the child is aged 16 or over, see below.
5 Section 20(11).

there is a residence order in force, or an order made under the High Court's inherent jurisdiction giving care of the child to a person, that person alone determines whether the child should be accommodated. Thus, where parents divorce and the mother obtains a residence order, the fact that the father objects to the child's being accommodated has no legal effect on the capacity of the authority to continue to provide that accommodation. The father would have to go to court to seek a residence order in his favour to change the position.[6]

The position of the child in all this is not entirely clear. We have seen that a child aged 16 may be accommodated against the parents' wishes. It is open to question whether, if such a child refused to be accommodated, a parent or other person with parental responsibility could override that refusal, on the basis that *Re W (a minor) (Medical Treatment; Court's Jurisdiction)*[7] is of general application. In any case, s 20(6) requires the authority to give due consideration to the child's wishes, and it might be a futile exercise to seek to prevent the child leaving. If there were a doubt about the child's competence, it would seem that he or she could not validly agree to or refuse being accommodated, and those with parental responsibility would be able to determine the question. Local authorities have a *duty* to accommodate such children only where they consider their welfare likely to be seriously prejudiced otherwise, although they also have a power to do so where they consider this would safeguard or promote the child's welfare. Although the duty is therefore a qualified one, it does at least recognise that not all young people have harmonious family lives and homes in which to see out their adolescence, which may be contrasted with the social security position which we discussed in Chapter 10.

As regards children under 16 who object to being accommodated, s 20(6) could be relevant to an authority rejecting a parent's request to accommodate a child, but again the decision in *Re W* may govern the matter, and the child's view could be overridden by the parents. But where a parent objects under s 20(7), then the local authority could not accommodate the child under the section, even if the child wanted to live away from home. The remedy would have to lie in the child seeking leave to obtain a residence order under s 8 (although not in order to be accommodated by the local authority itself),[8] or in the

---

6 Query whether a prohibited steps order could be made to prevent a parent from either agreeing to have a child accommodated by the authority, or objecting to such accommodation: cf *D v D (County Court Jurisdiction: Injunctions)* [1993] 2 FLR 802 – prohibited steps order could have been made to prevent father agreeing to medical examination of child as part of local authority investigations.

7 [1993] Fam 64; see Ch 6.

8 Children Act 1989, s 9(2) (see Ch 7); a residence order may not be made in favour of the child him or herself: *Re SC (a minor) (Leave to Seek Residence Order)* [1994] 1 FLR 96.

authority possibly taking care proceedings, which we discuss in the next Chapter.[9]

Even before the changes in the law made by the Children Act, the number of children in public care, either with the agreement of parents or compulsorily, had fallen steadily during the 1980s, as policy and practice shifted further towards attempting to keep families together and expanding family support services. The child care population fell from over 90,000 in 1981 to about 60,000 by 1991.[10] As might have been expected, it continued to drop after the Children Act came into force. On 31 March 1993, there were about 52,000 children being looked after by local authorities, compared with 54,400 in 1992. But the position is complicated by the fact that more children are being accommodated under s 20, and fewer under compulsory powers: there were 41,638 children subject to care orders and 17,615 in voluntary care in March 1991. By 1993, the number of children under care orders had dropped by 10,000, but those in s 20 accommodation had increased by 2,000.[11]

Children may be accommodated for very short periods, or for several years, depending on the reason why their own parents cannot care for them. The majority of children in accommodation will be there for a short time only, while a parent is in hospital, for example, and they may never need accommodating again. Others may be accommodated periodically, perhaps as a respite for parents, where the child has behavioural problems, or a disability which requires constant attention by carers. For those children whose parents are not capable of providing satisfactory levels of care or guidance, accommodation may be provided from time to time or in the medium-term, perhaps while parents are given the opportunity to sort themselves out or to receive advice or counselling, or as a long-term substitute for home. Whatever the reason for requiring accommodation, and whatever form it is to take, regulations require that local authorities negotiate a written agreement with the parents or those with parental responsibility, and in consultation with the child. The planning for the agreement should take place preferably before the child is accommodated, and it must be reviewed regularly.[12] The agreement is not legally binding and hence unenforceable, but it provides an opportunity to think through what is required for the child, and what will be the role

---

9 See V Smith, 'Children Act 1989: The Accommodation Trap' [1992] Fam Law 349 for the limitations of this course of action.

10 *Social Trends 24* (1994) Table 7.35. The total number of children in care fell from 92,270 in 1981 to 59,834 in 1991; Department of Health, *Children in the Care of Local Authorities 1991* (1993) A/F91/12, p 7.

11 *Children Act Report 1993*, Table 4.1.

12 *Arrangements for Placement of Children (General) Regulations 1991*, SI 1991/890 and *Review of Children's Cases Regulations 1991*. See *Children Act 1989 Guidance and Regulations Volume 3, Family Placements* (1991) Ch 2.

of the parents while the child is away. It will be important for the agreement to specify who can take decisions, such as consent to medical treatment, since the local authority (and any carers recruited to look after the child) will not have parental responsibility where the child is accommodated under s 20.[13] The agreement should also include arrangements for the child leaving accommodation, such as a notice period, thus going some way to plugging the gap left by the repeal of the notice requirement under the old law. The use of such an agreement provides a practical demonstration of the partnership principle, since it will be drawn up after full consultation and is subject anyway to the parent's rejection and removal or retention of the child. At the same time, it may be recognised that there is scope to use agreements as carrots in preference to the stick of compulsory intervention. Parents may be persuaded that agreement to their child being accommodated is preferable to a care or supervision order being obtained by the authority, the former of which would result in the authority acquiring, and sharing parental responsibility. An example is provided in *KS v GS (a minor: Sexual Abuse)*, where Thorpe J noted the influence of the local authority in a private law case concerning alleged sexual abuse;

'behind the scenes their role was crucially influential. For what they determined was then imposed upon the family under the open or veiled threat that if the family did not accept then there might be intervention.'[14]

No research is yet available to determine whether the apparent increase (noted above) in the number of children looked after under voluntary agreements reflects such practices in general.

The local authority have a number of duties to fulfil in respect of children whom they are looking after. This term includes both children being accommodated under s 20, and those subject to care orders, and we consider these duties after we have examined the route to compulsory care in the next chapter.

---

13 Although s 3(5) empowers a person caring for a child to 'do what is reasonable ... for the purpose of safeguarding or promoting the child's welfare'.
14 [1992] 2 FLR 361 at 367D.

Compulsory intervention to protect children

1. INTRODUCTION

The state's interest in the protection of its more vulnerable citizens may require compulsory intervention in the family. Where different life styles and modes of child upbringing can no longer be regarded as legitimate within a range of acceptable practices, the family may become an object of scrutiny and judgment as well as assistance. Michael King and Judith Trowell[1] have argued that taking legal proceedings to protect the child ironically has the effect of relegating the child's needs to second place while the circumstances of the case are fitted – and distorted – into the legal framework. They advocate European approaches which apparently rely much more upon persuasion rather than coercion and adjudication. Yet their argument contradicts their recognition that, since parents are not in an equal position with social workers, the principle that parents and social workers can truly work in 'partnership' is a hollow one. There is always the *potential* for coercive action behind the relationship, as we noted in the previous chapter.

The extent to which parents' own rights are recognised is governed in part by international obligations. Article 9 of the United Nations Convention on the Rights of the Child provides that states must ensure:

> 'that a child shall not be separated from his or her parents against their will, except when competent authorities subject to judicial review determine, in accordance with applicable law and procedures, that such separation is necessary for the best interests of the child. ... all interested parties shall be given an opportunity to participate in the proceedings and make their views known'.

These requirements are also implicit in the European Convention on Human Rights, in particular in Articles 6 (the right to a fair judicial

---

1 *Children's Welfare and the Law: The Limits of Legal Intervention* (1992)

hearing) and 8 (the right to respect for one's private and family life). While the European Commission and Court have generally rejected complaints based on the *merits* of a decision to remove a child, or to seek a long-term substitute home for a child, they have been more willing to scrutinise the ways in which such decisions are taken. In *R v United Kingdom, O v United Kingdom*,[2] for example, the Court held that the lack of any procedure, under laws pertaining before 1983, for challenging a decision to refuse a parent contact with a child in care, amounted to a breach of both Articles. Furthermore, the assumption of parental rights by administrative resolution was similarly flawed. One of the less-often stated, but nonetheless important, aims and achievements of the Children Act was to ensure that in future, procedures were compatible with these international rights.[3]

Social workers are not the prime movers in the initial suspicion or detection of parental or family conduct which reaches the level of abuse or neglect. Relatives or neighbours may be concerned about a child and inform police, social services departments or the NSPCC. Health visitors or community midwives visiting new mothers may have suspicions. GPs or hospital doctors may treat children brought to them either in respect of 'accidents' or for other medical complaints, and may become doubtful about explanations given, or the quality of care being given to the child. Teachers may regard a child's disruptive or passive behaviour in class as worthy of concern. The child may actually tell someone that he or she is suffering at the hands of parents, family or friends. Dingwall, Eekelaar and Murray, in a study of local authorities' child protection services, found that health service personnel, and health visitors in particular, were responsible for 53% of children aged under five who were referred to social services because of concern.[4] However, the authors' study suggested that, rather than ever-vigilant professionals eagerly on the lookout for signs of abuse, a 'rule of optimism' operates, influencing them (and social workers) to take a positive view of parents, and to seek an innocent explanation for what might have gone wrong.

> 'The liberal order ... is maintained by a comprehensive system of moral inquiry. Such surveillance, however, seems to be sustainable only by its starting assumption that the surveyed are of sound character.... [There is] a liberal compromise, that the family will be laid open for inspection provided that the state undertakes to make the best of what its agents find'.[5]

---

2   [1988] 2 FLR 445, (1987) 10 EHRR 82. See G Douglas, 'The Family and the State under the European Convention on Human Rights' (1988) 2 *International Journal of Law and the Family* 76, pp 97-100. See also *Eriksson v Sweden* (1989) 12 EHRR 183.

3   A Bainham, *Children – The New Law* (1990) para 1.12.

4   R Dingwall, J Eekelaar and T Murray, *The Protection of Children: State Intervention and Family Life* (1983) Chs 1, 3.

5   *Ibid* pp 78, 91.

It may be that this rule of optimism is an essential price to pay for allowing scrutiny of the family. On the other hand, the price may often be too high – as for example in the case of Jasmine Beckford, where the inquiry found that social workers seized on any apparent improvement in parenting as a meaningful advance.[6] Yet the failure or refusal of professionals to abide by this 'rule of optimism' in the Cleveland child abuse affair in 1987 may explain the enormous controversy which resulted and the public refusal to countenance such 'interference'.[7]

Alternatively, the family may already have been known to social services through voluntarily seeking the family support facilities described in Chapter 12. If such facilities prove inadequate to safeguard the child, the authority may decide to take further action through the courts. In fact, even where suspicion is aroused before any prior contact with social services, the local authority, alerted to the problem and instigating investigations, might well attempt support if possible before resorting to compulsion. It will be recalled that s 1(5) of the Children Act requires the court, in any family proceedings, not to make an order unless it considers that doing so would be better for the child than making no order at all. Local authorities contemplating action must therefore be able to show the court that either there is no point in trying non-coercive measures first (perhaps because the level of abuse or neglect is so great), or that they have been tried and failed; otherwise, they will fail to have shown that making an order is better than not doing so.[8] Thus, if a health visitor or teacher suspects that a child is being neglected, the social worker is likely to try to work with the parents first, rather than rush to remove the child. Of course, the seriousness and degree of risk involved will dictate the reaction when alerted to the potential problem. One of the (weaker) criticisms of the events in Cleveland was that the social workers removed children from their families on an emergency basis even though sexual abuse, albeit gravely serious, is generally not life-threatening and proceedings could have been taken in a more planned way which would have allowed the parents due process.[9] The dilemma for the law and policy makers is to provide a range of powers available to social workers to facilitate investigation of the problem and protection of the child, while at the same time to preserve the family from 'unwarranted' interference. The difficulty is that one person's 'unwarranted interference'

6 *A Child in Trust: the Report of the Panel of Enquiry into the circumstances surrounding the death of Jasmine Beckford* (1985) p 78.
7 R Harris develops a similar argument: 'A matter of balance: power and resistance in child protection policy' [1990] JSWL 332.
8 See also *Children Act 1989 Guidance and Regulations Volume 1 Court Orders* (1991) para 3.2.
9 *Report of the Inquiry into Child Abuse in Cleveland 1987* (1988) Cm 412, Ch 10, para 16.14.

is another's 'necessary investigation'. The retrenchment since Cleveland has ostensibly redressed the balance in favour of parental autonomy and privacy, but there is still scope to invoke compulsion.

2. INVESTIGATION OF ABUSE AND NEGLECT

(a) 'Working together'

The fact that so many different professional groups may have a role to play in the detection and treatment of abuse or neglect of children makes their co-operation essential. We consider in Chapters 15 and 16 some of the professional personnel involved in the application of the law relating to parenthood, and we focus here on the particular context of child protection. There is no 'mandatory reporting law' in the United Kingdom, such as is common in the United States, imposing a statutory duty upon any professional to refer a concern about a child to the social services department.[10] However, it has been held that there is no breach of confidentiality if a doctor discloses confidential information in order to safeguard a child's interests,[11] and other professionals are expected to report their concerns.[12] Numerous inquiries into deaths of abused children have pinpointed the failure of the professionals to work together closely enough.[13] The Department of Health's study of such inquiry reports suggested that whereas in the 1970s, the problem was perceived as a duplication of functions, in the 1980s, concern centred upon the separate viewpoints of the different groups.[14] The Cleveland affair is a striking example of this problem. There were sharp divisions of opinion as to the accuracy of the medical diagnosis between the paediatricians and the police surgeons involved. There were difficulties in working relationships between predominantly male police officers, and predominantly female social workers.[15] Guidance to professionals on how to work together in the child protection 'system' is given in the document, *Working Together*.[16]

10 Such a law was regarded as unnecessary by the Inter-departmental *Review of Child Care Law* (1985) paras 12.1-12.4, but for a contrary view, and overview of the arguments and evidence of the efficacy of mandatory reporting, see L Bell and P Tooman, 'Mandatory Reporting Laws: A Critical Overview' (1994) 8 *International Journal of Law and the Family* 337.
11 *Re C (a minor) (Evidence: Confidential Information)* [1991] 2 FLR 478.
12 See *Working Together* (1991) paras 3.10-3.15 and Part 4.
13 For a critical appraisal of the value of such reports, see R Dingwall, 'The Jasmine Beckford Affair' (1986) 49 MLR 489.
14 *Child Abuse: A Study of Inquiry Reports 1980-1989* (1991) para 41.
15 See B Campbell, *Unofficial Secrets* (1988).
16 (1991). This is produced jointly by the Home Office, Department of Health, Department for Education, Welsh Office, epitomising its message of inter-disciplinary co-operation. See John Williams 'Working Together II' (1992) 4 *Journal of Child Law* 68.

It is an important document because it outlines the arrangements, all non-statutory, which underpin the legislation in the Children Act. Three mechanisms, in particular, require discussion here.

(i) Area Child Protection Committees

These are intended to provide a 'recognised joint forum for developing, monitoring and reviewing child protection policies' in the area.[17] The aim is to establish a team of senior members of each of the relevant agencies to produce guidelines on how to handle cases, to identify issues arising from such cases, to recommend improvements to the systems in place, and to promote suitable training to be given to those who have to implement them. The Committees therefore function at a policy and supervisory level, concerned not with the running of individual cases, but with procedures and systems.[18] They are also required to review cases of child death found or suspected to be the result of abuse in their area. The purpose of such reviews is ostensibly to identify lessons which can be learnt for the future, but interestingly, the Department of Health comments that they can also satisfy the need 'to ensure that public concern is allayed and media comment is addressed in a positive manner'.[19]

Research into the functioning of the Committees reveals inevitable variations in their effectiveness and in their own satisfaction with what they have achieved. There is a risk that the demands of investigation into abuse and neglect swamp the attention which Committees, and their constituent agencies, can give to preventive work, and that the Committee may be in an anomalous position when seeking to ensure that its recommendations are translated into action by these agencies. It has been suggested that there might be a place at the national, rather than local level, for a body which can oversee the needs of child protection work, but this would fundamentally alter the nature of delivery of the service, with its local focus and accountability.[20]

(ii) Child protection registers

Each social services department (or the NSPCC) must maintain a register listing children in the area 'who are considered to be suffering from or likely to suffer significant harm and for whom there is a child protection plan'.[1] Entry of a name on to the register does not of itself offer the child

17 *Working Together* (1991) para 2.4.
18 For critical discussion of their predecessors, area review committees, see R Dingwall, J Eekelaar and T Murray, *The Protection of Children: State Intervention and Family Life* (1983).
19 *Working Together* (1991) para 8.1.
20 D Campbell, *Report into the Workings of Area Child Protection Committees* (1994) p xiv.
 1 *Working Together* (1991) para 6.36.

any protection; the purpose is rather to ensure a record of those children who must be monitored, and to enable a check to be made by each agency to see if a child it is dealing with is already on the register. The register is broken down into different categories: neglect, physical injury, sexual or emotional abuse. It appears that only a third of child protection investigations results in registration, although the non-registered cases may receive support, or 'be monitored informally'.[2] Registration is more likely where the police have been involved in the investigation, the alleged abuser is a male parent figure or outsider, the case is one of sexual abuse, there is a family history of abuse or of criminal behaviour, or the family is chaotic, or is joined by a known abuser.

There were 32,500 children on registers in England in March 1993 (although this figure includes children registered more than once because they were considered at risk of more than one type of harm), of whom 3.2% had no social worker allocated to deal with their case. In a survey of selected authorities, two were found to have over 19% of children on their registers with no allocated social worker, meaning that these cases could not be monitored properly, and making a mockery of registration.[3]

Authorities are also encouraged to include in their registers information about members of the household and 'regular visitors'. The information might relate to known convictions for offences against children, but it may go beyond convictions, to suspicions and allegations. In *R v Norfolk County Council Social Services Department, ex p M*,[4] a plumber was accused by a girl of molesting her when he came to the house to carry out repairs. His name was placed on the child protection register as the girl's abuser, and the local authority informed his employer. He had been given no opportunity to answer the allegation before registration. Not surprisingly, therefore, his application for judicial review to quash the registration was granted. It can be seen that registration has considerable implications for civil liberties and represents a major form of surveillance over families and individuals. Where registration occurs, parents may feel extremely ashamed and resentful, and this can damage the relationship with the social workers.

On the other hand, as the *Norfolk* decision shows, at least registration requires that some attempt be made to hear the alleged abuser's side of the story. Control over such people may go beyond registration. In *R v Devon County Council, ex p L*,[5] social workers suspected a man of child sexual abuse on a number of occasions. Over a period of about a year,

---

2 D Gough, *Child Abuse Interventions: A Review of the Research Literature* (1993) p 205.

3 *Children Act Report 1993,* Tables 3.4, 3.5 and para 3.16. The total rose to 34,900 by March 1994: *The Guardian,* 3 February, 1995.

4 [1989] QB 619.

5 [1991] 2 FLR 541.

they informed three women with whom he began relationships of their suspicions, and implied that if the women continued to see him, their children might become the subjects of intervention. Eastham J held that the social workers had acted correctly to protect the children in the light of the unreasonable belief about the man, even though they had not interviewed him themselves, and no criminal charges had ever been brought against him, despite police investigation.

(iii) Child protection conferences[6]

A child protection, or case, conference, is called by the social services department, or NSPCC if that is the lead child protection body in the area, following any investigation into alleged abuse or neglect of a particular child or children under s 47 of the Children Act.[7] The aim of the conference is to:

'share and evaluate the information gathered during the investigation, to make decisions about the level of risk to the child(ren), to decide on the need for registration and to make plans for the future'.[8]

All relevant professional groups should be represented at a case conference, and advice from the local authority's legal section should be available to it. The conference is not a judicial proceeding although the rules of natural justice apply to it, and the decisions taken at it will have lasting significance for the family. In keeping with the emphasis on partnership, *Working Together* advises that exclusion of parents from the conference should only take place on exceptional occasions, and must be especially justified.[9] Children of appropriate age and understanding should also be given the opportunity to attend. Obviously arrangements will have to be carefully worked out where there is a clear conflict between the parents and child, and the child might ask for his or her own friend or supporter to be present. This culture of openness and participation is recent; it was not, until the guidance, the general practice to permit parents (or children) to be present at the conference. Before implementation of the Children Act, June Thoburn found that in only 21% of cases did parents attend the whole of case conferences, and a further 40% attended part, even though the research was conducted in authorities stating a wish to involve parents. Other research has found 'pre-meetings' taking place before the actual case conference at which

6 *Working Together* (1991) Part 6.
7 See below.
8 *Working Together* (1991) para 6.5.
9 For discussion of parents' involvement, see J Thoburn, '"Working Together" and parental attendance at case conferences' (1992) 4 *Journal of Child Law* 11.

parents are admitted.[11] Yet the courts accepted that less than full parental participation was adequate. In *R v East Sussex County Council, ex p R*[11] a teacher discovered that a boy had been hit on the thigh with a wooden spoon by his mother for being 'lippy'. A child protection conference was held and the boy and his sister were placed on the child protection register. The Queen's Bench Division held that it was sufficient for a parent to be given the opportunity to make representations, either in writing or through a social worker, to the conference, on the basis that the procedure was not analagous to a criminal procedure or complaint of misbehaviour leading to a finding of guilt. 'Indeed, the matter did not involve specific criticism of the applicant.'[12] It may be doubted that the mother would have regarded the conference quite so equably. One would expect that, in the wake of the official guidance, exclusion from the conference should be rare, but it is unclear whether guidance has yet been turned into general practice.[13] However, any blanket policy of exclusion should now be regarded as amenable to judicial review, and might well fall foul of Articles 6 and 8 of the European Convention on Human Rights, as an interference with the right to a fair hearing in the determination of one's civil rights, and the right to respect for one's privacy and family life.

Once a decision has been taken to register the child, a child protection plan must be drawn up, specifying the courses of action for each of the relevant agencies, and preferably with the agreement of all concerned.

> 'It will make clear the part to be played by parents, what expectations they may have of agencies and what expectations agencies may have of them. ... must include consideration of the wishes of the child and parents, local resources, the suitability of specialist facilities, their availability for addressing the particular needs of the child and his or her family'.[14]

A review conference should be held every six months to monitor the plan and to decide if registration is still warranted.

The devices of the conference and the register provide an administrative mechanism to establish whether a family should be the object of agency concern, and, if so, to monitor action taken, and any 'progress' achieved. A ratchet effect may be discerned in this process. The threat of registration may be expected to act as a potent encouragement to 'partnership' and co-operation with what is being proposed, as for example, in the *Devon*

---

10 See Gough, *Child Abuse Interventions: A Review of the Research Literature* (1993) pp 205-206.

11 [1991] 2 FLR 358. See also *R v Harrow London Borough Council, ex p D* [1990] Fam 133.

12 *Per* Sir Stephen Brown P at 364B.

13 See S Davies, 'Dilemmas of practice': Review of M Ryan, *The Children Act 1989: Putting it into Practice* (1994) 18 *Adoption and Fostering* (3) 55.

14 *Working Together* (1991) para 5.17.

case (above) where the mothers terminated their relationships with the alleged abuser. Acceptance of Part III services may be seen as the price for no further intervention. Where entry on to the register is decided upon, there is further scope for persuasion; if the family co-operates with the child protection plan, court proceedings may be unnecessary and there is the possibility of de-registration. If registration and co-operation without court action prove inadequate, the family may face court proceedings for care or supervision orders.

(b) Investigation

The legal basis for local authority investigation of allegations of abuse or neglect is contained in two sections of the Children Act 1989. Under s 47, where a local authority:

> '(a) are informed that a child who lives, or is found, in their area—
>   (i) is the subject of an emergency protection order; or
>   (ii) is in police protection;[15] or
> (b) have reasonable cause to suspect that a child who lives, or is found, in their area is suffering, or is likely to suffer, significant harm, the authority shall make, or cause to be made, such enquiries as they consider necessary to enable them to decide whether they should take any action to safeguard or promote the child's welfare.'

A particular concern revealed in a number of inquiry reports was the inability of social workers and others to gain access to a child thought to be at risk. In the case of one child, Doreen Aston, social workers were permitted only to talk to the parents on the front doorstep, while in the case of Kimberley Carlile, the social worker had to observe her through an obscure glass door.[16] Section 47(4) requires the investigating authority to take such steps as are reasonably practicable to obtain access to the child, unless satisfied that they already have sufficient information, and s 47(6) provides that where access is refused, or information about the child's whereabouts is denied to the authority, then there is a duty to seek a court order unless they are satisfied that the child's welfare can be satisfactorily safeguarded without doing so. It will be a brave, or extremely foolish, local authority who decide not to seek an order where difficulty is experienced in gaining access to the child.

In cases of real danger, police protection under s 46 may be utilised. This empowers a constable, who has reasonable cause to believe that a

---

15 Police protection and emergency protection orders are discussed below.
16 Department of Health *Child Abuse: Study of Inquiry Reports 1980-1989* (1991), p 70; London Borough of Greenwich, *A Child in Mind: Report of the Commission of Inquiry into the Circumstances Surrounding the Death of Kimberley Carlile* (1987) p 115.

child would otherwise be likely to suffer significant harm, to remove the child to suitable accommodation, or prevent the child's removal from the place where he or she is currently being accommodated. The parents or other carers, and the local authority must be informed. The child may remain in police protection for up to 72 hours. The purpose of this provision is to enable the police lawfully to remove children from situations of emergency, for example on being found alone at home.

The outcome of the investigation is for the local authority to determine. If they decide not to seek a court order, they must consider whether to review the case at a later date.[18] The position is slightly different where the second investigative duty arises, under s 37 of the Act. There, where family proceedings are pending, and it appears to the court that it may be appropriate for a care or supervision order to be made with respect to a child, the court has the power to direct the local authority to investigate the child's circumstances. There were 1,890 directions made from January to June 1993, compared with 1,205 for the same period in 1992. The rise appears to have been due in part to a desire to obtain a report on a child more speedily than could be arranged in the private law proceedings.[19] This would not be an appropriate use of the power to direct an investigation. Should the authority decide not to apply for an order, they must inform the court of their reasons for this decision, any services they have provided or will offer for the child and the family, and any other action taken, or proposed, with respect to the child.[20] John Eekelaar has suggested that the duty to report back to the court is at least a means of holding the authority to account which is lacking under s 47.[1] However, as he goes on to note, the duty is an empty one since the authority cannot be compelled by the court to seek an order, even where the court is convinced they should do so.[2] The repeal of the court's power to make a care or supervision order of its own motion in pending proceedings was controversial at the time the Children Act was passed, and there have continued to be calls for such a reserve power to be reinstated,[3] but this would significantly weaken the aim of the Act to place responsibility for the application of public law powers upon local authority social services departments. Indeed, those firmly wedded to a family autonomy model of the law relating to parenthood could argue that the power of the court, to direct an investigation by social services departments of a matter

---

17 Section 47(7).
18 See Children Act Advisory Committee, *Annual Report 1992/93*, p 32.
19 Section 37(3). *Re CE (Section 37 Direction)* [1995] 1 FLR 26.
 1 J Eekelaar, 'Investigation under the Children Act 1989' [1990] Fam Law 486, 487.
 2 As demonstrated in *Nottinghamshire County Council v P* [1994] Fam 18.
 3 G Brasse, 'The Section 31 Monopoly' [1993] Fam Law 691.

arising in the context of quite separate proceedings, is itself a significant enough intrusion by the state.[4]

(c) Orders facilitating protection and investigation

(i) Child assessment orders

The need to examine and assess a child who may be at risk of abuse or neglect is obvious. Even something as simple as weighing and measuring a child may reveal cause for concern. Equally obviously, parents with something to hide may attempt to prevent their children being seen, as noted above. The Kimberley Carlile inquiry recommended that a new order should be enacted which would require parents to produce their children to be examined or assessed.[5] There was a strong division of opinion between those who favoured such orders, as offering a lesser form of intervention than the forced removal of a child from home for examination, and those who felt that if parents would not voluntarily allow their children to be examined, an order sanctioning removal would be more effective and less confusing than yet another order representing some sort of half-way house.[6]

Eventually, an order along the lines recommended by the Inquiry was enacted in s 43 of the Children Act 1989. This permits the court to grant an order on the application of a local authority or the NSPCC, where it is satisfied that the applicant has reasonable cause to suspect that the child is suffering, or is likely to suffer significant harm; that an assessment is required to determine whether there are grounds for this suspicion; and that it is unlikely that an assessment will be made, or be satisfactory, in the absence of the order.[7] If granted, the order may last for up to seven days from a date specified,[8] and requires the child to be produced for an assessment. The assessment may involve a medical or psychological examination,[9] or other form of investigation, and the court may sanction

---

4 See, eg, *Re H (a minor) (Section 37 Direction)* [1993] 2 FLR 541: s 37 direction ordered where lesbian couple caring for child handed over at birth, in part because of judge's concern at their ability, as lesbians, to care adequately for the child in the long-term future.
5 *A Child In Mind* (1987) Ch 25.
6 See the account by N Parton, *Governing the Family: Child Care, Child Protection and the State* (1991) pp 188-190.
7 Compare the test in s 31 for a full care order, and the meaning of 'significant harm', which are both discussed below.
8 So that, eg, the order could begin to run from a date of a future appointment at a specialist clinic.
9 Section 43(8) provides that a child of sufficient understanding to make an informed decision may refuse to submit to such an examination or assessment, but in *South*

the child's being kept away from home in order for it to be carried out. Situations where such an order might be appropriate could include cases of apparent failure to thrive, or alleged sexual abuse, where, although the matter is serious, the child is not in immediate serious danger.

However, the availability of these orders has not proved popular with social workers. Only 94 applications were made for child assessment orders in the period 1 October 1992 to 30 September 1993, compared with 2,508 applications for the more draconian emergency protection orders (discussed below).[10] Jonathan Dickens[11] has argued that child assessment orders represent a further attempt by the state to control how social workers go about their work and exercise their own professional judgment in deciding how to respond to situations of concern. He suggests that social workers' reluctance to seek such orders may therefore reflect a resistance to such control. This is interesting, but seems over-elaborate. A simpler explanation may be that, as opponents of the proposed order had predicted, rather than a half-way house, the child assessment order falls between two stools; on the one hand perhaps being avoided for fear of alienating parents who might otherwise have co-operated with an investigation, and on the other being regarded as inadequate to deal with serious cases. There would be a particular risk in seeking and failing to obtain the order, in terms of the message which this would send to non-co-operating parents.

(ii) Emergency protection orders

Before the enactment of the Children Act, it had become common for care proceedings to be initiated by means of a place of safety order. It was found that between one-third and one-fifth of children going into care were subject to such orders, and in some parts of the country, up to 90% of care proceedings were begun in this way.[12] They were used not only for young children in imminent physical danger, but for teenagers in moral danger or beyond parental control. As Jean Packman put it:

'to the protective function of an emergency removal, a sharp demonstration of control on the part of the local authority has been added. Families and children whose behaviour is chaotic and reprehensible are thereby forcibly reminded that the

Glamorgan County Council v W and B [1993] 1 FLR 574, it was held, surely wrongly, in the context of an equivalent provision relating to examinations directed to take place during interim care or supervision orders, that the High Court could exercise its inherent jurisdiction to override this refusal. See further below.
10 *Children Act Report 1993*, Table 3.1.
11 J Dickens, 'Assessment and the Control of Social Work: An Analysis of Reasons for the Non-Use of the Child Assessment Order' [1993] JSWL 88.
12 T Norris and N Parton, 'The administration of place of safety orders' [1987] JSWL 1; Second Report of the Social Services Committee *Children in Care* (HC 360) para 123.

social services department has the power to arrest such conduct in a dramatic fashion'.[13]

Place of safety orders could be granted, *ex parte*, on the application of any person, by a single magistrate, even in his or her own homes authorising the removal of the child to a place of safety for up to 28 days, and with no possibility of appeal. Such an order did not give parental rights to the person obtaining it, but this was not well understood. Although the continuing need for a power of removal of some sort was recognised, the criticisms levelled at place of safety orders meant that the replacement emergency protection orders have important differences. Nonetheless, they are still significant erosions of family autonomy.[14]

As under the law before the Children Act, and unlike the position for child assessment orders under s 43, under s 44(1)(a), any person may apply for an emergency protection order. The order may be made if the court is satisfied that there is reasonable cause to believe that the child is likely to suffer significant harm if he is not removed to accommodation provided by or on behalf of the applicant, or if he does not remain where he is being accommodated. Unlike the test for child assessment orders, the court, not the applicant, must have reasonable cause to believe that there is the likelihood of harm, and only the danger of future harm is relevant. Further, under s 44(1)(b)(c) where investigation by the local authority or authorised person (the NSPCC) is being frustrated because access to the child is being unreasonably refused, the court may grant an emergency protection order where the applicant authority or authorised person has reasonable cause to believe that access to the child is required as a matter of urgency. For any application, the welfare test under s 1 must also be satisfied, although s 1(3) does not apply.

The order requires the child to be produced to the applicant, and for the child to be removed (or prevented from being removed). The court may also authorise the applicant to enter premises in order to search for the child, and require a person to disclose any information he or she may have about the child's whereabouts.[15] The order may last for up to eight days, but it may be extended once for up to a further seven days. It is therefore of shorter duration than under the old law, requiring the local authority to move quickly in assessing whether further court proceedings should be taken, and in assembling sufficient evidence to justify such proceedings.

Given the emergency nature of the order, it can be made *ex parte* as under the old law, although the rules do provide for notice of one clear

13 J Packman, *The Child's Generation* (2nd ed, 1981) p 184. See also S Millham *et al*, *Lost in Care* (1986) p 47.
14 2,512 applications for emergency protection orders were made in 1993 of which about 90% were granted: *Judicial Statistics, England and Wales 1993*, Cm 2623 Table 5.2.
15 Section 48. See *Volume 1, Court Orders* (1991) paras 4.52-4.57.

day to be given.[16] Application to discharge the order may be made after 72 hours, but there is no provision for appeal, either against the making of, or the refusal to make, an order, and this may render either the parents, or the local authority, impotent in the face of an apparently irrational decision by the bench.[17]

The Cleveland events showed a general misunderstanding of the legal consequences of making a place of safety order. Social workers wrongly assumed that they had authority to withhold contact from the parents, and to consent to medical examination of the child. The position under emergency protection orders is clear. The order gives the applicant parental responsibility to enable him or her to take important decisions, such as those relating to medical examination, in respect of the child[18] unless the child is of sufficient understanding to make an informed decision and refuses.[19] On the other hand, there is a presumption that reasonable contact between the child and parents be permitted, and if there is a dispute over this the court may make a direction about contact, either when it makes the order, or while it is in force.[20]

3. PROCEEDINGS FOR CARE OR SUPERVISION ORDERS

Assuming that further intervention through court proceedings is felt to be warranted by the local authority after completing their investigations, it is necessary to consider the grounds upon which the court may make an order sanctioning continuing and compulsory control over the parents' or carers' upbringing of the child. We noted in Chapter 12 that the grounds for making care or supervision orders prior to the Children Act appeared to focus upon the circumstances of the *child*, even though the real concern was the care being given by the *parents*. Meanwhile, parental rights resolutions, which had the same effect of removing parental responsibility from the parent or parents, could be passed on grounds more closely tied to parental unfitness. Furthermore, the courts in matrimonial or wardship proceedings could make care or supervision orders where they regarded the circumstances as

---

16 Family Proceedings Courts (Children Act 1989) Rules 1991, SI 1991/1395, r 4(4) and Sch 2.
17 Section 45(9)(10); *Essex County Council v F* [1993] 1 FLR 847.
18 But s 44(5)(b) requires that action in meeting that responsibility should be limited to what is reasonably required to safeguard or promote the welfare of the child, having regard to the duration of the order.
19 Section 44(7). But note *South Glamorgan County Council v W and B* [1993] 1 FLR 574 (above).
20 Section 44(6)(13).

'exceptional'.[1] The 1989 Act simplified the law by allowing only one route to a care or supervision order – that the criteria set out in s 31 are satisfied, and that the child's welfare requires the making of the order within s 1.[2]

A local authority or authorised person[3] may apply to the court for a care or supervision order, which may be granted where the court is satisfied:

> '(a)that the child concerned is suffering, or is likely to suffer, significant harm; and
> (b) that the harm, or likelihood of harm, is attributable to—
> (i) the care given to the child, or likely to be given to him if the order were not made, not being what it would be reasonable to expect a parent to give to him; or
> (ii) the child's being beyond parental control.'

These grounds are known as the 'threshold criteria', because without satisfying them, no order can be made. However, the court must still go on to consider the child's welfare under s 1 and in so doing, have regard to the welfare checklist in s 1(3) and the no order principle in s 1(5).[4]

The section gives only limited guidance on the meaning of the threshold criteria. While harm is defined as meaning 'ill-treatment or the impairment of health or development', and ill-treatment, health and development are in turn defined in s 31(9), 'significant' is not defined. Guidance advises that it means 'considerable, noteworthy or important'.[5] Of more value to a court perhaps, s 31(10) provides that where the question of whether harm is significant turns on the child's health or development, these should be compared with the health or development which could reasonably be expected of a similar child. Thus, the development of a child with a known learning difficulty should not be compared with that of a child of average intelligence. But the extent to which one must construct a hypothetical similar child is problematic. Does one have to control for every relevant variable? In *Re O (a minor) (Care Proceedings: Education)*, Ewbank J ruled that, in the context of a truanting 15 year old, a similar child meant:

> 'a child of equivalent intellectual and social development, who has gone to school, and not merely an average child who may or may not be at school'.[6]

1 See Law Com WP No 100, *Care, Supervision and Interim Orders in Custody Proceedings*, Part II, No 101, *Wards of Court*, paras 3.30-3.47. In 1991, 8% of children in care were there under matrimonial care orders, and 15% under wardship committals; *Children in Care of Local Authorities 1991*, p 8.
2 It is possible for a care or supervision order to be made in other family proceedings, but only where the local authority or authorised person apply for such an order, and only on satisfaction of s 31(2) etc.
3 So far, only the NSPCC: s 31(9).
4 *Humberside County Council v B* [1993] 1 FLR 257.
5 *Volume 1, Court Orders* (1991) para 3.19.
6 [1992] 1 WLR 912 at 917 G-H.

It is not clear what his lordship meant by social development. Michael Freeman argues[7] that it should include an assessment of the child's cultural background, so that children from ethnic or other minorities should not be compared with those of the majority culture. Andrew Bainham, on the other hand, argues that the threshold criteria set minimally acceptable levels of behaviour towards children, and that culture is relevant only at the welfare test stage of the process.[8] Bainham's approach appears more convincing, especially since s 1(3)(d) expressly requires account to be taken of the child's background.

One of the major difficulties in obtaining a care order under the Children and Young Persons Act 1969, was that the main primary ground for so doing was phrased in the present tense; it had to be shown under s 1(2)(a) that:

> 'the child's proper development is being avoidably prevented or neglected or his health is being avoidably impaired or neglected or he is being ill-treated'.

The problem with this test was first, that a future prospect of harm was not covered, and secondly, that past harm which might recur if action were not taken also appeared to be excluded. The House of Lords minimised these difficulties by ruling, in *Re D (a minor)*[9] that the court could look back at the state of affairs existing immediately before the process of protecting the child had begun, and that the present tense covered a continuing situation which involved consideration of past, present and future development of the child. The original clause in the Children Bill dealt with the first problem by including reference to a likelihood of harm, and it addressed the second by using the words 'has suffered', to ensure that the argument that the child was no longer in danger and hence could not be suffering significant harm, could not be put. However, the wording was amended to stress the need to show continuing or future risk rather than evidence only of past harm, and this caused the Court of Appeal, in *Re M (a minor) (Care Orders: Threshold Conditions)*[10] to interpret the provision as requiring a finding of present or future harm at the time of the full hearing for the care order and not just at the time when the initial proceedings were set in train. The case concerned a young child whose father had murdered his mother. The child was placed in foster care and the local authority sought a care order with a view to finding an adoptive family for him. The mother's cousin, who was already looking after his half-siblings, sought a residence order to take over his care. The Court of Appeal considered that, since the father was in prison, and the cousin could provide adequate substitute

---

7 *Children, Their Families and the Law* (1992) at p 153.
8 See A Bainham, *Children: The modern law* (1993) at p 389.
9 [1987] AC 317.
10 [1994] Fam 95.

care for the child, he could not be said to be suffering, or likely to suffer significant harm, by the time of the hearing. This approach would have rendered it extremely difficult for local authorities to prove *present* significant harm where the child had been removed from danger, although it would have reflected a view, expressed especially after the Cleveland events, that *past* parental failings should not, *of themselves*, be sufficient to justify coercive action against the parents. The House of Lords reversed the Court of Appeal decision, and confirmed the *Re D* approach.[11] It will thus be possible for a local authority to obtain an order on the basis of the events which triggered their intervention, so long as, according to Lord Mackay, arrangements to protect the child have been continuously in place since then.[12] Oddly, the House made a care order in the local authority's favour, even though they accepted that the cousin (who had taken over care after the Court of Appeal judgment) was an excellent carer for the child. The supposed advantages of continuing monitoring of the child's progress, and the ability to intervene 'with speed if anything goes wrong'[13] show a clear policy preference for state scrutiny over family autonomy, although it may be significant that here, the 'family' was not that of the traditional nuclear family of parents and child.

It is not enough to show that the child is suffering, or is likely to suffer significant harm. The court must also be satisfied that the cause of this is that the care given, or likely to be given, to the child is not what it would be reasonable to expect a parent to give, or that the child is beyond parental control. In *Re M*, and more clearly in *Oldham Metropolitan Borough Council v E*,[14] the Court of Appeal had taken the view that this requirement was not limited to consideration of care actually provided *by a parent*. If an alternative carer was available who could provide a reasonable standard of care for the child, there could not be a finding of a likelihood of significant harm due to the care to be given. This argument had previously failed in *Northamptonshire County Council v S*[15] where Ewbank J had held that it is the parent's or existing carer's care which is relevant at the threshold stage; the quality of substitute care being considered only when deciding what order should be made. The House of Lords in *Re M*, in expressly overruling the *Oldham* decision and upholding *Northamptonshire*, appear to have adopted Ewbank J's reasoning. In so doing, the House reasserted the state's power to scrutinise and judge care arrangements for children who have come to the social

11 [1994] 2 AC 424.
12 At 433 H. But it is doubtful that the Lord Chancellor was thereby seeking to restrict the test; rather, he appears simply to have been addressing the problem caused by the inevitable passage of time between initial proceedings and the full care hearing.
13 *Per* Lord Templeman at 440 F.
14 [1994] 1 FLR 568.
15 [1993] Fam 136.

services' attention, whereas the Court of Appeal had adopted a much more *laissez faire*, family autonomy approach, stigmatising the making of public law orders in circumstances where the wider family could provide an alternative carer as 'social engineering'.[16] The House's preferred approach clearly implies that, notwithstanding the rhetoric of partnership between parents and authority, and the placement of s 20 accommodation within Part III of the Children Act, there is still a risk that acceptance of such services may make it harder to resist compulsory intervention in the future.

On the other hand, the legislative scheme may appear to have a gap where, although the child is not at risk of harm, there is no one available to take parental responsibility for him or her.[17] In *Birmingham City Council v D; Birmingham City Council v M*[18] Thorpe J ruled that orphans in local authority accommodation could not be made the subjects of care orders, simply because they were orphans, as there was no evidence that they were suffering, or likely to suffer significant harm. He rejected the authority's argument that the fact that there was no-one with parental responsibility for the children placed them at risk. In fact, the children were going to be adopted, so that, in the future, they would have adults with parental responsibility for them, but nonetheless, the similar situation could arise where there is no one to take important decisions for the child's future, since accommodation under s 20 does not give the local authority parental responsibility. In that situation, the authority would have to invoke the High Court's inherent jurisdiction so that the decision could be taken, or seek leave for a specific issue order under s 8. Since both courses of action would be a form of state intervention, it would seem sensible that there be some more appropriate mechanism available whereby the authority could acquire parental responsibility for the child.[19]

The court may make an order where the significant harm, or risk of it, is due to the child's being beyond parental control. Under the law before the Children Act 1989, parents could ask the local authority to initiate proceedings on this basis, and at one time, parents could take proceedings themselves.[20] The requirements that only the state, through the local

16 [1994] Fam 95 at 105 B *per* Balcombe LJ.

17 Under the old law, a parental rights resolution could have been passed.

18 [1994] 2 FLR 502.

19 In Re S *(minors)(Care Proceedings: Power to make care orders in respect of orphans)* [1994] Fam Law 356, care orders were made in the county court, where the testamentary guardians of the children sought to disclaim their appointments (on which, see Ch 5). The facts are distinguishable from *Re JD and BM* (above), but the reasoning and result are clearly inconsistent.

20 This was abolished by the Children and Young Persons Act 1963, although parents could ask the court to direct local authorities to take proceedings: s 3(1). See also P Meyer, *The Child and the State: The Intervention of the State in Family Life* (1983) p 28 , describing the ancient French power of fathers to require the state to imprison their recalcitrant children.

authority, may bring proceedings, and that harm or the risk of harm must be shown, can be seen as either the assertion by the state that it alone has the right to judge that a child cannot be handled by his or her parents, or as a benevolent realisation that it is undesirable to pit parents against child in the courts in such cases.

It seems strange that the law currently appears to provide that the state may *share* parental responsibility with those parents it deems unfit to care for their children, but it may not be able to *acquire* parental responsibility where no one else has it.

4. ORDERS WHICH CAN BE MADE

Once the threshold conditions have been satisfied,[1] the court still has to determine the outcome in the light of the child's welfare. The local authority must submit a plan to the court, setting out what it proposes for the child.[2] This will build upon any previous agreement reached with the parents, and after consultation with them and, if appropriate, the child. The views of the guardian *ad litem* will also be taken into account. It is at this stage that the particular circumstances of the family, including cultural or ethnic background, can be given weight. For example, the court might conclude that although the parents are unduly rigid in their upbringing of the child, it is not appropriate to make a care order, and that lesser intervention, or none, is called for in the context of the other benefits the child receives from the home.

The rationale for requiring a plan is clear – to enable the court to know what the consequences of the order for the child are expected to be. But it is by no means certain that a plan developed at that particular stage in the child's life will prove workable or sensible in the future; children's perceived needs may change, and there may be disagreement between professionals over how they are best met.[3] However, it is not open to courts to impose conditions in care orders whereby they might monitor or determine what happens after, since this would be to interfere in the exercise of parental responsibility by the local authority.[4]

---

1 Where the court is not in a position to make a final decision, it may make an interim care or supervision order under s 38.
2 In *Manchester City Council v F* [1993] 1 FLR 419, it was said that plans should be set out as indicated in the Guidance, *Volume 3, Family Placements* (1991) para 2.62.
3 Social Services Inspectorate, *Planning Long Term Placement Study* (1994) para 4.6.
4 *Re B (minors) (Termination of Contact: Paramount Consideration)* [1993] Fam 301; *Re J (minors) (Care: Care Plan)* [1994] 1 FLR 253. For a case illustrating the contrast between a care order without conditions, and a s 8 order with conditions attached, see *Re T (a minor) (Care Order: Conditions)* [1994] 2 FLR 423 (guardian *ad litem* argued for care order with condition that child live at home; residence order rather than care order made, on condition that father did not share bed with the child).

It is open to the court to make a care or supervision order; a s 8 order, with or without conditions attached to it; or no order at all, depending upon the court's view of whether, and how much, continuing state involvement in the child's life is required.

A care order gives the local authority parental responsibility, which it shares with the parents (or guardian). The order continues in effect, unless discharged, until the child reaches the age of 18.[5] In the wake of European Court decisions such as *R v United Kingdom*, and Article 9 of the United Nations Convention, noted above, the decision as to the extent to which the parents and other relatives can continue to enjoy contact with the child, as opposed to other aspects of the child's life in care, *is* reviewable by the court. We consider the effects of a care order and the question of contact further in the next chapter.

A supervision order requires the supervisor, who will usually be a social worker, to advise, assist and befriend the child. It may last for up to one year in the first instance, and may be renewed for a further two years.[6] The focus of the order is upon work with the child, but in many cases, it is the parents who require the help or control. There is some means of meeting this need in Sch 3, para 3. This provides that the court may require a 'responsible person' (a person with parental responsibility for the child, or with whom the child is living) who consents, to take all reasonable steps to ensure that the child complies with any directions given by the supervisor, or with any requirements included in the order to undergo medical or psychiatric examinations or treatment; or require the responsible person to comply with directions to attend at a specified place to take part in activities. It was held, in *Croydon London Borough Council v A (No 3)*[7] that this power extends to requiring a parent to live in a residential home with the child where attempts could be made to rehabilitate them. On the other hand, it will usually be for the supervisor, and not the court, to give directions to the responsible person,[8] and it may be queried whether it is desirable for the state, in the guise of the social worker as supervisor, to require that person to undergo psychotherapy, for example, when they have little real option but to consent.

As an alternative to either of these orders, or in addition to a supervision order, the court might decide to make a s 8 order in favour of the parent or relative of the child. For example, as we saw in the facts of *Re M* (above), there might be a relative who can care for the child rather than require that foster parents be found, and such a solution would be firmly in keeping with the philosophy of the legislation to promote the care of children within their own families.

---

5 Section 91(12).

6 *M v Warwickshire County Council* [1994] 2 FLR 593. Sched 3 para 6.

7 [1992] 2 FLR 350.

8 *Re H (minors) (Terms of Supervision Order)* [1994] Fam Law 486.

The courts are not required to apply a strictly 'tariff' approach to the issue, starting with minimum interference and working their way up to a full care order. In *Re D (a minor) (Care or Supervision Order)*,[9] for example, the court made a care order even though the local authority feared that this would undermine the partnership it had developed with the child's parents and had sought a supervision order only. The father had been suspected of causing fatal injuries to a son from his previous marriage, and the court preferred to ensure that the *court* evaluate whether there was a continuing risk to his new son, by placing the onus on the parents to seek a discharge of the care order, rather than require the supervisor to have to decide to seek an extension of a supervision order. As Bracewell J put it in *Re T (a minor) (Care or Supervision Order)*:

'The limits [of a supervision order] do not, in my judgment, begin to address the problems of these parents who continue, to date, to exercise their parental responsibilities in a way which still merits some criticism'.[10]

The message from these varying decisions on the criteria for public law orders and intervention is that there is still a strong belief by the courts in the role of the state as intervenor in family life where this is considered necessary to safeguard the child. There is still a reluctance to 'trust' the family, and especially the wider family, to provide adequate care without some form of monitoring. This attitude does not fit particularly neatly with the political 'story' of the working of the Children Act. The *Children Act Reports* show a reduced (though increasing) level of resort by local authorities to the courts for care or other orders since the Act was brought into force in 1991, and proclaim this as proof of the Act's success in encouraging parental responsibility for child care through voluntary partnership with the state. It may be that, as social services departments find courts more willing to make orders, they will return to their former levels of application, with the implication that the Act will then have 'failed'.[11]

On the other hand, there may have been undue caution on the part of local authorities about the chances of success in obtaining an order, and some second thoughts at central government level about the possible implications of the 'partnership' principle. Thus, the Social Services Inspectorate for England, reviewing policies in four local authorities in the wake of the Children Act, stated that:

'it was never the Act's intention to deny access to legal proceedings where situations required this. The threshold criteria of section 31, ie "significant harm",

9 [1993] 2 FLR 423.
10 [1994] 1 FLR 103.
11 *Children Act Report 1993*, para 3.11.

are at a level which would not be satisfied in trivial cases, but are not so high that would prevent well-argued cases succeeding'.[12]

5. THE INHERENT JURISDICTION AND WARDSHIP[13]

The powers and procedures set out in Parts IV and V of the Children Act present a formidable array of methods for obtaining effective degrees of control over parents or carers who are placing their children's welfare at risk. They are intended to provide a comprehensive package which should not need to be supplemented. Generally speaking, local authorities are expected, and required, to make use of these parts of the Act, the 'public law' parts, and to leave Part II to private individuals. Local authorities may, however, seek leave to apply for a specific issue or prohibited steps order, although this will not be appropriate where the result sought could have been obtained by the making of a residence or contact order, which local authorities may not seek.[14]

However, there will always be an exceptional case which does not fit the statutory scheme. Local authorities increasingly had recourse to the High Court's wardship jurisdiction as a means of circumventing the defects of the law before the Children Act. We saw in Chapter 10 that wardship is a manifestation of the *parens patriae* duty of the Crown to protect minors. It originated as a means of protecting the property of wealthy orphans from exploitation by guardians or other relatives, but it became a jurisdiction exercised to safeguard the general welfare of children by the beginning of the twentieth century.[15] The effect of making a child a ward of court is to vest control over the child in the High Court, which then has the power to direct how aspects of parental responsibility are to be exercised. For example, the court might determine that the child live with one parent rather than another. The court may also issue injunctions, such as to prohibit a third party (perhaps an undesirable boyfriend) from having contact with the ward.[16] Wardship had been

---

12 Social Services Inspectorate, *Planning Long Term Placement Study* (1994) para 8.5.
13 See M Parry, 'The Children Act 1989: Local Authorities, Wardship and the Revival of the Inherent Jurisdiction' [1992] JSWL 212.
14 Section 9(2). *Nottinghamshire County Council v P* [1994] Fam 18. Cf *Re R (a minor) (Blood Transfusion)* [1993] 2 FLR 757.
15 See N V Lowe and R A H White, *Wards of Court* (2nd ed, 1986); J Seymour, '*Parens Patriae* and Wardship Powers: Their Nature and Origins' (1994) 14 OJLS 159.
16 Wardship proceedings, as part of the inherent jurisdiction of the High Court, are 'family proceedings' within the Children Act, so that s 8 orders may be made in them: s 8(3)(a). A child may ward him or herself: see N Lowe and R A H White *Wards of Court* (2nd ed, 1986) at paras 3-4, 3-5; cf the power under s 10(8) to seek leave for a s 8 order.

primarily concerned with private disputes between parents over their children, or between parents and rebellious teenagers, but with the growing emphasis upon child protection by the state, by 1988 over 60% of wardship summonses were issued by local authorities.[17] The High Court had both a statutory and inherent power to commit a ward to the care of the local authority, or to make a supervision order in respect of the ward. Where the ward was committed to care, the court could issue directions to the authority on how it was to handle the case; for example, the Court could direct contact, or direct that a child be placed with prospective adopters. The jurisdiction was also used to sanction contraceptive sterilisations, and abortions, of children being cared for by local authorities.

The use of wardship in cases of abuse or neglect became controversial for a number of reasons. First, it was argued that, since Parliament had laid down a statutory code by which parental rights could be removed because of unfitness, it was wrong to permit local authorities to bypass the code where they could not satisfy its requirements. For example, since future harm was not clearly covered by s 1 of the Children and Young Persons Act 1969, the authority, fearing a child to be at risk, could ward the child and obtain care through wardship when it could not do so through the juvenile court. Parents could never be sure that they were beyond the reach of the state. The unfairness was compounded by the fact that the House of Lords had ruled, in *A v Liverpool City Council*,[18] that where a child was in local authority care (meaning subject to compulsory care), wardship could not be used by the parents as a means of challenging local authority decisions. Most importantly, if the local authority decided that a child's long-term future lay with a new family and that the child should be placed for adoption, parents could not invoke wardship to challenge that decision, and there was no statutory mechanism available to do so. On the other hand, where a ward was committed to local authority care, every important decision affecting the child had to be referred back to the court, impeding the authority's ability to develop plans, and change them in the light of new circumstances. Finally, the use of wardship was slow, with long delays in reaching a final decision, and thus detrimental to the child's welfare, and expensive for everyone involved.[19]

Concern had also been expressed during the Cleveland Inquiry about the use of wardship after the removal of children under place of safety

---

17 J Masson and S Morton, 'The use of wardship by local authorities' (1989) 52 MLR 762.

18 [1982] AC 363.

19 See J Hunt, *Local Authority Wardships before the Children Act: The baby or the bathwater?* (1993).

orders. The report favoured the retention of the ability of local authorities to use wardship, but also the overturning of the *Liverpool* principle, so that parents too could make use of the jurisdiction.[1] However, the legislation adopted the approach preferred by the Law Commission,[2] which had sought to achieve a comprehensive code relating to children, of preventing both local authorities and others from invoking wardship in relation to children in care or who are going into care.

Section 100 of the Children Act abolished the statutory power of the High Court to place a ward into care or under supervision. It also prohibited the use of the High Court's inherent jurisdiction to make orders with the effect of granting the local authority powers which it could otherwise only obtain through the provisions in Parts III and IV of the Act. However, it left a reserve power to the court to make orders under its inherent jurisdiction on the application of the local authority, where the result to be achieved could not be achieved through any statutory order. The effect is that, while *wardship*, which is to be seen as a particular manifestation of the inherent jurisdiction of the High Court, may not be used by the local authority, the general inherent power may still be called upon, provided that there is no alternative statutory route available. This looks a little like the safety-net approach which the Children Act was intended to curtail, but in practice, it leaves only a very limited range of decisions which can be taken by the Court outside the statutory scheme. For example, orders restraining publication of material relating to a child are not available under the Children Act, and would have to be made under the inherent jurisdiction.[3] More problematically, decisions about consent to medical treatment have been held to be available under both the statutory or the inherent power, depending upon the precise circumstances.[4] A more obvious case for resort to the inherent jurisdiction, albeit one with important civil liberties implications, was *Devon County Council v S (Inherent Jurisdiction)*, where Thorpe J gave leave to a local authority to apply under the inherent jurisdiction for an order to prohibit a family friend with convictions for child sexual abuse from visiting a woman with nine children, who refused to accept that he represented a serious risk.[5] In some respects, this resembles the classic

1 *Report of the Inquiry into Child Abuse in Cleveland 1987* (1988) Cm 412, para 16.65.
2 Law Com WP No 101, *Wards of Court* (1987).
3 See M Nicholls, 'Publicity and Children's Cases' [1993] Fam Law 108; N Fricker, 'Injunctive Orders relating to Children' [1993] Fam Law 226.
4 Compare *Re R (a minor) (Blood Transfusion)* [1993] 2 FLR 757 with *Re O (a minor) (Medical Treatment)* [1993] 2 FLR 149. In the former case, the local authority could apply, with leave, for a specific issue order under s 8, since the child was not in their care; in the latter, the child was the subject of an interim care order, so that a specific issue order could not be made: s 9(1).
5 [1994] Fam 169. Cf *Re S (minors) (Inherent Jurisdiction: Ouster)* [1994] 1 FLR 623, where the High Court used its inherent jurisdiction to order a *father*, who had been

mid-century use of wardship to restrain undesirable relationships of teenagers, but is being used because of a much more serious perceived risk. It is understandable, and in keeping with the modern philosophy of preserving children in their families, that a court would prefer to make such an order rather than see the local authority having to take Part IV proceedings to remove the children (assuming the threshold criteria could be satisfied). But it represents a subtle twist to the state's powers of surveillance and control.

In the next chapter, we consider the future of that relationship in the aftermath of state intervention.

found to have sexually abused his step-daughter, to vacate the family home; *quaere* if the exercise of such a power was compatible with the House of Lords' ruling in *Richards v Richards* [1984] AC 174?

CHAPTER 14

Children in the public care

1. INTRODUCTION

The major question to be answered about the public care system has been whether state assumption of responsibility for children's welfare represents a net improvement over what would have been forthcoming for the children if the family had been left alone.

Expectations of what the state could or should achieve have changed. As Roy Parker *et al* point out,[1] at one time, it would have been regarded as a success that children of the workhouses survived infancy and emerged able to find employment and independence. But when the emphasis shifted to the emotional and educational needs of children, and there were moves to increase use of foster care rather than institutional care, the task of achieving success became much harder. Where children are 'hard to place', for example, they suffer severe emotional problems, or have disabilities, finding them a foster home at all may be counted as a success – except that it fails to take into account what happens next. Does the placement 'work'? And will the child leaving care[2] be better off, or at least as well off, than if he or she had never entered it?

2. FORM OF PLACEMENT

The 'administrative parent'[3] is not required to provide the perfect upbringing for every child; no child can expect so much from any parent. But the aim, according to Parker, is 'to ensure that children encounter the

1 R Parker (ed) *Looking After Children: Assessing Outcomes in Child Care* (1991) p 78.
2 We use this term to include both children accommodated under s 20 and those subject to care orders under s 33.
3 Ie the state. The phrase is taken from a study of assumption of parental rights resolutions by M Adcock and R A H White, *The Administrative Parent* (1983).

type of experiences that are generally considered to be necessary if a satisfactory outcome to child-rearing is to be achieved'.[4]

Underlying this aim would seem to be the assumption that children should live in as family-like a situation as possible, and so, where possible, care within the child's own, or another family should be preferred to care within a residential home. Section 23(6) of the Children Act requires authorities to arrange for the child to live with a parent or other person with parental responsibility; or a relative, friend or other person connected with him, unless this would not be reasonably practicable or consistent with his welfare. Further, they must seek to provide accommodation near the child's home, and keep siblings together, under s 23(7). If such placements are not possible, then although there is no statutory preference, foster care in another family may be regarded as the best substitute. The age and needs of the child, however, may indicate that residential care, either in a home maintained by the authority, or in a charitable home or school, should be arranged.[5] It is estimated that, as at 31 March 1993, of the 52,000 children being looked after by local authorities, 62% were in foster placements, 15% in residential homes, and 10% at home with parents.[6]

In fact, Bullock *et al* note that institutional care has fallen out of favour throughout the Western world, and not just for children subject to state intervention; the use of boarding schools, and entry of young people into the armed forces, have also fallen. The number of children in residential placements fell from 60,000 in 1970 to 13,000 in 1990. They are now more likely to be older children, and to be disturbed or damaged.[7] But residential care is still used extensively for children who stay in care long term: 'four-fifths of children long separated have a taste of residential care'.[8] The effects of such care, so far as they have been documented, are mixed. Earlier research studies found that:

'Good residential care can provide children with a stable home and a stimulating educational environment. It can widen their cultural horizons and create a framework for emotionally secure relationships with adults. It can also provide a basis for more intensive therapeutic work. The weaknesses of residential settings lie in their inability to give unconditional love, the constraints they place on a child's emotional development, their inability to ensure staff continuity and the peripheral role they allocate to children's families.'[9]

---

4 *Looking After Children: Assessing Outcomes in Child Care* (1991) p 61.
5 Section 23(2).
6 *Children Act Report 1993*, Table 4.2.
7 R Bullock, M Little and S Millham, *Residential Care for Children: A Review of the Research* (1993) pp 11-12.
8 *Ibid* p 16.
9 *Ibid* p 8.

The trend towards foster care in preference to residential care has meant a need to find people willing to take on a varied range of tasks. We may distinguish between short-term foster placements to cover immediate receptions into local authority care; short-term arrangements to provide respite for families with special problems, for example, where a child is severely disabled; short-term placements while longer-term arrangements are being worked out; long-term fostering where links are to be maintained with the child's family; and fostering with a view to the child being adopted.[10] We discuss adoption later in this chapter.

The skills and attributes needed by foster carers in the public care system will vary, but the most essential one, which requires what may be an extraordinary level of altruism, is the ability to provide a loving home for a child while at the same time recognising that it will be necessary to let the child leave the placement whenever asked to do so. The expert recruitment, assessment and selection of foster carers by social workers may still be insufficient to ensure satisfactory results, unless there is also continuing support from the social workers, and training and advice for the carers. As we noted in Chapter 5, there is a tension between the altruistic essence of fostering, and the need to provide a professional, often paid, service for children in need. The latter is demonstrated by the fact that foster carers will usually be paid allowances (which are not intended to import a profit element) for their care, which vary from one local authority to another. (The National Foster Care Association recommends minimum allowances which ranged, for 1993/94, from £49.56 per week for a child aged under five outside London, to £116.41 for a child aged 16 to 18 in London.) But the end of the story is not finding the placement for a child, but preventing its breakdown; it seems that up to 50% of placements may fail.[11]

In fact, it appears that nine out of ten children do return to their families from care[12] and at least some of these will have been allowed to stay at home 'on trial', to see if it is safe for them to do so. Concern at the power of local authorities to return children or leave them at home without any control by the courts, even where care orders had been made, and with the possibility that serious errors of judgment might be made, led to the passing of regulations to impose extra requirements and safeguards before such placement decisions could be implemented.[13] Clearly, where

---

10 Detailed regulations governing foster placements are contained in the Foster Placement (Children) Regulations 1991, SI 1991/910.

11 D Berridge and H Cleaver, *Foster home breakdown* (1987) p 55. J Fratter, J Rowe, D Sapsford and J Thoburn, *Permanent family placement* (1991) Ch 3.

12 R Bullock, M Little and S Millham, *Going Home: The Return of Children Separated from their Families* (1993).

13 Accommodation of Children (Charge and Control) Regulations 1988; now see the Placement of Children with Parents etc Regulations 1991, SI 1991/893. These were

a child subject to a care order is returned home successfully, consideration must be given to the possibility of the order being discharged.[14]

Article 20 of the United Nations Convention provides that:

'A child, temporarily or permanently deprived of his or her family environment, or in whose own best interests cannot be allowed to remain in that environment, shall be entitled to special protection and assistance provided by the state.'

States have further duties under Article 9 to respect the right of the child to maintain personal relations and contact on a regular basis with the child's parents, except if this is contrary to the child's best interests, and under Article 25 to carry out a periodic review of the placement of the child. Duties are accordingly imposed upon local authorities to try to fulfil this intention as discussed below.

3. DECISION-MAKING WHILE THE CHILD IS BEING LOOKED AFTER

Whatever the legal status of the stay in accommodation, while the child is being looked after, the local authority is under a duty to:

'safeguard and promote his welfare; and ... to make such use of services available for children cared for by their own parents as appears to the authority reasonable in his case'.[15]

If the child is the subject of a care order, both the local authority and the parents[16] (or guardian) have parental responsibility, although the authority are in the driving seat and may, under s 33(3)(b) 'determine the extent to which a parent or guardian of the child may meet his parental responsibility for' the child. It is for the authority in such cases, and not the parents, to have the final say in where the child will live, what school the child attends, and so on. The partnership of local authority and parents in this situation is therefore inevitably an unequal one. The authority cannot, however, take certain decisions which may be regarded as going to the essence of being a parent; they cannot change the child's religion,[17] agree to the child's adoption or being freed for adoption, or appoint a guardian.[18] Certain other decisions require either the written

introduced following recommendations in the Jasmine Beckford Inquiry, *A Child in Trust* (1985), although it should be noted that part of the problem in that case was the *magistrates'* view that the child should be returned home.

14 Section 23(5); Placement of Children with Parents etc Regulations 1991 (above).
15 Section 22 (3).
16 Excluding a non-marital father who does not have a s 4 order or agreement in his favour.
17 This perhaps has a rather nineteenth century flavour about it.
18 Section 33(6).

agreement of the parents or guardian, such as changing the child's name, or the approval of the court, such as placement of a child in secure accommodation.[19]

Whenever they are looking after a child, the authority must, under s 22, consult the child and the parents, anyone else with parental responsibility for the child, and any other person whose wishes and feelings the authority consider relevant before making any decision. They must take into account the child's religious persuasion, racial origin and cultural and linguistic background. In this way, the upbringing that the parents wish the child to have may be accommodated, if this is thought desirable, and the parents' and child's right to respect for their family life under Article 8 of the European Convention is respected. In particular, the local authority will want to find a placement for the child which is compatible with these matters, but this can lead to a risk that the child lingers in an ostensibly short-term foster placement or residential care while the appropriate match of cultural and ethnic background is sought.[20]

The child's case must be reviewed within four weeks of the date when the child is first accommodated by the authority, the second review must be held within three months of the first, and thereafter, reviews must take place every six months. The reviews:

'form part of a continuous planning process – reviewing decisions to date and planning future work. The purpose of the review is to ensure that the child's welfare is safeguarded and promoted in the most effective way throughout the period he is looked after or accommodated. Progress ... should be examined and monitored at every review and the plan for the child amended as necessary to reflect any significant change.'[1]

Parents and child should be involved in the review, and, if not present when it is held, certainly consulted beforehand. The review must consider, whether, if an order is in force, an application should be made to discharge it; whether any changes in contact arrangements should be made; the placement of the child, and whether a permanent substitute

---

19 Section 33(7)(a): s 25. Where the child is being accommodated under s 20, a parent may object to continuing the accommodation and hence prevent the child's being placed or remaining in secure accommodation: s 25(9). The welfare checklist in s 1(3) of the Children Act 1989 does not apply to the decision whether to keep a child in secure accommodation, and welfare is not the paramount consideration: *Re M (a minor) (Secure Accommodation Order)* (1994) Times, 15 November.

20 Until increased awareness of the significance of ethnic and cultural identity had become a part of social work practice, few foster parents from minority communities were actively recruited. There has therefore been a dearth of such parents offering their services, which has only gradually, and not entirely successfully, been addressed. See, eg, *Re JK (Adoption: Transracial Placement)* [1991] 2 FLR 340: child placed at six days old, remaining with 'short-term' foster carers until aged three.

1 *Children Act 1989 Guidance and Regulations, Volume 3, Family Placements* (1991) para 8.1.

family should be found; whether an independent visitor should be appointed for a child who has no contact with his or her family; the child's educational needs and any aftercare which may be needed.[2] The focus is upon the child, but in many cases it will be the parents' conduct and progress which will determine the outcome of the review. For example, have the parents maintained contact with the child by keeping promises to visit? Have they worked on their relationship or their parenting skills so that they can be entrusted with the child's care?

The most crucial decision will be whether the child has a future with the birth family, or needs placement in a substitute family on a permanent basis. Yet, it has been pointed out that professionals have a low level of accuracy in predicting future risks for children, and that, as circumstances in the family change over time, there may need to be a continuing reassessment which renders a once-and-for-all decision highly problematic.[3] The question of how local authority decision-making can be challenged therefore becomes of central importance.

4. CHALLENGING THE LOCAL AUTHORITY

The cases[4] before the European Court of Human Rights revealed the lack of effective procedures open to either parents or children to challenge decisions taken by local authorities in respect of children in compulsory care. In particular, the decision to limit or terminate parents' contact with their children, which is taken in order to facilitate the child's move to a permanent substitute family, was not challengeable in the courts, either through a statutory mechanism, or through wardship.[5] The crucial decision that rehabilitation was not feasible and that a permanent placement be sought was also not challengeable. The European Court condemned the lack of effective remedies revealed by this state of affairs.[6] The United Nations Convention is not as clear as it might be on this point. Article 9(1) requires that decisions which result in the separation of the

---

2 Section 26; Review of Children's Cases Regulations 1991, SI 1991/895, r 3, Sch 2.

3 D Gough, *Child Abuse Interventions: A Review of the Research Literature* (1993) pp 197-198; Family Rights Group, *Reuniting Children and Their Families* (1993) p 5. The Social Services Inspectorate, *Planning Long Term Placement Study* (1994) concluded *inter alia* that the sheer complexity of some cases can make long-term planning difficult: para 5.5.

4 *R v United Kingdom* [1988] 2 FLR 445, *O v United Kingdom* (1987) 10 EHRR 82.

5 *A v Liverpool City Council* [1982] AC 363. It is true that judicial review was, and is, available to challenge the illegality, impropriety or irrationality of a decision, but this is an unsatisfactory and often slow mechanism, requiring leave and merely requiring a flawed decision to be taken again, without the court ruling on its merits.

6 *R v United Kingdom* [1988] 2 FLR 445, *O v United Kingdom* (1987) 10 EHRR 82.

child from the parents be subject to a judicial review in which all interested parties can participate. Article 9(3) requires states to respect the right of the separated child to maintain personal relations and direct contact with his or her parents, except if this is contrary to the child's best interests. It does not expressly require that the question of whether contact is in the child's best interests be subject to judicial scrutiny, and it is arguable that, since contact is dealt with expressly in paragraph (3), it is not embraced within the requirement of paragraph (1). However, since a decision regarding contact directly relates to the question of separation of the child from the parents, it would seem that paragraph (1) could be read so as to include such decisions. If so, then English law is not wholly compatible with this obligation, for while decisions on contact are subject to court review, the specific decision to place the child with a permanent substitute family is still not directly reviewable.[7] It has also been argued that other local authority decisions taken in the exercise of their parental responsibility while a child is in care should be amenable to judicial scrutiny, in order to avoid breach of the right to a judicial determination of parents' civil rights under Article 6 of the European Convention.[8]

(a) Complaints procedures

The difficulty for policy makers is to strike a balance, on the one hand allowing the local authority, entrusted by the courts or the parents themselves to look after the child, or to provide services for the family, to do so using their own judgment without constant recourse to another body for permission to act. On the other, there must be ways in which decisions which appear wrong to those affected by them can be reviewed to ensure that errors are not allowed to go uncorrected.

English law does offer some means of striking this balance, through a combination of judicial and other review processes, depending upon the type of decision in issue. There is the possibility first, of taking part in the periodic statutory reviews, which we have discussed. Secondly, s 26(3) requires local authorities to establish 'a procedure for considering any representations (including any complaint) made to them' by children in need or being looked after by them, parents, persons with parental responsibility, local authority foster parents, and any other person who they consider has a sufficient interest in the child's welfare. The Guidance defines 'representations' as including enquiries and statements about the availability, delivery and nature of services which 'will not necessarily

---

7 See below for discussion of proposed 'placement orders' in adoption.
8 J Eekelaar, 'The role of the courts under the Children Bill' (1989) NLJ 217.

be critical', while a complaint 'is a written or oral expression of dissatisfaction or disquiet in relation to an individual child' which:

'may arise as a result of an unwelcome or disputed decision, concern about the quality or appropriateness of services, delay in decision-making about services or about their delivery or non-delivery'.[9]

Before the Children Act, there was no statutory duty to provide such a procedure, and few local authorities did so. The utility of these mechanisms is open to doubt; early experiences suggested that they may be slow and local authorities may underestimate the importance of ensuring procedural fairness in their implementation.[10] There may also be a lack of publicity of the availability of the procedure, and a lack of awareness of when it should be used. For example, in *R v London Borough of Brent, ex p S*,[11] grandparents caring for an autistic child had been waiting to be rehoused by the council in more suitable accommodation for five years. They wrote to the council complaining that they were not taking the problem seriously enough. The council, according to the Court of Appeal, should have recognised that this letter was a complaint under s 26(3) and have advised the grandparents of the procedure, but failed to do so. Perhaps the reality in many cases will be that a local authority will attempt to solve the problem raised without encouraging the complainant to invoke the formal procedure; or one department, for example, the housing authority, will not recognise that a complaint may be raising an issue about responsibilities usually handled by social services.

(b) Challenging decisions on contact

Not only is the prevailing philosophy of child-care law one of 'normalisation' of care, but of the maintenance of family ties with the hope that the child can return home when it is safe or desirable to do so. However, the value judgment implicit in this approach must be recognised. The courts draw a distinction between private and public law disputes. Simon Jolly has noted how there is a strong presumption in the private law that where parents separate, the child should continue to have contact with the absent parent, notwithstanding that there may be no likelihood

---

9 *Children Act 1989 Guidance and Regulations, Volume 3, Family Placements* (1991) para 10.5. The consumerist language appears an attempt to incorporate the Citizen's Charter philosophy into the exercise.

10 B Rubenstein, 'An independent experience' (1992) NLJ 866. The *Children Act Report 1993*, para 4.63 presents a more positive picture: 'Social services departments were found to have done well in [eg]... encouraging positive staff views about complaints and users' rights ... handling complaints sensitively and confidentially'.

11 [1994] 1 FLR 203.

of the child going to live permanently with him or her. But in the public law context, he identifies a view of contact as being justified solely for its potential rehabilitative value, so that where resumption of care has been ruled out, contact is not supported and may well be positively discouraged or terminated.[12] We discuss further below the desirability of continuing links with the birth family where the child cannot return home to live. Here, we concentrate upon the legal mechanisms for promoting or terminating contact during care.

Section 34(11) of the Children Act requires the court to consider the contact arrangements being proposed by the local authority, and to invite the parties to comment upon them, before making a care order. Schedule 2, para 15 requires an authority looking after a child (under s 20 or a care order) to endeavour to promote contact between the child and parents, family and friends unless this is not reasonably practicable or consistent with the child's welfare. Section 34(1) also requires an authority looking after a child under a care order to allow reasonable contact with the child's parents, guardian, any person who had a residence order before the care order was made, or anyone who had care of the child by virtue of an order made under the inherent jurisdiction of the High Court. All these provisions reinforce the weight given to family contact by the legislation.

Studies carried out prior to the Children Act, however, noted a high level of failure to maintain contact and the diminishing likelihood of the child returning home. Millham *et al* found that a child still in care after six weeks had a 78% chance of remaining in care for more than six months, and a 63% chance of still being in care two years later.[13] Inevitably, the chance of a return home diminished if contact with the family was not maintained, but social workers could impose both specific and non-specific 'barriers to contact'. For example, not only might a social worker decline to permit a parent to see a child at certain times, but by placing a child in a foster-home which was difficult to reach by public transport, or by the foster parents appearing unwelcoming, the incentive to keep up contact could be lost. After children had been in care for a year, parents seemed 'increasingly disinclined to visit, they feel de-skilled, diminished and stigmatised.'[14]

In the face of this, the focus of legislative attention concerning local authority decision-making in child care has been primarily directed to questions of contact, not least because these appeared the most crucial and least open to challenge before the law was changed by the Health and Social Services and Social Security Adjudications Act 1983. This

12 S Jolly, 'Cutting the Ties – the Termination of Contact in Care' [1994] JSWFL 299.
13 S Millham *et al, Lost in Care* (1986) p 180. See also J Rowe and L Lambert *Children Who Wait* (1973).
14 *Ibid* p 134.

permitted parents of children subject to care orders to apply to courts to override local authority refusals or terminations of contact with their children, but not to complain about *restrictions* of contact. Furthermore, the onus was on the parent to challenge the local authority's decision, since there was no requirement on the authority to obtain court approval before notifying the parent of the decision. The inadequacies of this scheme were intended to be addressed in the Children Act, so that the fundamental principle of encouraging continuing links and the aim of restoring a child to the family could be upheld. Parents whose children were in voluntary care could at least in theory remove them if dissatisfied with the level of contact being enjoyed. Under the Children Act, parents whose children are being accommodated under s 20 may likewise require the return of the child, so no special mechanism to control contact is provided – but the 'non-specific' barriers identified by Millham *et al* may still apply.

Section 34 provides a means of applying to the court for orders allowing, or refusing contact with a child subject to a care order. Contact between the child and those listed in s 34(1) may not be refused without court approval, except as a matter of urgency and for a period of under seven days.[15] Where contact is sought by or on behalf of the child, or by others, application may be made to the court (with leave, if the person applying is not listed in s 34(1)) for an order for appropriate contact. But while it is possible to challenge specific restrictions on contact, such as the number of visits permitted, the times at which they take place, and the persons who may see the child, it is still difficult to challenge non-specific restrictions. For example, if a child has been placed in a foster home which is awkward for the family to reach, a court order requiring contact to be allowed does not solve the problem of how it is to be implemented. The authority has the power to provide financial assistance to facilitate visits where these could not otherwise be made without undue financial hardship, but no duty to do so.[16] Yet the court cannot require that a new foster placement nearer to home be arranged.

Furthermore, it appears that an order under s 34(4) authorising refusal of contact to a child in care may 'trump' an application to allow such contact under s 34(2). In *Birmingham City Council v H (a minor)*,[17] the House of Lords held that where the court determined that it would not be in a baby's best interests to have contact with his mother (herself a child in care), an order authorising the local authority to refuse contact could be made, in which case, 'it was of no value' to make an order for the

---

15 Section 34(6).
16 Schedule 2, para 16.
17 [1994] 2 AC 212, discussed by G Douglas in, 'In Whose Best Interests?' (1994) 110 LQR 379.

mother to be allowed to have contact, even though it appeared to be in *her* best interests.

Nor should it be assumed that providing recourse to a court is always an adequate remedy where contact is in issue. Millham *et al* found, under the old law, that parents going to court to challenge refusals of contact were generally in a weak position to resist the arguments of the local authority, and the most experienced solicitors tended to work for authorities rather than families. Of 309 children whose parents received notices terminating their contact, only 146 sets of parents took any action. 120 consulted solicitors, 106 applied to the court for an order permitting contact, and there were 96 hearings. But only 16 orders were made in the parents' favour (of which seven were later successfully appealed by the local authority).

The position for families should theoretically be better under the Children Act, because parents anxious about obstacles to contact may seek court orders at an earlier stage, before the decision to stop *all* contact in the light, usually, of a diminishing pattern of visits, is taken. The statistics for 1993 suggest that parents may still face hurdles in challenging contact decisions, however, for while about 13% of applications for contact were refused (or an order of 'no order' within s 1(5) of the Children Act was made), only 5% of applications for *refusal* of contact were similarly disposed of.[18] Furthermore, the research by Millham *et al* found that for every one *de jure* termination carried out by notice under the old legislation, there were two *de facto* terminations of contact. The message is that unless parents vigorously exercise their rights to be consulted and to make representations and complaints, there is still ample scope for them to be cut out of the child's life. Yet they will generally be:

> 'among a disadvantaged subsection of the poorest groups in society and are very insecure in legal situations. They cannot match the skills of the more prosperous in eliciting help and presenting a cogent case.'[19]

(c) Seeking a discharge of the care order

Notwithstanding the weak position of many parents whose children are in care, there is, at least in theory, the possibility of seeking a discharge of the care order and hence a return home. There are two ways in which this can be done. An application may either be made to discharge the order under s 39 of the Children Act, or a residence order may be sought

18 *Judicial Statistics: England and Wales 1993*, Cm 2623, from Table 5.2.
19 S Millham, R Bullock, K Hosie and M Little, *Access Disputes in Child-Care* (1989) *passim* and p 13.

under s 8, the effect of making which is automatically to bring the care order to an end.[20] The former route may be taken by any person who has parental responsibility for the child (ie parents or a guardian); the child him or herself; or the local authority. The latter is available to others, for example, an unmarried father who did not have parental responsibility, or a relative who wishes to take over the care of the child. It might also be used by a parent who is separated from the other and who wishes to resolve the care issue with both the local authority and the other parent at the same time. In either case, the child's welfare is the paramount consideration, and there are no 'threshold conditions' to be satisfied. The court may, if it wishes to preserve the local authority's role in the case, substitute a supervision order for the care order. But there is no direct power to order a 'phased return' of the child to the home so that, for example, the child could be gradually reintroduced to the family over a period of time of increasing contact. The Children Act Guidance, *Volume 1 Court Orders* suggests that the court might achieve this by varying the contact arrangements under s 34, or by attaching conditions to the residence order under s 11(7).[1]

To avoid the possibility of repeated applications for discharges, s 91(15) provides that no further application may be made within six months, without the leave of the court. Where an application for discharge is refused then, the local authority are left to continue implementing their care plan for the child free of constant interruption by court proceedings.[2] Of course, if the consultation and partnership provisions of the legislation work properly, this should be a rare problem since the local authority will be working with the family and making plans in the light of their, and the child's views. Indeed, if things are truly working well, the discharge of the order is likely to be sought by the authority themselves on the basis that it is no longer needed in the light of successful rehabilitation. It will be recalled that the periodic statutory reviews of the child's case must always consider whether the order should be discharged.

(d) Suing the local authority

Social workers, like everyone else, including the courts, make mistakes. This is abundantly clear from the history of inquiries into tragedies where

---

20 Section 91(1).
1 *Volume 1 Court Orders* (1991) para 3.57.
2 Additionally, s 91(14) empowers a court, disposing of any application for an order under the Children Act, to order that no application for a specified order be made in the future in respect of the child without the leave of the court. Such an order is to be made sparingly, where the child would otherwise suffer: *F v Kent County Council* [1993] 1 FLR 432. For an example where an order was made, see *Re W (minors) (Sexual Abuse: Standard of Proof)* [1994] 1 FLR 419.

children who should have been protected were not, and from inquiries and case law revealing that children were removed from their parents on flimsy grounds, and kept separated long after they should have been returned. The question arises whether, in addition to the administrative mechanisms, such as the possibility of challenging through the representations procedures, or through the Commissioner for Local Administration (the local government ombudsman) it is possible for parents, or their children, to seek compensation in damages through the courts, for the wrongs they may have suffered in the child care system.

The law is complicated on this point. It distinguishes between the interests of the children who are the subjects of intervention, and their parents, but in relation to either, the courts have adopted a restrictive attitude to allowing claims.

(i) Claims by the child

If a child sustains injuries at the hands of foster parents, it has been held that the local authority are not vicariously liable to the child, because the foster parents are not their agents.[3] In *Surtees v Kingston-upon-Thames Borough Council*,[4] the plaintiff, who suffered severe injuries to her foot through falling into scalding hot water when in the care of foster parents, conceded that if the foster parents were not found negligent, the local authority could not be liable in negligence to her either. The Court of Appeal held that the injury suffered was unforeseeable, hence there was no negligence on the part of the foster parents and hence none by the authority. However, the court went on to consider that only if the injury had been *deliberately* inflicted by the foster parent could the authority be liable to her, as a matter of causation, even if it could be shown that their approval and supervision of the foster parents had been negligent. Similarly, in *T (a minor) v Surrey County Council*, the Court of Appeal held that a local authority who failed to warn a parent that a child-minder was suspected of having inflicted non-accidental injury on another child, were liable to the child for negligent misstatement, but not for negligence or breach of statutory duty when the child suffered brain damage at the hands of the child-minder.[5]

It remains debatable whether *negligently placing* a child in a generally unsuitable placement which causes him or her physical or psychological injury, is actionable by the child. On the one hand, in *Holtom v Barnet London Borough Council*,[6] it was held that a local authority could be sued

3 *S v Walsall Metropolitan Borough Council* [1986] 1 FLR 397.
4 [1991] 2 FLR 559.
5 [1994] 4 All ER 577.
6 (1993) Times, 30 September.

by a person formerly in their care for breach of obligations while *in loco parentis*, although not as a local education authority for negligence in providing educational facilities. The authority had wrongly assessed the child as being severely mentally subnormal and had sent her to a special residential school. But in *M (a minor) v Newham London Borough Council, X (minors) v Bedfordshire County Council*,[7] the Court of Appeal upheld the striking out of a claim by a child (and her mother), for damages for negligence after the local authority obtained a place of safety order to remove a child from the mother. A psychiatrist had interviewed the child in the presence of a social worker, and together they had concluded, wrongly, that the mother's partner had sexually abused the child. The child was committed to care in wardship, and remained separated from her for a year until the wardship was discharged. It was held (Sir Thomas Bingham MR dissenting) that the only remedy open to either plaintiff was within the statutory code or by judicial review.

It has also been held that a *failure to act* to remove children from danger and place them in care is not actionable by the children.[8] Local authorities, it was held, owe them no duty of care in negligence, nor are they liable for breach of statutory duty. Their duties are imposed by statute, and so decisions taken in fulfilment or otherwise of those duties should be challengeable by judicial review or the complaints mechanisms only. The court appeared to fear the floodgates opening, not only to allow claims against local authorities, but also education, police and health authorities for their parts in the decision-making process. Yet where a local authority have taken to themselves, or had placed upon them, the responsibility for a child's upbringing, why should they not be liable to that child for negligently carrying out that responsibility? The difficulty, according to the Court of Appeal in *Surtees*, is to ensure that all *parents*, as well as state authorities, are not at risk of being sued by their children for not doing their best for them. But, as we discussed in Chapter 6, the law does not, as yet, impose the same obligation, to safeguard and promote the child's welfare, upon parents as it does upon local authorities, and there are other precedents for distinguishing between parents and strangers when it comes to questions of liability.[9]

7 [1994] 2 WLR 554. Compare *E (a minor) v Dorset County Council* [1994] 3 WLR 853, where the Queen's Bench Division allowed a claim to proceed to trial, alleging negligence by psychologists and teachers in failing to identify children's learning difficulties.

8 *X (minors) v Bedfordshire County Council*, above. The US Supreme Court has rejected a similar claim, on the basis that the public authorities had no constitutional duty to protect the child from a father's violence and that they could not be held causally responsible for the injuries suffered such as would establish violation of civil rights: *Deshaney v Winnebago County Department of Social Services* 109 S Ct 998 (1989).

9 Eg, Congenital Disabilities (Civil Liability) Act 1976 which generally excludes liability to children damaged in the womb by their mother's, but not others' negligence. In *Seymour v Williams* (1994) Guardian, 2 December, the Court

(ii) Claims by the parents

Where claims by parents, rather than by children, are concerned, it was held in the highly significant case of *F v Wirral Metropolitan Borough Council*[10] that there is no tort of interference with parental rights or responsibility which may be relied upon. Parents whose children went into voluntary care, and who were then made subject to parental rights resolutions and placed with long-term foster parents, sued the local authority, claiming that their parental rights had been infringed. But it was held that the common law recognised only the right of the father to control the child's religious upbringing, apprenticing and training, and to the child's services. This right did not include the right to 'consortium', or to enjoying the child's company. Further, the court held, obiter, that there was no right to sue in negligence or for breach of statutory duty to the parents, and that any remedy lay only within the public law sphere.

The *Wirral* decision shows the limited significance now accorded to the proprietary model of parenthood in the law. But the concern of the courts to protect local authorities and child care professionals from liability for negligence may be excessive. The argument that social work practitioners will practise 'defensively' if at risk of being sued for failure to take action, or will decline to act at all for fear of making an error of judgment, could be met by providing a test similar to that relied upon by medical professionals – if a body of responsible opinion would have done likewise, there is no actionable negligence on the part of the actor. Failure to accept such a test is perhaps a symptom of the uncertainty surrounding social work as a body of knowledge and practice.

5. LEAVING CARE

For the minority of children who cannot return to their families during their childhood, but for whom adoption is not feasible, the state, through social services departments and fostering or residential care, will assume the overall role of parent. The evidence suggests that it does a poor job. It is estimated that, in England, one in seven women leaving care is pregnant, or already has a child;[11] that more than a third of young prisoners have been in care; and that up to 40% of homeless young people are products of the care system. Further, such young people are expected

---

of Appeal ruled that a woman could sue her mother for failing to protect her when a child from her father's sexual abuse; the action against the father was statute-barred.

10 [1991] Fam 69.

to move out into independence at a lower age than is the norm for young people generally.[12] About a third of care leavers leave at the age of 16, and another third by their eighteenth birthday.

'So young people who are already more likely than their peers to have problems and lack family support are expected to fend for themselves at an unusually early age.'[13]

The time spent in care is all too often a deeply unsatisfactory experience,[14] and the prospects once out of care are not encouraging. Government social policy, which presupposes that young people will remain in their homes at least until they are working, is not designed to cope with such a disadvantaged group, and yet the state, by taking responsibility for them in the first place, should be expected to ensure they achieve secure independence.

The difficulties facing young people leaving care have been recognised in s 24 of the Children Act 1989, which requires authorities to provide advice and assistance before and after the person leaves care. However, a survey of local authorities found that 7% admitted that they did not monitor what happened to their care leavers, 9% only recorded the immediate position of care leavers, and only 34% monitored for more than two years. Without such monitoring, it is impossible for authorities to devise an appropriate service to fulfil their duty under s 24.[15]

6. ADOPTION AS AN OUTCOME

It is scarcely surprising, in the light of this picture, that it may be decided, either right from the time of the first care plan, or later if rehabilitation proves unlikely, that a permanent substitute family will be needed for the child, either through long-term fostering, or through adoption, and either with continuing contact of some kind with the child's birth family, or without.

Realisation that so many children were drifting in care, with no long-term stability or even coherent plan made for them, led to a drive in the 1970s and 1980s to encourage adoption as an alternative to foster or residential care. The Children Act 1975 and the Adoption Act 1976, which consolidated the law, were passed in the wake of the Maria

---

11 Ie about 14%. Cf the teenage conception rate of 4.34% at age 16 and 9.6% at age 19 in England and Wales as a whole in 1991: *Social Trends 24* (1994) Table 2.18.
12 See the account in *The Guardian*, 7 September 1994.
13 *Community Care* 4-10 August 1994.
14 B Kahan, *Growing Up in Care* (1979); P Mann, *Children in Care Revisited* (1984); M Stein and K Carey, *Leaving Care* (1986).
15 *Community Care* 4-10 August 1994.

Colwell inquiry, and in the light of the recommendations of the Houghton Committee, whose basic aim was to restrict the possibility of private adoption arrangements and to ensure instead that adoption became a service offered by all local authorities as part of their child care responsibilities. Local authorities are required to establish and maintain an adoption service within their area, by providing the service themselves or ensuring that an approved adoption society does so.[16] There are exchange arrangements intended to ensure that the small supply of people willing and able to adopt children with a history of special problems and needs are matched most appropriately. Indeed, the role of adoption has shifted substantially from a service for childless couples wishing to have a family, which we discussed in Chapter 4, to a service for children needing to find a permanent family to care for them. The total number of adoptions has declined substantially, from about 25,000 in 1968, to 6,751 in 1993.[17] At the same time, adoption has become commonly used for children in care. One representative study, *Pathways to Adoption*, found that almost half of all adoptions involved children who were in either voluntary or compulsory care.[18]

(a) Parental agreement to adoption

Since adoption means the irrevocable severing of all legal links between the child and the birth family, agreement to one's child being adopted is one of the most serious decisions a parent can ever take. Accordingly, the law permits the parents[19] to refuse their agreement, right up to the last moment, in the court proceedings for the application to adopt. It is however possible for the court to dispense with the parents' agreement on a number of grounds contained in s 16(2) of the Adoption Act 1976. Most of the grounds r late to various forms of parental unfitness, but the one usually relied upon is that the parent is withholding agreement unreasonably.[20] The House of Lords held, in *Re W (an infant)*,[1] that this

---

16 Adoption Act 1976, s 1.
17 Department of Health, Welsh Office, Home Office, Lord Chancellor's Department, *Adoption: The Future* (1993) Cm 2288, p 4; *Judicial Statistics: England and Wales 1993*, Table 5.6.
18 M Murch *et al, Pathways to Adoption* (1993) p 241, ie being accommodated or subject to care orders.
19 The parents whose agreement to adoption is required are the birth mother of a child born outside marriage, the father of such a child if he has parental responsibility, and both parents of a child born within marriage.
20 Section 16(2)(b).
 1 [1971] AC 682.

lays down an objective test, which does not require a finding that the parent has acted culpably:

> 'the test is reasonableness and not anything else. It is not culpability. It is not indifference. It is not failure to discharge parental duties. It is reasonableness in the context of the totality of the circumstances.'[2]

It has been held that s 6, which provides that:

> 'In reaching any decision relating to the adoption of a child a court or adoption agency shall have regard to all the circumstances, first consideration being given to the need to safeguard and promote the welfare of the child throughout his childhood'

does not apply to decisions under s 16(2),[3] and that the court should decide whether adoption would be in the child's interests *before* it decides whether to dispense with agreement.[4] However, in deciding whether the parent is acting reasonably, the court will inevitably have regard to the welfare of the child, for 'the fact that a reasonable parent does pay regard to the welfare of his child must enter into the question of reasonableness as a relevant factor'.[5] Thus, the House of Lords upheld the dispensing of the agreement of a homosexual father to his son's adoption, on the basis, *inter alia*, that, as the first instance judge had put it, 'A reasonable man would say "I must protect my boy even if this means parting from him for ever so that he can be free of this danger"'. It is quite likely that a modern court would take a different view,[6] but the case shows the scope for different opinions on what is reasonable. Furthermore, notwithstanding an important Court of Appeal decision, *Re H, Re W (Adoption: Parental Agreement)*,[7] where the court refused to dispense with the agreement of a mother whose son had been taken into care nine years earlier because of her alcoholism, the general trend since *Re D* has been towards dispensing with agreement, and in practice, it appears that it will be difficult for a parent to resist such dispensation. The *Pathways to Adoption* research project found that 95% of contested adoption applications were granted.[8]

Unease that the reasonableness test gives insufficient weight to the rights of parents has been expressed both by the judiciary and the Government. In *Re C (a minor) (Adoption: Parental Agreement: Contact)*,[9] the Court of Appeal upheld the decision of the trial judge that the mother's agreement was being unreasonably withheld. The mother was

2 *Per* Lord Hailsham at 699.
3 *Re P (an infant) (Adoption: Parental Agreement)* [1977] Fam 25.
4 *Re D (a minor) (Adoption: Freeing Order)* [1991] 1 FLR 48.
5 Lord Hailsham in *Re W* (above) at 700.
6 See *Re C (a minor) (Residence Order: Lesbian Co-Parents)* [1994] Fam Law 468.
7 [1983] 4 FLR 614.
8 Murch *et al*, *Pathways to Adoption* (1993) p 28.
9 [1993] 2 FLR 260.

of low intelligence and unable to care adequately for her child, K, who appeared emotionally and socially deprived; the unmarried father was at work most of the time and unable to provide much support, but he prevented the mother from sending the child to a day nursery. The child was removed after suspicions (later rejected by the judge) of sexual abuse and placed with foster parents where she thrived. After attempts at rehabilitation it was decided that the child should be placed for adoption. Balcombe LJ, while agreeing that the trial judge had correctly dispensed with the mother's consent to a freeing for adoption application,[10] found himself

> 'left with a feeling of distinct unease about the result of this case.... While I accept that a reasonable parent does pay regard to the welfare of his child, in my experience a decision to dispense with the agreement of the parent to the adoption of a child who is in care usually occurs when the child is in care because of some failure on the part of the parent. In this case, ... the only failure on the part of the parents was their inability to give K the standard of parental care necessary for her social and emotional development, which was primarily attributable to the mother's limited intellectual capacity, and the father's inability to comprehend the effect of this or himself to provide an acceptable alternative. If normal social work intervention should prove ineffective, this could well justify K being taken into care and placed during the remainder of her childhood with long-term foster parents, but I doubt whether Parliament intended that it should be a ground for irrevocably terminating the parents' ... legal relationship with the child. It has the flavour of social engineering.'[11]

Steyn and Hoffmann LJJ disagreed with his lordship's approach, pointing out that the statutory test is not one of inadequacy of parenting, but of unreasonable withholding of agreement. They also suggested that the 'reasonable parent' is simply an 'anthropomorphic conception of justice', and that the issue could equally be put in terms of asking whether:

> 'having regard to the evidence and applying the current values of our society, the advantages of adoption for the welfare of the child appear sufficiently strong to justify overriding the views and interests of the objecting parent'.[12]

The Government's inter-departmental review proposed a new test intended to place greater emphasis upon the parents' position and very similar to that put forward by their lordships. It might:

> 'be expressed in terms of the court being satisfied that the advantages to a child of becoming part of a new family and having a new legal status are so significantly greater than the advantages to the child of any alternative option as to justify overriding the wishes of a parent or guardian... where adoption would only be *marginally* better than another option, the court should allow the fact that a parent does not agree to adoption to tip the balance in favour of the other option'.[13]

10 Discussed in Ch 5 and below.
11 At 269E-H.
12 At 272D,G-H.
13 *Review of Adoption Law Consultation Document* (1992) at paras 12.6, 12.8.

The Government's White Paper[14] endorsed this test, which fits in well with the general thrust of their family policy to assert the rights and responsibilities of natural parents.

(b) Adoption *v* fostering; contact with the birth family

But such an approach also makes the decision on agreement much more clearly one based on competing claims to fulfilling the child's welfare, and it goes to the heart of the fundamental question of whether adoption into a new family, as opposed to long-term fostering, is a better option for children who cannot live with their own families. At one time, it might have been argued that the added security of adoption, the ability of the adoptive parents to take all decisions for the child free from having to consider the views of the birth family or the local authority, the giving to the child a new surname symbolising his or her integration into the new family, all combined to make adoption generally preferable. But the population of children being adopted has changed, from the stereotype of the baby born out of wedlock, to a much more mixed age range, and the proportion of children who have meaningful links with their birth families has accordingly risen, both in respect of children in care, and step-children whose parents have divorced. The desirability of always severing all links has become questionable. The approach of the Houghton Committee to this conundrum was to discourage adoption and to promote alternatives instead. For example, they proposed a form of guardianship, later enacted as 'custodianship',[15] which would give foster parents or others parental responsibility for the child until the age of 18, without granting them parental status. However, custodianship proved unpopular with prospective applicants, or at least was perceived by the courts as generally less satisfactory than adoption because it did not give the same permanent security to the foster family, and it was abolished by the Children Act 1989.[16] Nonetheless, the Government proposed introducing yet another form of 'inter vivos guardianship' in their White Paper, to give foster parents 'Foster-plus' status, yet seemingly ignoring the criticism which had led to the abolition of custodianship in the first place.[17]

At the same time, there has been greater emphasis in recent years upon the desirability of combining an adoption order with a continuing link

---

14 *Adoption: The Future* (1993) Cm 2288, para 5.4.
15 Children Act 1975, s 33.
16 E Bullard, E Malos and R Parker, *Custodianship: Caring for other people's children* (1991); *Re W (a minor) (Adoption: Custodianship)* [1992] Fam Law 64.
17 *Adoption: The Future* (1993) Cm 2288, para 5.24. See C Barton 'Adoption Law Reform' (1993) 137 Sol Jo 1198.

with the birth family, through some form of contact. Such forms of 'open adoption' are the norm in New Zealand, where openness extends both to involvement of the birth parent in the selection of the adopter, and to continuing contact through exchange of photographs, school reports, presents or visits.[18] In English law, it is possible for the court to attach conditions to an adoption order, under the Adoption Act 1976, s 12(6), or to make a s 8 order under the Children Act at the same time. The House of Lords approved the use of such means to maintain contact between the child and birth family in *Re C (a minor) (Adoption Order: Conditions)*,[19] at least where all parties are content for this to occur, but in practice, it seems to be done rarely. The *Pathways to Adoption* research study found that conditions were attached to only 1% of adoption orders.[20] It is probable that informal arrangements for some types of contact are more common, and much will depend upon the age of the child and the extent of the existing links with the birth family. The Government proposed[1] to introduce regulations requiring courts and adoption agencies to assess the most suitable arrangements for contact after the adoption, presumably in the same way that local authorities must set out their proposals for contact under s 34(11) of the Children Act before the court makes a care order. But once adoption ceases to be the irrevocable severance of all links with the birth family during the adoptee's childhood, the extent to which it can be viewed as preferable to long-term fostering becomes unclear. It is arguable that the child should remain legally part of the birth family so that his or her origins are not distorted by absorption into a new legal unit. On the other hand, if parenthood derives from the acceptance of the duties and responsibilities of bringing up a child rather than from biological (or marital) ties, legal parenthood should reflect the social reality, and the child should be regarded as part of the family where he or she is actually being raised. We have seen that the general trend in the law has been to accept the intention to perform the social role of parenthood as of greater significance, and on that basis, one might expect to see an accommodation of the child's need to maintain emotional ties

---

18 E France, *Inter-Departmental Review of Adoption Law: Background Paper No 1: International Perspectives* (1990) paras 80-87; A Mullender (ed) *Open adoption: the philosophy and the practice* (1991).

19 [1989] AC 1.

20 Murch *et al, Pathways to Adoption* (1993) p 216. Other sorts of conditions, which would control the exercise of parental responsibility by the adopters, are not approved: *Re S (a minor) (Blood Transfusion: Adoption Order Condition)* [1994] 2 FLR 416 (condition that Jehovah's Witnesses undertake to consent to blood transfusions should adoptive child so require should not have been imposed). Such disapproval is consonant with the view of adoption as a complete mechanism for acquiring parental status and authority.

 1 *Adoption: The Future* (1993) Cm 2288, para 4.16.

with the birth family alongside recognition of the social parents' position, through greater use of such open adoptions.

(c) Freeing for adoption

Even though parental refusal to agree is rarely an obstacle to an eventual adoption order, the prospective adopters do not know, until the adoption order is actually made, whether a parent will successfully be able to thwart their application, leading to great uncertainty and anxiety. As we discussed in Chapter 5, a procedure, known as freeing for adoption, was introduced in 1984 whereby the consent of the birth parents could be obtained, in principle, to the child's being adopted, in advance of an actual placement being made. This enables the prospective adopters (and the child and agency) to see if the placement would work, in the security that the birth parents could not turn round and object to the eventual adoption application. It also enables birth parents, having taken the decision to have the child adopted, to withdraw from the scene and feel able to get on with their lives. It involves the adoption agency applying to the court for a freeing order, to be made either with the consent of the birth parents, or, where the child is subject to a care order, after that consent is dispensed with under the grounds referred to above. Where the freeing order is made, the birth parents lose their parental responsibility, though not parental status, and become 'former parents'.

It was expected that freeing would become a normal step in the process of arranging adoption of children in care, but research found wide variations in its use between different agencies. It is also used in a significant number of cases where adoption will be contested, as a means of dispensing with parental consent, rather than where the parents voluntarily withdraw from involvement with the child. In a representative survey, 67% of freeing applications were made without the mother's consent[2] compared with 21% of adoption applications. Twenty-two per cent of freeing hearings were contested, compared with just 4% of hearings for non-relative adoptions.[3] Freeing, far from speeding up the adoption process, was found to make it much slower; it took on average nine months to obtain a freeing order from the time the application was made, compared with six months where application for adoption itself was made. And it must be remembered that freeing is only the first stage in the process – once the child has been placed (only 21% of children who were the subjects of freeing applications were in adoptive placements at

---

2 29% of freeing applications were accompanied by applications to dispense with fathers' consent: N Lowe *et al*, *Freeing for Adoption Provisions* (1993) p 72.
3 *Ibid.*

the time), there must then be a probationary period to see if the placement is suitable, and then an application for the adoption order itself. It was the delay in the proceedings which led social workers and solicitors interviewed for the research study seriously to qualify their view that freeing was, in principle, a good idea . However, freeing also requires the parent to decide if consent should be given for a child to be adopted, not by people actually chosen, whose strengths and attributes can be assessed, but by someone, perhaps, at some point in the future, while the child becomes the responsibility of the state in every sense of the word in the meantime. It must be much harder for a parent, who may feel intensely guilty about 'signing away' the child at all, to agree to this in the abstract.

The Government's Consultation Document in 1992 recommended that freeing should be abolished, and replaced, in the case of agency adoptions, by a 'placement order', whereby a court would sanction any proposed placement of a child with prospective adopters, *before* the placement occurred.[4] This would address what is the most important issue in the conduct of child care cases by authorities; the decision to place a child for adoption rather than return him or her to the family or in some other way preserve birth links. However, the difficulty of finding an appropriate means of balancing the need to plan children's futures and embrace the possible need for them to be adopted, while recognising birth parents' interests in retaining links with their children was demonstrated by the Department of Health issuing another consultation document on placement orders, which complicated matters still further. It suggested the introduction of two different placement procedures depending upon whether the birth parents were contesting the adoption or not, and yet a further distinction between approval of adoption in principle and approval of specific placements.[5]

The use of adoption as a remedy for the problem of children who cannot be brought up in their own families goes to the heart of the state's role as protector of its present, or future citizens. As long as the state regards the upbringing of children as best done within families, it must seek to find suitable substitute families for children who, for whatever reason, need them. So long as it regards the function of legal parenthood as being to provide a medium for the fulfilment of the responsibilities of upbringing, it must use adoption as a primary option in the range of measures available to it. Inevitably, the 'social engineering' which Balcombe LJ feared could take place is to some extent a reality; the

---

4 Department of Health and Welsh Office, *Review of Adoption Law, Report to Ministers of an Inter-departmental Working Group, Consultation Document* (1992) paras 14.4-15.4. See N V Lowe, 'Adoption Placement Orders – Freeing by another name?' (1993) 5 *Journal of Child Law* 62.

5 Department of Health, *Placement Orders: Consultation Document* (1994). Uncontested applications could be dealt with by notification rather than court hearing.

alternative would be to disclaim the state's interest in ensuring that children are brought up in adequate conditions and with reasonable standards of care.

PART V

Law and parenthood in litigation

CHAPTER 15

Outside court proceedings

1. INTRODUCTION

The next two chapters deal with those lawyers, mediators and court personnel whose work involves them with parenthood.

Their work alone brings millions of people into contact with other people's children. Although virtually everyone has some vicarious contact with parenthood, we deal here only with some of those who do so 'professionally'. A chronological taxonomy would start with an advance guard of fertility specialists, surrogates, ward assistants and adoption agency workers. Another shift is on hand for the 'birth' – midwives, doctors, even judges.[1] Paid early watchers and helpers, on the other hand, are thinner on the ground, and most parents will look more to family, rather than to (public) health visitors or (private) employees. The numbers soon explode, to include workers from the National Health Service, lollipop men and women, school teachers, social workers and police officers.

It will be apparent, to take a different perspective, that many of these people are only generically implicated in parenthood, and that this aspect of their work is subsumed within a wider role; the general medical practitioner and his or her receptionist, for example, are only tangentially involved. Even those who work within a relevant specialism may have a prior perspective: the school dinner assistant is primarily concerned with the child, and not the parent; the Relate counsellor sees his client *qua* partner, rather than as parent. It can be seen that many of the specialists play a more agreeable role than do lawyers in that their link with parenting is not probably as divisive, or pathological, in nature. The paediatrician, the patient and the parent(s) will normally be united against some extrinsic illness which ails the child; a schoolteacher's

---

1 By virtue of adoption orders (which can also be made by magistrates): see Ch 4.

work with his pupils and their parents may encounter nothing negative at all.

As we saw in Chapter 2, the United Nations Convention on the Rights of the Child is laced with provisions relevant to this Part of the book. Many of the 54 Articles require the states parties to deploy resources, and thus personnel, for the benefit of children. Article 6, for example, covers ongoing support:

'1. States Parties recognise that every child has the inherent right to life.
2. States Parties shall ensure to the maximum extent possible the survival and development of the child.'

Even such general duties as these, which are mainly aimed at children as such rather than at their relationship with their parents, are going to be supportive of the functioning family. Not that our domestic system is discharging them very well: the introduction to a Royal College of Physicians Report baldly states that:

'Without the necessary resources, many babies who could have been rescued will die and, as was the case 25 years ago, a high proportion of the survivors will have avoidable handicaps.'[2]

In these next two chapters we focus on those people most implicated in the *law* of parenthood and parenting. We look at the judges, solicitors and barristers, mediators, social workers, court welfare officers and guardians *ad litem* who, with varying levels of specificity, may influence, assist or encroach upon parenthood. Then we look at their ultimate arena of operation – the court system. A suggested *pro forma* letter[3] shows how some of this might be described to a young child:

Dear Sarah,
I am writing to you to let you know that I am your very own solicitor. Jane Rogers, your guardian *ad litem*, has explained to you who I am, and what my job is and that I need to come and see you. Now, I thought it was the right time to write to you about this.
  Where there are some worries about boys and girls, there is a special place called court. There, wise people listen to these worries and learn about the children and their families. The wise people also listen very carefully to what the children want, if they are able to say.
Yours sincerely
Children's Solicitor

The first persons we are going to look at are, respectively, the lawyer and the mediator. We shall see that their roles have become even more intertwined since this 1988[4] description of their roles:

'[Lawyers]... enjoy high status and have their own special language. Their responsibilities lie exclusively with one party to the conflict, although it has to be

2 *Medical Care of the Newborn in England and Wales* (1988).
3 P King and I Young, *The Child As Client* (1992) p 32, and see generally.
4 G Davis, *Partisans and Mediators* (1988) p 2.

understood that their tasks include negotiation as well as advocacy, the former responsibility being one which they share with another group of "helpers" who are of more recent origin and, generally speaking, have lower status.

The second group – the new mediators – offer themselves to both sides to the dispute, saying to them in effect, 'we see you cannot agree – why not let us help you sort out the problem?' Their claim to specialist expertise lies in the area of negotiating skill, although some will also be 'expert' in other areas, for example in counselling or in knowledge of child developmental psychology. The partisan may likewise be a skilled negotiator, although the negotiations in which he engages will be of a rather different kind. But the professional partisan will also be expert (and have qualifications) in law and legal processes. The mediator's knowledge of these matters is likely to have been built up informally.'

We might add that mediators are cheaper than lawyers;[5] we proceed to ask which are 'better'. But we make one preliminary criticism of the above analysis. It is not always true that parents, or others who approach mediators (or, indeed, lawyers) only do so in the wake of a previous failure to reach agreement. Some will do so in the very hope that they will be able to uncouple consensually. It is also important to note that disputes concerning children are often not concerned with assessing parental 'blame'. They are prospective, rather than retrospective in focus, ie regardless of blame, they are concerned with settling arrangements for the future. Hence, the 'traditional' focus of lawyers and courts, upon the assignment of blame for past events may be inappropriate.

2. LAWYERS

In the early 1970s it seemed that most reported 'family' cases were concerned with the main petition of divorce, as the courts worked at the interpretation of 'irretrievable breakdown', the new ground for dissolution of marriage introduced by s 1(1) of the Divorce Reform Act 1969. By 1977, the 'special procedure' was available to all undefended petitions for divorce and judicial separation, allowing time for the development of the 'new' (Matrimonial Proceedings and Property Act 1970) law on ancillary financial relief. Only now, in the 1990s, have such developments as the Children Act 1989 triggered many cases about parenthood. It would therefore seem that these are early days in which to talk of 'parent', rather than 'family', lawyers. The 1993 Government Green Paper on Divorce[6] stressed the difficulty of detaching issues affecting the

---

5 *Looking to the Future: Mediation and the Ground for Divorce* (1993) Cm 2424, paras 9.28, 29.
6 *Looking to the Future: Mediation and the Ground for Divorce* (1993) Cm 2424.

children from 'other' important issues about accommodation, income and property.[7] It would be tempting to assume, and perhaps pleasing to discover, that in dealing with parenting issues the family lawyer displays a particular sensitivity; and even more so where the child is the client. Yet in the maintenance context at least, the potential is *reversed*, as, since the Child Support Act 1991,[8] only spouses will usually be subject to the sort of discretionary regime which provides scope for something other than the impersonal approach. Ancillary financial relief for these adults, which still encourages lawyers to haggle over 'all the circumstances',[9] permits the sort of passionate involvement inimical to the mechanical calculation of the child maintenance requirement.

It is easy to trawl the surveys for uncomplimentary – and conflicting – examples of solicitor-client and client-solicitor attitudes.

(a) The parental view of lawyers

In one survey,[10] a father was disappointed by the pessimism evinced by his solicitor with regard to parenting after divorce:

> 'He started talking in terms of, oh well, a kind of pro forma arrangement straight away... He said, well, you know, obviously you're forty or whatever it was, you need to rebuild your life again... I said... I want a much more active relationship with my daughter, even if it is ultimately the case that my marriage is ended.'

Yet despite the fatalism which that parent discerned in his solicitor, half of those surveyed in another study found them 'approachable, friendly, helpful'.[11] One mother was asked how hers reacted when she cried in his office:

> 'Oh, he is very good. He has obviously seen many people like this. He tries to make me laugh. He's very understanding.'

One father had had a depressive illness after the break-up of his marriage and separation from his children:

> 'She thought I would harden up, but I didn't. When she realised this she was very kind. I think she can adapt to the sort of person she is dealing with'.

In the same survey, almost 30% – the highest number – of those parents who were asked, thought that residence and contact issues were the solicitors' main concern (less than 4% divined it as 'getting their fees paid'!)[12] and over 60% expressed themselves as being either 'satisfied'

---

7 *Ibid* para 7.17.
8 See Ch 9.
9 Matrimonial Causes Act 1973, s 25(1).
10 G Davis and M Murch, *Grounds for Divorce* (1988) p 58.
11 M Murch, *Justice and Welfare in Divorce* (1980) p 14.
12 *Ibid* at p 27.

or 'very satisfied' by their solicitors.[13] As regards simple *efficiency*, only a minority of those canvassed were unimpressed. But one parent thought that her solicitor, 'sometimes seemed to mix my case up with someone else's'; and one mother said:

> 'I can go to him after I've been to see him three or four times and he'll say "Is it two children you've got?" One feels then you are just a number rather than a person.'

Now, in the era of quality assurance and 'interpersonal skills' clients should not reasonably come away with such impressions. Much 'family work' is legally aided; even more so where children are involved. If the Solicitors Family Law Association Code of Practice (see below) may be said to be concerned with a professional philosophy and attitude, then the 'Transaction Criteria',[14] which govern work done by solicitors in partnership with the Legal Aid Board, represent the detailed mechanics. In requiring solicitors to consider the potential need for welfare benefits advice in 'family' matters, the Criteria have echoed similar calls dating from the Finer Report[15] onwards. A number of the Criteria[16] come into play if there are children *'affected by the relationship'* which is breaking down. These particular Criteria are heavily influenced by the terms of the statutory welfare checklist,[17] and other substantive issues such as the criteria for financial relief,[18] as well as by the dictates of office efficiency. The requirements concern both the information to be elicited and the advice offered. (We deal with the Legal Aid Scheme itself later in this chapter.)

The full names and ages of each child should be recorded, together with the identities of their natural parents, details of any maintenance orders or payments, state of health, schools, and any 'strong' religious faith or national identity. The solicitor must also establish the client's intentions for the children: whether he wants them to live with him; the children's views (unless they are of 'pre-school' age); and the other party's views. Finally, any fear that the child(ren) may be abducted by the other side must be noted, as must any contact with the social services, or other welfare organisation, together with the names of the social workers involved.

Naturally, the advice to be proffered to the client is a more direct (if unacknowledged) reflection of substantive law. In apprising the client as to whether a residence or contact order should be sought, much is made of the statutory checklist,[19] although without the qualification in the

---

13 *Ibid* at p 30.
14 *Transaction Criteria* (1993).
15 (1974) Cd 6478. See Ch 9.
16 *Transaction Criteria* (1993) pp 13-14 and 18-19.
17 Children Act 1989, s 1(3); see Ch 8.
18 Eg s 25 (3),(4) of the Matrimonial Causes Act 1973.
19 The guidelines laid out in s 1(3) which elaborate the welfare principle of s 1 (1).

Children Act 1989 which renders it inapplicable to non-contested s 8 proceedings.[20] The lawyer is also expected to explain Part 1 of the 1989 Act, and whether a s 8 application[1] is necessary in view of the 'principle of non-intervention' in s 1(5). In particular, an explanation of 'parental responsibility' is required: who has it, its continuing nature, the effect of residence and contact orders, and what the father of a non-marital child has to do to obtain parental responsibility. We suspect that, until all parents take the trouble to discover their legal position at the outset, parts of this standard lecture are going to come as an unwelcome surprise to some of them. Two such parents might, respectively, be the 'non-marital' father and the residence mother on divorce; the father discovering that he has no automatic parental responsibility, and the mother that hers is not exclusive.

Today, the improved training of *barristers*, together with the greater restraint required in the cross-examination of child-witnesses[2] may have combined to improve matters. Although child law, once the equivalent of geriatrics for doctors, has now achieved both a higher profile and a greater earning capacity, it remains a matter for regret that, despite the creation of the Family Law Bar Association, the 'cab rank' principle still permits any barrister to take any case. Solicitors who act for children must be members of the Child Panel, but this is not a necessary prerequisite for those who act for parents despite the obvious significance for their children.

(b) Lawyers' views of parents

In the early 1980s, the perceived view from the *other* side of the family practitioner's desk was said by Carol Smart[3] to be one of lazy women and irresponsible or hard-done-by men.

Only when parenting issues arose did Smart's solicitors 'recognise that a particular structure to family life might have consequences beyond individual self-determination'.[4] One explained why women are more likely to 'get custody':

> 'Well, its partly emotional and partly practical. If the husband is to have custody...
> it means he's got to give up work and the wife – you couldn't make the wife go out
> and earn as much money as the husband in most cases. Again this is part of the

---

20 Section 1(4)(a).
 1 For 'residence', 'contact', 'specific issue' and 'prohibited steps' orders; see Ch 8.
 2 See Ch 16.
 3 *The Ties That Bind: Law, Marriage and the Reproduction of Patriarchal Relations*
    (1984) pp 189-190. Smart's interviews took place in 1981. Virtually all of them
    specialised in 'matrimonial' work; only eight were women.
 4 *Ibid* p 190.

general social picture and many women would say this is wrong.... But of course we musn't go too far along with this Women's Lib and everything else and sex equality. There is in fact a difference between a man and a woman and it is the woman's natural role to look after the children.'[5]

Another solicitor explained matters in more detail:

'I think fathers can, particularly as children get older perform a very valuable function as fathers and indeed exceed mothers in their ability to understand what children are after. But it rather depends, if you are talking about children who are under shall we say seven or eight most fathers haven't the faintest idea what children of that age are and I think there should be a natural bias. You can't alter the biological fact that women bear children and it isn't just a matter of can you put a nappy on efficiently or otherwise, it is a matter of understanding children. I am quite certain that if a mother's particular relationship, having carried the child for nine months and probably breast fed it and so on, had all its needs as her immediate responsibility, it gives her a special relationship, there is no way that father can, it is very regrettable in many ways, that he can have the same relationship at that age.'[6]

Others mistook what, even at that time, was a stereotype for a general pattern. 'Usually the wife doesn't work... fathers' working hours will not coincide with children's school hours'. Yet the tendency for women with dependent children to go out to work had increased by about 20% between 1971 and 1976.[7] In Chapter 6 we noted some, more recent, *judicial,* ie *legal,* attitudes to mothering and fathering. They are certainly less stereotyped and one may expect that the new generation of lawyers is following their lead: below, we look at the more enlightened attitude displayed by the Solicitors Family Law Association.

In a later study,[8] gender was reported as being an issue *between* solicitor and client. Several men had been disconcerted to find that their 'man' was a woman, particularly if she was seen by the client as a campaigner for women's rights. (Today, when more females than males are being admitted as solicitors, their successors are either getting used to it or asking to see a man.[8a]) The more traditional converse was also in evidence:

'I felt that there were attitudes that came across that made me feel that perhaps he was more sympathetic to my husband's side of it. I mentioned being a single parent and doing a course and he just seemed very unsympathetic about that and women going out to work or doing any further education when they had children. The impression I got was that he thought that women should be at home and that I was going to be judged on the standard of care of my children as if there were two people looking after the children – it wasn't going to be taken into account that I was one person looking after them on very little finances and I think possibly a woman solicitor with children herself might have been more sympathetic to my case.'[9]

5 *Ibid* p 176.
6 *Ibid* p 179.
7 *Population Trends 13* (1978).
8 Of 299 people involved in contested applications; G Davis, *Partisans and Mediators* (1988); see, generally, Ch 8.
8a See *Trends in the Solicitors' Profession: Annual Statistical Report 1994* J Jenkins (1994); and passim.
9 *Ibid* p 87.

If this was an accurate perception of the solicitor's attitude, it must have been difficult for him to represent his client successfully, or for the children to have benefited from his work.

(c) An improving relationship?

In the light of such accounts of how lawyers and their family law clients have viewed each other, we might reflect on the inevitable limitations on the relationship, and consider what each might do to improve it. The separated parent must recognise that there is no remedy for the pain of having less contact with children than he would like and that the law, and thus the lawyer, may not be able to deliver his needs. Gwynn Davis develops this further by pointing out that the client may lack those personal resources necessary to the healing process: 'Instead they use the law as a pumice stone, endlessly rubbing away at their own wounds, never allowing them to heal'.[10] Yet the lawyer (and indeed other advisers/treaters) must not promise omniscience. Although Glin Bennet[11] refers specifically to doctors, nurses, social workers and clergy, perhaps his idea, of the 'wounded healers' needing to recognise their own vulnerability, is also applicable to lawyers. His thesis is that these professionals are themselves part-client, and that coming to terms with the fact of their being less than 100% competent and healthy will improve their work. The willingness of lawyers to direct the client to extra-legal services may act as a helpful acknowledgement of their own professional limitations.

The year after Carol Smart's survey (above) of what used to be called 'matrimonial' work, saw the 1982 formation of the Solicitors Family Law Association (SFLA). At that time there was a widespread belief, if only of folklore status, that adversarially inclined lawyers were exacerbating, indeed creating that 'bitterness, distress and humiliation' which had been identified in 1966 as avoidable under a good divorce law.[12] Whether they were all quite as bad as that may be doubted; it was also the time of the supposed 'civilised divorce', after which the spouses remained good friends and only the lawyers tried to stir things up. Perhaps the truth is that the relationship, for good or for bad, between family lawyer and client, has been symbiotic; one of them suggesting a morally dubious idea, the lawyer carrying it out and the client reaping the advantage.

---

10 *Partisans and Mediators* (1988) p 209.
11 *The Wound and the Doctor* (1987). The author is a consultant psychiatrist.
12 Law Commission, *Reform of the Grounds of Divorce: the Field of Choice* (1966) Cm 3123.

There is evidence to suggest[13] that a combination of 'elusive' parents on one side, and 'dilatory' solicitors on the other, can result in an abuse of the parental divorce process. In one survey[14] a husband queried whether the children were 'of the family', solely as a stratagem to postpone the decree,[15] and thus win an 18-month delay in the dispute over the family home. The status of the children would not have affected the property order, but the court did not have the power to set aside the question of their status.

It has been argued that lawyers, 'peddle the language of the law, legal symbols...[and] coerce the experience and life situations of their clients',[16] and that they are constrained by a procedure not designed to mitigate the intensity of disputes. One of the reasons for setting up the 1982 Matrimonial Causes Procedure Committee,[17] the purpose of which was the reduction of tension in divorce, was to provide further for the welfare of the children of the family.[18] Of those participating in a 1973/74 survey,[19] 22% said that the stance taken by the solicitor – that of either fighter or conciliator – should depend on the circumstances between the parties and the children.

In dealing with parties who were professionally unrepresented, some solicitors may have been guilty of writing letters in unduly technical language,[20] a particularly unhelpful practice if related to future parenting arrangements. SFLA members, who numbered about 3,500 by 1994, subscribe to a Code of Practice, which the Law Society recommends to all solicitors practising family law, and about which members, as a condition of membership, are required to inform their clients. The Code cannot be prescriptive because rules of law, or the duty owed to the client, may require departure from it. This may be contrasted with the duty owed

13 G Davis *et al*, *Simple Quarrels – Negotiating Money and Property Disputes on Divorce* (1994) p 151.
14 *Ibid* pp 152-3.
15 This was under the pre-Children Act 1989 law, whereby the divorce court had to certify its satisfaction with the arrangements made for the children of the family before a decree could be made absolute.
16 M Cain, 'The General Practice Lawyer and the Client; Towards a Radical Conception' (1979) 7 IJSL, 333.
17 Set up by Lord Hailsham LC, and chaired by Booth J, to undertake an overall examination of matrimonial procedure in the light of the development of conciliation.
18 Its 1985 Report recommended, eg, that the word 'application' should replace 'petition' (paras 4.2-4.4). So far as parental divorce was concerned, the suggestion was that the petitioner and respondent be encouraged to file a joint statement as to the arrangements for the children of the family.
19 See M Murch, *Justice and Welfare in Divorce* (1980) p 40.
20 A failing now deprecated by the SFLA Code.

to patients by the medical profession, which is largely allowed by the courts to set its own standards.[1]

The Code[2] has much to say about the client as parent, and even more about the child, both generally and as client. The solicitor should encourage both the client and other family members to regard the welfare of the child as the paramount consideration;[3] promote co-operation between parents in decisions concerning the child;[4] deal with arrangements for the children in separate letters;[5] and remember that the interests of the child may not always coincide with those of either one of the parents.[6] The client must be led to an understanding of the likely impact of his/her decisions upon the children.[7]

SFLA members are informed[8] that 'in exceptional cases it may be appropriate for the child to be separately represented; this may be by the Official Solicitor, a panel guardian[9] (in specified proceedings) or in the case of a mature child, by a solicitor direct'. In such cases para (7) of the Code, 'The Child as Client', is applicable:

> (7.1) A solicitor should only accept instructions from a child direct if the solicitor has the requisite training in this field. The solicitor should make a personal commitment to undertake all preparation and advocacy for the child and give the child the same respect afforded to an adult as client.
> (7.2) A difficult and continuing duty for the solicitor is to assess the child's capacity for giving instructions.
> (7.3) The solicitor should ensure that the child has sufficient information throughout the proceedings to make informed decisions; advice and information should be presented in a clear and understandable form. The solicitor must be aware that certain information may be harmful to the child.
> (7.4) The child's solicitor should maintain a neutral approach as between each parent, the local authority and other parties.

In 1994, the SFLA produced its *Guide to Good Practice for Solicitors Acting for Children.*[10] It applies in private law cases and, where there is the possibility of conflict between the guardian *ad litem* and the 'mature'

---

1 In *Bolam v Friern Hospital Management Committee* [1957] 2 All ER 118, a doctor had administered electro-convulsive therapy to a patient without a relaxant drug and without restraining convulsive movements. The patient suffered a fractured jaw. It was held that as the doctor had conformed with current medical practice he was not liable in negligence.
2 Re-drafted in 1994.
3 Para 6.1.
4 Para 6.2.
5 Para 6.3.
6 Para 6.4.
7 Para 2.2.
8 Para 6.4.
9 See Ch 16 for a discussion of these roles.
10 See Ch 7 for the child's right to ask for leave to apply for an order under s 8 of the Children Act 1989.

child, in public law proceedings also. It moves carefully amongst such competing issues as, the need to treat the child with the same respect as any other client, the practical needs of children, their autonomy versus their welfare, the spectre of their parents and confidentiality. It follows that meetings, which should be short and taken at the child's pace, should be held in an appropriate setting. A child who approaches a solicitor directly ought to be seen immediately, and it should be established whether or not the parent/carers know he or she is there; if not, there should be discussion as to whether they be told.[11] The young client is entitled to independent advice on a particular issue without those other people knowing about it. On the other hand, should there be a referral from an adult, the solicitor should question the motive, and establish whether the child is being seen as a potential ally to buttress an existing claim. Yet if a matter goes to mediation, the solicitor should ensure that, in using his or her voice on the child's behalf, trust between the child and the family is not undermined.

In 'taking instructions',[12] the solicitor should ensure that the mature minor has sufficient information to be able to make informed decisions, yet be aware that such a client may feel under pressure to agree to a course of action in order to please:

> 'It is important to proceed at the child's pace and to allow the child sufficient 'space' and 'permission' to change course or ultimately withdraw. It is easy for the solicitor effectively to take over the litigation and the solicitor should be sensitive to the risk.'

We note here the importance attached to maintaining an appropriate 'professional' distance, and to ensuring that the child will not feel deserted when the matter is done with:

1. A solicitor should ensure that he remains accessible to the child and is sympathetic yet professional. Over-dependence by either the child or the solicitor on the other should be discouraged.
2. It is important that the solicitor prepare the child for the end of the relationship and begin telling the child, before the end of the case, that the solicitor's role will shortly be over.

---

11 For a discussion of the concept of the 'mature minor', see Ch 6 and the references there to *Gillick v West Norfolk Wisbech Area Health Authority* [1986] AC 112. The level of understanding required of a child to give instructions to a solicitor is much lower than that required to make an informed decision regarding psychiatric examination: *Re H (a minor) (Care Proceedings: Child's Wishes)* [1993] 1 FLR 440. But participating as a party extends to giving evidence, taking decisions as matter arise and being cross-examined: *Re H (a minor) (Role of Official Solicitor)* [1993] 2 FLR 552. The court, rather than the solicitor, has the ultimate right to decide whether the child has the requisite level of understanding to instruct a solicitor: *Re CT (a minor) (Wardship: Representation)* [1993] 2 FLR 278.
12 See Ch 7.

We have seen how family lawyers have recently acknowledged the need for a specialist attitude to their work: later in this chapter, we look at how they relate to other workers in the family breakdown field, such as mediators. But whilst solicitors' pre-qualification training may now be more vocational, and involve oral and interviewing skills plus associated role-play, it should be remembered that unless their previous degrees are other than the traditional LLB, they will have little or no formal knowledge of the other disciplines which inform family life. This may well set them aside from their opposite numbers in some other European countries and in North America, as might their (possible) extreme youth[13] at first qualification – an accusation more commonly levelled at social workers – which in turn makes it likely that they themselves have experienced only one role within the family. Even worse, points out Professor Birks,[14] is the possibility that *they may have never studied family law* at all. The Family Law option on the Bar Finals course is of the 'black letter' variety, with a heavy reliance on drafting skills. Those qualifying as solicitors in the 1990s, or at least those of them who *opted* to study family law for six weeks or so as part of their Legal Practice Course, are given this early description of the role:

> 'If a relationship has finally broken down, it is fair to assume that a family client's ultimate objective is to be able to unravel the legal ties of that relationship and to begin life afresh with the minimum of pain and bitterness. This will apply particularly where children are involved. There will be times when a client may be so involved in the detail of a particular dispute that he loses sight of this wider aim. It is here that the good family practitioner can make a positive contribution: by maintaining a sufficiently detached viewpoint the professional may enable a client to refocus on his goal and to regard matters in the round.... A healthy measure of commonsense and a sense of humour are... invaluable.'[15]

Lawyers' possible ignorance at the point of qualification is compounded by the subsequent lack of compulsory specialist education afterwards. The generic qualification suffices: although the comparison with medical doctors needs to be pursued with caution, the thought of the houseman proceeding to an immediate practice in obstetrics – or even pathology – is a telling one. The 'continuing education' now required of solicitors often includes the opportunity to 'do' family law but provided the required number of points are obtained, the courses attended need not accord with the solicitor's specialism; membership of the SFLA (often

---

13 When four 'O Levels' was the minimum educational qualification for those wishing to become 'articled clerks', the Law Society's regulations restricted admission to the Roll to those aged over 21. The education/training system is now such that solicitors, and those called to the Bar, would normally be at least 23.

14 'Short Cuts', a Paper to the Society of Public Teachers of Law Seminar, 'Reviewing Legal Education' (1994). Birks' general thesis is that professional qualification (for non-LLB graduates) after only two academic years' study is inappropriate.

15 The College of Law, *Family Law and Practice* (1993).

specified in advertisements as a condition of appointment for 'matrimonial' solicitors) requires only proposal and seconding, not proven expertise: 'Membership is not a guarantee of excellence or specialisation... there is no test of legal ability'.[16]

In the public law area, there is some official guidance[17] for solicitors, be they acting for the local authority, the child or the parent. At child protection conferences,[18] the local authority employee may be required to advise the Chair, particularly when proceedings under the Children Act 1989 are under consideration. Yet the solicitor should not be a full participant in the conference, or ask questions directly of the parents or other participants; legal advice to the local authority on initiating legal proceedings should be given outside the case conference. The Law Society's Family Law Committee also suggest that it is good practice for parents' solicitors to attend with them 'to avoid the stressful situation of having to face a meeting of professionals without any professional assistance themselves'.[19] If court proceedings are a possible outcome, the solicitor should discuss with the clients the implications of giving information to the conference. Finally, the solicitor for the child, making three lawyers in all, should either accompany the child to the conference or be there on the child's behalf.

There is nothing to prevent any barrister from being involved in child work, whereas Law Society Children Panel practitioners acting for children must undertake to conduct the case themselves, and this includes conducting the advocacy.[20] If they are unable to do so, the case must be transferred to another Panel member, rather than a colleague or counsel. The Law Society has set up regional Children Panel Support Groups for this purpose. Whilst the pre-qualification education of solicitors may leave them ill-prepared for professional dealings with parenthood, the Law Society's Children Panel, established in 1984,[1] goes some way towards rectifying this. With selection and reselection carried out by the Law Society's Specialisation Family Casework Committee, it ensures that referral agencies, guardians *ad litem* and others, can identify solicitors appropriate to the task of representing children. It is equally important to remember that, whilst their use is not obligatory, Panel members are also available to represent parents, grandparents and any other parties joined to care proceedings.[2]

---

16 *Introduction and Code of Practice* (1994).
17 Law Society's Family Law Committee, *Attendance of Solicitors at Child Protection Conferences* (1994).
18 See Ch 13.
19 *Ibid.*
20 See D Hodson and L Dunmall, *The Business of Family Law* (1992) p 213 and Ch 15, 'Children', generally.
 1 Under the name of the Child Care Panel: see the Children Act Advisory Committee *Annual Report 1993/4* at pp 34-35 for an account of the present practices in selection and re-selection.
 2 See P King and I Young, *The Child As Client* (1992) pp 99-101.

'Children Panel practitioners learn special skills in dealing with children... all... must ensure that they can set children at ease and are able to talk to them and understand them on their own terms. Wearing trendy clothes and a Jason Donovan badge does not help – a 30 year old is a generation away from a 12 year old... However the practitioner must remain a lawyer and must not get emotionally involved – some children are remarkably perceptive, adept and manipulative.... The solicitor should be cautious, be on his guard, try to see the child's point of view but also be relaxed, good humoured and interesting.'[3]

This last point seems to involve a lesser duty than that owed to adults, parents or otherwise, for whom solicitors must do rather more than 'try and see' their point of view.

It is said that the traumatic nature of the work is such that the work load within a given practice should be shared, and that a solicitor should not concentrate on Child Panel business to the exclusion of other work.[4]

If practitioners do develop 'right-on' *attitudes* – which one undergraduate crammer[5] cynically recommends family law students to *affect* – such as a distaste for gladiatorial combat and a motivation to help children, they do so by chance. This contrasts with other workers in the field who, in the United Kingdom, are (more) likely to be employed within the public sector. These may *necessarily* be expected to take a caring role – unlike lawyers, of whom one father said:[6]

'They're businessmen same as anyone else – they have to think of themselves. A lot of people seem to think they're like chaplains but they're not!'

Members of all relevant 'professions' in this area need to be dispassionate, if only to be more effective: personal involvement may militate against the necessary objectivity. Quite apart from the constraints upon an officer of the court, the solicitor should avoid heightening the personal emotions associated with family disputes,[7] and ensure that the relationship with the client 'is such that... objectivity is preserved and [the solicitor's] personal emotions do not cloud the issue.'[8] *Re K (minors) (Incitement to Breach Contact Order)*[9] may demonstrate the dangers of acting otherwise. A father had obtained an order for Saturday contact with the two young children of his family. One weekend the meeting failed to take place. It so happened that the father was a taxi driver and that before he left the family home he had rigged the telephone in order

3 D Hodson and L Dunmall, *The Business of Family Law* (1992) p 208.
4 *Ibid* p 216.
5 C Barton *et al*, *Questions and Answers in Family Law* (1994) p 10, 'Be right on! Family lawyers, at least those who teach, tend to an attitude of "social responsibility". Get a copy of the SFLA Code of Practice (it is all on one card) and trot out its content as appropriate.'
6 M Murch, *Justice and Welfare in Divorce* (1980) p 26.
7 SFLA Code of Practice, para 1.5.
8 *Ibid* para 2.1.
9 [1992] 2 FLR 108.

to listen to calls in his cab. The day before the missed meeting, his equipment recorded an exchange between the mother and a legal executive at her solicitors' office. The device recorded the mother complaining about the court order; the legal executive said:[10]

'if you want to avoid it, then just go away for the weekend and then after Monday we can make an application to the court – it's a way of avoiding contact this week'.

Hollis J found a *prima facie* case, as against both the legal executive and her supervising partner, that they had incited or encouraged the mother to break the contact order, which: 'for an officer of the court and/ or his employee [is] as grave an offence as can be imagined'.[11]

(d) The nature of the work

We turn now to the technical nature of the interaction between lawyer and 'family' client. Smart (no great friend of family lawyers, as we have seen) nevertheless describes their role in neutral terms:

'Solicitors are central to the whole process of and operation of matrimonial law. They perform the function of gatekeepers, allowing lay people limited access to law, and they also act as mediators and translators. They mediate between parties and between individuals and the courts, and they translate personal conflicts into legally recognisable categories of dispute.'[12]

In the wake of the Children Act 1989, family law solicitors may well be limiting 'access' by anticipating the likely application by the court of the 'no order' principle of s 1(5),[13] and may well be 'translating' for their parent-clients by, for example, explaining that the term 'residence' is rightly preferred to that of 'custody'. Davis develops the theme further:[14]

'It is through the solicitor that the client sees her experience translated for the first time into legal terms. She is advised of the limits within which she can operate in this framework and she may be introduced to a new set of assumptions which do not match her original expectations. It is difficult for her to question the way in which her situation is interpreted; she has no point of comparison. The solicitor therefore has considerable control over the route that is pursued. She has to find out what her client wants, what matters are in dispute, and whether these issues are negotiable. There is pressure on the solicitor to translate a complicated personal story into a plan of legal action.'

10 At 110.
11 At 115. Hollis J reported the matter to the Law Society.
12 *The Ties That Bind: Law Marriage and the Reproduction of Patriarchal Relations* (1984) p 160.
13 See Ch 8.
14 *Partisans and Mediators: The Resolution of Divorce Disputes* (1988) p 92. See also Davis *et al, Simple Quarrels* (1994) Ch 4; W Felstiner and A Sarat, 'Negotiation Between Lawyer and Client in an American Divorce' in R Dingwall and J Eekelaar (eds) *Divorce Mediation and the Legal Process* (1988).

(i) Legal aid and lawyers' costs

Any discussion of the *de facto* nature of the lawyer's role must involve an early understanding of the Legal Aid Scheme. Most parents', and virtually all children's exchanges with lawyers will start with an explanation of the Scheme; few mothers[15] and children will proceed much further without obtaining legal aid. The essence of the present state scheme, dating from 1950, is that the sufficiently poor are provided with financial assistance which may subsequently be repaid[16] from costs or property recovered in court proceedings. The scheme affords three relevant forms of assistance: 'Legal Aid and Advice'; Assistance by Way of Representation; and Civil Legal Aid. There are competing interests:

> 'The stakeholders are the applicant (or assisted person), the legal adviser, the court and the Government (the taxpayer).... The decision must be capable of being justified to the unsuccessful stakeholder in any particular case.'[17]

Legal Advice and Assistance ('Green Form') covers advice, writing letters, negotiation and drafting documents. It includes family matters, where those who are financially eligible obtain free help until the solicitor's charges reach two hours work, or three hours if a matrimonial causes petition is drafted. (Legal aid *per se* is generally unavailable for undefended divorce and judicial separation petitions,[18] although it can still be obtained for associated orders in relation to children.) Child support advice may be included but it must be subsumed within the three hours allowed for matrimonial proceedings, and completion of the Child Support Agency's forms will only be covered if there is a legal element.

Minors are eligible for Green Form advice, and a solicitor may accept instructions directly from a *child under 16*[19] provided that there is, for example, a conflict of interest with the parent, or the child is in care, and he or she is old enough to 'give instructions' and understand the advice. (We suggest that this brings into question the extent to which any client, of whatever age and understanding, can be truly said to 'give instructions' to the solicitor.) Under s 10(8) of the Children Act 1989, the court could then proceed to grant leave to the child to make an application under s 8 of the Children Act 1989, if the child (no age specified) 'has sufficient understanding to make the proposed application'.[20]

---

15 In 1984 Smart (above) found that most women were legally aided (p 164). The reason is that their resources are unlikely to be aggregated with those of their partners in family law cases because they are likely to have a 'contrary interest', Legal Advice and Assistance Regulations 1989, SI 1989/340, Sch 2.

16 The 'statutory charge' does not apply in 'children only' cases.

17 *Legal Aid Handbook 1993*, p v.

18 See, eg, *Bromley's Family Law* (8th ed, 1992) at p 234 for further details.

19 Legal Advice and Assistance Regulations 1989, reg 14.

20 See Ch 7.

Legal aid may also be granted to 'any other person'.[1] The requirements are that the parent must be unable to make the application (for example, because of conflict of interest); the applicant must have sufficient connection with the child to ensure that he is acting responsibly in the child's interests; and the applicant must know enough about the problem to give proper 'instructions' to the solicitor. So far as the *law* is concerned, applications by such people for leave to make s 8 applications, require[2] the *court* to consider, not just the 'connection' with the child but also any risk that the child might be harmed by the application. If the child is being looked after by a local authority, then the latter's plans for the child, and the 'wishes and feelings' of the parents come into play. Such private and public connections as relatives, neighbours, teachers and doctors seem the most likely to take such initiatives. Guardians *ad litem* are ineligible for legal aid.[3]

An important use of Assistance by Way of Representation (normally known by its acronym, ABWOR), is in the family proceedings court,[4] with the crucial qualification that anyone requiring financial help for Children Act 1989 proceedings must apply for Civil Legal Aid instead. Each of these forms of assistance is subject to both a means, and a merits, test. The latter requires the applicant to satisfy the area officer that there are 'reasonable grounds'[5] for involving himself in the proceedings in question. This may be judged by reference to the 'private client' criterion: would a solicitor advise the applicant to go ahead if the client had adequate means to meet the likely cost? The same principle applies to limit the advice actually given:

'In discharging his responsibilities to his client, the solicitor owes a duty of care to the Legal Aid Board and should only give such advice to his legally aided client as he would give to a privately paying client of moderate means.'[6]

Practitioners were given a stern warning in *Evans v Evans*[7] in which Booth J, with the concurrence of the President of the Family Division, Sir Stephen Brown, laid down a series of guidelines[8] to be followed in preparing 'substantial' ancillary relief cases. The mother's case was that £100,000 could be taken from the father's business without endangering it – yet his costs amounted to £35,000 and hers (legally aided) to £25,000:

1 Legal Advice and Assistance Regulations 1989, SI 1989/340, reg 14(3)(d).
2 Section 10(9)(a)–(d).
3 See the next chapter.
4 In the magistrates' court. We look at this, and other courts, in the next chapter.
5 Legal Aid Act 1988, s 15(2).
6 *Per* Booth J in *Clark v Clark (No 2)* [1991] 1 FLR 179, 187-8.
7 [1990] 1 FLR 319.
8 At 321-322.

'The conduct of this case has resulted in an enormous amount of documentation much of which has been copied and incorporated into bundles which have served little useful purpose... it has been easy to extract the small number of relevant documents with ... the valuation of the properties involved. All this has led to the most appalling waste of time and money: the family assets have been unnecessarily dissipated and both parties, but particularly the wife, will suffer as a result.'[9]

Booth J would have done better to say that the two minor children of the family would suffer the most. They and their mother had to leave the family home, the sale of which might have been avoided had it not been for the (avoidable) costs. Davis is derisory about some solicitors' unspoken assumption that the house will pay for (their) costs:

'We were occasionally left wondering whether solicitors regard capital derived from the sale of the matrimonial home as somehow not real money or at least, not to be regarded in the same light as other income. Even though it has to be used to buy other accommodation, there may still be a tendency to regard it as profit, rather as if the matrimonial home were a demented fruit machine, permanently on jackpot.'[10]

The Transaction Criteria[11] require the solicitor to inform, in writing, the legally-aided 'family' client about the statutory charge[12] and whether or not she will have to make a contribution to the case, but Davis *et al* found many solicitors uncertain of how to do so.[13]

In a number of important circumstances the usual means and merits tests are inapplicable.[14] Children, parents (including 'unmarried' fathers) and others with parental responsibility are exempt for the purposes of the following public law proceedings:[15] applications for care and supervision orders; child assessment orders; and emergency protection orders. The child is also entitled to non-means, non-merits tested civil legal aid in applications by local authorities for the use of secure accommodation.

These provisions would seem to facilitate, at least for the financing[16]

---

9 At 324.
10 *Partisans and Mediators: The Resolution of Divorce Disputes* (1988) p 98.
11 These are the criteria used in the granting and retaining of legal aid franchises, ie the partnership between the Legal Aid Board and solicitors providing legal aid services. See A Sherr *et al*, *Transaction Criteria* (1992) p 15 for further details of what the solicitor should tell the legally aided 'family' client.
12 Under s 16(6) of the Legal Aid Act 1988, the Board has a charge, to the extent of its costs, over property 'recovered or preserved'. The first £2,500 of any property adjustment order is exempt. Part XI of the Civil Legal Aid (General) Regulations 1989, SI 1989/339, allows enforcement to be deferred, at 10.5% simple interest per annum, if the property is to be used as a home for the assisted person or 'his' dependants.
13 *Simple Quarrels* (1994) p 136.
14 Section 15 of the Legal Aid Act 1988 as amended and the Civil Legal Aid (General) Regulations 1989 as amended.
15 *Seriatim*, ss 31, 43, 44 and 45. All others required, or applying, to be joined to such proceedings have to satisfy only the civil aid means test, and not the merit test.
16 For the child's ability to obtain leave from the court to institute the proceedings themselves, see the treatment of s 10(8) of the Children Act 1989 in Ch 7.

of proceedings to which they apply, the operation of Article 12 (2) of the United Nations Convention on the Rights of the Child:

'the child shall in particular be provided the opportunity to be heard in any judicial and administrative proceedings affecting the child, either directly or through a representative or an appropriate body, in a manner consistent with the procedural rules of national law'.

Human nature being what it is, the solicitor's work for any client may vary in its commitment and success according to the former's sympathy with the latter's case; in family law, clients may feel particularly inclined to justify their actions and attitudes to the solicitor. In concluding any matter, the professional may reassure the client that the proposed deal is a good one; financial support in particular may best be settled by presenting the matter in terms of children's needs, thus making the payer's obligations more acceptable to him. Perhaps it was for that reason that, even in the 1970s, some 'registrars', as district judges were then termed, would allocate the larger proportion of the husband's payments to the children at the notional expense of the wife.[17]

(ii) 'Bargaining in the Shadow of the Law'

In 1979, Robert Mnookin and Lewis Kornhauser published their seminal article 'Bargaining in the Shadow of the Law: The Case of Divorce'.[18] It deals with why so much of what happens to children after family division has always been left to parental agreement,[19] and with 'the impact of the legal system on negotiation and bargaining that occur *outside* the courtroom'.[20] The study leant heavily on English law and experience.[1]

'A study of custody in England suggests, for example, that courts rarely set aside an arrangement acceptable to the parents...

The parents' broad discretion is not surprising for several reasons. First getting information is difficult when there is no dispute. The state usually has very limited resources for a thorough and independent investigation of the family's circumstances. Furthermore, parents may be unwilling to provide damaging information that may upset their agreed arrangements. Second the applicable legal standards are extremely vague and give judges very little guidance as to what circumstances justify overruling a parental decision. Finally, there are obvious limitations on a court's practical power to control the parents once they leave the courtroom.... When there is no dispute, busy judges or registrars are typically quite willing to rubber stamp a private agreement, in order to conserve resources for disputed cases.'

17 Barrington, Baker, Eekelaar, Gibson and Raikes, *The Matrimonial Jurisdiction of Registrars* (1977) para 3.6.
18 (1979) 88 *Yale Law Journal* 950: in the passages quoted, all footnotes have been omitted.
19 Similar arguments are utilised by J Goldstein, A Freud and A Solnit; see Ch 2.
20 At p 950; emphasis in original.
 1 It originated from Professor Mnookin's lecture at University College, London in November 1978.

Any supervisory aspirations which English family law may have had were open to the criticisms of being both ineffective and intrusive:[2] the only way to inform the court independently of the parties was to commission a welfare investigation, which was rarely done;[3] now divorce is commonplace, it no longer justifies compulsory state investigation into private life.

Mnookin and Korhhauser argued[4] that the child's best interest[5] is anyway largely incalculable, as it requires predictions beyond the capacity of the behavioural sciences. Therefore, the decision is normally best left to the mother and father.[6] They will know more about the child than will the judge. A process that leads to agreement between the parties is better than having a winner and a loser, and is the more likely to ensure a better parent-child relationship in the future. Given that it will be the parents, and not state officials, who will be caring for the child both before and after divorce, the former should have the primary authority to agree the arrangements.

We have argued[7] that the legal interest in parents and children is at its most desultory and least demanding when they stay together, as most do. But, for Mnookin and Kornhauser, the preferred approach is to 'round down',[8] ie to perpetuate this minimalism *after* separation. Whilst the law should strive for consistency and continuity, perhaps the standard should be set at the highest, not the lowest, attainable level. English law gives the parent(s) an effective choice between *either* (low-level) tending of the child *or* maintenance – 'care or pay'[9] – but perhaps this difference is best addressed by 'rounding up', by raising, not lowering standards. There are clear advantages to the private ordering of parental division, but consigning children to a low level of parental care is not amongst them.

Ingleby saw his mid-1980s survey[10] of the interaction between solicitors and family clients in terms of Galanter's[11] 'litigotiation':

---

2   R Dingwall and J Eekelaar 'A Wider Vision' in R Dingwall and J Eekelaar (eds) *Divorce Mediation in the Legal Process* (1988) pp 177-8.

3   This occurred in about 10% of undefended divorces in one survey: J Eekelaar, 'Children and Divorce: Some Further Data' (1982) 2 *Oxford Journal of Legal Studies* pp 63-85.

4   (1979) 88 *Yale Law Journal* at pp 957-8.

5   See Ch 8.

6   This is tacitly acknowledged by the 'no-order presumption' of s 1(5) of the Children Act 1989.

7   In Ch 7.

8   '... courts should not second-guess parental agreements unless judicial intervention is required by the narrow child-protection standard implicit in neglect laws.': (1979) 88 *Yale Law Journal* at p 956.

9   See Ch 8.

10 See R Ingleby, *Solicitors and Divorce* (1992); 60 matrimonial clients' files (12 each from five solicitors) were continuously monitored over an 18-month period in 1985-87.

11 M Galanter, 'World of Deals: Using Negotiation to Teach about Legal Process' (1984) 34 *Journal of Legal Education* 268 (emphasis in original).

'The negotiation of disputes is not an alternative to litigation. It is only a slight exaggeration to say that it *is* litigation. There are not two distinct processes, negotiation and litigation; there is a simple process of disputing in the vicinity of official tribunals that we might call *litigotiation*, that is, the strategic pursuit of a settlement through mobilising the court process.'

Ingleby himself advances a litigotiation 'scale', somewhat reminiscent of Chou-en-Lai's dictum that diplomacy is war carried on by other means:

(1) self-help;
(2) agreement negotiated without legal advice;
(3) agreement negotiated without express invocation of the court;
(4) telephone threat to use the court;
(5) written threat to use the court;
(6) application to use the court;
(7) door of the court agreement/undertakings;
(8) contested court hearing;
(9) contempt, enforcement proceedings.

Ingleby noted some regular patterns early in the proceedings, ie in the interim child care arrangements.[12] Solicitors were often called upon to advise on contact with the non-residence parent. This usually concerned its very existence and not merely its extent. The most common objections were those based upon disapproval of the new partner and, disjunctively, the fear of physical harm to the child. The former elicited the advice, from both sides, that the child's need for contact outweighed feelings about relationship breakdown; the latter that denial would be justified.

The interaction between the solicitors provided many illustrations of arrangements being made at the higher end of the 'scale', in unconscious anticipation of the 'no order' presumption of s 1(5) of the Children Act 1989. In some cases they tried to reduce conflict by keeping the parents apart during the exercise of contact, suggesting the use of relatives for the hand-over and their homes for the visits themselves. Reassuringly, and perhaps contrary to myth, there were no clear cases of the resident parent using the issue of contact as leverage in the financial negotiations. One matter frequently obtruded with regard to the semi-traditional weekend contact, with unwaged mothers tending to welcome the break but those in work seeing it as a deprivation of their own 'quality time' with the children. Further up the litigotiation scale, there were 'offensive' uses of the spectre of court proceedings, such as where one parent would not let the other take the child abroad. 'Defensive' advancements, where one solicitor invited, or challenged, the other to take proceedings in the confidence that they would not be successful, were also noted.[13]

12 *Solicitors and Divorce* (1992) Ch 5.
13 *Ibid* pp 62-3.

So far as final child-care arrangements on divorce are concerned, much of Ingleby's study has been rendered otiose by the Children Act 1989,[14] but we might again note the extent to which previous practice foreshadowed the non-intervention principle by way of pre-emptive private action. At least three earlier studies had already indicated that the court is only rarely determinative of child residence post-divorce.[15] More pertinent to the present context is that the solicitors in Ingleby's study were only informed after the event when children moved from the care of one divorcing parent to the other. In fact there were only two such incidents, a girl who had had her first period and wanted to be with her mother, and a teenager who took the option of living with the other parent rather than go into care. Both these transfers took place with, and by, the agreement of the three people concerned. Where they could not agree, and one invoked court proceedings, there is evidence that neither parent believed that the judge knew enough about them and their children to make the right decision.[16] Consequently:

> 'It is the existence of... three basic ground-rules – presumption in favour of the mother; do not disturb the status quo; accept the welfare officer's recommendation – which enables legal advisers to "settle" a good many otherwise intractable child care disputes.'[17]

(e) The holistic lawyer

Solicitors are not necessarily, or exclusively, adversarial in their approach to family law practice. Even clients have seen that it is a false dichotomy to present them as having to be *either* gladiatorial *or* conciliatory in approach.[18] We have certainly seen that negotiation, or at least 'litigotiation', can be central to their family law work. Ingleby's survey[19] of the interaction between solicitors produced some examples of 'non-contentious' negotiation, ie 'speedy settlement of an issue without the mention of the possibility of court proceedings'. (Admittedly, they often involved child-free marriages in which one party bought the other out of the former family home, a fact consistent with the unpalatable suggestion

14 In that much of the solicitors' work involved explaining the meaning of such concepts as 'custody', 'joint custody', and 'care and control'. These expressions have now been abrogated and replaced by the 1989 Act.
15 S Maidment, 'A Study of Child Custody' (1976) 6 *Family Law* 196 and 236; J M Eekelaar, 'Children in Divorce: Some Further Data' (1982) 2 *Oxford Journal of Legal Studies* 63; and A K Mitchell, *Children in the Middle: Living Through Divorce* (1984).
16 Children in Divorce: Some Further Data (above).
17 G Davis *et al*, *Simple Quarrels* (1994) p 191.
18 G Davis, *Partisans and Mediators: The Resolution of Divorce Disputes* (1988) p 92.
19 *Solicitors and Divorce* (1992) p 80.

that the existence of children exacerbates marital conflict.[20]) There was no bargaining at all in these cases. 'The solicitors' function of providing a forum and guaranteeing the acceptability of a settlement was of itself enough to resolve the issues.'[1] Naturally, there were also some incidents of 'contentious negotiation, in which agreement only ensued after a period of bargaining. Interestingly, this may subsequently lead to three of the four people, ie both solicitors and one of the parent-clients, involved being agreed as to the outcome, the negotiations then taking place between one solicitor and his and her client.

Although Davis was content to refer to a 'relatively small group of difficult or needlessly aggressive solicitors who are readily identified by their fellow practitioners',[2] Smart saw professional relationships as being *generally* determinative of the outcome of negotiations:

'The practice of matrimonial law is therefore primarily about negotiations between solicitors according to sets of mutually agreed rules. The practice of matrimonial law, particularly in provincial cities, is an on-going negotiation between solicitors who are well-known to one another. The clients are to some extent incidental to the process because solicitors will know the rules by which their colleagues operate.... Where specialised knowledge is power the client is at a disadvantage and has very little option except to take the advice of the specialist.'[3]

And yet:

'As well as being legal advisers they were frequently ascribed a counselling role. In this respect they were, surprisingly, viewed more favourably than most other professional workers.... Unlike various kinds of social worker – probation officers, local authority social workers and marriage guidance counsellors particularly – solicitors appeared to have the important advantage of being free from stigmatic associations.... They were consequently seen as offering a more acceptable form of social support.'[4]

Clients' (especially female clients') generally favourable views of their solicitors were also noted by Davis *et al*, who further found most of the solicitors they were studying had understood the limitations of an adversarial approach.[5]

---

20 Law Com No 192, *The Ground for Divorce* (1990) Appendix C, para 7, referred to the 'greater tendency to use fault-based facts amongst petitioners with children'; see Table 4, 'Facts Relied upon by Petitioners with Children, by Social Group.'

1 *Ibid* at p 81.

2 *Partisans and Mediators: The Resolution of Divorce Disputes* (1988) p 121.

3 *The Ties That Bind: Law, Marriage and the Reproduction of Patriarchal Relations* (1984) p 162.

4 M Murch, *Justice and Welfare in Divorce* (1980) p 35.

5 *Simple Quarrels* (1994) pp 92 and 94.

3. MEDIATION

(a) Introduction

Since, as we have seen, parents generally *negotiate* a settlement of their disputes, processes which aid the production of settlements are an important aspect of the setting in which the law operates. Significant to this is the development of mediation as a means of alternative dispute resolution. As its history has been insufficiently long to develop the same sort of distinction between mediators and their function as is often drawn between lawyers and law, the topic of this section is 'mediation' rather than 'mediators'.

In *Re D (minors) (Conciliation: Disclosure of Information)*,[6] Sir Thomas Bingham MR adverted to the value of mediation in resolving parental disputes:

> 'It is notorious that when marriages break down the victims not only include the spouses themselves but also, and particularly, their children, who are swept into the vortex of their parents' embittered emotions at the cost of much unhappiness and, not infrequently, lasting psychological damage. It is also notorious that when marriages break down and problems arise affecting the children, resolution of those problems through the ordinary processes of adversarial litigation often leads to exaggerated accusations and counter-accusations with, in consequence, an exacerbation of feelings and heightening of tension. In the interests of the children there is everything to be gained and nothing lost if the parents can be induced, through the good offices of an intermediary, to compose their differences so as to achieve a working compromise which may be wholly welcome to neither parent but acceptable to each. This interest is shared by the public at large, which not only wishes to spare children unnecessary suffering but also to reduce the great burden of cost and delay which contested litigation of this kind necessarily imposes on an already overloaded legal system.'

The American writers, Lee Teitelbaum and Laura Dupaix, argue that[7]:

> 'Adjudication is ill-suited to the interests of children in custody matters. A mediated agreement is more likely than a judicial decision to match the parents' capacity and desires with a child's needs... the litigative process is more likely to create adjustment problems for the children and their parents.... Compliance with adjudication is based on force or its threat.... Mediated results... are the result of participatory activity and the disputants are likely to have a strong commitment to the results reached.'

There is no settled (and certainly no statutory) definition of mediation. We use John Haynes'[8] suggestion as a starting point:

> 'Mediation is a process in which a third person helps the parties in a dispute to resolve it. The outcome of a successful mediation is an agreement that is satisfactory

6 [1993] 1 FLR 933.
7 'Alternative dispute resolution and divorce; natural experimentation in family law', in J Eekelaar and M Maclean (eds) *A Reader on Family Law* (1994) p 363 at p 364.
8 *Alternative Dispute Resolution; The Fundamentals of Family Mediation* (1993) p 1.

to all the disputants. The agreement addresses the problem with a mutually acceptable solution and is structured in a way that helps to maintain the relationships of the people involved. *Mediation is ideally suited to family disputes'* (emphasis added).

This seems to lack explicit recognition of the theoretically 'non-coercive' nature of the process, whereby the mediator has no power to impose a settlement.[9] It should also be acknowledged that, whilst not primarily directed towards reconciliation, it is probably a better means of identifying those relationships which are capable of being saved, than are adversarial proceedings.[10] Beneficent characteristics of mediation should include: enabling parents to accept responsibility for the family breakdown; to address questions of fault and blame on a face-to-face basis; and to deal with the feelings, at least so far as the adults are concerned, of hurt and anger.[11] It is said[12] that consumer choice of mediation is much influenced by the attractions of speed, cost and privacy (the traditional claims made for magistrates' courts and arbitration). So far as parenthood is concerned, mediation, as a catalytic aid to self-ordering, sits well with the non-interventionist policy of the Children Act 1989. *Looking to the Future: Mediation and the Ground for Divorce*,[13] in announcing that children are often amongst the first casualties of divorce,[14] acknowledged the existing claims made on behalf of mediation, specifically[15] that it encourages the spouses to focus upon their children's needs rather than their own, that it is likely to ensure that arrangements are made before,[16] and not during or even after, the dissolution, and that it tends to result in more durable results, with better prospects of renegotiation when circumstances change.[17]

In considering the mediators, we start by making a clear point about these relative newcomers to the field of family breakdown and re-allocation of parenting. It is that mediation provides them with a living, just as law does for lawyers. In a chapter entitled, 'Starting and Building Your Practice' (which counsels the mediator not to 'expect many referrals from solicitors') one text[18] remarks that:

9 G Davis, *Partisans and Mediators: The Resolution of Divorce Disputes* (1988) p 51.
10 *Looking to the Future: Mediation and the Ground for Divorce* (1993) Cm 2424, para 7.4.
11 *Ibid* para 7.5.
12 J Haynes, *Alternative Dispute Resolution; The Fundamentals of Family Mediation* (1993) p 2.
13 (1993) Cm 2424.
14 Para 7.2.
15 Para 7.7.
16 Para 7.9.
17 Para 7.20.
18 J Haynes, *Alternative Dispute Resolution; The Fundamentals of Family Mediation* (1993) p 1. As regards his dismissal of solicitors, Haynes would appear, at best, to be

'Even the perfect product needs careful marketing, and mediation is no exception to this rule. A mediation service needs to generate a client flow and this chapter suggests ways of getting the client to contact you.'

Fearing that solicitors may be reluctant to spread the business around, the chapter recommends[19] that others such as clergy, therapists, 'medical professionals', personnel officers and accountants, should be courted. Leafleting, presentations, press releases, the yellow pages and networking should all be used. It is a *business*. It has also become *institutionalised*, with two umbrella organisations, National Family Mediation and the Family Mediators Association respectively.[20] The Academy of British Experts includes mediators in its generic register of 'Qualified Dispute Resolvers', and there are journals dedicated to the subject.[1] There has even been time for a change of name; we will follow the domestic practice of using the terms 'conciliation' and 'mediation' interchangeably. In some other countries the expressions may not be used synonymously.[2] In this country, the distinction is more historical in nature; what used to be called conciliation is now called mediation. Or at least, those who used to be called conciliators are now called mediators; clearly there remain important semantic differences such that, for example, anyone professionally involved in family breakdown can adopt a conciliatory *approach*, whereas a lawyer *qua* lawyer, or a judge, cannot be a mediator because it would conflict with the main role.

Christopher Clulow has argued[3] that:

'The role of professionals is being redefined from experts who 'know best' to specialists who can be consulted about different aspects of the human condition, each with a different sphere of competence. The language of the market place now pervades all professional activities. 'Product', 'cost-effectiveness', 'value for money', 'competitive tendering' – these and other phrases have become common parlance in places which would have been unthinkable 15 years ago. The symbolism of money is highly emotive and transforms relationships, as 'clients', 'patients', 'passengers' or whoever, are renamed 'customers'. If the customer is always right, what price professional judgment? If the professional is always right, what price

out of date: The Joseph Rowntree Foundation Social Policy Research Findings Paper No 48 (1994) states that, 'Solicitors continue to be influential in mediation. They recommend or suggest use of the services; act as lawyer mediators and consultants in the process'.

19 *Ibid* p 133.
20 NFM's services are primarily child-related, and funded largely from charitable sources. FMA offers a comprehensive service, and its mediators usually operate in pairs, a lawyer with a 'non-lawyer'. The two organisations have a joint Code of Practice. Dame Maragaret Booth has urged, extra-judicially, that *one* body be established; [1994] Fam Law 661.
1 Such as *Mediation Quarterly* and *Negotiations Journal*.
2 See L Parkinson, *Conciliation and Separation in Divorce* (1986), for an account of the distinctions in Australia (conciliation involves a more *profound* interaction with the parties) and the USA (where conciliation is, or was, a publicly-funded service).
3 'Why difficult Solicitors?' [1992] Fam Law 398.

client rights? Will the unholy alliance between the profit motive of professionals and the psychological motives of clients, support the expenditure of vast sums on campaigns which, at best, can only result in Pyrrhic victories, change as markets open up?'

Similarly, one solicitor's admiring view of a conciliation service was based partly on cost:[4]

'It has time to counsel, advise and warn. It is generally much too expensive to treat your solicitor as a father confessor.'

Further, in 1990, the then Lord Chancellor, Lord Havers LC praised 'conciliators' for their championing of children against an unholy alliance of lawyers and parents:

'One problem is that too many parents (and sadly their solicitors) welcome a good, rough, stand-up court fight and conciliators have to deal with this problem all too frequently.'[5]

We will see below that although mediation has its advocates (as it were) as a tool for child welfare, it is also distrusted as being a Trojan Horse for the mere reduction of state cost in divorce, parental or otherwise.

(b) The journey to the 1990s

It should not be thought that mediation was invented in 1970s California, or that it first arrived in a grateful England and Wales shortly thereafter. It was apparently the major forum for resolving disputes in ancient China;[6] it was originally Confucian teaching that agreements reached by the protagonists themselves stick longer than those imposed on them after confrontational exchanges, and the reported[7] injunction of a modern Chinese conciliator, 'You can't wrap fire in paper', is a striking one. Historically, the *noblesse oblige* of a Cheyenne Indian Chief required him to mediate in disputes amongst his camp-followers;[8] the Ndendueli of what is now Tanzania would convene a meeting of kinsmen in order to resolve differences, looking for settlements by reminding the disputants of their duties to each other, and the importance of those duties to the continued harmony of the community as a whole.[9] However, Gwynn

4 A view of the Bristol Courts Family Conciliation Service, quoted in G Davis, *Partisans and Mediators: The Resolution of Divorce Disputes* (1988) p 3.
5 In T Fisher (ed) *Family Conciliation Within the UK; Policy and Practice* (1992) p iii.
6 D Brown, 'Divorce and Family Counselling: History, Review and Future Directions' (1982) 20 *Conciliation Courts Review* pp 1-37. See L Parkinson, *Conciliation in Separation and Divorce* (1986) for a further account.
7 *Ibid* at p 53.
8 G Grinnell, *The Cheyenne Indians* (1923).
9 P Gulliver, *Neighbours and Networks* (1971).

Davis sees the long *anthropological* history[10] of 'mediation' as being irrelevant to its current potential in family matters. Unlike those characteristics commonly found[11] in 'alternative dispute resolution' in non-industrial societies, he points out that current family mediation takes place in private, with the mediator reliant on personal professional wisdom rather than upon any embodiment of community pressure.

Religious *imprimaturs* abound. The contemporary English judge Christopher Humphreys wrote of his Zen Buddhism:

> 'Most of our time is spent in analysing differences. Now concentrate on similarities, on what is common between two things which are habitually regarded as antagonistic opposites. In other words, look for the higher two-thirds above all opposites... look for this relationship and you will be kinder to each of the pairs.'[12]

The Jewish *Beth Din*[13] has been used universally and ubiquitously as a forum for the private settlement of disputes, in order to avoid 'solutions' imposed by the perceivedly alien rules of the host society. Quakers (The Society of Friends) continue to use mediation to settle commercial and family *contretemps* in order to pre-empt reliance on litigation.

This link with the diffusion of commercial tensions is reflected in the existence of the Advisory, Conciliation and Arbitration Service whose definition of 'collective conciliation' has a transferable, and again familiar, ring:

> 'A means whereby employers and trade unions can be helped to reach mutually acceptable settlements of their disputes by a neutral and independent third party, ACAS. Its essential characteristics are that its use is voluntary and that agreements reached in conciliation are the responsibility of the disputing parties.'[14]

Martin Richards has since criticised[15] current practices in family mediation as being polarised between those who come from the pragmatic dispute resolution tradition of labour disputes, and those who draw on more therapeutic frameworks.

With regard to family conciliation our domestic history[16] is modest, and reflective of our legal tradition of limiting curial interest to inter-

10 *Partisans and Mediators: The Resolution of Divorce Disputes* (1988) at pp 51-2.
11 S Merry, 'The Social Organisation of Mediation in Non-Industrial Societies; Implications for Informal Community Justice in America', in R Abel (ed) *The Politics of Informal Justice* (1982) vol 2, identified such factors as: lengthy deliberation; publicly-held; conducted by leaders of the community known to both parties; and culminating in an award of damages.
12 *Zen Buddhism* (Re-issued 1984).
13 An arbitration body.
14 ACAS 1979, para 10.
15 'Divorcing children: roles for parents and the state', in J Eekelaar and M Maclean (eds) *A Reader on Family Law* (1994) p 247 at p 257.
16 See J Eekelaar and R Dingwall, 'The Development of Conciliation in England' in J Eekelaar and R Dingwall (eds) *Divorce Mediation and the Legal Process* (1988) pp 3-22.

spousal matters. In an effort to create a suitably specialised procedure, three 'Courts of Domestic Relations Bills' were read (albeit unsuccessfully) in the House of Commons between 1928 and 1930. In 1934, a magistrate could still observe:[17]

> 'Police courts do not appear to be the proper tribunal, if a tribunal at all is needed, to unravel the tangled threads of matrimonial trouble. They are concerned chiefly with the administration of the criminal law and maintenance of public order. Their business is with offences against the public order, not with domestic squabbles.'

In truth, such nods as were made in the direction of 'conciliation' tended, as the Finer Report pointed out,[18] to concern *reconciliation*. The Report of the Departmental Committee on Social Services of Summary Jurisdiction[19] said of the 'conciliation' practised in matrimonial cases coming before the magistrates':

> 'We cannot help feeling that under the present system there is a real risk that conciliation may be carried too far. The practice adopted in so many courts of allowing the probation officers to see all persons who come to them in matrimonial difficulties may well tend to lead to some denial of justice.... There is a strong temptation to the zealous officer to settle as many cases as he can out of court and he may even be actuated by personal convictions as to the sanctity of the marriage tie.'

Even today, the mediation process is represented as being 'much better adapted to identifying those marriages which are capable of being saved than is the adversarial legal process'.[20] But in such happy circumstances its role is self-terminating as the mediator(s) will then refer the matter, with the approval of both spouses, to a counsellor. It is the latter who will help the couple, married or otherwise, to strengthen or maintain their relationship or, if separated, to reunite them.

Yet in 1932, Alfred Fellows could already bemoan the institutionalised reluctance to acknowledge, even then, that some stricken marriages were beyond resuscitation:

> 'This ostrich policy of pretending that we have a system of Christian monogamy might be regarded as a harmless one, and a normal product of unctuous rectitude, save for the fact that it results in real and grievous hardship.'[1]

An early example of domestic legal recognition of the value of conciliation was a *Practice Direction*[2] issued in 1971 by the then President of the Family Division, Sir George Baker. When a court

---

17 J Cairns, *Drab Street Glory* (1934) p 131; see generally, C Gibson, *Dissolving Wedlock* (1994) pp 93-6.
18 Para 4.295, note 7.
19 (1936) Cm 9678, p 12; see Ch 16 for the history of the Divorce Court Welfare Service.
20 *Looking to the Future: Mediation and the Ground for Divorce* (1993) Cm 2424, para 7.4.
1 *The Case Against the English Divorce Law* (1932).
2 [1971] 1 All ER 894.

decided that 'conciliation' might be useful in ancillary proceedings, the matter might be reported to the court welfare officer. Following consultation with the parties, either the court welfare officer or an appropriate referee would assist them accordingly. Ultimately, a report on the success of the exercise was to be made to the court.

Lisa Parkinson, formerly Training Officer of the National Family Conciliation Council, praised the Direction as being ahead of its time, whilst deprecating the fact that many judges seemed to be unaware of it.[3] The Finer Committee[4] concluded that nothing had come of it, the report envisaging that the future of conciliation lay in an overall reform of family law. Yet not all of those who gathered under the banner of the Family Court Campaign had the same high aspirations for conciliation:

> 'Some lawyers and Court Officials evidently hoped that conciliation would streamline the court's production line and reduce court waiting lists and some saw conciliators as "charitable ladies" (as they were described in one part of the country, until they politely declined the description), who would pacify distressed and angry people and clear the way for effective action by solicitors or the court.'[5]

By 1978 two subsequently well-chronicled initiatives had originated in Bristol, the 'In Court' and 'Out-of-Court' conciliation systems. They were both concerned with divorce proceedings. The former was operated by the probation service (Divorce Court Welfare Service) and chiefly concerned parental disputes. 'Out-of-Court' conciliation was an independent service which accepted referrals from solicitors, which were normally made before a potentially contested case was taken to court. By the end of the next decade, a Report[6] to the Lord Chancellor found that these were the two main types of conciliation service available in the jurisdiction. The most oft-quoted finding of that Report best explains the subsequent explosion of establishment interest in the subject: at £150, the average 'in-court' cost of resolving a child dispute was 40% less than its 'out-of-court' parallel.[7]

(c) The mechanics of mediation

In 1992/93 the family court welfare service and the National Family Mediation network completed over 19,000 adult- and 6,500 child-related

---

3 *Conciliation in Separation and Divorce – Finding Common Ground* (1986) p 64.
4 *Report of the Committee on One-Parent Families* (1974) Cm 5629, para 4.288.
5 L Parkinson, *Conciliation in Separation and Divorce – Finding Common Ground* (1986) p 66-7.
6 A Ogus *et al*, *The Costs and Effectiveness of Conciliation in England and Wales* (1989).
7 See the judgment of Sir Thomas Bingham MR in *Re D (minors) (Conciliation: Privilege)* [1993] 1 FLR 932, 936-8 for a summary of 'Recent Practices' in conciliation since 1982.

mediations respectively. The Family Mediators Association concluded some 1,500 'comprehensive' (money, property *and* children) cases.[8] What are the mechanics of mediation, as a form of alternative dispute resolution?[9] John Haynes identifies nine stages to the overall process:[10]

(1) recognising the problem;
(2) choosing the arena;
(3) selecting the mediator;
(4) gathering the data;
(5) defining the problem;
(6) defining options;
(7) redefining positions;
(8) bargaining;
(9) drafting the agreement.

He argues that so far as parenting is concerned, mediators should make careful use of language. They should not, for example, refer to a 'failed marriage' or a 'broken home' but to 'ending the spousal relationship' and 'mum's house and dad's house'. Even though s 8 Children Act 1989 orders have not (yet) acquired the opprobrium of 'custody' and 'access', they are still best avoided because they are the names of court orders:

'The mediator has a choice. She can use the legal, adversarial language and provoke adversarial behaviour, or she can use everyday language that speaks of a couple's future parenting responsibilities and encourage co-operative behaviour'.[11]

Perhaps it is only mediators, and not lawyers, who are currently supplying such encouragement. Yet a one-stop approach – even if it involves seeing two people at once – is increasingly possible, with dual training of the 'professionals' concerned. The task of communicating the following information does not seem any more difficult than explaining the legal process.

It is easy to understand, for example, that each age group of children has its own typical reaction[12] to parental division (discussed in Chapter 8) and that it will be of value to all concerned to prepare the parents for these reactions. Regression may be expected in three to five year olds; parental patience may help the child to get over it. A boy aged between six and eight may tend to a strong loyalty towards his absent father, and

---

8 *Looking to the Future: Mediation and the Ground for Divorce* (1993) Cm 2424, paras 7.13,14.
9 For detailed descriptions see, eg: L Parkinson, *Conciliation and Separation in Divorce* (1986), Chs 5 and 6; G Davis, *Partisans and Mediators: The Resolution of Divorce Disputes* (1988); and, generally, J Haynes, *Alternative Dispute Resolution: The Fundamentals of Family Mediation* (1993).
10 *Alternative Dispute Resolution: The Fundamentals of Family Mediation* (1993) pp 1-5.
11 *Ibid* p 75.
12 J Wallerstein and J Kelly, *Surviving the Breakup, How Children and Parents Cope with Divorce* (1980).

be difficult with his mother; she might be advised to help him to understand the time scale of visits. Until s/he is 12, the child may continue to long for the absent parent while expressing anger at the resident parent; and the peer group becomes important. Adolescent reaction may be marked by financial worries, although 'strategic withdrawal' – where a youngster lives and eats in his or her bedroom – is a not-unusual teenage development which may actually help by facilitating an escape from the parents' world during the division. Similarly, a mediator might be the best person to warn the 'client(s)' of how they might exacerbate their children's problems: sharing with the children their anger at the other parent, even *displacing* that anger; becoming self-absorbed and forgetting the children's needs; using them as peers; using older children as caretakers; and viewing them as property.[13]

Haynes has described how and what the mediator might best explain to the children themselves:

> 'I know this is the last place in the world you want to be and I appreciate you coming here, as do Mum and Dad. As they have told you I have been working with them for the last few weeks helping them negotiate their separation (divorce) agreement. In those talks you have been at the centre of most of the discussions as your parents have tried to reach an agreement that, as far as possible, meets your needs. We have spent most of the time talking about your best interests and how things could work best for you because both parents love you very much.'

The mediator might then proceed to explain to younger children what a divorce is, before proceeding to assure them that they did not cause it and that whilst the children will not be able to re-unite the family, their parents' love for them will not change.[14] It may also be possible to relieve their anxieties with respect to prevailing folklore amongst children about what happens to them on divorce, for example that they are automatically taken into care.[15] But what does the mediator do to procure an agreement between the parties which they could not reach for, or by, themselves? In an early analysis,[16] Lisa Parkinson suggested that it could provide a 'positive reframing' of the parties' positions. Haynes[17] suggests that the mediator first demonstrates to the parties the possibility that their

---

13 See Ch 2.
14 *Alternative Dispute Resolution: The Fundamentals of Family Mediation* (1993) pp 85-8.
15 A fear identified by J Collinson and K Gardner, 'Conciliation and Children' in T Fisher (ed) *Family Conciliation within the UK: Policy and Practice* (1992) p 109.
16 'Conciliation: A New Approach to Family Conflict Resolution' (1983) *British Journal of Social Work* 13. For a discussion of theoretical frameworks for 'conciliation', see *Conciliation in Separation and Divorce* (1986) at pp 123-9; and J Haynes, *Alternative Dispute Resolution: The Fundamentals of Family Mediation* (1993) at pp 98-121, for a further account of practical skills.
17 'The Process of Negotiations', (1983) *Mediation Quarterly* 1.

opening stances may be unfair, before helping them to see the issue as a shared problem to be jointly solved. It may be doubted whether the mediator frequently comes up with solutions which have previously eluded those with most to gain from them. It seems just as likely that the parties wish to be well-regarded by the mediator, whose presence enables them to make concessions which they might otherwise have seen as a sign of weakness:[18]

'I'd made my decision in my mind. He'd made his choice, another woman. She's got two children. Let him have her and her two kids, you know... we went to this Family Reconciliation (*sic*)... very good... I could see when somebody else was telling it's not fair from his point of view. I then saw it, but until that point I wouldn't.'[19]

Despite the arguments in favour of mediation, it is possible that a traditional resistance to 'counsellors' in Britain may subsequently be transferred to mediators. The American terminology of 'displacement', 'strategic withdrawal', even 'peer-group', may begin to alienate some, in the same way that 'petition' and 'ancillary relief' have long confused others. Yet in facilitating agreement between parting parents, it seems that the mediator's major skill is her vicarious experience of the sorts of matters which will need to be addressed anyway. She merely *manages* the negotiations:

'Managers do not evaluate, judge, rate, parenting competency, or decide who is the better parent. Neither are they advocates of one form of family structure over another. Managers organise the agenda, determine the order in which the items are to be taken up, help the parents define the problem and develop options to solve the problem.'[20]

For mediators, particularly if they have come from other professions, the realisation that they are not there to solve problems, that they are not working towards preferred solutions, may be a demanding discipline: 'most adults assume the role of problem solvers when faced with distressed children'.[1] But mediators should take positive steps to avoid what Robert Dingwall and David Greatbach call 'invisible knowledge'; if, for example, they are relying on expert knowledge of child welfare to encourage particular arrangements for residence and/or contact, then the parties should be told as much.[2]

---

18 See *Partisans and Mediators: The Resolution of Divorce Disputes* (1988) pp 74-5 and the references cited therein. (Later in this chapter, we look at the possibility that a desire to please the mediator may lead to a party giving *too much* away.)
19 Quoted at p 74.
20 J Haynes, *Alternative Dispute Resolution: The Fundamentals of Family Mediation* (1993) at p 77.
1 J Collinson and K Gardner, 'Conciliation and Children' in T Fisher (ed) *Family Conciliation within the UK: Policy and Practice* (1992) p 108.
2 'Divorce Mediation – the Virtues of Formality?' from J Eekelaar and M Maclean (eds) *A Reader on Family Law* (1994).

It is all very reminiscent of the lawyer's role in domestic partnership contracts at the *outset* of the relationship. Perhaps the only significant difference is that the division of the family necessarily renders the division of labour more difficult, and thus potentially harder to agree about. In each case, it is difficult to guarantee that the agreement reached will be 'judge-proof'. The law casts a long shadow over both sorts of arrangement; given the omniscience of both the Child Support Act and the welfare principle, it is a longer one for the parties *qua* parents – despite the non-intervention principle – than *qua* partners.[3]

Where issues concerning the children are not a major matter, then: 'The mediator's interventions with the family are minimal and designed to strengthen the two families that will emerge from the decision to divorce'.[4]   Matters that the parents might not anticipate, but are subsequently likely to encounter unprepared if they are not raised prospectively, include: birthdays; open telephone contact; extended family rights; moving; and the death or re-partnering of a parent. Where disputes over future parenting threaten to go to court, the mediator might help by assisting the parties to separate out their roles as continuing parents from that of former partners. The mother might, for example, say, 'He left *us*' when, in truth, the father left *her* and wants to continue his role as parent. The path to progress might be unblocked by leading each to acknowledge the other's good points as parent. Universal strategies include the reduction of defensiveness and creating dissonance. In the former case, each might be asked to admit to their worst fears for the outcome of the mediation; if it is 'losing the children', each might be asked to affirm that he or she does not wish such loss upon the other; the fear may then be exposed as untenable. 'Creating dissonance' involves helping each parent to think about what the other really wants; in apparently incorrigible disputes, the participants typically ascribe unreal views to each other. By 'walking a mile in the other's moccasins', each may then work out what it is needed from the other to agree to the other's position – and what might be offered to the other in order to obtain an agreement.

In one survey,[5] almost half of the parents involved in mediation indicated that they did not feel a sense of joint parental responsibility for their children after separation. The mediators first attempted to counter this by querying the relevance of pre-separation responsibility; 'He wasn't a caring husband – you are denying him the right to attempt to be

---

3 Some parts of pre-partnership arrangements may well be legally binding, so far as the adults are concerned, particularly for those who do not marry. See generally C Barton, 'Pre-Nuptial And Cohabitation Contracts: in at the Birth?' [1992] Fam Law 47.

4 J Haynes, *Alternative Dispute Resolution: The Fundamentals of Family Mediation* (1993) p 78.

5 C Piper, *The Responsible Parent* (1993) pp 91-94 and generally.

a caring father'.[6] Then the residence parent would be encouraged to acknowledge the innate difficulties suffered by a contact parent, and *vice versa*: the father who has to bring the children back at a particular time should remember that the mother has to prepare them for school in the morning.[7] To this extent, the mediator's role goes beyond a mere facilitation of agreement; it shapes the parties' attitudes and responses in a manner based on the mediator's own values.

(d) The future?

Positive descriptions of parental conciliation come mainly from mediators themselves: but there is some objective evidence as to its value. We will balance out these views below, after we look at the proposed expansion of the mediators' role. In 1990, a Law Commission Report, *The Ground for Divorce*[8] followed the majority of its respondents[9] in rejecting any idea of mandatory mediation, 'whatever its benefits in some cases, there are many issues or relationships in which it is quite unsuitable'.[10] One example would be where violence has occurred, or is likely to as a result of the initiation of the divorce proceedings; in any event the success rate with pressed attenders is likely to be low.[11] Instead, the Commission recommended[12] that the court should have two additional means of encouraging mediation. First, a power to direct that the parties meet a specified conciliator with whom to discuss the possible benefits which might accrue from mediation. In relation to children, the court would be able to act of its own motion even if not already seised of the case. Secondly, where the parties are in dispute, the court should have the power to adjourn the proceedings for the purpose of enabling the parties to take part in mediation; the interests of the children – whether they would be more helped by the resolution of the dispute than harmed by the delay – would be taken into account in ordering such adjournment. It was also noted that, in contrast to reconciliation,[13] there is no settled law relating to privilege in mediation.[14] Yet in recommending that a statutory

6 *Ibid* p 93.
7 *Ibid* p 94.
8 Law Com No 192 (1990).
9 To Law Com No 170 *Facing the Future – A Discussion Paper on the Ground for Divorce* (1988).
10 At para 5.34, which notes that practitioners in the field thought mandatory mediation might actually be counter-productive.
11 *Looking to the Future: Mediation and the Ground for Divorce* (1993) Cm 2424, para 7.27.
12 Paras 5.38,39.
13 See s 6 of the Matrimonial Causes Act 1973.
14 Other than in-court mediation (above) where exchanges *are* privileged: *Practice Direction: (Conciliation Procedure)* [1982] 1 WLR 1420.

privilege be conferred upon any statements made by the parties,[15] the Commission added a rider in the case of parental mediation. A distinction should be drawn between evidential privilege and confidentiality. Whilst the former would continue to apply even in respect of allegations of abuse, or any other matters relating to the protection of children, the latter would clearly be inappropriate. In *Re D (minors) (Conciliation: Privilege)*,[16] the Court of Appeal held that:

> 'the law is that evidence may not be given in proceedings under the Children Act 1989 of statements made by one or other of the parties in the course of meetings held by or communications made for the purpose of conciliation save in the very unusual case where a statement is made clearly indicating that the maker has in the past caused or is likely to cause serious harm to the well-being of a child.'[17]

The reason for the main rule is clear:

> 'It is... plain that parents will not succeed in composing their differences or achieving a working compromise through the good offices of a third party unless they approach the process of conciliation in an open and unreserved manner, prepared to give as well as to take and to make admissions and conciliatory gestures with a view to reaching an accord. If the parties remain in their entrenched positions no armistice will be reached in no-man's land. But it is plain that the parties will not make admissions or conciliatory gestures, or dilute their claims, or venture out of their entrenched positions unless they can be confident that their concessions and admissions cannot be used as weapons against them if conciliation fails and full-blooded litigation follows. To be effective, any attempt at conciliation must be off the record.'[18]

In 1993, three years after the publication of *The Ground for Divorce*, the Lord Chancellor's Department produced a Consultation Paper[19] which brought the matter firmly into the public and political domain. 'The aim would be for mediation to become the norm rather than the exception.'[20] Threaded throughout the Government thoughts on divorce, children and mediation were the consequences for the public purse. The stated objectives for a good divorce law now[1] included keeping 'to the minimum the cost to the parties and the taxpayer' as well as to 'reduce the trauma for the children'.[2] *Looking to the Future*'s attempts to address

---

15 *Looking to the Future: Mediation and the Ground for Divorce* (1993) Cm 2424, para 5.44.
16 [1993] 1 FLR 933.
17 *Per* Sir Thomas Bingham MR, at 938.
18 Sir Thomas Bingham MR at 933-4.
19 *Looking to the Future: Mediation and the Ground for Divorce* (1993) Cm 2424.
20 *Ibid,* para 7.11.
 1 In the Law Commission Report, *Reform of the Ground of Divorce: the Field of Choice* (1966) Cm 3123, which led to the Divorce Reform Act 1969, it was asserted at para 15 that a good divorce law should: (i) seek to buttress the stability of marriage; and (ii) minimise the bitterness suffered on irretrievable breakdown.
 2 *Looking to the Future: Mediation and the Ground for Divorce* (1993) Cm 2424, para 4.1.

this conflict are unimpressive. Unexceptionally, it states that although the costs of dissolving a marriage, like those of forming one, should be borne by the parties themselves, there are occasions in which this approach would put at risk the interests of the children of the marriage and therefore, 'In such circumstances there is a clear case for public assistance with the costs'.[3] Yet its stated criteria for public assistance – itself to be mediation-based on the belief that this will be cheaper[4] – include the requirement that the recipients 'should behave reasonably in all the circumstances'.[5] This seems to ignore the probability that the worse the parents behave during the divorce process, the greater the threat to children's interests.

If Government really had faith in parental divorce mediation, it should surely assume that persistence in it will eventually move even the unreasonable, but still participating, parent. This in turn should therefore save expenditure from other pockets in the public purse. Children suffering from stress or other ailments, and the additional educational or social work thus generated, contributed to the £1.3 billion which marital breakdown is estimated to have cost the state in 1987/88.[6] So far as cost is concerned, it appears that the bill for child-related mediation is considerably less anyway than the 'comprehensive' variety.[7] And as *Looking to the Future* itself says:

> 'If the children of today's divorcing parents are to develop into well-balanced adults, capable of forming and sustaining a committed relationship themselves and of being responsible parents, then it will be necessary to ensure that their development is not weakened by the way in which the divorce process works. This is a crucial factor in ensuring the stability of the family and family life after divorce.... With help [the parents] may find a means of renegotiating their relationship so that they and their children may have a life together.'[8]

(e) Some reservations

It must be asked whether this vested, and now establishment, support for parental mediation is justified. Even the establishment has acknowledged[9]

---

3 *Ibid* para 9.7.
4 The average cost of mediation is assumed (as of December 1993) to be £550 per case (para 9.29). This is contrasted with an average cost to the Legal Aid Fund of £1,565 per matrimonial bill in 1992/3 (para 9.30).
5 *Looking to the Future: Mediation and the Ground for Divorce* (1993) Cm 2424, para 9.8.
6 As estimated by Relate; *The Times*, 8 March, 1994.
7 National Family Mediation estimate the cost of an average comprehensive service at £550 per mediation – and the average child-related version at some £350 less. (*Looking to the Future: Mediation and the Ground for Divorce* (1993) Cm 2424, para 9.28).
8 Paras 4.11,12.
9 See *ibid* para 7.21.

some of the disquiet which has been expressed about the mediation process. A poor mediator may become over-influential, with parties wanting to please her rather than to reach a genuine agreement between themselves. This may be particularly characteristic of the American experience, where the 'fee for service' (payment by results) model may lead the mediator to invoke the children's interests in the hope of shifting the adults' negotiating position, rather than for the children's sake *per se*.[10] This (English) mother found the experience patronising:

'the Conciliation Bureau went on explaining to me how important it is for the children to see their father and to keep contact and I thought "Don't you bloody tell me that. I know all that"'.[11]

Such an approach might be inaccurate: unblinking commitment to the idea of contact with the non-resident parent has anyway been questioned,[12] at least in cases where the two parents themselves are not in positive contact. More generally:

'Any attempt to push conciliators into the role of a superior expert or authority figure who automatically knows better than natural parents what their children need introduces a paternalistic, child-saving philosophy which runs counter to the main principles of conciliation'.[13]

But perhaps the most worrying, and certainly most oft-expressed concern about mediation is that:

'It can disadvantage a weak or inarticulate party, who may be relatively easily led to settlement because of fear of the other party'.[14]

This is similar to the feminist critique[15] that mediation conceals and continues pre-existing male dominance, thereby putting at risk the recent *legal* advances made by women in the context of violence and property. Yet if men still have the greater economic power, women may feel more able to rally the children to their side and, as Gwynn Davis points out:

'It is also slightly incongruous to find our notoriously male-dominated legal institutions being presented as upholders of women's rights in opposition to mediation services with their predominantly female staff. However "bourgeois" the latter may be, they probably have a better appreciation of, say, the problems of single parenthood than do most judges.'[16]

10 R Dingwall 'Some Observations on Divorce Mediation in Britain and the United States', (1986) *Mediation Quarterly* 11.

11 Quoted in G Davis,*Partisans and Mediators: The Resolution of Divorce Disputes* (1988) p 81.

12 J Goldstein, A Freud and A Solnit, *Beyond the Best Interests of the Child* (1973) p 38.

13 L Parkinson, *Conciliation and Separation in Divorce* (1986) at p 160.

14 *Looking to the Future: Mediation and the Ground for Divorce* (1993) Cm 2424, para 7.21.

15 For a detailed account, see A Bottomley, 'Resolving Family Disputes: A Critical View' in M Freeman (ed) *State Law and the Family* (1984).

16 *Partisans and Mediators: The Resolution of Divorce Disputes* (1988) p 6.

One difficulty is that the mediation model of co-parenting is 'joint', and thus at odds with what we might term the 'several' approach of the Children Act 1989:

> 'There is no legal mechanism in the Act to ensure that both parents are involved in making decisions... either before or after separation.... There is, in effect, a non-convergence of practical responsibility and control. Mediation, by constructing as joint what is only marginally so, and by constructing the responsible duty to care and protect as less important than the responsible right to make parenting decisions, reinforces those notions of the family which have been shown to "silence" the mother. It also acts as a diversion from other solutions: by further "privatising" the family it makes it less likely that the level of community support for the family is strengthened.'[17]

That one-time phenomenon, 'inequality of bargaining power' is still cited as a danger of the mediation process, despite its subsequent deletion[18] (as a vitiating factor) from the law of contract, its original base. We might further milk the analogy (if that is all it is) by remembering that the husband-and-wife relationship is not subject to the rebuttable presumption of undue influence.[19] It is inevitable that people will bring their respective strengths and weaknesses to a bargaining session and that, in this context, these will include the present residence of the children, as well the ever-present questions of personal resource and the psychological baggage carried by any existing relationship. In any case, what a party hopes to *obtain* as a parent will vary from one to another:[20]

> 'Many individuals like spending time with their children and are willing to sacrifice a great deal to have child-rearing responsibilities. Sadly, some parents might pay a great deal to avoid child-rearing responsibilities altogether[1].... A parent may value very highly some tasks like reading the child a bedtime story, and place negative values on others, like shopping for school clothes. Preferences may vary depending on how much custody a parent has... Informed bargaining requires a parent to assess accurately his or her own preferences. Yet the assessments are difficult and complicated. The information each parent has relates to the actual division of child-rearing tasks in an on-going family... the parent may discover new advantages or disadvantages to child-rearing responsibilities. Moreover the parents' own needs may alter drastically after divorce.... Additionally a parent's interest in children may vary according to their age... projecting parental preferences for custody ten years into the future is a formidable task. Nevertheless, most parents have some self-awareness, however imperfect, and no third party... is likely to have better information about a parent's tastes, present or future.'

---

17 C Piper, *The Responsible Parent* (1993) p 201.
18 *National Westminster Bank v Morgan* [1985] AC 686 (HL).
19 *Midland Bank plc v Shephard* [1988] 3 All ER 17; *Barclays Bank plc v O'Brien* [1994] AC 180.
20 'Bargaining in the Shadow of the Law' (1979) 88 Yale Law Journal 950 at 967.
 1 In the Len Deighton novel *Violent Ward* (1993), the parents respectively petition the court to order the other to house their child.

Although the Conservative Government was anyway prepared to recommend mediation 'blind',[2] there is now some empirical evidence with which to stiffen the theorising and speculation. In concluding her 1986 review of the results of conciliation in Australia, New Zealand, Canada the United States of America and England and Wales, Lisa Parkinson wrote:[3]

> 'There is... substantial evidence that conciliation can enable even very hostile couples to reach workable agreements and that the level of conflict at the outset is not a reliable predictor of the outcome. Generally speaking, a positive outcome seems to depend on the interplay of various factors, including both parties' motivation and emotional resources, the skills and methods used by the conciliators, and the co-operation of other professionals and third parties with the conciliation process.'

More recently, there has been an evaluation[4] of over 500 couples who were involved with the mediation services. The general findings were encouraging. Eighty per cent reached some agreement, of whom about half achieved a settlement on *all* the issues. The parties were less likely to be in conflict about the children's future than they were about finance and property issues, and yet, when the former were in contention, the couple were more likely to reach agreement about them than they were with the other issues. On the other hand, comprehensive mediation 'seemed to do better than child-based mediation in terms of improving communication between couples'.[5]

This survey's other findings provide an encouraging analysis of the lawyer's role in mediation, bringing together both of the actors whose roles we have studied in this chapter:

> 'Lawyers have played an influential role in the development of mediation, and many people first heard of mediation through their solicitors... the occasional presence of a lawyer in the mediation process seemed neither to cause difficulty to clients nor to disrupt the flow of negotiations. Their legal expertise was appreciated by clients who felt the presence of lawyers gave the process and outcomes greater validity.... Their role was essentially one of ratification of the Memoranda of Understanding and, if necessary, converting agreements into legally acceptable documents. However, most clients felt the support of their own solicitors was helpful and they tended to look to them for reassurance about decisions they were taking, and for protection against particularly unfavourable settlements.'

It should be remembered that, given matrimonial legal work is itself mainly geared towards settlement, it is misleading to present mediation and litigation as stark alternatives to one another. Yet parenting

2 *Looking to the Future: Mediation and the Ground for Divorce* (1993) Cm 2424, para 7.21 acknowledged the then 'lack of empirical evidence in England and Wales about mediation's effectiveness and long-term outcomes'.

3 L Parkinson, *Conciliation and Separation in Divorce* (1986) at p 192.

4 Joseph Rowntree Foundation: Social Policy Research Findings No 48 (1994).

5 *Ibid.*

agreements, whether reached by the couple acting alone,[6] or through mediators, lawyers, or both, cannot be guaranteed legally binding. Such outcome can only be achieved by the courts (and even then, only until further order) whose function we examine in the next chapter.

6 Para 7.27 of *Looking to the Future: Mediation and the Ground for Divorce* (1993) Cm 2424, states that 'some couples prefer to obtain a divorce without the help of outside professionals. They are able to resolve any issues to their mutual satisfaction.... The Government believes that it would remain entirely appropriate for couples to act in this way under the proposed system where they decide to do so'.

CHAPTER 16

Court proceedings

1. INTRODUCTION

For the layperson, this chapter title may have a criminal ring about it; the 'juvenile'[1] court as a shared nemesis for young wrong-doers and their parents. In fact, parenthood is most likely to attract the attention of the courts by way of private dispute *between* mother and father,[2] or in public law proceedings invoked by the local authority.[3] Most recently, we have seen parents responding to children's own suits about their upbringing[4] – and in both civil[5] and criminal courts[6] as suspected abusers.

We will be examining the courts, and their personnel, in all these roles but we start with a reminder that private ordering in parental disputes long preceded the arrival of alternative dispute resolution.[7] In the mid-seventeenth century, the reason for this was simple: a *dearth* of courts:

> 'Informal private separation agreements sprang up in the 1650s as a response to the administrative chaos during the interregnum. This sort of *ad hoc* improvisation was made necessary by the abolition of the old ecclesiastical court system and the failure of the Commonwealth or Protectorate to put anything in its place. The judicial administration of separation and divorce virtually collapsed from about 1644 to 1660'.[8]

This early private ordering took the form of lawyer-drafted separation deeds, many of which, according to Lawrence Stone, 'Lastly... contained

1 The name was changed to the 'Youth Court' by the Criminal Justice Act 1991.
2 Eg, on divorce or separation; see Ch 8.
3 See Ch 13.
4 See Ch 7.
5 Eg, in *Re C* [1992] 2 FCR 65, allegations were made in care proceedings that five siblings had all been sexually abused by their father. See Chapter 7.
6 Section 1(1) of the Children and Young Persons Act 1933 lists five types of cruel conduct for which a person with parental responsibility will be criminally liable: assault; ill-treatment; neglect; abandonment or exposure; and unnecessary suffering or injury to health. See Ch 7.
7 For a discussion of modern-day negotiation and settlement, see the previous chapter.
8 L Stone, *Road to Divorce* (1992) p 149.

a clause which transferred the custody of one or more of the younger children from the father to the mother'.[9] For wives generally, private separation agreements had the advantages of freeing them from both legal harassment and forcible seizure;[10] for the mothers there was the further attraction of freeing them and their children from the law's patriarchy. By the end of the eighteenth century, the wish to do so may have been compounded by the growing ideal of domesticity, whereby motherhood was deemed an end in itself, and not merely a means of making heirs.[11] Yet such agreements, if challenged, might not be upheld: far from the mid-seventeenth century shortage of courts, even a late nineteenth century Lord Chancellor could say:

> 'I do not think... that the bargain between parties, whereby he surrenders his paternal rights, is worth the parchment on which it is engrossed. The law would not give effect to it. Nor is the paternal right capable of being bargained away.'[12]

The Custody of Infants Act 1839 had long since enabled the Court (of Chancery) to transfer 'legal custody' of marital children under seven to their mother. (Based on her supposed greater suitability to care for the very young, the 1839 Act stands in ironic counterpoint to the reluctance of *some* modern judges to admit to any such presumption.[13]) In those early Victorian times, the promulgation of the Bill owed much to the campaigning within the legislature of the well-connected Mrs Caroline Norton, whose own three children had been taken from her by their father, despite her own 'acquittal' on 'charges' of adultery. 'I endured... pain, exasperation, helplessness and despair, under the evil law which suffered any man, for vengeance and for interest, to take baby children from the mother'.[14]

Once safely past seven (time enough, by Jesuitic theory, to have moulded the child for ever) legal patriarchy[15] still prevailed. Private ordering, despite the weakness of its legal base, remained, 'a remarkable example of how an officially non-divorcing society could devise its own quasi-legal instruments to cope with the fact of irremediable marital breakdowns'.[16] In the wife-support negotiations, the legal default position

9 *Ibid* p 153.
10 It was finally held in *R v Jackson* [1891] 1 QB 671 that a husband was not entitled to confine his wife even whilst the right to consortium was extant.
11 J Lewis, *In the Family Way: Child-bearing in the British Aristocracy, 1760-1860* (1986) pp 55-6.
12 J Roberts, *Divorce Bills in the Imperial Parliament* (1906) p 93. The Lord Chancellor concerned was Lord Halsbury LC.
13 See Chapter 6.
14 C Norton, *A Letter to the Queen on Lord Chancellor Cranworth's Marriage and Divorce Bill* (1855) pp 68-9. For a biography of Caroline Norton, and the background to the 1839 Act, see A Chedzoy, *A Scandalous Woman* (1992).
15 *'Pater'*, father, *'archein'*, to rule.
16 L Stone, *Road to Divorce* (1992) p 182.

left the father well-armed. Additionally, many men did not actually want to burden themselves, or even their 'mistresses', with their children. Stone reports[17] that 'some of the great custody battles among the well-to-do were concerned as much with which parent was going to pay for upkeep as they were with which parent would obtain custody and control'.

2. PRIVACY

A continuing reason for avoiding court proceedings is the protection of privacy. Generally, the public interest in open justice permits the personal presence of such strangers who wish to attend and for whom there is room, with the press (including law reporters) free to report the proceedings. But in the present century, there is no 'open house' in proceedings relating to parenthood. Deliberations in the 'juvenile' court have been heard in private since the Children and Young Persons Act 1933.[18] In matrimonial proceedings, the Judicial Proceedings (Regulation of Reports) Act 1926 permits the publication of the names and addresses of the parties and the judgment, but not the evidence. The magistrates' family proceedings courts may hear any Children Act 1989 proceedings in private, if the child's interests so require,[19] and superior court hearings take place in chambers unless the court directs otherwise.[20] It is these dull rules which lie at the heart of that frequent media announcement, 'whose name cannot be revealed for legal reasons to protect the identity of the child'. Only the evidence in those few tens of divorces which are annually defended remains subject to media review. The Booth Committee observed:[1]

'The extreme press coverage which some defended cases attract is often distasteful and may be very damaging for the parties themselves and their children.'

Why is 'respect for privacy... one of the key social values that underpins the emergent family justice'?[2] Perhaps because it protects the intimacy of relationships, which is brought about by the sharing of personal information amongst the members, their conduct, thoughts and emotions. After all, these are matters which:

17 *Ibid* p 174.
18 Section 47; now covered by s 144 of the Magistrates' Court Act 1980 and s 97 of the Children Act 1989.
19 Family Proceedings Courts (Children Act 1989) Rules 1991, SI 1991/1395, r 16(7).
20 Family Proceedings Rules 1991, SI 1991/1247, r 4.16(7).
 1 *Report of Matrimonial Causes Procedure Committee* (1985) para 4.100; as the matter went beyond its terms of reference, the Committee made no recommendation on the issue.
 2 M Murch and D Hooper, *The Family Justice System* (1992) p 33 (and see generally).

'One does not share with all and which one has the right not to share with anyone. By conferring this right, privacy creates the moral capital which we spend in love and friendship.'[3]

Yet it is notorious that such privacy, and the institutional encouragement afforded to it, may mask such wickedness within the family as child abuse. Jan Pahl points out that:[4]

'reducing the power of outsiders to control what goes on within the family can have the effect of increasing the significance of power differentiations within the family'.

It can therefore be argued that a court system which colludes in the protection of family privacy may thereby conflict with those other social controls which monitor family life.[5]

Whilst the seventeenth century did not provide courts for the resolution of parental disputes, and subsequent protagonists avoided them, the twentieth century has yet to see the 'Child Courtroom', as imagined here for use in criminal proceedings:

'The Child Courtroom is designed to take a victim's testimony in an informal and relaxed manner, while the child can see only four persons around him: the judge, the prosecutor, the defence counsel, and the child examiner, who will all be seated in a "judge's room", arranged in a way which contributes to the security and psychological comfort of the child. The accused, the jury and the audience should be seated behind a one-way glass, separating them from the judge's room, but enabling them to observe everything which occurs there. In this manner the defendant's right to trial by jury is secured and the jury can view the accused's demeanour while the child is testifying. In addition, the accused will have microphone and earphone by means of which he and his counsel, who is in the judge's room, will be able to communicate with each other. The proceedings are transmitted to the accused's box by suitable electronic methods which would not interfere with the accused's capacity to communicate with his counsel.'[6]

The lack of such a forum seems particularly regrettable, given that even where the child is 'recognised' as having committed a crime, the United Nations Convention on the Rights of the Child requires[7] states parties to establish, where appropriate, 'measures for dealing with such children without resorting to judicial proceedings'. Spencer and Flin point out[8] that one reason why such a place has not (yet) been built, is the impossibility of using it as a normal courtroom.

---

3 C Fried, *An Anatomy of Values* (1992) p 142.
4 *Private Violence and Public Policy* (1985) p 190.
5 M March and D Hooper, *The Family Justice System* (1992) p 34.
6 D Libai, 'The Protection of the Child Victim of a Sexual Offence in the Criminal System' (1969) 15 WLR p 977.
7 Article 40(3)(b).
8 *The Evidence of Children: the Law and the Psychology* (2nd ed, 1993) p 102.

3. THE TECHNICAL STRUCTURE OF THE COURT SYSTEM

Below, we look at some accounts of the physical, social and near-philosophical aspects of the court scene; first, we analyse its formal structure.

Under the Children Act 1989, there is a three-tier court system.[9] The magistrates' court is the base of the hierarchy of courts, and the most geographically widespread. Specially selected justices drawn from the new 'family' (previously 'domestic') panels sit in the 'family proceedings court'. Rather surprisingly, their 'selection' takes the form of election by their peers; perhaps less surprisingly, their 'training' includes case studies centred round Open University videos.[10] The court sits in comparative privacy[11] with a maximum of three magistrates, both sexes to be represented if possible.

Although every first-year law student is taught the traditional 'advantages' of the local bench (convenience, speed, informality and cost) it is depressing to discover that northern parents have far greater recourse to the 'bargain basement' of family law than do their south-eastern counterparts. This is supposedly a reflection of such factors as the social class of the participants, the taste of individual practitioners and their legal aid area committees, and the policies of local DSS offices.[12]

The magistrates' courts also house that discrete system of criminal justice which has been provided for young offenders for most of the century.[13] In normal cases it replaces the adult magistrates' court or the Crown Court. Formerly known as the 'juvenile court', it is now termed the youth court[14] in a nomenclatural change wrought more by a recognition of the increased age,[15] rather than the likely gender, of those appearing

9 As implemented by the Children (Allocation of Proceedings) Order 1991, SI 1991/1677.
10 Such as the six-minute tale of Toby and Rosie whose divorced parents seem set to involve lawyers and courts in whether the father and his boyfriend should now take them on a month-long tour of the Far East and the USA; the story invokes a discussion of continuing parental responsibility, s 8 of the Children Act 1989, and the 'no-order presumption' (s1(5)). See the Children Act Advisory Committee *Annual Report 1993/4* at pp 47-50 for an account of the appointment and training of members of the family panel. In 1994, magistrates received 38% of all private law cases and 81% of all public law cases under the Children Act 1989: Table 1A *op cit.*
11 See s 69 of the Magistrates' Courts Act 1980 for a list of those allowed in: the privacy issue is discussed earlier in this chapter.
12 J Priest and J Whybrow, *Custody Law in Practice in the Divorce and Domestic Courts* (1986). More recently, Table 1 of the Children Act Advisory Committee, *Annual Report for 1992/93* (1994) details the total number of applications by county (*pro rata* of population, Mid-Glamorgan topped, and Warwickshire tailed, the list for private law applications).
13 See H K Bevan, *Child Law* (1989) para 12. 01 *et seq* for an historical account.
14 Since the Criminal Justice Act 1991.
15 For most purposes, s 68 of the Criminal Justice Act 1991 now brings 17 year olds within the ambit of the youth court.

before it. A contributing factor to that age rise has been the departure of care proceedings to the family proceedings court. In an echo of the latter, youth court justices are drawn from the youth court panel for the area. There will usually be a three-member court of whom at least one will be female.

There are no fewer than three types of county courts now seised of jurisdiction for 'family proceedings'. Some are divorce courts for administrative purposes only, ie in which all 'matrimonial causes' must first be put down for hearing, and for cases which can be heard by the district judge. 'Family hearing' centres decide contested private law applications under s 8 of the 1989 Act and injunctions in domestic violence and matrimonial proceedings. Some of these are further designated 'care centres' and hear public law cases transferred from the family proceedings court.

Since the Administration of Justice Act 1970, the Family Division of the High Court has been in exclusive possession of the High Court's family jurisdiction, an improvement upon the previous practice whereby all three Divisions might be simultaneously engaged in dividing one family: the marriage in Probate Divorce and Admiralty, the house in Queen's Bench, and the children in Chancery.

These three courts have a concurrent jurisdiction: any of them may make an order under s 8 of the Children Act 1989 in any family proceedings. Most public law cases must be heard in the family proceedings court, but there is a free choice for private law cases; and cases of exceptional complexity or importance will be transferred (see below). Most will be self-allocating in that many orders will be made in the course of divorce proceedings, and thus in the divorce county court.

The regulations[16] permit magistrates to transfer private law cases to the county court, and the county court to the High Court, where this is appropriate and in the interests of the child. The 'transfer system' between these courts is a crucial expression of both the need for specialism – the Lord Chancellor is empowered[17] to create a nominated group of circuit and district judges who will specialise in specific types of family proceedings – and the implementation of the 'no-delay' principle of the Children Act 1989.[18]

Public law cases may be transferred from a magistrates' court in three circumstances. First, if the issues are 'exceptionally grave, important or complex', ie there is conflicting evidence, a large number of parties, a conflict of laws, a novel point of law, or matters of public interest. A second reason is to consolidate the case with other family proceedings

16 The Children (Allocation of Proceedings) Order 1991, SI 1991/1677.
17 Courts and Legal Services Act 1990, s 9.
18 Section 1(2).

pending in another court. Finally, the case will be transferred if delay would prejudice the child and the receiving court can deal with the case more quickly. At the next tier, matters will be transferred from a county court to the High Court if they are likely to have an important impact beyond the instant case.

Perhaps this structure, which the Children Act 1989 built largely out of the existing buildings and system, produces a form of the fabled 'family court', for which there has been a near-incessant call since the 1974 Finer Report.[19] The Government view at the time of the 1989 Act was that substantive reform should precede mere procedural change, although it was claimed that the latter had made a step in the direction of the family court.[20] With its, at least apparently, agreeable connotation of non-adversariality, 'family court' is to 'court', what 'conciliators' are to 'lawyers', and the two debates,[1] which have produced similar arguments, have been intertwined. Some idealists might imagine inter-disciplinarily trained arbitrators, sitting down with the parties in non-confrontational triangular fashion the better to resolve family breakdown problems previously found to be intractable in any other system: 'some utopian tribunal capable of dealing with a whole array of family problems as well as meeting some of the deficiencies of the welfare agencies'.[2] Yet the Finer Report saw the family court as 'an impartial judicial institution, regulating the rights of citizens and settling their disputes according to law... the individual in the family court must... remain the subject of rights, not the object of assistance'.[3] Whilst its American meaning may be therapeutic, it appears that the Australian experience, which dates from 1975,[4] was initially met with some scepticism, even including public dismay at the disrobing of judges.[5]

---

19 *Report of the Committee on One-Parent Families*, Cmnd 5629, Pt 4.
20 See *Hansard* (HC) Vol 158, col 547.
 1 See, eg, *Bromley's Family Law* (8th ed, 1992) pp 16-18; J Dewar *Law and the Family* (2nd ed, 1992) pp 15-17; and A Bainham *Children, The Modern Law* (1994) pp 67-70 (together, in each case, with the references cited therein) for a history of the 'campaign', the possible models for such a court, and the extent to which the Children Act 1989 has achieved it.
 2 E Szwed, 'The Family Court' in M Freeman (ed) *State, Law and the Family* (1984) p 266.
 3 (1974) paras 4.283 and 285.
 4 Family Law Act 1975; New Zealand followed with the Family Courts (New Zealand) Act 1980.
 5 See A Dickey *Family Law* (2nd ed, 1990) at Ch 4 for a record of the hostility generated.

4. USER PERSPECTIVE

Some of the courtrooms presently dedicated to the hearing of parenthood issues are widely seen as wanting. Recent official reports are, at least in part, condemnatory:[6]

'those attending and working within the family proceedings court at Bolton have to put up with near intolerable conditions... for instance the waiting area consists of a corridor which leads to three criminal courts on one side, with the family proceedings court on the other side. People attending the family proceedings court, whether parties, social workers, guardians, welfare officers or advocates must wait in this corridor, together with defendants, witnesses and others waiting to appear in the criminal courts. The seating is inadequate and it is not unusual to see parties sitting on the stone steps leading to an upper floor.... There are inadequate facilities for advocates to take instructions... and a windowsill is frequently pressed into service for this purpose.... Justices allocated to the family proceedings court must walk through this public area'.

In the mid-1980s, it was clear that family litigants themselves recognised these shortcomings. Some of those surveyed[7] felt that the courts in which they appeared were so constructed as to separate them, physically and metaphorically from their representatives and adjudicators. They wanted more interviewing rooms in which to consult with their lawyers, rather than the 'corridors, halls and stairways' of their actual experiences. Sensible appointment systems and friendly court officials to explain things to them were also at a premium.

To some extent these horror stories for parents and children are increasingly historical in nature. By 1993:

'A good deal of work [had] been done to improve privacy by way of better arrangements in reception, at court office counters, and by the provision of interview rooms. Decor has been generally improved, particularly in public areas and waiting rooms, and more children's rooms with books and toys have been made available. In some courts it has been possible to create mother and baby rooms'.[8]

This referred to county courts; but although there have also been improvements in the family proceedings courts, 'It would take well into the next century to bring all magistrates' courthouses up to modern standards'.[9]

Yet if the Bolton experience is, or was, the nadir, perhaps the 1993 Havant Family Court Centre is the way of the future:

'The reception area is especially "user-friendly" and the decor throughout is in soft pastel colours and fabrics. The ancillary accommodation is equipped to meet the

6 Children Act Advisory Committee, *Annual Report*,1992/93 (1994) at p 56.
7 M Murch, M Borkowski, R Copner and K Griew, *The Overlapping Family Jurisdictions of Magistrates' Courts and County Courts* (1987).
8 Children Act Advisory Committee, *Annual Report 1992/93* (1994) at p 54.
9 *Ibid* p 55.

need of families by provision of a creche area and baby changing facilities. There are private interview rooms for welfare officers and additional facilities for disabled people and for video links. A clever arrangement of portable furnishings and curtaining enables the court room to be a formal magistrates' court and a youth court or a family proceedings court as required.'[10]

We noted earlier that, in reinforcing privacy values, the family justice system may conflict with other state mechanisms. An example of the latter are those very criminal courts with which participants in the family justice system have been so dismayed to find themselves physically associated, by way of shared waiting rooms and the like. Predictably, such people say that they would rather avoid the stigma of criminality. They do not want to feel on trial, or perceived deviant, or as belonging to a lower social class.[11] Equally, perhaps, they do not wish it to be assumed that they are necessarily in need of some kind of treatment, with its unwelcome connotation of ubiquitous, therapy dispensing, counsellors. But it must be acknowledged that the criminality nexus can never be completely abandoned. If, for example, there is insufficiently weighty evidence to initiate a prosecution for (familial) child abuse, it would be unrealistic to expect those administering the relevant family proceedings to be dispassionate about the matter. Indeed:

'there is an argument that it is against the public interest for the civil courts to appear morally neutral when faced with social deviance considered harmful to children and other family members'.[12]

It seems that the social dynamics of the conflict start well in advance of the formal proceedings, and that they are particularly inappropriate to the resolution of parenting difficulties:

'In English courts there is a well-established ritual which precedes most child care hearings. Almost as soon as the lawyers, litigants and witnesses arrive at the court, under the lawyers' stewardship, they form themselves into separate camps. The parents, their lawyers and their witnesses cluster in one part of the corridor or waiting room while the social workers, their lawyers and expert witnesses huddle together in another part. The senior lawyers – in English courts usually barristers – now take charge of their respective camps. No talking with 'the enemy', even if they were, until today, your patients or clients. The only permissible contact is through the medium of the lawyers'.[13]

We now turn to the social *nature* of family court proceedings, and other proceedings involving family relations. It is a matter which some professional witnesses, at least, have felt a need to address:

10 *Ibid* p 55.
11 These were some of the findings of M Murch, M Borkowski, R Copner and K Griew, *The Overlapping Family Jurisdictions of Magistrates' Courts and County Courts* (1987).
12 M Murch and D Hooper, *The Family Justice System* (1992) p 35.
13 M King and C Piper, *Children's Welfare and the Law: The Limits of Legal Intervention* (1992) p 98.

'psychiatrists learn to prepare themselves for the courtroom.... They may read books and articles on court procedures and the art of giving expert evidence.... Little of this... has anything to do with the clinical judgment that the psychiatrists apply in their assessment of children and their family situations; it has everything to do with giving a good performance in the legal arena'.[14]

Other psychiatrists refuse, even though their profession has brought them to the witness box, to enter the legal 'domain', contenting themselves with a statement of clinical judgment, and an acknowledgement that it is for the court to decide whether or not this constitutes sufficient evidence.[15] The health care system itself is a domain to be entered by the family in trouble; social welfare is a third. Psychiatry itself may have even more in common with courts as a 'domain' in that 'the primary health care system and the local solicitor's office are both much less demanding of the commitment of the complainant than the much more formal structures of hospital clinic or court'.[16]

As a term of art in this context, 'domains' may be cross-referenced with 'ghettoes', which invoke the image of 'a group of people who are trained to use the same universe of discourse and who feel more at home with each other than with practitioners from other ghettoes'.[17] This latter analogy is imperfect in that membership of the professional ghetto, unlike that of its racial counterpart, is chosen by the members themselves; and each analogy contrasts with the other in that the area of the 'domain' is broadly physical – here, the courtroom and its environs – whilst that of the 'ghetto' is essentially social. The ambivalent value (for parents in our case) of the ghetto has been recognised for 70 years:

'Another great fact confronting the modern world is the... method of training professionals who specialise in particular regions of thought. Effective knowledge is professional knowledge supported by a restricted acquaintance with useful subjects subservient to it. This situation has its dangers. It produces minds in a groove.... But there is no groove of abstractions which is adequate for the comprehension of modern life.'[18]

Perhaps psychiatrists (whom, it is said, one should see only out of boredom[19]) would approve of the hospice analogy as a model for reform:

'the most important conceptual advance resulting from the creation of the hospice movement was to redefine death and dying as living processes and to focus the new facility together with the professional roles around that paradoxical view. Law and legal professionals probably have more difficulty in recognising the importance of processes rather than structure. By definition, the law seeks to regulate affairs – and

14 *Ibid* p 96.
15 *Ibid* pp 97-8.
16 M Murch and D Hooper, *The Family Justice System* (1992) p 42.
17 *Ibid* p 43.
18 A Whitehead, *Science and the Modern World* (1925).
19 Attributed to Muriel Spark (*The Penguin Dictionary of Modern Humorous Quotations* (1986)).

in family struggles this may be very difficult indeed. New thinking is badly needed here and may (as in the hospice analogy) have to take place outside the normal framework.'[20]

Contributions to such 'new thinking' may well come from some of the professionals to be found working in the courts.

5. THE COURTS' WELFARE PROFESSIONALS

In the previous chapter we looked specifically at two groups of people, lawyers and mediators, who may impinge upon those parents and children who come near the courtroom. In this chapter, we look at the judges and magistrates who await them there. But there is another group of people, perhaps best generically described as 'welfare professionals' who may also be encountered at such times. They include divorce court welfare officers, the obscurely-entitled 'Official Solicitor' and the latinesque 'guardian *ad litem*'. In so far as they come from the 'caring professions', the first and last of these are clearly set aside from lawyers and judges, and even mediators, but their titles and roles may confuse their 'clients'. A need to rationalise 'the family justice system's various welfare support systems' has already been identified.[1]

(a) The Official Solicitor

The oldest of these entities is the 'Office of the Official Solicitor to the Supreme Court' which was established in 1875 after the Judicature Acts 1873-5. The Official Solicitor is likely to be appointed to represent a ward of court, although this is not an automatic step.[2] 'He' (all holders so far have been male) was preceded by his linear ancestor, the intriguingly named 'solicitor to the suitors'[3] who had existed in the previous century. He has been judicially described as 'not only an officer of the court and the ward's guardian, but... a solicitor [with] the ward as his client',[4] and by one incumbent[5] as one who:

20 M Murch and D Hooper, *The Family Justice System* (1992) p 49.
 1 *Ibid* p 65 and pp 110-124.
 2 See *Practice Direction* [1982] 1 All ER 319. Appointment is particularly likely in conflict of law cases, those involving health or medical issues and, more traditionally, those of older children in dispute with their parents, perhaps arising out of the ward's associations with others.
 3 See O Stone, *The Child's Voice in the Court of Law* (1982) p 60 *et seq* for a brief history of this office, which, in 1871, was re-named the Official Solicitor to the High Court of Chancery.
 4 *Re R (PM) (an infant)* [1968] 1 All ER 691, per Goff J at 692. For wardship generally, see Ch 13.
 5 Mr Peter Venables (quoted by M Murch and D Hooper, *The Family Justice System* (1992) p 70).

'makes such submissions to the court, having due regard to the expressed views and wishes of the child concerned, as he thinks consistent with the child's welfare and best interests'.

Ironically, although the 'office' is the oldest entity charged with the supervision of children's interests in civil cases, it is the least 'professional' in the specific sense that its civil servants, drawn from the Lord Chancellor's court service and yet called upon to deal directly with children, are unlikely to be qualified social workers.[6] The conflict (inherent in the self-description above) between the child's actual wishes and the Official Solicitor's perception of what will actually serve his or her interests might even lead to subsequent litigation between *them*. *In Re S (a minor) (Independent Representation)*,[7] the Court of Appeal held that an 11 year old could not instruct his own solicitor, following the evidence of a child psychiatrist that he lacked the necessary maturity to do so. It was subsequently reported[8] that the boy was later refused permission to sue for damages the Official Solicitor, who, *qua* his guardian *ad litem* and solicitor, had allegedly mishandled his desire for contact with the American side of his family.

A certain preoccupation with the more difficult cases is also apparent, with over 91% of all new work in 1987 involving either wardship or contested adoptions, mostly in the High Court.[9] Section 41(8) of the Children Act 1989 perpetuated this trend by allowing for the appointment of the Official Solicitor as guardian *ad litem* (see below) in High Court cases: the Department of Health Guidance[10] stresses the Office's experience in important and complex cases and its nationwide links with expert paediatricians and child psychiatrists. The Office can act very quickly, at least in London. In *Re B (Wardship; Abortion)*,[11] a case which involved an application for an abortion to be performed on a 12 year old girl, the judge telephoned the Official Solicitor at 12:45 pm. The latter briefed counsel to appear before the court at 2:00 pm and the child was interviewed one hour later.

6 Situated in London, its staff consists 'mostly [of] lawyers and civil servants': D Venables, 'The Official Solicitor: Outline and Aspects of his work' [1990] Fam Law 53. Their lack of special training in dealing with children means that they rely heavily on consultants, especially psychiatrists; J Masson 'The Official Solicitor as the Child's Guardian *ad litem* under the Children Act 1989" (1992) 4 JCL 58.
7 [1993] Fam 263; see below.
8 H Stephens (in fact a pseudonym for the boy's father), 'Independent Representation' (1994) NLJ 1 July. In December 1994, Johnson J dismissed the Official Solicitor from the case and gave S, now 13, permission to move to the United States with his father in July 1995. S remains a ward of court until the age of 18; [1995] Fam Law 59.
9 *Report of the Official Solicitor to the Cleveland Child Abuse Enquiry* (1988) p 108.
10 *The Children Act 1989 Guidance and Regulations*, Volume 7 *Guardians ad Litem and other Court Related Issues* (1991).
11 [1991] 2 FLR 426.

(b) The Divorce Court Welfare Service

The historical involvement of the Probation Service rather than the Official Solicitor, in what is now the Divorce Court Welfare Service, may stem from the former's involvement in the magistrates' courts' matrimonial jurisdiction, which dates from the turn of the century. Between the wars, it was feared that the practice of allowing probation officers to see applicants before the hearing could deny justice by obstructing access to the courts.[12] The Summary Procedure (Domestic Proceedings) Act 1937 ensured that all complainants should be seen first by the courts, which would then decide which cases should be referred to the Probation Service. After the 1939-45 war, the Denning Committee,[13] set up in the light of the highest-ever number of divorces (52,249 decrees nisi in 1947, a number not exceeded until 1969[14]) recommended that there should be a welfare report for *every* divorce involving children under 16. It seems that, as a matter of practice, the divorce court first started to ask probation officers to report in cases of parental *dispute* from the 1950s onwards.[15] The Divorce Court Welfare Service was established in 1959 and, following the Matrimonial Causes Act 1967, a court welfare officer was assigned to every divorce county court. The early development of the Service was marked by a struggle for appropriate resources (the Home Office allocated to the Service's civil work 10% of that provided for its criminal jurisdiction) and by policy tensions. Both issues were sparked by the primary need for social work with criminal offenders: 'The higher the incidence of divorce and the higher the crime rate, the more concerned and ambivalent the Home Office became'.[16] The priority given by the Service to children in family break-up has varied. In the 1960s, Service interest was drawn to such children as a result of the declining scope[17] for spousal reconciliation in the magistrates' courts, yet officers' actual *experience* with children was reduced by the loss of juvenile delinquency work to local authority social services departments under the Children and Young Persons Act 1963. In the period leading up to the Children Act 1989, it was thought that the officers were allowing attempts at inter-spousal conciliation to distract them from the preparation of welfare reports, their work with adult offenders having

---

12 See J Eekelaar and R Dingwall, 'The Development of Conciliation in England' in J Eekelaar and R Dingwall (eds) *Divorce Mediation and the Legal Process* (1988) p 4.

13 *Procedure in Matrimonial Causes* (1947) HC 7024.

14 54,151: *Judicial Statistics, passim.*

15 M Murch and D Hooper, *The Family Justice System* (1992) p 67.

16 *Ibid* p 67.

17 As a result of divorce jurisdiction being extended to designated county courts by the Matrimonial Causes Act 1967; and see C Clulow and C Vincent, *In the Child's Best Interests – Divorce Court Welfare and the Search for Settlement* (1987) p 49 and generally.

left them better prepared for the former role. In *Re H (Conciliation: Welfare Reports)*,[18] Ewbank J said it was 'fundamental' that:

'conciliation and reporting as a court welfare officer are different functions. Conciliation is the helping of parties to resolve their disputes. The duty of a court welfare officer is to help the court to resolve disputes that the parties are unable to resolve... they are not functions which are to be mixed up. Probation officers who are involved in conciliation are not subsequently to investigate and write welfare officers' reports.'

He castigated as 'useless and unacceptable',[19] reports which declined, on the basis that one parent had refused to meet the officer in the presence of the rest of the family, to proffer information to the court.

We should note that the courts can, instead, ask the local authority for welfare reports, and that this was often done when the child was in care or otherwise 'known to' the local authority.[20] Yet the social services departments could hardly be seen as impartial, least of all by the families concerned: the two sides might even be in downright opposition, as where, pre-Children Act 1989, the local authority terminated access to children in care.

(c) Guardians *ad Litem*

As we shall shortly see, the 1989 Act brought the work of the Divorce Court Welfare Service into sharper focus. The Act did the same for the (Panels of) Guardians *ad Litem*[1] and Reporting Officers. Formed in 1984, these 'GALRO Panels' have a much shorter history than the Divorce Court Welfare Service and yet, being concerned with separate representation for children, have most in common with the Office of the Official Solicitor – the oldest of these three 'welfare professional' groups. Their independence means that they have least in common with the local authority social services departments, despite apparent background links:

'The role of the guardian *ad litem* revolves principally around assessment, protection and representation of children. Court welfare work... is essentially about investigating on behalf of the court issues relevant to determining what is in the best interests of the child, including ascertaining their wishes and feelings, with a view to communicating information about them to the court.'[2]

---

18 [1986] 1 FLR 476, 476. The Court of Appeal made similar points in *Scott v Scott* [1986] 2 FLR 320.
19 At 477.
20 D Murch and D Hooper, *The Family Justice System* (1992) p 69.
 1 It means 'for the proceedings'.
 2 A James and W Hay, *Court Welfare in Action* (1993) p 204. James and Hay proceed to argue that these distinctions militate against any integration of their functions. See C Lyon and P de Cruz, *Child Abuse* (2nd ed, 1993) p 174 *et seq* for a more detailed account of the role of guardians *ad litem*.

At first, this independence was achieved by a 'swopping' arrangement (sometimes known as 'reciprocators') whereby neighbouring authorities used each other's care staff. Increasingly, guardians *ad litem* now work as freelancers. Yet the perceived link with the local authority is as worrying for them as the probation connection is for divorce court welfare officers. John Eekelaar's suggestion[3] that their work be changed to focus on childrens' *rights* (and that they be renamed 'children's officers'), might bring more attention to bear on parental divorce whilst bringing them closer to the guardian *ad litem* role.

(d) Welfare professionals and the Children Act 1989

The Children Act 1989 has influenced the roles of these groups in several of its provisions. Section 7 of the Act is very general, both in regard to who may be *required*[4] to make report to the court, ie probation officers and the local authority;[5] and in its scope, ie 'any question with respect to a child under this Act'.[6] Significantly, the local authority is free to appoint not only one of its own officers, but anyone 'appropriate',[7] thereby opening the door to GALRO Panel members (who will, of course, have to be paid by the authority). Under s 7(1)(b), the report to the court will deal with any matters 'relating to the welfare of that child as are required'.

By s 37, the local authority can be required (at the discretion of the court) to make its own assessment in private law cases. Under the old law, the court could make care or supervision orders on its own initiative but s 37, although triggered when private proceedings incidentally uncover the possibility of some threat to the child, effectively limits the court to inviting the local authority, after due consideration, to make its own application for such orders.[8] This is a rare example of the Children Act favouring the state over the court in child-parent relations. Even so, it represents a higher degree of intervention than a 'family assistance order'[9] whereby the court, in any family proceedings, may require a probation officer or a local authority officer to 'advise assist and (where appropriate) befriend any person named in the order'; 'exceptional circumstances' are required, as is the consent of everyone named in the order other than the child.

---

3 *Regulating Divorce* (1991) p 170.
4 Section 7(5).
5 Section 7(1)(b)(i),(ii).
6 Section 7(1).
7 Section 7(1)(b)(ii).
8 Cf *Nottinghamshire County Council v P* [1993] 2 FLR 134; see Ch 12.
9 Section 16.

If the 1989 Act leaves both the Divorce Court Welfare Service and guardians *ad litem* with a role to play in private law proceedings, s 41 puts public law matters firmly in the hands of the latter.[10] The court 'shall' appoint a guardian *ad litem* in all cases where a care order is being sought or discharged and where a supervision order is sought or varied, 'unless satisfied that it is not necessary [in order] to safeguard [the child's] interests'.[11] Guardians *ad litem* seem well-favoured by the Act:

> 'their professional role as advisers to and officers of the court has been emphasised; a role which is central to the notion of the more proactive "managerial court" which follows from the provisions of [the Act]'.[12]

Whatever the future holds for these various services, it appears that the Divorce Court Welfare Service and the GALRO Panels share some similar difficulties[13] such as a need for improved information systems, specialist core teams, accurate costings – and completing their reports on time. This last seems particularly unfortunate in view of the statutory 'no delay' principle[14] with regard to the welfare of the child. For the guardian *ad litem*, other difficulties survive the 1989 Act. Their independence from the authority bringing the proceedings is not clear, the criteria for appointment to the relevant panel may be inadequate, and their numbers are insufficient. In *R v Cornwall County Council, ex p Cornwall and Isles of Scilly Guardians ad litem and Reporting Officers Panel*,[15] an attempt by the local authority to limit payment to 65 hours per matter, was quashed on judicial review. Guardians *ad litem* are entitled to legal representation but not to legal aid, which brings us to the related question of whether guardians *ad litem* and their solicitors are agents for the child, for each other, or for the court: child's rights or child's best interests? We discussed the solicitor's role in the previous chapter, and the child's autonomy throughout the book, but the position here is that the guardian reports on what she thinks is right for the child whilst the solicitor represents the latter's wishes.

Such a dichotomy need not necessarily arise. Under s 41[16] of the 1989 Act, a solicitor may be appointed for the child in public law cases, but only if no guardian *ad litem* has already been appointed. But a procedural

---

10 As recommended by the Department of Health and Social Security, *Review of Child Care Law* (1985) paras 14.10-14.18.
11 Section 41(1).
12 M Murch and D Hooper, *The Family Justice System* (1992) p 75.
13 As identified by 1990 inspections by, respectively, the Probation Inspectorate of the Home Office and the Social Services of the Department of Health. For a detailed account and discussion, see M Murch and D Hooper, *ibid* pp 75-78.
14 Children Act 1989, s 1(2).
15 [1992] 2 All ER 471.
16 If the court considers that the child has sufficient understanding to give instructions: s 41(3),(4),(5).

development has since created the possibility that the guardian and the child will be *separately* represented. The Family Proceedings Courts (Children Act 1989) Rules 1991[17] state that the solicitor originally appointed by the guardian must follow the latter's instructions unless the solicitor thinks that 'the child... is able... having regard to his understanding, to give such instructions on his own behalf'. If that happens, leave may be given for the guardian to be represented by another solicitor.[18]

If, in private law cases,[19] proceedings have already begun with a guardian *ad litem* but the child now wishes to proceed alone, the court will remove the guardian if the court thinks that the child has sufficient understanding to instruct a solicitor.[20] We have already seen the case[1] of the 11 year old who wished to intervene in the divorce proceedings between his parents; the court refused to allow him to discharge the Official Solicitor (who was acting as guardian *ad litem*) on the basis that the boy lacked the necessary understanding. But in *Re T (a minor) (Child: Representation)*,[2] where a 13 year old adopted girl was seeking an order allowing her to live with her natural aunt, the court, having found that she was capable of instructing a solicitor, held that she should not subsequently have a guardian imposed upon her. In a third case, *Re H (a minor) (Role of the Official Solicitor)*,[3] a 15 year old boy who wished to live apart from his family was allowed to discharge as his guardian the Official Solicitor – whom the court then retained as *amicus curiae*, with a concomitant investigative role. Given that court-ordered investigations have all but disappeared in private law when the parents are in agreement, it would be ironic were such enquiries to reappear as a by-product of the representation of children.[4]

6. THE JUDGES

The Courts and Legal Services Act 1990 empowers the Lord Chancellor to develop a pool of specialist district and circuit judges to adjudicate

17 Rule 12(1)(a).
18 *Re H (a minor) (Care proceedings: Child's Wishes)* [1993] 1 FLR 440.
19 By the Family Proceedings (Amendment) Rules 1992, SI 1992/456, a minor who wishes to *initiate* private law proceedings must be allowed to do so if the court thinks the child has sufficient understanding to participate.
20 *Re S (a minor) (Independent Representation* [1993] Fam 263
1 *Ibid*; see the section on the Official Solicitor above.
2 [1993] 4 All ER 518.
3 [1993] 2 FLR 552.
4 J Eekelaar, 'A Jurisdiction in Search of a Mission: Family Proceedings in England and Wales' (1994) MLR 57 839 at p 857. See Ch 7 for a discussion of children's ability to take legal initiatives against their parent(s) with regard to their upbringing.

family matters. Perhaps their expertise, aided by training from the Judicial Studies Board, will help to address the sort of criticism diffidently expressed here by Simon Lee:[5]

'So from where do judges derive their conflicting interpretations of public policy? In *Gillick*,[6] as I have said, they did not draw on any evidence, either in the form of facts and statistics or in the form of evidence from medical and ethical experts. The judges are merely offering their own views, the hunches of five wise old men. Any group of five wise old men might have split 3-2, as did the Law Lords, on the public policy... the judges' differing hunches as to the desirability of the likely consequences determined the result and indeed the conflict... I have yet to meet anyone who is particularly interested in what the seventeenth century cases say about the very recent phenomenon of teenagers being prescribed the contraceptive pill. What worries people is that they disagree vehemently over the best strategy for dealing with early sexual activity. That is how they judged the judges in the *Gillick* case. That is how the judges probably judged the matter for themselves.'

Lee dismisses[7] any idea that, in *Gillick*, the judges can be seen as necessarily either left or right wing: the decision is as consistent with conservatism (support for DSS and the medical profession) as it is with liberalism (children's rights to contraception). With regard to a deeper analysis of the nature of judicial 'hunches' our system has yet (so far as the authors are aware) to follow the American example, perhaps first practised[8] as early as 1948, of psychoanalysing judges in an attempt to explain their decisions. 'Judge Z', mercurial, demanding of deference and 'agitational', was found to be soft with the youthful, severe on the middle-aged and lenient with the aged.[9] Other American researchers have claimed to identify various personality types amongst the judiciary. Many of these are inconsistent with either the English system of appointment – like, perhaps, the 'political adventurer-careerist' – or with our culture, such as the 'judicial pensioners', 'routineer hacks', 'hatchet men', 'tyrant-showboat-benevolent-despots'.[10]

---

5 *Judging Judges* (1989) pp 85-87.

6 [1986] AC 112; we discuss this case at length (together with the sort of associated data whose omission from the judgments Lee so deprecates) in Ch 6.

7 *Judging Judges* (1989), pp 36-7. Lee uses this argument as part of his attack on the assumption (most readily expressed in J Griffith's, *The Politics of the Judiciary* (4th ed, 1991) that the establishment background of judges has created an unremittingly conservative judiciary.

8 N Kerr and R Bray (eds) *The Psychology of the Courtroom* (1988) p 262 and generally.

9 H Lasswell, *Power and Personality* (1948).

10 A Smith and A Blumberg, 'The problem of objectivity in judicial decision-making' (1967) 46 *Social Forces* 96.

7. THE CHILD IN COURT

In so far as the Children 1989 Act produced a cohesive system (admittedly out of existing materials) for familial proceedings concerning *children*, together with concomitant training for all adjudicators from lay magistrates to superior court judges, perhaps it is presently other family law matters which remain the furthest from the idealised image of the 'family court'. In recent years, greater adult sensitivity to children's experiences has generated considerable change.[11] The matter has also stimulated quite recent entries in the judicial book of gaffes, with Christmas Humphreys J (whose more liberal thoughts on conciliation we quoted approvingly in the previous chapter) once saying that those with long experience 'know that the evidence of a girl giving evidence of indecency by a man is notoriously unreliable'.[12] In a recent American survey, some young American children returned the compliment, describing lawyers as people who 'sit around', 'play golf' and 'lie'.[13]

In civil proceedings, the competence of a child under 14 who is to be 'sworn in' as a witness, is subject to the *Hayes*[14] test, ie whether he or she has:

'a sufficient appreciation of the solemnity of the occasion and the added responsibility to tell the truth, which is involved in taking a oath, over and above the duty to tell the truth which is an ordinary duty of normal social conduct'.

Of increasingly greater significance to family proceedings is the Children Act's own criterion[15] for the admission of unsworn evidence, which is borrowed from the previous test for the adduction of evidence of children of 'tender years' in criminal proceedings.[16] Where the court considers that children do not understand the nature of an oath, the evidence can be heard provided the children understand that there is a duty to speak the truth, and that their understanding is sufficient to make their evidence useful to the court.

Although the child-witness is an unusual sight in care cases, the magistrates (as they are likely to be, see above) may well wish to explain their order to the child concerned. We have mentioned both sworn and unsworn *evidence* given to the *court*, but there is also the possibility of an exclusive exchange between judge and child:

11 See generally, J Spencer and R Flin, *The Evidence of Children – the Law and the Psychology* (2nd ed, 1993).
12 *R v Gammon* (1959) 43 Cr App Rep 155, 159.
13 Quoted by R Flin in 'Child Witnesses: the Psychological Evidence' (1988) 138 NLJ p 608 at p 610.
14 *R v Hayes* [1977] 1 WLR 234, *per* Bridge LJ at 237.
15 Section 96(2).
16 Children and Young Persons Act 1933, s 38.

'The judge's private interview with the child is mainly thought of as a means of informing the judge about the child's views and wishes. In practice, however, it sometimes ends up with the judge and the child discussing disputed matters of fact that lie at the heart of the case.'[17]

It is this last prospect which takes the matter beyond the statutory requirement that the court have regard to (and therefore establish) 'the ascertainable wishes and feelings of the child... considered in the light of his age and understanding'.[18] The potential of this contrasts sharply with their lack of legal standing, although some diverse points have been established[19] *ad hoc*. Seeing the child is a matter for individual judicial discretion[20] constrained by the age of the child, who should not be less than eight years old according to one decided case.[1]

The interview should be in chambers with at least one other person present, preferably of the same sex as the child; the first instance judge who went off on his own to see the child at school was subsequently criticised by the Court of Appeal.[2] The judge should tell the court welfare officer and the parties of his intentions beforehand, and subsequently tell the latter what was said (subject always to the welfare principle[3]).

In the interests of their welfare, is it possible to distance children from the formal court proceedings whilst keeping faith with the rules of evidence, the legitimate interests of other parties and, in criminal cases, the presumption of innocence? It is worth noting that the child may be hurt by prosecutors who value youthful distress as a tactic, as well as by zealous defence counsel. These matters have been so recently addressed that the use of screens and video links to facilitate the testimony of the child-witness have been developed at about the same time. Some of the cases have involved that nadir of parent-child relations in which the father is accused of physical or sexual attacks upon his son or daughter. The search for a validating authority has led to the disinterring[4] of *R v Smellie*[5] in which the trial judge ordered a defendant, accused of assaulting his 11 year old daughter, to sit on the stairs leading to the dock so that she could not see him (nor he her) as she gave evidence. The Court of Appeal

---

17 J Spencer and R Flin, *The Evidence of Children – the Law and the Psychology* (2nd ed, 1993) p 98.
18 Children Act 1989, s 1(3)(a).
19 See J Spencer and R Flin, *The Evidence of Children – the Law and the Psychology* (2nd ed, 1993) p 97 for a detailed collation.
20 *Re R (a minor) (Residence Order)*, (1992) Times, 3 November.
1 *Ingham v Ingham* [1976] LS Gaz R 486.
2 *L v L* [1991] FCR 547.
3 *Re B* [1992] 2 FCR 617.
4 Both Spencer and Flin in J Spencer and R Flin, *The Evidence of Children – the Law and the Psychology* (2nd ed, 1993) p 100 and A Bainham in *Children – the Modern Law* (1993) p 470) describe as 'laconic', Lord Coleridge's dismissal of the appeal.
5 (1919) 14 Cr App Rep 128.

dismissed his appeal against conviction, with a broad ruling that the prospect of intimidation will justify the court in removing the 'prisoner' from the presence of the witness. In 1990, the same court approved[6] the use of wooden screens to hide young victims and their alleged abusers from each other whilst the former gave evidence; in such cases the court of first instance must orchestrate matters justly, for example warning the jury against prejudice and ensuring that counsel can see the children. Magistrates' courts are now officially[7] encouraged to make use of screens.

If adults and children are going to be hidden from each other inside the courtroom, perhaps the court could simply send one of them outside. In the youth court, the parents' normal entitlement to be present may be curtailed whilst the child gives evidence or makes a statement.[8] The parent (or anyone else) as defendant in a criminal case is irremovable in English law (at least during good behaviour) although Spencer and Flin argue[9] that other jurisdictions see the continued presence of his counsel as being a sufficient bulwark against injustice.

One such jurisdiction is Queensland where, in an interesting reversal of current domestic developments, the possible injustice to the accused is reduced by relaying the proceedings to him live on video.[10] Under s 32(1)(b) of the Criminal Justice Act 1988 as amended[11] the Crown and youth courts may give leave for a child to give evidence 'by a live television link' in prosecutions for either sexual violence (when the age limit is 17) or personal violence (14). Some of these constraints have been criticised as unnecessarily cautious: why, for example, are these cases restricted to prosecutions related to sex and violence when the child might just as reasonably be frightened of a defendant accused of Fagin-type offences?[12]

We may assume that the child is thankfully spared undue anxiety by the video link, but is his or her credibility as a witness reduced or enhanced? Perhaps the answer depends on how the watchers rate television *generally*, ie whether they believe what they see on it or not.

'Overall, the verdict on the live link in England seems to be that it is helpful. It enables more children to give more and clearer evidence, and whilst suffering less stress: though at the possible cost – if it is a cost – of reducing the emotional impact

6 *R v X, Y and Z* [1990] Crim LR 515.
7 Home Office Circular No 61/1990.
8 Magistrates' Courts (Children and Young Persons) Rules 1992, r 19.
9 J Spencer and R Flin, *The Evidence of Children – the Law and the Psychology* (2nd ed, 1993) at p 112.
10 Evidence Act 1977, s 21A(2), (4).
11 By s 55 of the Criminal Justice Act 1991.
12 J Spencer and R Flin, *The Evidence of Children – the Law and the Psychology* (2nd ed, 1993) at p 104.

of their evidence. It would be a mistake, however to think that with the live link all problems of children's evidence are solved. In the first place, what it cannot do is relieve the stress involved in having to wait for the case to come to trial. Furthermore, such advantages as it does have at the trial can still be thrown away if the judge and lawyers are clumsy with the technology, the child is repeatedly cut off from contact with the court for no apparent reason, is ill-prepared for court appearance and is examined and cross-examined in a clumsy, inept and overbearing manner as still happens in some cases'.[13]

Many of these objections (but not some others) would be met by the use of pre-recorded video tapes. In two important instances such evidence may be adduced without difficulty. First, if it records the event in question, rather than an alleged conversation about it: thankfully, the audiotape Brady and Hindley made of themselves abusing one of their victims helped to convict them of their wicked deeds. Secondly, in one of the earliest implemented provisions of the Children Act 1989, the Lord Chancellor made provision for the admissibility of evidence otherwise rendered inadmissible by the hearsay rule:[14] *ex hypothesi* recorded video tapes with such children may be adduced in evidence, leaving the court with the sole question of the weight to be attached to them. In the criminal courts, however, the rule against hearsay evidence is retained. The Pigot Committee[15] said that children:[16]

'ought never to be required to appear in public as witnesses in the Crown Court, whether in open court or protected by screens or closed circuit television unless they wish to do so. This principle, we believe, is not only absolutely necessary for their welfare, but is also essential in overcoming the reluctance of children and their parents to assist the authorities. It would create a certainty which... would enable many more prosecutions to be pursued successfully and therefore enhance the protection afforded to the very young by the courts.'

The Committee made detailed proposals for a replacement system. Faced with a suspected offence, a trained person should interview the child, a video tape being shown to the suspect. A second recording would be made of a preliminary hearing before the judge in chambers, with the defence putting questions to the child. If further matters came to light, there could be a third interview with the child, also taped. In any subsequent trial, the three tapes would replace the live evidence of the child.[17]

13 *Ibid* p 111.
14 Section 96(3)–(7). The Children (Admissibility of Hearsay Evidence) Order 1993, SI 1993/621, made by the Lord Chancellor under s 96(3) now permits hearsay evidence in virtually any civil matter involving children, including proceedings brought under the Child Support Act 1991.
15 *Report of the Advisory Group on Video Evidence* (1989).
16 *Ibid* para 2.26.
17 For the definitive marshalling of arguments for and against video tapes (11 against (all rebutted) and 8 or so in favour) see J Spencer and R Flin, *The Evidence of Children – the Law and the Psychology* (2nd ed, 1993) pp 191-200.

The ensuing legislative action was mild by comparison. Section 32A[18] of the Criminal Justice Act 1988 gives the judge a discretion to allow videos of pre-trial interviews in cases involving sexual offences or violence. Crucially, and in major diminution of the Pigot proposals, it may only take the place of evidence-in-chief, with the child having to be available for cross-examination – at the hands of a defence lawyer whose duty it may be to discredit the child. The Government did, however, undertake to monitor the working of this 'reform' with a view to further reconsideration where appropriate. For the moment, any advocates who really are up to discomforting little children may still have scope for their skills.

8. CONCLUSION

In these last two chapters, we have discussed the role of legal and other professionals who are closely involved in the legal regulation of parenthood. We have noted how there is a theoretical (and often actual) conflict between the concept of family privacy and intimacy on the one hand, and the scrutiny of outsiders through court proceedings often *initiated by family members themselves* on the other. Negotiation and settlement with the aid of lawyers and mediators may obviate the need for close scrutiny in many private law cases and, with the non-intervention principle of the Children Act 1989, one would expect the number of such cases to grow. In the public law sphere, the emphasis on partnership between local authority and parents is intended to produce the same shift away from formal court proceedings, to 'voluntary' arrangements and acceptance of 'support' from social workers.

There is a further possibility of conflict between the interests of parents on the one hand, and those of children on the other, and yet a further complication in drawing a distinction between a child's wishes and feelings, and welfare. We have seen how an attempt is made to steer a course between all these difficulties, through the use of 'independent' experts such as welfare officers and guardians *ad litem*, but with the residual possibility of the child's being able to appoint his or her own legal representatives to counteract the 'objective' case based on welfare.

It is doubtful that a full-blown 'family court', or adoption of the Scottish children's hearing system[19] would solve these difficulties much more effectively than is being currently attempted. There is a fundamental

18 Inserted by s 54 of the Criminal Justice Act 1991. See *Practice Note 'Video Recordings of Children's Evidence'* [1992] 3 All ER 909, for the editing arrangements.
19 See Ch 13.

problem in family proceedings in ensuring due process for parties of differing articulacy, and this is exacerbated when one of the parties is a child who is still viewed in law as presumptively 'belonging' to the parents.

PART IV

Conclusion

CHAPTER 17

From nature to nurture?

In this concluding chapter, we seek to draw out the themes arising from our discussion of how parenthood is regulated by law and to offer some thoughts on possible future developments.

1. TRENDS IN LEGAL DEVELOPMENT

We have traced and discussed various trends in the legal approach to the parent-child relationship, in particular, the move away from a focus upon parental rights towards an emphasis upon child welfare. This can also be seen as shifting the law away from a proprietorial view of children towards recognising them as persons and rights-bearers to whom duties and responsibilities are owed. Secondly, we have seen recognition of the equal claims of mothers at the start of this century, and of the equal claims of the 'new fathers' at the end of it, to undertake the care of their children. Thirdly, it is possible to trace an increasing readiness to attach the status of parent to those playing the social role and to minimise the importance of the genetic contribution.

These developments can be seen as reflecting a gradually changing understanding of parenthood, from a focus upon the procreative, biological role, to the caring and nurturing aspect. Since socialisation of the child is crucial for the continuity of order in society, it is unsurprising that the state should attach weight to it. We see this both through the interest the state takes in the formal education of children, and also in the development of legal rules which emphasise the paramountcy of the child's welfare and which recognise the intention to assume the social role as justifying parental status.

But the trend is not a clear-cut one, and there are still problems and tensions inherent in the law which have yet to be resolved.

2. COMPLICATIONS AND CONTRADICTIONS

(a) Parental rights *vs* parental responsibilities

First, although it may have become politically convenient in this country to focus on parents' responsibilities rather than rights, we sought to argue in Part I of this book that philosophically, it is still appropriate to recognise parents as having rights in respect of their children which go beyond those required to fulfil their duties. Intuitively, people assert quasi-proprietorial claims over, and to, their children, and morally these can be defended as aspects of the worthwhile project of human procreation and child-rearing. A failure to recognise this in the law may help to explain how, for example, the procedures intended to deal with the consequences of divorce and family breakdown fail to provide satisfaction to those personally involved (both parents and children alike), to public opinion or to the state. It may be that asking parents to act responsibly, and to put their children first when it comes to arrangements for residence and contact, without giving due weight to the feelings that parents have for their children, becomes mere exhortation which parents do not 'hear'. Even more strikingly, and notwithstanding all the legislative changes, care procedures designed to protect children from their parents' abuse or neglect may still be applied in ways which fail to respect the fundamental point that, in English law, parents are presumptively deemed fit to care for their children until proved otherwise, and even if unfit, are still classed as parents until the child is adopted. The attempt to import a trustee model of parenthood runs the risk of sending a 'social engineering' message that parents may be judged unfit - or unworthy - to care for their children, and thus of driving them away from seeing the public care system as a positive form of help.

(b) Parental equality: aspiration *v* reality

Secondly, formal equality of mothers and fathers' rights and duties is meaningless while mothers still assume the primary caretaking role with the consequent opportunity loss in income and earning capacity and poverty if the relationship with the father breaks down. Parliament effectively recognises this in its treatment of non-marital, if not divorced, fathers. Where formal equality does exist, it has, moreover, led fathers who wish to claim residence to have unrealistic expectations of their legal position, since, in the majority of cases, it is likely that mothers will continue to be granted the residence of their children if this reflects the existing position, and yet it leaves mothers feeling insecure and compelled reluctantly to compromise on contact arrangements by being told that 'fathers have rights too'.[1]

(c) Maximal welfare for the few: minimal standards for the many

Thirdly, the greater significance attached to caring and welfare must be set alongside the fact that the rules focusing on the child's best interests are invoked only with regard to *some* of those *few* children to whom the court's attention is drawn; not, for example, to all the children of divorcing parents (and still less, to all those whose unmarried parents split up). Even where the rules are invoked, there are question marks surrounding how well the courts can, and do, judge issues of welfare.

(d) Resistance to increased opportunities for parenthood

Continuing uncertainty over the balance to be struck between the procreative and social roles is also apparent in two other areas.

There is controversy surrounding access to assisted reproduction treatment. This raises issues of morality in terms of family form and sexual preference, and of the commodification of children. Opponents of new reproductive techniques may argue on the one hand that use of donated gametes distorts family relationships by creating, and then concealing, a gap between genetic and social parenthood. Such an approach focuses upon the centrality of procreation and 'nature' in parenthood. Additionally, they might object that it is wrong to permit single persons or same-sex partnerships to have children and thereby create 'undesirable' family structures. They may add that it is doubly wrong where the facility is paid for. Such arguments focus upon the social family created as a result of treatment. The legal mechanisms governing the provision of treatment do little to satisfy such concerns but do create extra hurdles in the way of those seeking treatment.

(e) Children's awareness *v* parental security

Children's rights to knowledge about their background have yet to be satisfactorily accommodated within the setting of increased recognition of the social role of parenthood. There is uncertainty over this problem, apparent both in relation to whether there should be continuing contact

1 C Piper, *The Responsible Parent* (1993); C Smart and S Sevenhuijsen, *Child Custody and the Politics of Gender* (1989).

with the birth family after a child's adoption into a new social family, and in relation to whether children born as a result of gamete donation should have the right to discover their genetic identity. We would argue that to sustain a presumption against contact in the former case,[2] or to permit gamete donors to maintain anonymity in the latter case, is to confuse the *child's* right to knowledge and security of identity with the *social parent's* right to a relationship with the child. It needs to be recognised in the law that both rights can co-exist successfully.

3. DIVERSITY IN FAMILY FORM

Interestingly, a focus on the caring role of parenthood *should* enable a more flexible approach to be taken towards styles of parenting and varying family forms. If procreation is no longer the central feature of parenthood, there is no *necessary* requirement for a 'traditional' family of mother and father to carry out the caring function. To some extent, this has been recognised in the law: parental responsibility is a collection of rights and duties which can be held by a multiplicity of persons; there is no rule of law forbidding same-sex partners from caring for children and the courts have used residence orders to award parental responsibility to such partners.[3] Exhortations are made regarding the importance of respect for varying ethnic and cultural practices in child-rearing in the Children Act, for example.[4]

But such instances are significant only up to a point. It is still not possible for a child to have more than two legal parents at a time, and shared parental responsibility at a distance is not easy to put into practice.[5] While the extended West Indian family is admired, the mother-headed nuclear unit is not; the 'traditional' values Asian unit is admired, but not so its alien, and demanding, religious dimension. And the Child Support Act might be viewed as an attempt to reinstate the genetic tie at the cost of ignoring or undermining the social bond, although this legal development has met with particular resistance.

4. PARENTS *V* CHILDREN IN DECISION-MAKING

Possibly the most problematic area of legal development lies in the extent of recognition of children's autonomy to take decisions at odds with their

---

2 See the analysis by S Jolly, 'Cutting the Ties – The Termination of Contact in Care' [1994] JSWL 299.

3 *Re C (a minor) (Residence Order: Lesbian Co-parents)* [1994] Fam Law 468.

4 Section 22(5); Sch 2, paras 11, 12.

5 A Bainham, 'The Privatisation of the Public Interest in Children' (1990) 53 MLR 206.

parents' (and the state's) wishes. It is clear that there are major conflicting principles here, which have yet to be fully resolved in the case law and legislation. The concept of the 'mature minor' or '*Gillick* competent' minor has been diminished both in relation to common law principles[6] and in defiance of clear statutory provision in the Children Act.[7] This reflects a reluctance by the courts to follow through their own logic and to accept that where minors can truly be said to be mature enough to take their own decisions, they must be allowed to do so. Perhaps it also mirrors the fundamental dilemma of parenthood - how can the creative enterprise involved in bringing up a child be respected while at the same time recognising that the child is not simply the product of that enterprise? At the same time, there continues to exist the seemingly eternal perception of children as being beyond both parental and legal influence, as out of control and threats to society. The 'Children's Act' (sic) has almost taken the place of the 'permissive sixties', in being blamed for causing this (mythical) situation.

5. A LIFE-LONG RELATIONSHIP

There is a further complication. In this book, we have focused on the parent-child relationship in the first sense we explained in Chapter 1, ie where the child is a minor. We noted that in many cultures, parents have children so that they can provide support for the parents in old age. Such 'selfish' motives are rejected in our society, where the development of the retirement pension and comprehensive social insurance were intended to ensure that relief of need should not be dependent upon the chance of family support or the whim of charity. As the population ages and working adults are advised to take steps to ensure that their eventual pensions will be adequate to save them from destitution, suggestions are beginning to be made that children might one day be legally required to support their parents, a re-enactment of the Poor Law obligation abolished in 1948, and commonly found in civil law jurisdictions.[8] Indeed, 'community care' of the aged is already premised on family support. These developments turn the parent-child relationship on its head, and might be justified on the basis that children should show gratitude for their parents' efforts in bringing them up by caring for them in turn when they become dependent.

6 *Re R (a minor) (Wardship: Consent to Treatment)* [1992] Fam 11, *Re W (a minor) (Medical Treatment: Court's Jurisdiction)* [1993] Fam 64.

7 *South Glamorgan County Council v W and B* [1993] 1 FLR 574.

8 See the discussion by J Twigg in 'Carers, Families, Relatives: Socio-legal Conceptions of Care-giving Relationships' [1994] JSWFL 279.

Yet Janet Finch has shown how, in contemporary British society, there is usually a net transmission of goods and services from the older generation to the younger - throughout life and on death - reflecting a continuation of the obligation felt by parents towards their children (a moral obligation which remains squarely on the parents where the child is disabled, of course[9]) and a wish to respect the autonomy and independence of the children, perhaps in part because of a sense that children have no choice in determining their parents and so should not be placed under an equivalent obligation.[10] Yet oddly, there have been numerous judicial pronouncements that parental obligations to support children last only during their dependency,[11] and English inheritance law has never required that a parent make provision for a child (either as a dependent or simply as the parent's offspring) by will. Such examples suggest a legal approach to parenthood which may take an unduly narrow view of the relationship with the child.

6. PARENTHOOD AND POLICY

Finally, there is a limit to the extent to which political claims to 'support the family', to uphold 'children's rights' and to respect 'parental choice' can become translated into action through family law, or indeed through law in general. As the rationale of the series in which this book appears makes clear, law cannot be understood without an understanding of the wider context of which it is a part. A true political desire to promote the objective of successful parenting of children would require much greater attention to the consequences of policy initiatives far removed from the family sphere. True partnership with parents facing difficulties in rearing their children would require a much greater attempt at empowering them through the provision of services without strings attached. The problems of children in one-parent families cannot be tackled simply through child support formulae or civics lessons in the national curriculum but through meaningful attempts to raise children out of poverty and to develop a whole society which shares moral values and practises their messages.

Such an approach can be achieved without necessarily incorporating greater state involvement in family choices, and it does not seem likely

---

9 See, eg, *Bate v Chief Adjudication Officer*, (1994) Times, 12 December. The Court of Appeal ruled that a mentally handicapped woman was entitled to severe disability premium, because she lived with her parents, rather than, as the relevant regulations excluding entitlement suggested, they lived with her. Millett LJ said that while parents might be expected to look after her 'because, after all, she is their daughter', they were not giving their help *in return for* accommodation.

10 J Finch, *Family Obligations and Social Change* (1989) esp pp 36-41.

11 See, eg, *Lilford (Lord) v Glynn* [1979] 1 WLR 78.

that such involvement would be sought. There has not yet been an attempt by Government, in this country at least, to do very much in practice to encourage a particularly favoured family form, or to control what transpires within it. Methods of procreation are regulated, but the growing interest in the quality of parenting is unlikely to result in blanket monitoring of parental conduct. Whether children are smacked, brought up within Islam, and what sort of school they go to, are matters likely to remain dependent upon who their parents are; and whether people of any age enjoy cricket, take to crime, or become writers about parenthood, is also likely to remain much influenced by the values and attitudes inculcated in them by those who were, or acted as, their parents.

Bibliography

Abbott, M *Family Ties: English Families 1540-1920* (1993) Routledge

Abercrombie, N and Warde, A *Contemporary British Society* (2nd ed, 1994) Polity Press

Aberle, O *et al* 'The Incest Taboo and the Mating Pattern of Animals' (1963) 65 *American Anthropologist* 15

Adcock, M and White, R 'The use of s 3 resolutions' (1982) 6 *Adoption and Fostering* 9

Adcock, M and White, R A H *The Administrative Parent: A Study of the Assumption of Parental Rights and Duties* (1983) BAAF

Adcock, M and White, R (eds) *Good-Enough Parenting* (1985) State Mutual

Advisory Conciliation and Arbitration Service *The ACAS Role in Conciliation, Arbitration and Mediation* (1979) HMSO

Allen, M J *Criminal Law* (1991) Blackstone

Almond, B 'Human Bonds' (1988) 5 *Journal of Applied Philosophy* 3

Almond, B 'Parenthood – Social Construct or Fact of Nature?' in Morgan, D and Douglas, G *Constituting Families: A Study in Governance* (1994)

Alston, P *et al* (eds) *Children, Rights and the Law* (1992) OUP

Alston, P 'The Best Interests Principle: Towards a Reconciliation of Culture and Human Rights' in Alston, P (ed) *The Best Interests of the Child* (1994)

Alston, P (ed) *The Best Interests of the Child* (1994) 8 *International Journal of Law and the Family: Special Issue*

Archard, D 'Child abuse, parental rights and the interests of the child' (1990) 7 *Journal of Applied Philosophy* 183

Archard, D *Children, Rights and Childhood* (1993) Routledge
Ariès, P *Centuries of Childhood* (1962,1979) Penguin
Ashworth, A *et al The Youth Court* (1992) Waterside Press
Asquith, S and Hill, M *Justice for Children* (1994) Martinus Nijhoff
Association of Metropolitan Authorities *Special Child, Special Needs* (1994)
Atkinson, C and Horner, A 'Private fostering – legislation and practice' (1990) 14 *Adoption and Fostering* (3) 17
Audit Commission *Seen but Not Heard - executive summary* (1994)

Bainham, A *Children, Parents and the State* (1988) Sweet & Maxwell
Bainham, A 'When is a Parent not a Parent?' (1989) 2 *International Journal of Law and the Family* 209
Bainham, A 'The Privatisation of the Public Interest in Children' (1990) 53 MLR 206
Bainham, A 'The Judge and the Competent Minor' (1992) 108 LQR 194
Bainham, A 'Growing up in Britain: Adolescence in the Post-Gillick Era' in Eekelaar, J and Sarcevic, P (eds) *Parenthood in Modern Society)* (1993) Martinus Nijhoff
Bainham, A *Children – The Modern Law* (1993) Family Law
Baker, J H *An Introduction to English Legal History* (1990) Butterworths
Barrington Baker, W, Eekelaar, J, Gibson, C and Raikes, S *The Matrimonial Jurisdiction of Registrars* (1977) Oxford Centre for Socio-Legal Studies
Bartlett, K 'Rethinking Parenthood as an Exclusive Status: The Need for Legal Alternatives When the Premise of the Nuclear Family has Failed' (1984) 70 *Virginia Law Review* 879
Barton, C 'Incest and the Prohibited Degrees' (1987) 137 NLJ 502
Barton, C 'Those who are First ... shall one Day be Last' (1988) 1 *Journal of Child Law* 24
Barton, C 'Legal Family Favourites: the Man, then the Couple – now the Child' (1989) 2 *Journal of Child Law* (1) 29
Barton, C 'Emigration after Divorce: (Not) the Children Act 1989' (1989) 24 JALT 81
Barton, C 'Pre-Nuptial and Cohabitation Contracts: in at the Birth?' [1992] Fam Law 47
Barton, C 'Tell me off and I'll 'phone my Lawyer' *The Times,* 17 November 1992
Barton, C 'Money and Sex' (1992) 26 *Law Teacher* 255
Barton, C 'Adoption Law Reform' (1993) 137 Sol Jo 1198
Barton, C 'Child Support Act 1991' (1993) 137 Sol Jo 213
Barton, C '"Guidance", Childminding and Smacking' [1994] Fam Law 284

Barton, C and Moss, K 'Who can smack children now?' (1994) 6 *Journal of Child Law* (1) 32

Barton, C *et al Questions and Answers in Family Law* (1994) Blackstone

Bean, P and Melville, J *Lost Children of the Empire* (1989) Unwin

Beck, C *et al* 'The Rights of Children: A Trust Model' (1978) 46 *Fordham Law Review* 669

Becker, S and Macphearson, S *Public Issues, Private Pain: Poverty, Social Work and Social Policy* (1988) Care Matters

Bell, L and Tooman, P 'Mandatory Reporting Laws: A Critical Overview' (1994) 8 *International Journal of Law and the Family* 337

Bennet, G *The Wound and the Doctor* (1987) Secker and Warburg

Bennett Woodhouse, B '"Who Owns the Child?" *Meyer* and *Pierce* and the Child as Property' (1992) 33 *William and Mary Law Review* 996

Berridge, D and Cleaver, H *Foster home breakdown* (1987) Blackwell

Bevan, H *Child Law* (1989) Butterworths

Bigelow, J *et al* 'Parental Autonomy' (1988) 5 *Journal of Applied Philosophy* 183

Bigner, J J *Parent-Child Relations – an Introduction to Parenting* (3rd ed, 1989) Macmillan

Bilton, T *et al Introductory Sociology* (2nd ed, 1987) Macmillan Educational

Bingley-Miller, L and McNeish, D 'Paramountcy or partnership? Applicants attending adoption panels' (1993) 17 *Adoption and Fostering* (4) 15

Bird, R *Child Maintenance – The Child Support Act 1991* (2nd ed, 1993) Family Law

Birks, P 'Short Cuts' in Birks, P (ed) *Reviewing Legal Education* (1994) OUP

Bissett-Johnson, A 'Children in Subsequent Marriages – Questions of Access, Name and Adoption' in Eekelaar, J and Katz, S *Marriage and Cohabitation in Contemporary Societies* (1980) Butterworths

Blom-Cooper, L *A Child in Trust: the Report of the Panel of Enquiry into the circumstances surrounding the death of Jasmine Beckford* (1985) London Borough of Brent

Blom-Cooper, L *A Child in Mind: Report of the Commission of Inquiry into the Circumstances Surrounding the Death of Kimberley Carlile* (1987) London Borough of Greenwich

Boisard, P 'Le système français de prestations familiales' in Meulders-Klein, M-T and Eekelaar, J (eds) *Family, State and Individual Economic Security* (1985) E Story Scientia

Booth, Dame M *Report of the Matrimonial Causes Procedure Committee* (1985) HMSO

Borkowski, A *Textbook on Roman Law* (1994) Blackstone

Bottomley, A 'Resolving Family Disputes: A Critical View' in Freeman M D A (ed) *State, Law and the Family* (1984) Tavistock

Bouchier, P, Lambert, L and Triseliotis, J *Parting with a child for adoption* (1991) BAAF

Bowlby, J *Child Care and the Growth of Love* (2nd ed, 1965) Penguin

Boyd, D 'Blaming the Parents' (1990) 2 *Journal of Child Law* (1) 65

Bradney, A 'Blood Tests, Paternity and the Double Helix' [1986] Fam Law 378

Bradshaw, J *Child Poverty and Deprivation in the UK* (1990) National Children's Bureau

Bradshaw, J *et al Support for Children: A comparison of arrangements in fifteen countries* (1993) Department of Social Security

Brasse, G 'The Section 31 Monopoly' [1993] Fam Law 691

Braye, S and Preston-Shoot, M 'Honourable Intentions: Partnership and Written Agreements in Welfare Legislation' [1992] JSWFL 511

Brinich, P 'Adoption, ambivalence and mourning' (1990) 14 *Adoption and Fostering* (1) 6

Bromley, P M *Family Law* (1957) Butterworths

Bromley, P M and Lowe, N V *Bromley's Family Law* (8th ed, 1992) Butterworths

Brophy, J '"State and the Family": the Politics of Child Custody' (1987) University of Sheffield PhD thesis

Brophy, J 'Custody Law, Child Care, and Inequality in Britain' in Smart, C and Sevenhuijsen, S (eds) *Child Custody and the Politics of Gender* (1989)

Brown, D 'Divorce and Family Counselling: History, Review and Future Directions' (1992) 20 *Conciliation Courts Review* (2) 1

Bruch, C 'The Anatomy of a Success Story: the Hague Convention on International Child Abduction', paper presented to International Society of Family Law 8th World Conference, Cardiff (1994)

Buist, M and Gentleman, H *The Legal Capacity of Minors and Pupils – Experiences and Attitudes to Change* (1987) Scottish Office Central Research Unit

Bull, J *Housing Consequences of Relationship Breakdown* (1993) HMSO

Bullard, E, Malos, E and Parker, R *Custodianship: Caring for Other People's Children* (1991) HMSO

Bullock, R, Little, M and Millham, S *Going Home: The Return of Children Separated from their Families* (1993) Dartmouth

Bullock, R, Little, M and Millham, S *Residential Care for Children: A Review of the Research* (1993) HMSO

Burrows, D 'Anyone Remember Finer?' [1993] Fam Law 699

Butler I *et al* 'The Children Act 1989 and the Unmarried Father' (1993) 5 *Journal of Child Law* (4) 157

Butler-Sloss, Dame E *Report of the Inquiry into Child Abuse in Cleveland 1987* (1988) Cm 412, HMSO

Cain, M 'The General Practice Lawyer and the Client: Towards a Radical Conception' (1979) 7 *International Journal of the Sociology of Law* 333

Cairns, J *Drab Street Glory* (1934) Hutchinson

Campbell, B *Unofficial Secrets; child sexual abuse – the Cleveland case* (1988) Virago

Campbell, D *Report into the Workings of Area Child Protection Committees* (1994) Department of Health

Cashmore, E 'Re-writing the Script' (1985) *New Society*, December, 511

Cass, B 'The Limits of the Public/Private Dichotomy: A Comment on Coady and Coady' in Alston, P *et al* (eds) *Children, Rights and the Law* (1992) OUP

Central Statistical Office *Social Trends 1993* (1993) HMSO

Central Statistical Office *Social Trends 1994* (1994) HMSO

Chedzoy, A *A Scandalous Woman* (1992) Allison and Busby

Chief Child Support Officer *Annual Report 1993-94* (1994) HMSO

Children Act Advisory Committee *Annual Report 1992/93* (1994) Lord Chancellor's Department

Children's Legal Centre 'Information Sheet: Child Abduction' (1992) 89 *Childright* 9

Clevenger, N 'Statute of Limitations: Childhood Victims of Sexual Abuse Bringing Civil Actions Against their Perpetrators After Attaining the Age of Maturity' (1991/92) 30 *Journal of Family Law* 447

Clulow, C 'Why "difficult" solicitors?' [1992] Fam Law 398

Clulow, C and Vincent, C *In the Child's Best Interests? Divorce court welfare and the search for settlement* (1987) Tavistock

Coady, M and Coady, C '"There Ought to be a Law against It": Reflections on Child Abuse, Morality and Law' in Alston, P *et al* (eds) *Children, Rights and the Law* (1992) OUP

Cobley, C 'Child abuse, child protection and the criminal law' (1992) 4 *Journal of Child Law* 78

Cobley, C and Lowe, N V 'Ousting Abusers – Public or Private Law Solution?' (1994) 110 LQR 38

Cobbe, F *The Philosophy of the Poor Laws* (1865) Trubner

College of Law *Family Law and Practice* (1993) Jordans

Collinson, J and Gardner, K 'Conciliation and Children' in Fisher T (ed) *Family Conciliation within the UK* (1992) Family Law

Cooper, D *The Death of the Family* (1972) Penguin

Cowan, D and Fionda, J 'Back to Basics: the Government's Homelessness Consultation Paper' (1994) 57 MLR 610

Cowan, D and Fionda, J 'New Angles on Homelessness' [1993] JSWFL 403

Cranston, R *Legal Foundations of the Welfare State* (1985) Weidenfeld and Nicolson

Croll, E *et al* (eds) *China's One Child Family Policy* (1985) Macmillan

Crook, H '*In loco parentis*: Time for a Reappraisal?' [1989] Fam Law 447

Curtis, M *Report of the Care of Children Committee* (1946) Cmd 6922, HMSO

David, M 'Moral and Maternal: The Family in the Right' in Levitas, R (ed) *The Ideology of the New Right* (1986) Polity Press

Davies, S 'Dilemmas of practice' (1994) 18 *Adoption and Fostering* (3) 55

Davis, G *Partisans and Mediators: The Resolution of Divorce Disputes* (1988) Clarendon Press

Davis, G, Cretney, S and Collins, J *Simple Quarrels* (1994) Clarendon Press

Davis, G, Macleod, A and Murch, M 'Undefended Divorce; Should s 41 of the Matrimonial Causes Act 1973 be repealed?' (1983) 46 MLR 121

Davis, G and Murch, M *Grounds for Divorce* (1988) OUP

Davis, K *Human Society* (1970) Macmillan International

Deech, R 'The unmarried father and human rights' (1992) 4 *Journal of Child Law* 3

Deighton, L *Violent Ward* (1993) HarperCollins

Department of the Environment *Access to Local Authority and Housing Association Tenancies* (1994)

Department of the Environment and Welsh Office *Homelessness: Code of Guidance for Local Authorities* (3rd ed, 1991) HMSO

Department of Health *Inter-Departmental Review of Child Care Law* (1985)

Department of Health *The Law on Child Care and Family Services* (1987) Cm 62, HMSO

Department of Health *Inter-Departmental Review of Adoption Law, Discussion Paper No 1, The Nature and Effect of Adoption* (1990)

Department of Health *Child Abuse: A Study of Inquiry Reports 1980-1991* (1991) HMSO

Department of Health *Children Act 1989: Guidance and Regulations: Family Support, Court Orders* Vol 1 (1991) HMSO

Department of Health *Children Act 1989: Guidance and Regulations: Family Support, Day Care and Educational Provision for Young Children* Vol 2 (1991) HMSO

Department of Health *Children Act 1989: Guidance and Regulations: Family Placements* Vol 3 (1991) HMSO

Department of Health *Children Act 1989: Guidance and Regulations: Guardians ad Litem and other Court Related Issues* Vol 7 (1991) HMSO

Department of Health *Private Fostering and Place of Safety Orders* (1991)

Department of Health *Child Protection: Guidance for Senior Nurses, Health Visitors and Midwives* (1992) HMSO

Department of Health *Children in the Care of Local Authorities 1991* (1993)

Department of Health *Placement Orders: Consultation Document* (1994)

Department of Health *The Future of Adoption Panels: Consultation Document* (1994)

Department of Health *The UK's First Report to the UN Committee on the Rights of the Child* (1994) HMSO

Department of Health and Welsh Office *Review of Adoption Law: Consultation Document* (1992)

Department of Health and Welsh Office *Children Act Report 1992* (1993)

Department of Health and Welsh Office *Children Act Report 1993* (1994)

Department of Health, Welsh Office, Home Office, Lord Chancellor's Department *Adoption: The Future* (1993) Cm 2288, HMSO

Department of Social Security *Social Security Statistics 1993* (1993) HMSO

Dewar, J *Law and the Family* (2nd ed, 1992) Butterworths

Dickens, J 'Assessment and the Control of Social Work: An Analysis of the Reasons for the Non-Use of the Child Assessment Order' [1993] JSWFL 88

Dickey, A *Family Law* (2nd ed, 1990) Law Books

Dingwall, R 'The Jasmine Beckford Affair' (1986) 49 MLR 489

Dingwall, R 'Some Observations on Divorce Mediation in Britain and the United States' (1986) *Mediation Quarterly* 11

Dingwall, R, Eekelaar, J and Murray, T *The Protection of Children: State Intervention and Family Life* (1983) Basil Blackwell

Dingwall, R and Eekelaar, J 'Families and the State: An Historical Perspective on the Public Regulation of Private Conduct' (1988) 10 *Law and Policy* 341

Dingwall, R and Eekelaar, J 'A Wider Vision?' in Dingwall, R and Eekelaar, J (eds) *Divorce Mediation and the Legal Process* (1988) Clarendon Press

Dingwall, R and Greatbach, D 'Divorce Mediation – The Virtues of Formality?' in Eekelaar, J and Maclean, M *A Reader on Family Law* (1994) OUP

Donzelot, J *The Policing of Families* (1979) Hutchinson

Douglas, G 'Justice or Welfare in Financial Proceedings on Divorce?' (1987) 50 MLR 516

Douglas, G 'The Family and the State under the European Convention on Human Rights' (1988) 2 *International Journal of Law and the Family* 76

Douglas, G *Law, Fertility and Reproduction* (1991) Sweet & Maxwell

Douglas, G *Access to Assisted Reproduction – Legal and other Criteria for Eligibility* (1992) Cardiff Law School

Douglas, G 'The Retreat from *Gillick*' (1992) 55 MLR 569

Douglas, G 'Assisted reproduction and the welfare of the child' in Freeman M D A and Hepple B A (eds) *Current Legal Problems 1993* (1993) Vol 46, Part 2: Collected Papers

Douglas, G 'In Whose Best Interests?' (1994) 110 LQR 379

Douglas, G 'The In1tention to be a Parent and the Making of Mothers' (1994) 57 MLR 636

Douglas, G and Lowe, N V 'Becoming a Parent in English Law' (1992) 108 LQR 414

Duquette, D 'Scottish Children's Hearings and Representation for the Child' in Asquith, S and Hill, M (eds) *Justice for Children* (1994)

Dwork, D *War is Good for Babies and Other Young Children* (1987) Tavistock

Economic and Social Committee of the European Community 'Opinion on Adoption' *Official Journal of the European Communities* No C 287/18, 4 November 1992

Edwards, S, Gould, C and Halpern, A, 'The Continuing Saga of Maintaining the Family After Divorce' [1990] Fam Law 31

Eekelaar, J 'What are Parental Rights?' (1973) 89 LQR 210

Eekelaar, J and Clive, E with Clarke, K and Raikes, S *Custody After Divorce: The Disposition of Custody in Divorce Cases in Great Britain* (1977) Oxford Centre for Socio-Legal Studies

Eekelaar, J 'Children and Divorce: Some Further Data' (1982) 2 *Oxford Journal of Legal Studies* 63

Eekelaar, J 'The Emergence of Children's Rights' (1986) 6 *Oxford Journal of Legal Studies* 161.

Eekelaar, J 'The role of the courts under the Children Bill' (1989) NLJ 217

Eekelaar, J 'What is "Critical" Family Law?' (1989) 105 LQR 244

Eekelaar, J 'Investigation under the Children Act 1989' [1990] Fam Law 486

Eekelaar, J *Regulating Divorce* (1991) Clarendon Press

Eekelaar, J 'Are Parents Morally Obliged to Care for their Children?'(1991) 11 Oxford Journal of Legal Studies 51.

Eekelaar, J 'Parental Responsibility: State of Nature or Nature of the State?' [1991] JSWFL 37

Eekelaar, J 'The Importance of Thinking that Children Have Rights' (1992) 6 *International Journal of Law and the Family* 221

Eekelaar, J 'White Coats or Flak Jackets? Doctors, Children and the Courts – Again' (1993) 109 LQR 182

Eekelaar, J 'Third Thoughts on Child Support' [1994] Fam Law 99

Eekelaar, J 'A Jurisdiction in Search of a Mission: Family Proceedings in England and Wales' (1994) 57 MLR 839

Eekelaar, J 'Parenthood, Social Engineering and Rights' in Morgan, D and Douglas, G (eds) *Constituting Families: A Study in Governance* (1994)

Eekelaar, J '"The chief Glory": The Export of Children from the United Kingdom' (1994) 21 JLS 487

Eekelaar, J 'The Interests of the Child and the Child's Wishes: The Role of Dynamic Self-Determinism' (1994) 8 *International Journal of Law and the Family* 42

Eekelaar, J and Dingwall, R *Human Rights, Report to the Council of Europe* (1987) Council of Europe

Eekelaar, J and Dingwall, R 'The Development of Conciliation in England' in Dingwall, R and Eekelaar, J *Divorce Mediation and the Legal Process* (1988) Clarendon Press

Elliott, J *et al* 'Divorce and Children: A British Challenge to the Wallerstein view' [1990] Fam Law 309

Elliott, J and Richards, M 'Parental Divorce and the Life Chances of Children' [1991] Fam Law 481

Evans, K *The Development and Structure of the English School System* (1985) Hodder and Stoughton

Family Law Action Group *Policy Paper No 2: The Case Against the Child Support Agency* (1994)

Family Rights Group *Reuniting Children and their Families* (1993)

Farmer, M *The Family* (2nd ed, 1979) Longman

Farson, R *Birthrights* (1978) Penguin

Fellows, A *The Case Against the English Divorce Law* (1932) Lane

Felstiner, W and Sarat, A 'Negotiation between Lawyer and Client in an American Divorce' in Dingwall R and Eekelaar J (eds) *Divorce Mediation and the Legal Process* (1988) Clarendon Press

Ferri, E *Growing Up in a One-Parent Family* (1976) NFER Publishing

Field-Fisher, T G *Report of the Committee of Inquiry into the care and supervision provided in relation to Maria Colwell* (1974) HMSO

Finch, J *Family Obligations and Social Change* (1989) Polity Press

Finer Report *Report of the Committee on One Parent Families* (1974) Cmnd 5629, HMSO

Firestone, S *The Dialectic of Sex: the case for feminist revolution* (1979) Women's Press

Fisher T, (ed) *Family conciliation within the UK: Policy and Practice* (1992) Family Law

Flekkoy, M G *Children's Rights* (1993) Children's Rights Centre, Universiteit Gent

Flin, R 'Child Witnesses: the Psychological Evidence' (1988) 138 NLJ 608

Fortin, J *'Re F*: "The Gooseberry Bush Approach"' (1994) 57 MLR 296

Fragonard, B 'L'aid à la famille: Politiques de préstations et politiques fiscales' in Meulders-Klein, M-T and Eekelaar, J (eds) *Family, State and Individual Economic Security* (1985) E Story Scientia

France, E *Inter-Departmental Review of Adoption Law: Background Paper No 1: International Perspectives* (1990) Department of Health

Frank, G 'American and International Responses to International Child Abduction' (1984) *New York University Journal of International Law and Politics* 415

Fratter, J, Rowe, J, Sapsford, D and Thoburn, J *Permanent Family Placement* (1991) BAAF

Freeman, M D A *The Rights and Wrongs of Children* (1983) Frances Pinter

Freeman, M D A 'Towards a Critical Theory of Family Law' (1985) *Current Legal Problems* 153

Freeman, M D A *Children, Their Families and the Law* (1992) Macmillan

Freeman, M D A 'The Private and the Public' in Morgan, D and Douglas, G (eds) *Constituting Families: A Study in Governance* (1994)

Fricker, N 'Injunctive Orders relating to Children' [1993] Fam Law 226

Fried, C *An Anatomy of Values* (1992) Books Demand

Foucault, M *Discipline and Punish* (1975, trans 1977) Penguin

Gahagan, J 'The Foundations of Social Behaviour' in Radford, J and Govier, E (eds) *A Textbook of Psychology* (1980) Sheldon Press

Galanter, M 'World of Deals: using negotiation to teach about legal process' (1984) 34 *Journal of Legal Education* 368

Gardner, J *Women in Roman Law and Society* (1986) Croom Helm

Geis, G and Binder, A 'Sins of their Children: Parental Responsibility for Juvenile Delinquency' (1991) 5 *Notre Dame Journal of Law, Ethics and Public Policy* 303

Giddens, A *Sociology* (1989) Polity Press

Gibson, C *Dissolving Wedlock* (1994) Routledge

Gill, O and Jackson, B *Adoption and Race: black, Asian and mixed race children in white families* (1993) Batsford Academic and Educational in association with BAAF

Gilligan, C *In a Different Voice: Psychological Theory and Women's Development* (1982) Harvard University Press

Goldstein, J, Freud, A, Solnit, A, *Before the Best Interests of the Child* (1979) Burnett Books

Goldstein, J, Freud, A, Solnit, A, *Beyond the Best Interests of the Child* (1973, 1980) Burnett Books

Goody, J *The development of the family and marriage in Europe* (1983) CUP

Gough, D *Child Abuse Interventions: A Review of the Research Literature* (1993) HMSO

Griffith, J A G *The Politics of the Judiciary* (4th ed, 1991) Fontana

Grinnell, G *The Cheyenne Indians* (1923) University of Nebraska Press

Grubb, A and Pearl, D *Blood Testing, AIDS and DNA Profiling* (1990) Family Law

Gulliver, P *Neighbours and Networks* (1971) University of California Press

Gutmann, A 'Children, Paternalism and Education: A Liberal Argument' (1980) 9 *Philosophy and Public Affairs* 33

Haldane, J 'Children, Families, Autonomy and the State' in Morgan, D and Douglas, G *Constituting Families: a Study in Governance* (1994)

Hall, J C 'The Waning of Parental Rights' [1972B] 31 CLJ 248

Hamilton, C 'The Right to a Religious Education' in Lowe, N V and Douglas, G (eds) *Families across Frontiers* (forthcoming)

Haralambos, M and Holborn, M *Sociology – Themes and Perspectives* (3rd ed, 1990) Collins Educational

Harris, N *Law and Education, Regulation, Consumerism and the Education System* (1993) Sweet & Maxwell

Harris, N 'Testing choice: parents, children and the National Curriculum' (1993) 5 *Journal of Child Law* (3) 125

Harris, N and Van Bijsterveld, S 'Parents as "Consumers" of Education in England and Wales and the Netherlands: A Comparative Analysis' (1993) 7 *International Journal of Law and the Family* 178

Harris, R 'A matter of balance: power and resistance in child protection policy' [1990] JSWL 332

Haskey, J *Children in Families Broken by Divorce: Population Trends No 61* (1990) HMSO

Haynes, J 'The Process of Negotiations' (1983) *Mediation Quarterly* 1

Haynes, J *Alternative Dispute Resolution: The Fundamentals of Family Mediation* (1993) Old Bailey Press

Held, V 'The Equal Obligations of Mothers and Fathers' in O'Neill, O and Ruddick, W (eds) *Having Children* (1979)

Helmholz, R H 'Bastardy Litigation in Medieval England' (1969) 13 *American Journal of Legal History* 360

Helmholz, R H *Canon Law and the Law of England* (1987) Hambledon

Helmholz, R H 'And were there children's rights in early modern England?' (1993) 1 *International Journal of Children's Rights* 23

Hennessy, P *Never Again: Britain 1945-1951* (1993) Vintage

Human Fertilisation and Embryology Authority *Sex Selection: Public Consultation Document* (1993)

Herman, J *Father-Daughter Incest* (1981) Harvard University Press

Hershman, D and McFarlane, A *Children: Law and Practice* (1993) Family Law

Hill, J 'What does it mean to be a "parent"? The claims of biology as the basis for parental rights' (1991) 66 *New York University Law Review* 353

Hill, M 'Concepts of parenthood and their application to adoption' (1991) 15 *Adoption and Fostering* (4) 16

Hodson, D and Dunmall, L *The Business of Family Law* (1992) Family Law

Hoggett, B *Parents and Children – The Law of Parental Responsibility* (4th ed, 1993) Sweet & Maxwell

Hoggett, B 'Joint Parenting Systems: the English experiment' (1994) 6 *Journal of Child Law* (1) 8

Holgate, G 'Housing Dependent Children' [1994] Fam Law 582

Holman, R *Trading in Children: A Study of Private Fostering* (1973) Routledge and Kegan Paul

Holman, R 'The twilight zone' *Community Care* 28 August 1986

Holt, J *Escape from Childhood* (1975) Dutton

Home Office *Crime, Justice and Protecting the Public* (1990) Cm 965, HMSO

Home Office *Criminal Statistics England and Wales 1992* (1993) Cm 2401, HMSO

Home Office, Department of Health, Department for Education, Welsh Office *Working Together under the Children Act 1989: A guide to arrangements for inter-agency co-operation for the protection of children from abuse* (1991) HMSO

Hopkinson Report *Report of the Committee on Child Adoption* (1921) Cmd 1254, HMSO

Houghton Report *Report of the Departmental Committee on the Adoption of Children* (1972) Cmnd 5107, HMSO

House of Commons Select Committee on Education *Third Report, Special Educational Needs: Implementation of the Education Act 1981* (1987) HC 201-1 and (1993) HC 287-1

House of Commons Social Security Committee *First Report of the Social Security Committee: The Operation of the Child Support Act*, Session 1993/94 (1993) HC 69

House of Commons Social Services Committee *Second Report, Children in Care* (1983-84) HC 360

Hughes, C *Step-Parents: Wicked or Wonderful?* (1991) Avebury

Humphreys, C *Zen Buddhism* (re-issued 1984) Routledge, Chapman and Hall

Hunt, J *Local Authority Wardships before the Children Act: The baby or the bathwater?* (1993) HMSO

Hurst Report *Report of the Departmental Committee on the Adoption of Children* (1954) Cmd 9248, HMSO

Ingleby, R *Solicitors and Divorce* (1992) OUP

Jacobs, E and Douglas, G *Child Support: The Legislation* (1993) Sweet & Maxwell

Jacobs, E and Douglas, G *Child Support: The Legislation, First Supplement* (1994) Sweet & Maxwell

James, A and Hay, W *Court Welfare in Action* (1993) Harvester Wheatsheaf

Jary, D and Jary, J *Collins Dictionary of Sociology* (1991) Collins

Johnson, A 'Practical Guide to Contact' [1991] Fam Law 536

Jolly, S 'Cutting the Ties – the Termination of Contact in Care' [1994] JSWFL 299

Jolly, S and Sandland, R 'Political Correctness and the Adoption White Paper' [1994] Fam Law 30

Jones, G and Wallace, C *Family and Citizenship* (1992) Open University Press

Kahan, B *Growing Up in Care* (1979) Basil Blackwell

Kelly, W 'Evolution of the Concept of the Rights of the Child in the Western World' (1978) 21 *The Review* (International Commission of Jurists) 43

Kerr, N and Bray, R *The Psychology of the Courtroom* (1988) Academic Press

Kiernan, K E 'The Impact of Family Disruption and Transitions made in Family Life' (1992) 46 *Population Studies* (2) 213

King, M and Piper, *How the Law Thinks about Children* (1990) Gower

King, M and Trowell, J *Children's Welfare and the Law: The Limits of Legal Intervention* (1992) Sage

King, P and Young, I *The Child as Client* (1992) Family Law

Killerby, M 'The Council of Europe's Contribution to Family Law' in Lowe, N V and Douglas, G (eds) *Families across Frontiers* (forthcoming)

Krafft-Ebing *Psychopathia Sexualis* (1886) Verlag von Ferdinand Erker

Kymlicka, W 'Rethinking the Family' (1991) 20 *Philosophy and Public Affairs* 77

Lacey, N, Wells, C and Meure, D *Reconstructing Criminal Law* (1990) Weidenfeld and Nicolson

Lafollette, H 'Licensing Parents' (1980) 9 *Philosophy and Public Affairs* 182

Laing, R D *The Politics of the Family* (1976) Penguin

Lamm, J B 'Easing Access to the Courts for Incest Victims: Toward an Equitable Application of the Delayed Discovery Rule' (1991) *Yale Law Journal* 2189

Lasch, C *Haven in a Heartless World: The Family Besieged* (1977) Basic Books

Laslett, P and Wall, R *Household and Family in Past Time* (1972) CUP

Laslett, P *et al* (eds) *Bastardy and its Comparative History* (1980) Edward Arnold

Lasswell, H *Power and Personality* (1948) Greenwood

Law Commission *Reform of the Grounds of Divorce: the Field of Choice* (1966) Cmnd 3123, HMSO

Law Commission Discussion Paper No 103 *The Financial Consequences of Divorce: The Basic Policy* (1980) HMSO

Law Commission Discussion Paper No 170 *Facing the Future: A Discussion Paper on the Ground for Divorce* (1988) HMSO

Law Commission Report No 112 *The Financial Consequences of Divorce* (1982) HMSO

Law Commission Report No 118 *Illegitimacy* (1982) HMSO

Law Commission Report No 157 *Illegitimacy (Second Report)* (1986) HMSO

Law Commission Report No 172 *Review of Child Law: Guardianship and Custody* (1988) HMSO

Law Commission Report No 187 *Distribution on Intestacy* (1990) HMSO

Law Commission Report No 192 *The Ground for Divorce* (1990) HMSO

Law Commission Report No 207 *Domestic Violence and Occupation of the Family Home* (1992) HMSO

Law Commission Working Paper No 74 *Illegitimacy* (1979) HMSO

Law Commission Working Paper No 90 *Transfer of Money between Spouses – the Married Women's Property Act 1964* (1985) HMSO

Law Commission Working Paper No 91 *Review of Child Law: Guardianship* (1985) HMSO

Law Commission Working Paper No 96 *Review of Child Law: Custody* (1986) HMSO

Law Commission Working Paper No 100 *Care, Supervision and Interim Orders in Custody Proceedings* (1987) HMSO

Law Commission Working Paper No 101 *Wards of Court* (1987) HMSO

Law Society *Guidance on Confidentiality and Privilege* (1991)

Law Society Family Law Committee *Maintenance and Capital Provision on Divorce* (1991) Law Society

Law Society Family Law Committee *Attendance of Solicitors at Child Protection Conferences* (1994) Law Society

Lee, S *Judging Judges* (1989) Faber

Legal Aid Board *Legal Aid Handbook* (1993) Sweet & Maxwell

Levitas, R 'Ideology and the New Right' in Levitas R, (ed) *The Ideology of the New Right* (1986) Polity Press

Lewis, J *In the Family Way: Child-bearing in the British Aristocracy 1760-1860* (1986) Rutgers University Press

Libai, D 'The Protection of the Child Victim of a Sexual Offence in the Criminal Justice System' (1969) 15 *Wayne Law Review* 977

Linton, R 'Present Conditions in Cultural Perspective' in Linton R, (ed) *The Science of Man in World Crisis* (1945) Columbia University Press

Local Government Board *Relief to Widows and Children* (1914) Local Government Board Circular *BPP C 744* (1920) vol XXVII

Locke, J *Second Treatise of Civil Government* (P Laslett ed, 1963) CUP

Lockyer, A 'The Scottish Children's Hearings System; Internal Developments and the UN Convention' in Asquith, S and Hill, M (eds) *Justice for Children* (1994)

Lord Chancellor's Department *Judicial Statistics: England and Wales 1993* (1993) Cm 2268, HMSO

Lord Chancellor's Department *Judicial Statistics: England and Wales 1993* (1994) Cm 2623, HMSO

Lord Chancellor's Department *Looking to the Future: Mediation and the ground for divorce* (1993) Cm 2424, HMSO

Loveland, I 'Square Pegs, Round Holes: The "Right" to Council Housing in the Post-War Era' (1992) 19 JLS 339

Lowe, N V 'Adoption Placement Orders – Freeing by Another Name?' (1993) 5 *Journal of Child Law* 62

Lowe, N V *et al Freeing for Adoption Provisions* (1993) HMSO

Lowe, N V and Douglas, G (eds) *Families across Frontiers* (forthcoming) Martinus Nijhoff

Lowe, N and Juss S, 'Medical Treatment – Pragmatism and the Search for Principle' (1993) 56 MLR 865

Lowe, N and White, R A H *Wards of Court* (2nd ed, 1986) Barry Rose

Lyon, C and de Cruz, P *Child Abuse* (2nd ed, 1993) Family Law

MacCormick, N 'Children's Rights: A Test-Case for Theories of Right' (1976) 62 *Archiv fur Rechts-und Sozialphilosophie* 305

Macfarlane, A 'Illegitimacy and illegitimates in English history' in Laslett, P *et al Bastardy and its Comparative History* (1980)

Maclean, M 'The Making of the Child Support Act 1991: Policy Making at the Intersection of Law and Social Policy' (1994) 21 *Journal of Law and Society* 505

Maclean, M and Eekelaar, J 'Child Support: The British Solution' (1993) 7 *International Journal of Law and the Family* 205

Maclean, M and Weitzman, L J 'The Way Ahead: A Policy Agenda' in Weitzman, L J and Maclean, M (eds) *Economic Consequences of Divorce: the International Perspective* (1992) OUP

Maidment, S 'A Study of Child Custody' (1976) 6 Fam Law 196

Maidment, S 'Step-Parents and Step-Children: Legal Relationships in Serial Unions' in Eekelaar, J and Katz, S *Marriage and Cohabitation in Contemporary Societies* (1980)

Maidment, S 'The Fragmentation of Parental Rights' (1981) CLJ 135

Mair, L *Marriage* (1971) Penguin

Mann, P *Children in Care Revisited* (1984) Batsford Academic and Educational in association with BAAF

Marsh, P 'Social Work and Fathers – an Exclusive Practice?' in Lewis, C and O'Brien, M (eds) *Reassessing Fatherhood* (1987) Sage

Masson, J 'The Official Solicitor as the Child's Guardian *ad Litem* under the Children Act 1989' (1992) 4 *Journal of Child Law* (4) 58

Masson, J '*Re W*: Appealing from a Golden Cage' (1993) 5 *Journal of Child Law* 37

Masson, J and Harrison, C 'Identity: Mapping the Frontiers' in Lowe, N V and Douglas, G (eds) *Families across Frontiers* (forthcoming)

Masson, J and Morton, S 'The use of wardship by local authorities' (1989) 52 MLR 762

McCall Smith, A 'Is Anything Left of Parental Rights?' in Sutherland, E and McCall Smith, A (eds) *Family Rights: Family Law and Medical Advance* (1990) Edinburgh University Press

McGoldrick, D 'The United Nations Convention on the Rights of the Child' (1991) 5 *International Journal of Law and the Family* 132

McGoldrick, D *The Human Rights Committee: Its Role in the Development of the International Covenant on Civil and Political Rights* (1991) Clarendon Press

McKee, L and O'Brien, M (eds) *The Father Figure* (1982) Tavistock

McLellan, D *Engels* (1977) Fontana/Collins

Meadows, H 'Child Maintenance After the 1991 Act – The Residual Functions of the Court' [1994] Fam Law 96

Meiselman, K *Incest* (1978) Jossey-Bass

Melli, M 'Toward a Restructuring of Custody Decision-making at Divorce: an Alternative Approach to the Best Interests of the Child' in Eekelaar, J and Sarcevic, P (eds) *Parenthood in Modern Society* (1993)

Merry, S 'The Social Organisation of Mediation in Non-Industrial societies: Implications for Informal Community Justice in America' in Abel, R (ed) *The Politics of Informal Justice* Vol 2 (1982) Academic Press

Meyer, P *The Child and the State: The Intervention of the State in Family Life* (1983) CUP

Midgley, M 'Rights-talk Will Not Sort Out Child-abuse: comment on Archard on parental rights' (1991) 8 *Journal of Applied Philosophy* 103

Miller, J G 'Children and Family Capital on Divorce' (1993) 5 *Journal of Child Law* (3) 113

Millham, S, Bullock, R, Hosie, K and Haak, M *Lost in Care: The problems of maintaining links between children in care and their families* (1986) Gower

Millham, S, Bullock, R, Hosie, K and Little, M *Access Disputes in Child-Care* (1989) Gower

Mitchell, A K *Children in the Middle: Living Through Divorce* (1984) Tavistock

Mnookin, R 'Child Custody Adjudication: Judicial Functions in the face of Indeterminacy' (1975) 39 *Law and Contemporary Problems* 226

Mnookin, R and Kornhauser, L 'Bargaining in the Shadow of the Law: The Case of Divorce' (1979) 88 *Yale Law Journal* 950

Moller Okin, S *Justice, Gender and the Family* (1989) Basic Books

Montgomery, J 'Children as Property' (1988) 51 MLR 323

Morgan, D 'A Surrogacy Issue: Who is the Other Mother?' (1994) 8 *International Journal of Law and the Family* 386

Morgan, D and Douglas, G (eds) *Constituting Families: A Study in Governance* (1994) 57 *Archiv fur Rechts-und Sozialphilosophie* Franz Steiner Verlag

Morgan, T *Somerset Maugham* (1980) Jonathan Cape

Morris, A and Giller, H *Understanding Juvenile Justice* (1987) Croom Helm

Mount, F *The Subversive Family: An Alternative History of Love and Marriage* (1982) Jonathan Cape

Mulkay, M 'Science and Family in the Great Embryo Debate' (1994) 28 *Sociology* (3) 699

Mullender, A (ed) *Open Adoption: the philosophy and the practice* (1991) BAAF

Murch, M *Justice and Welfare in Divorce* (1980) Sweet & Maxwell

Murch, M, Borkowski, M, Copner, R and Griew, K, *The Overlapping Family Jurisdictions of Magistrates' Courts and County Courts* (1987) University of Bristol

Murch, M and Hooper, D *The Family Justice System* (1992) Family Law

Murch, M *et al Pathways to Adoption* (1993) HMSO

Murdock, G P *Social Structure* (1965) Collier-Macmillan

Murphy, W 'Come Whoam to Thi Childer An' Me' (1983) 46 MLR 363

Murray, C *The Emerging British Underclass* (1990) IEA Health and Welfare Unit

NCH Action for Children *A lost generation?* (1993)

Newell, P *Children are People Too* (1989) Bedford Square Press

Newell, P *The UN Convention and Children's Rights in the UK* (1991) National Children's Bureau

Newson, J and Newson, E 'The Extent of Parental Physical Punishment in the UK' (1986) paper presented to Children's Legal Centre seminar on 'Protecting Children from Parental Physical Punishment'

Nicholls, M 'Publicity and Children's Cases' [1993] Fam Law 108

Norrie, K McK 'Medical Treatment of Children and Young Persons' in Morgan, D and Douglas, G (eds) *Constituting Families: A Study in Governance* (1994)

Norris, T and Parton, N 'The administration of place of safety orders' [1987] JSWL 1

Norton, C *A Letter to the Queen on Lord Chancellor Cranworth's Marriage and Divorce Bill* (1855) London

O'Donnell, K 'Parent-Child Relationships within the European Convention' in Lowe, N V and Douglas, G *Families across Frontiers* (forthcoming)

O'Donovan, K *Sexual Divisions in Law* (1985) Weidenfeld and Nicolson

O'Donovan, K *Family Law Matters* (1993) Pluto Press

Ogus, A *et al Report to the Lord Chancellor on the Costs and Effectiveness of Conciliation in England and Wales* (1989) University of Newcastle Conciliation Project Unit

Oldfield, N and Yu, A *The Cost of a Child* (1993) CPAG

O'Neill, O and Ruddick, W (eds) *Having Children: Philosophical and Legal Reflections on Parenthood* (1979) OUP

Olsen, F 'Children's Rights: Some Feminist Approaches to the United Nations Convention on the Rights of the Child' in Alston, P *et al* (eds) *Children, Rights and the Law* (1992)

OPCS *Birth Statistics 1991* (1993) HMSO

OPCS *Population Trends 13* (1978) HMSO

OPCS *Population Trends 70* (1993) HMSO

OPCS *Population Trends 73* (1993) HMSO

OPCS *General Household Survey 1992* (1994) HMSO

Oppenheim, C 'Families and the Recession' (1993) *Childright* 11 November

Packman, J *The Child's Generation: Child Care Policy in Britain* (2nd ed, 1981) Basil Blackwell

Page, E 'Parental Rights' (1984) 1 *Journal of Applied Philosophy* 187

Pahl, J (ed) *Private Violence and Public Policy: The Needs of Battered Women and the Reponse of the Public Services* (1985) Routledge and Kegan Paul

Painter, K *Wife-Rape, Marriage and the Law* (1991) Manchester University Press

Parker, R (ed) *Looking After Children: Assessing Outcomes in Child Care* (1991) HMSO

Parker, S 'Child Support in Australia: Children's Rights or Public Interest?' (1991) 5 *International Journal of Law and the Family* 24

Parker, S 'The Best Interests of the Child – Principles and Problems' in Alston, P (ed) *The Best Interests of the Child* (1994)

Parker, S, Parkinson, P and Behrens, J, *Australian Family Law in Context* (1994) Law Book Company

Parkinson, L 'Conciliation – A New Approach to Family Conflict Resolution' (1983) 13 *British Journal of Social Work* 19

Parkinson, L *Conciliation in Separation and Divorce – Finding Common Ground* (1986) Croom Helm

Parry, M 'The Children Act 1989: Local Authorities, Wardship and the Revival of the Inherent Jurisdiction' [1992] JSWFL 212

Parton, N *The Politics of Child Abuse* (1985) Macmillan

Parton, N *Governing the Family: Child Care, Child Protection and the State* (1991) Macmillan Education

Parton, N 'The Contemporary Politics of Child Protection' [1992] JSWFL 100

Pateman, C *The Sexual Contract* (1988) Stanford University Press

Pearson, G *Hooligan: a history of respectable fears* (1983) Macmillan

Phoenix, A, Woollett, A, and Lloyd, E (eds) *Motherhood: Meanings, Practices and Ideologies* (1991) Sage

Pigot, Judge T, QC *Report of the Advisory Group on Video Evidence* (1989) Home Office

Pinchbeck, I and Hewitt, M *Children in English Society* Vol 1 (1969) and Vol 2 (1973) Routledge and Kegan Paul

Piper, C *The Reponsible Parent* (1993) Harvester Wheatsheaf

Piper, C 'Parental Responsibility and the Education Acts' [1994] Fam Law 146

Plato *The Republic* (1981, trans Grube, G M A) Pan

Polansky, N A *et al Damaged Parents: An Anatomy of Neglect* (1981) University of Chicago Press

Pollock, L *Forgotten Children: Parent-Child Relations from 1500-1900* (1983) CUP

Poor Law Commissioners *Report from His Majesty's Commissioners for Inquiring into the Administration and Practical Operation of the Poor Laws* (1834) (44) XXVII, London

Priest, J and Whybrow, J *Custody Law in Practice in the Divorce and Domestic Courts* (1986) Supplement to Law Commission Working Paper No 96, HMSO

Radford, J and Govier, E *A Textbook of Psychology* (1980) Sheldon Press

Report of the Departmental Committee on Social Services in Courts of Summary Jurisdiction (1936) Cmd 5122, HMSO

Rhodes, P 'Charitable vocation or "proper job"? The role of payment in foster care' (1993) 17 *Adoption and Fostering* (1) 8

Richards, M *Adoption* (1989) Jordans

Richards, M 'Post Divorce Arrangements for Children: A Psychological Perspective' [1982] JSWL 133

Richards, M 'Divorcing children: roles for parents and the state' in Eekelaar, J and Maclean, M (eds) *A Reader on Family Law* (1994) OUP

Richardson, D *Women, Motherhood and Childrearing* (1993) Macmillan

Roberts, J *Divorce Bills in the Imperial Parliament* (1906) Dublin

Rose, L *The Erosion of Childhood* (1991) Routledge

Rowe, J and Lambert, L *Children Who Wait* (1973) ABAFA (now BAAF)

Royal College of Physicians *Medical Care of the Newborn in England and Wales* (1988)

Royal Society of Arts *Start Right* (1994)

Rubenstein, B 'An independent experience' (1992) NLJ 866

Ruddick, W 'Parents and Life Prospects' in O'Neill, O and Ruddick, W (eds) *Having Children* (1979)

Rutter, M 'Parent-child separation: psychological effects on the children' (1971) 12 *Journal of Child Psychology and Psychiatry*

Rutter, M *Maternal Deprivation Re-Assessed* (1972) Penguin

Sandland, R 'Adoption, Law and Homosexuality: Can Gay People Adopt a Child?' [1993] JSWFL 321

Saunders, J *Parental Responsibility for the Sixteen and Seventeen Year Old: Practically Redundant?* (1994) University of East Anglia LLM thesis (unpublished)

Scourfield, F and Hendry, A *et al* 'Unfinished business – the experience of a birth mothers' group' (1991) 15 *Adoption and Fostering* (2) 36

Scottish Law Commission Report No 82 *Illegitimacy* (1984) HMSO

Scottish Law Commission Report No 135 *Report on Family Law* (1992) HMSO

Scottish Office *Scotland's Children: Proposals for Child Care Policy and Law* (1993) Cm 2286, HMSO

Selbourne, D *The Principle of Duty* (1994) Sinclair-Stevenson

Selwyn, J 'Applying to adopt: the experience of rejection' (1991) 15 *Adoption and Fostering* (3) 26

Seymour, J '*Parens Patriae* and Wardship Powers: Their Nature and Origins' (1994) 14 Oxford Journal of Legal Studies 159

Shalev, C *Birth Power: The Case for Surrogacy* (1989) Yale University Press

Sherr, A *et al Transaction Criteria* (1992) HMSO

Sherrin, C H *et al Williams on Wills* (6th ed, 1987) Butterworths

Shimazu I 'Japan: Trailing the West in Family Law' (1988-89) 27 *Journal of Family Law* 185

Shultz, M 'Reproductive technology and intent-based parenthood: an opportunity for gender neutrality' (1990) *Wisconsin Law Review* 297

Smart, C *The Ties that Bind: Law, marriage and the reproduction of patriarchal relations* (1984) Routledge and Kegan Paul

Smart, C '"There is of course the distinction dictated by nature": Law and the Problem of Paternity' in Stanworth, M (ed) *Reproductive Technologies: Gender, Motherhood and Medicine* (1987) Polity Press

Smart, C and Sevenhuijsen, S (eds) *Child Custody and the Politics of Gender* (1989) Routledge

Smith, A and Blumberg, A 'The problem of objectivity in judicial decision-making' (1967) 46 *Social Forces* 96

Smith, L 'Children, Parents and the European Convention on Human Rights' in Eekelaar, J and Sarcevic, P (eds) *Parenthood in Modern Society* (1993)

Smith, V 'Children Act 1989: The Accommodation Trap' [1992] Fam Law 349

Social and Community Planning Research, Jowell, R *et al British Social Attitudes Cumulative Sourcebook* (1991) Gower

Social Fund Commissioner *Annual Report for 1993/94 on the standards of reviews of Social Fund Inspectors* (1994) HMSO

Social Services Inspectorate *Planning Long Term Placement Study: A study of experiences in local authorities of planning and achieving long term placements for children* (1994) Department of Health

Solicitors' Family Law Association *The Introduction and Code of Practice* (1994)

Spencer, J and Flin, R *The Evidence of Children: the Law and the Psychology* (2nd ed, 1993) Blackstone

Stacey, M 'The Division of Labour Revisited: Overcoming the Two Adams' in Abrahams, P *et al* (eds) *Practice and Progress – British Sociology 1950-1980* (1981) Allen and Unwin

Standley, C *Confidentiality and the Immature Minor* (1994) Cardiff Law School LLM thesis (unpublished)

Standley, K *Family Law* (1993) Macmillan

Stein, M and Carey, K *Leaving Care* (1986) Blackwell

Stephens, H 'Independent Representation' (1994) NLJ 907

Stevenson, K 'The provision of sex education in schools: the new DfE guidelines' (1994) *Childright*, 11 September

Stone, L *The Family, Sex and Marriage in England 1500-1800* (1977) Penguin

Stone, L *Road to Divorce* (1990) OUP

Stone, O *The Child's Voice in the Court of Law* (1982) Butterworths

Strathern, M *Reproducing the Future: Essays on Anthropology, Kinship and the New Reproductive Technologies* (1992) Manchester University Press

Szwed, E 'The Family Court' in Freeman, M D A (ed) *State, Law and the Family* (1984) Tavistock

Teitelbaum, L and Dupaix, L 'Alternative dispute resolution and divorce: natural experimentation in family law' in Eekelaar, J and Maclean, M (eds) *A Reader on Family Law* (1994) OUP

Thandabantu Nhlapo, R 'Biological and Social Parenthood in African Perspective: The Movement of Children in Swazi Family Law' in Eekelaar, J and Sarcevic, P (eds) *Parenthood in Modern Society* (1993)

Thoburn, J '"Working Together" and parental attendance at case conferences' (1992) 4 *Journal of Child Law* 11

Thomas, P and Costigan, R *Promoting Homosexuality: Section 28 of the Local Government Act 1988* (1990) Cardiff Law School

Thornton, R 'Multiple Keyholders – Wardship and Consent to Medical Treatment' (1992) 51 CLJ 34

Toffler, A *Future Shock* (1971) Bodley Head

Tomlin Report *First Report of the Child Adoption Committee* (1924-25) Cmd 2401, HMSO

Triseliotis, J 'Obtaining birth certificates' in Bean, P (ed) *Adoption: Essays in Social Policy, Law and Sociology* (1984) Tavistock

Twigg, J 'Carers, Families, Relatives: Socio-legal Conceptions of Care-giving Relationships' [1994] JSWFL 279

Van Beuren, G *The Best Interests of the Child – International Co-Operation on Child Abduction* (1993) British Institute of Human Rights

Venables, D 'The Official Solicitor: Outline and Aspects of his Work' [1990] Fam Law 53

Wagner, G *Children of the Empire* (1982) Weidenfeld & Nicolson

Walker, J *et al Social Policy Research Findings Paper No 48: An Evaluation of Comprehensive Mediation Services for Divorcing Couples* (1994) Joseph Rowntree Foundation

Wallerstein, J and Blakeslee, S *Second Chances* (1990) Corgi

Wallerstein, J and Kelly, J *Surviving the Breakup: How Children and Parents Cope with Divorce* (1980) Grant McIntyre

Walsh, B 'The United Nations Convention on the Rights of the Child: A British View' (1991) 5 *International Journal of Law and the Family* 170

Warnock, M *Special Educational Needs: Report of the Committee of Enquiry into the Education of Handicapped Children and Young Persons* (1978) Cmnd 7212, HMSO

Warnock, M *Report of the Committee of Inquiry into Human Fertilisation and Embryology* (1984) Cmnd 9314, HMSO

Weitzman, L J *The Marriage Contract* (1981) Free Press

Weitzman, L J *The Divorce Revolution – The Unexpected Social Consequences for Women and Children in America* (1985) Free Press

Wells, S 'What do birth mothers want?' (1993) 17 *Adoption and Fostering* (4) 22

Welsh Office *Education: A Charter for Parents in Wales* (1994) HMSO

Whitehead, A *Science and the Modern World* (1925) Free Association Books

Willetts, D *The Family* (1993) WH Smith Contemporary Papers No 14, London

Wright, J 'Negligent Parenting – Can my Child Sue?' (1994) 6 *Journal of Child Law* (3) 104

Index